Introduction to Parallel Processing

Algorithms and Architectures

PLENUM SERIES IN COMPUTER SCIENCE

Series Editor: **Rami G. Melhem**
University of Pittsburgh
Pittsburgh, Pennsylvania

FUNDAMENTALS OF X PROGRAMMING
Graphical User Interfaces and Beyond
Theo Pavlidis

INTRODUCTION TO PARALLEL PROCESSING
Algorithms and Architectures
Behrooz Parhami

Introduction to
Parallel Processing
Algorithms and Architectures

Behrooz Parhami
University of California at Santa Barbara
Santa Barbara, California

Plenum Press • New York and London

Library of Congress Cataloging-in-Publication Data

Parhami, Behrooz.
    Introduction to parallel processing : algorithms and architectures
/ Behrooz Parhami.
        p.   cm. -- (Plenum series in computer science)
    Includes bibliographical references and index.
    ISBN 0-306-45970-1
    1. Parallel processing (Electronic computers)   I. Title.
    II. Series.
    QA76.58.P3798   1998
    004'.35--dc21   98-45719
                                                                   CIP

ISBN 0-306-45970-1

© 1999 Plenum Press, New York
A Division of Plenum Publishing Corporation
233 Spring Street, New York, N.Y. 10013

http://www.plenum.com

10 9 8 7 6 5 4 3 2 1

Printed in the United States of America

To the four parallel joys in my life,

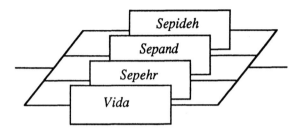

for their love and support.

Preface

THE CONTEXT OF PARALLEL PROCESSING

The field of digital computer architecture has grown explosively in the past two decades. Through a steady stream of experimental research, tool-building efforts, and theoretical studies, the design of an instruction-set architecture, once considered an art, has been transformed into one of the most quantitative branches of computer technology. At the same time, better understanding of various forms of concurrency, from standard pipelining to massive parallelism, and invention of architectural structures to support a reasonably efficient and user-friendly programming model for such systems, has allowed hardware performance to continue its exponential growth. This trend is expected to continue in the near future.

This explosive growth, linked with the expectation that performance will continue its exponential rise with each new generation of hardware and that (in stark contrast to software) computer hardware will function correctly as soon as it comes off the assembly line, has its down side. It has led to unprecedented hardware complexity and almost intolerable development costs. The challenge facing current and future computer designers is to institute simplicity where we now have complexity; to use fundamental theories being developed in this area to gain performance and ease-of-use benefits from simpler circuits; to understand the interplay between technological capabilities and limitations, on the one hand, and design decisions based on user and application requirements on the other.

In computer designers' quest for user-friendliness, compactness, simplicity, high performance, low cost, and low power, parallel processing plays a key role. High-performance uniprocessors are becoming increasingly complex, expensive, and power-hungry. A basic trade-off thus exists between the use of one or a small number of such complex processors, at one extreme, and a moderate to very large number of simpler processors, at the other. When combined with a high-bandwidth, but logically simple, interprocessor communication facility, the latter approach leads to significant simplification of the design process. However, two major roadblocks have thus far prevented the widespread adoption of such moderately to massively parallel architectures: the interprocessor communication bottleneck and the difficulty, and thus high cost, of algorithm/software development.

The above context is changing because of several factors. First, at very high clock rates, the link between the processor and memory becomes very critical. CPUs can no longer be designed and verified in isolation. Rather, an integrated processor/memory design optimization is required, which makes the development even more complex and costly. VLSI technology now allows us to put more transistors on a chip than required by even the most advanced superscalar processor. The bulk of these transistors are now being used to provide additional on-chip memory. However, they can just as easily be used to build multiple processors on a single chip. Emergence of multiple-processor microchips, along with currently available methods for glueless combination of several chips into a larger system and maturing standards for parallel machine models, holds the promise for making parallel processing more practical.

This is the reason parallel processing occupies such a prominent place in computer architecture education and research. New parallel architectures appear with amazing regularity in technical publications, while older architectures are studied and analyzed in novel and insightful ways. The wealth of published theoretical and practical results on parallel architectures and algorithms is truly awe-inspiring. The emergence of standard programming and communication models has removed some of the concerns with compatibility and software design issues in parallel processing, thus resulting in new designs and products with mass-market appeal. Given the computation-intensive nature of many application areas (such as encryption, physical modeling, and multimedia), parallel processing will continue to thrive for years to come.

Perhaps, as parallel processing matures further, it will start to become invisible. Packing many processors in a computer might constitute as much a part of a future computer architect's toolbox as pipelining, cache memories, and multiple instruction issue do today. In this scenario, even though the multiplicity of processors will not affect the end user or even the professional programmer (other than of course boosting the system performance), the number might be mentioned in sales literature to lure customers in the same way that clock frequency and cache size are now used. The challenge will then shift from making parallel processing work to incorporating a larger number of processors, more economically and in a truly seamless fashion.

THE GOALS AND STRUCTURE OF THIS BOOK

The field of parallel processing has matured to the point that scores of texts and reference books have been published. Some of these books that cover parallel processing in general (as opposed to some special aspects of the field or advanced/unconventional parallel systems) are listed at the end of this preface. Each of these books has its unique strengths and has contributed to the formation and fruition of the field. The current text, *Introduction to Parallel Processing: Algorithms and Architectures*, is an outgrowth of lecture notes that the author has developed and refined over many years, beginning in the mid-1980s. Here are the most important features of this text in comparison to the listed books:

1. *Division of material into lecture-size chapters.* In my approach to teaching, a lecture is a more or less self-contained module with links to past lectures and pointers to what will transpire in the future. Each lecture must have a theme or title and must

proceed from motivation, to details, to conclusion. There must be smooth transitions between lectures and a clear enunciation of how each lecture fits into the overall plan. In designing the text, I have strived to divide the material into chapters, each of which is suitable for one lecture (1–2 hours). A short lecture can cover the first few subsections, while a longer lecture might deal with more advanced material near the end. To make the structure hierarchical, as opposed to flat or linear, chapters have been grouped into six parts, each composed of four closely related chapters (see diagram on page xi).

2. *A large number of meaningful problems.* At least 13 problems have been provided at the end of each of the 24 chapters. These are well-thought-out problems, many of them class-tested, that complement the material in the chapter, introduce new viewing angles, and link the chapter material to topics in other chapters.

3. *Emphasis on both the underlying theory and practical designs.* The ability to cope with complexity requires both a deep knowledge of the theoretical underpinnings of parallel processing and examples of designs that help us understand the theory. Such designs also provide hints/ideas for synthesis as well as reference points for cost–performance comparisons. This viewpoint is reflected, e.g., in the coverage of problem-driven parallel machine designs (Chapter 8) that point to the origins of the butterfly and binary-tree architectures. Other examples are found in Chapter 16 where a variety of composite and hierarchical architectures are discussed and some fundamental cost–performance trade-offs in network design are exposed. Fifteen carefully chosen case studies in Chapters 21–23 provide additional insight and motivation for the theories discussed.

4. *Linking parallel computing to other subfields of computer design.* Parallel computing is nourished by, and in turn feeds, other subfields of computer architecture and technology. Examples of such links abound. In computer arithmetic, the design of high-speed adders and multipliers contributes to, and borrows many methods from, parallel processing. Some of the earliest parallel systems were designed by researchers in the field of fault-tolerant computing in order to allow independent multichannel computations and/or dynamic replacement of failed subsystems. These links are pointed out throughout the book.

5. *Wide coverage of important topics.* The current text covers virtually all important architectural and algorithmic topics in parallel processing, thus offering a balanced and complete view of the field. Coverage of the circuit model and problem-driven parallel machines (Chapters 7 and 8), some variants of mesh architectures (Chapter 12), composite and hierarchical systems (Chapter 16), which are becoming increasingly important for overcoming VLSI layout and packaging constraints, and the topics in Part V (Chapters 17–20) do not all appear in other textbooks. Similarly, other books that cover the foundations of parallel processing do not contain discussions on practical implementation issues and case studies of the type found in Part VI.

6. *Unified and consistent notation/terminology throughout the text.* I have tried very hard to use consistent notation/terminology throughout the text. For example, n always stands for the number of data elements (problem size) and p for the number of processors. While other authors have done this in the basic parts of their texts, there is a tendency to cover more advanced research topics by simply borrowing

the notation and terminology from the reference source. Such an approach has the advantage of making the transition between reading the text and the original reference source easier, but it is utterly confusing to the majority of the students who rely on the text and do not consult the original references except, perhaps, to write a research paper.

SUMMARY OF TOPICS

The six parts of this book, each composed of four chapters, have been written with the following goals:

- Part I sets the stage, gives a taste of what is to come, and provides the needed perspective, taxonomy, and analysis tools for the rest of the book.
- Part II delimits the models of parallel processing from above (the abstract PRAM model) and from below (the concrete circuit model), preparing the reader for everything else that falls in the middle.
- Part III presents the scalable, and conceptually simple, mesh model of parallel processing, which has become quite important in recent years, and also covers some of its derivatives.
- Part IV covers low-diameter parallel architectures and their algorithms, including the hypercube, hypercube derivatives, and a host of other interesting interconnection topologies.
- Part V includes broad (architecture-independent) topics that are relevant to a wide range of systems and form the stepping stones to effective and reliable parallel processing.
- Part VI deals with implementation aspects and properties of various classes of parallel processors, presenting many case studies and projecting a view of the past and future of the field.

POINTERS ON HOW TO USE THE BOOK

For classroom use, the topics in each chapter of this text can be covered in a lecture spanning 1–2 hours. In my own teaching, I have used the chapters primarily for 1-1/2-hour lectures, twice a week, in a 10-week quarter, omitting or combining some chapters to fit the material into 18–20 lectures. But the modular structure of the text lends itself to other lecture formats, self-study, or review of the field by practitioners. In the latter two cases, the readers can view each chapter as a study unit (for 1 week, say) rather than as a lecture. Ideally, all topics in each chapter should be covered before moving to the next chapter. However, if fewer lecture hours are available, then some of the subsections located at the end of chapters can be omitted or introduced only in terms of motivations and key results.

Problems of varying complexities, from straightforward numerical examples or exercises to more demanding studies or miniprojects, have been supplied for each chapter. These problems form an integral part of the book and have not been added as afterthoughts to make the book more attractive for use as a text. A total of 358 problems are included (13–16 per chapter). Assuming that two lectures are given per week, either weekly or biweekly homework can be assigned, with each assignment having the specific coverage of the respective half-part

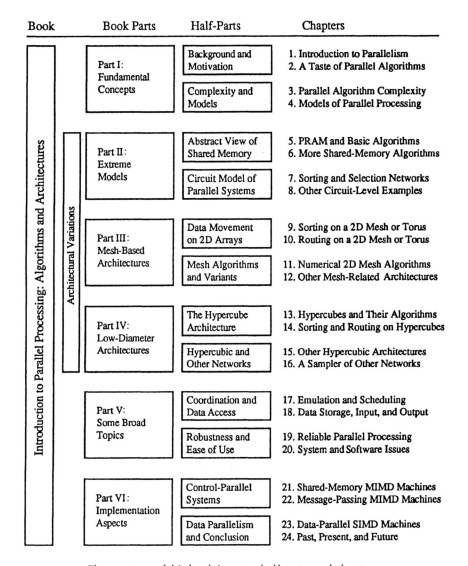

Book	Book Parts	Half-Parts	Chapters
Introduction to Parallel Processing: Algorithms and Architectures	Part I: Fundamental Concepts	Background and Motivation	1. Introduction to Parallelism 2. A Taste of Parallel Algorithms
		Complexity and Models	3. Parallel Algorithm Complexity 4. Models of Parallel Processing
	Part II: Extreme Models	Abstract View of Shared Memory	5. PRAM and Basic Algorithms 6. More Shared-Memory Algorithms
		Circuit Model of Parallel Systems	7. Sorting and Selection Networks 8. Other Circuit-Level Examples
	Part III: Mesh-Based Architectures	Data Movement on 2D Arrays	9. Sorting on a 2D Mesh or Torus 10. Routing on a 2D Mesh or Torus
		Mesh Algorithms and Variants	11. Numerical 2D Mesh Algorithms 12. Other Mesh-Related Architectures
	Part IV: Low-Diameter Architectures	The Hypercube Architecture	13. Hypercubes and Their Algorithms 14. Sorting and Routing on Hypercubes
		Hypercubic and Other Networks	15. Other Hypercubic Architectures 16. A Sampler of Other Networks
	Part V: Some Broad Topics	Coordination and Data Access	17. Emulation and Scheduling 18. Data Storage, Input, and Output
		Robustness and Ease of Use	19. Reliable Parallel Processing 20. System and Software Issues
	Part VI: Implementation Aspects	Control-Parallel Systems	21. Shared-Memory MIMD Machines 22. Message-Passing MIMD Machines
		Data Parallelism and Conclusion	23. Data-Parallel SIMD Machines 24. Past, Present, and Future

(Architectural Variations spans Parts II–IV)

The structure of this book in parts, half-parts, and chapters.

(two chapters) or full part (four chapters) as its "title." In this format, the half-parts, shown above, provide a focus for the weekly lecture and/or homework schedule.

An instructor's manual, with problem solutions and enlarged versions of the diagrams and tables, suitable for reproduction as transparencies, is planned. The author's detailed syllabus for the course ECE 254B at UCSB is available at http://www.ece.ucsb.edu/courses/syllabi/ece254b.html.

References to important or state-of-the-art research contributions and designs are provided at the end of each chapter. These references provide good starting points for doing in-depth studies or for preparing term papers/projects.

New ideas in the field of parallel processing appear in papers presented at several annual conferences, known as FMPC, ICPP, IPPS, SPAA, SPDP (now merged with IPPS), and in archival journals such as *IEEE Transactions on Computers* [TCom], *IEEE Transactions on Parallel and Distributed Systems* [TPDS], *Journal of Parallel and Distributed Computing* [JPDC], *Parallel Computing* [ParC], and *Parallel Processing Letters* [PPL]. Tutorial and survey papers of wide scope appear in *IEEE Concurrency* [Conc] and, occasionally, in *IEEE Computer* [Comp]. The articles in *IEEE Computer* provide excellent starting points for research projects and term papers.

ACKNOWLEDGMENTS

The current text, *Introduction to Parallel Processing: Algorithms and Architectures*, is an outgrowth of lecture notes that the author has used for the graduate course "ECE 254B: Advanced Computer Architecture: Parallel Processing" at the University of California, Santa Barbara, and, in rudimentary forms, at several other institutions prior to 1988. The text has benefited greatly from keen observations, curiosity, and encouragement of my many students in these courses. A sincere thanks to all of them! Particular thanks go to Dr. Ding-Ming Kwai who read an early version of the manuscript carefully and suggested numerous corrections and improvements.

GENERAL REFERENCES

[Akl89]   Akl, S. G., *The Design and Analysis of Parallel Algorithms*, Prentice–Hall, 1989.
[Akl97]   Akl, S. G., *Parallel Computation: Models and Methods*, Prentice–Hall, 1997.
[Alma94]   Almasi, G. S., and A. Gottlieb, *Highly Parallel Computing*, Benjamin/Cummings, 2nd ed., 1994.
[Bert89]   Bertsekas, D. P., and J. N. Tsitsiklis, *Parallel and Distributed Computation: Numerical Methods*, Prentice–Hall, 1989.
[Code93]   Codenotti, B., and M. Leoncini, *Introduction to Parallel Processing*, Addison–Wesley, 1993.
[Comp]   *IEEE Computer*, journal published by IEEE Computer Society; has occasional special issues on parallel/distributed processing (February 1982, June 1985, August 1986, June 1987, March 1988, August 1991, February 1992, November 1994, November 1995, December 1996).
[Conc]   *IEEE Concurrency*, formerly *IEEE Parallel and Distributed Technology*, magazine published by IEEE Computer Society.
[Cric88]   Crichlow, J. M., *Introduction to Distributed and Parallel Computing*, Prentice–Hall, 1988.
[DeCe89]   DeCegama, A. L., *Parallel Processing Architectures and VLSI Hardware*, Prentice–Hall, 1989.
[Desr87]   Desrochers, G. R., *Principles of Parallel and Multiprocessing*, McGraw-Hill, 1987.
[Duat97]   Duato, J., S. Yalamanchili, and L. Ni, *Interconnection Networks: An Engineering Approach*, IEEE Computer Society Press, 1997.
[Flyn95]   Flynn, M. J., *Computer Architecture: Pipelined and Parallel Processor Design*, Jones and Bartlett, 1995.
[FMPC]   *Proc. Symp. Frontiers of Massively Parallel Computation*, sponsored by IEEE Computer Society and NASA. Held every 1 1/2–2 years since 1986. The 6th FMPC was held in Annapolis, MD, October 27–31, 1996, and the 7th is planned for February 20–25, 1999.
[Foun94]   Fountain, T. J., *Parallel Computing: Principles and Practice*, Cambridge University Press, 1994.
[Hock81]   Hockney, R. W., and C. R. Jesshope, *Parallel Computers*, Adam Hilger, 1981.
[Hord90]   Hord, R. M., *Parallel Supercomputing in SIMD Architectures*, CRC Press, 1990.
[Hord93]   Hord, R. M., *Parallel Supercomputing in MIMD Architectures*, CRC Press, 1993.
[Hwan84]   Hwang, K., and F. A. Briggs, *Computer Architecture and Parallel Processing*, McGraw-Hill, 1984.
[Hwan93]   Hwang, K., *Advanced Computer Architecture: Parallelism, Scalability, Programmability*, McGraw-Hill, 1993.

[Hwan98]   Hwang, K., and Z. Xu, *Scalable Parallel Computing: Technology, Architecture, Programming*, McGraw-Hill, 1998.

[ICPP]   *Proc. Int. Conference Parallel Processing*, sponsored by The Ohio State University (and in recent years, also by the International Association for Computers and Communications). Held annually since 1972.

[IPPS]   *Proc. Int. Parallel Processing Symp.*, sponsored by IEEE Computer Society. Held annually since 1987. The 11th IPPS was held in Geneva, Switzerland, April 1–5, 1997. Beginning with the 1998 symposium in Orlando, FL, March 30–April 3, IPPS was merged with SPDP. **

[JaJa92]   JaJa, J., *An Introduction to Parallel Algorithms*, Addison–Wesley, 1992.

[JPDC]   *Journal of Parallel and Distributed Computing*, Published by Academic Press.

[Kris89]   Krishnamurthy, E. V., *Parallel Processing: Principles and Practice*, Addison–Wesley, 1989.

[Kuma94]   Kumar, V., A. Grama, A. Gupta, and G. Karypis, *Introduction to Parallel Computing: Design and Analysis of Algorithms*, Benjamin/Cummings, 1994.

[Laks90]   Lakshmivarahan, S., and S. K. Dhall, *Analysis and Design of Parallel Algorithms: Arithmetic and Matrix Problems*, McGraw-Hill, 1990.

[Leig92]   Leighton, F. T., *Introduction to Parallel Algorithms and Architectures: Arrays, Trees, Hypercubes*, Morgan Kaufmann, 1992.

[Lerm94]   Lerman, G., and L. Rudolph, *Parallel Evolution of Parallel Processors*, Plenum, 1994.

[Lipo87]   Lipovski, G. J., and M. Malek, *Parallel Computing: Theory and Comparisons*, Wiley, 1987.

[Mold93]   Moldovan, D. I., *Parallel Processing: From Applications to Systems*, Morgan Kaufmann, 1993.

[ParC]   *Parallel Computing*, journal published by North-Holland.

[PPL]   *Parallel Processing Letters*, journal published by World Scientific.

[Quin87]   Quinn, M. J., *Designing Efficient Algorithms for Parallel Computers*, McGraw-Hill, 1987.

[Quin94]   Quinn, M. J., *Parallel Computing: Theory and Practice*, McGraw-Hill, 1994.

[Reif93]   Reif, J. H. (ed.), *Synthesis of Parallel Algorithms*, Morgan Kaufmann, 1993.

[Sanz89]   Sanz, J. L. C. (ed.), *Opportunities and Constraints of Parallel Computing* (IBM/NSF Workshop, San Jose, CA, December 1988), Springer-Verlag, 1989.

[Shar87]   Sharp, J. A., *An Introduction to Distributed and Parallel Processing*, Blackwell Scientific Publications, 1987.

[Sieg85]   Siegel, H. J., *Interconnection Networks for Large-Scale Parallel Processing*, Lexington Books, 1985.

[SPAA]   *Proc. Symp. Parallel Algorithms and Architectures*, sponsored by the Association for Computing Machinery (ACM). Held annually since 1989. The 10th SPAA was held in Puerto Vallarta, Mexico, June 28–July 2, 1998.

[SPDP]   *Proc. Int. Symp. Parallel and Distributed Systems*, sponsored by IEEE Computer Society. Held annually since 1989, except for 1997. The 8th SPDP was held in New Orleans, LA, October 23–26, 1996. Beginning with the 1998 symposium in Orlando, FL, March 30–April 3, SPDP was merged with IPPS.

[Ston93]   Stone, H. S., *High-Performance Computer Architecture*, Addison–Wesley, 1993.

[TCom]   *IEEE Trans. Computers*, journal published by IEEE Computer Society; has occasional special issues on parallel and distributed processing (April 1987, December 1988, August 1989, December 1991, April 1997, April 1998).

[TPDS]   *IEEE Trans. Parallel and Distributed Systems*, journal published by IEEE Computer Society.

[Varm94]   Varma, A., and C. S. Raghavendra, *Interconnection Networks for Multiprocessors and Multicomputers: Theory and Practice*, IEEE Computer Society Press, 1994.

[Zoma96]   Zomaya, A. Y. (ed.), *Parallel and Distributed Computing Handbook*, McGraw-Hill, 1996.

*The 27th ICPP was held in Minneapolis, MN, August 10–15, 1998, and the 28th is scheduled for September 21–24, 1999, in Aizu, Japan.

**The next joint IPPS/SPDP is sceduled for April 12–16, 1999, in San Juan, Puerto Rico.

Contents

Introduction to
Parallel Processing
Algorithms and Architectures

Fundamental Concepts

The field of parallel processing is concerned with architectural and algorithmic methods for enhancing the performance or other attributes (e.g., cost-effectiveness, reliability) of digital computers through various forms of concurrency. Even though concurrent computation has been around since the early days of digital computers, only recently has it been applied in a manner, and on a scale, that leads to better performance, or greater cost-effectiveness, compared with vector supercomputers. Like any other field of science/technology, the study of parallel architectures and algorithms requires motivation, a big picture showing the relationships between problems and the various approaches to solving them, and models for comparing, connecting, and evaluating new ideas. This part, which motivates us to study parallel processing, paints the big picture, and provides some needed background, is composed of four chapters:

- Chapter 1: Introduction to Parallelism
- Chapter 2: A Taste of Parallel Algorithms
- Chapter 3: Parallel Algorithm Complexity
- Chapter 4: Models of Parallel Processing

1

Introduction to Parallelism

This chapter sets the context in which the material in the rest of the book will be presented and reviews some of the challenges facing the designers and users of parallel computers. The chapter ends with the introduction of useful metrics for evaluating the effectiveness of parallel systems. Chapter topics are

1.1. WHY PARALLEL PROCESSING?

The quest for higher-performance digital computers seems unending. In the past two decades, the performance of microprocessors has enjoyed an exponential growth. The growth of microprocessor speed/performance by a factor of 2 every 18 months (or about 60% per year) is known as Moore's law. This growth is the result of a combination of two factors:

1. Increase in complexity (related both to higher device density and to larger size) of VLSI chips, projected to rise to around 10 M transistors per chip for microprocessors, and 1B for dynamic random-access memories (DRAMs), by the year 2000 [SIA94]
2. Introduction of, and improvements in, architectural features such as on-chip cache memories, large instruction buffers, multiple instruction issue per cycle, multithreading, deep pipelines, out-of-order instruction execution, and branch prediction

Moore's law was originally formulated in 1965 in terms of the doubling of chip complexity every year (later revised to every 18 months) based only on a small number of data points [Scha97]. Moore's revised prediction matches almost perfectly the actual increases in the number of transistors in DRAM and microprocessor chips.

Moore's law seems to hold regardless of how one measures processor performance: counting the number of executed instructions per second (IPS), counting the number of floating-point operations per second (FLOPS), or using sophisticated benchmark suites that attempt to measure the processor's performance on real applications. This is because all of these measures, though numerically different, tend to rise at roughly the same rate. Figure 1.1 shows that the performance of actual processors has in fact followed Moore's law quite closely since 1980 and is on the verge of reaching the GIPS (giga IPS = 10^9 IPS) milestone.

Even though it is expected that Moore's law will continue to hold for the near future, there is a limit that will eventually be reached. That some previous predictions about when the limit will be reached have proven wrong does not alter the fact that a limit, dictated by physical laws, does exist. The most easily understood physical limit is that imposed by the finite speed of signal propagation along a wire. This is sometimes referred to as the speed-of-light argument (or limit), explained as follows.

The Speed-of-Light Argument. The speed of light is about 30 cm/ns. Signals travel on a wire at a fraction of the speed of light. If the chip diameter is 3 cm, say, any computation that involves signal transmission from one end of the chip to another cannot be executed faster than 10^{10} times per second. Reducing distances by a factor of 10 or even 100 will only increase the limit by these factors; we still cannot go beyond 10^{12} computations per second. To relate the above limit to the instruction execution rate (MIPS or FLOPS), we need to estimate the distance that signals *must* travel within an instruction cycle. This is not easy to do, given the extensive use of pipelining and memory-latency-hiding techniques in modern high-performance processors. Despite this difficulty, it should be clear that we are in fact not very far from limits imposed by the speed of signal propagation and several other physical laws.

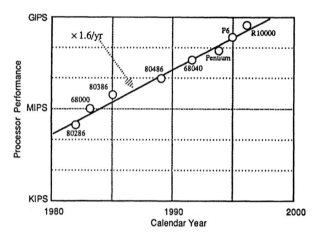

Figure 1.1. The exponential growth of microprocessor performance, known as Moore's law, shown over the past two decades.

The speed-of-light argument suggests that once the above limit has been reached, the only path to improved performance is the use of multiple processors. Of course, the same argument can be invoked to conclude that any parallel processor will also be limited by the speed at which the various processors can communicate with each other. However, because such communication does not have to occur for every low-level computation, the limit is less serious here. In fact, for many applications, a large number of computation steps can be performed between two successive communication steps, thus amortizing the communication overhead.

Here is another way to show the need for parallel processing. Figure 1.2 depicts the improvement in performance for the most advanced high-end supercomputers in the same 20-year period covered by Fig. 1.1. Two classes of computers have been included: (1) Cray-type pipelined vector supercomputers, represented by the lower straight line, and (2) massively parallel processors (MPPs) corresponding to the shorter upper lines [Bell92].

We see from Fig. 1.2 that the first class will reach the TFLOPS performance benchmark around the turn of the century. Even assuming that the performance of such machines will continue to improve at this rate beyond the year 2000, the next milestone, i.e., PFLOPS (peta FLOPS = 10^{15} FLOPS) performance, will not be reached until the year 2015. With massively parallel computers, TFLOPS performance is already at hand, albeit at a relatively high cost. PFLOPS performance within this class should be achievable in the 2000–2005 time frame, again assuming continuation of the current trends. In fact, we already know of one serious roadblock to continued progress at this rate: Research in the area of massively parallel computing is not being funded at the levels it enjoyed in the 1980s.

But who needs supercomputers with TFLOPS or PFLOPS performance? Applications of state-of-the-art high-performance computers in military, space research, and climate modeling are conventional wisdom. Lesser known are applications in auto crash or engine combustion simulation, design of pharmaceuticals, design and evaluation of complex ICs, scientific visualization, and multimedia. In addition to these areas, whose current computational needs are met by existing supercomputers, there are unmet computational needs in

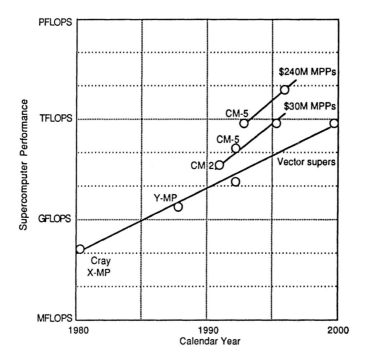

Figure 1.2. The exponential growth in supercomputer performance over the past two decades [Bell92].

aerodynamic simulation of an entire aircraft, modeling of global climate over decades, and investigating the atomic structures of advanced materials.

Let us consider a few specific applications, in the area of numerical simulation for validating scientific hypotheses or for developing behavioral models, where TFLOPS performance is required and PFLOPS performance would be highly desirable [Quin94].

To learn how the southern oceans transport heat to the South Pole, the following model has been developed at Oregon State University. The ocean is divided into 4096 regions E–W, 1024 regions N–S, and 12 layers in depth (50 M 3D cells). A single iteration of the model simulates ocean circulation for 10 minutes and involves about 30B floating-point operations. To carry out the simulation for 1 year, about 50,000 iterations are required. Simulation for 6 years would involve 10^{16} floating-point operations.

In the field of fluid dynamics, the volume under study may be modeled by a $10^3 \times 10^3 \times 10^3$ lattice, with about 10^3 floating-point operations needed per point over 10^4 time steps. This too translates to 10^{16} floating-point operations.

As a final example, in Monte Carlo simulation of a nuclear reactor, about 10^{11} particles must be tracked, as about 1 in 10^8 particles escape from a nuclear reactor and, for accuracy, we need at least 10^3 escapes in the simulation. With 10^4 floating-point operations needed per particle tracked, the total computation constitutes about 10^{15} floating-point operations.

From the above, we see that 10^{15}–10^{16} floating-point operations are required for many applications. If we consider 10^3–10^4 seconds a reasonable running time for such computations, the need for TFLOPS performance is evident. In fact, researchers have already begun working toward the next milestone of PFLOPS performance, which would be needed to run the above models with higher accuracy (e.g., 10 times finer subdivisions in each of three dimensions) or for longer durations (more steps).

The motivations for parallel processing can be summarized as follows:

1.   Higher speed, or solving problems faster. This is important when applications have "hard" or "soft" deadlines. For example, we have at most a few hours of computation time to do 24-hour weather forecasting or to produce timely tornado warnings.
2.   Higher throughput, or solving more instances of given problems. This is important when many similar tasks must be performed. For example, banks and airlines, among others, use transaction processing systems that handle large volumes of data.
3.   Higher computational power, or solving larger problems. This would allow us to use very detailed, and thus more accurate, models or to carry out simulation runs for longer periods of time (e.g., 5-day, as opposed to 24-hour, weather forecasting).

All three aspects above are captured by a figure-of-merit often used in connection with parallel processors: the computation *speed-up* factor with respect to a uniprocessor. The ultimate efficiency in parallel systems is to achieve a computation speed-up factor of p with p processors. Although in many cases this ideal cannot be achieved, *some* speed-up is generally possible. The actual gain in speed depends on the architecture used for the system and the algorithm run on it. Of course, for a task that is (virtually) impossible to perform on a single processor in view of its excessive running time, the computation speed-up factor can rightly be taken to be larger than p or even infinite. This situation, which is the analogue of several men moving a heavy piece of machinery or furniture in a few minutes, whereas one of them could not move it at all, is sometimes referred to as *parallel synergy*.

This book focuses on the interplay of *architectural* and *algorithmic* speed-up techniques. More specifically, the problem of algorithm design for *general-purpose* parallel systems and its "converse," the incorporation of architectural features to help improve algorithm efficiency and, in the extreme, the design of algorithm-based special-purpose parallel architectures, are considered.

1.2.   A MOTIVATING EXAMPLE

A major issue in devising a parallel algorithm for a given problem is the way in which the computational load is divided between the multiple processors. The most efficient scheme often depends both on the problem and on the parallel machine's architecture. This section exposes some of the key issues in parallel processing through a simple example [Quin94].

Consider the problem of constructing the list of all prime numbers in the interval $[1, n]$ for a given integer $n > 0$. A simple algorithm that can be used for this computation is the sieve of Eratosthenes. Start with the list of numbers $1, 2, 3, 4, \ldots, n$ represented as a "mark" bit-vector initialized to $1000 \ldots 00$. In each step, the next unmarked number m (associated with a 0 in element m of the mark bit-vector) is a prime. Find this element m and mark all multiples of m beginning with m^2. When $m^2 > n$, the computation stops and all unmarked elements are prime numbers. The computation steps for $n = 30$ are shown in Fig. 1.3.

2	3	4	5	6	7	8	9	10	11	12	13	14	15	16	17	18	19	20	21	22	23	24	25	26	27	28	29	30
2	3		5		7		9		11		13		15		17		19		21		23		25		27		29	
2	3		5		7				11		13				17		19				23		25				29	
2	3		5		7				11		13				17		19				23						29	

$m=2$ (under 2, first row), $m=3$ (under 3, second row), $m=5$ (under 5, third row), $m=7$ (under 7, fourth row)

Figure 1.3. The sieve of Eratosthenes yielding a list of 10 primes for $n = 30$. Marked elements have been distinguished by erasure from the list.

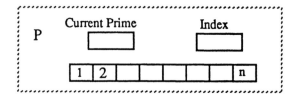

Figure 1.4. Schematic representation of single-processor solution for the sieve of Eratosthenes.

Figure 1.4 shows a single-processor implementation of the algorithm. The variable "current prime" is initialized to 2 and, in later stages, holds the latest prime number found. For each prime found, "index" is initialized to the square of this prime and is then incremented by the current prime in order to mark all of its multiples.

Figure 1.5 shows our first parallel solution using p processors. The list of numbers and the current prime are stored in a shared memory that is accessible to all processors. An idle processor simply refers to the shared memory, updates the current prime, and uses its private index to step through the list and mark the multiples of that prime. Division of work is thus self-regulated. Figure 1.6 shows the activities of the processors (the prime they are working on at any given instant) and the termination time for $n = 1000$ and $1 \le p \le 3$. Note that using more than three processors would not reduce the computation time in this control-parallel scheme.

We next examine a data-parallel approach in which the bit-vector representing the n integers is divided into p equal-length segments, with each segment stored in the private memory of one processor (Fig. 1.7). Assume that $p < \sqrt{n}$, so that all of the primes whose multiples have to be marked reside in Processor 1, which acts as a coordinator: It finds the next prime and broadcasts it to all other processors, which then proceed to mark the numbers in their sublists. The overall solution time now consists of two components: the time spent on transmitting the selected primes to all processors (communication time) and the time spent by individual processors marking their sublists (computation time). Typically, communication time grows with the number of processors, though not necessarily in a linear fashion. Figure 1.8 shows that because of the abovementioned communication overhead, adding more processors beyond a certain optimal number does not lead to any improvement in the total solution time or in attainable speed-up.

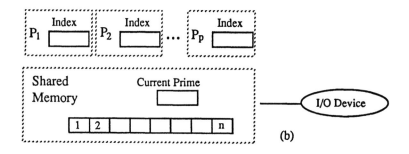

(b)

Figure 1.5. Schematic representation of a control-parallel solution for the sieve of Eratosthenes.

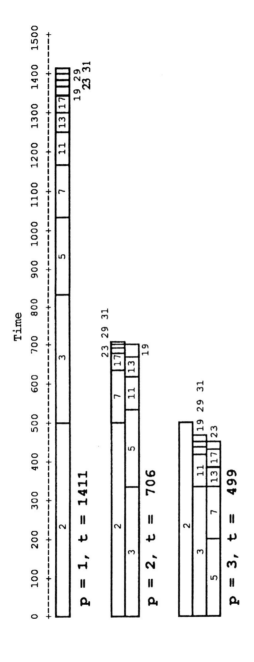

Figure 1.6. Control-parallel realization or the sieve of Eratosthenes with $n = 1000$ and $1 \leq p \leq 3$.

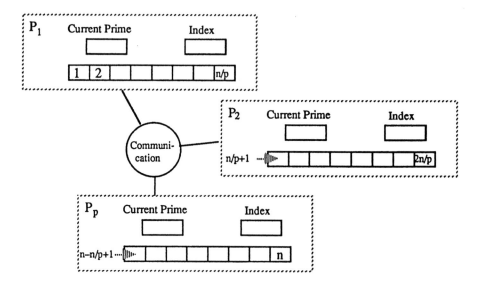

Figure 1.7. Data-parallel realization of the sieve of Eratosthenes.

Finally, consider the data-parallel solution, but with data I/O time also included in the total solution time. Assuming for simplicity that the I/O time is constant and ignoring communication time, the I/O time will constitute a larger fraction of the overall solution time as the computation part is speeded up by adding more and more processors. If I/O takes 100 seconds, say, then there is little difference between doing the computation part in 1 second or in 0.01 second. We will later see that such "sequential" or "unparallelizable" portions of computations severely limit the speed-up that can be achieved with parallel processing. Figure 1.9 shows the effect of I/O on the total solution time and the attainable speed-up.

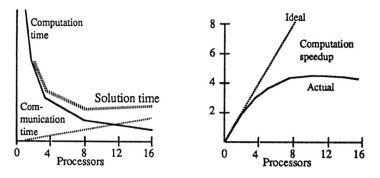

Figure 1.8. Trade-off between communication time and computation time in the data-parallel realization of the sieve of Eratosthenes.

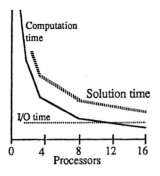 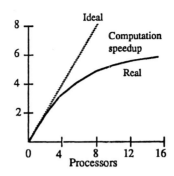

Figure 1.9. Effect of a constant I/O time on the data-parallel realization of the sieve of Eratosthenes.

1.3. PARALLEL PROCESSING UPS AND DOWNS

L. F. Richardson, a British meteorologist, was the first person to attempt to forecast the weather using numerical computations. He started to formulate his method during the First World War while serving in the army ambulance corps. He estimated that predicting the weather for a 24-hour period would require 64,000 slow "computers" (humans + mechanical calculators) and even then, the forecast would take 12 hours to complete. He had the following idea or dream:

> Imagine a large hall like a theater. . . . The walls of this chamber are painted to form a map of the globe. . . . A myriad of computers are at work upon the weather on the part of the map where each sits, but each computer attends to only one equation or part of an equation. The work of each region is coordinated by an official of higher rank. Numerous little 'night signs' display the instantaneous values so that neighbouring computers can read them. . . . One of [the conductor's] duties is to maintain a uniform speed of progress in all parts of the globe. . . . But instead of waving a baton, he turns a beam of rosy light upon any region that is running ahead of the rest, and a beam of blue light upon those that are behindhand. [See Fig. 1.10.]

Parallel processing, in the literal sense of the term, is used in virtually every modern computer. For example, overlapping I/O with computation is a form of parallel processing, as is the overlap between instruction preparation and execution in a pipelined processor. Other forms of parallelism or *concurrency* that are widely used include the use of multiple functional units (e.g., separate integer and floating-point ALUs or two floating-point multipliers in one ALU) and multitasking (which allows overlap between computation and memory load necessitated by a page fault). Horizontal microprogramming, and its higher-level incarnation in very-long-instruction-word (VLIW) computers, also allows some parallelism. However, in this book, the term *parallel processing* is used in a restricted sense of having multiple (usually identical) processors for the main computation and not for the I/O or other peripheral activities.

The history of parallel processing has had its ups and downs (read company formations and bankruptcies!) with what appears to be a 20-year cycle. Serious interest in parallel processing started in the 1960s. ILLIAC IV, designed at the University of Illinois and later

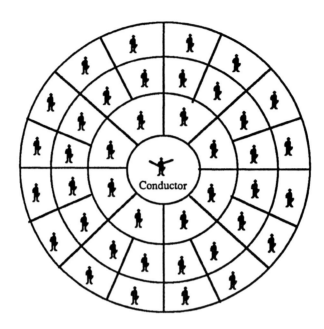

Figure 1.10. Richardson's circular theater for weather forecasting calculations.

built and operated by Burroughs Corporation, was the first large-scale parallel computer implemented; its 2D-mesh architecture with a common control unit for all processors was based on theories developed in the late 1950s. It was to scale to 256 processors (four quadrants of 64 processors each). Only one 64-processor quadrant was eventually built, but it clearly demonstrated the feasibility of highly parallel computers and also revealed some of the difficulties in their use.

Commercial interest in parallel processing resurfaced in the 1980s. Driven primarily by contracts from the defense establishment and other federal agencies in the United States, numerous companies were formed to develop parallel systems. Established computer vendors also initiated or expanded their parallel processing divisions. However, three factors led to another recess:

1. Government funding in the United States and other countries dried up, in part related to the end of the cold war between the NATO allies and the Soviet bloc.
2. Commercial users in banking and other data-intensive industries were either saturated or disappointed by application difficulties.
3. Microprocessors developed so fast in terms of performance/cost ratio that custom-designed parallel machines always lagged in cost-effectiveness.

Many of the newly formed companies went bankrupt or shifted their focus to developing software for distributed (workstation cluster) applications.

Driven by the Internet revolution and its associated "information providers," a third resurgence of parallel architectures is imminent. Centralized, high-performance machines may be needed to satisfy the information processing/access needs of some of these providers.

1.4. TYPES OF PARALLELISM: A TAXONOMY

Parallel computers can be divided into two main categories of control flow and data flow. Control-flow parallel computers are essentially based on the same principles as the sequential or von Neumann computer, except that multiple instructions can be executed at any given time. Data-flow parallel computers, sometimes referred to as "non-von Neumann," are completely different in that they have no pointer to active instruction(s) or a locus of control. The control is totally distributed, with the availability of operands triggering the activation of instructions. In what follows, we will focus exclusively on control-flow parallel computers.

In 1966, M. J. Flynn proposed a four-way classification of computer systems based on the notions of instruction streams and data streams. Flynn's classification has become standard and is widely used. Flynn coined the abbreviations SISD, SIMD, MISD, and MIMD (pronounced "sis-dee," "sim-dee," and so forth) for the four classes of computers shown in Fig. 1.11, based on the number of instruction streams (single or multiple) and data streams (single or multiple) [Flyn96]. The SISD class represents ordinary "uniprocessor" machines. Computers in the SIMD class, with several processors directed by instructions issued from a central control unit, are sometimes characterized as "array processors." Machines in the MISD category have not found widespread application, but one can view them as generalized pipelines in which each stage performs a relatively complex operation (as opposed to ordinary pipelines found in modern processors where each stage does a very simple instruction-level operation).

The MIMD category includes a wide class of computers. For this reason, in 1988, E. E. Johnson proposed a further classification of such machines based on their memory structure (global or distributed) and the mechanism used for communication/synchronization (shared variables or message passing). Again, one of the four categories (GMMP) is not widely used. The GMSV class is what is loosely referred to as (*shared-memory*) *multiprocessors*. At the

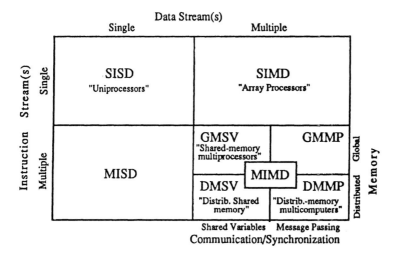

Figure 1.11. The Flynn–Johnson classification of computer systems.

other extreme, the DMMP class is known as *(distributed-memory) multicomputers*. Finally, the DMSV class, which is becoming popular in view of combining the implementation ease of distributed memory with the programming ease of the shared-variable scheme, is sometimes called *distributed shared memory*. When all processors in a MIMD-type machine execute the same program, the result is sometimes referred to as *single-program multiple-data* [SPMD (spim-dee)].

Although Fig. 1.11 lumps all SIMD machines together, there are in fact variations similar to those suggested above for MIMD machines. At least conceptually, there can be shared-memory and distributed-memory SIMD machines in which the processors communicate by means of shared variables or explicit message passing.

Anecdote. The Flynn–Johnson classification of Fig. 1.11 contains eight four-letter abbreviations. There are many other such abbreviations and acronyms in parallel processing, examples being CISC, NUMA, PRAM, RISC, and VLIW. Even our journals (JPDC, TPDS) and conferences (ICPP, IPPS, SPDP, SPAA) have not escaped this fascination with four-letter abbreviations. The author has a theory that an individual cannot be considered a successful computer architect until she or he has coined at least one, and preferably a group of two or four, such abbreviations! Toward this end, the author coined the acronyms SINC and FINC (Scant/Full Interaction Network Cell) as the communication network counterparts to the popular RISC/CISC dichotomy [Parh95]. Alas, the use of these acronyms is not yet as widespread as that of RISC/CISC. In fact, they are not used at all.

1.5. ROADBLOCKS TO PARALLEL PROCESSING

Over the years, the enthusiasm of parallel computer designers and researchers has been counteracted by many objections and cautionary statements. The most important of these are listed in this section [Quin87]. The list begins with the less serious, or obsolete, objections and ends with Amdahl's law, which perhaps constitutes the most important challenge facing parallel computer designers and users.

1. *Grosch's law* (economy of scale applies, or computing power is proportional to the square of cost). If this law did in fact hold, investing money in p processors would be foolish as a single computer with the same total cost could offer p^2 times the performance of one such processor. Grosch's law was formulated in the days of giant mainframes and actually did hold for those machines. In the early days of parallel processing, it was offered as an argument against the cost-effectiveness of parallel machines. However, we can now safely retire this law, as we can buy more MFLOPS computing power per dollar by spending on micros rather than on supers. Note that even if this law did hold, one could counter that there is only one "fastest" single-processor computer and it has a certain price; you cannot get a more powerful one by spending more.

2. *Minsky's conjecture* (speed-up is proportional to the logarithm of the number p of processors). This conjecture has its roots in an analysis of data access conflicts assuming random distribution of addresses. These conflicts will slow everything down to the point that quadrupling the number of processors only doubles the performance. However, data access patterns in real applications are far from

random. Most applications have a pleasant amount of data access regularity and locality that help improve the performance. One might say that the log p speed-up rule is one side of the coin that has the perfect speed-up p on the flip side. Depending on the application, real speed-up can range from log p to p (p/log p being a reasonable middle ground).

3. *The tyranny of IC technology* (because hardware becomes about 10 times faster every 5 years, by the time a parallel machine with 10-fold performance is designed and implemented, uniprocessors will be just as fast). This objection might be valid for some special-purpose systems that must be built from scratch with "old" technology. Recent experience in parallel machine design has shown that off-the-shelf components can be used in synthesizing massively parallel computers. If the design of the parallel processor is such that faster microprocessors can simply be plugged in as they become available, they too benefit from advancements in IC technology. Besides, why restrict our attention to parallel systems that are designed to be only 10 times faster rather than 100 or 1000 times?

4. *The tyranny of vector supercomputers* (vector supercomputers, built by Cray, Fujitsu, and other companies, are rapidly improving in performance and additionally offer a familiar programming model and excellent vectorizing compilers; why bother with parallel processors?). Figure 1.2 contains a possible answer to this objection. Besides, not all computationally intensive applications deal with vectors or matrices; some are in fact quite irregular. Note, also, that vector and parallel processing are complementary approaches. Most current vector supercomputers do in fact come in multiprocessor configurations for increased performance.

5. *The software inertia* (billions of dollars worth of existing software makes it hard to switch to parallel systems; the cost of converting the "dusty decks" to parallel programs and retraining the programmers is prohibitive). This objection is valid in the short term; however, not all programs needed in the future have already been written. New applications will be developed and many new problems will become solvable with increased performance. Students are already being trained to think parallel. Additionally, tools are being developed to transform sequential code into parallel code automatically. In fact, it has been argued that it might be prudent to develop programs in parallel languages even if they are to be run on sequential computers. The added information about concurrency and data dependencies would allow the sequential computer to improve its performance by instruction prefetching, data caching, and so forth.

6. *Amdahl's law* (speed-up $\leq 1/[f + (1 - f)/p] = p/[1 + f(p - 1)]$; a small fraction f of inherently sequential or unparallelizable computation severely limits the speed-up that can be achieved with p processors). This is by far the most important of the six objections/warnings. A unit-time task, for which the fraction f is unparallelizable (so it takes the same time f on both sequential and parallel machines) and the remaining $1 - f$ is fully parallelizable [so it runs in time $(1 - f)/p$ on a p-processor machine], has a running time of $f + (1 - f)/p$ on the parallel machine, hence Amdahl's speed-up formula.

Figure 1.12 plots the speed-up as a function of the number of processors for different values of the inherently sequential fraction f. The speed-up can never exceed $1/f$, no matter how

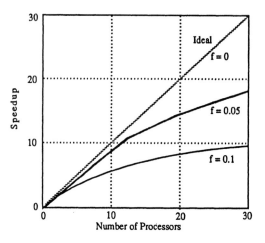

Figure 1.12. The limit on speed-up according to Amdahl's law.

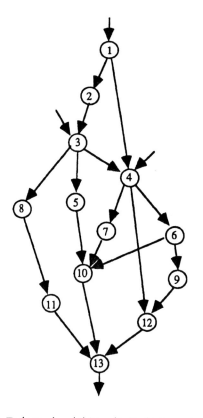

Figure 1.13. Task graph exhibiting limited inherent parallelism.

many processors are used. Thus, for $f = 0.1$, speed-up has an upper bound of 10. Fortunately, there exist applications for which the sequential overhead is very small. Furthermore, the sequential overhead need not be a constant fraction of the job independent of problem size. In fact, the existence of applications for which the sequential overhead, as a fraction of the overall computational work, diminishes has been demonstrated.

Closely related to Amdahl's law is the observation that some applications lack inherent parallelism, thus limiting the speed-up that is achievable when multiple processors are used. Figure 1.13 depicts a task graph characterizing a computation. Each of the numbered nodes in the graph is a unit-time computation and the arrows represent data dependencies or the prerequisite structure of the graph. A single processor can execute the 13-node task graph shown in Fig. 1.13 in 13 time units. Because the critical path from input node 1 to output node 13 goes through 8 nodes, a parallel processor cannot do much better, as it needs at least 8 time units to execute the task graph. So, the speed-up associated with this particular task graph can never exceed 1.625, no matter how many processors are used.

1.6. EFFECTIVENESS OF PARALLEL PROCESSING

Throughout the book, we will be using certain measures to compare the effectiveness of various parallel algorithms or architectures for solving desired problems. The following definitions and notations are applicable [Lee80]:

p	Number of processors
$W(p)$	Total number of unit operations performed by the p processors; this is often referred to as computational work or energy
$T(p)$	Execution time with p processors; clearly, $T(1) = W(1)$ and $T(p) \leq W(p)$
$S(p)$	Speed-up $= \dfrac{T(1)}{T(p)}$
$E(p)$	Efficiency $= \dfrac{T(1)}{pT(p)}$
$R(p)$	Redundancy $= \dfrac{W(p)}{W(1)}$
$U(p)$	Utilization $= \dfrac{W(p)}{pT(p)}$
$Q(p)$	Quality $= \dfrac{T^3(1)}{pT^2(p)W(p)}$

The significance of each measure is self-evident from its name and defining equation given above. It is not difficult to establish the following relationships between these parameters. The proof is left as an exercise.

$$1 \leq S(p) \leq p$$

$$U(p) = R(p)E(p)$$

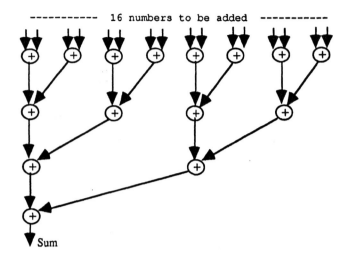

Figure 1.14. Computation graph for finding the sum of 16 numbers.

$$E(p) = \frac{S(p)}{p}$$

$$Q(p) = E(p)\,\frac{S(p)}{R(p)}$$

$$\frac{1}{p} \leq E(p) \leq U(p) \leq 1$$

$$1 \leq R(p) \leq \frac{1}{E(p)} \leq p$$

$$Q(P) \leq S(p) \leq p$$

Example. Finding the sum of 16 numbers can be represented by the binary-tree computation graph of Fig. 1.14 with $T(1) = W(1) = 15$. Assume unit-time additions and ignore all else. With $p = 8$ processors, we have

$W(8) = 15$	$T(8) = 4$	$E(8) = 15/(8 \times 4) = 47\%$
$S(8) = 15/4 = 3.75$	$R(8) = 15/15 = 1$	$Q(8) = 1.76$

Essentially, the 8 processors perform all of the additions at the same tree level in each time unit, beginning with the leaf nodes and ending at the root. The relatively low efficiency is the result of limited parallelism near the root of the tree.

Now, assuming that addition operations that are vertically aligned in Fig. 1.14 are to be performed by the same processor and that each interprocessor transfer, represented by an oblique arrow, also requires one unit of work (time), the results for $p = 8$ processors become

$$W(8) = 22 \qquad\qquad T(8) = 7 \qquad\qquad E(8) = 15/(8 \times 7) = 27\%$$

$$S(8) = 15/7 = 2.14 \qquad R(8) = 22/15 = 1.47 \qquad Q(8) = 0.39$$

The efficiency in this latter case is even lower, primarily because the interprocessor transfers constitute overhead rather than useful operations.

PROBLEMS

1.1. Ocean heat transport modeling
     Assume continuation of the trends in Figs. 1.1 and 1.2:

   a. When will a single microprocessor be capable of simulating 10 years of global ocean circulation, as described in Section 1.1, overnight (5:00 PM to 8:00 AM the following day), assuming a doubling of the number of divisions in each of the three dimensions? You can assume that a microprocessor's FLOPS rating is roughly half of its MIPS rating.
   b. When will a vector supercomputer be capable of the computation defined in part (a)?
   c. When will a $240M massively parallel computer be capable of the computation of part (a)?
   d. When will a $30M massively parallel computer be capable of the computation of part (a)?

1.2. Micros versus supers
     Draw the performance trend line for microprocessors on Fig. 1.2, assuming that a microprocessor's FLOPS rating is roughly half of its MIPS rating. Compare and discuss the observed trends.

1.3. Sieve of Eratosthenes
     Figure 1.6 shows that in the control-parallel implementation of the sieve of Eratosthenes algorithm, a single processor is always responsible for sieving the multiples of 2. For $n = 1000$, this is roughly 35% of the total work performed. By Amdahl's law, the maximum possible speed-up for $p = 2$ and $f = 0.35$ is 1.48. Yet, for $p = 2$, we note a speed-up of about 2 in Fig. 1.6. What is wrong with the above reasoning?

1.4. Sieve of Eratosthenes
     Consider the data-parallel implementation of the sieve of Eratosthenes algorithm for $n = 10^6$. Assume that marking of each cell takes 1 time unit and broadcasting a value to all processors takes b time units.

   a. Plot three speed-up curves similar to Fig. 1.8 for $b = 1, 10$, and 100 and discuss the results.
   b. Repeat part (a), this time assuming that the broadcast time is a linear function of the number of processors: $b = \alpha p + \beta$, with $(\alpha, \beta) = (5, 1), (5, 10), (5, 100)$.

1.5. Sieve of Eratosthenes
     Consider the data-parallel implementation of the sieve of Eratosthenes algorithm for $n = 10^6$. Assume that marking of each cell takes 1 time unit and broadcasting m numbers to all processors takes $b + cm$ time units, where b and c are constants. For each of the values 1, 10, and 100 for the parameter b, determine the range of values for c where it would be more cost-effective for Processor 1 to send the list of all primes that it is holding to all other processors in a single message before the actual markings begin.

1.6. Sieve of Eratosthenes

    a. Noting that 2 is the only even prime, propose a modification to the sieve of Eratosthenes algorithm that requires less storage.

    b. Draw a diagram, similar to Fig. 1.6, for the control-parallel implementation of the improved algorithm. Derive the speed-ups for two and three processors.

    c. Compute the speed-up of the data-parallel implementation of the improved algorithm over the sequential version.

    d. Compare the speed-ups of parts (b) and (c) with those obtained for the original algorithm.

1.7. Amdahl's law

Amdahl's law can be applied in contexts other than parallel processing. Suppose that a numerical application consists of 20% floating-point and 80% integer/control operations (these are based on operation counts rather than their execution times). The execution time of a floating-point operation is three times as long as other operations. We are considering a redesign of the floating-point unit in a microprocessor to make it faster.

    a. Formulate a more general version of Amdahl's law in terms of selective speed-up of a portion of a computation rather than in terms of parallel processing.

    b. How much faster should the new floating-point unit be for 25% overall speed improvement?

    c. What is the maximum speed-up that we can hope to achieve by only modifying the floating-point unit?

1.8. Amdahl's law

    a. Represent Amdahl's law in terms of a task or computation graph similar to that in Fig. 1.13. *Hint*: Use an input and an output node, each with computation time $f/2$, where f is the inherently sequential fraction.

    b. Approximate the task/computation graph of part (a) with one having only unit-time nodes.

1.9. Parallel processing effectiveness

Consider two versions of the task graph in Fig. 1.13. Version U corresponds to each node requiring unit computation time. Version E/O corresponds to each odd-numbered node being unit-time and each even-numbered node taking twice as long.

    a. Convert the E/O version to an equivalent V version where each node is unit-time.

    b. Find the maximum attainable speed-up for each of the U and V versions.

    c. What is the minimum number of processors needed to achieve the speed-ups of part (b)?

    d. What is the maximum attainable speed-up in each case with three processors?

    e. Which of the U and V versions of the task graph would you say is "more parallel" and why?

1.10. Parallel processing effectiveness

Prove the relationships between the parameters in Section 1.6.

1.11. Parallel processing effectiveness

An image processing application problem is characterized by 12 unit-time tasks: (1) an input task that must be completed before any other task can start and consumes the entire bandwidth of the single-input device available, (2) 10 completely independent computational tasks, and (3) an output task that must follow the completion of all other tasks and consumes the entire bandwidth of the single-output device available. Assume the availability of one input and one output device throughout.

    a. Draw the task graph for this image processing application problem.

    b. What is the maximum speed-up that can be achieved for this application with two processors?

    c. What is an upper bound on the speed-up with parallel processing?

    d. How many processors are sufficient to achieve the maximum speed-up derived in part (c)?

    e. What is the maximum speed-up in solving five independent instances of the problem on two processors?

    f. What is an upper bound on the speed-up in parallel solution of 100 independent instances of the problem?

    g. How many processors are sufficient to achieve the maximum speed-up derived in part (f)?

    h. What is an upper bound on the speed-up, given a steady stream of independent problem instances?

1.12. Parallelism in everyday life

    Discuss the various forms of parallelism used to speed up the following processes:

    a. Student registration at a university.

    b. Shopping at a supermarket.

    c. Taking an elevator in a high-rise building.

1.13. Parallelism for fame or fortune

    In 1997, Andrew Beale, a Dallas banker and amateur mathematician, put up a gradually increasing prize of up to U.S. \$50,000 for proving or disproving his conjecture that if $a^q + b^r = c^s$ (where all terms are integers and $q, r, s > 2$), then $a, b,$ and c have a common factor. Beale's conjecture is, in effect, a general form of Fermat's Last Theorem, which asserts that $a^n + b^n = c^n$ has no integer solution for $n > 2$. Discuss how parallel processing can be used to claim the prize.

REFERENCES AND SUGGESTED READING

[Bell92]   Bell, G., "Ultracomputers: A Teraflop Before Its Time," *Communications of the ACM*, Vol. 35, No. 8, pp. 27–47, August 1992.

[Flyn96]   Flynn, M. J., and K. W. Rudd, "Parallel Architectures," *ACM Computing Surveys*, Vol. 28, No. 1, pp. 67–70, March 1996.

[John88]   Johnson, E. E., "Completing an MIMD Multiprocessor Taxonomy," *Computer Architecture News*, Vol. 16, No. 3, pp. 44–47, June 1988.

[Lee80]   Lee, R. B.-L., "Empirical Results on the Speed, Efficiency, Redundancy, and Quality of Parallel Computations," *Proc. Int. Conf. Parallel Processing*, 1980, pp. 91–96.

[Parh95]   Parhami, B., "The Right Acronym at the Right Time" (The Open Channel), *IEEE Computer*, Vol. 28, No. 6, p. 120, June 1995.

[Quin87]   Quinn, M. J., *Designing Efficient Algorithms for Parallel Computers*, McGraw-Hill, 1987.

[Quin94]   Quinn, M. J., *Parallel Computing: Theory and Practice*, McGraw-Hill, 1994.

[Scha97]   Schaller, R. R., "Moore's Law: Past, Present, and Future," *IEEE Spectrum*, Vol. 34, No. 6, pp. 52–59, June 1997.

[SIA94]   Semiconductor Industry Association, *The National Roadmap for Semiconductors*, 1994.

2

A Taste of Parallel Algorithms

In this chapter, we examine five simple building-block parallel operations (defined in Section 2.1) and look at the corresponding algorithms on four simple parallel architectures: linear array, binary tree, 2D mesh, and a simple shared-variable computer (see Section 2.2). This exercise will introduce us to the nature of parallel computations, the interplay between algorithm and architecture, and the complexity of parallel computations (analyses and bounds). Also, the building-block computations are important in their own right and will be used throughout the book. We will study some of these architectures and algorithms in more depth in subsequent chapters. Chapter topics are

- 2.1. Some simple computations
- 2.2. Some simple architectures
- 2.3. Algorithms for a linear array
- 2.4. Algorithms for a binary tree
- 2.5. Algorithms for a 2D mesh
- 2.6. Algorithms with shared variables

2.1. SOME SIMPLE COMPUTATIONS

In this section, we define five fundamental building-block computations:

1. Semigroup (reduction, fan-in) computation
2. Parallel prefix computation
3. Packet routing
4. Broadcasting, and its more general version, multicasting
5. Sorting records in ascending/descending order of their keys

Semigroup Computation.   Let $\otimes$ be an associative binary operator; i.e., $(x \otimes y) \otimes z$ $= x \otimes (y \otimes z)$ for all x, y, $z \in S$. A semigroup is simply a pair $(S, \otimes)$, where S is a set of elements on which $\otimes$ is defined. *Semigroup* (also known as *reduction* or *fan-in*) *computation* is defined as: Given a list of n values $x_0, x_1, \ldots, x_{n-1}$, compute $x_0 \otimes x_1 \otimes \ldots \otimes x_{n-1}$. Common examples for the operator $\otimes$ include $+$, $\times$, $\wedge$, $\vee$, $\oplus$, $\cap$, $\cup$, max, min. The operator $\otimes$ may or may not be commutative, i.e., it may or may not satisfy $x \otimes y = y \otimes x$ (all of the above examples are, but the carry computation, e.g., is not). This last point is important; while the parallel algorithm can compute chunks of the expression using any partitioning scheme, the chunks must eventually be combined in left-to-right order. Figure 2.1 depicts a semigroup computation on a uniprocessor.

Parallel Prefix Computation.   With the same assumptions as in the preceding paragraph, a parallel prefix computation is defined as simultaneously evaluating all of the prefixes of the expression $x_0 \otimes x_1 \ldots \otimes x_{n-1}$; i.e., x_0, $x_0 \otimes x_1$, $x_0 \otimes x_1 \otimes x_2, \ldots, x_0 \otimes x_1 \otimes \ldots \otimes x_{n-1}$. Note that the ith prefix expression is $s_i = x_0 \otimes x_1 \otimes \ldots \otimes x_i$. The comment about commutativity, or lack thereof, of the binary operator $\otimes$ applies here as well. The graph representing the prefix computation on a uniprocessor is similar to Fig. 2.1, but with the intermediate values also output.

Packet Routing.   A packet of information resides at Processor i and must be sent to Processor j. The problem is to route the packet through intermediate processors, if needed,

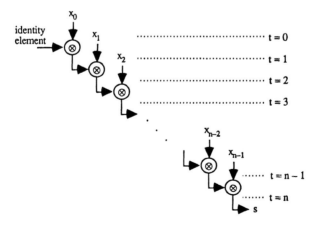

Figure 2.1. Semigroup computation on a uniprocessor.

such that it gets to the destination as quickly as possible. The problem becomes more challenging when multiple packets reside at different processors, each with its own destination. In this case, the packet routes may interfere with one another as they go through common intermediate processors. When each processor has at most one packet to send and one packet to receive, the packet routing problem is called *one-to-one communication* or *1–1 routing*.

Broadcasting.   Given a value a known at a certain processor i, disseminate it to all p processors as quickly as possible, so that at the end, every processor has access to, or "knows," the value. This is sometimes referred to as *one-to-all communication*. The more general case of this operation, i.e., one-to-many communication, is known as *multicasting*. From a programming viewpoint, we make the assignments $x_j := a$ for $1 \leq j \leq p$ (broadcasting) or for $j \in G$ (multicasting), where G is the multicast group and x_j is a local variable in processor j.

Sorting.   Rather than sorting a set of records, each with a key and data elements, we focus on sorting a set of keys for simplicity. Our sorting problem is thus defined as: Given a list of n keys $x_0, x_1, \ldots, x_{n-1}$, and a total order $\leq$ on key values, rearrange the n keys as $x_{i_0}, x_{i_1}, \ldots, x_{i_{n-1}}$, such that $x_{i_0} \leq x_{i_1} \leq \ldots \leq x_{i_{n-1}}$. We consider only sorting the keys in nondescending order. Any algorithm for sorting values in nondescending order can be converted, in a straightforward manner, to one for sorting the keys in nonascending order or for sorting records.

2.2. SOME SIMPLE ARCHITECTURES

In this section, we define four simple parallel architectures:

1.   Linear array of processors
2.   Binary tree of processors
3.   Two-dimensional mesh of processors
4.   Multiple processors with shared variables

Linear Array.   Figure 2.2 shows a linear array of nine processors, numbered 0 to 8. The *diameter* of a p-processor linear array, defined as the longest of the shortest distances between pairs of processors, is $D = p - 1$. The (*maximum*) *node degree*, defined as the largest number of links or communication channels associated with a processor, is $d = 2$. The ring variant, also shown in Fig. 2.2, has the same node degree of 2 but a smaller diameter of $D = \lfloor p/2 \rfloor$.

Binary Tree.   Figure 2.3 shows a binary tree of nine processors. This binary tree is *balanced* in that the leaf levels differ by at most 1. If all leaf levels are identical and every nonleaf processor has two children, the binary tree is said to be *complete*. The diameter of a

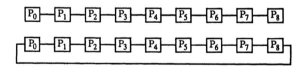

Figure 2.2. A linear array of nine processors and its ring variant.

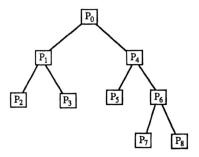

Figure 2.3. A balanced (but incomplete) binary tree of nine processors.

p-processor complete binary tree is $2 \log_2(p + 1) - 2$. More generally, the diameter of a p-processor balanced binary tree architecture is $2\lfloor \log_2 p \rfloor$ or $2\lfloor \log_2 p \rfloor - 1$, depending on the placement of leaf nodes at the last level. Unlike linear array, several different p-processor binary tree architectures may exist. This is usually not a problem as we almost always deal with complete binary trees. The (maximum) node degree in a binary tree is $d = 3$.

2D Mesh.   Figure 2.4 shows a square 2D mesh of nine processors. The diameter of a p-processor square mesh is $2\sqrt{p} - 2$. More generally, the mesh does not have to be square. The diameter of a p-processor $r \times (p/r)$ mesh is $D = r + p/r - 2$. Again, multiple 2D meshes may exist for the same number p of processors, e.g., 2×8 or 4×4. Square meshes are usually preferred because they minimize the diameter. The torus variant, also shown in Fig. 2.4, has end-around or wraparound links for rows and columns. The node degree for both meshes and tori is $d = 4$. But a p-processor $r \times (p/r)$ torus has a smaller diameter of $D = \lfloor r/2 \rfloor + \lfloor p/(2r) \rfloor$.

Shared Memory.   A shared-memory multiprocessor can be modeled as a complete graph, in which every node is connected to every other node, as shown in Fig. 2.5 for $p = 9$. In the 2D mesh of Fig. 2.4, Processor 0 can send/receive data directly to/from P_1 and P_3. However, it has to go through an intermediary to send/receive data to/from P_4, say. In a shared-memory multiprocessor, every piece of data is directly accessible to every processor (we assume that each processor can simultaneously send/receive data over all of its $p - 1$ links). The diameter $D = 1$ of a complete graph is an indicator of this direct access. The node

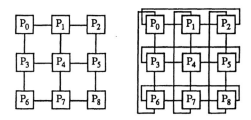

Figure 2.4. A 2D mesh of nine processors and its torus variant.

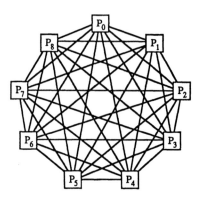

Figure 2.5. A shared-variable architecture modeled as a complete graph.

degree $d = p - 1$, on the other hand, indicates that such an architecture would be quite costly to implement if no restriction is placed on data accesses.

2.3. ALGORITHMS FOR A LINEAR ARRAY

Semigroup Computation.   Let us consider first a special case of semigroup computation, namely, that of maximum finding. Each of the p processors holds a value initially and our goal is for every processor to know the largest of these values. A local variable, max-thus-far, can be initialized to the processor's own data value. In each step, a processor sends its max-thus-far value to its two neighbors. Each processor, on receiving values from its left and right neighbors, sets its max-thus-far value to the largest of the three values, i.e., max(left, own, right). Figure 2.6 depicts the execution of this algorithm for $p = 9$ processors. The dotted lines in Fig. 2.6 show how the maximum value propagates from P_6 to all other processors. Had there been two maximum values, say in P_2 and P_6, the propagation would have been faster. In the worst case, $p - 1$ communication steps (each involving sending a processor's value to both neighbors), and the same number of three-way comparison steps, are needed. This is the best one can hope for, given that the diameter of a p-processor linear array is $D = p - 1$ (diameter-based lower bound).

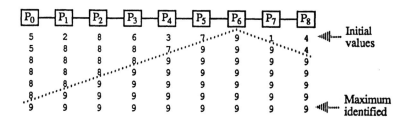

Figure 2.6. Maximum-finding on a linear array of nine processors.

For a general semigroup computation, the processor at the left end of the array (the one with no left neighbor) becomes active and sends its data value to the right (initially, all processors are dormant or inactive). On receiving a value from its left neighbor, a processor becomes active, applies the semigroup operation $\otimes$ to the value received from the left and its own data value, sends the result to the right, and becomes inactive again. This wave of activity propagates to the right, until the rightmost processor obtains the desired result. The computation result is then propagated leftward to all processors. In all, $2p - 2$ communication steps are needed.

Parallel Prefix Computation.   Let us assume that we want the ith prefix result to be obtained at the ith processor, $0 \le i \le p - 1$. The general semigroup algorithm described in the preceding paragraph in fact performs a semigroup computation first and then does a broadcast of the final value to all processors. Thus, we already have an algorithm for parallel prefix computation that takes $p - 1$ communication/combining steps. A variant of the parallel prefix computation, in which Processor i ends up with the prefix result up to the $(i - 1)$th value, is sometimes useful. This *diminished prefix computation* can be performed just as easily if each processor holds onto the value received from the left rather than the one it sends to the right. The diminished prefix sum results for the example of Fig. 2.7 would be 0, 5, 7, 15, 21, 24, 31, 40, 41.

Thus far, we have assumed that each processor holds a single data item. Extension of the semigroup and parallel prefix algorithms to the case where each processor initially holds several data items is straightforward. Figure 2.8 shows a parallel prefix sum computation with each processor initially holding two data items. The algorithm consists of each processor doing a prefix computation on its own data set of size n/p (this takes $n/p - 1$ combining steps), then doing a diminished parallel prefix computation on the linear array as above ($p - 1$ communication/combining steps), and finally combining the local prefix result from this last computation with the locally computed prefixes (n/p combining steps). In all, $2n/p + p - 2$ combining steps and $p - 1$ communication steps are required.

Packet Routing.   To send a packet of information from Processor i to Processor j on a linear array, we simply attach a *routing tag* with the value $j - i$ to it. The sign of a routing tag determines the direction in which it should move ($+$ = right, $-$ = left) while its magnitude indicates the action to be performed (0 = remove the packet, nonzero = forward the packet). With each forwarding, the magnitude of the routing tag is decremented by 1. Multiple packets

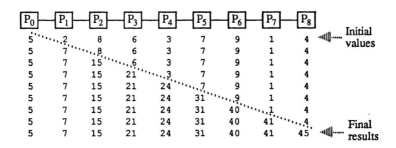

Figure 2.7. Computing prefix sums on a linear array of nine processors.

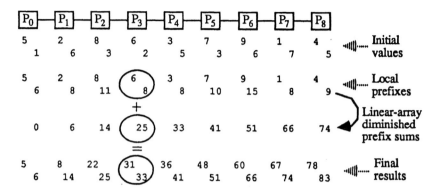

Figure 2.8. Computing prefix sums on a linear array with two items per processor.

originating at different processors can flow rightward and leftward in lockstep, without ever interfering with each other.

Broadcasting.   If Processor i wants to broadcast a value a to all processors, it sends an rbcast(a) (read r-broadcast) message to its right neighbor and an lbcast(a) message to its left neighbor. Any processor receiving an rbcast(a) message, simply copies the value a and forwards the message to its right neighbor (if any). Similarly, receiving an lbcast(a) message causes a to be copied locally and the message forwarded to the left neighbor. The worst-case number of communication steps for broadcasting is $p - 1$.

Sorting.   We consider two versions of sorting on a linear array: with and without I/O. Figure 2.9 depicts a linear-array sorting algorithm when p keys are input, one at a time, from the left end. Each processor, on receiving a key value from the left, compares the received value with the value stored in its local register (initially, all local registers hold the value +∞). The smaller of the two values is kept in the local register and larger value is passed on to the right. Once all p inputs have been received, we must allow $p - 1$ additional communication cycles for the key values that are in transit to settle into their respective positions in the linear array. If the sorted list is to be output from the left, the output phase can start immediately after the last key value has been received. In this case, an array half the size of the input list would be adequate and we effectively have zero-time sorting, i.e., the total sorting time is equal to the I/O time.

If the key values are already in place, one per processor, then an algorithm known as *odd–even transposition* can be used for sorting. A total of p steps are required. In an odd-numbered step, odd-numbered processors compare values with their even-numbered right neighbors. The two processors exchange their values if they are out of order. Similarly, in an even-numbered step, even-numbered processors compare–exchange values with their right neighbors (see Fig. 2.10). In the worst case, the largest key value resides in Processor 0 and must move all the way to the other end of the array. This needs $p - 1$ right moves. One step must be added because no movement occurs in the first step. Of course one could use even–odd transposition, but this will not affect the worst-case time complexity of the algorithm for our nine-processor linear array.

Note that the odd–even transposition algorithm uses p processors to sort p keys in p compare–exchange steps. How good is this algorithm? Let us evaluate the odd–even

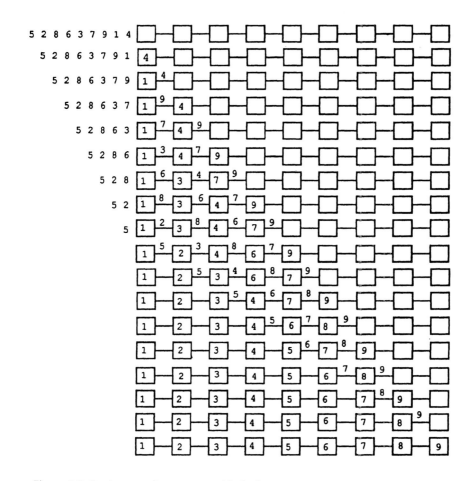

Figure 2.9. Sorting on a linear array with the keys input sequentially from the left.

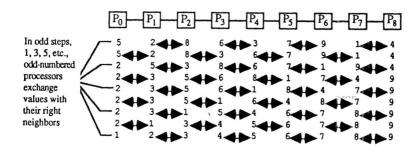

Figure 2.10. Odd–even transposition sort on a linear array.

transposition algorithm with respect to the various measures introduced in Section 1.6. The best sequential sorting algorithms take on the order of $p \log p$ compare–exchange steps to sort a list of size p. Let us assume, for simplicity, that they take exactly $p \log_2 p$ steps. Then, we have $T(1) = W(1) = p \log_2 p$, $T(p) = p$, $W(p) = p^2/2$, $S(p) = \log_2 p$ (Minsky's conjecture?), $E(p) = (\log_2 p)/p$, $R(p) = p/(2 \log_2 p)$, $U(p) = 1/2$, and $Q(p) = 2(\log_2 p)^3/p^2$.

In most practical situations, the number n of keys to be sorted (the *problem size*) is greater than the number p of processors (the *machine size*). The odd–even transposition sort algorithm with n/p keys per processor is as follows. First, each processor sorts its list of size n/p using any efficient sequential sorting algorithm. Let us say this takes $(n/p)\log_2(n/p)$ compare–exchange steps. Next, the odd–even transposition sort is performed as before, except that each compare–exchange step is replaced by a merge–split step in which the two communicating processors merge their sublists of size n/p into a single sorted list of size $2n/p$ and then split the list down the middle, one processor keeping the smaller half and the other, the larger half. For example, if P_0 is holding $(1, 3, 7, 8)$ and P_1 has $(2, 4, 5, 9)$, a merge–split step will turn the lists into $(1, 2, 3, 4)$ and $(5, 7, 8, 9)$, respectively. Because the sublists are sorted, the merge–split step requires n/p compare–exchange steps. Thus, the total time of the algorithm is $(n/p)\log_2(n/p) + n$. Note that the first term (local sorting) will be dominant if $p < \log_2 n$, while the second term (array merging) is dominant for $p > \log_2 n$. For $p \geq \log_2 n$, the time complexity of the algorithm is linear in n; hence, the algorithm is more efficient than the one-key-per-processor version.

One final observation about sorting: Sorting is important in its own right, but occasionally it also helps us in data routing. Suppose data values being held by the p processors of a linear array are to be routed to other processors, such that the destination of each value is different from all others. This is known as a *permutation routing* problem. Because the p distinct destinations must be $0, 1, 2, \ldots, p - 1$, forming records with the destination address as the key and sorting these records will cause each record to end up at its correct destination. Consequently, permutation routing on a linear array requires p compare–exchange steps. So, effectively, p packets are routed in the same amount of time that is required for routing a single packet in the worst case.

2.4. ALGORITHMS FOR A BINARY TREE

In algorithms for a binary tree of processors, we will assume that the data elements are initially held by the leaf processors only. The nonleaf (inner) processors participate in the computation, but do not hold data elements of their own. This simplifying assumption, which can be easily relaxed, leads to simpler algorithms. As roughly half of the tree nodes are leaf nodes, the inefficiency resulting from this assumption is not very great.

Semigroup Computation. A binary-tree architecture is ideally suited for this computation (for this reason, semigroup computation is sometimes referred to as *tree computation*). Each inner node receives two values from its children (if each of them has already computed a value or is a leaf node), applies the operator to them, and passes the result upward to its parent. After $\lfloor \log_2 p \rfloor$ steps, the root processor will have the computation result. All processors can then be notified of the result through a broadcasting operation from the root. Total time: $2\lfloor \log_2 p \rfloor$ steps.

Parallel Prefix Computation.   Again, this is quite simple and can be done optimally in $2\lfloor\log_2 p\rfloor$ steps (recall that the diameter of a binary tree is $2\lfloor\log_2 p\rfloor$ or $2\lfloor\log_2 p\rfloor - 1$). The algorithm consists of an upward propagation phase followed by downward data movement. As shown in Fig. 2.11, the upward propagation phase is identical to the upward movement of data in semigroup computation. At the end of this phase, each node will have the semigroup computation result for its subtree. The downward phase is as follows. Each processor remembers the value it received from its left child. On receiving a value from the parent, a node passes the value received from above to its left child and the combination of this value and the one that came from the left child to its right child. The root is viewed as receiving the identity element from above and thus initiates the downward phase by sending the identity element to the left and the value received from its left child to the right. At the end of the downward phase, the leaf processors compute their respective results.

It is instructive to look at some applications of the parallel prefix computation at this point. Given a list of 0s and 1s, the rank of each 1 in the list (its relative position among the 1s) can be determined by a prefix sum computation:

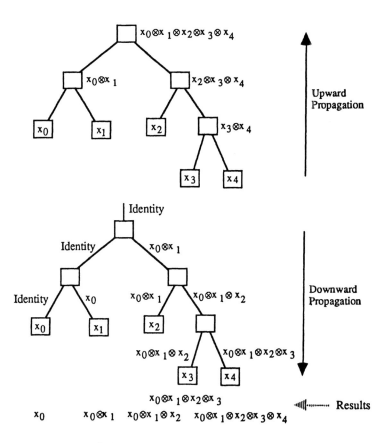

Figure 2.11. Parallel prefix computation on a binary tree of processors.

Data:	0	0	1	0	1	0	0	1	1	1	0
Prefix sums:	0	0	1	1	2	2	2	3	4	5	5
Ranks of 1s:			1		2			3	4	5	

A priority circuit has a list of 0s and 1s as its inputs and picks the first (highest-priority) 1 in the list. The function of a priority circuit can be defined as

Data: 0	0	1	0	1	0	0	1	1	1	0
Diminished prefix logical ORs: 0	0	0	1	1	1	1	1	1	1	1
Complement: 1	1	1	0	0	0	0	0	0	0	0
AND with data: 0	0	1	0	0	0	0	0	0	0	0

As a final example, the carry computation in the design of adders can be formulated as a parallel prefix computation in the following way. Let "g," "p," and "a" denote the event that a particular digit position in the adder generates, propagates, or annihilates a carry. For a decimal adder, e.g., these correspond to the digit sums being greater than 9, equal to 9, and less than 9, respectively. Therefore, the input data for the carry circuit consists of a vector of three-valued elements such as

$$p \quad g \quad a \quad g \quad g \quad p \quad p \quad p \quad g \quad a \quad c_{in}$$

direction of indexing   g or a

Final carries into the various positions can be determined by a parallel prefix computation using the *carry operator* "¢" defined as follows (view $x \in \{g, p, a\}$ as the incoming carry into a position):

$$p \; ¢ \; x = x \qquad x \text{ propagates over } p$$
$$a \; ¢ \; x = a \qquad x \text{ is annihilated or absorbed by } a$$
$$g \; ¢ \; x = g \qquad x \text{ is immaterial because a carry is generated}$$

In fact, if each node in the two trees of Fig. 2.11 is replaced by a logic circuit corresponding to the carry operator, a five-digit carry-lookahead circuit would result.

Packet Routing.   The algorithm for routing a packet of information from Processor i to Processor j on a binary tree of processors depends on the processor numbering scheme used. The processor numbering scheme shown in Fig. 2.3 is not the best one for this purpose but it will be used here to develop a routing algorithm. The indexing scheme of Fig. 2.3 is known as "preorder" indexing and has the following recursive definition: Nodes in a subtree are numbered by first numbering the root node, then its left subtree, and finally the right subtree. So the index of each node is less than the indices of all of its descendants. We assume that each node, in addition to being aware of its own index (*self*) in the tree, which is the smallest in its subtree, knows the largest node index in its left (*maxl*) and right (*maxr*) subtrees. A packet on its way from node i to node *dest*, and currently residing in node *self*, is routed according to the following algorithm.

```
if dest = self
then remove the packet {done}
else if dest < self or dest > maxr
    then route upward
    else if dest ≤ maxl
        then route leftward
        else route rightward
        endif
    endif
endif
```

This algorithm does not make any assumption about the tree except that it is a binary tree. In particular, the tree need not be complete or even balanced.

Broadcasting.   Processor i sends the desired data upwards to the root processor, which then broadcasts the data downwards to all processors.

Sorting.   We can use an algorithm similar to bubblesort that allows the smaller elements in the leaves to "bubble up" to the root processor first, thus allowing the root to "see" all of the data elements in nondescending order. The root then sends the elements to leaf nodes in the proper order. Before describing the part of the algorithm dealing with the upward bubbling of data, let us deal with the simpler downward movement. This downward movement is easily coordinated if each node knows the number of leaf nodes in its left subtree. If the rank order of the element received from above (kept in a local counter) does not exceed the number of leaf nodes to the left, then the data item is sent to the left. Otherwise, it is sent to the right. Note that the above discussion implicitly assumes that data are to be sorted from left to right in the leaves.

The upward movement of data in the above sorting algorithm can be accomplished as follows, where the processor action is described from its own viewpoint. Initially, each leaf has a single data item and all other nodes are empty. Each inner node has storage space for two values, migrating upward from its left and right subtrees.

```
if you have 2 items
then do nothing
else if you have 1 item that came from the left (right)
    then get the smaller item from the right (left) child
    else get the smaller item from each child
    endif
endif
```

Figure 2.12 shows the first few steps of the upward data movement (up to the point when the smallest element is in the root node, ready to begin its downward movement). The above sorting algorithm takes linear time in the number of elements to be sorted. We might be interested to know if a more efficient sorting algorithm can be developed, given that the diameter of the tree architecture is logarithmic (i.e., in the worst case, a data item has to move $2\lfloor \log_2 p \rfloor$ steps to get to its position in sorted order). The answer, unfortunately, is that we cannot do fundamentally better than the above.

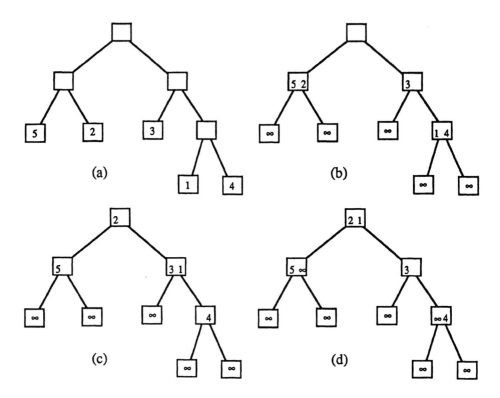

Figure 2.12. The first few steps of the sorting algorithm on a binary tree.

The reasoning is based on a lower bound argument that is quite useful in many contexts. All we need to do to partition a tree architecture into two equal or almost equal halves (composed of $\lfloor p/2 \rfloor$ and $\lceil p/2 \rceil$ processors) is to cut a single link next to the root processor (Fig. 2.13). We say that the *bisection width* of the binary tree architecture is 1. Now, in the worst case, the initial data arrangement may be such that all values in the left (right) half of the tree must move to the right (left) half to assume their sorted positions. Hence, all data elements must pass through the single link. No matter how we organize the data movements,

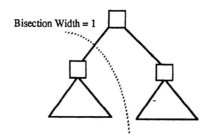

Figure 2.13. The bisection width of a binary tree architecture.

it takes linear time for all of the data elements to pass through this bottleneck. This is an example of a *bisection-based lower bound*.

2.5. ALGORITHMS FOR A 2D MESH

In all of the 2D mesh algorithms presented in this section, we use the linear-array algorithms of Section 2.3 as building blocks. This leads to simple algorithms, but not necessarily the most efficient ones. Mesh-based architectures and their algorithms will be discussed in great detail in Part III (Chapters 9–12).

Semigroup Computation.   To perform a semigroup computation on a 2D mesh, do the semigroup computation in each row and then in each column. For example, in finding the maximum of a set of p values, stored one per processor, the row maximums are computed first and made available to every processor in the row. Then column maximums are identified. This takes $4\sqrt{p} - 4$ steps on a p-processor square mesh, per the results in Section 2.3. The same process can be used for computing the sum of p numbers. Note that for a general semigroup computation with a noncommutative operation, the p numbers must be stored in row-major order for this algorithm to work correctly.

Parallel Prefix Computation.   Again, this is quite simple and can be done in three phases, assuming that the processors (and their stored values) are indexed in row-major order: (1) do a parallel prefix computation on each row, (2) do a diminished parallel prefix computation in the rightmost column, and (3) broadcast the results in the rightmost column to all of the elements in the respective rows and combine with the initially computed row prefix value. For example, in doing prefix sums, first-row prefix sums are computed from left to right. At this point, the processors in the rightmost column hold the row sums. A diminished prefix computation in this last column yields the sum of all of the preceding rows in each processor. Combining the sum of all of the preceding rows with the row prefix sums yields the overall prefix sums.

Packet Routing.   To route a data packet from the processor in Row r, Column c, to the processor in Row r', Column c', we first route it within Row r to Column c'. Then, we route it in Column c' from Row r to Row r'. This algorithm is known as *row-first routing*. Clearly, we could do column-first routing, or use a combination of horizontal and vertical steps to get to the destination node along a shortest path. If the mesh nodes are indexed as in Fig. 2.4, rather than in terms of row and column numbers, then we simply determine the index of the intermediate Processor l where the row-first path has to turn. The problem is then decomposed into two problems: route horizontally from i to l, then route vertically from l to j. When multiple packets must be routed between different source and destination nodes, the above algorithm can be applied to each packet independently of others. However, multiple packets might then compete for the same outgoing link on their paths to their respective destinations. The processors must have sufficient buffer space to store the packets that must wait at their turning points before being forwarded along the column. Details will be discussed in Chapter 10.

Broadcasting.   Broadcasting is done in two phases: (1) broadcast the packet to every processor in the source node's row and (2) broadcast in all columns. This takes at most $2\sqrt{p} - 2$ steps. If multiple values are to be broadcast by a processor, then the required data

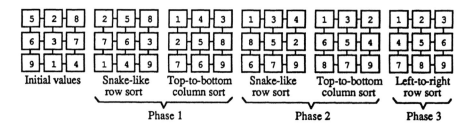

Figure 2.14. The shearsort algorithm on a 3 × 3 mesh.

movements can be pipelined, such that each additional broadcast requires only one additional step.

Sorting. We describe, without proof, the simple version of a sorting algorithm known as *shearsort*. Complete proof and more efficient variants will be provided in Chapter 9. The algorithm consists of $\lceil \log_2 r \rceil + 1$ phases in a 2D mesh with r rows. In each phase, except for the last one, all rows are independently sorted in a snakelike order: even-numbered rows 0, 2, . . . from left to right, odd-numbered rows 1, 3, . . . from right to left. Then, all columns are independently sorted from top to bottom. For example, in a 3 × 3 mesh, two such phases are needed, as shown in Fig. 2.14. In the final phase, rows are independently sorted from left to right. As we already know that row-sort and column-sort on a p-processor square mesh take $\sqrt{p}$ compare–exchange steps, the shearsort algorithm needs $(2\lceil \log_2 p \rceil + 1)\sqrt{p}$ compare–exchange steps for sorting in row-major order.

2.6. ALGORITHMS WITH SHARED VARIABLES

Again, in this section, we focus on developing simple algorithms that are not necessarily very efficient. Shared-memory architectures and their algorithms will be discussed in more detail in Chapters 5 and 6.

Semigroup Computation. Each processor obtains the data items from all other processors and performs the semigroup computation independently. Obviously, all processors will end up with the same result. This approach is quite wasteful of the complex architecture of Fig. 2.5 because the linear time complexity of the algorithm is essentially comparable to that of the semigroup computation algorithm for the much simpler linear-array architecture and worse than the algorithm for the 2D mesh.

Parallel Prefix Computation. Similar to the semigroup computation, except that each processor only obtains data items from processors with smaller indices.

Packet Routing. Trivial in view of the direct communication path between any pair of processors.

Broadcasting. Trivial, as each processor can send a data item to all processors directly. In fact, because of this direct access, broadcasting is not needed; each processor already has access to any data item when needed.

Sorting. The algorithm to be described for sorting with shared variables consists of two phases: ranking and data permutation. ranking consists of determining the relative order of each key in the final sorted list. If each processor holds one key, then once the ranks are determined, the jth-ranked key can be sent to Processor j in the data permutation phase, requiring a single parallel communication step. Processor i is responsible for ranking its own key x_i. This is done by comparing x_i to all other keys and counting the number of keys that are smaller than x_i. In the case of equal key values, processor indices are used to establish the relative order. For example, if Processors 3 and 9 both hold the key value 23, the key associated with Processor 3 is deemed smaller for ranking purposes. It should be clear that each key will end up with a unique rank in the range 0 (no key is smaller) to $p - 1$ (all other $p - 1$ keys are smaller).

Again, despite the greater complexity of the shared-variable architecture compared with the linear-array or binary-tree architectures, the linear time required by the above sorting algorithm is comparable to the algorithms for these simpler architectures. We will see in Chapter 6 that logarithmic-time sorting algorithms can in fact be developed for the shared-variable architecture, leading to linear speed-up over sequential algorithms that need on the order of $n \log n$ compare–exchange steps to sort n items.

PROBLEMS

2.1. Lower bounds based on bisection width
For each of the following problem/architecture pairs, find a lower bound based on the bisection width. State if the derived bound is useful.

   a. Semigroup computation on linear array.
   b. Parallel prefix computation on linear array.
   c. Semigroup computation on 2D mesh.
   d. Sorting on shared-variable architecture.

2.2. Semigroup or parallel prefix computation on a linear array

   a. Semigroup computation can be performed on a linear array in a recursive fashion. Assume that p is a power of 2. First, semigroup computation is performed on the left and right halves of the array independently. Then the results are combined through two half-broadcast operations, i.e., broadcasting from each of the middle two processors to the other side of the array. Supply the details of the algorithm and analyze its complexity. Compare the result with that of the algorithm described in Section 2.3.
   b. Can an algorithm similar to that in part (a) be devised for parallel prefix computation? If so, how does its performance compare with the algorithm described in Section 2.3?

2.3. Parallel prefix computation on a linear array
Given n data items, determine the optimal number p of processors in a linear array such that if the n data items are distributed to the processors with each holding approximately n/p elements, the time to perform the parallel prefix computation is minimized.

2.4. Multicasting on a linear array
Suppose processors in a linear array compose messages of the form mcast(x, a, b) with the meaning that the data value x must be sent (multicast) to all processors with indices in the interval $[a, b]$. Packet routing and broadcasting correspond to the special cases mcast(x, j, j) and mcast(x, 0, $p - 1$) of this more general mechanism. Develop the algorithm for handling such a multicast message by a processor.

2.5. Sorting on a linear array
      Determine the speed-up, efficiency, and other effectiveness measures defined in Section 1.6
      for linear-array sorting with more than one data item per processor.

2.6. Parallel prefix computation

      a. In determining the ranks of 1s in a list of 0s and 1s (Section 2.4), what happens if a
          diminished parallel prefix sum computation is performed rather than the regular one?
      b. What is the identity element for the carry operator "¢" defined in Section 2.4?
      c. Find another example of parallel prefix computation (besides carry computation) involving
          a noncommutative binary operation.

2.7. Algorithms for a linear array
      In Section 2.3, we assumed that the communication links between the processors in the linear
      array are full-duplex, meaning that they can carry data in both directions simultaneously (in
      one step). How should the algorithms given in Section 2.3 be modified if the communication
      links are half-duplex (they can carry data in either directions, but not in the same step)?

2.8. Algorithms for a ring of processors
      Develop efficient algorithms for the five computations discussed in this chapter on a p-proc-
      essor ring, assuming:

      a. Bidirectional, full-duplex links between processors.
      b. Bidirectional, half-duplex links between processors.
      c. Unidirectional links between processors.

2.9. Measures of parallel processing effectiveness
      Compute the effectiveness measures introduced in Section 1.6 for the parallel prefix compu-
      tation algorithm on a linear array, binary tree, 2D mesh, and shared-variable architecture.
      Compare and discuss the results.

2.10. Parallel prefix computation on a binary tree
      Develop an algorithm for parallel prefix computation on a binary tree where the inner tree
      nodes also hold data elements.

2.11. Routing on a binary tree of processors

      a. Modify the binary tree routing algorithm in Section 2.4 so that the variables *maxl* and *maxr*
          are not required, assuming that we are dealing with a complete binary tree.
      b. Each processor in a tree can be given a name or label based on the path that would take us
          from the root to that node via right (R) or left (L) moves. For example, in Fig. 2.3, the root
          will be labeled Λ (the empty string), P_3 would be labeled LR (left, then right), and P_7 would
          be labeled RRL. Develop a packet routing algorithm from Node A to Node B if node labels
          are specified as above.

2.12. Sorting on a binary tree of processors

      a. Develop a new binary-tree sorting algorithm based on all-to-all broadcasting. Each leaf
          node broadcasts its key to all other leafs, which compare the incoming keys with their own
          and determine the rank of their keys. A final parallel routing phase concludes the algorithm.
          Compare this new algorithm with the one described in Section 2.4 and discuss.
      b. Modify the binary tree sorting algorithm in Section 2.4 so that it works with multiple keys
          initially stored in each leaf node.

2.13. Algorithms on 2D processor arrays

Briefly discuss how the semigroup computation, parallel prefix computation, packet routing, and broadcasting algorithms can be performed on the following variants of the 2D mesh architecture.

a. A 2D torus with wraparound links as in Fig. 2.4 (simply ignoring the wraparound links is not allowed!).

b. A Manhattan street network, so named because the row and column links are unidirectional and, like the one-way streets of Manhattan, go in opposite directions in adjacent rows or columns. Unlike the streets, though, each row/column has a wraparound link. Assume that both dimensions of the processor array are even, with links in even-numbered rows (columns) going from left to right (bottom to top).

c. A honeycomb mesh, which is a 2D mesh in which all of the row links are left intact but every other column link has been removed. Two different drawings of this architecture are shown below.

2.14. Shearsort on 2D mesh of processors

a. Write down the number of compare–exchange steps required to perform shearsort on general (possibly nonsquare) 2D mesh with r rows and p/r columns.

b. Compute the effectiveness measures introduced in Section 1.6 for the shearsort algorithm based on the results of part (a).

c. Discuss the best aspect ratio for a p-processor mesh in order to minimize the sorting time.

d. How would shearsort work if each processor initially holds more than one key?

REFERENCES AND SUGGESTED READING

[Akl85]   Akl, S. G., *Parallel Sorting Algorithms*, Academic Press, 1985.

[Akl97]   Akl, S. G., *Parallel Computation: Models and Methods*, Prentice–Hall, 1997.

[Corm9O]   Cormen, T. H., C. E. Leiserson, and R. L. Rivest, *Introduction to Algorithms*, McGraw-Hill, 1990.

[JaJa96]   JaJa, J. F., "Fundamentals of Parallel Algorithms," Chapter 12 in *Parallel and Distributed Computing Handbook*, Edited by A. Y. Zomaya, McGraw-Hill, 1996, pp. 333–354.

[Knut73]   Knuth, D. E., *The Art of Computer Programming: Vol. 3—Sorting and Searching*, Addison–Wesley, 1973.

[Laks94]   Lakshmivarahan, S., and S. K. Dhall, *Parallel Computing Using the Prefix Problem*, Oxford University Press, 1994.

[Leig92]   Leighton, F. T., *Introduction to Parallel Algorithms and Architectures: Arrays, Trees, Hypercubes*, Morgan Kaufmann, 1992.

3

Parallel Algorithm Complexity

Having seen several examples of parallel algorithms in Chapter 2, we are ready to embark on a general discussion of parallel algorithm complexity. This chapter deals with basic notions of complexity as well as time and time-cost optimality of parallel algorithms. The ideas and methods covered here lead to tools for comparing various algorithms or for making given parallel algorithms faster and/or more efficient. Chapter topics are

- 3.1. Asymptotic complexity
- 3.2. Algorithm optimality and efficiency
- 3.3. Complexity classes
- 3.4. Parallelizable tasks and the NC class
- 3.5. Parallel programming paradigms
- 3.6. Solving recurrences

3.1. ASYMPTOTIC COMPLEXITY

Algorithms can be analyzed in two ways: precise and approximate. In precise analysis, we typically count the number of operations of various types (e.g., arithmetic, memory access, data transfer) performed in the worst or average case and use these counts as indicators of algorithm complexity. If each of these operations takes a constant amount of time, then a weighted sum of these counts will constitute a numerical measure of algorithm complexity that can be compared with other algorithms for the same task.

Such a precise analysis is quite tedious and at times impossible to perform. We thus resort to various approximate analysis methods to compare algorithms, always keeping in mind the error margin of the method applied. For example, if such an approximate analysis indicates that Algorithm A is 1.2 times slower than Algorithm B, we may not be able to conclude with certainty that Algorithm B is better for the task at hand.

A useful form of approximate analysis, which we will use extensively throughout this book, is *asymptotic analysis*. Suppose that a parallel sorting algorithm requires $(\log_2 n)^2$ compare–exchange steps, another one $(\log_2 n)^2/2 + 2 \log_2 n$ steps, and a third one $500 \log_2 n$ steps (assume these are the results of exact analyses). Ignoring lower-order terms and multiplicative constants, we may say that the first two algorithms take *on the order of* $\log^2 n$ steps while the third one takes on the order of $\log n$ steps. The logic behind ignoring these details is that when n becomes very large, eventually $\log n$ will exceed any constant value. Thus, for such large values of n, an algorithm with running time $c \log n$ is *asymptotically better* than an algorithm with running time $c' \log^2 n$ for any values of the constants c and c'.

Of course, n must indeed be very large for $\log n$ to overshadow the constant 500 in the above example. Thus, in practice, we do not totally ignore the constant factors but rather take a two-step approach. First, through asymptotic analysis, we determine which algorithm is likely to be better for large problem sizes: An algorithm of order $\log n$ is usually, but not always, better than an algorithm of order $\log^2 n$. If we have reason to doubt this conclusion, then we resort to an exact analysis to determine the constant factors involved.

We will see later that there are practical situations when we use an algorithm of order $\log^2 n$ even though the existence of algorithms of order $\log n$ has been demonstrated (albeit with very large constant factors that make the algorithm worse for any problem size of practical interest). However, and this is a key observation, once an asymptotically better algorithm has been found that happens to have a large constant factor as above, it is often possible to modify or fine-tune the algorithm to reduce its constant factor; if not in all cases, at least for some special cases of common interest.

To make our discussions of asymptotic analysis more precise, we introduce some notations that are commonly used in the study of computational complexity. Given two functions $f(n)$ and $g(n)$ of an independent variable n (usually, the problem size), we define the relationships "O" (big-oh), "Ω" (big-omega), and "Θ" (theta) between them as follows:

$$f(n) = O(g(n)) \text{ if } \exists c, n_0 \text{ such that } \forall n > n_0 \text{ we have } f(n) < c \, g(n)$$

$$f(n) = \Omega(g(n)) \text{ if } \exists c, n_0 \text{ such that } \forall n > n_0 \text{ we have } f(n) > c \, g(n)$$

$$f(n) = \Theta(g(n)) \text{ if } \exists c, c', n_0 \text{ such that } \forall n > n_0 \text{ we have } c \, g(n) < f(n) < c' \, g(n)$$

Thus,

$$f(n) = \Theta(g(n)) \text{ iff } f(n) = O(g(n)) \text{ and } f(n) = \Omega(g(n))$$

These notations essentially allow us to compare the growth rates of different functions.

For example, $f(n) = O(g(n))$ means that $f(n)$ grows no faster than $g(n)$, so that for n sufficiently large (i.e., $n > n_0$) and a suitably chosen constant c, $f(n)$ always remains below $c\,g(n)$. This relationship is represented graphically in the left panel of Fig. 3.1.

Similarly, $f(n) = \Omega(g(n))$ means that $f(n)$ grows at least as fast as $g(n)$, so that eventually $f(n)$ will exceed $c\,g(n)$ for all n beyond n_0 (middle panel of Fig. 3.1).

Finally, $f(n) = \Theta(g(n))$ means that $f(n)$ and $g(n)$ grow at about the same rate so that the value of $f(n)$ is always bounded by $c\,g(n)$ and $c'\,g(n)$ for $n > n_0$ (right panel of Fig. 3.1).

Loosely speaking, the above notations, and two new ones introduced below, define ordering relationships between the growth rates of functions. In other words, in the statement

"The rate of growth of $f(n)$ is ___ that of $g(n)$."

we can fill in the blank with the relational symbol ($<$, $\leq$, $=$, $\geq$, $>$) to the left of the defined relations shown below:

$<$	$f(n) = o(g(n))$	$\lim_{n\to\infty} f(n)/g(n) = 0$ {read little-oh of $g(n)$}
$\leq$	$f(n) = O(g(n))$	{big-oh}
$=$	$f(n) = \Theta(g(n))$ or $\theta(g(n))$	{theta}
$\geq$	$f(n) = \Omega(g(n))$	{big-omega}
$>$	$f(n) = \omega(g(n))$	$\lim_{n\to\infty} f(n)/g(n) = \infty$ {little-omega}

Of the above, the big-oh notation will be used most extensively, because it can express an upper bound on an algorithm's time or computational complexity and thus helps us establish whether or not a given algorithm is feasible for a given architecture.

For example, an algorithm with running time $O(n \log n)$ or $O(n^2)$ might be feasible today; one that takes $O(n^3)$ time might be just beyond the limit of practicality on today's hardware and quite practical in 5–10 years, say, when processor speeds have improved by

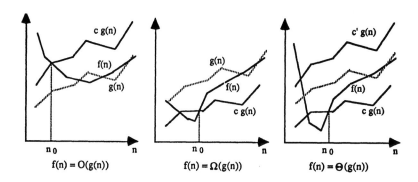

Figure 3.1. Graphical representation of the notions of asymptotic complexity.

Table 3.1. Comparing the Growth Rates of Sublinear and Superlinear Functions (K = 1000, M = 1,000,000)

Sublinear		Linear	Superlinear	
$\log^2 n$	$\sqrt{n}$	n	$n \log^2 n$	$n^{3/2}$
9	3	10	90	30
36	10	100	3.6 K	1 K
81	31	1K	81 K	31 K
169	100	10 K	1.7 M	1 M
256	316	100 K	26 M	31 M
361	1 K	1 M	361 M	1000 M

one or two orders of magnitude; an algorithm with $O(2^n)$ running time will likely remain impractical.

At a very coarse level, we sometimes talk about algorithms with *sublinear*, *linear*, and *superlinear* running times or complexities. These coarse categories can be further subdivided or refined as illustrated by the following examples:

Sublinear	$O(1)$	constant-time
	$O(\log \log n)$	double logarithmic
	$O(\log n)$	logarithmic
	$O(\log^k n)$	polylogarithmic; k is a constant
	$O(n^a)$	$a < 1$ is a constant; e.g., $O(\sqrt{n})$ for $a = 1/2$
	$O(n / \log^k n)$	k is a constant
Linear	$O(n)$	
Superlinear	$O(n \log^k n)$	
	$O(n^c)$	polynomial; $c > 1$ is a constant; e.g., $O(n\sqrt{n})$ for $c = 3/2$
	$O(2^n)$	exponential
	$O(2^{2^n})$	double exponential

Table 3.2. Effect of Constants on the Growth Rates of Selected Functions Involving Constant Factors (K = 1000, M = 1,000,000)

n	$\frac{n}{4} \log^2 n$	$n \log^2 n$	$100\sqrt{n}$	$n^{3/2}$
10	22	90	300	30
100	900	3.6 K	1 K	1 K
1 K	20 K	81 K	3.1 K	31 K
10 K	423 K	1.7 M	10 K	1 M
100 K	6 M	26 M	32 K	32 M
1 M	90 M	361 M	100 K	1000 M

Table 3.3. Effect of Constants on the Growth Rates of Selected Functions Using Larger Time Units and Round Figures

n	$\frac{n}{4}\log^2 n$	$n\log^2 n$	$100\sqrt{n}$	$n^{3/2}$
10	20 s	2 min	.5 min	30 s
100	15 min	1 hr	15 min	15 min
1 K	6 hr	1 day	1 hr	9 hr
10 K	5 days	20 days	3 hr	10 days
100 K	2 mo	1 yr	1 yr	1 yr
1 M	3 yr	11 yr	3 yr	32 yr

Table 3.1 helps you get an idea of the growth rates for two sublinear and two superlinear functions, as the problem size n increases. Table 3.2 shows the growth rates of a few functions, including constant multiplicative factors, to give you a feel for the contribution of such constants. Table 3.3 presents the same information using larger time units and rounded figures which make the differences easier to grasp (assuming that the original numbers of Table 3.2 showed the running time of an algorithm in seconds).

3.2. ALGORITHM OPTIMALITY AND EFFICIENCY

One way in which we use the big-oh and big-omega notations, introduced in Section 3.1, is as follows. Suppose that we have constructed a *valid* algorithm to solve a given problem of size n in $g(n)$ time, where $g(n)$ is a known function such as $n \log_2 n$ or n^2, obtained through exact or asymptotic analysis. A question of interest is whether or not the algorithm at hand is the *best* algorithm for solving the problem. Of course, algorithm quality can be judged in many different ways, with running time, resource requirements, simplicity (which affects the cost of development, debugging, and maintenance), and portability being some of the factors in this evaluation. Let us focus on running time for now. The question then becomes

What is the running time $f(n)$ of the fastest algorithm for solving this problem?

If we are interested in asymptotic comparison, then because an algorithm with running time $g(n)$ is already known, $f(n) = O(g(n))$; i.e., for large n, the running time of the best algorithm is upper bounded by $cg(n)$ for some constant c. If, subsequently, someone develops an asymptotically faster algorithm for solving the same problem, say in time $h(n)$, we conclude that $f(n) = O(h(n))$. The process of constructing and improving algorithms thus contributes to the establishment of *tighter upper bounds* for the complexity of the best algorithm (Fig. 3.2).

Concurrently with the establishment of upper bounds as discussed above, we might work on determining lower bounds on a problem's time complexity. A lower bound is useful as it tells us how much room for improvement there might be in existing algorithms. Lower bounds can be established by a variety of methods. Examples include

1. Showing that, in the worst case, solution of the problem requires data to travel a certain distance or that a certain volume of data must pass through a limited-bandwidth interface. An example of the first method is the observation that any sorting algorithm on a p-processor square mesh needs at least $2\sqrt{p} - 2$ communication steps in the worst case (diameter-based lower bound). The second method is exemplified by the worst-case linear time required by any sorting algorithm on a binary tree architecture (bisection-based lower bound).

2. Showing that, in the worst case, solution of the problem requires that a certain number of elementary operations be performed. This is the method used for establishing the $\Omega(n \log n)$ lower bound for comparison-based sequential sorting algorithms. Consider n distinct (unequal) keys. These n keys can be arranged in $n!$ different ways. The goal of sorting is to identify the one permutation (among $n!$) that corresponds to the sorted order. Each comparison has only two possible outcomes, and thus narrows down our choice by at most a factor of 2. Thus, $\log_2(n!)$ $= \Theta(n \log n)$ comparisons are needed in the worst case.

3. Showing that any instance of a previously analyzed problem can be converted to an instance of the problem under study, so that an algorithm for solving our problem can also be used, with simple pre- and postprocessing steps, to solve the previous problem. Any lower bound for the previous problem then becomes a lower bound for our new problem. For example, we saw in Section 2.4 that the carry computation problem can be converted to a parallel prefix computation. Thus, any lower bound established for carry computation is also a lower bound for general parallel prefix computation. Also, trivially, any upper bound for the prefix computation problem is an upper bound for the carry problem.

As shown in Fig. 3.2, a known lower bound can be viewed as a barrier against algorithmic speed improvements. When a wide gap exists between the best known lower and upper bounds, further efforts in raising the lower bound, or lowering the upper bound, might be warranted. The lower bound can be raised by applying the methods in the above list in novel ways. The upper bound can be lowered by designing new algorithms and showing them to be faster than the best previously known algorithms.

If and when the known upper bound and lower bound for a given problem converge, we say that we have an *optimal algorithm*. At this point, no asymptotic improvement is possible and the focus changes to improving the constant factors involved (e.g., reducing the algorithm's running time from $3\sqrt{n}$ to $2\sqrt{n}$).

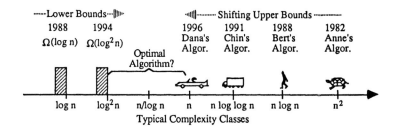

Figure 3.2. Upper and lower bounds may tighten over time.

Now, let us broaden our attention and consider the cost of the machine on which the algorithm runs in addition to the running time. Unfortunately, a simple, accurate, and time-invariant cost model for parallel machines does not exist. So, in the interest of tractability, we often take the number p of processors used for a given algorithm as a very rough indicator of cost. If we are allowed to vary the number of processors used (either by choosing/designing our own parallel machine or else by limiting the algorithm's execution to a subset of processors (a partition) of a larger parallel machine, then the running time will be a function of both the problem size n and the number p of processors used.

Now, because of the additional cost factor introduced, different notions of optimality can be entertained. Let $T(n, p)$ be our algorithm's running time when solving a problem of size n on a machine with p processors. The algorithm is said to be

- Time-optimal if $T(n, p) = g(n, p)$, where $g(n, p)$ is an established time lower bound.
- Cost-time optimal (cost-optimal for short) iff $p\,T(n, p) = T(n, 1)$.
  Redundancy = Utilization = 1
- Cost-time efficient (efficient for short) iff $p\,T(n, p) = \Theta(T(n, 1))$.
  Redundancy = Utilization = $\Theta(1)$

One final observation is in order. Just as we took a simplified view of cost by equating it with the number p of processors, we can simplify our view of time by counting computation and/or communication steps instead of measuring real time. So, rather than saying that a parallel matrix multiplication algorithm terminates in so many seconds, we may say that it executes so many floating-point operations and transmits so many messages between the processors. With this simplified view, one must be careful in comparing algorithm complexities across different machines. A speed-up of 5 in terms of step counts may correspond to a speed-up of 2 or 3, say, when real time is considered (Fig. 3.3).

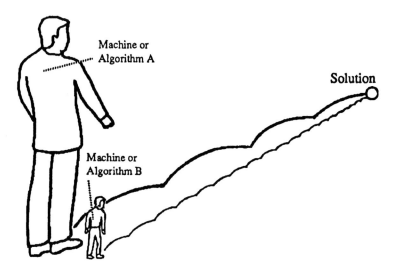

Figure 3.3. Five times fewer steps does not necessarily mean five times faster.

3.3. COMPLEXITY CLASSES

Complexity theory is a branch of computer science that deals with the ease or difficulty of solving various computational problems of interest. In complexity theory, problems are divided into several complexity classes according to their running times on a single-processor system (or a deterministic Turing machine, to be more exact). Problems whose running times are upper bounded by polynomials in n are said to belong to the P class and are generally considered to be tractable. Even if the polynomial is of a high degree, such that a large problem requires years of computation on the fastest available supercomputer, there is still hope that with improvements in the algorithm or in computer performance, a reasonable running time may be obtained.

On the other hand, problems for which the best known deterministic algorithm runs in exponential time are intractable. For example, if solving a problem of size n requires the execution of 2^n machine instructions, the running time for $n = 100$ on a GIPS (giga IPS) processor will be around 400 billion centuries! A problem of this kind for which, when given a solution, the correctness of the solution can be verified in polynomial time, is said to belong to the NP (nondeterministic polynomial) class.

An example of an NP problem is the *subset-sum problem*: Given a set of n integers and a target sum s, determine if a subset of the integers in the given set add up to s. This problem looks deceptively simple, yet no one knows how to solve it other than by trying practically all of the 2^n subsets of the given set. Even if each of these trials takes only 1 ps, the problem is virtually unsolvable for $n = 100$. This does not mean that we cannot solve specific instances of the subset-sum problem, or even most instances of practical interest, efficiently. What it implies is that an efficient general algorithm for solving this problem is not known. Neither has anyone been able to prove that an efficient (polynomial-time) algorithm for the subset-sum problem does not exist.

In fact, the P =? NP question is an open problem of complexity theory. A positive answer to this question would mean that the subset-sum and a host of other "hard" problems can be solved efficiently even if we do not yet know how to do it. A negative answer, on the other hand, would imply that there exist problems for which efficient algorithms can never be found. Despite a lack of proof in either direction, researchers in complexity theory believe that in fact P ≠ NP. Furthermore, they have defined the class of *NP-complete* problems, meaning that any problem in NP can be transformed, by a computationally efficient process, to any one of these problems. The subset-sum problem is known to be NP-complete. Thus, if one ever finds an efficient solution to the subset-sum problem, this is tantamount to proving P = NP. On the other hand, if one can prove that the subset-sum problem is not in P, then neither is any other NP-complete problem (leading to the conclusion P ≠ NP).

Figure 3.4 depicts the relationships of these classes as we currently understand them. The details and subclasses shown inside the class P will be explained in Section 3.4. The class NP-hard is explained below.

Given the large class of problems of practical interest that are in NP and the vast amount of time and other resources spent over the years in trying to find efficient solutions to these problems, proving that a computational problem is NP-complete virtually removes any hope of ever finding an efficient algorithm for that problem. Thus, in a sense, NP-complete problems are the "hardest" problems in the NP class. Besides the subset-sum problem

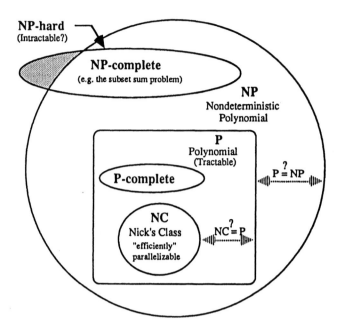

Figure 3.4. A conceptual view of complexity classes and their relationships.

mentioned above, the following problems of practical interest (and many others) are known to be NP-complete:

1. Determining if there exists an assignment of truth values to the variables in a Boolean expression, written as the AND of several OR clauses, such that the resulting value of the expression is "true" (the *satisfiability* problem). This problem is in NP even if each OR clause is restricted to have exactly 3 literals (true or complemented variables).
2. Determining if there exists an assignment of 0s and 1s to the inputs of a logic circuit that makes the output 1 (the *circuit satisfiability* problem).
3. Deciding if a graph contains a cycle or loop with all of the nodes in it (the *Hamiltonian cycle* problem).
4. Finding a lowest-cost or shortest-distance tour of a number of cities, given the travel cost or distance between all pairs of cities (the *traveling salesman* problem).

One final bit of terminology: As difficult as NP problems may seem, there exist problems that are not even in NP, meaning that even verifying that a claimed solution to such a problem is correct is currently intractable. An *NP-hard* problem is one that we do not know to be in NP but do know that any NP problem can be reduced to it by a polynomial-time algorithm. The name of this class implies that such problems are at least as hard as any NP problem.

Typically, the proof that a problem of interest is NP-complete consists of two parts: (1) proving that it is in NP by showing that a given solution for it can be verified in polynomial time and (2) proving that it is NP-hard by showing that some NP-complete (and thus any

NP) problem can be reduced to it. For the latter part of the proof, we have a wide array of NP-complete problems to choose from. But how was this process bootstrapped; i.e., where did the first NP-complete problem come from? The first seed was the satisfiability problem that was established to be NP-complete by Cook in 1971 [Cook71] using a rather tedious proof.

3.4. PARALLELIZABLE TASKS AND THE NC CLASS

Based on the discussion in Section 3.3, parallel processing is generally of no avail for solving NP problems. A problem that takes 400 billion centuries to solve on a uniprocessor, would still take 400 centuries even if it can be perfectly parallelized over 1 billion processors. Again, this statement does not refer to specific instances of the problem but to a general solution for all instances. Thus, parallel processing is primarily useful for speeding up the execution time of the problems in P. Here, even a factor of 1000 speed-up can mean the difference between practicality and impracticality (running time of several hours versus 1 year).

In 1979, Niclaus Pippenger [Pipp79] suggested that efficiently parallelizable problems in P might be defined as those problems that can be solved in a time period that is at most polylogarithmic in the problem size n, i.e., $T(p) = O(\log^k n)$ for some constant k, using no more than a polynomial number $p = O(n^l)$ of processors. This class of problems was later named *Nick's Class* (NC) in his honor. The class NC has been extensively studied and forms a foundation for parallel complexity theory.

Pippenger used a parallel machine model known as *parallel random-access machine* (PRAM) in formulating his complexity results. We will define PRAM in Chapter 5, but knowledge of the PRAM model is not essential for understanding the NC class, as the NC class is closed under virtually all transformations of practical interest.

A weaker form of NC, known as the *parallel computation thesis*, is stated as follows:

> Anything that can be computed on a Turing machine using polynomially (polylogarithmically) bounded space in unlimited time can be computed on a parallel machine in polynomial (polylogarithmic) time using an unlimited number of processors, and vice versa.

The problem with this thesis is that it places no bound on computational resources other than time. The significance of NC, and its popularity, stems from its establishing simultaneous bounds on time and hardware resources, while at the same time being relatively insensitive to architectural and technological variations in parallel machine implementations.

At present, the question NC = ? P is an open problem of parallel complexity theory. Just as was the case for the P = ? NP question, no one knows the answer to this question, but there is strong suspicion that NC ≠ P. The reason behind this suspicion is also quite similar to that for P ≠ NP. A P-complete problem in P is a problem such that any other problem in P can be transformed to it in polylogarithmic time using a polynomial number of processors. So, if a polylogarithmic-time algorithm with a polynomial number of processors is ever found for any P-complete problem, then all problems in P are efficiently parallelizable and NC = P. Some of these problems have been around for years and studied extensively by numerous researchers. Thus, the lack of efficient algorithms for these problems strongly supports the conclusion that NC ≠ P.

Sorting is a good example of an NC problem. In Chapter 7, we will see that several techniques are available for building an n-input sorting network from $O(n \log^2 n)$ two-input compare–exchange circuit blocks, with the critical path across the network going through $O(\log^2 n)$ comparison–exchange levels. Hence, polylogarithmic time is achieved for sorting using a number of circuit blocks (processors) that is upper bounded by $O(n^{1+\epsilon})$ for any $\epsilon > 0$.

An example of a P-complete problem is the *circuit-value* problem: Given a logic circuit with known inputs, determine its output. The fact that the circuit-value problem is in P should be obvious. It is a simple problem that we routinely solve in logic simulation packages. Yet no general algorithm exists for the efficient parallel evaluation of a circuit's output. This rather surprising fact limits the speed-ups that can be achieved in parallel logic simulation.

3.5. PARALLEL PROGRAMMING PARADIGMS

Several methods are used extensively in devising efficient parallel algorithms for solving problems of interest. A brief review of these methods (divide and conquer, randomization, approximation) is appropriate at this point as they are important to complexity analysis efforts.

Divide and Conquer. Some problems in P can be solved in parallel as follows. Decompose the problem of size n into two or more "smaller" subproblems. Suppose that the required decomposition, when done in parallel, takes $T_d(n)$ time. Solve the subproblems independently and obtain the corresponding results. As the subproblems are smaller than the original one, the time T_s to solve them will likely be less than $T(n)$. Finally, combine the results of the subproblems to compute the answer to the original problem. If the combining phase can be done in time $T_c(n)$, the total computation time is given by $T(n) = T_d(n) + T_s + T_c(n)$.

For example, in the case of sorting a list of n keys, we can decompose the list into two halves, sort the two sublists independently in parallel, and merge the two sorted sublists into a single sorted list. If we can perform each of the decomposition and merging operations in $\log_2 n$ steps on some parallel computer, and if the solution of the two sorting problems of size $n/2$ can be completely overlapped in time, then the running time of the parallel algorithm is characterized by the recurrence $T(n) = T(n/2) + 2 \log_2 n$. We will discuss the solution of such recurrences in Section 3.6. The divide-and-conquer paradigm is perhaps the most important tool for devising parallel algorithms and is used extensively in the rest of this book.

Randomization. Often it is impossible, or computationally difficult, to decompose a large problem into smaller problems in such a way that the solution times of the subproblems are roughly equal. Large decomposition and combining overheads, or wide variations in the solution times of the subproblems, may reduce the effective speed-up achievable by the divide-and-conquer method. In these cases, it might be possible to use random decisions that lead to good results with very high probability. The field of randomized parallel algorithms has grown significantly over the past few years and has led to the solution of many otherwise unsolvable problems.

Again, sorting provides a good example. Suppose that each of p processors begins with a sublist of size n/p. First each processor selects a random sample of size k from its local sublist. The kp samples from all processors form a smaller list that can be readily sorted, perhaps on a single processor or using a parallel algorithm that is known to be efficient for small lists. If this sorted list of samples is now divided into p equal segments and the beginning values in the p segments used as thresholds to divide the original list of n keys into p sublists, the lengths of these latter sublists will be approximately balanced with high probability. The n-input sorting problem has thus been transformed into an initial random sampling, a small sorting problem for the kp samples, broadcasting of the p threshold values to all processors, permutation of the elements among the processors according to the p threshold values, and p independent sorting problems of approximate size n/p. The average case running time of such an algorithm can be quite good. However, there is no useful worst-case guarantee on its running time.

Besides the *random sampling* method used in the above example, randomization can be applied in several other ways [Gupt94]. *Input randomization* is used to avoid bad data patterns for which a particular algorithm, known to be efficient on the average, might have close to worst-case performance. For example, if a routing algorithm is known to have good performance when the source/destination nodes are randomly distributed but suffers from excessive resource contentions, and thus degraded performance, for certain regular data movement patterns, it might be possible to handle the problematic routing patterns by using a randomly selected intermediate node for each source–destination pair.

To complete the picture, we briefly review the three other classes of randomization methods that have been found useful in practice:

1. *Random search.* When a large space must be searched for an element with certain desired properties, and it is known that such elements are abundant, random search can lead to very good average-case performance. A deterministic linear search, on the other hand, can lead to poor performance if all of the desired elements are clustered together.
2. *Control randomization.* To avoid consistently experiencing close to worst-case performance with one algorithm, related to some unfortunate distribution of inputs, the algorithm to be applied for solving a problem, or an algorithm parameter, can be chosen at random.
3. *Symmetry breaking.* Interacting deterministic processes may exhibit a cyclic behavior that leads to deadlock (akin to two people colliding when they try to exit a room through a narrow door, backing up, and then colliding again). Randomization can be used to break the symmetry and thus the deadlock.

Approximation.   Iterative numerical methods often use approximation to arrive at the solution(s). For example, to solve a system of n linear equations, one can begin with some rough estimates for the answers and then successively refine these estimates using parallel numerical calculations. Jacobi relaxation, to be covered in Section 11.4, is an example of such approximation methods. Under proper conditions, the iterations converge to the correct solutions; the larger the number of iterations, the more accurate the solutions.

The strength of such approximation methods lies in the fact that fairly precise results can be obtained rather quickly, with additional iterations used to increase the precision if desired. Provided that the required computations for each iteration can be easily parallelized over any number p of processors, we have at our disposal a powerful method for time/cost/accuracy trade-offs. If time and hardware resources are limited by deadlines or concurrent running of more urgent tasks, the computation can still be performed, albeit at lower precision. The analysis of complexity is somewhat more difficult here as the number of iterations required often cannot be expressed as a simple function of the desired accuracy and/or the problem size. Typically, an upper bound on the number of iterations is established and used in determining the algorithm's worst-case running time.

3.6. SOLVING RECURRENCES

In our discussion of the divide-and-conquer method in Section 3.5, we presented the recurrence $T(n) = T(n/2) + 2 \log_2 n$ as an example of what might transpire in analyzing algorithm complexity. Because such recurrences arise quite frequently in the analysis of (parallel) algorithms, it is instructive to discuss methods for their solution. As no general method exists for solving recurrences, we will review several methods along with examples.

The simplest method for solving recurrences is through *unrolling*. The method is best illustrated through a sequence of examples. In all examples below, $f(1) = 0$ is assumed.

1. $f(n) = f(n-1) + n$ {rewrite $f(n-1)$ as $f((n-1)-1) + n - 1$}
   $= f(n-2) + n - 1 + n$
   $= f(n-3) + n - 2 + n - 1 + n$
   . . .
   $= f(1) + 2 + 3 + \cdots + n - 1 + n$
   $= n(n+1)/2 - 1$
   $= \Theta(n^2)$

2. $f(n) = f(n/2) + 1$ {rewrite $f(n/2)$ as $f((n/2)/2) + 1$}
   $= f(n/4) + 1 + 1$
   $= f(n/8) + 1 + 1 + 1$
   . . .
   $= f(n/n) + 1 + 1 + 1 + \cdots + 1$
   $\qquad\qquad$ --- $\log_2 n$ times ---
   $= \log_2 n$
   $= \Theta(\log n)$

3. $f(n) = 2f(n/2) + 1$
   $= 4f(n/4) + 2 + 1$
   $= 8f(n/8) + 4 + 2 + 1$
   . . .
   $= nf(n/n) + n/2 + \cdots + 4 + 2 + 1$
   $= n - 1$
   $= \Theta(n)$

4. $f(n) = f(n/2) + n$
   $= f(n/4) + n/2 + n$
   $= f(n/8) + n/4 + n/2 + n$
   . . .
   $= f(n/n) + 2 + 4 + \cdots + n/4 + n/2 + n$
   $= 2n - 2$
   $= \Theta(n)$

5. $f(n) = 2f(n/2) + n$
$\qquad = 4f(n/4) + n + n$
$\qquad = 8f(n/8) + n + n + n$
$\qquad \cdots$
$\qquad = nf(n/n) + n + n + n + \cdots + n$
$\qquad\qquad$ --- $\log_2 n$ times ---
$\qquad = n \log_2 n$
$\qquad = \Theta(n \log n)$

Alternate solution for the recurrence $f(n) = 2f(n/2) + n$:
Rewrite the recurrence as

$$\frac{f(n)}{n} = \frac{f(n/2)}{n/2} + 1$$

and denote $f(n)/n$ by $h(n)$ to get

$$h(n) = h(n/2) + 1$$

This is the same as Example 2 above and leads to

$$h(n) = \log_2 n \Rightarrow f(n) = n \log_2 n$$

6. $f(n) = f(n/2) + \log_2 n$
$\qquad = f(n/4) + \log_2(n/2) + \log_2 n$
$\qquad = f(n/8) + \log_2(n/4) + \log_2(n/2) + \log_2 n$
$\qquad \cdots$
$\qquad = f(n/n) + \log_2 2 + \log_2 4 + \cdots + \log_2(n/2) + \log_2 n$
$\qquad = 1 + 2 + 3 + \cdots + \log_2 n$
$\qquad = \log_2 n (\log_2 n + 1)/2$
$\qquad = \Theta(\log^2 n)$

Another method that we will find useful, particularly for recurrences that cannot be easily unrolled, is guessing the answer to the recurrence and then verifying the guess by substitution. In fact, the method of substitution can be used to determine the constant multiplicative factors and lower-order terms once the asymptotic complexity has been established by other methods.

As an example, let us say that we know that the solution to Example 1 above is $f(n) = \Theta(n^2)$. We write $f(n) = an^2 + g(n)$, where $g(n) = o(n^2)$ represents the lower-order terms. Substituting in the recurrence equation, we get

$$an^2 + g(n) = a(n - 1)^2 + g(n - 1) + n$$

This equation simplifies to

$$g(n) = g(n - 1) + (1 - 2a)n + a$$

Choose $a = 1/2$ in order to make $g(n) = o(n^2)$ possible. Then, the solution to the recurrence $g(n) = g(n - 1) + 1/2$ is $g(n) = n/2 - 1$, assuming $g(1) = 0$. The solution to the original recurrence then becomes $f(n) = n^2/2 + n/2 - 1$, which matches our earlier result based on unrolling.

Unrolling recurrences can be tedious and error-prone in some cases. The following general theorem helps us establish the order of the solution to some recurrences without unrolling [Bent80].

THEOREM 3.1 (basic theorem for recurrences). *Given the recurrence* $f(n) = a\,f(n/b) + h(n)$, *where a and b are constants and h is an arbitrary function, the asymptotic solution to the recurrence is*

$$f(n) = \Theta(n^{\log_b a}) \qquad \text{if } h(n) = O(n^{\log_b a - \varepsilon}) \text{ for some } \varepsilon > 0$$

$$f(n) = \Theta(n^{\log_b a} \log n) \qquad \text{if } h(n) = \Theta(n^{\log_b a})$$

$$f(n) = \Theta(h(n)) \qquad \text{if } h(n) = \Omega(n^{\log_b a + \varepsilon}) \text{ for some } \varepsilon > 0$$

The recurrence given in the statement of Theorem 3.1 arises, for example, if we decompose a given problem of size n into b problems of size n/b, with these smaller problems solved in a batches (e.g., because the available resources, typically processors, are inadequate for solving all subproblems concurrently).

The function $h(n)$ represents the time needed to decompose the problem and for obtaining the overall solution from the solutions to the subproblems. Therefore, $a = 1$ typically means that we have enough processors to solve all b subproblems concurrently, $a = b$ means we have just one processor, so the subproblems are solved sequentially, and $1 < a < b$ means we can solve some of the problems concurrently but that the number of processors is inadequate to deal with all of them concurrently. An example of this last situation might be when the number of processors required is sublinear in problem size (problems with $1/b = 1/4$ the size require half as many processors, say, when $p = \sqrt{\text{size}}$ thus dictating $a = 2$ passes for solving the four subproblems).

Note that the first and third cases in the statement of Theorem 3.1 are separated from the middle case by $\pm\varepsilon$ in the exponent of n. Let us consider the middle case first. Unrolling the recurrence in this case will be done $\log_b n$ times before getting to $f(1)$. As $b^{\log_b a} = a$, each of the $\log_b n$ terms resulting from the unrolling is on the order of $\Theta(h(n)) = \Theta(n^{\log_b a})$; so, one can say that the decomposition/merging overhead is more or less constant across the recursive iterations. In the third case, the overhead decreases geometrically, so the first term in the unrolling, i.e., $h(n)$, dictates the complexity. Finally, in the first case, the unrolled terms form an increasing geometric progression, making the last term in the unrolling dominant. This last term can be obtained as follows:

$$f(n) \; = a\,f(n/b) + h(n)$$

$$= a^2 f(n/b^2) + \ldots$$

$$\ldots$$

$$= a^{\log_b n} f(1) + \ldots \qquad \text{Use } \log_b n = \log_2 n / \log_2 b$$

$$= a^{\log_2 n / \log_2 b} f(1) + \ldots \qquad \text{Use } a = 2^{\log_2 a}$$

$$= 2^{\log_2 a \log_2 n / \log_2 b} f(1) + \ldots \qquad \text{Use } 2^{\log_2 n} = n$$

$$= n^{\log_2 a / \log_2 b} f(1) + \cdots$$

$$= \Theta(n^{\log_b a})$$

Theorem 3.1 only provides an asymptotic solution in cases where the theorem's conditions are met. However, as noted earlier, once the order of the solution is known, substitution in the recurrence can be used to determine the constant factors and lower-order terms if desired.

PROBLEMS

3.1. Asymptotic complexity

For each of the following pairs of functions $f(n)$ and $g(n)$, determine which of the relationships $f(n) = o(g(n))$, $f(n) = O(g(n))$, $f(n) = \Theta(g(n))$, $f(n) = \Omega(g(n))$, or $f(n) = \omega(g(n))$, if any, holds. Explain your reasoning.

a. $f(n) = 10n^2$, $g(n) = n^2 + 100$.

b. $f(n) = n^{5/2}$, $g(n) = 2^{n/2}$.

c. $f(n) = \sqrt{n}$, $g(n) = 2^{(\log n)/3}$.

d. $f(n) = 25 \, |\sin n|^n$, $g(n) = n$.

e. $f(n) = n \, |\sin n|$, $g(n) = n/100$.

f. $f(n) = 2^{(\log n)^{1/2}}$, $g(n) = \sqrt{n}$.

3.2. Asymptotic complexity

Order the following functions with respect to their growth rates, from the slowest growing to the fastest growing. Explain your reasoning.

a. $2^{\sqrt{\log n}}$

b. $\sqrt{n}$

c. $(\sqrt{2})^{\log n}$

d. $(\log n)^{\sqrt{2}}$

e. $2^{\log \log n}$

f. $(\log \log n)^{\log \log n}$

3.3. Computational complexity

Assume that the pairs of functions $f(n)$ and $g(n)$ of Problem 3.1 correspond to the running times of two different algorithms A and B, respectively, for solving a given problem when the input size is n (do not worry about the fact that some of the instances do not represent real problems). Determine, for each pair of functions, the problem sizes for which Algorithm A is better than Algorithm B.

3.4. Computational complexity

With reference to the data in Table 3.2, suppose that a running time of 3 hours or less is tolerable in a given application context. Assuming that Moore's law holds (see Section 1.1), for each of the five functions shown in Table 3.2, determine the factor by which the problem size can increase in 10 years.

3.5. Comparing algorithms

Suppose two different parallel algorithms for solving a given problem lead to the following recurrences for the computation time. Which algorithm is asymptotically faster and why?

a. $T(n) = 2T(n/2) + n$.

b. $T(n) = T(n/2) + n^2$.

3.6. Solving recurrences

    a. Derive an exact solution to the recurrence $T(n) = T(n/2) + cn$ assuming that n is a power of 2, c is a constant, and $T(1) = 0$.

    b. More generally, the problem size (initially or in intermediate steps) is not necessarily even. Consider the recurrence $T(n) = T(\lceil n/2 \rceil) + cn$ and use it to derive an upper bound for $T(n)$. *Hint:* The worst case occurs when n is 1 more than a power of 2.

    c. Repeat part (b) for the more general recurrence $T(n) = aT(\lceil n/b \rceil) + cn$.

3.7. System of two recurrences

    a. Find exact solutions for $A(n)$ and $B(n)$ if $A(n) = B(n/2) + gn$ and $B(n) = A(n/2) + hn$, assuming n to be a power of 2, g and h known constants, and $A(1) = B(1) = 0$.

    b. Repeat part (a) with $A(n) = 2B(n/2) + gn$ and $B(n) = A(n/2) + hn$.

    c. Repeat part (a) with $A(n) = 2B(n/2) + gn$ and $B(n) = 2A(n/2) + hn$.

    d. Formulate a general theorem for the asymptotic solution of system of two recurrences of the form $A(n) = cB(n/a) + gn$ and $B(n) = dA(n/b) + hn$, where a, b, c, and d are constants.

3.8. Solving recurrences

Apply the method of Theorem 3.1 to the solution of Examples 1 through 6 that precede it, where applicable.

3.9. Solving recurrences

Apply the method of Theorem 3.1 to the solution of the recurrence $f(n) = 2f(n/4) + cn$, where c is a known constant. Then, find the constant factor and the order of residual terms through substitution.

3.10. Basic theorem for recurrences

In the proof of the first case of Theorem 3.1, we implicitly assumed that $f(1)$ is a nonzero constant. Would the proof fall apart if $f(1) = 0$?

3.11. Solving recurrences

Solve the recurrence $f(n) = f(3n/4) + f(n^{1-b}) + cn^b$, where b and c are constants and $0 < b < 1$.

3.12. Asymptotic complexity

A *rough set S* is characterized by a lower bound set S_{lb} consisting of elements that are certain to be members of S and an upper bound set S_{ub} which also contains a *boundary region* consisting of possible elements of S (the possibility is not quantified) [Pawl97]. Define the basic set operations on rough sets and determine if they are asymptotically more complex than ordinary set operations in sequential and parallel implementations.

3.13. Computational complexity

Consider the following results from number theory [Stew97]: (a) x is not prime iff some number in $[2, \lfloor \sqrt{x} \rfloor]$ divides it. (b) x is prime iff it divides $(x - 1)! + 1$. (c) If x is prime, then it divides $2^x - 2$ (the converse is not true). A large number x, with hundreds of digits, is given and we would like to prove that it is not a prime. We do not need the factors; just a confirmation that it is not a prime. Which of the above three methods would lead to a more efficient parallel implementation and why? Note that in computing a large number whose divisibility by x is to be tested, we can do all of the calculations modulo x.

3.14. NP-completeness

In our discussion of NP-completeness, we stated that the satisfiability problem for OR–AND

Boolean expressions is NP-complete and that even the special case where each of the ORed terms consists of exactly 3 literals (known as the 3-satisfiability problem) is not any easier.

a. Show that the AND–OR version of the satisfiability problem, i.e., when the Boolean expression in question consists of the OR of AND terms, is in P.

b. Show that 2-satisfiability is in P. *Hint:* Use the equivalence of x OR y with (NOT x) IMPLIES y to reduce the 2-satisfiability problem to a problem on a directed graph.

3.15. NP-completeness

Consider a set S of integers. The set partition problem is that of determining if the set S can be partitioned into two disjoint subsets such that the sum of the integers in each subset is the same. Show that the set partition problem is NP-complete.

REFERENCES AND SUGGESTED READING

[Cook71]   Cook, S., "The Complexity of Theorem Proving Procedures," *Proc. 3rd ACM Symp. Theory of Computing*, 1971, pp. 151–158.

[Corm90]   Cormen, T. H., C. E. Leiserson, and R. L. Rivest, *Introduction to Algorithms*, McGraw-Hill, 1990, Chapter 36, pp. 916–963.

[Gupt94]   Gupta, R., S. A. Smolka, and S. Bhaskar, "On Randomization in Sequential and Distributed Algorithms," *ACM Computing Surveys*, Vol. 26, pp. 7–86, March 1994.

[Kris96]   Krishnamurthy, E. V., "Complexity Issues in Parallel and Distributed Computing," Chapter 4 in *Parallel and Distributed Computing Handbook*, edited by A. Y. Zomaya, McGraw-Hill, 1996, pp. 89–126.

[Parb87]   Parberry, I., *Parallel Complexity Theory*, Pitman, 1987.

[Pawl97]   Pawlak, Z., J. Grzymala-Busse, R. Slowinski, and W. Ziarko, "Rough Sets," *Communications of the ACM*, Vol. 38, No. 11, pp. 89–95, November 1995.

[Pipp79]   Pippenger, N., "On Simultaneous Resource Bounds," *Proc. 20th Symp. Foundations of Computer Science*, 1979, pp. 307–311.

[Stew97]   Stewart, I., "Mathematical Recreations: Big Game Hunting in Primeland," *Scientific American*, Vol. 276, No. 5, pp. 108–111, May 1997.

4

Models of Parallel Processing

Parallel processors come in many different varieties. It would not be possible to discuss all of these varieties, including their distinguishing features, strong points within application contexts, and drawbacks, in a single book. Thus, we often deal with abstract models of real machines. The benefits of using abstract models include technology-independent theories and algorithmic techniques that are applicable to a large number of existing and future machines. Disadvantages include the inability to predict the actual performance accurately and a tendency to simplify the models too much, so that they no longer represent any real machine. However, even oversimplified models do offer some benefits. The conceptual simplicity of such models makes the development of algorithms and the analysis of various trade-offs more manageable. If automatic translation of these abstract algorithms into efficient programs for real machines is possible through the use of intelligent or optimizing compilers, then these models can indeed be enormously helpful. Chapter topics are

- 4.1. Development of early models
- 4.2. SIMD versus MIMD architectures
- 4.3. Global versus distributed memory
- 4.4. The PRAM shared-memory model
- 4.5. Distributed-memory or graph models
- 4.6. Circuit model and physical realizations

4.1. DEVELOPMENT OF EARLY MODELS

Associative processing (AP) was perhaps the earliest form of parallel processing. Associative or content-addressable memories (AMs, CAMs), which allow memory cells to be accessed based on contents rather than their physical locations within the memory array, came into the forefront in the 1950s when advances in magnetic and cryogenic memory technologies allowed the construction of, and experimentation with, reasonably sized prototypes. However, the origins of research on AM/AP technology and applications actually go back to the 1943 sketch of a relay-based associative memory by Konrad Zuse and the 1945 visionary assessment of the need for associative access to information by Vannevar Bush (see Table 4.1).

AM/AP architectures are essentially based on incorporating simple processing logic into the memory array so as to remove the need for transferring large volumes of data through the limited-bandwidth interface between the memory and the processor (the *von Neumann bottleneck*). Early associative memories provided two basic capabilities: (1) masked search, or looking for a particular bit pattern in selected fields of all memory words and marking those for which a match is indicated, and (2) parallel write, or storing a given bit pattern into selected fields of all memory words that have been previously marked. These two basic capabilities, along with simple logical operations on mark vectors (e.g., ORing them together) suffice for the programming of sophisticated searches or even parallel arithmetic operations [Parh97].

Over the past half-century, the AM/AP model has evolved through the incorporation of additional capabilities, so that it is in essence converging with SIMD-type array processors. Early examples of APs included the Goodyear STARAN processor, a relatively successful commercial product of the 1970s, whose design was motivated by the computation-intensive problem of aircraft conflict detection; $O(n^2)$ pairwise checks are required to avoid collisions and near misses for n aircraft in the vicinity of a busy airport. Modern incarnations of this model are seen in processor-in-memory (PIM) chips, which are basically standard DRAM chips with a large number of very simple processors added on their data access paths, and intelligent RAM (IRAM) architectures, which have been shown to have advantages in both performance and power consumption [From97].

Another early model, introduced in the 1950s, dealt with parallel processing for image understanding applications. In those days, interest in artificial intelligence, and particularly its subfield of computer vision, was quite high. The development of *perceptrons* (a neuronlike device in charge of processing a single pixel in a digital image) was based on the pioneering

Table 4.1. Entering the Second Half-Century of Associative Processing

Decade	Events and advances	Technology	Performance
1940s	Formulation of need & concept	Relays	
1950s	Emergence of cell technologies	Magnetic, cryogenic	Mega-bit-OPS
1960s	Introduction of basic architectures	Transistors	
1970s	Commercialization & applications	ICs	Giga-bit-OPS
1980s	Focus on system/software issues	VLSI	Tera-bit-OPS
1990s	Scalable & flexible architectures	ULSI, WSI	Peta-bit-OPS?

work of McCulloch and Pitts in the 1940s. The perceptron convergence theorem of Rosen-
blatt, along with Minsky's work on the limitations of such devices in the 1960s, created a
flurry of research activities that laid the foundation for the modern field of *neural networks*.
Hopfield's energy approach and the introduction of the back propagation learning algorithm
put neural networks on the fast track so that today they are used for the solution of complex
decision problems in a wide class of applications [Jain96].

The 1960s saw the introduction of a model of fundamental importance. *Cellular
automata* formed natural extensions of the types of abstract machines that were studied as
theoretical models of von Neumann-type sequential computers. Cellular automata machines
are typically viewed as a collection of identical finite-state automata that are interconnected,
through their input–output links, in a regular fashion, with the state transitions of each
automaton controlled by its own state, the states of the neighbors to which it is connected,
and its primary inputs, if any [Garz95]. Systolic arrays, which form the basis of
high-performance VLSI-based designs in some application areas, can be viewed as
cellular automata. In recent years, we have witnessed a resurgence of interest in cellular
automata as theoretical models of massively parallel systems and as tools for modeling
physical phenomena [PPCA].

In the subsequent sections of this chapter, we will review some of the commonly used
models in the field of parallel processing. Before doing so, it is instructive to revisit the
Flynn–Johnson classification of computer systems. Figure 4.1 depicts the classification
along with the two major dichotomies that we will consider in the next two sections.

The SISD class encompasses standard uniprocessor systems, including those that
employ pipelining, out-of-order execution, multiple instruction issue, and several functional
units to achieve higher performance. Because the SIMD and MIMD classes will be examined
in detail in the remainder of this book, here we say a few words about the class of MISD
parallel architectures for completeness. As mentioned in Section 1.4, the MISD (miss-
dee) class has not found widespread application. One reason is that most application

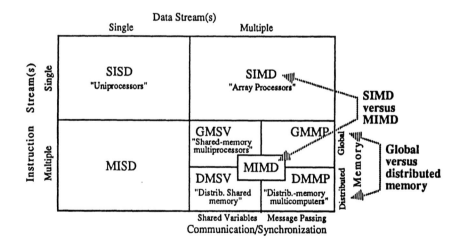

Figure 4.1. The Flynn–Johnson classification of computer systems.

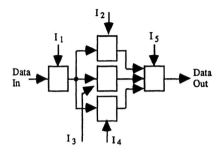

Figure 4.2. Multiple instruction streams operating on a single data stream (MISD).

problems do not map easily onto a MISD architecture, making it impossible to design a general-purpose architecture of this type. However, one can quite properly envisage MISD-type parallel processors for specific applications.

Figure 4.2 shows an example parallel processor with the MISD architecture. A single data stream enters the machine consisting of five processors. Various transformations are performed on each data item before it is passed on to the next processor(s). Successive data items can go through different transformations, either because of data-dependent conditional statements in the instruction streams (control-driven) or because of special control tags carried along with the data (data-driven). The MISD organization can thus be viewed as a flexible or high-level pipeline with multiple paths and programmable stages.

Even though we often view conventional pipelines as linear structures, pipelines with multiple paths and the capability to selectively bypass various stages are in fact used in high-performance CPU design. For example, the block diagram of a floating-point arithmetic pipeline may resemble Fig. 4.2, where the entry block is used for unpacking of the inputs and detection of special operands, the three parallel branches perform various floating-point arithmetic operations (say add, multiply, and divide), and the exit block normalizes and packs the results into the standard format. The key difference between the above pipeline and a MISD architecture is that the floating-point pipeline stages are not programmable.

4.2. SIMD VERSUS MIMD ARCHITECTURES

Most early parallel machines had SIMD designs. The ILLIAC IV computer, briefly mentioned in Section 1.3, and described in more detail in Section 23.2, is a well-known example of such early parallel machines. SIMD implies that a central unit fetches and interprets the instructions and then broadcasts appropriate control signals to a number of processors operating in lockstep. This initial interest in SIMD resulted both from characteristics of early parallel applications and from economic necessity. Some of the earliest applications, such as air traffic control and linear-algebra computations, are pleasantly parallel (at times researchers have characterized these as "embarrassingly parallel," referring to the extreme ease with which they can be parallelized). From the user's perspective, such applications tend to be much easier to program in SIMD languages and lead to more cost-effective SIMD hardware. On the economics front, full-fledged processors with reasonable speed were quite expensive in those days, thus limiting any highly parallel system to the SIMD variety.

Within the SIMD category, two fundamental design choices exist:

1. *Synchronous versus asynchronous SIMD.* In a SIMD machine, each processor can execute or ignore the instruction being broadcast based on its local state or data-dependent conditions. However, this leads to some inefficiency in executing conditional computations. For example, an "if-then-else" statement is executed by first enabling the processors for which the condition is satisfied and then flipping the "enable" bit before getting into the "else" part. On the average, half of the processors will be idle for each branch. The situation is even worse for "case" statements involving multiway branches. A possible cure is to use the asynchronous version of SIMD, known as SPMD (spim-dee or single-program, multiple data), where each processor runs its own copy of the common program. The advantage of SPMD is that in an "if-then-else" computation, each processor will only spend time on the relevant branch. The disadvantages include the need for occasional synchronization and the higher complexity of each processor, which must now have a program memory and instruction fetch/decode logic.

2. *Custom- versus commodity-chip SIMD.* A SIMD machine can be designed based on commodity (off-the-shelf) components or with custom chips. In the first approach, components tend to be inexpensive because of mass production. However, such general-purpose components will likely contain elements that may not be needed for a particular design. These extra components may complicate the design, manufacture, and testing of the SIMD machine and may introduce speed penalties as well. Custom components (including ASICs = application-specific ICs, multichip modules, or WSI = wafer-scale integrated circuits) generally offer better performance but lead to much higher cost in view of their development costs being borne by a relatively small number of parallel machine users (as opposed to commodity microprocessors that are produced in millions). As integrating multiple processors along with ample memory on a single VLSI chip becomes feasible, a type of convergence between the two approaches appears imminent.

Judging by what commercial vendors have introduced in the 1990s, the MIMD paradigm has become more popular recently. The reasons frequently cited for this shift of focus are the higher flexibility of the MIMD architectures and their ability to take advantage of commodity microprocessors, thus avoiding lengthy development cycles and getting a free ride on the speed improvement curve for such microprocessors (see Fig. 1.1). MIMD machines are most effective for medium- to coarse-grain parallel applications, where the computation is divided into relatively large subcomputations or *tasks* whose executions are assigned to the various processors. Advantages of MIMD machines include flexibility in exploiting various forms of parallelism, relative ease of partitioning into smaller independent parallel processors in a multiuser environment (this property also has important implications for fault tolerance), and less difficult expansion (scalability). Disadvantages include considerable interprocessor communication overhead and more difficult programming.

Within the MIMD class, three fundamental issues or design choices are subjects of ongoing debates in the research community.

1. *MPP—massively or moderately parallel processor.* Is it more cost-effective to build a parallel processor out of a relatively small number of powerful processors or a massive number of very simple processors (the "herd of elephants" or the "army of ants" approach)? Referring to Amdahl's law, the first choice does better on the inherently sequential part of a computation while the second approach might allow a higher speed-up for the parallelizable part. A general answer cannot be given to this question, as the best choice is both application- and technology-dependent. In the 1980s, several massively parallel computers were built and marketed (massive parallelism is generally taken to include 1000 or more processors). In the 1990s, however, we have witnessed a general shift from massive to moderate parallelism (tens to hundreds of processors), but the notion of massive parallelism has not been altogether abandoned, particularly at the highest level of performance required for Grand Challenge problems.

2. *Tightly versus loosely coupled MIMD.* Which is a better approach to high-performance computing, that of using specially designed multiprocessors/ multicomputers or a collection of ordinary workstations that are interconnected by commodity networks (such as Ethernet or ATM) and whose interactions are coordinated by special system software and distributed file systems? The latter choice, sometimes referred to as *network of workstations* (NOW) or cluster computing, has been gaining popularity in recent years. However, many open problems exist for taking full advantage of such network-based loosely coupled architectures. The hardware, system software, and applications aspects of NOWs are being investigated by numerous research groups. We will cover some aspects of such systems in Chapter 22. An intermediate approach is to link tightly coupled clusters of processors via commodity networks. This is essentially a hierarchical approach that works best when there is a great deal of data access locality.

3. *Explicit message passing versus virtual shared memory.* Which scheme is better, that of forcing the users to explicitly specify all messages that must be sent between processors or to allow them to program in an abstract higher-level model, with the required messages automatically generated by the system software? This question is essentially very similar to the one asked in the early days of high-level languages and virtual memory. At some point in the past, programming in assembly languages and doing explicit transfers between secondary and primary memories could lead to higher efficiency. However, nowadays, software is so complex and compilers and operating systems so advanced (not to mention processing power so cheap) that it no longer makes sense to hand-optimize the programs, except in limited time-critical instances. However, we are not yet at that point in parallel processing, and hiding the explicit communication structure of a parallel machine from the programmer has nontrivial consequences for performance.

4.3. GLOBAL VERSUS DISTRIBUTED MEMORY

Within the MIMD class of parallel processors, memory can be global or distributed.

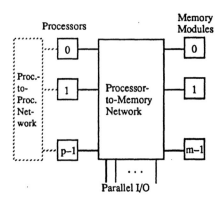

Figure 4.3. A parallel processor with global memory.

Global memory may be visualized as being in a central location where all processors can access it with equal ease (or with equal difficulty, if you are a half-empty-glass type of person). Figure 4.3 shows a possible hardware organization for a global-memory parallel processor. Processors can access memory through a special processor-to-memory network. As access to memory is quite frequent, the interconnection network must have very low latency (quite a difficult design challenge for more than a few processors) or else *memory-latency-hiding* techniques must be employed. An example of such methods is the use of multithreading in the processors so that they continue with useful processing functions while they wait for pending memory access requests to be serviced. In either case, very high network bandwidth is a must. An optional processor-to-processor network may be used for coordination and synchronization purposes.

A global-memory multiprocessor is characterized by the type and number p of processors, the capacity and number m of memory modules, and the network architecture. Even though p and m are independent parameters, achieving high performance typically requires that they be comparable in magnitude (e.g., too few memory modules will cause contention among the processors and too many would complicate the network design).

Examples for both the processor-to-memory and processor-to-processor networks include

1. Crossbar switch; $O(pm)$ complexity, and thus quite costly for highly parallel systems
2. Single or multiple buses (the latter with complete or partial connectivity)
3. Multistage interconnection network (MIN); cheaper than Example 1, more bandwidth than Example 2

The type of interconnection network used affects the way in which efficient algorithms are developed. In order to free the programmers from such tedious considerations, an abstract model of global-memory computers, known as PRAM, has been defined (see Section 4.4).

One approach to reducing the amount of data that must pass through the processor-to-memory interconnection network is to use a private cache memory of reasonable size within each processor (Fig. 4.4). The reason that using cache memories reduces the traffic through

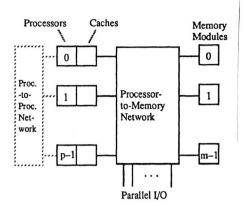

Figure 4.4. A parallel processor with global memory and processor caches.

the network is the same here as for conventional processors: locality of data access, repeated access to the same data, and the greater efficiency of block, as opposed to word-at-a-time, data transfers. However, the use of multiple caches gives rise to the *cache coherence* problem: Multiple copies of data in the main memory and in various caches may become inconsistent. With a single cache, the write-through policy can keep the two data copies consistent. Here, we need a more sophisticated approach, examples of which include

1. Do not cache shared data at all or allow only a single cache copy. If the volume of shared data is small and access to it infrequent, these policies work quite well.
2. Do not cache "writeable" shared data or allow only a single cache copy. Read-only shared data can be placed in multiple caches with no complication.
3. Use a cache coherence protocol. This approach may introduce a nontrivial consistency enforcement overhead, depending on the coherence protocol used, but removes the above restrictions. Examples include *snoopy caches* for bus-based systems (each cache monitors all data transfers on the bus to see if the validity of the data it is holding will be affected) and *directory-based schemes* (where writeable shared data are "owned" by a single processor or cache at any given time, with a directory used to determine physical data locations). See Sections 18.1 and 18.2 for more detail.

Distributed-memory architectures can be conceptually viewed as in Fig. 4.5. A collection of p processors, each with its own private memory, communicates through an interconnection network. Here, the latency of the interconnection network may be less critical, as each processor is likely to access its own local memory most of the time. However, the communication bandwidth of the network may or may not be critical, depending on the type of parallel applications and the extent of task interdependencies. Note that each processor is usually connected to the network through multiple links or *channels* (this is the norm here, although it can also be the case for shared-memory parallel processors).

In addition to the types of interconnection networks enumerated for shared-memory parallel processors, distributed-memory MIMD architectures can also be interconnected by

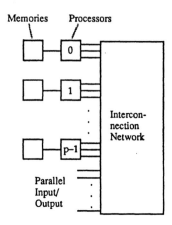

Figure 4.5. A parallel processor with distributed memory.

a variety of *direct networks*, so called because the processor channels are directly connected to their counterparts in other processors according to some interconnection pattern or *topology*. Examples of direct networks will be introduced in Section 4.5.

Because access to data stored in remote memory modules (those associated with other processors) involves considerably more latency than access to the processor's local memory, distributed-memory MIMD machines are sometimes described as nonuniform memory access (NUMA) architectures. Contrast this with the uniform memory access (UMA) property of global-memory machines. In a UMA architecture, distribution of data in memory is relevant only to the extent that it affects the ability to access the required data in parallel, whereas in NUMA architectures, inattention to data and task partitioning among the processors may have dire consequences. When coarse-grained tasks are allocated to the various processors, load-balancing (in the initial assignment or dynamically as the computations unfold) is also of some importance.

It is possible to view Fig. 4.5 as a special case of Fig. 4.4 in which the global-memory modules have been removed altogether; the fact that processors and (cache) memories appear in different orders is immaterial. This has led to the name *all-cache* or *cache-only* memory architecture (COMA) for such machines.

4.4. THE PRAM SHARED-MEMORY MODEL

The theoretical model used for conventional or sequential computers (SISD class) is known as the *random-access machine* (RAM) (not to be confused with random-access memory, which has the same acronym). The parallel version of RAM [PRAM (pea-ram)], constitutes an abstract model of the class of global-memory parallel processors. The abstraction consists of ignoring the details of the processor-to-memory interconnection network and taking the view that each processor can access any memory location in each machine cycle, independent of what other processors are doing.

Thus, for example, PRAM algorithms might involve statements like "for $0 \leq i < p$, Processor i adds the contents of memory location $2i + 1$ to the memory location $2i$" (different

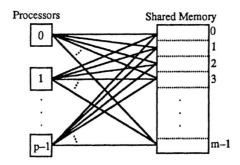

Figure 4.6. Conceptual view of a parallel random-access machine (PRAM).

locations accessed by the various processors) or "each processor loads the contents of memory location x into its Register 2" (the same location accessed by all processors). Obviously, the problem of multiple processors attempting to write into a common memory location must be resolved in some way. A detailed discussion of this issue is postponed to Chapter 5. Suffice it to say at this point that various inhibition, priority, or combining schemes can be employed when concurrent write operations to a common location are attempted.

In the formal PRAM model, a single processor is assumed to be active initially. In each computation step, each active processor can read from and write into the shared memory and can also activate another processor. Using a recursive doubling scheme, $\lceil \log_2 p \rceil$ steps are necessary and sufficient to activate all p processors. In our discussions, the set of active processors is usually implied. We do not explicitly activate the processors.

Even though the global-memory architecture was introduced as a subclass of the MIMD class, the abstract PRAM model depicted in Fig. 4.6 can be SIMD or MIMD. In the SIMD variant, all processors obey the same instruction in each machine cycle; however, because of indexed and indirect (register-based) addressing, they often execute the operation that is broadcast to them on different data. In fact, the shared-memory algorithms that we will study in Chapters 5 and 6 are primarily of the SIMD variety, as such algorithms are conceptually much simpler to develop, describe, and analyze.

In view of the direct and independent access to every memory location allowed for each processor, the PRAM model depicted in Fig. 4.6 is highly theoretical. If one were to build a physical PRAM, the processor-to-memory connectivity would have to be realized by an interconnection network. Because memory locations are too numerous to be assigned individual ports on an interconnection network, blocks of memory locations (or modules) would have to share a single network port. Let us ignore this practical consideration for now in order to make a fundamental point. Suppose we do in fact design a network connecting the processors to individual memory locations, as shown in Fig. 4.7. If this network is built from elements with constant fan-in and fan-out, then the depth of the network, and thus its latency, will be at least logarithmic in mp. This implies that each instruction cycle would have to consume $\Omega(\log p)$ real time.

The above point is important when we try to compare PRAM algorithms with those for distributed-memory models. An $O(\log p)$-step PRAM algorithm may not be faster than an

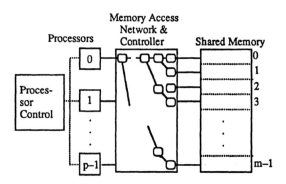

Figure 4.7. PRAM with some hardware details shown.

$O(\log^2 p)$-step algorithm for a hypercube architecture, say. We should always have Fig. 3.3 in mind when making such comparisons.

It is interesting to note that the above logarithmic latency is of no consequence in most theoretical studies of parallel algorithms. Recall that the class NC of efficiently parallelizable problems was defined as those that would require polylogarithmic running times. The formal definition of NC is in fact in terms of PRAM steps rather than real time. However, if an algorithm is executed in a polylogarithmic number of PRAM steps and if each step is realized in logarithmic real time, the actual running time is still polylogarithmic.

There is a way in which the log-factor slowdown implied by the above discussion can be hidden, leading to higher algorithm efficiency. Suppose that the memory access latency is exactly $\log_2 p$ clock cycles. A p-processor physical machine of the type shown in Fig. 4.7 can be used to emulate a $(p \log_2 p)$-processor "logical PRAM." A PRAM instruction cycle begins by issuing a memory access request, followed by some computation in the processor (e.g., an arithmetic operation), and ends by storing the result in memory. Suppose that the physical Processor 0, emulating logical Processors 0 through $\log_2 p - 1$, issues the $\log_2 p$ memory access requests in turn, one per clock cycle, with these requests pipelined through the network. When the last access request has been issued, the data for the first request arrive at the processor, followed, in consecutive clock cycles, by those for the other requests. In this way, the processor will be busy at all times and the $\log_2 p$ memory latency does not slow it down, provided that the memory access network possesses the aggregate bandwidth required by all of the $p \log_2 p$ in-transit memory requests.

Recall the graph representation of a shared-variable architecture introduced in Fig. 2.5, where each node of the p-node complete graph K_p contains one of the p processors plus m/p of the m memory locations. This would be an accurate model of the abstract PRAM if each node can honor p simultaneous memory access requests (one from the local processor and $p - 1$ coming from the node's communication ports), with multiple requests potentially addressing the same memory location. If only one or a small constant number of memory access requests can be processed in each cycle, then PRAM is not accurately represented. However, with additional effort, it is sometimes possible to structure a PRAM algorithm such that simultaneous accesses to the same block of memory locations are never attempted.

4.5. DISTRIBUTED-MEMORY OR GRAPH MODELS

Given the internal processor and memory structures in each node, a distributed-memory architecture is characterized primarily by the network used to interconnect the nodes (Fig. 4.5). This network is usually represented as a graph, with vertices corresponding to processor–memory nodes and edges corresponding to communication links. If communication links are unidirectional, then directed edges are used. Undirected edges imply bidirectional communication, although not necessarily in both directions at once. Important parameters of an interconnection network include

1. *Network diameter*: the longest of the shortest paths between various pairs of nodes, which should be relatively small if network latency is to be minimized. The network diameter is more important with store-and-forward routing (when a message is stored in its entirety and retransmitted by intermediate nodes) than with wormhole routing (when a message is quickly relayed through a node in small pieces).
2. *Bisection (band)width*: the smallest number (total capacity) of links that need to be cut in order to divide the network into two subnetworks of half the size. This is important when nodes communicate with each other in a random fashion. A small bisection (band)width limits the rate of data transfer between the two halves of the network, thus affecting the performance of communication-intensive algorithms.
3. *Vertex or node degree*: the number of communication ports required of each node, which should be a constant independent of network size if the architecture is to be readily scalable to larger sizes. The node degree has a direct effect on the cost of each node, with the effect being more significant for parallel ports containing several wires or when the node is required to communicate over all of its ports at once.

Table 4.2 lists these three parameters for some of the commonly used interconnection networks. Do not worry if you know little about the networks listed in Table 4.2. They are there to give you an idea of the variability of these parameters across different networks (examples for some of these networks appear in Fig. 4.8).

The list in Table 4.2 is by no means exhaustive. In fact, the multitude of interconnection networks, and claims with regard to their advantages over competing ones, have become quite confusing. The situation can be likened to a sea (Fig. 4.8). Once in a while (almost monthly over the past few years), a new network is dropped into the sea. Most of these make small waves and sink. Some produce bigger waves that tend to make people seasick! Hence, there have been suggestions that we should stop introducing new networks and instead focus on analyzing and better understanding the existing ones. A few have remained afloat and have been studied/analyzed to death (e.g., the hypercube).

Even though the distributed-memory architecture was introduced as a subclass of the MIMD class, machines based on networks of the type shown in Fig. 4.8 can be SIMD- or MIMD-type. In the SIMD variant, all processors obey the same instruction in each machine cycle, executing the operation that is broadcast to them on local data. For example, all processors in a 2D SIMD mesh might be directed to send data to their right neighbors and receive data from the left. In fact, the distributed-memory algorithms that we will study in Chapters 9–14 are primarily of the SIMD variety, as such algorithms are conceptually much simpler to develop, describe, and analyze.

Table 4.2. Topological Parameters of Selected Interconnection Networks

Network name(s)	No. of nodes	Network diameter	Bisection width	Node degree	Local links?
1D mesh (linear array)	k	$k-1$	1	2	Yes
1D torus (ring, loop)	k	$k/2$	2	2	Yes
2D mesh	k^2	$2k-2$	k	4	Yes
2D torus (k-ary 2-cube)	k^2	k	$2k$	4	Yes[1]
3D mesh	k^3	$3k-3$	k^2	6	Yes
3D torus (k-ary 3-cube)	k^3	$3k/2$	$2k^2$	6	Yes[1]
Pyramid	$(4k^2-1)/3$	$2\log_2 k$	$2k$	9	No
Binary tree	2^l-1	$2l-2$	1	3	No
4-ary hypertree	$2^l(2^{l+1}-1)$	$2l$	2^{l+1}	6	No
Butterfly	$2^l(l+1)$	$2l$	2^l	4	No
Hypercube	2^l	l	2^{l-1}	l	No
Cube-connected cycles	$2^l l$	$2l$	2^{l-1}	3	No
Shuffle–exchange	2^l	$2l-1$	$\geq 2^{l-1}/l$	4 unidir.	No
De Bruijn	2^l	l	$2^l/l$	4 unidir.	No

[1]With folded layout.

The development of efficient parallel algorithms suffers from the proliferation of available interconnection networks, for algorithm design must be done virtually from scratch for each new architecture. It would be nice if we could abstract away the effects of the interconnection topology (just as we did with PRAM for global-memory machines) in order to free the algorithm designer from a lot of machine-specific details. Even though this is not

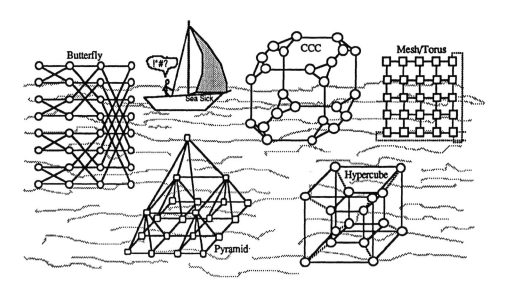

Figure 4.8. The sea of interconnection networks.

completely possible, models that replace the topological information reflected in the inter-connection graph with a small number of parameters do exist and have been shown to capture the effect of interconnection topology fairly accurately.

As an example of such abstract models, we briefly review the LogP model [Cull96]. In LogP, the communication architecture of a parallel computer is captured in four parameters:

L *Latency* upper bound when a small message (of a few words) is sent from an arbitrary source node to an arbitrary destination node

o The *overhead*, defined as the length of time when a processor is dedicated to the transmission or reception of a message, thus not being able to do any other computation

g The *gap*, defined as the minimum time that must elapse between consecutive message transmissions or receptions by a single processor ($1/g$ is the available per-processor communication bandwidth)

P *Processor* multiplicity (p in our notation)

If LogP is in fact an accurate model for capturing the effects of communication in parallel processors, then the details of interconnection network do not matter. All that is required, when each new network is developed or proposed, is to determine its four LogP parameters. Software simulation can then be used to predict the performance of an actual machine that is based on the new architecture for a given application. On most early, and some currently used, parallel machines, the system software overhead (o) for message initiation or reception is so large that it dwarfs the hop-to-hop and transmission latencies by comparison. For such machines, not only the topology, but also the parameters L and g of the LogP model may be irrelevant to accurate performance prediction.

Even simpler is the bulk-synchronous parallel (BSP) model which attempts to hide the communication latency altogether through a specific parallel programming style, thus making the network topology irrelevant [Vali90]. Synchronization of processors occurs once every L time steps, where L is a periodicity parameter. A parallel computation consists of a sequence of *supersteps*. In a given superstep, each processor performs a task consisting of local computation steps, message transmissions, and message receptions from other processors. Data received in messages will not be used in the current superstep but rather beginning with the next superstep. After each period of L time units, a global check is made to see if the current superstep has been completed. If so, then the processors move on to executing the next superstep. Otherwise, the next period of L time units is allocated to the unfinished superstep.

A final observation: Whereas direct interconnection networks of the types shown in Table 4.2 or Fig. 4.8 have led to many important classes of parallel processors, bus-based architectures still dominate the small-scale-parallel machines. Because a single bus can quickly become a performance bottleneck as the number of processors increases, a variety of multiple-bus architectures and hierarchical schemes (Fig. 4.9) are available for reducing bus traffic by taking advantage of the locality of communication within small clusters of processors.

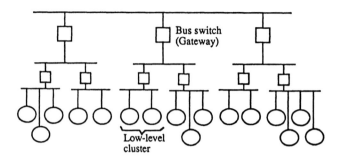

Figure 4.9. Example of a hierarchical interconnection architecture.

4.6. CIRCUIT MODEL AND PHYSICAL REALIZATIONS

In a sense, the only sure way to predict the performance of a parallel architecture on a given set of problems is to actually build the machine and run the programs on it. Because this is often impossible or very costly, the next best thing is to model the machine at the circuit level, so that all computational and signal propagation delays can be taken into account. Unfortunately, this is also impossible for a complex supercomputer, both because generating and debugging detailed circuit specifications are not much easier than a full-blown implementation and because a circuit simulator would take eons to run the simulation.

Despite the above observations, we can produce and evaluate circuit-level designs for specific applications. The example of sorting networks will be covered in Chapter 7, where we take the number of two-input compare–exchange circuits as a measure of cost and the depth of the circuit as being indicative of delay. Additional examples, covering the fast Fourier transform, parallel prefix computations, and dictionary operations, will be provided in Chapter 8 where similar cost and delay criteria are used.

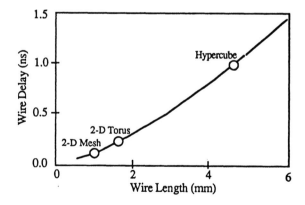

Figure 4.10. Intrachip wire delay as a function of wire length.

A more precise model, particularly if the circuit is to be implemented on a dense VLSI chip, would include the effect of wires, in terms of both the chip area they consume (cost) and the signal propagation delay between and within the interconnected blocks (time). In fact, in modern VLSI design, wire delays and area are beginning to overshadow switching or gate delays and the area occupied by devices, respectively.

The rightmost column in Table 4.2 indicates which network topologies have local or short links, thus being less likely to suffer from long interprocessor signal propagation delays. Figure 4.10 depicts the expected wire delays on a 1B-transistor chip of the future as a function of wire length, assuming the use of copper wires that are less resistive, and thus faster, than today's aluminum wires [Parh98]. The circles designate the estimated wire lengths, and thus interprocessor propagation delays, for a 256-processor chip with three different architectures. It is seen that for the hypercube architecture, which has nonlocal links, the interprocessor wire delays can dominate the intraprocessor delays, thus making the communication step time much larger than that of the mesh- and torus-based architectures.

Determining the area requirements and maximum wire lengths for various interconnection topologies has been a very active research area in the past two decades. At times, we can determine bounds on area and wire-length parameters based on network properties, without having to resort to detailed specification and layout with VLSI design tools. For example, in 2D VLSI implementation, the bisection width of a network yields a lower bound on its layout area in an asymptotic sense. If the bisection width is B, the smallest dimension of the chip should be at least Bw, where w is the minimum wire width (including the mandatory interwire spacing). The area of the chip is thus $\Omega(B^2)$. If the bisection width is $\Theta(\sqrt{p})$, as in 2D meshes, then the area lower bound will be linear in the number p of processors. Such an architecture is said to be scalable in the VLSI layout sense. On the other hand, if the bisection width is $\Theta(p)$, as in the hypercube, then the area required is a quadratic function of p and the architecture is not scalable.

The following analogy is intended to reinforce the importance of the above discussion of physical realizations and scalability [Hart86]. You have all read science-fiction stories, or seen sci-fi movies, in which scaled up ants or other beasts destroy entire towns (top panel of Fig. 4.11). Let us say that a 0.5-cm ant has been scaled up by a factor of 10^4 so that its new length is 50 m. Assuming linear scaling, so that the enlarged ant looks exactly like an ordinary ant, the ants leg has thickened by the same factor (say from 0.01 cm to 1 m). The weight of the ant, meanwhile, has increased by a factor of 10^{12}, say from 1 g to 1 M tons! Assuming that the original ant legs were just strong enough to bear its weight, the leg thickness must in fact increase by a factor of $\sqrt{10^{12}} = 10^6$, from 0.01 cm to 100 m, if the ant is not to collapse under its own weight. Now, a 50-m-long ant with legs that are 100 m thick looks nothing like the original ant!

Power consumption of digital circuits is another limiting factor. Power dissipation in modern microprocessors grows almost linearly with the product of die area and clock frequency (both steadily rising) and today stands at a few tens of watts in high-performance designs. Even if modern low-power design methods succeed in reducing this power by an order of magnitude, disposing of the heat generated by 1 M such processors is indeed a great challenge.

$O(10^4)$

Scaled up ant on the rampage!
What is wrong with this picture?

Scaled up ant collapses under own weight.

Figure 4.11. Pitfalls of scaling up.

PROBLEMS

4.1. Associative processing

A bit-serial associative memory is capable of searching, in one memory access cycle, a single bit slice of all active memory words for 0 or 1 and provides the number of responding words in the form of an unsigned integer. For example, the instruction Search(0, i) will yield the number of active memory words that store the value 0 in bit position i. It also has instructions for activating or deactivating memory words based on the results of the latest search (i.e., keep only the responders active or deactivate the responders). Suppose that initially, all words are active and the memory stores m unsigned integers.

a. Devise an AM algorithm to find the largest number stored in the memory.
b. Devise an AM algorithm for finding the kth largest unsigned integer among the m stored values.
c. Extend the algorithm of part (b) to deal with signed integers in signed-magnitude format.
d. Extend the algorithm of part (b) to deal with signed integers in 2's-complement format. *Hint*: In a 2's-complement number, the sign bit carries a negative weight so that 1010 represents $-8 + 2 = -6$.

4.2. Associative processing
With the same assumptions as in Problem 4.1:

a. Devise an AM algorithm to find the exclusive-OR (checksum) of the values in all memory words.
b. Devise an AM algorithm for finding the arithmetic sum of the values stored in all memory words. Assume unsigned or 2's-complement numbers, with all results representable in a single word.
c. Repeat part (b), this time assuming that some results may not be representable in a single word.

4.3. Cellular automata synchronization
Cellular automata form abstract models of homogeneous massively parallel computers. Consider the special case of a linear array of finite automata viewed as modeling a firing squad. All cells are identical and the length of the linear array is unknown and unbounded. We would like to synchronize this firing squad so that all cells enter the special "fire" state at exactly the same time. The synchronization process begins with a special input to the leftmost cell of the array (the general). Cells (soldiers) can only communicate with their left and right neighbor in a synchronous fashion and the only global signal is the clock signal, which is distributed to all cells. *Hint*: Try to identify the middle cell, or the middle two cells, of the array, thus dividing the problem into two smaller problems of exactly the same size.

4.4. Image-processing computer
Two types of operations are commonly used in image processing. Assume that an image is represented by a 2D matrix of 0s and 1s corresponding to dark and light pixels, respectively. Noise removal has the goal of removing isolated 0s and 1s (say those that have at most one pixel of the same type among their eight horizontally, vertically, or diagonally adjacent neighbors). Smoothing is done by replacing each pixel value with the median of nine values consisting of the pixel itself and its eight neighbors.

a. Discuss the design of a 2D array of simple cells capable of noise removal or smoothing.
b. Propose suitable generalizations for noise removal and smoothing if each pixel value is a binary integer (say 4 bits wide) representing a gray level.
c. Sketch the modifications required to the cells of part (a) if part (b) is to be implemented.

4.5. MISD architecture
In the MISD architecture depicted in Fig. 4.2, the rate of data flow or throughput in a synchronous mode of operation is dictated by the execution time of the slowest of the five blocks. Suppose that the execution times for the five blocks are not fixed but rather have uniform distributions in the interval from a lower bound l_i to an upper bound u_i, $1 \le i \le 5$, where l_i and u_i are known constants. Discuss methods for improving the throughput beyond the throughput $1/\max(u_i)$ of a synchronous design.

4.6. Cache coherence protocols
Study the snooping and directory-based cache coherence protocols (see, e.g., [Patt96], pp. 655–666 and 679–685). Then pick one example of each and do the following exercises:

a. Present one advantage for each protocol over the other.
b. Discuss an application, or a class of applications, for which the chosen snooping cache coherence protocol would perform very poorly.
c. Repeat part (b) for the chosen directory-based protocol.

4.7. Topological parameters of interconnection networks
Add entries corresponding to the following topologies to Table 4.2.

   a. An X-tree; a complete binary tree with nodes on the same level connected as a linear array.
   b. A hierarchical bus architecture with a maximum branching factor b ($b = 4$ in Fig. 4.9).
   c. A degree-4 chordal ring with skip distance s; i.e., a p-node ring in which Processor i is also connected to Processors $i \pm s$ mod p, in addition to Processors $i \pm 1$ mod p.

4.8. Hierarchical-bus architectures
Consider the hierarchical multilevel bus architecture shown in Fig. 4.9, except that each of the low-level clusters consists of four processors. Suppose that we want to emulate a 4×6 or 6×4 mesh architecture on this bus-based system. Consider the shearsort algorithm described in Section 2.5 and assume that each transfer over a shared bus to another processor or to a switch node takes unit time. Ignore computation time as well as any control overhead, focusing only on communication steps.

   a. How long does this system take to emulate shearsort on a 4×6 mesh if each processor holds a single data item and each cluster emulates a column of the mesh?
   b. How long does this system take to emulate shearsort on a 6×4 mesh (cluster = row)?
   c. Devise a method for performing a parallel prefix computation on this architecture.

4.9. The LogP model
Using the LogP model, write an equation in terms of the four parameters of the model for the total time needed to do a "complete exchange," defined as each processor sending $p - 1$ distinct messages, one to each of the other $p - 1$ processors.

4.10. The BSP and LogP models
A $k\sqrt{p} \times k\sqrt{p}$ array holds the initial data for an iterative computation. One iteration involves computing a new value for each array element based on its current value and the current values of its eight horizontally, vertically, and diagonally adjacent array elements. Each of the p processors stores a $k \times k$ block of the array at the center of a $(k + 2) \times (k + 2)$ local matrix, where the top/bottom rows and leftmost/rightmost columns represent data acquired from neighboring blocks and available at the beginning of an iteration. Processors dealing with blocks at the edge of the large array simply copy values from edge rows/columns in lieu of receiving them from a neighboring block.

   a. Formulate the above as a BSP computation.
   b. If you could choose the BSP parameter L at will, how would you go about the selection process for the above computation?
   c. Estimate the running time for m iterations, assuming the BSP model.
   d. Repeat Part (c) for the LogP model.

4.11. Physical realizations
Consider the column labeled "Local Links?" in Table 4.2. It is obvious how a 2D mesh can be laid out so that all links are local or short.

   a. Describe a 2D layout for a 2D torus that has short local links. *Hint*: Use folding.
   b. The 3D mesh and torus networks have also been characterized as having short local links. However, this is only true if a 3D realization is possible. Show that a 3D mesh (and thus torus) cannot be laid out with short local links in two dimensions.
   c. Show that any network whose diameter is a logarithmic function of the number of nodes cannot be laid out in two or three dimensions using only short local links.

4.12. Physical realizations

    a. Describe the network diameter, bisection width, and node degree of each of the networks listed in Table 4.2 as an asymptotic function of the number p of nodes (e.g., the 1D mesh has diameter, bisection, and degree of $\Theta(p)$, $\Theta(1)$, and $\Theta(1)$, respectively).

    b. Using the results of part (a), compare the architectures listed in terms of the composite figure of merit "degree × diameter," in an asymptotic way.

    c. Obtain an asymptotic lower bound for the VLSI layout area of each architecture based on its bisection width.

    d. The area–time product is sometimes regarded as a good composite figure of merit because it incorporates both cost and performance factors. Assuming that delay is proportional to network diameter, compute the asymptotic area–time figure of merit for each of the architectures, assuming that the area lower bounds of part (c) are in fact achievable.

4.13. Physical realizations

The average internode distance of an interconnection network is perhaps a more appropriate indicator of its communication latency than its diameter. For example, if the network nodes are message routers, some of which are randomly connected to processors or memory modules in a distributed shared-memory architecture, then the average internode distance is a good indicator of memory access latency.

    a. Compute the average internode distance d_{avg} for as many of the interconnection networks listed in Table 4.2 as you can.

    b. If a processor issues a memory access request in every clock cycle, there is no routing or memory access conflict, and the memory access time is t_{ma} cycles, then, on the average, each processor will have $2d_{avg} + t_{ma}$ outstanding memory access requests at any given time. Discuss the implications of the above on the scalability of the architectures in part (a).

REFERENCES AND SUGGESTED READING

[Cull96]   Culler, D. E., et al., "A Practical Model of Parallel Computation," *Communications of the ACM*, Vol. 39, No. 11, pp. 78–85, November 1996.

[From97]   Fromm, R., et al., "The Energy Efficiency of IRAM Architectures," *Proc. Int. Conf. Computer Architecture*, 1997, pp. 327–337.

[Garz95]   Garzon, M., *Models of Massive Parallelism: Analysis of Cellular Automata and Neural Networks*, Springer, 1995.

[Hart86]   Hartmann, A. C., and J. D. Ullman, "Model Categories for Theories of Parallel Systems," Microelectronics and Computer Corporation, Technical Report PP-341-86; reprinted in *Parallel Computing: Theory and Comparisons*, by G. J. Lipovski and M. Malek, Wiley, 1987, pp. 367–381.

[Jain96]   Jain, A. K., J. Mao, and K. M. Mohiuddin, "Artificial Neural Networks: A Tutorial," *IEEE Computer*, Vol. 29, No. 3, pp. 31–44, March 1996.

[Parh95]   Parhami, B., "Panel Assesses SIMD's Future," *IEEE Computer*, Vol. 28, No. 6, pp. 89–91 June 1995. For an unabridged version of this report, entitled "SIMD Machines: Do They Have a Significant Future?," see *IEEE Computer Society Technical Committee on Computer Architecture Newsletter*, pp. 23–26, August 1995, or *ACM Computer Architecture News*, Vol. 23, No. 4, pp. 19–22, September 1995.

[Parh97]   Parhami, B., "Search and Data Selection Algorithms for Associative Processors," in *Associative Processing and Processors*, edited by A. Krikelis and C. Weems, IEEE Computer Society Press, 1997, pp. 10–25.

[Parh98]   Parhami, B., and D.-M. Kwai, "Issues in Designing Parallel Architectures Using Multiprocessor and Massively Parallel Microchips," in preparation.

[Patt96]   Patterson, D. A., and J. L. Hennessy, *Computer Architecture: A Quantitative Approach*, 2nd ed., Morgan Kaufmann, 1996.

[PPCA]   *Proc. Int. Workshop on Parallel Processing by Cellular Automata and Arrays*, 3rd, Berlin, 1986; 6th, Potsdam, Germany (Parcella'94).
[Vali90]   Valiant, L. G., "A Bridging Model for Parallel Computation," *Communications of the ACM*, Vol. 33, No. 8, pp. 103–111, August 1990.

II

Extreme Models

The models of parallel computation range from very abstract to very concrete, with real parallel machine implementations and user models falling somewhere between these two extremes. At one extreme lies the abstract shared-memory PRAM model, briefly introduced in Section 4.4, which offers a simple and familiar programming model but is quite removed from what transpires at the hardware level as a parallel computation unfolds. At the other extreme is the circuit model of parallel processing where a computational task is considered in terms of what happens to individual bits, in order to gain an appreciation for actual hardware complexities (e.g., circuit depth or VLSI chip layout area). After covering the two extremes of very abstract (the PRAM model) and very concrete (the circuit model), we proceed to explore various intermediate models in the rest of the book. This part consists of the following four chapters:

- Chapter 5: PRAM and Basic Algorithms
- Chapter 6: More Shared-Memory Algorithms
- Chapter 7: Sorting and Selection Networks
- Chapter 8: Other Circuit-Level Examples

5

PRAM and Basic Algorithms

In this chapter, following basic definitions and a brief discussion of the relative computational powers of several PRAM submodels, we deal with five key building-block algorithms that lay the foundations for solving various computational problems on the abstract PRAM model of shared-memory parallel processors. We will continue with more algorithms and implementation considerations in Chapter 6. The example algorithms provided should be sufficient to convince the reader that the PRAM's programming model is a natural extension of the familiar sequential computer (RAM) and that it facilitates the development of efficient parallel algorithms using a variety of programming paradigms. Chapter topics are

- 5.1. PRAM submodels and assumptions
- 5.2. Data broadcasting
- 5.3. Semigroup or fan-in computation
- 5.4. Parallel prefix computation
- 5.5. Ranking the elements of a linked list
- 5.6. Matrix multiplication

5.1. PRAM SUBMODELS AND ASSUMPTIONS

As mentioned in Section 4.4, the PRAM model prescribes the concurrent operation of p processors (in SIMD or MIMD mode) on data that are accessible to all of them in an m-word shared memory. In the synchronous SIMD or SPMD version of PRAM, which is of primary interest in our subsequent discussions, Processor i can do the following in the three phases of one cycle:

1. Fetch an operand from the source address s_i in the shared memory
2. Perform some computations on the data held in local registers
3. Store a value into the destination address d_i in the shared memory

Not all three phases need to be present in every cycle; a particular cycle may require no new data from memory, or no computation (just copying from s_i to d_i, say), or no storing in memory (partial computation result held in a local register, say).

Because the addresses s_i and d_i are determined by Processor i, independently of all other processors, it is possible that several processors may want to read data from the same memory location or write their values into a common location. Hence, four submodels of the PRAM model have been defined based on whether concurrent reads (writes) from (to) the same location are allowed. The four possible combinations, depicted in Fig. 5.1, are

- EREW: Exclusive-read, exclusive-write
- ERCW: Exclusive-read, concurrent-write
- CREW: Concurrent-read, exclusive-write
- CRCW: Concurrent-read, concurrent-write

The classification in Fig. 5.1 is reminiscent of Flynn's classification (Fig. 1.11 or 4.1) and offers yet another example of the quest to invent four-letter abbreviations/acronyms in computer architecture! Note that here, too, one of the categories is not very useful, because if concurrent writes are allowed, there is no logical reason for excluding the less problematic concurrent reads.

EREW PRAM is the most realistic of the four submodels (to the extent that thousands of processors concurrently accessing thousands of memory locations within a shared-memory address space of millions or even billions of locations can be considered realistic!). CRCW PRAM is the least restrictive submodel, but has the disadvantage of requiring a conflict resolution mechanism to define the effect of concurrent writes (more on this below). The default submodel, which is assumed when nothing is said about the submodel, is CREW PRAM. For most computations, it is fairly easy to organize the algorithm steps so that concurrent writes to the same location are never attempted.

CRCW PRAM is further classified according to how concurrent writes are handled. Here are a few example submodels based on the semantics of concurrent writes in CRCW PRAM:

- Undefined: In case of multiple writes, the value written is undefined (CRCW-U).
- Detecting: A special code representing "detected collision" is written (CRCW-D).

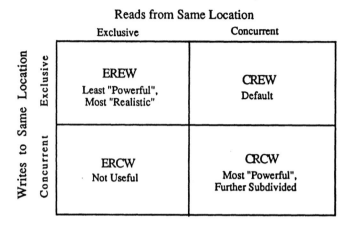

Figure 5.1. Submodels of the PRAM model.

- Common: Multiple writes allowed only if all store the same value (CRCW-C). This is sometimes called the *consistent-write submodel*.
- Random: The value written is randomly chosen from among those offered (CRCW-R). This is sometimes called the *arbitrary-write submodel*.
- Priority: The processor with the lowest index succeeds in writing its value (CRCW-P).
- Max/Min: The largest/smallest of the multiple values is written (CRCW-M).
- Reduction: The arithmetic sum (CRCW-S), logical AND (CRCW-A), logical XOR (CRCW-X), or some other combination of the multiple values is written.

These submodels are all different from each other and from EREW and CREW. One way to order these submodels is by their computational power. Two PRAM submodels are equally powerful if each can emulate the other with a constant-factor slowdown. A PRAM submodel is (strictly) less powerful than another submodel (denoted by the "<" symbol) if there exist problems for which the former requires significantly more computational steps than the latter. For example, the CRCW-D PRAM submodel is less powerful than the one that writes the maximum value, as the latter can find the largest number in a vector A of size p in a single step (Processor i reads $A[i]$ and writes it to an agreed-upon location x, which will then hold the maximum value for all processors to see), whereas the former needs at least $\Omega(\log n)$ steps. The "less powerful or equal" relationship "$\leq$" between submodels can be similarly defined.

The following relationships have been established between some of the PRAM submodels:

$$\text{EREW} < \text{CREW} < \text{CRCW-D} < \text{CRCW-C} < \text{CRCW-R} < \text{CRCW-P}$$

Even though all CRCW submodels are strictly more powerful than the EREW submodel, the latter can simulate the most powerful CRCW submodel listed above with at most logarithmic slowdown.

THEOREM 5.1. *A p-processor CRCW-P (priority) PRAM can be simulated by a p-processor EREW PRAM with a slowdown factor of $\Theta(\log p)$.*

The proof of Theorem 5.1 is based on the ability of the EREW PRAM to sort or find the smallest of p values in $\Theta(\log p)$ time, as we shall see later. To avoid concurrent writes, each processor writes an ID-address-value triple into its corresponding element of a scratch list of size p, with the p processors then cooperating to sort the list by the destination addresses, partition the list into segments corresponding to common addresses (which are now adjacent in the sorted list), do a reduction operation within each segment to remove all writes to the same location except the one with the smallest processor ID, and finally write the surviving address-value pairs into memory. This final write operation will clearly be of the exclusive variety.

5.2. DATA BROADCASTING

Because data broadcasting is a fundamental building-block computation in parallel processing, we devote this section to discussing how it can be accomplished on the various PRAM submodels. Semigroup computation, parallel prefix computation, list ranking, and matrix multiplication, four other useful building-block computations, will be discussed in the next four sections.

Simple, or one-to-all, broadcasting is used when one processor needs to send a data value to all other processors. In the CREW or CRCW submodels, broadcasting is trivial, as the sending processor can write the data value into a memory location, with all processors reading that data value in the following machine cycle. Thus, simple broadcasting is done in $\Theta(1)$ steps. Multicasting within groups is equally simple if each processor knows its group membership(s) and only members of each group read the multicast data for that group. All-to-all broadcasting, where each of the p processors needs to send a data value to all other processors, can be done through p separate broadcast operations in $\Theta(p)$ steps, which is optimal.

The above scheme is clearly inapplicable to broadcasting in the EREW model. The simplest scheme for EREW broadcasting is to make p copies of the data value, say in a broadcast vector B of length p, and then let each processor read its own copy by accessing $B[j]$. Thus, initially, Processor i writes its data value into $B[0]$. Next, a method known as *recursive doubling* is used to copy $B[0]$ into all elements of B in $\lceil \log_2 p \rceil$ steps. Finally, Processor j, $0 \leq j < p$, reads $B[j]$ to get the data value broadcast by Processor i. The recursive doubling algorithm for copying $B[0]$ into all elements of the broadcast vector B is given below.

Making p copies of $B[0]$ by recursive doubling

    for $k = 0$ to $\lceil \log_2 p \rceil - 1$ Processor j, $0 \leq j < p$, do
        Copy $B[j]$ into $B[j + 2^k]$
    endfor

In the above algorithm, it is implied that copying will not occur if the destination address is outside the list (Fig. 5.2). Alternatively, the list B might be assumed to extend beyond

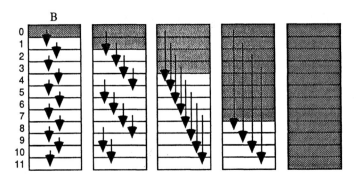

Figure 5.2. Data broadcasting in EREW PRAM via recursive doubling.

$B[p − 1]$ with dummy elements that are written into but never read. However, it is perhaps more efficient to explicitly "turn off" the processors that do not perform useful work in a given step. This approach might allow us to use the idle processors for performing other tasks in order to speed up algorithm execution, or at the very least, reduce the memory access traffic through the processor-to-memory interconnection network when the algorithm is ported to a physical shared-memory machine. Note that in Step k of the above recursive doubling process, only the first 2^k processors need to be active. The complete EREW broadcast algorithm with this provision is given below.

EREW PRAM algorithm for broadcasting by Processor i

> Processor i write the data value into $B[0]$
> $s := 1$
> while $s < p$ Processor j, $0 \le j < \min(s, p − s)$, do
>   Copy $B[j]$ into $B[j + s]$
> $s := 2s$
> endwhile
> Processor j, $0 \le j < p$, read the data value in $B[j]$

The parameter s can be interpreted as the "span" of elements already modified or the "step" for the copying operation (Fig. 5.3).

The following argument shows that the above $\Theta(\log p)$-step broadcasting algorithm is optimal for EREW PRAM. Because initially a single copy of the data value exists, at most one other processor can get to know the value through a memory access in the first step. In the second step, two more processors can become aware of the data value. Continuing in this manner, at least $\lceil \log_2 p \rceil$ read–write cycles are necessary for p-way broadcasting.

To perform all-to-all broadcasting, so that each processor broadcasts a value that it holds to each of the other $p − 1$ processors, we let Processor j write its value into $B[j]$, rather than into $B[0]$. Thus, in one memory access step, all of the values to be broadcast are written into the broadcast vector B. Each processor then reads the other $p − 1$ values in $p − 1$ memory accesses. To ensure that all reads are exclusive, Processor j begins reading the values starting with $B[j + 1]$, wrapping around to $B[0]$ after reading $B[p − 1]$.

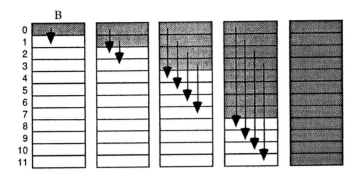

Figure 5.3. EREW PRAM data broadcasting without redundant copying.

EREW PRAM algorithm for all-to-all broadcasting

> Processor j, $0 \le j < p$, write own data value into $B[j]$
> for $k = 1$ to $p - 1$ Processor j, $0 \le j < p$, do
>   Read the data value in $B[(j + k) \bmod p]$
> endfor

Again the above all-to-all broadcasting algorithm is optimal as the shared memory is the only mechanism for interprocessor communication and each processor can read but one value from the shared memory in each machine cycle.

Given a data vector S of length p, a naive sorting algorithm can be designed based on the above all-to-all broadcasting scheme. We simply let Processor j compute the rank $R[j]$ of the data element $S[j]$ and then store $S[j]$ into $S[R[j]]$. The rank $R[j]$ of $S[j]$, loosely defined as the total number of data elements that are smaller than $S[j]$, is computed by each processor examining all other data elements and counting the number of elements $S[l]$ that are smaller than $S[j]$. Because each data element must be given a unique rank, ties are broken by using the processor ID. In other words, if Processors i and j ($i < j$) hold equal data values, the value in Processor i is deemed smaller for ranking purposes. Following is the complete sorting algorithm.

Naive EREW PRAM sorting algorithm using all-to-all broadcasting

> Processor j, $0 \le j < p$, write 0 into $R[j]$
> for $k = 1$ to $p - 1$ Processor j, $0 \le j < p$, do
> $l := (j + k) \bmod p$
>   if $S[l] < S[j]$ or $S[l] = S[j]$ and $l < j$
>   then $R[j] := R[j] + 1$
>   endif
> endfor
> Processor j, $0 \le j < p$, write $S[j]$ into $S[R[j]]$

Unlike the broadcasting algorithms discussed earlier, the above sorting algorithm is not optimal in that the $O(p^2)$ computational work involved in it is significantly greater than the

O($p \log p$) work required for sorting p elements on a single processor. The analysis of this algorithm with regard to speed-up, efficiency, and so forth is left as an exercise. Faster and more efficient PRAM sorting algorithms will be presented in Chapter 6.

5.3. SEMIGROUP OR FAN-IN COMPUTATION

Semigroup computation was defined in Section 2.1 based on associative binary operator ⊗. This computation is trivial for a CRCW PRAM of the "reduction" variety if the reduction operator happens to be ⊗. For example, computing the arithmetic sum (logical AND, logical XOR) of p values, one per processor, is trivial for the CRCW-S (CRCW-A, CRCW-X) PRAM; it can be done in a single cycle by each processor writing its corresponding value into a common location that will then hold the arithmetic sum (logical AND, logical XOR) of all of the values.

Here too the recursive doubling scheme can be used to do the computation on an EREW PRAM (much of the computation is in fact the same for all PRAM submodels, with the only difference appearing in the final broadcasting step). Interestingly, the computation scheme is virtually identical to that of Fig. 5.2, with the copying operation replaced by a combining (⊗) operation. Figure 5.4 illustrates the process, where the pair of integers $u{:}v$ shown in each memory location represents the combination (e.g., sum) of all input values from $X[u]$ to $X[v]$. Initially, $S[i]$ holds the ith input $X[i]$, or $i{:}i$ according to our notation. After the first parallel combining step involving adjacent elements, each element $S[i]$, except $S[0]$, holds $(i-1){:}i$. The next step leads to the computation of the sums of 4 adjacent elements, then 8, and eventually all 10. The final result, which is available in $S[p-1]$, can then be broadcast to every processor.

EREW PRAM semigroup computation algorithm

> Processor j, $0 \le j < p$, copy $X[j]$ into $S[j]$
> $s := 1$
> while $s < p$ Processor j, $0 \le j < p - s$, do
> $S[j + s] := S[j] \otimes S[j + s]$
> $s := 2s$

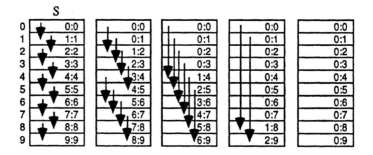

Figure 5.4. Semigroup computation in EREW PRAM.

endwhile
Broadcast $S[p - 1]$ to all processors

The $\Theta(\log p)$ computation time of the above algorithm is optimal, given that in each machine cycle, a processor can combine only two values and the semigroup computation requires that we combine p values to get the result.

When each of the p processors is in charge of n/p elements, rather than just one element, the semigroup computation is performed by each processor first combining its n/p elements in n/p steps to get a single value. Then, the algorithm just discussed is used, with the first step replaced by copying the result of the above into $S[j]$.

It is instructive to evaluate the speed-up and efficiency of the above algorithm for an n-input semigroup computation using p processors. Because the final broadcasting takes $\log_2 p$ steps, the algorithm requires $n/p + 2 \log_2 p$ EREW PRAM steps in all, leading to a speed-up of $n/(n/p + 2 \log_2 p)$ over the sequential version. If the number of processors is $p = \Theta(n)$, a sublinear speed-up of $\Theta(n/\log n)$ is obtained. The efficiency in this case is $\Theta(n/\log n)/\Theta(n) = \Theta(1/\log n)$. On the other hand, if we limit the number of processors to $p = O(n/\log n)$, we will have

$$\text{Speed-up}(n, p) = n/O(\log n) = \Omega(n/\log n) = \Omega(p)$$

Hence, linear or $\Theta(p)$ speed-up and $\Theta(1)$ efficiency can be achieved by using an appropriately smaller number p of processors compared with the number n of elements.

The above can be intuitively explained as follows. The semigroup computation is representable in the form of a binary tree, as shown in Fig. 5.5. When the number of processors is comparable to the number of leaves in this binary tree, only the first few computation levels possess enough parallelism to utilize the processors efficiently, with most of the processors sitting idle, or else doing redundant computations, in all subsequent levels. On the other hand, when $p \ll n$, we achieve perfect speed-up/efficiency near the leaves, where the bulk of the computation occurs. The inefficiency near the root is not enough to significantly affect the overall efficiency. The use of *parallel slack*, i.e., having more processors than items to be processed, is a recurring theme in parallel processing and is often a prerequisite for efficient parallel computation.

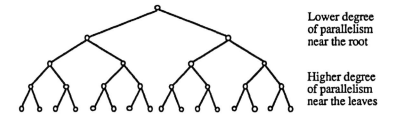

Lower degree
of parallelism
near the root

Higher degree
of parallelism
near the leaves

Figure 5.5. Intuitive justification of why parallel slack helps improve the efficiency.

5.4. PARALLEL PREFIX COMPUTATION

Just as was the case for a linear array (Section 2.3), parallel prefix computation consists of the first phase of the semigroup computation. We see in Fig. 5.4 that as we find the semigroup computation result in $S[p-1]$, all partial prefixes are also obtained in the previous elements of S. Figure 5.6 is identical to Fig. 5.4, except that it includes shading to show that the number of correct prefix results doubles in each step.

The above algorithm is quite efficient, but there are other ways of performing parallel prefix computation on the PRAM. In particular, the divide-and-conquer paradigm leads to two other solutions to this problem. In the following, we deal only with the case of a p-input problem, where p (the number of inputs or processors) is a power of 2. As in Section 5.3, the pair of integers $u:v$ represents the combination (e.g., sum) of all input values from x_u to x_v.

Figure 5.7 depicts our first divide-and-conquer algorithm. We view the problem as composed of two subproblems: computing the odd-indexed results $s_1, s_3, s_5, \ldots$ and computing the even-indexed results $s_0, s_2, s_4, \ldots$.

The first subproblem is solved as follows. Pairs of consecutive elements in the input list (x_0 and x_1, x_2 and x_3, x_4 and x_5, and so on) are combined to obtain a list of half the size. Performing parallel prefix computation on this list yields correct values for all odd-indexed results. The even-indexed results are then found in a single PRAM step by combining each even-indexed input with the immediately preceding odd-indexed result. Because the initial combining of pairs and the final computation of the even-indexed results each takes one step, the total computation time is given by the recurrence

$$T(p) = T(p/2) + 2$$

whose solution is $T(p) = 2 \log_2 p$.

Figure 5.8 depicts a second divide-and-conquer algorithm. We view the input list as composed of two sublists: the even-indexed inputs $x_0, x_2, x_4, \ldots$ and the odd-indexed inputs $x_1, x_3, x_5, \ldots$. Parallel prefix computation is performed separately on each sublist, leading to partial results as shown in Fig. 5.8 (a sequence of digits indicates the combination of elements with those indices). The final results are obtained by pairwise combination of adjacent partial results in a single PRAM step. The total computation time is given by the recurrence

$$T(p) = T(p/2) + 1$$

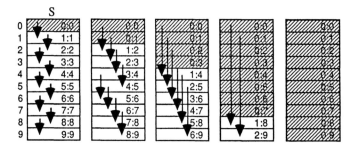

Figure 5.6. Parallel prefix computation in EREW PRAM via recursive doubling.

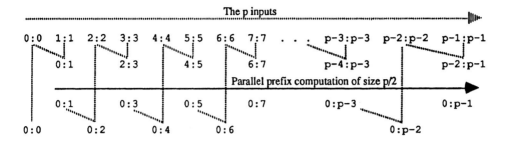

Figure 5.7. Parallel prefix computation using a divide-and-conquer scheme.

whose solution is $T(p) = \log_2 p$.

Even though this latter algorithm is more efficient than the first divide-and-conquer scheme, it is applicable only if the operator $\otimes$ is commutative (why?).

5.5. RANKING THE ELEMENTS OF A LINKED LIST

Our next example computation is important not only because it is a very useful building block in many applications, but also in view of the fact that it demonstrates how a problem that seems hopelessly sequential can be efficiently parallelized.

The problem will be presented in terms of a linear linked list of size p, but in practice it often arises in the context of graphs of the types found in image processing and computer vision applications. Many graph-theoretic problems deal with (directed) paths between various pairs of nodes. Such a path essentially consists of a sequence of nodes, each "pointing" to the next node on the path; thus, a directed path can be viewed as a linear linked list.

The problem of list ranking can be defined as follows: Given a linear linked list of the type shown in Fig. 5.9, rank the list elements in terms of the distance from each to the terminal

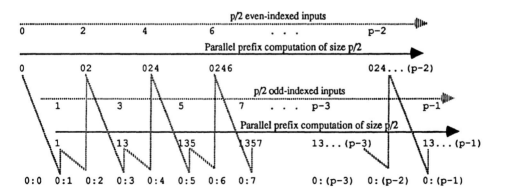

Figure 5.8. Another divide-and-conquer scheme for parallel prefix computation.

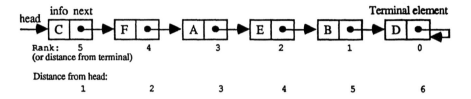

Figure 5.9. Example linked list and the ranks of its elements.

element. The terminal element is thus ranked 0, the one pointing to it 1, and so forth. In a list of length p, each element's rank will be a unique integer between 0 and $p - 1$.

A sequential algorithm for list ranking requires $\Theta(p)$ time. Basically, the list must be traversed once to determine the distance of each element from the head, storing the results in the linked list itself or in a separate integer vector. This first pass can also yield the length of the list (six in the example of Fig. 5.9). A second pass, through the list, or the vector of p intermediate results, then suffices to compute all of the ranks.

The list ranking problem for the example linked list of Fig. 5.9 may be approached with the PRAM input and output data structures depicted in Fig. 5.10. The *info* and *next* vectors are given, as is the *head* pointer (in our example, *head* = 2). The *rank* vector must be filled with the unique element ranks at the termination of the algorithm.

The parallel solution method for this problem is known as *pointer jumping*: Repeatedly make each element point to the successor of its successor (i.e., make the pointer jump over the current successor) until all elements end up pointing to the terminal node, keeping track of the number of list elements that have been skipped over. If the original list is not to be modified, a copy can be made in the PRAM's shared memory in constant time before the algorithm is applied.

Processor j, $0 \leq j < p$, will be responsible for computing *rank*[j]. The invariant of the list ranking algorithm given below is that initially and after each iteration, the partial computed rank of each element is the difference between its rank and the rank of its successor. With the difference between the rank of a list element and the rank of its successor available, the rank of an element can be determined as soon as the rank of its successor becomes known. Again, a doubling process takes place. Initially, only the rank of the terminal element (the only node that points to itself) is known. In successive iterations of the algorithm, the ranks

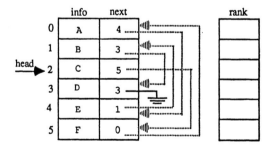

Figure 5.10. PRAM data structures representing a linked list and the ranking results.

of two elements, then four elements, then eight elements, and so forth become known until the ranks of all elements have been determined.

PRAM list ranking algorithm (via pointer jumping)

Processor j, $0 \le j < p$, do {initialize the partial ranks}
  if $next[j] = j$
  then $rank[j] := 0$
  else $rank[j] := 1$
  endif
  while $rank[next[head]] \ne 0$ Processor j, $0 \le j < p$, do
    $rank[j] := rank[j] + rank[next[j]]$
    $next[j] := next[next[j]]$
  endwhile

Figure 5.11 shows the intermediate values in the vectors $rank$ (numbers within boxes) and $next$ (arrows) as the above list ranking algorithm is applied to the example list of Fig. 5.9. Because the number of elements that are skipped doubles with each iteration, the number of iterations, and thus the running time of the algorithm, is logarithmic in p.

List-ranking appears to be hopelessly sequential, as no access to list elements is possible without traversing all previous elements. However, the list ranking algorithm presented above shows that we can in fact use a recursive doubling scheme to determine the rank of each element in optimal time. The problems at the end of the chapter contain other examples of computations on lists that can be performed just as efficiently. This is why intuition can be misleading when it comes to determining which computations are or are not efficiently parallelizable (formally, whether a computation is or is not in NC).

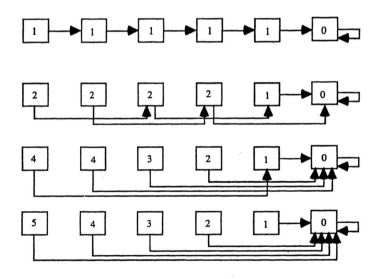

Figure 5.11. Element ranks initially and after each of the three iterations.

5.6. MATRIX MULTIPLICATION

In this section, we discuss PRAM matrix multiplication algorithms as representative examples of the class of numerical problems. Matrix multiplication is quite important in its own right and is also used as a building block in many other parallel algorithms. For example, we will see in Section 11.5 that matrix multiplication is useful in solving graph problems when the graphs are represented by their adjacency or weight matrices.

Given $m \times m$ matrices A and B, with elements a_{ij} and b_{ij}, their product C is defined as

$$c_{ij} = \sum_{k=0}^{m-1} a_{ik} b_{kj}$$

The following $O(m^3)$-step sequential algorithm can be used for multiplying $m \times m$ matrices:

Sequential matrix multiplication algorithm

```
for i = 0 to m − 1 do
  for j = 0 to m − 1 do
    t := 0
    for k = 0 to m − 1 do
      t := t + a_{ik}b_{kj}
    endfor
    c_{ij} := t
  endfor
endfor
```

If the PRAM has $p = m^3$ processors, then matrix multiplication can be done in $\Theta(\log m)$ time by using one processor to compute each product $a_{ik}b_{kj}$ and then allowing groups of m processors to perform m-input summations (semigroup computation) in $\Theta(\log m)$ time. Because we are usually not interested in parallel processing for matrix multiplication unless m is fairly large, this is not a practical solution.

Now assume that the PRAM has $p = m^2$ processors. In this case, matrix multiplication can be done in $\Theta(m)$ time by using one processor to compute each element c_{ij} of the product matrix C. The processor responsible for computing c_{ij} reads the elements of Row i in A and the elements of Column j in B, multiplies their corresponding kth elements, and adds each of the products thus obtained to a running total t. This amounts to parallelizing the i and j loops in the sequential algorithm (Fig. 5.12). For simplicity, we label the m^2 processors with

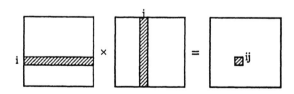

Figure 5.12. PRAM matrix multiplication by using $p = m^2$ processors.

two indices (i, j), each ranging from 0 to $m - 1$, rather than with a single index ranging from 0 to $m^2 - 1$.

PRAM matrix multiplication algorithm using m^2 processors

```
Processor (i, j), 0 ≤ i, j < m, do
begin
    t := 0
    for k = 0 to m − 1 do
        t := t + a_{ik}b_{kj}
    endfor
    c_{ij} := t
end
```

Because multiple processors will be reading the same row of A or the same column of B, the above naive implementation of the algorithm would require the CREW submodel. For example, in a given iteration of the k loop, all processors (i, y), $0 \le y < m$, access the same element a_{ik} of A and all processors (x, j) access the same element b_{jk} of B. However, it is possible to convert the algorithm to an EREW PRAM algorithm by skewing the memory accesses (how?).

Next, assume that the PRAM has $p = m$ processors. In this case, matrix multiplication can be done in $\Theta(m^2)$ time by using Processor i to compute the m elements in Row i of the product matrix C in turn. Thus, Processor i will read the elements of Row i in A and the elements of all columns in B, multiply their corresponding kth elements, and add each of the products thus obtained to a running total t. This amounts to parallelizing the i loop in the sequential algorithm.

PRAM matrix multiplication algorithm using m processors

```
for j = 0 to m − 1 Processor i, 0 ≤ i < m, do
    t := 0
    for k = 0 to m − 1 do
        t := t + a_{ik}b_{kj}
    endfor
    c_{ij} := t
endfor
```

Because each processor reads a different row of the matrix A, no concurrent reads from A are ever attempted. For matrix B, however, all m processors access the same element b_{kj} at the same time. Again, one can skew the memory accesses for B in such a way that the EREW submodel is applicable. Note that for both $p = m^2$ and $p = m$ processors, we have efficient algorithms with linear speed-ups.

In many practical situations, the number of processors is even less than m. So we need to develop an algorithm for this case as well. We can let Processor i compute a set of m/p rows in the result matrix C; say Rows $i, i + p, i + 2p, \ldots, i + (m/p - 1)p$. Again, we are parallelizing the i loop as this is preferable to parallelizing the k loop (which has data dependencies) or the j loop (which would imply m synchronizations of the processors, once at the end of each i iteration, assuming the SPMD model). On a lightly loaded Sequent Symmetry shared-memory multiprocessor, this last algorithm exhibits almost linear speed-up, with the speed-up of about 22 observed for 24 processors when multiplying two 256×256 floating-point matrices [Quin94]. This is typical of what can be achieved on UMA multiprocessors with our simple parallel algorithm. Recall that the UMA (uniform memory access) property implies that any memory location is accessible with the same amount of delay.

The drawback of the above algorithm for NUMA (nonuniform memory access) shared-memory multiprocessors is that each element of B is fetched m/p times, with only two arithmetic operations (one multiplication and one addition) performed for each such element. Block matrix multiplication, discussed next, increases the computation to memory access ratio, thus improving the performance for NUMA multiprocessors.

Let us divide the $m \times m$ matrices A, B, and C into p blocks of size $q \times q$, as shown in Fig. 5.13, where $q = m/\sqrt{p}$. We can then multiply the $m \times m$ matrices by using $\sqrt{p} \times \sqrt{p}$ matrix multiplication with $(\sqrt{p})^2 = p$ processors, where the terms in the algorithm statement $t := t + a_{ik}b_{kj}$ are now $q \times q$ matrices and Processor (i, j) computes Block (i, j) of the result matrix C. Thus, the algorithm is similar to our second algorithm above, with the statement $t := t + a_{ik}b_{kj}$ replaced by a sequential $q \times q$ matrix multiplication algorithm.

Each multiply–add computation on $q \times q$ blocks needs $2q^2 = 2m^2/p$ memory accesses to read the blocks and $2q^3$ arithmetic operations. So q arithmetic operations are performed for each memory access and better performance will be achieved as a result of improved locality. The assumption here is that Processor (i, j) has sufficient local memory to hold Block (i, j) of the result matrix C (q^2 elements) and one block-row of the matrix B; say the q elements in Row $kq + c$ of Block (k, j) of B. Elements of A can be brought in one at a time. For example, as element in Row $iq + a$ of Column $kq + c$ in Block (i, k) of A is brought in, it is multiplied in turn by the locally stored q elements of B, and the results added to the appropriate q elements of C (Fig. 5.14).

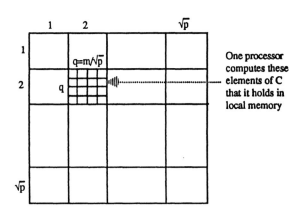

Figure 5.13. Partitioning the matrices for block matrix multiplication.

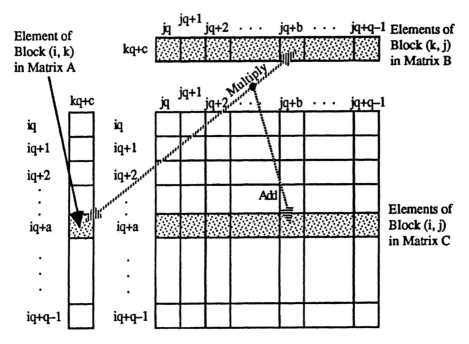

Figure 5.14. How Processor (i, j) operates on an element of A and one block-row of B to update one block-row of C.

On the Cm* NUMA-type shared-memory multiprocessor, a research prototype machine built at Carnegie-Mellon University in the 1980s, this block matrix multiplication algorithm exhibited good, but sublinear, speed-up. With 16 processors, the speed-up was only 5 in multiplying 24×24 matrices. However, the speed-up improved to about 9 (11) when larger 36×36 (48×48) matrices were multiplied [Quin94].

It is interesting to note that improved locality of the block matrix multiplication algorithm can also improve the running time on a uniprocessor, or distributed shared-memory multiprocessor with caches, in view of higher cache hit rates.

PROBLEMS

5.1. Ordering of CRCW PRAM submodels
      Complete the ordering relationships between the various CRCW PRAM submodels briefly discussed in Section 5.1, i.e., place the remaining submodels in the linear order. If you cannot provide formal proofs, try to guess where the missing submodels belong and describe the intuition behind your guess.

5.2. The power of various PRAM submodels
      State and prove a result similar to Theorem 5.1 for the CRCW-M (max/min) and CRCW-S (summation) PRAM submodels (and more generally for the reduction submodel, where the reduction operation is a semigroup computation).

5.3. Broadcasting on a PRAM

    a. Find the speed-up, efficiency, and the various other measures defined in Section 1.6 for each of the PRAM broadcasting algorithms presented in Section 5.2.

    b. Show how two separate broadcasts, by Processors i_0 and i_1, can be completed in only one or two extra EREW PRAM steps compared with a single broadcast.

    c. Can you do p-way broadcasting through a broadcast vector B of length $p/2$?

    d. Modify the broadcasting algorithms such that a processor that obtains the value broadcast by Processor i keeps it in a register and does not have to read it from the memory each time.

5.4. Naive sorting on a PRAM

    a. Find the speed-up, efficiency, and the various other measures defined in Section 1.6 for the naive PRAM sorting algorithm presented in Section 5.2.

    b. Present a more efficient sorting algorithm when the elements of the list to be sorted are two-valued (e.g., each is 0 or 1).

    c. Generalize the method proposed in part (b) to the case when the inputs are d-valued and indicate when the resulting algorithm would be faster than the naive algorithm.

5.5. Semigroup computation on a PRAM
In order to avoid the final broadcasting phase, which essentially doubles the execution time of the semigroup computation algorithm in the EREW PRAM, it has been suggested that we replace the indices $i + s$ in the algorithm with $i + s$ mod p (i.e., allow the computations to wrap around). Under what conditions would this method yield correct results in all processors?

5.6. Parallel prefix computation on a PRAM
For each of the PRAM parallel prefix algorithms presented in Section 5.4:

    a. Determine the speed-up, efficiency, and the various other measures defined in Section 1.6.

    b. Extend the algorithm to the case of n inputs, where $n > p$.

    c. Repeat part (a) for the extended algorithms of part (b).

5.7. Parallel prefix on a PRAM
Show that a p-processor PRAM needs at least $2n/(p + 1)$ steps for an n-input parallel prefix computation, where $n = mp(p + 1)/2 + 1$ and $m \geq 1$ [Wang96].

5.8. Parallel prefix computation on a PRAM

    a. Modify the algorithms given in Section 5.4 so that they perform the diminished parallel prefix computation; the ith element of the result is obtained from combining all elements up to $i - 1$.

    b. Develop a PRAM algorithm for an *incomplete parallel prefix computation* involving p or fewer elements in the input vector $X[0:p - 1]$. In this variant, some elements of X may be marked as being invalid and the ith prefix result is defined as the combination of all valid elements up to the ith entry.

    c. Develop a PRAM algorithm for a *partitioned parallel prefix computation* defined as follows. The input X consists of p elements. A partition vector Y is also given whose elements are Boolean values, with $Y[i] = 1$ indicating that the $X[i]$ is the first element of a new partition. Parallel prefix computation must be performed independently in each partition, so that the kth result in a partition is obtained by combining the first k elements in that partition. *Hint:* Convert the problem to an ordinary parallel prefix computation by defining a binary operator for which each operand is a pair of values from X and Y.

     d. Extend the algorithm of part (c) so that its input size is n rather than p ($n > p$).

5.9. List-ranking on a PRAM

Modify the list ranking algorithm of Section 5.5 so that it works with a circular list. The *head* pointer points to an arbitrary list element and the rank of an element is defined as the distance from *head* to that element (so the head element itself has a rank of 1, its successor has a rank of 2, and so on).

5.10. List-ranking on a PRAM

     a. Show that the CREW submodel is implicit in the list ranking algorithm of Section 5.5.

     b. Modify the algorithm so that it uses the EREW PRAM submodel.

     c. Extend the algorithm so that it ranks a list of size n, with $n > p$.

     d. Suppose that the *info* part of a linked list (see Fig. 5.10) is a value from a set S on which an associative binary operator $\otimes$ has been defined. Develop an algorithm for parallel prefix computation that fills a *value* vector with the prefix computation result on all elements of the list from the head element up to the current element.

5.11. Maximum-sum-subsequence problem

Given a vector composed of n signed numbers, we would like to identify the indices u and v such that the sum of all vector elements from element u to element v is the largest possible.

     a. Develop a sequential algorithm for this problem that has linear running time.

     b. Develop an efficient EREW PRAM algorithm for this problem.

5.12. Matrix multiplication

Our first parallel matrix multiplication algorithm in Section 5.6 used $p = m^3$ processors and achieved $\Theta(\log m)$ running time. Show how the same asymptotic running time can be obtained with a factor of $\log m$ fewer processors.

5.13. Vector operations on a PRAM

Devise PRAM algorithms for the following operations on m-vectors using p ($p < m$) processors:

     a. Inner product of two vectors.

     b. Convolution of two vectors.

5.14. Matrix multiplication

Based on what you learned about matrix–matrix multiplication in Section 5.6, devise efficient PRAM algorithms for the following:

     a. Matrix–vector multiplication.

     b. Multiplication of large nonsquare matrices.

     c. Raising a square matrix to a given integer power.

5.15. The all-pairs-shortest-path problem on a PRAM

An n-node weighted directed graph can be represented by an $n \times n$ matrix W, with $W[i, j]$ denoting the weight associated with the edge connecting Node i to Node j. The matrix element will be ∞ if no such edge exists. Elements of W can be interpreted as the length of the shortest path between Nodes i and j, where the number of edges in the path is restricted to be ≤ 1.

     a. Show that W^2 represents the length of the shortest path with ≤ 2 edges, if "matrix multiplication" is done by using "min" instead of addition and "+" instead of multiplication.

b. Using the result of part (a), develop an efficient PRAM algorithm for finding the lengths of the shortest paths between all node pairs in the graph. *Hint:* What do W^4, W^8, ... represent?

5.16. Maximum-finding on CRCW PRAM

Consider the problem of finding the maximum of p numbers on a p-processor CRCW PRAM. Show that this can be done in sublogarithmic time using the following scheme. Divide the p numbers and processors into $p/3$ groups of size 3. Select the maximum number in each group in constant time, thus reducing the problem to that of determining the maximum of $p/3$ numbers using p processors. Next, use groups of 21 processors to determine the maximum values in groups of 7 numbers in constant time. Show how the process continues, what rule is used by a processor to determine the numbers it will process in a given phase, how many phases are needed, and which CRCW submodel(s) must be assumed.

REFERENCES AND SUGGESTED READING

[Akl97]   Akl, S. G., *Parallel Computation: Models and Methods*, Prentice–Hall, 1997.
[Fort78]   Fortune, S., and J. Wyllie, "Parallelism in Random Access Machines," *Proc. 10th Annual ACM Symp. Theory of Computing*, 1978, pp. 114–118.
[JaJa92]   JaJa, J., *An Introduction to Parallel Algorithms*, Addison–Wesley, 1992.
[Kron96]   Kronsjo, L. I., "PRAM Models," Chapter 6 in *Parallel and Distributed Computing Handbook*, edited by A.Y. Zomaya, McGraw-Hill, 1996, pp. 163–191.
[Quin94]   Quinn, M. J., *Parallel Computing: Theory and Practice*, McGraw-Hill, 1994.
[Reid93]   Reid-Miller, M., G. L. Miller, and F. Modugno, "List Ranking and Parallel Tree Contraction," Chapter 3 in *Synthesis of Parallel Algorithms*, edited by J. H. Reif, Morgan Kaufmann, 1993, pp. 115–194.
[Wang96]   Wang, H., A. Nicolau, and K.-Y. S. Siu, "The Strict Time Lower Bound and Optimal Schedules for Parallel Prefix with Resource Constraints," *IEEE Trans. Computers*, Vol. 45, No. 11, pp. 1257–1271, November 1996.

6

More Shared-Memory Algorithms

In this chapter, following the same notation and basic methods introduced in Chapter 5, we develop PRAM algorithms for several additional problems. These problems are somewhat more complex than the building-block computations of Chapter 5, to the extent that the reader may not know efficient sequential algorithms for the problems that would allow one to obtain the PRAM version by simply parallelizing the sequential algorithm or to deduce the speed-up achieved by the parallel version. For this reason, some background material is provided in each case and a separate section (Section 6.1) is devoted to the sequential version of the first algorithm, complete with its analysis. Chapter topics are

- 6.1. Sequential rank-based selection
- 6.2. A parallel selection algorithm
- 6.3. A selection-based sorting algorithm
- 6.4. Alternative sorting algorithms
- 6.5. Convex hull of a 2D point set
- 6.6. Some implementation aspects

6.1. SEQUENTIAL RANK-BASED SELECTION

Rank-based selection is the problem of finding a (the) kth smallest element in a sequence $S = x_0, x_1, \ldots, x_{n-1}$ whose elements belong to a linear order. Median, maximum, and minimum finding are special cases of this general problem. Clearly the (rank-based) selection problem can be solved through sorting: Sort the sequence in nondescending order and output the kth element (with index $k - 1$, if 0-origin indexing is used) of the sorted list. However, this is wasteful in view of the fact that any sorting algorithm requires $\Omega(n \log n)$ time, whereas $O(n)$-time selection algorithms are available. The following is an example of a recursive linear-time selection algorithm.

Sequential rank-based selection algorithm *select(S, k)*

1. if $|S| < q$ {q is a small constant}
   then   sort S and return the kth smallest element of S
   else   divide S into $|S|/q$ subsequences of size q
            Sort each subsequence and find its median
            Let the $|S|/q$ medians form the sequence T
   endif
2. $m = select(T, |T|/2)$ {find the median m of the $|S|/q$ medians}
3. Create 3 subsequences
   L: Elements of S that are $< m$
   E: Elements of S that are $= m$
   G: Elements of S that are $> m$
4. if $|L| \geq k$
   then return *select(L, k)*
   else if $|L| + |E| \geq k$
         then return m
         else return *select(G, k - |L| - |E|)*
   endif

An analysis of the above selection algorithm follows. If S is small, then its median is found through sorting in Step 1 (the size threshold constant q will be defined later). This requires constant time, say c_0. Otherwise, we divide the list into a number of subsequences of length q, sort each subsequence to find its median, and put the medians together into a list T. These operations require linear time in $|S|$, say $c_1|S|$ time. Step 2 of the algorithm that finds the median of the medians constitutes a smaller, $|S|/q$-input, selection problem. Given the median m of the medians, Step 3 of the algorithm takes linear time in $|S|$, say $c_3 |S|$, as it involves scanning the entire list, comparing each element to m, and putting it in one of three output lists according to the comparison result. Finally, Step 4 is another smaller selection problem. We will show that the size of this selection problem is $3|S|/4$ in the worst case. Assuming that this claim is true, the running time of the above selection algorithm is characterized by the recurrence

$$T(n) = T(n/q) + T(3n/4) + cn$$

where the term cn represents an amalgamation of all linear-order terms discussed above. This recurrence has a linear solution for any $q > 4$. For example, let the linear solution be $T(n) = dn$ for $q = 5$. Plugging into the recurrence, we get

$$dn = dn/5 + 3dn/4 + cn$$

The above leads to $d = 20c$ and $T(n) = 20cn$. Choosing a larger value for the threshold q leads to a multiplicative factor that is smaller than 20 but at the same time increases the value of c, so an optimal choice may exist for q.

All that is left to complete our analysis of the selection algorithm is to justify the term $T(3n/4)$ in the above recurrence. The reason that the selection problem in Step 4 of the algorithm involves no more than $3n/4$ inputs is as follows. The median m of the n/q medians is no smaller (no larger) than at least half, or $(n/q)/2$, of the medians, each of which is in turn no smaller (no larger) than $q/2$ elements of the original input list S. Thus, m is guaranteed to be no smaller (no larger) than at least $((n/q)/2) \times q/2 = n/4$ elements of the input list S.

The following example shows the application of the above sequential selection algorithm to an input list of size $n = 25$ using $q = 5$.

```
◄················································  n/q sublists of q elements  ································································►
S      6 4 5 6 7     1 5 3 8 2      1 0 3 4 5     6 2 1 7 1      4 5 4 9 5
              ─────              ─────                ─────            ─────              ─────
T         6              3              3              2              5

m                                              3

         1 2 1 0 2 1 1      3 3      6 4 5 6 7 5 8 4 5 6 7 4 5 4 9 5
         ───────────────    ─────    ───────────────────────────────
                L              E                    G

            |L| = 7        |E| = 2              |G| = 16
```

To find the 5th smallest element in S, select the 5th smallest element in L ($|L| \geq 5$) as follows

```
        S       1  2  1  0  2        1  1
                ──────────────       ─────
        T            1                 1
        m                              1

             0      1  1  1  1      2  2
             ─      ─────────      ─────
             L         E            G
```

leading to the answer 1, because in the second iteration, $|L| < 5$ and $|L| + |E| \geq 5$. The 9th smallest element of S is 3 ($|L| + |E| \geq 9$). Finally, the 13th smallest element of S is found by selecting the 4th smallest element in G ($4 = 13 - |L| - |E|$):

```
S     6  4  5  6  7     5  8  4  5  6     7  4  5  4  9     5
      ─────────────     ─────────────     ─────────────     ─
T           6                 5                 5           5
m                                               5

      4  4  4  4     5  5  5  5  5     6  6  7  8  6  7  9
      ──────────     ─────────────     ──────────────────
          L               E                    G
```

The preceding leads to the answer 4.

6.2. A PARALLEL SELECTION ALGORITHM

If a parallel computation model supports fast sorting, then the n-input parallel selection problem can be solved through sorting. This is the case, e.g., for the CRCW PRAM-S or "summation" submodel with $p = n^2$ processors as shown below. We will see in Chapter 9 that the more realistic 2D mesh model also supports fast sorting relative to its diameter-based lower bound.

In the CRCW PRAM-S model, let us number each of the $p = n^2$ processors by an index pair (i, j), with $0 \le i, j < n$. Processor (i, j) compares inputs $S[i]$ and $S[j]$ and writes a 1 into the memory location $rank[j]$ if $S[i] < S[j]$ or if $S[i] = S[j]$ and $i < j$. Because of the summation feature on concurrent writes, after this single-cycle operation, $rank[j]$ will hold the rank or index of $S[j]$ in the sorted list. In the second cycle, Processor $(0, j)$, $0 \le j < n$, reads $S[j]$ and writes it into $S[rank[j]]$. The selection process is completed in a third cycle when all processors read $S[k - 1]$, the kth smallest element in S.

It is difficult to imagine a faster selection algorithm. Unfortunately, however, this fast three-step algorithm is quite impractical: It uses both a large number of processors and a very strong PRAM submodel. One might say that this algorithm holds the record for the most impractical parallel algorithm described in this book!

Now, coming down to earth, the selection algorithm described in Section 6.1 can be parallelized to obtain a p-processor *PRAMselect* algorithm for selecting the kth smallest value in a list S of size n. List T of size n is used as working storage, in addition to L, E, and G, as discussed for the sequential selection algorithm in Section 6.1.

Parallel rank-based selection algorithm *PRAMselect(S, k, p)*
___

1. if $|S| < 4$
    then   sort S and return the kth smallest element of S
    else   broadcast $|S|$ to all p processors
            divide S into p subsequences $S^{(j)}$ of size $|S|/p$
            Processor j, $0 \le j < p$, compute the median $T_j := select(S^{(j)}, |S^{(j)}|/2)$
    endif
2. $m = PRAMselect(T, |T|/2, p)$ {find the median of the medians in parallel}
3. Broadcast m to all processors and create 3 subsequences
    L: Elements of S that are $< m$
    E: Elements of S that are $= m$
    G: Elements of S that are $> m$
4. if $|L| \ge k$
    then return *PRAMselect(L, k, p)*
    else   if $|L| + |E| \ge k$
            then return m
            else return *PRAMselect(G, k – |L| – |E|, p)*
    endif

Note that the parallel algorithm *PRAMselect* is quite similar in appearance, and underlying concepts, to the sequential algorithm *select* presented in Section 6.1. This familiarity of the shared-memory programming model is one of its key advantages. Figuring out the reason behind the choice of the constant 4 in Step 1 of *PRAMselect* is left as an exercise.

To analyze the *PRAMselect* algorithm, we assume that the number p of processors is sublinear in the number n of elements in the input list; namely, $p = n^{1-x}$, where x is a parameter that is known a priori. For example, $x = 1/2$ corresponds to $p = \sqrt{n}$ processors being applied to the solution of an n-input problem.

Step 1 of the algorithm involves broadcasting, which needs $O(\log p) = O(\log n)$ time, dividing into sublists, which is done in constant time by each processor independently computing the beginning and end of its associated sublist based on $|S|$ and x, and sequential selection on each sublist of length n/p, which needs $O(n/p) = O(n^x)$ time. Step 3 can be done as follows. First, each processor counts the number of elements that it should place in each of the lists L, E, and G in $O(n/p) = O(n^x)$ time. Then, three diminished parallel prefix computations are performed to determine the number of elements to be placed on each list by all processors with indices that are smaller than i. Finally, the actual placement takes $O(n^x)$ time, with each processor independently writing into the lists L, E, and G using the diminished prefix computation result as the starting address. Noting that logarithmic terms are negligible compared with $O(n^x)$ terms and using the knowledge that the parallel selection algorithm in Step 4 will have no more than $3n/4$ inputs, the running time of *PRAMselect* algorithm for $p = n^{1-x}$ can be characterized by the following recurrence, which is easily verified to have the solution $T(n, p) = O(n^x)$;

$$T(n, p) = T(n^{1-x}, p) + T(3n/4, p) + cn^x$$

The *PRAMselect* algorithm is quite efficient:

Speed-up $(n, p) = \Theta(n)/O(n^x) = \Omega(n^{1-x}) = \Omega(p)$

Efficiency $\quad = $ Speed-up $/ p = \Omega(1)$

Work $(n, p) \quad = pT(n, p) = \Theta(n^{1-x})O(n^x) = O(n)$

The above asymptotic analysis is valid for any $x > 0$. What if $x = 0$, i.e., we use $p = n$ processors for an n-input selection problem? Does the above analysis imply that in this case, we have a constant-time selection algorithm? The answer is negative. Recall that in the asymptotic analysis, we ignored several $O(\log n)$ terms in comparison with $O(n^x)$ terms. If $O(n^x) = O(1)$, then the logarithmic terms dominate and the recurrence would have an $O(\log n)$ solution.

One positive property of *PRAMselect* is that it is adaptable to any number of processors and yields linear speed-up in each case, provided that $p < n$. This is a desirable property in a parallel algorithm, as we do not have to adjust the algorithm for running it on different hardware configurations. It is self-adjusting. Even if the number of processors in the target machine is known a priori, it is still the case that the number available to the algorithm may vary, either because the algorithm must share the machine with other running programs (a machine partition is assigned to it) or because of dynamic variations caused by processor failures.

6.3. A SELECTION-BASED SORTING ALGORITHM

Here is one way to sort a list of size n via divide and conquer. First identify the $k - 1$ elements that would occupy positions $n/k, 2n/k, 3n/k, \ldots, (k - 1)n/k$ in the sorted list, for a suitably chosen small constant k. Call the values of these elements $m_1, m_2, m_3, \ldots, m_{k-1}$,

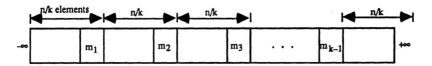

Figure 6.1. Partitioning of the sorted list for selection-based sorting.

and define $m_0 = -\infty$ and $m_k = +\infty$ for convenience (see Fig. 6.1). Now, if the above $k - 1$ elements are put in their proper places in the sorted list and all other elements are moved so that any element that is physically located between m_i and m_{i+1} in the list has a value in the interval $[m_i, m_{i+1}]$, the sorting task can be completed by independently sorting each of the k sublists of size n/k.

The assumptions here are quite similar to those for the parallel selection algorithm in Section 6.2. We have $p < n$ processors for sorting a list of size n, with $p = n^{1-x}$. Because x is known a priori, we can choose $k = 2^{1/x}$ as our partitioning constant. The algorithm thus begins by finding m_i, the (in/k)th smallest element in the sorted list, $0 < i < k$, and proceeds as discussed above.

Parallel selection-based sorting algorithm *PRAMselectionsort(S, p)*

1. if $|S| < k$ then return *quicksort(S)*
2. for $i = 1$ to $k - 1$ do
    $m_i := PRAMselect(S, i|S|/k, p)$
    {for notational convenience, let $m_o := -\infty$; $m_k := +\infty$}
    endfor
3. for $i = 0$ to $k - 1$ do
    make the sublist $T^{(i)}$ from elements of S that are between m_i and m_{i+1}
    endfor
4. for $i = 1$ to $k/2$ do in parallel
    $PRAMselectionsort(T^{(i)}, 2p/k)$
    {$p/(k/2)$ processors are used for each of the $k/2$ subproblems}
    endfor
5. for $i = k/2 + 1$ to k do in parallel
    $PRAMselectionsort(T^{(i)}, 2p/k)$
    endfor

The analysis of complexity for the *PRAMselectionsort* algorithm is as follows. Step 1 takes constant time. Step 2 consists of k separate and sequentially solved parallel selection problems with n inputs using n^{1-x} processors. From the analysis of Section 6.2, because k is a constant, the total time for Step 2 is $O(n^x)$. In Step 3, each processor compares its n^x values with the $k - 1$ threshold values and counts how many elements it will contribute to each of the k partitions. Then, k diminished parallel prefix computations, each taking $O(\log p) = O(\log n)$ time, are performed to obtain the starting index for each processor to store the elements that it contributes to each partition. The last part of Step 3 involves a processor writing its n^x elements to the various partitions. Thus, Step 3 takes a total of $O(n^x)$ time.

In Steps 4 and 5, the *PRAMselectionsort* algorithm is recursively called. The running time of the algorithm is thus characterized by the recurrence

$$T(n, p) = 2T(n/k, 2p/k) + cn^x$$

which has the solution $T(n, p) = O(n^x \log n)$. The above recurrence also gives us a clue as to why all of the k subproblems cannot be handled in Step 4 at once: Our algorithm assumes the availability of $p = n^{1-x}$ processors for n inputs. Thus, to solve each of the subproblems with $n/k = n/2^{1/x}$ inputs, the number of processors needed is

$$(\text{number of inputs})^{1-x} = (n/2^{1/x})^{1-x} = n^{1-x}/2^{1/x-1} = p/(k/2)$$

Thus, the number p of processors is adequate for solving $k/2$ of the subproblems concurrently, giving rise to the need for two recursive steps to solve all k subproblems.

It is straightforward to establish the asymptotic optimality of *PRAMselectionsort* among comparison-based sorting algorithms, keeping in mind that any sequential sorting algorithm requires $\Omega(n \log n)$ comparisons:

Speed-up(n, p) $= \Omega(n \log n) / O(n^x \log n) = \Omega(n^{1-x}) = \Omega(p)$

Efficiency $= \text{Speed-up} / p = \Omega(1)$

Work(n, p) $= pT(n, p) = \Theta(n^{1-x}) O(n^x \log n) = O(n \log n)$

As in the case of our *PRAMselect* algorithm in Section 6.2, the above asymptotic analysis is valid for any $x > 0$ but not for $x = 0$, i.e., *PRAMselectionsort* does not allow us to sort p keys using p processors in optimal $O(\log p)$ time. Furthermore, even in the case of $p < n$, the time complexity may involve large constant multiplicative factors. In most cases, the algorithms discussed in Section 6.4 might prove more practical.

Consider the following example of how *PRAMselectionsort* works on an input list with $|S| = 25$ elements, using $p = 5$ processors (thus, $x = 1/2$ and $k = 2^{1/x} = 4$).

$$S: 6\ 4\ 5\ 6\ 7\ 1\ 5\ 3\ 8\ 2\ 1\ 0\ 3\ 4\ 5\ 6\ 2\ 1\ 7\ 0\ 4\ 5\ 4\ 9\ 5$$

The threshold values needed for partitioning the list into $k = 4$ sublists are determined as follows:

$$m_0 = -\infty$$

$n/k = 25/4 \approx 6$ $m_1 = PRAMselect(S, 6, 5) = 2$

$2n/k = 50/4 \approx 13$ $m_2 = PRAMselect(S, 13, 5) = 4$

$3n/k = 75/4 \approx 19$ $m_3 = PRAMselect(S, 19, 5) = 6$

$$m_4 = +\infty$$

After these elements are placed in their respective positions, the working list T looks as follows, with the partition boundaries also shown for clarity:

$$T: - - - - - 2| - - - - - - 4| - - - - 6| - - - - -$$

Once all other 22 elements are placed in their respective partitions and the four partitions independently sorted, the sorted list T results:

$$T: 0\ 0\ 1\ 1\ 1\ 2|2\ 3\ 3\ 4\ 4\ 4\ 4|5\ 5\ 5\ 5\ 6|6\ 6\ 7\ 7\ 8\ 9$$

Note that for elements that are equal to one of the comparison thresholds, the proper place may be to the left or right of that value. The algorithm as described above, may not work properly if the input list contains repeated values. It is possible to modify the algorithm so that such repeated values are handled properly, but this would lead to higher algorithm complexity.

6.4. ALTERNATIVE SORTING ALGORITHMS

Much of the complexity of the parallel sorting algorithm described in Section 6.3 is related to our insistence that the k subproblems resulting at the end be exactly of the same size, thus allowing us to establish an optimal upper bound on the worst-case running time. There exist many useful algorithms that are quite efficient on the average but that exhibit poor worst-case behavior. Sequential *quicksort* is a prime example that runs in order $n \log n$ time in most cases but can take on the order of n^2 time for worst-case input patterns.

In the case of our selection-based sorting algorithm, if the comparison thresholds are picked such that their ranks in the sorted list are approximately, rather than exactly, equal to in/k, the same process can be applied for the rest of the algorithm, the only difference being that the resulting k subproblems will be of roughly the same size (in a probabilistic sense).

Given a large list S of inputs, a random sample of the elements can be used to establish the k comparison thresholds. In fact, it would be easier if we pick $k = p$, so that each of the resulting subproblems is handled by a single processor. Recall that this sorting algorithm was used as an example in our discussion of randomization methods in Section 3.5. Below is the resulting algorithm assuming $p \ll \sqrt{n}$.

Parallel randomized sorting algorithm *PRAMrandomsort(S, p)*

1. Processor j, $0 \leq j < p$, pick $|S|/p^2$ random samples of its $|S|/p$ elements and store them in its corresponding section of a list T of length $|S|/p$
2. Processor 0 sort the list T
   {the comparison threshold m_i is the $(i|S|/p^2)$th element of T}
3. Processor j, $0 \leq j < p$, store its elements that are between m_i and m_{i+1} into the sublist $T^{(i)}$
4. Processor j, $0 \leq j < p$, sort the sublist $T^{(j)}$

The analysis of complexity for the above algorithm (in the average case) is left as an exercise.

The next sorting algorithm that we will discuss is *parallel radixsort*. In the binary version of *radixsort*, we examine every bit of the k-bit keys in turn, starting from the least-significant bit (LSB). In Step i, bit i is examined, $0 \leq i < k$. All records with keys having a 0 in bit position i are shifted toward the beginning and keys with 1 toward the end of the list, keeping the relative order of records with the same bit value in the current position unchanged (this is sometimes referred to as *stable sorting*). Here is an example of how radixsort works (key values are followed by their binary representations in parentheses):

Input list	Sort by LSB	Sort by middle bit	Sort by MSB
5 (101)	4 (100)	4 (100)	1 (001)
7 (111)	2 (010)	5 (101)	2 (010)
3 (011)	2 (010)	1 (001)	2 (010)
1 (001)	5 (101)	2 (010)	3 (011)
4 (100)	7 (111)	2 (010)	4 (100)
2 (010)	3 (011)	2 (010)	5 (101)
7 (111)	1 (001)	7 (111)	7 (111)
2 (010)	7 (111)	3 (011)	7 (111)

It remains to be shown that the required data movements (upward and downward shifting) in each of the k steps can be done efficiently in parallel. Let us focus on the data movements associated with Bit 0. The new position of each record in the shifted list can be established by two prefix sum computations: a diminished prefix sum computation on the complement of Bit 0 to establish the new locations of records with 0 in bit position 0 and a normal prefix sum computation on Bit 0 to determine the location for each record with 1 in bit position 0 relative to the last record of the first category (2 in the following example).

Input list	Compl't of Bit 0	Diminished prefix sums	Bit 0	Prefix sums plus 2	Shifted list
5 (101)	0	—	1	1 + 2 = 3	4 (100)
7 (111)	0	—	1	2 + 2 = 4	2 (010)
3 (011)	0	—	1	3 + 2 = 5	2 (010)
1 (001)	0	—	1	4 + 2 = 6	5 (101)
4 (100)	1	0	0	—	7 (111)
2 (010)	1	1	0	—	3 (011)
7 (111)	0	—	1	5 + 2 = 7	1 (001)
2 (010)	1	2	0	—	7 (111)

Thus, the running time of the parallel radixsort algorithm consists mainly of the time needed to perform $2k$ parallel prefix computations, where k is the key length in bits. For k a constant, the running time is asymptotically $O(\log p)$ for sorting a list of size p using p processors.

6.5. CONVEX HULL OF A 2D POINT SET

The 2D convex hull algorithm presented in this section is a representative example of geometric problems that are encountered in image processing and computer vision applications. It is also an excellent case study of multiway divide and conquer. The convex hull problem for a 2D point set is defined as follows: Given a point set Q of size n on the Euclidean plane, with the points specified by their (x, y) coordinates, find the smallest convex polygon that encloses all n points. The inputs can be assumed to be in the form of two n-vectors X and Y. The desired output is a list of points belonging to the convex hall starting from an arbitrary point and proceeding, say, in clockwise order. The output list has a size of at most n. As an example, for the point set shown in Fig. 6.2, the convex hull may be represented by the list 0, 1, 7, 11, 15, 14, 8, 2.

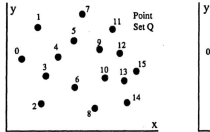 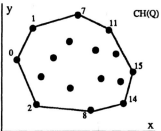

Figure 6.2. Defining the convex hull problem.

The following properties of the convex hull allow us to construct an efficient PRAM parallel algorithm ([Akl93], p. 28):

Property 1. Let q_i and q_j be consecutive points of CH(Q). View q_i as the origin of coordinates. The line from q_j to q_i forms a smaller angle with the positive (or negative) x axis than the line from q_j to any other q_k in the point set Q. Figure 6.3 illustrates this property.

Property 2. A segment (q_i, q_j) is an edge of CH(Q) iff all of the remaining $n - 2$ points fall to the same side of it. Again, Fig. 6.3 illustrates this property.

The following algorithm finds the convex hull CH(Q) of a 2D point set of size p on a p-processor CRCW PRAM.

Parallel convex hull algorithm *PRAMconvexhull(S, p)*

---

1. Sort the point set by the x coordinates
2. Divide the sorted list into $\sqrt{p}$ subsets $Q^{(i)}$ of size $\sqrt{p}$, $0 \le i < \sqrt{p}$
3. Find the convex hull of each subset $Q^{(i)}$ by assigning $\sqrt{p}$ processors to it
4. Merge the $\sqrt{p}$ convex hulls CH($Q^{(i)}$) into the overall hull CH(Q)

Figure 6.4 shows an example with a 16-element sorted point set ($p = 16$), the four subsets, and the four partial convex hulls. Step 4 is the heart of the algorithm and is described next.

Note that the convex hull of Q can be divided into the upper hull, which goes from the point with the smallest x coordinate to the one with the largest x coordinate, and the lower

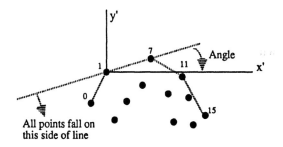

Fig. 6.3. Illustrating the properties of the convex hull.

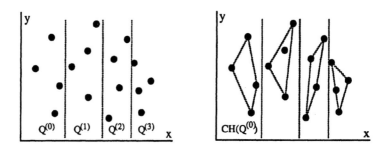

Figure 6.4. Multiway divide and conquer for the convex hull problem.

hull, which returns from the latter to the former. We will only show how the upper hull of Q is derived (the part from q_0 to q_{15} in the example of Fig. 6.2).

Each point subset of size $\sqrt{p}$ is assigned $\sqrt{p}$ processors to determine the upper tangent line between its hull and each of the other $\sqrt{p} - 1$ hulls. One processor finds each tangent in $O(\log p)$ steps using an algorithm of Overmars and van Leeuwen [Over81]. The algorithm resembles binary search. To determine the upper tangent from $CH(Q^{(i)})$ to $CH(Q^{(k)})$, the midpoint of the upper part of $CH(Q^{(k)})$ is taken and the slopes for its adjacent points compared with its own slope. If the slope is minimum, then we have found the tangent point. Otherwise, the search is restricted to one or the other half. Because multiple processors associated with various partial convex hulls read data from all hulls, the CREW model must be assumed.

Once all of the upper tangents from each hull to all other hulls are known, a pair of candidates are selected by finding the min/max slopes. Finally, depending on the angle between the two candidates being less than or greater than 180 degrees (Fig. 6.5), no point or a subset of points from $CH(Q^{(i)})$ belongs to $CH(Q)$.

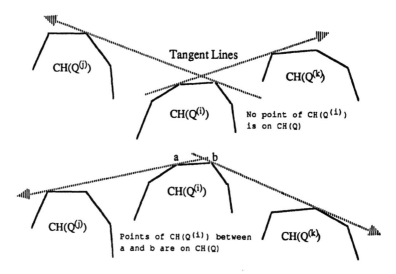

Figure 6.5. Finding points in a partial hull that belong to the combined hull.

The final step is to renumber the points in proper order for CH(Q). A parallel prefix computation on the list containing the number of points from each CH($Q^{(i)}$) that have been identified as belonging to the combined hull yields the rank or index of each node on CH(Q).

The complexity of the above parallel convex hull algorithm (excluding the initial sorting of the point set) is characterized by the following recurrence:

$$T(p, p) = T(p^{1/2}, p^{1/2}) + c \log p$$

which has the solution $T(p, p) \approx 2c \log p$. Given that sorting a list of size p can be performed in O($\log p$) time as well, the overall time complexity is O($\log p$).

Because the best sequential algorithm for a p-point convex hull problem requires $\Omega(p \log p)$ computation steps, the above parallel convex hull algorithm is asymptotically optimal.

6.6. SOME IMPLEMENTATION ASPECTS

In this section, we discuss a number of practical considerations that are important in transforming a PRAM algorithm into an efficient program for an actual shared-memory parallel computer. The most important of these relates to data layout in the shared memory. To discuss these issues, we need to look at hardware implementation aspects of shared memory.

In any physical implementation of shared memory, the m memory locations will be in B memory banks (modules), each bank holding m/B addresses. Typically, a memory bank can provide access to a single memory word in a given memory cycle. Even though memory units can be, and have been, designed to allow access to a few independently addressed words in a single cycle, such *multiport memories* tend to be quite expensive. Besides, if the number of memory ports is less than m/B (which is certainly the case in practice), these multiport memories still do not allow us the same type of access that is permitted even in the weakest PRAM submodel.

So, even if the PRAM algorithm assumes the EREW submodel where no two processors access the same memory location in the same cycle, memory bank conflicts may still arise. Depending on how such conflicts are resolved, moderate to serious loss of performance may result. An obvious solution is to try to lay out the data in the shared memory and organize the computational steps of the algorithm so that a memory bank is accessed at most once in each cycle. This is quite a challenging problem that has received significant attention from the research community and parallel computer designers.

The main ideas relating to data layout methods are best explained in connection with the matrix multiplication problem of Section 5.6. Let us take the $m \times m$ matrix multiplication algorithm in which $p = m^2$ processors are used. We identify each processor by an index pair (i, j). Then, Processor P_{ij} will be responsible for computing the element c_{ij} of the result matrix C. The m processors P_{iy}, $0 \le y < m$, would need to read Row i of the matrix A for their computation. In order to avoid multiple accesses to the same matrix element, we skew the accesses so that P_{iy} reads the elements of Row i beginning with A_{iy}. In this way, the entire Row i of A is read out in every cycle, albeit with the elements distributed differently to the processors in each cycle.

To ensure that conflict-free parallel access to all elements of each row of A is possible in every memory cycle, the data layout must assign different columns of A to different

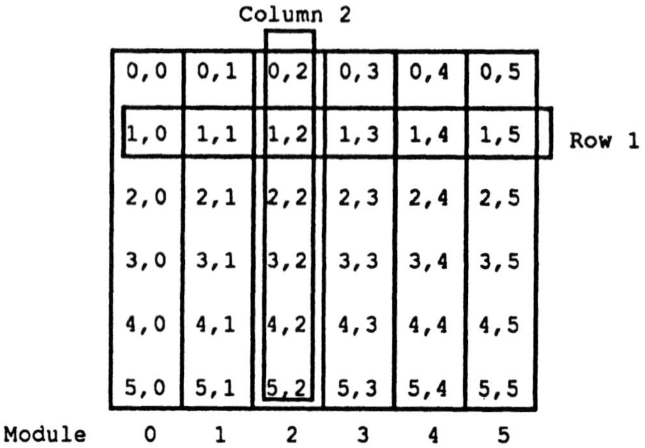

Column 2
0,0 0,1 0,2 0,3 0,4 0,5
1,0 1,1 1,2 1,3 1,4 1,5
Row 1
2,0 2,1 2,2 2,3 2,4 2,5
3,0 3,1 3,2 3,3 3,4 3,5
4,0 4,1 4,2 4,3 4,4 4,5
5,0 5,1 5,2 5,3 5,4 5,5
Module 0 1 2 3 4 5

Figure 6.6. Matrix storage in column-major order to allow concurrent accesses to rows.

memory banks. This is possible if we have at least m memory banks and corresponds to the data storage in column-major order, as shown in Fig. 6.6, where the matrix element (i, j) is found in location i of memory bank j. If fewer than m memory modules are available, then the matrix element (i, j) can be stored in location $i + m\lfloor j/B \rfloor$ of memory bank j mod B. This would ensure that the row elements can be read out with maximum parallelism.

However, also note that Processors P_{xj}, $0 \le x < m$, all access the jth column of B. Therefore, the column-major storage scheme of Fig. 6.6 will lead to memory bank conflicts for all such accesses to the columns of B. We can store B in row-major order to avoid such conflicts. However, if B is later to be used in a different matrix multiplication, say $B \times D$, then either the layout of B must be changed by physically rearranging it in memory or the algorithm must be modified, neither of which is desirable.

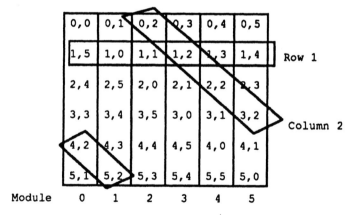

0,0 0,1 0,2 0,3 0,4 0,5
1,5 1,0 1,1 1,2 1,3 1,4
Row 1
2,4 2,5 2,0 2,1 2,2 2,3
3,3 3,4 3,5 3,0 3,1 3,2
Column 2
4,2 4,3 4,4 4,5 4,0 4,1
5,1 5,2 5,3 5,4 5,5 5,0
Module 0 1 2 3 4 5

Figure 6.7. Skewed matrix storage for conflict-free accesses to rows and columns.

Fortunately, a matrix can be laid out in memory in such a way that both columns and rows are accessible in parallel without memory bank conflicts. Figure 6.7 shows a well-known skewed storage scheme that allows conflict-free access to both rows and columns of a matrix. In this scheme, the matrix element (i, j) is found in location i of module $(i + j)$ mod B. It is clear from this formulation that all elements (i, y), $0 \leq y < m$, will be found in different modules, as are all elements (x, j), $0 \leq x < m$, provided that $B \geq m$. It is also clear that if all of the m diagonal elements (x, x) of the matrix were to be accessed in parallel, conflicts could arise, unless $B \geq 2m$ or else B is an odd number in the range $m \leq B < 2m$.

To generalize the above discussion and lay a foundation for a theoretical treatment of the memory layout problem for conflict-free parallel access, it is more convenient to deal with vectors rather than matrices. The 6×6 matrix of Figs. 6.6 and 6.7 can be viewed as a 36-element vector, as shown in Fig. 6.8, that may have to be accessed in some or all of the following ways:

Column:	$k, k + 1, k + 2, k + 3, k + 4, k + 5$	Stride of 1
Row:	$k, k + m, k + 2m, k + 3m, k + 4m, k + 5m$	Stride of m
Diagonal:	$k, k + m + 1, k + 2(m + 1), k + 3(m + 1), k + 4(m + 1), k + 5(m + 1)$	Stride of $m + 1$
Antidiagonal:	$k, k + m - 1, k + 2(m - 1), k + 3(m - 1), k + 4(m - 1), k + 5(m - 1)$	Stride of $m - 1$

where index calculations are assumed to be modulo m^2 (or, more generally, modulo the length l of the vector at hand). In this context, it does not matter whether we number the matrix elements in column-major or row-major order, as the latter will only interchange the first two strides.

Thus, the memory data layout problem is reduced to the following: Given a vector of length l, store it in B memory banks in such a way that accesses with strides $s_0, s_1, \ldots, s_{h-1}$ are conflict-free (ideal) or involve the minimum possible amount of conflict.

A *linear skewing scheme* is one that stores the kth vector element in the bank $a + kb$ mod B. The address within the bank is irrelevant to conflict-free parallel access, though it does affect the ease with which memory addresses are computed by the processors. In fact, the constant a above is also irrelevant and can be safely ignored. Thus, we can limit our attention to linear skewing schemes that assign V_k to memory module $M_{kb \bmod B}$.

With a linear skewing scheme, the vector elements $k, k + s, k + 2s, \ldots, k + (B - 1)s$ will be assigned to different memory modules iff sb is relatively prime with respect to the number B of memory banks. A simple way to guarantee conflict-free parallel access for all strides is to choose B to be a prime number, in which case $b = 1$ can be used for simplicity. But having

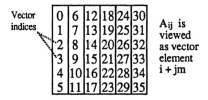

Figure 6.8. A 6×6 matrix viewed, in column-major order, as a 36-element vector.

a prime number of banks may be inconvenient for other reasons. Thus, many alternative methods have been proposed.

Now, even assuming conflict-free access to memory banks, it is still the case that the multiple memory access requests must be directed from the processors to the associated memory banks. With a large number of processors and memory banks, this is a nontrivial problem. Ideally, the memory access network should be a permutation network that can connect each processor to any memory bank as long as the connection is a permutation. However, permutation networks are quite expensive to implement and difficult to control (set up). Thus, we usually settle for networks that do not possess full permutation capability.

Figure 6.9 shows a multistage interconnection network as an example of a compromise solution. This is a butterfly network that we will encounter again in Chapter 8 where we devise a circuit for computing the fast Fourier transform (FFT) and again in Chapter 15, where it is shown to be related to the hypercube architecture. For our discussion here, we only note that memory accesses can be self-routed through this network by letting the ith bit of the memory bank address determine the switch setting in Column $i - 1$ ($1 \leq i \leq 3$), with 0 indicating the upper path and 1 the lower path. For example, independent of the source processor, any request going to memory bank 3 (0011) will be routed to the "lower," "upper," "upper," "lower" output line by the switches that forward it in Columns 0–3. A self-routing interconnection network is highly desirable as the ease of routing translates directly into simpler hardware, lower delay, and higher throughput.

The switches in the memory access network of Fig. 6.9 can be designed to deal with access conflicts by simply dropping duplicate requests (in which case the processors must rely on a positive acknowledgment from memory to ensure that their requests have been honored), buffering one of the two conflicting requests (which introduces nondeterminacy in the memory access time), or combining access requests to the same memory location.

When buffers are used to hold duplicate requests, determining the size of the buffers needed is a challenging problem. Large buffers increase the probability that no request has to be dropped because of buffer overflow, but lead to complex switches with attendant cost and speed penalties. Experience has shown that conflicts can usually be resolved in a few

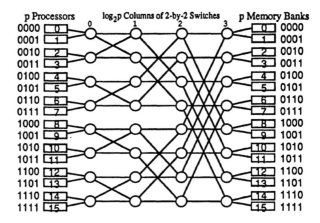

Figure 6.9. Example of a multistage memory access network.

rounds or handled with relatively small buffers. In other words, the worst case does not usually occur.

However, there are occasionally "hot spots" in memory that many processors may try to access simultaneously. If the hot spots are related to control mechanisms, such as locks and semaphores, that are typically accessed by many processors, then the use of switches with combining capability may help. For example, multiple read requests from the same location may be buffered in the switch, with only one forwarded to the next level. When the read result for such duplicate requests comes back to the switch from its memory side, the data will be broadcast to both processor-side ports. With combining switches, the powerful PRAM CRCW reduction submodels (e.g., maximum or summation) can be implemented with little additional cost in the memory access network relative to the EREW, provided that multiple accesses to a given memory bank are guaranteed to be to the same memory location.

PROBLEMS

6.1. Parallel sorting on CRCW-S PRAM
For the impractical sorting algorithm discussed at the beginning of Section 6.2, compute the speed-up, efficiency, and the other figures of merit introduced in Section 1.6.

6.2. Parallel rank-based selection
Develop a parallel selection algorithm by applying the ideas used in the radixsort algorithm of Section 6.4. Compare the performance of your algorithm to that of parallel radixsort and to the parallel selection algorithm of Section 6.2 and discuss.

6.3. Parallel rank-based selection
In the parallel selection algorithm of Section 6.2:

a. Why is the constant 4 used on the first line of the algorithm (e.g., why not "if $|S| < 3$"?)?
b. How would the algorithm complexity be affected if the constant 4 is increased to 6, say?
c. What if instead of a constant we use a value such as $p/\log_2 p$ or $n/\log_2 n$?

6.4. Parallel selection-based sorting
In the selection-based sorting algorithm of Section 6.3, the decomposition parameter k was chosen to be $2^{1/x}$ in order to allow us to solve the k subproblems in two passes (Steps 4 and 5 of the algorithm).

a. Justify the solution given for the recurrence characterizing the running time of the algorithm with the above choice for k.
b. What is the appropriate choice for k if the k subproblems are to be solved in no more than r passes?
c. How is the running time of the algorithm affected if $r = 4$ in part (b)?

6.5. Parallel selection-based sorting
At the end of Section 6.3, it was mentioned that rank-based selection algorithm becomes more complex if the input list contains repeated elements. Make the required modifications in the algorithm for this case.

6.6. Parallel randomized sorting
Analyze the average-case complexity of the parallel randomized sorting algorithm presented

in Section 6.4. Using your analysis, justify the choice of $|S|/p^2$ random samples in the first algorithm step.

6.7. **Parallel radixsort algorithm**

a. Extend the parallel radixsort algorithm given in Section 6.4 to the case where the number n of elements to be sorted is larger than the number p of processors.
b. Radixsort can be done in higher radices (e.g., radix 4 rather than 2). Describe a parallel radixsort algorithm using the radix of 4 and compare its running time with the radix-2 version.
c. Based on the results of part (b), would it be advantageous to use even higher radices?

6.8. **Parallel convex hull algorithm**

a. On Fig. 6.4, show how the next level of recursion would subdivide the four smaller problems.
b. In general, when does the recursion stop?
c. Express the number of recursion levels in terms of the problem size p.
d. Extend the algorithm to the general case of n data points and p processors, with $n > p$.

6.9. **Other geometric problems on point sets**
The convex hull problem is only one example of a rich collection of practical problems that involve point sets in the Cartesian coordinates. Propose algorithms for solving each of the following problems on point sets.

a. Determining the center of gravity of a 2D set of points, each having a positive weight.
b. Determining the subset of points that are not dominated by any other point, where a point (x_1, y_1) dominates another point (x_2, y_2) iff $x_1 \geq x_2$ and $y_1 \geq y_2$. As an example, the answer in the case of the point set in Fig. 6.2 should be 7, 11, 12, 15.
c. Dynamically updating the convex hull of a 2D point set as each point is added to, or removed from, the set.
d. Determining the largest circle centered at each point that does not have any other point inside it.
e. Determining the diameter of a 2D point set, defined as the diameter of the smallest circle that can enclose all of the points.
f. Determining a pair of points that are closest to, or farthest from, each other.

6.10. **Geometric problems on sets of line segments**
Given a set of straight line segments on a plane, each specified by the coordinates of its two endpoints, propose algorithms for solving each of the following problems.

a. Yes or no answer to the question of whether any pair of line segments intersect.
b. Determining all intersection points between pairs of line segments.
c. Detecting the existence of parallel line segments.
d. Determining which portion of each line segment would be visible to an observer located at the point $(x, y) = (0, \infty)$, where line segments are assumed to obstruct the visibility of line segments that are "behind" them.

6.11. **Polynomial interpolation**
We are given n points (x_i, y_i), $0 \leq i < n$, and asked to find an $(n-1)$th-degree polynomial $y = f(x)$ such that $f(x_i) = y_i$ for the given n data points. By Newton's interpolation method, the polynomial can be written as $f(x) = c_0 + c_1(x - x_0) + c_2(x - x_0)(x - x_1) + c_3(x - x_0)(x - x_1)(x - x_2) + \cdots + c_n(x - x_0)(x - x_1) \ldots (x - x_{n-1})$.

a. Show that c_i can be computed as the sum of $i + 1$ terms, the jth of which $(0 \le j \le i)$ constitutes a fraction with y_j in the numerator and a prefix product of length i in the denominator.

b. Based on the result of part (a), devise a PRAM algorithm that computes the coefficients c_i using n parallel prefix computations and additional arithmetic operations as needed.

c. Devise a PRAM algorithm to compute $f(x)$, given x and the coefficients c_i, $0 \le i \le n$.

6.12. Numerical integration

To compute the integral of $f(x)dx$ over the interval $[a, b]$ using the *trapezoidal rule*, the interval $[a, b]$ is divided into n subintervals of equal length $h = (b - a)/n$. The definite integral is then approximated by $h(f(a)/2 + f(a + h) + f(a + 2h) + \cdots + f(b - h) + f(b)/2)$.

a. Develop a PRAM algorithm implementing the trapezoidal rule.

b. To minimize the number of function evaluations, the following adaptive version of the trapezoidal rule, known as *adaptive quadrature*, can be used. Given a desired accuracy ε, the definite integral is evaluated using the trapezoidal rule with $n = 1$ and $n = 2$. Call the results I_1 and I_2. If $I_2 - I_1 \le \varepsilon$, then I_2 is taken to be the desired result. Otherwise, the same method is applied to each of the subintervals $[a, (a + b)/2]$ and $[(a + b)/2, b]$ with the accuracy $\varepsilon/2$. Discuss the parallel implementation of adaptive quadrature.

6.13. Linear skewing schemes for matrices

Consider the linear skewing scheme $s(i, j) = ai + bj \bmod B$ that yields the index of the memory bank where the element (i, j) of an $m \times m$ matrix is stored. Prove each of the following results.

a. In order to have conflict-free parallel access to rows, columns, diagonals, and antidiagonals, it is sufficient to choose B to be the smallest prime number that is no less than $\max(m, 5)$.

b. In order to have conflict-free parallel access to rows, columns, diagonals, and antidiagonals, the smallest number of memory banks required is m if $\gcd(m, 2) = \gcd(m, 3) = 1$, $m + 1$ if m is even and $m = 0 \bmod 3$ or $1 \bmod 3$, $m + 2$ if m is odd and a multiple of 3, and $m + 3$ if m is even and $m = 2 \bmod 3$.

c. If it is possible to have conflict-free parallel access to rows, columns, diagonals, and antidiagonals using a linear skewing scheme, then it is possible to achieve this using the scheme $s(i, j) = i + 2j \bmod B$.

6.14. Memory access networks

For the butterfly memory access network depicted in Fig. 6.9:

a. Show that there exist permutations that are not realizable.

b. Show that the shift permutation, where Processor i accesses memory bank $i + k \bmod p$, for some constant k, is realizable.

6.15. PRAM sorting by merging

Develop a parallel algorithm for sorting on the PRAM model of parallel computation that is based on merging the sublists held by the various processors into successively larger sublists until a sorted list containing all items is formed. Analyze your algorithm and compare its time complexity with those of the algorithms presented in this chapter.

REFERENCES AND SUGGESTED READING

[Akl93]   Akl, S., and K. A. Lyons, *Parallel Computational Geometry*, Prentice–Hall, 1993.

[Akl97]   Akl, S. G., *Parallel Computation: Models and Methods*, Prentice–Hall, 1997.

[Kron96]   Kronsjo, L. I., "PRAM Models," Chapter 6 in *Parallel and Distributed Computing Handbook*, edited by A. Y. Zomaya, McGraw-Hill, 1996, pp. 163–191.

[Mace87]   Mace, M. E., *Memory Storage Patterns in Parallel Processing*, Kluwer, 1987.
[Over81]   Overmars, M. H., and J. van Leeuwen, "Maintenance of Configurations in the Plane," *J. Computer and System Sciences*, Vol. 23, pp. 166–204, 1981.
[Prep85]   Preparata, F. P., and M. I. Shamos, *Computational Geometry: An Introduction*, Springer-Verlag, 1985.
[Wijs89]   Wijshoff, H. A. G., *Data Organization in Parallel Computers*, Kluwer, 1989.

7

Sorting and Selection Networks

Circuit-level designs for parallel processing are necessarily problem-specific or special-purpose. This arises in part from the relatively inflexible structure of a circuit (as compared with a stored program that can be easily modified or adapted to varying numbers of inputs) and in part from our limited ability to deal with complexity, making it virtually impossible to develop a complete circuit-level design individually and in a reasonable amount of time unless the problem at hand is simple and well-defined. The problem of sorting, which is the focus of this chapter, is an ideal example. Discussion of sorting networks or circuits touches on many of the important design methods and speed–cost trade-offs that are recurring themes in the field of parallel processing. A sampler of other interesting problems will be covered in Chapter 8. Chapter topics are

- 7.1. What is a sorting network?
- 7.2. Figures of merit for sorting networks
- 7.3. Design of sorting networks
- 7.4. Batcher sorting networks
- 7.5. Other classes of sorting networks
- 7.6. Selection networks

7.1. WHAT IS A SORTING NETWORK

A sorting network is a circuit that receives n inputs, $x_0, x_1, x_2, \ldots, x_{n-1}$, and permutes them to produce n outputs, $y_0, y_1, y_2, \ldots, y_{n-1}$, such that the outputs satisfy $y_0 \leq y_1 \leq y_2 \leq \ldots y_{n-1}$. For brevity, we often refer to such an n-input n-output sorting network as an *n-sorter* (Fig. 7.1). Just as many sorting algorithms are based on comparing and exchanging pairs of keys, we can build an n-sorter out of 2-sorter building blocks. A 2-sorter compares its two inputs (call them *input*$_0$ and *input*$_1$) and orders them at the output, by switching their order if needed, putting the smaller value, min(*input*$_0$, *input*$_1$), before the larger value, max(*input*$_0$, *input*$_1$).

Figure 7.2 shows the block diagram of a 2-sorter that always directs the smaller of the two input values to the top output. It also depicts simpler representations of the 2-sorter, where the rectangular box is replaced by a vertical line segment and the input-to-output direction is implied to be from left to right. Because, in some situations, we may want to place the smaller of the two inputs on the bottom, rather than top, output, we can replace the vertical line segment representing the 2-sorter by an arrow pointing in the direction of the larger output value. These schematic representations make it quite easy to draw large sorting networks. In particular, note that the heavy dots representing the I/O connections of a 2-sorter can be removed when there is no ambiguity. The schematic representations can be easily extended to larger building blocks. For example, a 3-sorter can be represented by a vertical line segment (or arrow) with three connecting dots.

The hardware realization of a 2-sorter is quite straightforward. If we view the inputs as unsigned integers that are supplied to the 2-sorter in bit-parallel form, then the 2-sorter can be implemented using a comparator and two 2-to-1 multiplexers, as shown in Fig. 7.3 (left panel). When the keys are long, or when we need to implement a sorting network with many inputs on a single VLSI chip, bit-parallel input becomes impractical in view of pin limitations. Figure 7.3 (right panel) also depicts a bit-serial hardware realization of the 2-sorter using two state flip-flops. The flip-flops are reset to 0 at the outset. This state represents the two inputs being equal thus far. The other two states are 01 (the upper input is less) and 10 (the lower input is less). While the 2-sorter is in state 00 or 01, the inputs are passed to the outputs straight through. When the state changes to 10, the inputs are interchanged, with the top input routed to the lower output and vice versa.

Figure 7.4 depicts a 4-sorter built of 2-sorter building blocks. For this initial example, we have shown both the block diagram and the schematic representation. In subsequent

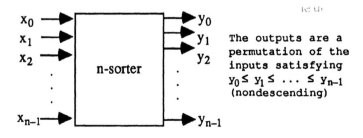

Figure 7.1. An *n*-input sorting network or an *n*-sorter.

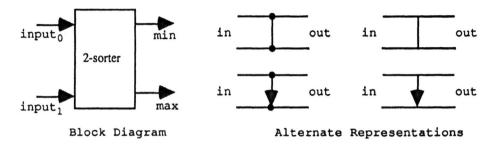

Figure 7.2. Block diagram and four different schematic representations for a 2-sorter.

examples, we will use only schematic diagrams. The schematic representation of the 4-sorter in Fig. 7.4 shows the data values carried on all lines when the input sequence 3, 2, 5, 1 is applied.

How do we verify that the circuit shown in Fig. 7.4 is in fact a valid 4-sorter? The answer is easy in this case. After the first two circuit levels, the top line carries the smallest and the bottom line the largest of the four input values. The final 2-sorter orders the middle two values. More generally, we need to verify the correctness of an n-sorter through tedious formal proofs or by time-consuming exhaustive testing. Neither approach is attractive. Fortunately, the *zero–one principle* allows us to do this with much less work.

The Zero–One Principle.   An n-sorter is valid if it correctly sorts all 0/1 sequences of length n.

Proof.   Clearly any n-sorter must also sort 0s and 1s correctly (necessity). Suppose that an n-sorter does not sort the input sequence $x_1, x_2, \ldots, x_n$ properly, i.e., there exist outputs y_i and y_{i+1} with $y_i > y_{i+1}$. We show that there is a 0/1 sequence that is not sorted properly also. Replace all inputs that are strictly less than y_i with 0s and all other inputs with 1s. The relative positions of the input values will not change at the output. Therefore, at the output we will have $y_i = 1$ and $y_{i+1} = 0$.

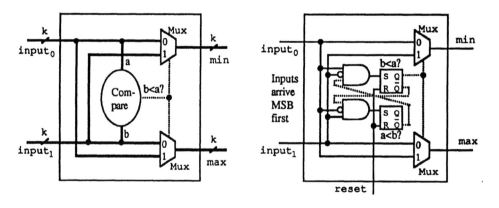

Figure 7.3. Parallel and bit-serial hardware realizations of a 2-sorter.

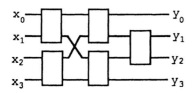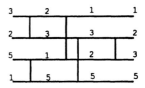

Figure 7.4. Block diagram and schematic representation of a 4-sorter.

Using the zero–one principle, the correctness of the 4-sorter in Fig. 7.4 can be verified by testing it for the 16 possible 0/1 sequences of length 4. The network clearly sorts 0000 and 1111. It sorts all sequences with a single 0 because the 0 "bubbles up" to the top line. Similarly, a single 1 would "sink down" to the bottom line. The remaining part of the proof deals with the sequences 0011, 0101, 0110, 1001, 1010, 1100, all of which lead to the correct output 0011.

7.2. FIGURES OF MERIT FOR SORTING NETWORKS

Is the sorting network shown in Fig. 7.4 the best possible 4-sorter? To answer this question, we need to specify what we mean by "the best n-sorter." Two figures of merit immediately suggest themselves:

- Cost: the total number of 2-sorter blocks used in the design
- Delay: the number of 2-sorters on the critical path from input to output

Of course, for VLSI implementation of an n-sorter, the wiring pattern between the 2-sorters is also important because it determines the layout area, which has an impact on cost. However, for simplicity, we will ignore this aspect of cost/complexity and use the number of 2-sorters as an approximate cost indicator. Each 2-sorter will thus be assumed to have unit cost, independent of its location in the network or its connectivity.

Similar observations apply to the delay of a sorting network. We will again assume that a 2-sorter has unit delay independent of its location or connectivity. In VLSI circuits, signal propagation delay on wires is becoming increasingly important. Longer wires, going from one chip to another or even from one side to the other side of the same chip, contribute nonnegligible delays, to the extent that signal propagation delays sometimes overshadow the device switching or computation delays. Therefore, our delay measure is also approximate.

We can also use composite figures of merit involving both cost and delay. For example, if we expect linear speed-up from more investment in the circuit, then minimizing cost × delay would be appropriate. According to the cost × delay measure, if we can redesign a sorting network so that it is 10% faster but only 5% more complex, the redesign is deemed to be cost-effective and the resulting circuit is said to be *time-cost-efficient* (or at least more so than the original one).

Figure 7.5 shows examples of low-cost sorting networks ([Knut73], p. 228) that have been discovered over the years by different researchers. Unfortunately, lowest-cost designs

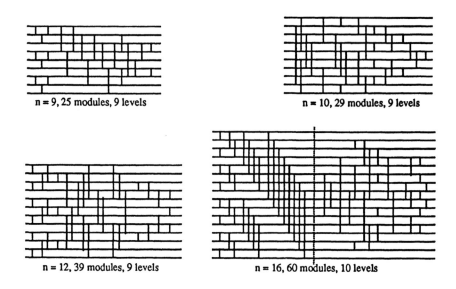

Figure 7.5. Some low-cost sorting networks.

are known only for small n and as yet there is no general method for systematically deriving low-cost designs.

Figure 7.6 depicts examples of fast sorting networks ([Knut73], p. 231). The fastest possible designs are also known only for small n.

Time-cost-efficient sorting networks are even harder to come by. For the 10-input examples in Figs. 7.5 and 7.6, the cost × delay products are

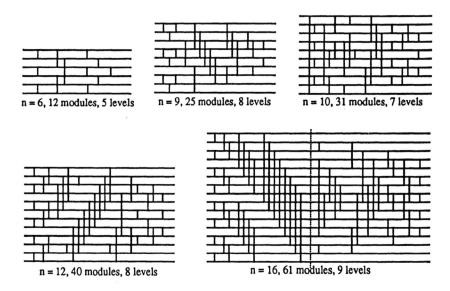

Fig. 7.6. Some fast sorting networks.

29 modules, 9 delay units   cost × delay = 261

31 modules, 7 delay units   cost × delay = 217

Thus, the 10-sorter in Fig. 7.6 has higher time-cost efficiency than its counterpart in Fig. 7.5. However, in general, the most time-cost-efficient design may be neither the fastest nor the least complex n-sorter.

7.3. DESIGN OF SORTING NETWORKS

There are many ways to design sorting networks, leading to different results with respect to the figures of merit defined in Section 7.2. For example, Fig. 7.7 shows a 6-sorter whose design is based on the odd–even transposition sorting algorithm discussed in connection with sorting on a linear array of processors in Section 2.3 (rotate Fig. 7.7 clockwise by 90 degrees and compare the result with the compare–exchange pattern of Fig. 2.10). This "brick wall" design offers advantages in terms of wiring ease (because wires are short and do not cross over). However, it is quite inefficient as it uses $n\lfloor n/2 \rfloor$ modules and has n units of delay. Its cost × delay product is $\Theta(n^3)$. So, a natural question is how one might design more efficient sorting networks.

Let us try a couple of other ideas. One way to sort n inputs is to sort the first $n - 1$ inputs, say, and then insert the last input in its proper place. This recursive solution based on insertion sort is depicted in the top left panel of Fig. 7.8. Another way is to select the largest value among the n inputs, output it on the bottom line, and then sort the remaining $n - 1$ values. This also is a recursive solution, as shown in the top right panel of Fig. 7.8. Both solutions are characterized by the following recurrences for delay and cost. In fact, both lead to the same design, which is in effect based on the parallel version of bubblesort.

$$C(n) = C(n - 1) + n - 1 = (n - 1) + (n - 2) + \cdots + 2 + 1 = n(n - 1)/2$$

$$D(n) = D(n - 1) + 2 = 2 + 2 + \cdots + 2 + 1 = 2(n - 2) + 1 = 2n - 3$$

$$\text{Cost} \times \text{Delay} = n(n - 1)(2n - 3)/2 = \Theta(n^3)$$

All three designs presented thus far in this section are quite inefficient. Lower bounds on the cost and delay of an n-sorter are $\Omega(n \log n)$ and $\Omega(\log n)$, respectively. These are established by the fan-in argument and the minimum number of comparisons needed for

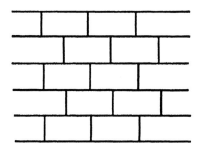

Figure 7.7. Brick-wall 6-sorter based on odd–even transposition.

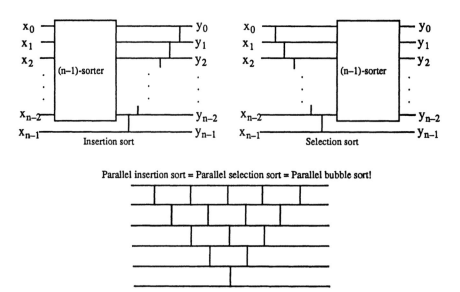

Figure 7.8. Sorting network based on insertion sort or selection sort.

sorting n values. Can we achieve these lower bounds? Note that even if both bounds are achieved simultaneously, the resulting cost $\times$ delay product will be $\Theta(n \log^2 n)$ which is more than the sequential lower bound on work, but this is the best we can hope for.

In 1983, Ajtai, Komlos, and Szemeredi [Ajta83] showed how $O(n \log n)$-cost, $O(\log n)$-delay sorting networks can be constructed. Their proposed design, which uses a sorting-by-splitting approach based on the notion of expander graphs, is known as the AKS sorting network. However, the AKS design is of theoretical interest only, as the asymptotic notation hides huge four-digit constants! The constants remain large despite further improvements and refinements by other researchers since 1983. A good exposition of the asymptotically optimal AKS sorting circuit was given by Akl ([Akl97], pp. 125–137).

Even though researchers have not given up hope on the prospects of practical, $O(n \log n)$-cost, $O(\log n)$-delay, sorting networks, work has diversified on several other fronts. One is the design of more efficient sorting networks with special inputs or outputs; for example, when inputs are only 0s and 1s, or they are already partially sorted, or we require only partially sorted outputs. Another is the design of networks that sort the input sequence with high probability but do not guarantee sorted order for all possible inputs [Leig97].

Practical sorting networks are based on designs by Batcher and others that have $O(n \log^2 n)$ cost and $O(\log^2 n)$ delay. These designs are a factor of $\log n$ away from being asymptotically optimal in cost or delay, but because $\log_2 n$ is only 20 when n is as large as 1 million, such networks are more practical than the asymptotically optimal designs mentioned above. Some of these designs will be discussed in Sections 7.4 and 7.5.

7.4. BATCHER SORTING NETWORKS

Batcher's ingenious constructions date back to the early 1960s (published a few years later) and constitute some of the earliest examples of parallel algorithms. It is remarkable that in more than three decades, only small improvements to his constructions have been made.

One type of sorting network proposed by Batcher is based on the idea of an (m, m')-merger and uses a technique known as even–odd merge or odd–even merge. An (m, m')-merger is a circuit that merges two sorted sequences of lengths m and m' into a single sorted sequence of length $m + m'$. Let the two sorted sequences be

$$x_0 \leq x_1 \leq \ldots \leq x_{m-1}$$

$$y_0 \leq y_1 \leq \ldots \leq y_{m'-1}$$

If $m = 0$ or $m' = 0$, then nothing needs to be done. For $m = m' = 1$, a single comparator can do the merging. Thus, we assume $mm' > 1$ in what follows. The odd–even merge is done by merging the even- and odd-indexed elements of the two lists separately:

$$x_0, x_2, \ldots, x_{2\lceil m/2\rceil-2} \text{ and}$$

$$y_0, y_2, \ldots, y_{2\lceil m'/2\rceil-2} \text{ are merged to get}$$

$$v_0, v_1, \ldots, v_{\lceil m/2\rceil+\lceil m'/2\rceil-1}$$

$$x_1, x_3, \ldots, x_{2\lfloor m/2\rfloor-1} \text{ and}$$

$$y_1, y_3, \ldots, y_{2\lfloor m'/2\rfloor-1} \text{ are merged to get}$$

$$w_0, w_1, \ldots, w_{\lfloor m/2\rfloor+\lfloor m'/2\rfloor-1}$$

If we now compare–exchange the pairs of elements $w_0{:}v_1$, $w_1{:}v_2$, $w_2{:}v_3$, ..., the resulting sequence $v_0 \, w_0 \, v_1 \, w_1 \, v_2 \, w_2 \ldots$ will be completely sorted. Note that v_0, which is known to be the smallest element overall, is excluded from the final compare–exchange operations.

An example circuit for merging two sorted lists of sizes 4 and 7 using the odd–even merge technique is shown in Fig. 7.9. The three circuit segments, separated by vertical dotted lines, correspond to a $(2, 4)$-merger for even-indexed inputs, a $(2, 3)$-merger for odd-indexed inputs, and the final parallel compare–exchange operations prescribed above. Each of the smaller mergers can be designed recursively in the same way. For example, a $(2, 4)$-merger consists of two $(1, 2)$-mergers for even- and odd-indexed inputs, followed by two parallel compare–exchange operations. A $(1, 2)$-merger is in turn built from a $(1, 1)$-merger, or a single comparator, for the even-indexed inputs, followed by a single compare–exchange operation. The final $(4, 7)$-merger in Fig. 7.9 uses 16 modules and has a delay of 4 units.

It would have been quite difficult to prove the correctness of Batcher's even–odd merger were it not for the zero–one principle that allows us to limit the proof of correctness to only 0 and 1 inputs. Suppose that the sorted x sequence has k 0s and $m - k$ 1s. Similarly, let there be k' 0s and $m' - k'$ 1s in the sorted y sequence. When we merge the even-indexed terms, the v sequence will have $k_{\text{even}} = \lceil k/2\rceil + \lceil k'/2\rceil$ 0s. Likewise, the w sequence resulting from the merging of odd-indexed terms will have $k_{\text{odd}} = \lfloor k/2\rfloor + \lfloor k'/2\rfloor$ 0s. Only three cases are possible:

Case a: $k_{\text{even}} = k_{\text{odd}}$ The sequence $v_0 \, w_0 \, v_1 \, w_1 \, v_2 \, w_2 \ldots$ is already sorted

Case b: $k_{\text{even}} = k_{\text{odd}} + 1$ The sequence $v_0 \, w_0 \, v_1 \, w_1 \, v_2 \, w_2 \ldots$ is already sorted

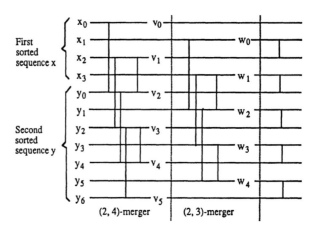

Figure 7.9. Batcher's even–odd merging network for 4 + 7 inputs.

Case c: $k_{even} = k_{odd} + 2$

In the last case, the sequence $v_0\, w_0\, v_1\, w_1\, v_2\, w_2 \ldots$ has only a pair of elements that are not in sorted order, as shown in the example below (the out-of-order pair is underlined).

$$v_0\ v_1\ v_2\ v_3\ v_4\ v_5\ v_6\ v_7\ v_8\ v_9\ v_{10}\ v_{11}$$
$$0\ \ 0\ \ 0\ \ 0\ \ 0\ \ 0\ \ 0\ \ \underline{0}\ \ 1\ \ 1\ \ 1\ \ \ 1$$

$$0\ \ 0\ \ 0\ \ 0\ \ 0\ \ 0\ \ \underline{1}\ \ 1\ \ 1\ \ 1\ \ 1$$
$$w_0\ w_1\ w_2\ w_3\ w_4\ w_5\ w_6\ w_7\ w_8\ w_9\ w_{10}$$

The problem will be fixed by the compare–exchange operations between w_i and v_{i+1}.

Batcher's (m, m) even–odd merger, when m is a power of 2, is characterized by the following delay and cost recurrences:

$$C(m) = 2C(m/2) + m - 1 = (m - 1) + 2(m/2 - 1) + 4(m/4 - 1) + \cdots = m \log_2 m + 1$$

$$D(m) = D(m/2) + 1 = \log_2 m + 1$$

$$\text{Cost} \times \text{Delay} = \Theta(m \log^2 m)$$

Armed with an efficient merging circuit, we can design an n-sorter recursively from two $n/2$-sorters and an $(n/2, n/2)$-merger, as shown in Fig. 7.10. The 4-sorter of Fig. 7.4 is an instance of this design: It consists of two 2-sorters followed by a $(2, 2)$-merger in turn built from two $(1, 1)$-mergers and a single compare–exchange step. A larger example, corresponding to an 8-sorter, is depicted in Fig. 7.11. Here, 4-sorters are used to sort the first and second halves of the inputs separately, with the sorted lists then merged by a $(4, 4)$-merger composed of an even $(2, 2)$-merger, an odd $(2, 2)$-merger, and a final stage of three comparators.

Batcher sorting networks based on the even–odd merge technique are characterized by the following delay and cost recurrences:

$$C(n) = 2C(n/2) + (n/2)(\log_2(n/2)) + 1 \approx n(\log_2 n\,)^2/\, 2$$

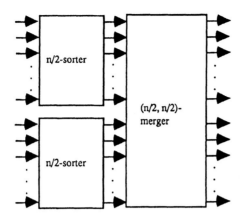

Figure 7.10.   The recursive structure of Batcher's even–odd merge sorting network.

$$D(n) = D(n/2) + \log_2(n/2) + 1 = D(n/2) + \log_2 n = \log_2 n\,(\log_2 n + 1)/2$$

$$\text{Cost} \times \text{Delay} = \Theta\,(n \log^4 n)$$

A second type of sorting network proposed by Batcher is based on the notion of bitonic sequences. A bitonic sequence is defined as one that "rises then falls" ($x_0 \le x_1 \le \ldots \le x_i \ge x_{i+1} \ge x_{i+2} \ge \ldots \ge x_{n-1}$), "falls then rises" ($x_0 \ge x_1 \ge \ldots \ge x_i \le x_{i+1} \le x_{i+2} \le \ldots \le x_{n-1}$), or is obtained from the first two categories through cyclic shifts or rotations. Examples include

1 3 3 4 6 6 6 2 2 1 0 0	Rises then falls
8 7 7 6 6 6 5 4 6 8 8 9	Falls then rises
8 9 8 7 7 6 6 6 5 4 6 8	The previous sequence, right-rotated by 2

Batcher observed that if we sort the first half and second half of a sequence in opposite directions, as indicated by the vertical arrows in Fig. 7.12, the resulting sequence will be bitonic and can thus be sorted by a special bitonic-sequence sorter. It turns out that a

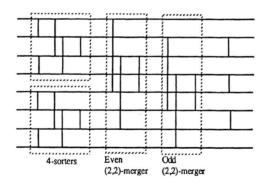

Figure 7.11.   Batcher's even–odd merge sorting network for eight inputs.

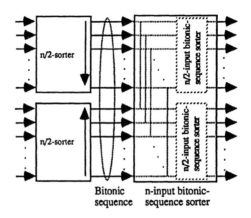

Figure 7.12.   The recursive structure of Batcher's bitonic sorting network.

bitonic-sequence sorter with n inputs has the same delay and cost as an even–odd ($n/2$, $n/2$)-merger. Therefore, sorters based on the notion of bitonic sequences (bitonic sorters) have the same delay and cost as those based on even–odd merging.

A bitonic-sequence sorter can be designed based on the assertion that if in a bitonic sequence, we compare–exchange the elements in the first half with those in the second half, as indicated by the dotted comparators in Fig. 7.12, each half of the resulting sequence will be a bitonic sequence and each element in the first half will be no larger than any element in the second half. Thus, the two halves can be independently sorted by smaller bitonic-sequence sorters to complete the sorting process. Note that we can reverse the direction of sorting in the lower n-sorter if we suitably adjust the connections of the dotted comparators in Fig. 7.12. A complete eight-input bitonic sorting network is shown in Fig. 7.13.

While asymptotically suboptimal, Batcher sorting networks are quite efficient. Attempts at designing faster or less complex networks for specific values of n have yielded only marginal improvements over Batcher's construction when n is large.

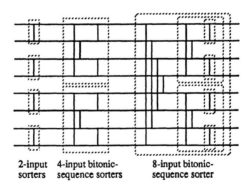

Figure 7.13.   Batcher's bitonic sorting network for eight inputs.

7.5. OTHER CLASSES OF SORTING NETWORKS

A class of sorting networks that possess the same asymptotic $\Theta(\log^2 n)$ delay and $\Theta(n \log^2 n)$ cost as Batcher sorting networks, but that offer some advantages, are the periodic balanced sorting networks [Dowd89]. An n-sorter of this type consists of $\log_2 n$ identical stages, each of which is a $(\log_2 n)$-stage n-input bitonic-sequence sorter. Thus, the delay and cost of an n-sorter of this type are $(\log_2 n)^2$ and $n(\log_2 n)^2/2$, respectively. Figure 7.14 shows an eight-input example. The 8-sorter of Fig. 7.14 has a larger delay (9 versus 6) and higher cost (36 versus 19) compared with a Batcher 8-sorter but offers the following advantages:

1. The structure is regular and modular (easier VLSI layout).
2. Slower, but more economical, implementations are possible by reusing the blocks. In the extreme, $\log_2 n$ passes through a single block can be used for cost-efficient sorting.
3. Using an extra block provides tolerance to some faults (missed exchanges).
4. Using two extra blocks provides tolerance to any single fault (a missed or incorrect exchange).
5. Multiple passes through a faulty network can lead to correct sorting (graceful degradation).
6. Single-block design can be made fault-tolerant by adding an extra stage to the block.

Just as we were able to obtain a sorting network based on odd–even transposition sort on a linear array, we can base a sorting network on a sorting algorithm for a 2D array. For example, the two 8-sorters shown in Figs. 7.15 and 7.16 are based on shearsort (defined in Section 2.5) with snakelike order on 2×4 and 4×2 arrays, respectively. Compared with Batcher 8-sorters, these are again slower (7 or 9 versus 6 levels) and more complex (24 or 32 versus 19 modules). However, they offer some of the same advantages enumerated for periodic balanced sorting networks.

In general, an rc-sorter can be designed based on shearsort on an $r \times c$ mesh. It will have $\log_2 r$ identical blocks, each consisting of r parallel c-sorters followed by c parallel r-sorters, followed at the end by a special block composed of r parallel c-sorters. However, such networks are usually not competitive when r is large.

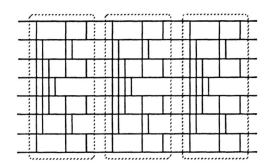

Figure 7.14. Periodic balanced sorting network for eight inputs.

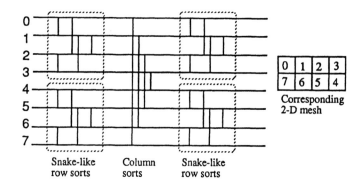

Figure 7.15. Design of an 8-sorter based on shearsort on 2 × 4 mesh.

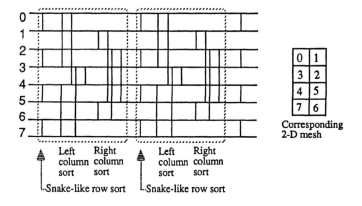

Figure 7.16. Design of an 8-sorter based on shearsort on 4 × 2 mesh.

7.6. SELECTION NETWORKS

If we need the kth smallest value among n inputs, then using a sorting network would be an overkill in that an n-sorter does more than what is required to solve our (n, k) selection problem. For example, the 8-sorter of Fig. 7.15 can still give us the third or fourth smallest element among its eight inputs if we remove the five comparators constituting the lower-right 4-sorter. A natural question is whether we can design selection networks that are significantly simpler than sorting networks. This is an interesting problem and we deal only with some aspects of it in this section.

Let us broaden our view a bit and define three selection problems [Knut73]:

I.   Select the k smallest values and present them on k outputs in sorted order.
II.   Select the kth smallest value and present it on one of the outputs.
III. Select the k smallest values and present them on k outputs in any order.

The above are listed in decreasing order of circuit and time complexity, i.e., (I) is the hardest and (III) the easiest. For example, the 8-sorter of Fig. 7.15 solves the first problem after removing the five comparators constituting the lower-right 4-sorter. If, additionally, we replace the upper-right 4-sorter in Fig. 7.15 with three comparators to choose the maximum value on the upper four lines, a type II (8, 4)-selector would result. Finally, if we remove the upper-right 4-sorter altogether, we obtain a type III (8, 4)-selector.

It can be proven ([Knut73], pp. 234–235) that the number of comparators needed for solving the third selection problem (and hence the second one) satisfies the following lower bound which is tight for $k = 1$ and $k = 2$:

$$C_{III}(n, k) \geq (n - k)\lceil \log_2(k + 1)\rceil$$

Figure 7.17 depicts a type III (8, 4)-selector. The pairs of integers shown on each line in Fig. 7.17 denote the minimum and maximum rank that is possible for the value carried by that line. Initially, each input value can have any rank in [0, 7]. When two inputs are compared, and possibly exchanged, the upper one will have a rank in [0, 6] and the lower one in [1, 7]. It is easily proven that if the two inputs of a comparator have ranks in $[l_i, u_i]$ and $[l_j, u_j]$, then the output rank intervals $[l_i', u_i']$ and $[l_j', u_j']$ satisfy $l_i' = \min(l_i, l_j)$ and $l_j' \geq l_i + l_j$. Similar results can be proven for the upper bounds u_i' and u_j'. The correctness of the type III (8, 4)-selector in Fig. 7.17 is evident from the output rank intervals.

Classifiers constitute a class of selection networks that can divide a set of n values into $n/2$ largest and $n/2$ smallest values, with possible overlap in case of repeated values at the input. The selection network of Fig. 7.17 is in fact an 8-input classifier. Generalizing the construction of Fig. 7.17, an n-input classifier can be built from two ($n/2$)-sorters followed by $n/2$ comparators. Using Batcher's designs for the ($n/2$)-sorters leads to a depth of O($\log^2 n$) and size of O($n \log^2 n$) for an n-input classifier. Of course, O($\log n$)-depth, O($n \log n$)-cost classifiers can be derived from AKS sorting networks, but the resulting designs are not practical. It has been shown that classifiers of depth O($\log n$) and size $Cn \log_2 n + $ O(n), where C is any number exceeding $3/\log_2 3 \approx 1.8927$, can be constructed [Jimb96].

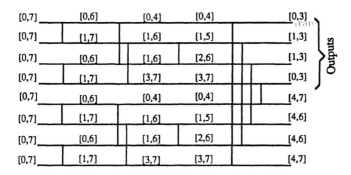

Figure 7.17. A type III (8, 4)-selector.

PROBLEMS

7.1. Design of 2-sorter and 3-sorter building blocks

  a. How should the 2-sorter designs shown in Fig. 7.3 be modified if they are to deal with signed, rather than unsigned, integer inputs?
  b. Design a 3-sorter building block with unsigned bit-serial inputs. Try to make the 3-sorter as fast as possible, e.g., do not use three 2-sorters inside the module.

7.2. The zero–one principle
  Using the zero–one principle, prove the validity of each of the following sorting networks. *Hint:* Noting that the designs begin with a set of smaller sorters reduces the amount of work needed for your proof.

  a. The 6-sorter in Fig. 7.6.
  b. The 9-sorter in Fig. 7.5.
  c. The 9-sorter in Fig. 7.6.
  d. The 12-sorter in Fig. 7.5.

7.3. Programmable sorters
  Consider the design of a sorting network that can sort in ascending or descending order, as dictated by a single control signal. Compare the following two design methods with respect to cost and delay.

  a. Sort in ascending order, then reverse the sequence if descending order is desired.
  b. Modify the building blocks of Fig. 7.3 so that the output order is switched by the control signal.

7.4. Bitonic-sequence sorters
  Show how an n-input bitonic-sequence sorter can be used to merge two sorted sequences with unequal lengths that add up to at most n; one sequence is of length m and the other is no longer than $n - m$.

7.5. Figures of merit for sorting networks
  Calculate the speed-up, efficiency, and other figures of merit introduced in Section 1.6 for each of the following sorting network designs.

  a. Sorting networks based on insertion or selection sort.
  b. Batcher sorting networks.
  c. Periodic balanced sorting networks.
  d. Sorting network based on shearsort on a $2 \times (n/2)$ mesh.
  e. Sorting network based on shearsort on an $(n/2) \times 2$ mesh.

7.6. Pruning of sorting networks

  a. Show that removing the top or bottom line, along with all of the comparators connected to it, converts an n-sorter to a valid $(n - 1)$-sorter.
  b. Experiment with the transformation given in part (a) to derive new sorting networks from the n-sorters in Figs. 7.5 and 7.6. For example, derive 6-sorters from the given 9-sorters and compare the results to the 6-sorters given.
  c. Show that the statement of part (a) is in general not valid for other lines in a sorting network.

7.7. Sorting networks

  a. Use the zero–one principle to prove that the following circuit is not a valid 6-sorter.

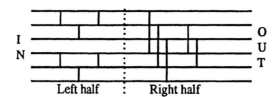

Left half   :   Right half

b. Based on the observations in part (a), show how a single comparator can be added to the circuit to turn it into a valid 6-sorter.

c. Use Batcher's odd–even merge method to redesign the right half of the sorter of part (b).

d. Compare the designs of parts (b) and (c) with respect to cost and delay.

7.8. Periodic balanced sorting networks

a. Give an example of an input sequence that is sorted after passing through the first two stages of the 8-sorter in Fig. 7.14 but that is still unsorted at the output of the first stage.

b. Give an example of an input sequence whose sorting requires all three stages of the 8-sorter in Fig. 7.14 (i.e., it is still unsorted at the output of the second stage).

c. Prove the correctness of the periodic balanced 8-sorter in Fig. 7.14.

d. Using the zero–one principle, prove the correctness of periodic balanced n-sorters in general.

7.9. Merging networks

Consider the merging of a single input value x with a sorted list of n values $y(i)$, $0 \le i \le n - 1$.

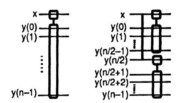

Let such a $(1, n)$-merger be depicted as in the left diagram above.

a. Prove that the diagram on the right above represents a valid way to construct a $(1, n)$-merger.

b. Find the delay and cost of a $(1, n)$-merger recursively constructed as in part (a).

c. Prove that the $(1, n)$-merger resulting from the construction suggested in Part (a) is optimal.

7.10. Sorting networks based on shearsort

Design 16-sorters based on shearsort on 2×8, 4×4, and 8×2 meshes and compare the resulting designs with respect to various figures of merit.

a. Design each smaller sorter that is needed by using the same shearsort-based approach.

b. Feel free to use the best 4-sorter and 8-sorter designs that you can get as building blocks.

7.11. Validity of sorting networks

Show that the following circuit built of 4-sorters is a valid 16-sorter.

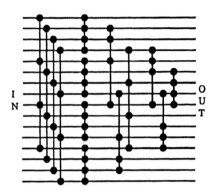

7.12. Synthesis of sorting networks

Define a pairwise $2n$-sorter as follows. There are $2n$ inputs and $2n$ outputs y_0 to y_{2n-1}. The outputs form n pairs $(y_0, y_1), (y_2, y_3), \ldots, (y_{2n-2}, y_{2n-1})$. The pairwise $2n$-sorter guarantees that $\max(y_{2k}, y_{2k+1}) \leq \min(y_{2k+2}, y_{2k+3})$ for all k. Prove or disprove the following assertion: The pairwise $2n$-sorter defined above is always a $2n$-sorter.

7.13. Merging networks

a. Prove or disprove: One can construct a $(2m, m)$ merging network from two (m, m)-mergers and no other component.

b. How many (m, m)-mergers are needed to build a $(3m, m)$-merger and why?

c. How many (m, m)-mergers are needed to build a $(2m, 2m)$-merger and why?

7.14. Synthesis of sorting networks

An n-sorter design can be converted to a kn-sorter design by replacing each line with k lines, replacing each 2-sorter by a (k, k)-merger, and preceding all of the above with n parallel k-sorters. The above procedure can be used, e.g., to construct a $3n$-sorter, given the design for an n-sorter. A $3n$-sorter can also be designed from three n-sorters, one (n, n)-merger, and one $(n, 2n)$-merger in the obvious way.

a. Design a 6-sorter, a 9-sorter, and a 12-sorter based on the first approach.

b. Repeat part (a) for the second approach.

c. Compare the results in parts (a) and (b) with each other and with the sorter designs appearing in this chapter and discuss.

d. For $k = n$, the first construction above yields an n^2-sorter based on a Batcher n-sorter. How does the resulting design compare with an n^2-sorter built directly based on Batcher's method?

7.15. Selection networks

a. Justify the labels assigned to various lines in Fig. 7.17.

b. A type III $(n, n/2)$-selector can be converted to an n-sorter by attaching two $(n/2)$-sorters to its upper-half and lower-half outputs. For example, applying this method to the $(8,4)$-selector of Fig. 7.17 yields the 8-sorter of Fig. 7.15. Using the information provided by the line labels in Fig. 7.17, show that the two additional 4-sorters can be somewhat simplified.

c. Prove the bound $C_{III}(n, k) \geq (n - k) \lceil \log_2(k + 1) \rceil$ given in Section 7.6 for the cost of a type III selection network. Hint: Label the lines in the selection network as follows. Label all inputs with 0. The upper output of each comparator is labeled by the smaller of its two input labels and the lower output by the larger input label plus 1. Show that the sum of the labels at the outputs of the selection network equals the total number of comparators in the network and that $n - k$ of the outputs have labels that are greater than or equal to $\lceil \log_2(k + 1) \rceil$.

    d. Show that the bound of part (a) is tight for $k = 1$ and $k = 2$.

7.16. Classifier networks

    a. Prove that an n-input classifier (defined at the end of Section 7.6) has a delay of $\Omega(\log n)$ and a cost of $\Omega(n \log n)$. *Hint:* A classifier is a type III selection network.

    b. Show how an n-sorter can be synthesized using classifier networks of various sizes as the only building blocks.

    c. Find the asymptotic delay and cost of the sorting networks derived in part (b) and compare the results with those of Batcher sorting networks.

    d. Show how an (n, k)-selector, where k is an arbitrary given number, can be synthesized using classifier networks of various sizes as the only building blocks.

    e. Determine the worst-case asymptotic delay and cost of the (n, k)-selector derived in part (d).

REFERENCES AND SUGGESTED READING

[Ajta83]   Ajtai, M., J. Komlos, and E. Szemeredi, "Sorting in $c \log n$ Parallel Steps," *Combinatorica*, Vol. 3, pp. 1–19, 1983.

[Akl97]   Akl, S. G., *Parallel Computation: Models and Methods*, Prentice–Hall, 1997.

[Batc68]   Batcher, K., "Sorting Networks and Their Applications," *Proc. AFIPS Spring Joint Computer Conf.*, Vol. 32, pp. 307–314, 1968.

[Dowd89]   Dowd, M., Y. Perl, L. Rudolph, and M. Saks, "The Periodic Balanced Sorting Network," *J. ACM*, Vol. 36, No. 4, pp. 738–757, October 1989.

[Jimb96]   Jimbo, S. and A. Maruoka, "A Method of Constructing Selection Networks with O(log n) Depth," *SIAM J. Computing*, Vol. 25, No. 4, pp. 709–739, August 1996.

[Knut73]   Knuth, D.E., *The Art of Computer Programming: Vol. 3—Sorting and Searching*, Addison–Wesley, 1973.

[Leig97]   Leighton, T., Y. Ma, and T. Suel, "On Probabilistic Networks for Selection, Merging, and Sorting," *Theory of Computing Systems*, Vol. 30, pp. 559–582, 1997.

[Pipp91]   Pippenger, N., "Selection Networks," *SAIM J. Computing*, Vol. 20, pp. 878–887, 1991.

[Sun94]   Sun, J., E. Cerny, and J. Gecsei, "Fault Tolerance in a Class of Sorting Networks," *IEEE Trans. Computers*, Vol. 43, No. 7, pp. 827–837, July 1994.

8

Other Circuit-Level Examples

In this chapter, we study three application areas along with parallel architectures that were developed to address their specific needs. The application areas are dictionary operations, parallel prefix computation, and fast Fourier transform. The resulting hardware structures (tree machine, parallel prefix networks, and butterfly network) are highly specialized to the application at hand and might be inappropriate for dealing with other problems. The common thread through this chapter is that, like sorting networks in Chapter 7, the architectures are fully specified at the circuit level; i.e., the internal structure of each processor can be drawn as a digital circuit, given the simplicity of its control functions and data manipulations. Similarly, the interprocessor links are fully defined and easily realizable with modest area overhead and delay. Chapter topics are

- 8.1. Searching and dictionary operations
- 8.2. A tree-structured dictionary machine
- 8.3. Parallel prefix computation
- 8.4. Parallel prefix networks
- 8.5. The discrete Fourier transform
- 8.6. Parallel architectures for FFT

8.1. SEARCHING AND DICTIONARY OPERATIONS

Searching is one of the most important operations on digital computers and consumes a great deal of resources. A primary reason for sorting, an activity that has been estimated to use up more than one-fourth of the running time on most computers, is to facilitate searching. Thus, it is safe to say that searching consumes at least 25% of the running time on most computers, directly or indirectly. Obviously, it would be desirable to speed up this operation through the application of parallelism.

Let us first see how searching for y in a list of n keys can be speeded up on a p-processor PRAM. Assume that the input list x is sorted in ascending order. Recall that a single processor uses the *binary search* algorithm to search a sorted list efficiently in $\lceil \log_2 (n+1) \rceil$ comparison steps. The given key y is compared with the key $x_{\lfloor n/2 \rfloor}$ at or near the middle of the list. If $y = x_{\lfloor n/2 \rfloor}$, then the search is over. Two other outcomes are possible:

$$y < x_{\lfloor n/2 \rfloor} \qquad \text{Restrict the search to } x_0 \text{ through } x_{\lfloor n/2 \rfloor - 1}$$

$$y > x_{\lfloor n/2 \rfloor} \qquad \text{Restrict the search to } x_{\lfloor n/2 \rfloor + 1} \text{ through } x_{n-1}$$

In either case above, the problem size is reduced to $n/2$, leading to a logarithmic number of steps. The extension of the binary search algorithm to $(p + 1)$-ary search on a p-processor PRAM is straightforward and leads to a running time of $k = \lceil \log_2(n + 1)/\log_2(p + 1) \rceil$ steps. The proof is by induction. Let $n = (p + 1)^k - 1$ for some k; otherwise find the smallest k such that $n \le (p + 1)^k - 1$. The claimed running time can clearly be achieved for $k = 1$ (p processors search a p-element list in one step). Assume that $k - 1$ steps are sufficient for any list of size not exceeding $(p + 1)^{k-1} - 1$. In Step 1, Processor i compares y with the $i(p + 1)^{k-1}$th element in x. Either one of the processors finds y or the search is restricted to a segment of the list of a size no larger than $(p + 1)^{k-1} - 1$. Hence, k steps are needed overall.

The above algorithm is optimal in that no comparison-based searching algorithm can be faster. We use induction on k to show that after k parallel comparisons, there must be one or more contiguous unexamined segments of the list x containing at least $(n + 1)/(p + 1)^k - 1$ keys. Equating this expression with 0 yields a lower bound on the number k of steps. The speed-up achieved by the above parallel search algorithm is

$$\lceil \log_2(n + 1) \rceil / \lceil \log_2(n + 1)/\log_2(p + 1) \rceil \approx \log_2(p + 1)$$

which is quite disappointing, given the optimality of the algorithm.

Even though single searches in a sorted list of keys cannot be significantly speeded up by parallel processing, all hope is not lost and parallel searching is still important. First, in applications where the list of keys changes quite frequently, the requirement of a sorted list is unrealistic and leads to significant overhead that must be accounted for in analyzing the overall application. Associative memories and processors can be quite efficient in searching unsorted lists and usually offer linear speed-up in this context (see Section 4.1). Second, and this is our primary focus here, when m different searches are to be performed in the same list of n keys, parallel searching might be quite efficient and can lead to much better speed-up. This problem, which is exemplified by a word processor's spelling checker having to verify that a list of document words appear in a standard dictionary, is known as *batch searching*.

To put the need for searching in a realistic application context, we define a set of *dictionary operations* on a given list of n records with keys $x_0, x_1, \ldots, x_{n-1}$. We want to be able to perform the following three basic operations efficiently. In most of what follows, "the record" can be replaced with "a record" or "all records" if multiple records with the same key value can exist among the stored records.

> *search(y)* Find the record with key y and return its associated data.
>
> *insert(y, z)* Augment the list with a record having the key y and the data part z.
>
> *delete(y)* Remove the record with key y [and, optionally, return the associated data].

The operation *delete(y)* is said to be *redundant* if no record with the key value y is found. In such a case, the operation can be simply ignored or it might signal an exception. Similarly, the operation *insert(y, z)* is said to be redundant if a record with the key value y is already stored and the list of records is restricted to hold only one record with a given key value. In this case, we often take "insert" to mean "update or change the data part of the record with the key value y to z," although ignoring the redundant insertion is also an option.

Additionally, some or all of the following operations might be of interest:

> *findmin* Find the record with the smallest key value and return its associated data.
>
> *findmax* Find the record with the largest key value and return its associated data.
>
> *findmed* Find the record with the median key value and return its associated data.
>
> *findbest(y)* Find the record with the *best* or *nearest* match to the key value y.
>
> *findnext(y)* Find the record whose key is the *successor* of the key value y.
>
> *findprev(y)* Find the record whose key is the *predecessor* of the key value y.
>
> *extractmin* Remove the record(s) with the smallest key value [return the record data].
>
> *extractmax* Remove the record(s) with the largest key value [return the record data].
>
> *extractmed* Remove the record(s) with the median key value [return the record data].

The *findmin* and *extractmin* (or *findmax* and *extractmax*) operations are sometimes referred to as *priority queue* operations. For example, the minimum key value might correspond to the highest-priority task in a queue of tasks that are ready for execution. Finding the priority level of the highest-priority task in the queue might be of interest when we want to decide if a currently running task can continue or must be preempted. Extracting the highest-priority task from the priority queue is required when we want to schedule the task to run on an idle processor.

8.2. A TREE-STRUCTURED DICTIONARY MACHINE

In dealing with circuit-level designs, we essentially proceed in a direction that is the reverse of what is done in the rest of the book: Rather than defining a "general-purpose" parallel architecture (e.g., PRAM, 2D mesh, hypercube) and developing algorithms for solving various problems of interest on it, we take a problem and deal with one or more circuit realizations or architectures that can solve it efficiently in parallel.

Tree-structured dictionary machines, an example of which is described in this section, were proposed by Bentley and Kung [Bent79], among others, and later expanded and refined by many other researchers. Others have proposed dictionary machines based on meshes, hypercubes, and so forth (see, e.g., [Parh90] and [Nara96] for references and latest developments in dictionary machines).

The tree machine consists of two back-to-back complete binary trees whose leaves have been merged (Fig. 8.1). The "circle" tree is responsible for broadcasting the dictionary operations that enter via the "input root" to all of the leaf nodes that hold the records. The "triangle" tree combines the results of individual operations by the leaf nodes into an overall result that emerges from the "output root." In an actual hardware implementation, the double tree might be *folded*, with circular and triangular nodes merged just like the leaf nodes. However, even with folding, two separate functions of broadcasting and combining will have to be performed, making the representation of Fig. 8.1 more appropriate than a simple binary tree.

Searches can be easily pipelined through the levels of the two trees in Fig. 8.1. As the first instruction, *search*(y_0), is passed from the input root to its two children, the next one, *search*(y_1), can be accepted. The two instructions are pipelined in lockstep, eventually reaching the leaf nodes in successive cycles. Each leaf processor then responds to the search instruction, with the search response (e.g., yes/no, leaf node ID, key value, data, or a match-degree indicator in the case of best-match search) combined, in the same pipelined fashion, in the lower tree.

The combining function of the triangular nodes depends on the search type. In the following operations, it is possible to pass a leaf node ID (indicating the location of the leaf node where a match was found), along with the control information and data, as part of the search result.

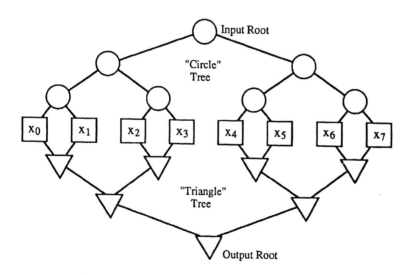

Figure 8.1. A tree-structured dictionary machine.

search(y)	Pass the logical OR of the "yes" signals, along with data from the "yes" side, or from one of the two sides if both indicate "yes" (the choice being arbitrary or by priority).
findmin	Pass the smaller of the two key values and its associated data.
findmax	Similar to *findmin*.
findmed	The median-finding operation is not supported by this particular design.
findbest(y)	Pass the larger of the two match-degree indicators along with the record.
findnext(y)	Leaf nodes generate a "larger" bit; *findmin* is done among the larger values.
findprev(y)	Similar to *findnext*.

If there are n leaf nodes, a *search* instruction reaches the leaves in $\lceil \log_2 n \rceil$ steps after it enters the input root node and its result will emerge from the output root node after $\lceil \log_2 n \rceil$ additional steps. The total latency is thus $2\lceil \log_2 n \rceil + 1$ steps, with one search result emerging in each subsequent cycle. Thus, the throughput can approach one search per cycle with a suitably large batch of searches. If searches were the only operations of interest and the list of records were static, the speed-up relative to sequential binary search would not be impressive. We are in effect using $3n - 2$ nodes or simple processors (circles, squares, and triangles) to reduce the running time per search from $\log_2 n$ to 1.

There are two redeeming factors, however. First, because the list of records does not have to be sorted, both insertion and deletion (extraction) are almost as simple as searching, as we shall see shortly. Second, each of our nodes is much simpler, and thus significantly faster, than a sequential processor with the need to calculate the address of the next comparison location, read data from memory, and then set new search-boundary addresses for every comparison.

Deleting a record is straightforward when there are no duplicate keys or the deletion is intended to remove all records with the given key y. The *delete(y)* instruction is broadcast to all leaf nodes, with those leaf nodes whose key values are equal to y marking their records as "deleted." Reclaiming the space occupied by such records will be discussed along with insertion. New searches can enter the tree immediately following a delete instruction, because by the time these search instructions reach the leaf nodes, the deletion will have already taken place.

Both *extractmin* and *extractmax* must be performed in two phases. First, the location of the leaf node holding the minimum or maximum key value is identified. Once this result has emerged from the output root node, an instruction is inserted for extracting the record. Thus, the latency of these instructions is twice as large. Furthermore, no search instruction should be allowed to enter the tree before the second phase has begun.

Insertion of a record is also straightforward. If duplicate keys are not allowed and we are not certain that a record with the key value y does not already exist, we may precede the *insert(y, z)* instruction with a *delete(y)* instruction. The main difference between the *insert* instruction and the previous ones is that the instruction is not broadcast to all leaf nodes, as we do not want every empty leaf node to insert the new record. Rather, a mechanism is needed to selectively route an *insert* instruction to one, and only one, empty leaf node.

A simple mechanism for routing an *insert* instruction is as follows. Suppose that each nonleaf node maintains two counters indicating the number of empty leaf nodes in its left and right subtrees, respectively. When an *insert* instruction is received by a nonleaf node, it is sent to one of the subtrees with a nonzero free-space count (perhaps to the one with the larger count if both are nonzero or always to the left subtree if possible). The corresponding subtree counter is then decremented by 1. Figure 8.2 shows an example eight-leaf tree machine with three empty leaves and the free-space counter values associated with each circular node. We see in Fig. 8.2 that as the insert instruction is passed to the left child of the root node, the left counter of the root node is decremented from 1 to 0.

The only remaining problem is to show how the counter values are updated on deleting a record. When a *delete* instruction is being sent down the upper tree, it is not yet known which leaf node will perform the deletion and, thus, which counters must be incremented. However, if we require that the deleting leaf's ID be provided to us at the output root, a second instruction can be inserted into the machine for the sole purpose of updating the free-space counters. The slight delay between a record being deleted and its space becoming usable again is not a serious problem unless the tree machine is almost full. Even in this latter case, the speed penalty is not paid unless an insertion is required shortly after a *delete* instruction.

An interesting variant of the tree machine for dictionary operations uses a systolic binary-tree data structure in which the root of each subtree contains the smallest, median value, and largest of the key values in that subtree (Fig. 8.3). When a subtree holds an odd number of keys, its root contains three values and its two subtrees contain the same number of keys. Otherwise, by convention, the left subtree contains one fewer key. This information is held in the root in the form of a single-bit flag, so that the next element inserted will be forwarded to the left subtree and the bit is flipped to indicate complete balance. With this data structure, the smallest, largest, and median of the stored values is readily accessible in one clock cycle via the root node. Specifying the details of the algorithms is left as an exercise.

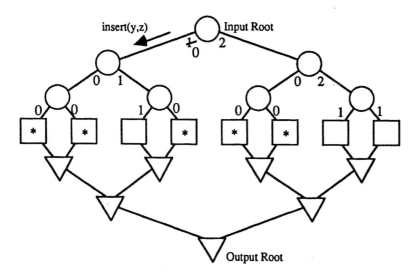

Figure 8.2. Tree machine storing five records and containing three free slots.

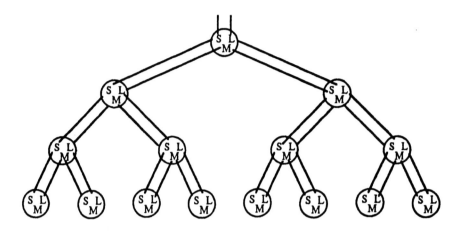

Figure 8.3. Systolic data structure for minimum, maximum, and median finding.

8.3. PARALLEL PREFIX COMPUTATION

Parallel prefix computation was defined in Section 2.1, with several algorithms provided subsequently in Sections 2.3 (linear array), 2.4 (binary tree), 2.5 (2D mesh), and 5.4 (PRAM). Here, we use an alternative formulation in terms of linear recurrences. Let $\otimes$ be an associative binary operator over S; i.e., $(x \otimes y) \otimes z = x \otimes (y \otimes z)$ for all $x, y, z \in S$. Given a sequence of n input values $x_1, x_2, \ldots, x_n$, solve the linear recurrence

$$s_i = s_{i-1} \otimes x_i$$

where s_0 is the identity element of the operator $\otimes$ (e.g., 0 for addition, 1 for multiplication). Note that the ith output value is $s_i = x_1 \otimes x_2 \otimes \cdots \otimes x_i$.

The linear recurrence formulation of the prefix computation immediately suggests a sequential circuit implementation shown in Fig. 8.4 (left). One input is provided to the circuit, and one output is produced, in every clock cycle. Obviously, the clock period must be long enough to accommodate the worst-case signal propagation delay in the circuit computing $\otimes$ plus the latch hold and setup times. Figure 2.1 represents a *computation dependence graph* or a *signal flow graph* for this scheme, if we take the clock period as a unit of time.

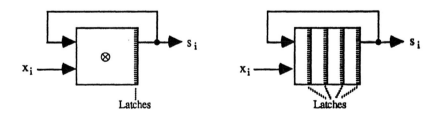

Figure 8.4. Prefix computation using a latched or pipelined function unit.

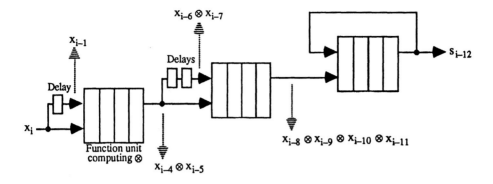

Figure 8.5. High-throughput prefix computation using a pipelined function unit.

A q-stage pipelined function unit does not help in speeding up the prefix computation, for even though the clock period is now much shorter, one input can be supplied after every q clock ticks. In fact, because of the added overhead for latching of the intermediate results, the pipelined function unit shown in Fig. 8.4 (right) actually slows the computation down.

Figure 8.5 shows how parallelism can be applied to improve the throughput to one input or result per clock tick. It is easy to generalize this scheme to use a pipelined function unit with more stages, leading to a correspondingly higher throughput with a greater investment in hardware. However, there is a limit beyond which throughput cannot be improved using this scheme. Namely, if the latching overhead per pipeline stage is c, then the throughput can never exceed $1/c$ no matter how many pipelined units are used or how they are arranged.

In Section 8.4, we will review some of the methods for designing faster prefix computation circuits. The prefix computation is quite important. We discussed some of its applications in Section 2.4. Many other interesting applications are reviewed by Lakshmivarahan and Dhall ([Laks94], pp. 5–35).

8.4. PARALLEL PREFIX NETWORKS

For the sake of brevity and concreteness, we will discuss the design of circuits for computing parallel prefix sums with unsigned integer inputs, i.e., the operator $\otimes$ is taken to be unsigned integer addition. The resulting circuits, which are built of two-input adders, will be referred to as *(parallel) prefix sum networks*. Replacing the two-input adders in these networks with blocks that compute the operator $\otimes$ will yield a general *parallel prefix network*.

There are many similarities between prefix sum networks and sorting networks that we discussed in Chapter 7. A two-input binary adder is roughly of the same complexity as a two-input comparator. Like comparators, these adders can be implemented with parallel inputs or with bit-serial inputs. In the latter case, the input order should be LSB-first, as opposed to MSB-first for two-input comparators. Note that if parallel inputs are used, the adders need not be of the fast variety (e.g., carry-lookahead). In most cases, a simple ripple-carry adder will do, because the rippling delays in a set of cascaded adders do not add up; the rippling in the next adder downstream can begin as soon as the LSB of the sum from the previous adder becomes available.

Several strategies can be used to synthesize a prefix sum network. The two divide-and-conquer methods discussed in connection with PRAM in Section 5.4, and depicted in Figs. 5.7 and 5.8, can form the basis for hardware prefix sum networks. Figures 8.6 and 8.7 depict the resulting networks. The analyses of Section 5.4 can be used to deduce the delays of $T(n) = 2 \log_2 n - 1$ and $T(n) = \log_2 n$ for these circuits, where the unit of time is the delay of a two-input adder. The cost recurrences for the networks of Figs. 8.6 and 8.7 are $C(n) = C(n/2) + n - 1 = 2n - 2 - \log_2 n$ and $C(n) = 2C(n/2) + n/2 = (n/2) \log_2 n$, respectively.

The two designs in Figs. 8.6 and 8.7 offer a clear speed–cost trade-off. The second design is faster ($\log_2 n$ as opposed to $2 \log_2 n - 1$ levels) but also much more expensive [$(n/2) \log_2 n$ adders as opposed to $2n - 2 - \log_2 n$ adder blocks]. Another problem with the second design is that it leads to large fan-out requirements if implemented directly. We will see shortly that intermediate designs, with costs and delays that fall between the above two extremes, are also possible.

The design shown in Fig. 8.6 is known as the Brent–Kung parallel prefix graph. The 16-input instance of this graph is depicted in Fig. 8.8. Note that even though the graph of Fig. 8.8 appears to have seven levels, levels 4 and 5 from the top have no data dependency and thus imply a single level of signal delay. In general, an n-input Brent–Kung parallel prefix graph has a delay of $2 \log_2 n - 2$ levels and a cost of $2n - 2 - \log_2 n$ blocks.

Figure 8.9 depicts a Kogge–Stone parallel prefix graph that has the same delay as the design shown in Fig. 8.7 but avoids its fan-out problem by distributing the required computations. An n-input Kogge–Stone parallel prefix graph has a delay of $\log_2 n$ levels and a cost of $n \log_2 n - n + 1$ blocks. The Kogge–Stone parallel prefix graph represents the fastest possible implementation of a parallel prefix computation if only two-input blocks are allowed. However, its cost can be prohibitive for large n, in terms of both blocks and the dense wiring between blocks.

Other parallel prefix network designs are also possible. For example, it has been suggested that the Brent–Kung and Kogge–Stone approaches of Figs. 8.8 and 8.9 can be combined to form hybrid designs [Sugl90]. Figure 8.10 shows an example where the middle

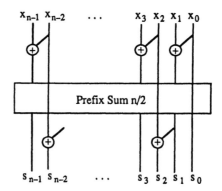

Figure 8.6. Prefix sum network built of one $n/2$-input network and $n - 1$ adders.

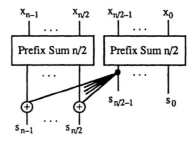

Figure 8.7. Prefix sum network built of two $n/2$-input networks and $n/2$ adders.

four of the six levels in the design of Fig. 8.8 (essentially doing an eight-input parallel prefix computation) have been replaced by an eight-input Kogge–Stone network. The resulting design has five levels and 32 blocks, placing it between the pure Brent–Kung (6, 26) and pure Kogge–Stone (4, 49) designs.

More generally, if a single Brent–Kung level is used along with an $n/2$-input Kogge–Stone design, the delay and cost of the hybrid network become $\log_2 n + 1$ and $(n/2)\log_2 n$, respectively. The resulting design is close to the minimum in terms of delay (only one more than Kogge–Stone) but costs roughly half as much.

The theory of parallel prefix graphs is quite well developed. There exist numerous theoretical bounds and actual designs with different restrictions on fan-in/fan-out and with

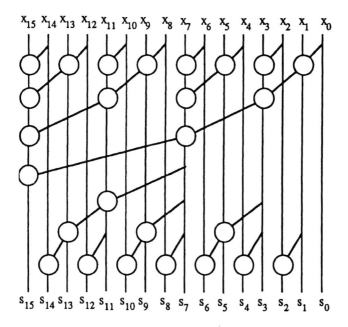

Figure 8.8. Brent–Kung parallel prefix graph for 16 inputs.

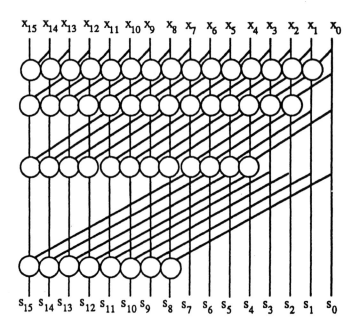

Figure 8.9. Kogge–Stone parallel prefix graph for 16 inputs.

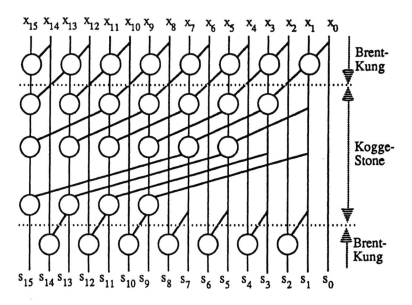

Figure 8.10. A hybrid Brent–Kung/Kogge–Stone parallel prefix graph for 16 inputs.

various optimality criteria in terms of network cost and delay. For a more detailed discussion, see Lakshmivarahan and Dhall ([Laks94], pp. 133–211).

8.5. THE DISCRETE FOURIER TRANSFORM

The discrete Fourier transform (DFT) is defined as follows. Given the sequence $x_0, x_1, \ldots, x_{n-1}$, compute the sequence $y_0, y_1, \ldots, y_{n-1}$ according to

$$y_i = \sum_{j=0}^{n-1} \omega_n^{ij} x_j$$

The DFT is expressed in matrix form as $y = F_n x$, which is shorthand for

$$\begin{bmatrix} y_0 \\ y_1 \\ \vdots \\ y_{n-1} \end{bmatrix} = \begin{bmatrix} 1 & 1 & 1 & \cdots & 1 \\ 1 & \omega_n & \omega_n^2 & \cdots & \omega_n^{n-1} \\ \vdots & \vdots & \vdots & \cdots & \vdots \\ 1 & \omega_n^{n-1} & \omega_n^{2(n-1)} & \cdots & \omega_n^{(n-1)^2} \end{bmatrix} \begin{bmatrix} x_0 \\ x_1 \\ \vdots \\ x_{n-1} \end{bmatrix}$$

In the above expressions, ω_n is the nth primitive root of unity, i.e., $\omega_n^n = 1$ and $\omega_n^j \neq 1$ for $1 \leq j < n$. For example, $\omega_3 = -1/2 + i\sqrt{3}/2$ and $\omega_4 = i$, where $i = \sqrt{-1}$. The following are easily derived:

$$\omega_n = e^{2\pi i/n}$$

$$\omega_n^j = e^{2\pi ji/n} = \cos(2\pi j/n) + i\sin(2\pi j/n)$$

The inverse DFT can be used to recover the x sequence, given the y sequence. It can be shown that the inverse DFT is essentially the same computation as the DFT. That is,

$$x_i = \frac{1}{n} \sum_{j=0}^{n-1} \omega_n^{-ij} y_j$$

Note that n processors can compute the DFT in $O(n)$ time steps, without any communication, if the jth processor computes y_j. Also, given the matrix formulation of the DFT, any matrix–vector multiplication algorithm can be used to compute DFTs. However, the special structure of F_n can be exploited to devise a much faster algorithm based on the divide-and-conquer paradigm. The resulting algorithm, described below, is known as the fast Fourier transform (FFT) algorithm.

Let us partition the DFT summation into odd- and even-indexed terms:

$$y_i = \sum_{j=0}^{n-1} \omega_n^{ij} x_j = \underbrace{\sum \omega_n^{ij} x_j}_{j \text{ even } (2r)} + \underbrace{\sum \omega_n^{ij} x_j}_{j \text{ odd } (2r+1)}$$

$$= \sum_{r=0}^{n/2-1} \omega_{n/2}^{ir} x_{2r} + \omega_n^i \sum_{r=0}^{n/2-1} \omega_{n/2}^{ir} x_{2r+1}$$

where we have used the identity $\omega_{n/2} = \omega_n^2$ in rewriting the two summation terms. The two terms in the last expression are $n/2$-point DFTs that can be written as

$$u = F_{n/2}\begin{bmatrix} x_0 \\ x_2 \\ \vdots \\ x_{n-2} \end{bmatrix} \qquad v = F_{n/2}\begin{bmatrix} x_1 \\ x_3 \\ \vdots \\ x_{n-1} \end{bmatrix}$$

Then:

$$y_i = \begin{cases} u_i + \omega_n^i v_i & 0 \le i < n/2 \\ u_{i-n/2} + \omega_n^i v_{i-n/2} & n/2 \le i < n \end{cases} \quad \text{or} \quad y_{i+n/2} = u_i + \omega_n^{i+n/2} v_i$$

Hence, the n-point FFT algorithm consists of performing two independent $n/2$-point FFTs and then combining their results using n multiply–add operations. The sequential time complexity of FFT is thus characterized by the recurrence

$$T(n) = 2T(n/2) + n = n \log_2 n$$

If the two $n/2$-point subproblems can be solved in parallel and the n multiply–add operations are also concurrent, with their required inputs transferred to the computing nodes instantly, then the recurrence for parallel time complexity becomes

$$T(n) = T(n/2) + 1 = \log_2 n$$

In both cases, the unit of time is the delay of performing one multiply–add operation.

Before discussing hardware circuits to implement the FFT algorithm, it is instructive to examine some applications of DFT to polynomial arithmetic. First, note that the DFT can be viewed as polynomial evaluation:

Given the polynomial $\quad f(x) = c_{n-1} x^{n-1} + \ldots + c_1 x + c_0$

Compute $\qquad\qquad f(\omega_n^0), f(\omega_n^1), \ldots, f(\omega_n^{n-1})$

In matrix form,

$$\begin{bmatrix} f(\omega_n^0) \\ f(\omega_n^1) \\ \vdots \\ f(\omega_n^{n-1}) \end{bmatrix} = F_n \begin{bmatrix} c_0 \\ c_1 \\ \vdots \\ c_{n-1} \end{bmatrix}$$

In a similar way, the inverse DFT can be used for polynomial interpolation:

$$\begin{bmatrix} c_0 \\ c_1 \\ \vdots \\ c_{n-1} \end{bmatrix} = F_n^{-1} \begin{bmatrix} f(\omega_n^0) \\ f(\omega_n^1) \\ \vdots \\ f(\omega_n^{n-1}) \end{bmatrix} \quad \text{with } F_n^{-1}[i,j] = \frac{1}{n}\omega_n^{-ij} = \frac{1}{n}(F_n[i,j])^{-1}$$

The problem of multiplying two polynomials f and g to obtain their product h, where

$$g(x) = a_{n'-1}x^{n'-1} + \cdots + a_1 x + a_0$$

$$h(x) = b_{n''-1}x^{n''-1} + \cdots + b_1 x + b_0$$

$$f(x) = g(x) \times h(x) = c_{n-1}x^{n-1} + \cdots + c_1 x + c_0 \quad \text{with} \quad n = n' + n'' - 1$$

that is, computing the c_js given the a_js and b_js, can be converted to three n-point DFTs and $n = n' + n'' - 1$ complex multiplications as follows:

1. Evaluate $g(x)$ and $h(x)$ at the n nth roots of unity (two n-point DFTs).
2. Evaluate $f(\omega_n^j) = g(\omega_n^j) \times h(\omega_n^j)$ for all j (n complex multiplications).
3. Interpolate to find the c_js (an n-point inverse DFT).

Thus, $T_{\text{poly-mult}} = 3T_{\text{DFT}} + 1$. If we use an O(log n)-time FFT algorithm, the overall time for polynomial multiplication will be O(log n).

Convolution of two n'-element sequences a and b, defined as computing the n-element sequence c with $c_j = a_j b_0 + a_{j-1} b_1 + \cdots + a_0 b_j$, for $0 \le j \le 2n' - 2$, is identical to polynomial multiplication.

Finally, integer multiplication is intimately related to polynomial multiplication, and thus to DFT. Straightforward k-bit integer multiplication circuits require O(log k) delay and O(k^2) cost (k^2 bit multipliers or AND gates, followed by a carry-save adder tree and a logarithmic-time fast adder). An O(log k)-time integer multiplication algorithm for k-bit numbers, using O($k \log^2 k \log \log k$) bit-level processors, is presented by Leighton ([Leig92], pp. 722–729). The resulting multiplication circuit can be used to multiply O(log k) pairs of k-bit integers in O(log k) time through pipelining, thus leading to O($k \log k \log \log k$) cost per multiplication, which is nearly optimal.

8.6. PARALLEL ARCHITECTURES FOR FFT

Figure 8.11 (left) shows an eight-point FFT network that is derived directly from the divide-and-conquer computation scheme of Section 8.5. Each circular node performs a multiply–add computation. An inductive proof that this network does indeed compute the FFT can be easily constructed. Assume that the u_j and v_j values, the results of $n/2$-point FFTs with even- and odd-indexed inputs, are obtained in the upper and lower parts of the circuit, as shown in Fig. 8.11. Then, it is easy to see that the last stage of the circuit has just the right connectivity to finish the computation by performing the required n multiply–adds.

By rearranging the nodes of our FFT circuit, which is known as the *butterfly* network, we obtain an equivalent representation, as shown in Fig. 8.11 (right). This representation is known as the *shuffle–exchange* network. This network, and the reason for its name, will be discussed in Section 15.5. For now, we view it as simply an equivalent representation of the FFT network that offers the advantage of identical connectivities between the various stages of nodes. In the original FFT network, the inputs are separated into even- and odd-indexed and provided to the top and bottom half of the circuit, respectively, with the outputs obtained in ascending index order. In the equivalent shuffle–exchange version, the inputs are in ascending index order from top to bottom, with the outputs obtained in *bit-reversal order*.

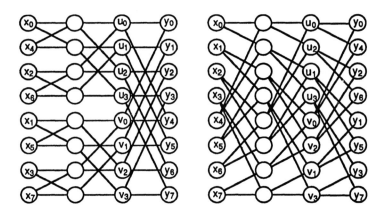

Figure 8.11. Butterfly network for computing an eight-point FFT.

This means that the order of the indices of the output elements is sorted by the reverse of their binary representations. For example, the binary representation of 4 is 100, with its reverse being 001. Thus, y_4 is the second output from the top.

More efficient FFT networks are possible. For example, Yeh and Parhami [Yeh96] present a class of FFT networks that are more modular than those in Fig. 8.11 and thus less costly in VLSI implementation. The shuffle–exchange circuit of Fig. 8.11 (right) can be somewhat simplified by removing half of the links, as shown in Fig. 8.12 (left). The arrows in Fig. 8.12 show the path of data movements (through an intermediate node) in lieu of the missing links.

The butterfly network, and its variants discussed above, can become quite complex for large n. In this case, more economical implementations may be sought. One way is to project the circuit of Fig. 8.12 (left) in the horizontal direction, so that a single multiply–add node

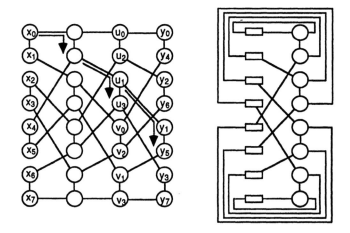

Figure 8.12. FFT network variant and its shared-hardware realization.

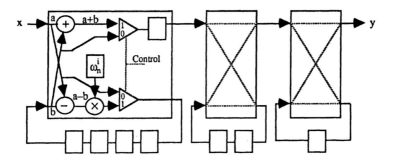

Figure 8.13. Linear array of $\log_2 n$ cells for n-point FFT computation.

performs, in successive time steps, the function of all of the nodes located in one row. The resulting circuit is shown in Fig. 8.12 (right). Here, the single column of multiply–add nodes alternately acts as the various columns of nodes in the diagram on the left, with the partial computation results that would be passed from one column to the next saved in registers or latches for use in the following time step. This approach reduces the cost of the network from $O(n \log n)$ to $O(n)$, without significantly increasing its delay.

An even more economical implementation results if the diagram is projected vertically instead of horizontally. Figure 8.13 shows the resulting linear-array circuit, with feedback shift registers inserted to maintain the proper timing of the various node inputs [Kwai96]. Discovering the details of how this design works is left as an exercise.

PROBLEMS

8.1. Parallel searching
      In Section 8.1, a lower bound for parallel searching of a sorted input list using comparison operations was obtained and an algorithm was given that matched the lower bound.

      a. Obtain a lower bound for parallel searching of an unsorted input list.
      b. Provide a parallel search algorithm that matches the lower bound of part (a).
      c. Can one improve the lower bound of part (a) or the algorithm of part (b) if the input list is known to be partially sorted in the sense that no element is more than m locations away from its correct position in a sorted input list, where $m << n$?

8.2. Tree machine
      This problem relates to the tree-structured dictionary machine of Section 8.2.

      a. We noted that both *extractmin* and *extractmax* must be performed in two phases, with no search instruction allowed to enter the tree before the second phase has begun. Can any instruction be entered immediately after the above instructions? Why (not)?
      b. Design bit-serial processors for a tree machine that performs only the three basic dictionary operations of *search*, *insert*, and *delete*.

8.3. Modified tree machine
      Consider a variant of the tree-structured dictionary machine of Section 8.2 in which the leaves

are interconnected as a linear array. Records are stored at the left end of the array; empty slots are at the right.

a. Discuss how this change affects the operation of the leaf nodes and the execution of the *insert* instruction.

b. Suppose that in the modified tree machine, the leaves are to hold the records in ascending order of the key values from left to right. Propose a method for executing the *insert* instruction that maintains the sorted order. Does the sorted order lead to any advantage?

8.4. **Systolic priority queue**
The systolic binary tree data structure, described at the end of Section 8.2 and depicted in Fig. 8.3, can perform *insert*, *extractmin*, *extractmax*, and *extractmed* operations at the rate of one per clock cycle.

a. Describe the insertion algorithm in detail.

b. Describe algorithms for the three *extract* operations in detail. Make sure that *extractmin* and *extractmax* lead to equal elements being output in FIFO order.

c. Describe a simplified version of the data structure, and its associated algorithms, if we only need to extract the smallest or largest value (median extraction is not needed).

d. A simple priority queue only needs the *insert* and *extractmin* operations. Can we further simplify the data structure and algorithms of part (c) in this case?

8.5. **Solving linear recurrences**
Show that a linear recurrence of the form $y_i = a_{i1}y_{i-1} + a_{i2}y_{i-2} + \cdots + a_{im}y_{i-m} + x_i$ can be solved by a parallel prefix computation involving vectors and matrices. *Hint:* Look ahead to the end of Section 11.3 where it is shown that the solution of a tridiagonal system of linear equations can be converted to a parallel prefix computation.

8.6. **Pipelined prefix computation**
Consider the prefix computation scheme of Fig. 8.4 (right) and its parallel version in Fig. 8.5.

a. Ignoring pipelining overhead and start-up time, the latter is 4 times faster than the former. Is this inconsistent with the assertion that we cannot achieve a speed-up of more than 3 with three processors?

b. Draw a similar diagram assuming a function unit pipeline that has eight stages.

c. Repeat part (b) for a three-stage pipeline.

d. Present a general method of implementation for any q-stage pipeline.

8.7. **Parallel prefix networks**

a. Determine the depth and cost of a 64-input hybrid parallel prefix network with two levels of the Brent–Kung scheme at each end and the rest built by the Kogge–Stone construction.

b. Compare the design of part (a) with pure Brent–Kung and Kogge–Stone schemes and discuss.

8.8. **Parallel prefix networks**

a. Obtain delay and cost formulas for a hybrid parallel prefix network that has l levels of Brent–Kung design at the top and bottom and an $n/2^l$-input Kogge–Stone network in the middle.

b. Use the delay–cost product figure of merit to find the best combination of the two approaches for the number n of inputs ranging from 8 to 64 (powers of 2 only).

8.9. Parallel prefix networks

a. Find delay and cost formulas for the Brent–Kung and Kogge–Stone parallel prefix networks when the number n of inputs is not a power of 2.
b. Draw Brent–Kung, Kogge–Stone, and hybrid parallel prefix graphs for 24 inputs.
c. Using the results of part (b), plot the cost, delay, and cost–delay product for the three types of networks for $n = 16, 24, 32$ inputs and discuss.

8.10. Parallel prefix networks
The large fan-out of $s_{n/2-1}$ in Fig. 8.7 can be replaced by a tree of constant fan-out logic elements. Show how this might be done to minimize the speed penalty.

8.11. Discrete Fourier transform

a. Write down the Fourier and inverse Fourier matrices, F_8 and F_8^{-1}, in terms of $a = \omega_8$.
b. Use DFT to multiply the polynomials $g(x) = x^3 + 2x^2 - 3x + 1$ and $h(x) = -x^4 + 5x^2 - x + 4$.
c. Describe the computation of part (b) as convolution of two sequences.
d. Can the computation of part (b) be interpreted as multiplying two integers? If so, what are the operands and what is the number representation base?

8.12. Butterfly FFT network
Consider the butterfly FFT computation network.

a. Write down the complete expression for the partial result evaluated at each node in both versions of the network shown in Fig. 8.11.
b. Consider the butterfly network in reverse order, i.e., with inputs entering at the rightmost column and outputs produced at the left. Show the ordering of the inputs and outputs in both versions of the network shown in Fig. 8.11.

8.13. Butterfly FFT network
Consider the butterfly FFT computation network of Fig. 8.11.

a. Draw both versions of the network for $n = 16$ inputs.
b. Repeat part (a) for $n = 12$ inputs.

8.14. Shuffle–exchange FFT network
Consider the FFT network variant depicted in Fig. 8.12. Each pair of circular nodes interconnected in the same column constitute a *butterfly processor*.

a. Redraw the left diagram in Fig. 8.12, showing the three columns of butterfly processors, the eight inputs, and the eight outputs.
b. Redraw the right diagram in Fig. 8.12, including the registers in the butterfly processors.
c. Present the complete design of a butterfly processor.

8.15. FFT on a linear array
This problem relates to the linear array of $\log_2 n$ cells for computing the n-point FFT (Fig. 8.13).

a. Explain how the three-cell linear array computes the eight-point FFT. *Hint:* In cycles 0–3, the inputs x_0, x_1, x_2, and x_3 are simply placed in the four-element feedback shift register and are subsequently combined with x_4, x_5, x_6, and x_7 in cycles 4–7.
b. How much time is needed to compute an n-point FFT on the $(\log_2 n)$-cell linear array?
c. Discuss the control scheme for setting the cell multiplexers in the proper state as required by your explanation for part (a).

    d. Show that the control settings of part (c) can be implemented by attaching a control tag to each input [Kwai96].

REFERENCES AND SUGGESTED READING

[Bent79]   Bentley, J. L., and H. T. Kung, "A Tree Machine for Searching Problems," *Proc. Int. Conf. Parallel Processing*, pp. 257–266, 1979.

[Kwai96]   Kwai, D.-M., and B. Parhami, "FFT Computation with Linear Processor Arrays Using a Data-Driven Control Scheme," *J. VLSI Signal Processing*, Vol. 13, pp. 57–66, 1996.

[Laks94]   Lakshmivarahan, S., and S.K. Dhall, *Parallel Computing Using the Prefix Problem*, Oxford University Press, 1994.

[Leig92]   Leighton, F. T., *Introduction to Parallel Algorithms and Architectures: Arrays, Trees, Hypercubes*, Morgan Kaufmann, 1992.

[Nara96]   Narayanan, T. S., "A Class of Semi-X Tree-Based Dictionary Machines," *The Computer J.*, Vol. 39, No. 1, pp. 45–51, 1996.

[Parh90]   Parhami, B., "Massively Parallel Search Processors: History and Modern Trends," *Proc. 4th Int. Parallel Processing Symp.*, pp. 91–104, 1990.

[Sugl90]   Sugla, B., and D. A. Carlson, "Extreme Area-Time Tradeoffs in VLSI," *IEEE Trans. Computers*, Vol. 39, No. 2, pp. 251–257, February 1990.

[Yeh96]   Yeh, C.-H., and B. Parhami, "A Class of Parallel Architectures for Fast Fourier Transform," *Proc. 39th Midwest Symp. Circuits and Systems*, 1996, pp. 856–859.

Mesh-Based Architectures

The bulk of this part is devoted to the study of 2D meshes and tori, a class of parallel architectures that can be built quite easily in VLSI and that are readily scalable to very large configurations. One might say that 2D meshes and tori occupy one end of the spectrum that has the physically unrealistic PRAM model at the other end. If the processors in a 2D mesh have simple circuit-level realizations and are driven by an external control unit in SIMD mode, then the mesh can be viewed as just another circuit-level model of parallel processing with the additional benefits of localized connectivity and regularity; properties that can lead to compact layout and high performance. However, we do not view meshes or tori in this way. Rather, we use more complex processors, or processing elements, to make our mesh-based parallel processors flexible and easier to use for a variety of computational problems. Sorting on 2D meshes is covered first, followed by data routing and numerical algorithms. We conclude with variations and extensions of the simple 2D mesh or torus, as well as certain related architectures. This part consists of the following four chapters:

- Chapter 9:   Sorting on 2D Mesh or Torus
- Chapter 10: Routing on 2D Mesh or Torus
- Chapter 11: Numerical 2D Mesh Algorithms
- Chapter 12: Other Mesh-Related Architectures

9

Sorting on a 2D Mesh or Torus

There are good reasons for beginning our discussion of 2D mesh and torus architectures through algorithms for the seemingly difficult sorting problem. First, sorting on the 2D mesh is nothing like its counterpart on the PRAM; it is easy to build fairly efficient sorting algorithms for the 2D mesh and the process of refining these algorithms into more efficient ones is also quite intuitive. Second, the discussion of sorting networks in Chapter 7 has given us all the background that we need for building, verifying, and evaluating mesh sorting algorithms. So we can delve right into the algorithms, and the fascinating methods and observations used in their designs, following a short introductory discussion of the machine model(s) assumed. Third, sorting is an ideal vehicle for exposing the strengths and weaknesses of mesh-based architectures in communication-intensive applications. Chapter topics are

- 9.1. Mesh-connected computers
- 9.2. The shearsort algorithm
- 9.3. Variants of simple shearsort
- 9.4. Recursive sorting algorithms
- 9.5. A nontrivial lower bound
- 9.6. Achieving the lower bound

9.1. MESH-CONNECTED COMPUTERS

A 2D mesh of processors was defined in Section 2.2 and some simple algorithms for it were presented in Section 2.5. This section covers a complete definition for the simple 2D mesh, including variations in control, interprocessor communication, input/output, and processor indexing. Extensions such as higher dimensions, stronger and weaker connectivities, inclusion of buses, addition of express channels, triangular or hexagonal shapes, variations in the wraparound links, and reconfigurable connectivity will be covered in Chapter 12.

Figure 9.1 shows the basic 2D mesh architecture. Each processor, other than the ones located on the boundary, has degree 4. The free links of the boundary processors can be used for input/output or to establish row and column wraparound connections to form a 2D torus. Variations in the wraparound links (such as connecting to the next row/column, rather than to the same row/column) will not be discussed here. A $k \times k$ mesh has diameter $2k - 2$ and bisection width k or $k + 1$. A $k \times k$ torus has diameter k or $k - 1$ and bisection width $2k$ or $2k + 2$.

A $k \times k$ torus is sometimes referred to as a k-ary 2-cube (or 2D "cube" of size k). The general form of this architecture is known as k-ary q-cube (q-D cube of size k). In particular, for $k = 2$, we get the class of 2-ary (or binary) q-cubes, also known as (binary) hypercubes. Thus, 2D torus and binary hypercube represent the two extremes of the k-ary q-cube architecture; fixing q at 2 gives us the 2D torus architecture with fixed node degree and $\Theta(\sqrt{p})$ diameter, while fixing k at 2 gives us the binary hypercube with logarithmic node degree and $\Theta(\log p)$ diameter.

A 2D mesh can be laid out on a VLSI chip in an area that increases linearly with the number of processors. Because of the short, local connections between processors, the area consumed by the wires is negligible and it would be quite realistic and fair to equate the complexity or implementation cost of a 2D mesh computer with the number p of processors that it contains. Furthermore, the signal propagation delay between adjacent processors is quite small, making it possible to perform communications at very high speed. A 2D torus, on the other hand, has long wraparound links that can slow down interprocessor communication. However, it is possible to lay out a 2D torus in such a way that it too uses only short, local links. Figure 9.2 depicts the method of *folding* that can be used for this purpose.

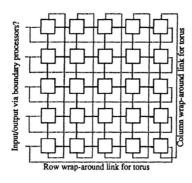

Figure 9.1. Two-dimensional mesh-connected computer.

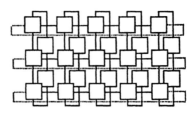

Figure 9.2. A 5×5 torus folded along its columns. Folding this diagram along the rows will produce a layout with only short links.

Unless otherwise stated, the links between processors in 2D meshes and tori are assumed to be bidirectional and capable of carrying data in both directions at the same time (full duplex). The four neighbors of a node are sometimes referred to as *north, east, west,* and *south,* leading to the name *NEWS mesh.* Alternatively, the neighbors may be identified as "top/up/above," "right," "left," and "bottom/down/below." For example, a communication action may be specified for a processor as "send x to north/south neighbor," "send x up/down," "receive x from south/north neighbor," or "receive x from below/above."

Various control schemes are possible. In a MIMD mesh, the processors run independent programs and communicate asynchronously with their four neighbors. A SPMD mesh is similar, except that the node programs are identical. In a SIMD mesh, all processor actions are dictated by a shared central control unit. SIMD mesh is the default model assumed in this book.

Various submodels of the SIMD mesh can be defined with respect to interprocessor communication. In the weakest submodel, all processors must communicate with a neighbor in the same direction, e.g., all send data to their "north" neighbor or "upward." In this weak SIMD submodel, there is never contention for the use of a link; thus, even half-duplex links will do. Next in terms of power is a mesh in which each processor can send a message to only one neighbor in each step, but the neighbor is determined locally based on data-dependent conditions. Of course, in this case, a processor must be able to receive data from all neighbors at once. The most powerful submodel allows transmission and reception to/from all neighbors at once, leading to what is known as the *all-port communication* model.

Processors in a 2D mesh can be indexed (numbered) in a variety of ways. The simplest and most natural is to identify or label each processor by its row and column indices, using either 0-origin or 1-origin indexing (we use 0-origin throughout this book). Thus, Processor $(0, 0)$ is at the upper left corner, Processor $(0, \sqrt{p} - 1)$ is at the upper right corner, and Processor $(\sqrt{p} - 1, \sqrt{p} - 1)$ is at the lower right corner of a p-processor square mesh.

It is at times more convenient to number the processors from 0 to $p - 1$. This puts the processors into a linear order that can be used to assign priorities or to define the order of data elements in processors when we sort them. Figure 9.3 shows some of the possible indexing schemes. You are already familiar with the row-major and snakelike row-major orders. Column-major and snakelike column-major orders can be defined similarly. The shuffled row-major order is a recursive indexing scheme where the mesh is divided into four quadrants and the quadrants are indexed in row-major order; numbering within each quadrant

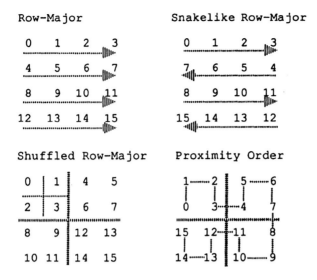

Figure 9.3. Some linear indexing schemes for the processors in a 2D mesh.

is done using the same scheme recursively. Finally, proximity order is also recursive but has the additional property that processors whose indices differ by 1 are neighbors.

A few words about interprocessor communication in a 2D mesh are in order. Each processor can communicate with its NEWS neighbors. The actual data transfer mechanism will be different depending on the communication style. We will take the simple view depicted in Fig. 9.4 where one or more registers in each processor are viewed as part of the register space of each of its NEWS neighbors. Hence, access to any of the Registers R_1 through R_4 in a processor is viewed as reading an element from a neighbor's register. Even this simple scheme can be implemented in a variety of ways. The left diagram in Fig. 9.4 depicts a scheme in which a single value placed in Register R_5 of a processor is made available to its NEWS neighbors. The right diagram in Fig. 9.4 allows more flexibility in that different values can be sent to the four neighbors. This is particularly helpful in routing of multiple independent messages through a node. To forward a message eastward, for example, a processor simply copies its Register R_3 into R_7.

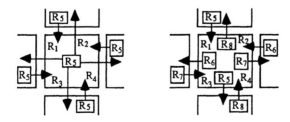

Figure 9.4. Reading data from NEWS neighbors via virtual local registers.

9.2. THE SHEARSORT ALGORITHM

The shearsort algorithm was described without proof, in Section 2.5. Here, we look at the algorithm in more detail and provide a proof of its convergence and correctness. As an algorithm, shearsort is not very efficient and we will see more efficient 2D mesh sorting algorithms later. However, shearsort is very easy to describe, prove, and analyze. Furthermore, it can be used as a building block in the synthesis of more efficient sorting algorithms. Thus, shearsort is important, both as a pedagogical tool and as a practical one.

We begin by assuming that each processor holds a single data item (key) and that the data should be arranged in nondescending order according to row-major or snakelike row-major order. Thus, there are p data items and p processors that form an $r \times (p/r)$ mesh (with r rows and p/r columns). In its simplest form, the shearsort algorithm consists of $\lceil \log_2 r \rceil + 1$ phases (Fig. 9.5). In each phase, except for the last one, all rows are independently sorted in snakelike order: even-numbered rows 0, 2, . . . from left to right, odd-numbered rows 1, 3, . . . from right to left. Then, all columns are independently sorted from top to bottom. In the final phase, rows are independently sorted in snakelike order, or from left to right, depending on the final sorted order desired.

The time complexity of shearsort is easily derived by noting that each row (column) sort takes p/r (r) compare–exchange steps, because rows (columns) are linear arrays for which the odd–even transposition sort is applicable (see Section 2.3):

$$T_{\text{shearsort}} = \lceil \log_2 r \rceil (p/r + r) + p/r$$

On a square $\sqrt{p} \times \sqrt{p}$ mesh, the time complexity of simple shearsort becomes (approximately) $\sqrt{p}(\log_2 p + 1)$.

To prove the convergence and correctness of shearsort, it suffices to show that any 0/1 pattern is properly sorted by the algorithm (the zero–one principle). Consider an arbitrary pattern of 0s and 1s and focus on the first column sort following the initial snakelike row sort. The end result of this column sort will not change if we precede it with a redundant

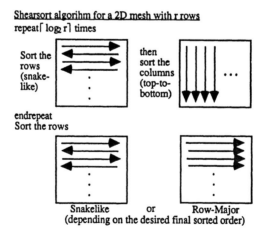

Figure 9.5. Description of the shearsort algorithm on an *r*-row 2D mesh.

compare–exchange between each even-indexed element and the odd-indexed element directly below it (0&1, 2&3, 4&5, . . .). A pair of rows affected by such exchanges can be in one of three classes:

a. They contain more 0s than 1s.
b. They contain more 1s than 0s.
c. They contain the same number of 0s and 1s.

In each case, the redundant exchange creates at least one "clean" row (containing only 0s or only 1s) and no more than one "dirty" row (containing both 0s and 1s), as shown in Fig. 9.6. In sorting the columns, such clean rows "bubble up" or "sink down" and lead to a total of at least $\lfloor r/2 \rfloor$ rows of the array being in their final sorted order. This reduction of the number of dirty rows by a factor of 2, from r to $\lceil r/2 \rceil$ to $\lceil \lceil r/2 \rceil /2 \rceil$ and so on (Fig. 9.7), continues until, after $\lceil \log_2 r \rceil$ iterations, we have at most one dirty row remaining. This last dirty row will be put in its proper sorted order by the final phase of the algorithm.

Figure 9.8 shows a complete example for the application of shearsort to sorting 16 keys on a 4×4 mesh. The initial data distribution is given at the top. Then we have two iterations of snakelike row sorts followed by column sorts. Finally, we end with row-major or snakelike row sorts, depending on the desired sorted order. Note, in particular, that with arbitrary keys, "clean" and "dirty" rows do not exist and thus the notions of clean and dirty rows cannot be used to measure the progress toward the eventual sorted order. In fact, we see in the example of Fig. 9.8 that none of the rows assumes its final sorted state until the very last step in the algorithm.

Note that sorting the rows in snakelike order is the key to being able to sort the array by independent row and column sorts. Take the example of a 4×4 mesh with each of its four rows initially containing the bit pattern 0111. Clearly, no amount of row/column sorting, with row-major order for row sorts, will sort this array.

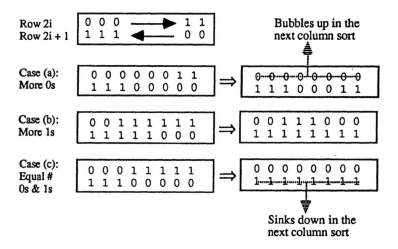

Figure 9.6. A pair of dirty rows create at least one clean row in each shearsort iteration.

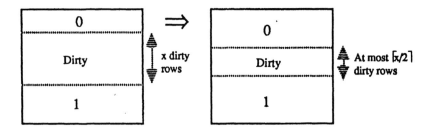

Figure 9.7. The number of dirty rows halves with each shearsort iteration.

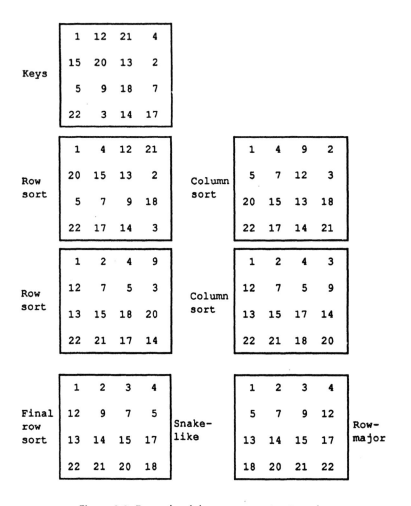

Figure 9.8. Example of shearsort on a 4 × 4 mesh.

9.3. VARIANTS OF SIMPLE SHEARSORT

Shearsort can be terminated earlier in some cases because sorting is complete when no exchange occurs during a row sort or a column sort. In practice, one cannot take advantage of this early termination feature unless some form of fast global combine operation is implemented in hardware.

It is, however, possible to speed up shearsort by a constant factor by taking advantage of the reduction of the number of dirty rows in each iteration. Note that in sorting a sequence of 0s and 1s on a linear array, the number of odd–even transposition steps can be limited to the number of dirty elements that are not already in their proper places (0s at the left/top, 1s at the right/bottom). For example, sorting the sequence 0000010111111 requires no more than two odd–even transposition steps. Therefore, we can replace the complete column sorts within the shearsort algorithm with successively fewer odd–even transposition steps; r in the initial step, $\lceil r/2 \rceil$ in the next step, and so forth. The time complexity of this optimized shearsort then becomes

$$T_{\text{opt shearsort}} = (p/r)(\lceil \log_2 r \rceil + 1) + r + \lceil r/2 \rceil + \lceil \lceil r/2 \rceil/2 \rceil + \cdots + 2$$

When r is a power of 2, the above simplifies to $(p/r)(\log_2 r + 1) + 2r - 2$. For a square $\sqrt{p} \times \sqrt{p}$ mesh, time complexity of the optimized version of shearsort is approximately $\sqrt{p}(\frac{1}{2}\log_2 p + 3) - 2$.

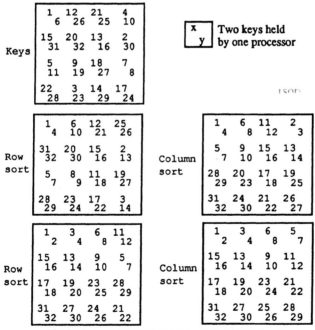

The final row sort (snakelike or row-major) is not shown.

Figure 9.9. Example of shearsort on a 4 × 4 mesh with two keys stored per processor.

Simple shearsort can be easily extended to the case where multiple keys are stored in each processor. The algorithm begins by presorting the sublists of size n/p within the processors, using any sequential sorting algorithm. It then proceeds with row and column sorts as in simple (p-input) shearsort, except that each compare–exchange step of the latter is replaced by a "merge–split" step involving lists of size n/p. For example, if $n/p = 4$ and the two processors doing the compare–exchange step in simple shearsort now hold the sublists {1, 5, 8, 8} and {2, 3, 5, 7}, the merge–split step will result in the two processors holding, in the sorting order, the sublists {1, 2, 3, 5} and {5, 7, 8, 8}. Performing a merge–split operation on two sorted lists of length n/p requires n/p compare–exchange steps in the worst case.

Figure 9.9 shows an example of shearsort with two keys stored per processor. The time complexity of the shearsort algorithm with n/p keys per processors is easily obtained from the $\Theta((n/p)\log(n/p))$ complexity of the presort phase and the $\Theta(n/p)$ complexity of each merge–split operation.

9.4. RECURSIVE SORTING ALGORITHMS

A recursive algorithm for sorting on a square $\sqrt{p}\times\sqrt{p}$ mesh, based on four-way divide-and-conquer strategy, is shown in Fig. 9.10. The algorithm consists of four phases.

First recursive sorting algorithm on a 2D mesh

   1.   Sort each of the four quadrants in snakelike order.
   2.   Sort the rows independently, in snakelike order.

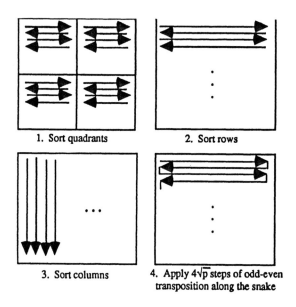

1. Sort quadrants   2. Sort rows

3. Sort columns   4. Apply $4\sqrt{p}$ steps of odd-even transposition along the snake

Figure 9.10. Graphical depiction of the first recursive algorithm for sorting on a 2D mesh based on four-way divide and conquer.

3. Sort the columns independently, from top to bottom.
4. Apply $4\sqrt{p}$ steps of odd–even transposition along the overall snake.

In the last phase, the mesh is viewed as a snakelike p-processor linear array for the application of the $4\sqrt{p}$ steps of odd–even transposition.

If the above algorithm is in fact correct, as we will show shortly, its running time is characterized by the following recurrence:

$$T(\sqrt{p}) = T(\sqrt{p}/2) + 5.5\sqrt{p} \approx 11\sqrt{p}$$

where $5.5\sqrt{p}$ is the sum of $0.5\sqrt{p}$ for row sort (with each half being already sorted, $\sqrt{p}/2$ steps of odd–even transposition suffice for row sort), $\sqrt{p}$ for column sort, and $4\sqrt{p}$ for the last phase.

As usual, we prove the algorithm correct by using the zero–one principle. Figure 9.11 (left side) shows the state of the array after sorting the four quadrants in Phase 1, with various numbers of clean 0 and 1 rows as indicated. The snakelike row sort in Phase 2 will spread the elements of these clean rows roughly evenly in the left and right halves of the array. After Phase 3, we end up with x clean 0 rows on the top and x' clean 1 rows at the bottom. Because at most one dirty row remains in each quadrant after sorting it, each of the sums $a + a'$, $b + b'$, $c + c'$, or $d + d'$ is either $\sqrt{p}/2$ or $\sqrt{p}/2 - 1$. Let $a > b$ and $c < d$, as shown in Fig. 9.11 (other cases are similar). Then, the row sorts of Phase 2 produce $b + c$ clean 0 rows outright and $\lfloor (a - b)/2 \rfloor + \lfloor (d - c)/2 \rfloor$ clean 0 rows as a result of the extra 0 half-rows being divided equally among the left and right halves of the array by the snakelike row sorts. Thus, the number of clean 0 rows at the end of Phase 3 of the algorithm satisfies

$$x \geq b + c + \lfloor (a - b)/2 \rfloor + \lfloor (d - c)/2 \rfloor$$

A similar inequality for x' leads to

$$x + x' \geq b + c + \lfloor (a - b)/2 \rfloor + \lfloor (d - c)/2 \rfloor + a' + d' + \lfloor (b' - a')/2 \rfloor + \lfloor (c' - d')/2 \rfloor$$

$$\geq b + c + a' + d' + (a - b)/2 + (d - c)/2 + (b' - a')/2 + (c' - d')/2 - 4 \times 1/2$$

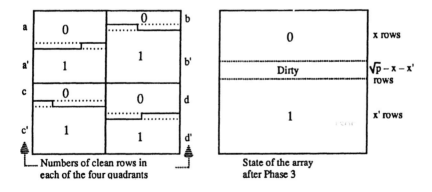

Numbers of clean rows in each of the four quadrants

State of the array after Phase 3

Figure 9.11. The proof of the first recursive sorting algorithm for 2D meshes.

$$= (a + a')/2 + (b + b')/2 + (c + c')/2 + (d + d')/2 - 2$$

$$\geq \sqrt{p} - 4$$

Hence, the number $\sqrt{p} - x - x'$ of dirty rows after Phase 3 is at most 4. Now, viewing the array as a p-processor snakelike linear array and applying $4\sqrt{p}$ steps of odd–even transposition will put the $4\sqrt{p}$ potentially out-of-position elements in their proper places.

A second, somewhat more efficient, recursive algorithm for sorting on a square $\sqrt{p} \times \sqrt{p}$ mesh is again based on four-way divide-and-conquer strategy. The algorithm consists of four phases.

Second recursive sorting algorithm on a 2D mesh

1. Sort each of the four quadrants in snakelike order.
2. Shuffle the columns, i.e., interlace the left- and right-half elements in each row.
3. Sort pairs of columns, 0 & 1, 2 & 3, etc., in snakelike row-major order.
4. Apply $2\sqrt{p}$ steps of odd–even transposition along the overall snake.

Figure 9.12 shows the four algorithm phases graphically. In the last phase, the mesh is viewed as a snakelike p-processor linear array for the application of the $2\sqrt{p}$ steps of odd–even transposition.

Again, assuming that the algorithm is in fact correct, its running time is characterized by the following recurrence:

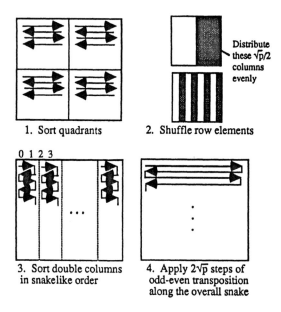

1. Sort quadrants

2. Shuffle row elements
Distribute these $\sqrt{p}/2$ columns evenly

3. Sort double columns in snakelike order

4. Apply $2\sqrt{p}$ steps of odd-even transposition along the overall snake

Figure 9.12. Graphical depiction of the second recursive algorithm for sorting on a 2D mesh based on four-way divide and conquer.

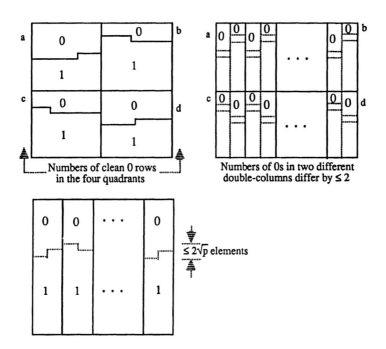

Figure 9.13. The proof of the second recursive sorting algorithm for 2D meshes.

$$T(\sqrt{p}) = T(\sqrt{p}/2) + 4.5\sqrt{p} \approx 9\sqrt{p}$$

where the term $4.5\sqrt{p}$ is the sum of $0.5\sqrt{p}$ for row shuffling (this is the maximum distance that an element needs to move to the right or to the left), $2\sqrt{p}$ for double-column sorts, and $2\sqrt{p}$ for the last phase.

By now you can probably guess that we need to use the zero–one principle in order to prove the above algorithm correct. The structure of the proof is depicted in Fig. 9.13. As in Fig. 9.11, representing the proof of the first recursive sorting algorithm, the numbers of clean 0 rows in the four quadrants have been indicated in Fig. 9.13. Filling in the remaining details of the correctness proof is left as an exercise.

9.5. A NONTRIVIAL LOWER BOUND

Because the diameter of a square $\sqrt{p} \times \sqrt{p}$ mesh is $2\sqrt{p} - 2$, a $\Theta(\sqrt{p})$-time algorithm is the best that we can hope for. However, our best $\Theta(\sqrt{p})$-time algorithm thus far is about 4.5 times slower that the diameter-based lower bound. Two natural questions at this point are

1. Can we raise the $2\sqrt{p} - 2$ lower bound?
2. Can we design a sorting algorithm with a lower execution time than $9\sqrt{p}$?

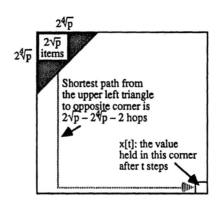

Figure 9.14. The proof of the $3\sqrt{p} - o(\sqrt{p})$ lower bound for sorting in snakelike row-major order.

In this section, we show that for sorting in snakelike row-major order, the lower bound can be raised to $3\sqrt{p} - o(\sqrt{p})$. Then, in Section 9.6, we present an algorithm that matches this lower bound asymptotically in that its execution time is $3\sqrt{p} + o(\sqrt{p})$.

Consider the square $\sqrt{p} \times \sqrt{p}$ mesh depicted in Fig. 9.14. The shaded triangular region at the upper left corner of this mesh contains $2\sqrt{p}$ processors and keys. Let the keys held by the $p - 2\sqrt{p}$ processors in the unshaded region be the numbers 1 through $p - 2\sqrt{p}$. Each of the keys in the shaded part is 0 or $p - 2\sqrt{p} + 1$ (i.e., all are smaller or larger than those in the unshaded region), with the number of 0s being z, $0 \le z \le 2\sqrt{p}$. We denote by $x[t]$ the key held by the processor at the lower right corner of the mesh at time step t, as the sorting algorithm is executed.

We now take an arbitrary sorting algorithm and show that it needs at least $3\sqrt{p} - o(\sqrt{p})$ steps to sort the above keys in snakelike row-major order. Consider the state of the mesh after the algorithm has run for $2\sqrt{p} - 2\sqrt[4]{p} - 3$ steps and, in particular, the value $x[2\sqrt{p} - 2\sqrt[4]{p} - 3]$ held by the processor at the lower right corner of the mesh. Because the shortest path from any processor in the shaded region to the corner processor contains at least $2\sqrt{p} - \sqrt[4]{p} - 2$ hops, this corner value can in no way depend on the number z of 0s in the shaded region. If we vary z from 0 to its maximum of $2\sqrt{p}$, the correct final position of the value $x[2\sqrt{p} - 2\sqrt[4]{p} - 3]$ in the sorted order can be made to be in any of the columns, and in particular in Column 0. Thus, in the worst case, the algorithm needs at least $\sqrt{p} - 1$ additional steps to complete the sorting. The total running time of the algorithm is thus lower bounded by

$$T(\sqrt{p}) \ge 2\sqrt{p} - 2\sqrt[4]{p} - 3 + \sqrt{p} - 1 = 3\sqrt{p} - \Theta(\sqrt[4]{p})$$

Consider, for example, a 9×9 square mesh ($p = 81$). By the above construction, each of the 18 processors in the shaded region holds a key value 0 or 64, while the remaining processors hold the key values 1 through 63. If $z = 18$, the initial state and final sorted order are as shown on the left side of Fig. 9.15. The other extreme of $z = 0$ is depicted on the right side of Fig. 9.15. It is clear from this example that as z gradually changes from 0 to 18, the final location of each of the key values 1–63 shifts through every column in the mesh.

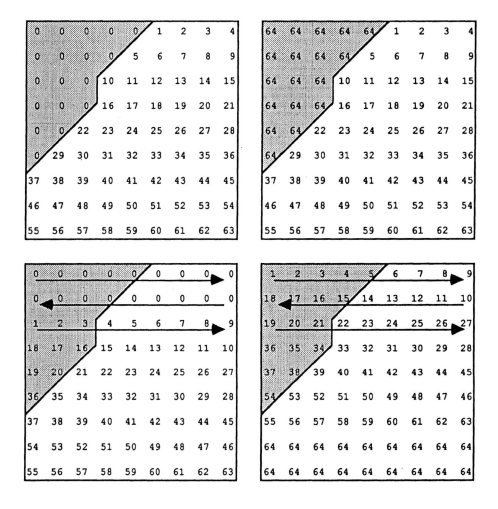

Figure 9.15. Illustrating the effect of fewer or more 0s in the shaded area.

If we run any given sorting algorithm for 10 steps, the key value that appears at the lower right corner will be independent of z. If after these 10 steps, the lower right value is 55, say, then choosing any of the values 0, 9, or 18 for z will force the algorithm to work for at least 8 more steps just to shift the key value 55 to column 0 where it belongs. So, the algorithm needs at least $10 + 8 = 18$ steps for this particular example (it will likely need more).

Note that the above proof only applies to the snakelike final order and is based on the implicit assumption that each processor holds one key initially and at each step of the algorithm. Nigam and Sahni [Niga95] have shown that by "folding" the keys into half of the columns, so that each processor in the central half of the mesh holds two keys, the above lower bound can be overcome and sorting done in roughly $2.5\sqrt{p}$ communication steps. More generally, folding the keys into $\sqrt{p}/k$ columns reduces the sorting time even further for $k > 2$. A different approach to obtaining a sorting algorithm that requires $2.5\sqrt{p} + o(\sqrt{p})$ communication steps on a p-processor square 2D mesh is provided by Kunde [Kund91].

9.6. ACHIEVING THE LOWER BOUND

In this section, we describe a sorting algorithm, reported by Schnorr and Shamir [Schn86], that comes very close to the $3\sqrt{p}$ lower bound of Section 9.5 in terms of its running time. However, the mesh has to be quite large for the algorithm to be significantly faster than the simpler algorithms presented earlier in this chapter. This is so because in the analysis of the algorithm, several terms on the order of $p^{3/8}$ or $p^{3/8} \log_2 p$ are ignored in comparison with $p^{1/2}$. For $p = 2^{32}$, or approximately 4 billion processors, we have $p^{3/8} \log_2 p = 2^{12} \times 32 = 128\text{K}$ compared with $p^{1/2} = 2^{16} = 64\text{K}$. Once the algorithm is described, the reader will see that the lower-order terms ignored in the analysis in fact constitute a significant portion of the running time even when the number of processors is in the billions. Hence, presently, this algorithm cannot be considered practical.

Figure 9.16 depicts the divide-and-conquer strategy, and some relevant notation, for presenting this asymptotically optimal sorting algorithm.

The eight-phase Schnorr–Shamir algorithm for snakelike sorting on a 2D mesh is based on dividing the $p^{1/2} \times p^{1/2}$ mesh into smaller $p^{3/8} \times p^{3/8}$ submeshes (blocks), sorting the blocks independently in Phase 1, and then merging the results through various data movement and sorting operations in the remaining seven phases.

The Schnorr–Shamir algorithm for snakelike sorting on a 2D mesh

1. Sort all of the blocks in snakelike order, independently and in parallel.

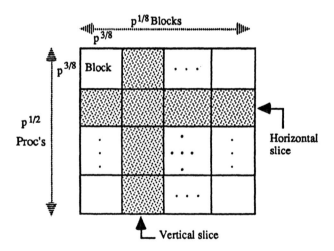

Figure 9.16. Notation for the asymptotically optimal sorting algorithm.

2. Permute the columns such that the columns of each vertical slice are evenly distributed among all vertical slices.
3. Sort each block in snakelike order.
4. Sort the columns independently from top to bottom.
5. Sort Blocks 0&1, 2&3, ... of all vertical slices together in snakelike order, i.e., sort within $2p^{3/8} \times p^{3/8}$ submeshes.
6. Sort Blocks 1&2, 3&4, ... of all vertical slices together in snakelike order again sorting is done within $2p^{3/8} \times p^{3/8}$ submeshes.
7. Sort the rows independently in snakelike order.
8. Apply $2p^{3/8}$ steps of odd–even transposition to the overall snake.

The proof of correctness for this algorithm is somewhat involved and is thus not presented here (like all other proofs in this chapter, it is based on the zero–one principle).

Each of Phases 1, 3, 5, and 6 of the algorithm can be executed in $O(p^{3/8} \log p)$ compare–exchange steps, say by using the shearsort algorithm. Each of Phases 2, 4, and 7 requires at most $p^{1/2}$ steps. Phase 8 obviously needs $2p^{3/8}$ steps. The total running time is thus upper bounded by $3p^{1/2} + o(p^{1/2})$, where the second term can be replaced by $\Theta(p^{3/8} \log p)$.

PROBLEMS

9.1. Topological properties of meshes and tori
 a. Write an expression for the diameter of an $r \times (p/r)$ mesh and show that it is minimized when the mesh is square.
 b. Repeat part (a) for an $r \times (p/r)$ torus.
 c. Write an expression for the bisection width of an $r \times (p/r)$ mesh and show that it is maximized when the mesh is square.
 d. Repeat part (c) for an $r \times (p/r)$ torus.

9.2. Topological properties of meshes and tori
 Diameter or worst-case distance is not the only indicator of communication delay. Average or expected distance is often of greater importance.
 a. What is the average distance from a given node to a random destination node in a p-node linear array?
 b. Repeat part (a) for a p-node ring.
 c. What is the average distance between two randomly selected nodes in a p-node linear array?
 d. Repeat part (c) for a p-node ring.
 e. Using the result of part (a), find the average distance from a given node to a random destination node in an $r \times (p/r)$ mesh.
 f. Repeat part (e) for an $r \times (p/r)$ torus, using the result of part (b).
 g. Using the result of part (c), find the average distance between two randomly selected nodes in an $r \times (p/r)$ mesh.
 h. Repeat part (g) for an $r \times (p/r)$ torus, using the result of part (d).

9.3. VLSI layout of a 2D mesh or torus
 Consider the problem of laying out a mesh or torus on a grid with unit distance between horizontal and vertical lines. Nodes or processors occupy no area (they are shown as dots) and wires are restricted to be nonoverlapping and routed on grid lines (intersecting wires are

acceptable). Let the number p of processors be an even power of 2. Clearly, a p-processor 2D mesh can be laid out in p units of area.

    a. What is the area needed for laying out a p-processor 2D torus with long wraparound links?

    b. What is the area needed for laying out a p-processor torus if it is folded along the rows and columns to make all interprocessor connections short?

9.4.   Interprocessor communication

Using the communication convention shown in the left side of Fig. 9.4 and assuming that each processor knows the number r of rows in the mesh, the total number p of processors, and its own row/column indices (i, j), write a complete program at the level of an assembly language to sort the elements of each row in snakelike order; i.e., even rows sorted from left to right, odd rows from right to left.

9.5.   Row and column sorts

    a. Show that if we sort the rows of a matrix from left to right and then sort the columns from top to bottom, the rows will remain in sorted order.

    b. Show that sorted rows and columns are necessary but not sufficient for a matrix being sorted in row-major order, while the condition is necessary and sufficient with snakelike ordering.

9.6.   The shearsort algorithm

Prove that if an array of integer keys is sorted by applying the shearsort algorithm, the state of the array just before the final row sort is such that if we pick an arbitrary threshold value t, replacing all keys that are less than t with 0 and all those that are greater than or equal to t with 1, the resulting array of 0s and 1s will have at most one dirty row.

9.7.   Optimized shearsort on a 2D mesh

    a. Considering the analysis of optimized shearsort, find a closed-form tight bound on the complexity when r is not a power of 2. *Hint:* The worst case occurs for $r = 2^a + 1$.

    b. Prove that your bound is tight by providing one example when the bound is actually reached.

    c. Can optimized shearsort be extended to the case when n/p keys are stored per processor? If it can, provide algorithm details and its time complexity. If not, state why.

9.8.   Recursive sorting on a 2D mesh

Show that in the first recursive sorting algorithm presented in Section 9.4, replacing Phase 4 (the one saying "apply $4\sqrt{p}$ steps of odd–even transposition along the overall snake") by row sorts and partial column sorts, as in optimized shearsort, would lead to a more efficient algorithm. Provide complexity analysis for the improved version of the algorithm.

9.9.   The shearsort algorithm

Show that on an $r \times 2$ mesh, shearsort requires only $3r/2 + 3$ steps. Then use this result to improve the performance of the second recursive sorting algorithm described in Section 9.4, providing the complexity analysis for the improved version.

9.10. The columnsort algorithm

Consider a seven-phase algorithm that sorts the p elements in an $r \times (p/r)$ matrix in column-major order. During Phases 1, 3, and 7, the columns are independently sorted from top to bottom. During Phase 5, the columns are sorted in snakelike column-major order. During Phase 2, we "transpose" the matrix by picking up the items in column-major order and setting them down in row-major order, while preserving the $r \times (p/r)$ shape of the matrix. During Phase 4, we reverse the permutation applied in Phase 2, picking up items in row-major order and setting them down in column-major order. During Phase 6, we apply two odd–even transposition steps to each row.

    a. Show that the above algorithm, known as *columnsort*, sorts the matrix into column-major order provided that $r^3 \geq p^2$.

    b. Find the time complexity of columnsort when performed on an $r \times (p/r)$ mesh.

    c. Find the time complexity of columnsort when the $r \times (p/r)$ matrix is mapped onto a $\sqrt{p} \times \sqrt{p}$ mesh, with each matrix column occupying $r/\sqrt{p}$ (an integer) consecutive mesh columns.

9.11. **Sorting on a ring of processors**
Using a method similar to that used in Section 9.5, prove that a p-processor ring requires at least $3p/4 - O(1)$ steps to sort p items if each processor is restricted to holding exactly one key in each step. The sorted order is defined as Processor 0 holding the smallest key and the keys appearing in nondescending order in clockwise direction. *Hint:* Consider the $p/2$ processors that are farthest away from Processor 0 and assume that the key values held by these processors are smaller or larger than the keys held by the other $p/2$ processors.

9.12. **Optimal snakelike sorting algorithm**
Using the zero–one principle, prove the correctness of the $(3p^{1/2} + o(p^{1/2}))$-step Schnorr–Shamir sorting algorithm described in Section 9.6 (see [Schn86] or [Leig92], pp. 148–151).

9.13. **Bounds for sorting**
The *bisection bound* on sorting on a square 2D mesh is $\sqrt{p}/2$ steps.

    a. Show that if interprocessor communication is restricted to be in one direction in each step, then a corresponding *multisection lower bound* of $\sqrt{p}$ applies [Kund91].

    b. Derive similar bound for k–k sorting, where each processor begins and ends with k records.

    c. Modify the above lower bounds for a p-processor 2D square torus.

9.14. **Mesh sorting by interleaved row/column sorts**
Consider a 2D mesh sorting algorithm based on row sorts and columns sorts, except that the row sorting and column sorting steps are interleaved (i.e., we perform one odd–even transposition step along the rows, then one along the columns, again one along the rows, and so on). As in shearsort, the row sort steps are done in opposite directions for adjacent rows. Analyze this algorithm and derive its worst-case performance.

9.15. **Average-case performance of sorting algorithms**
Our analyses of sorting algorithms in this chapter focused on worst-case performance. Mesh sorting algorithms that are asymptotically optimal in terms of their worst-case performance are clearly also optimal in terms of their average-case performance when applied to randomly ordered key values. Show that the average-case performance of shearsort is also asymptotically the same as its worst-case performance. *Hint:* Consider what happens to the k smallest keys as shearsort runs on a $k \times k$ mesh.

9.16. **The revsort sorting algorithm**
Consider a $k \times k$ torus sorting algorithm that is based on alternately sorting rows and columns. The ith row is cyclically sorted from left to right beginning at Processor rev(i), where rev(i) is the integer whose binary representation is the reverse of i; e.g., in an 8×8 torus, rev(1) = rev($(001)_{two}$) = $(100)_{two}$ = 4.

a. Prove that all numbers are close to their final row positions after $O(\log \log k)$ iterations of a row sort followed by a column sort.

b. Show that the time complexity of the revsort algorithm is $O(k \log \log k)$.

c. Show that the wraparound links of the torus are not needed and that a 2D mesh can achieve the same time complexity as in part (b).

REFERENCES AND SUGGESTED READING

[Chle90]   Chlebus, B. S., and M. Kukawka, "A Guide to Sorting on the Mesh-Connected Processor Array," *Computers and Artificial Intelligence*, Vol. 9, pp. 599–610, 1990.

[Kund91]   Kunde, M., "Concentrated Regular Data Streams on Grids: Sorting and Routing Near to the Bisection Bound," *Proc. Symp. Foundations of Computer Science*, 1991, pp. 141–150.

[Leig85]   Leighton, T., "Tight Bounds on the Complexity of Parallel Sorting," *IEEE Trans. Computers*, Vol. 34, No. 4, pp. 344–354, April 1985.

[Leig92]   Leighton, F. T., *Introduction to Parallel Algorithms and Architectures: Arrays, Trees, Hypercubes*, Morgan–Kaufmann, 1992.

[Niga95]   Nigam, M., and S. Sahni, "Sorting n^2 Numbers on $n{\times}n$ Meshes," *IEEE Trans. Parallel and Distributed Systems*, Vol. 6, No. 12, pp. 1221–1225, December 1995.

[Sche86]   Scherson, I., S. Sen, and A. Shamir, "Shear-sort: A True Two-Dimensional Sorting Technique for VLSI Networks," *Proc. Int. Conf. Parallel Processing*, 1986, pp. 903–908.

[Schn86]   Schnorr, C. P. and A. Shamir, "An Optimal Sorting Algorithm for Mesh Connected Computers," *Proc. Symp. Theory of Computing*, 1986, pp. 255–263.

10

Routing on a 2D Mesh or Torus

Data routing is needed to make a data item present or computed in one processor available to other processors. In PRAM, all memory words are directly accessible to all processors, so the data routing problem is nonexistent. In the circuit model (e.g., sorting networks), one directly connects the producer of each data word to all of its consumers, so data routing is hardwired into the design. For meshes and other network-based architectures, access to a nonlocal data item requires explicit routing of the access request to the processor where the data item resides and, in the case of reading, explicit routing of the accessed value back to the requesting processor. In this chapter we review methods for data routing on 2D meshes and analyze these methods with regard to their routing delays and resource requirements. Chapter topics are:

- 10.1. Types of data routing operations
- 10.2. Useful elementary operations
- 10.3. Data routing on a 2D array
- 10.4. Greedy routing algorithms
- 10.5. Other classes of routing algorithms
- 10.6. Wormhole routing

10.1. TYPES OF DATA ROUTING OPERATIONS

Most of our discussion will focus on *packet data routing* or *packet switching* where a packet is an atomic unit of data transfer. A packet may be a complete message, containing one or more data values, or a part of a longer message. In the latter case, the packet will have a sequence number indicating that it is the *i*th packet (out of *j* packets). Because we often deal with data transfers involving a single data element, we use *packet* and *message* interchangeably. A packet or message typically has a *header* that holds the destination address, plus possibly some routing information supplied by its sender, and a *message body* (sometimes called *payload*) that carries the actual data. Depending on the *routing algorithm* used, the routing information in the header may be modified by intermediate nodes. A message may also have various other control and error detection or correction information, which we will ignore for simplicity.

Depending on the multiplicity of data sources and destinations, data routing or communication can be divided into two classes: one-to-one (one source, one destination) and collective (multiple sources and/or multiple destinations).

A processor sending a message to another processor, independent of all other processors, constitutes a *one-to-one data routing* operation. Such a data routing operation may be physically accomplished by composing and sending a point-to-point message. Typically, multiple independent point-to-point messages coexist in a parallel machine and compete for the use of communication resources. Thus, we are often interested in the amount of time required for completing the routing operation for up to p such messages, each being sent by a different processor. We refer to a batch of up to p independent point-to-point messages, residing one per processor, as a *data routing problem instance*. If exactly p messages are sent by the p processors and all of the destinations are distinct, we have a *permutation routing* problem.

Collective data routing, as defined in the Message Passing Interface (MPI) Standard [MPIF94], may be of three types:

1. *One to many.*   When a processor sends the same message to many destinations, we call the operation *multicasting*. Multicasting to all processors (one to all) is called *broadcasting*. When different messages are sent from one source to many destinations, a *scatter* operation is performed. The multiple destination nodes may be dynamically determined by problem- and data-dependent conditions or be a topologically defined subset of the processors (e.g., a row of a 2D mesh).

2. *Many to one.*   When multiple messages can be merged as they meet at intermediate nodes on their way to their final common destination, we have a *combine* or *fan-in* operation (e.g., finding the sum of, or the maximum among, a set of values). Combining values from all processors (all to one) is called *global combine*. If the messages reach the destination intact and in their original forms, we have a *gather* operation. Combining saves communication bandwidth but is lossy in the sense that, in general, the original messages cannot be recovered from the combined version.

3. *Many to many.*   When the same message is sent by each of several processors to many destinations, we call the operation *many-to-many multicasting*. If all processors are involved as senders and receivers, we have *all-to-all broadcasting*. When

different messages are sent from each source to many (all) nodes, the operation performed is (*all-to-all*) *scatter-gather* (sometimes referred to as *gossiping*).

For 2D meshes and tori, we are particularly interested in the following three data routing operations:

1. *Data compaction or packing.* Many problems are solved by starting with a set of elements, as the parameters on which the final computation results depend, and successively removing some of the elements that are no longer useful or relevant. Rather than leave these elements in their original locations and pay the worst-case $\Omega(\sqrt{p})$ communication delay in all subsequent computations, we may want to compact or pack the useful or relevant data into the smallest possible submesh in order to speed up the rest of the process. Figure 10.1 shows an example where eight remaining elements in a 4×4 mesh are compacted or packed into a 3×3 submesh.

2. *Random-access write* (RAW). This operation can be viewed as emulating one memory write step of a PRAM having p processors and m memory locations on a distributed-memory machine that has p processors and m/p memory locations per processor. Each processor may have an address (consisting of destination processor ID and memory location within the processor) into which it wants to write its value. Thus, up to p write operations may be required that must be performed via routing of the destination/address/value messages to their destinations. Once there, the address/value part of the message is used for performing the write operation. Unique destination/address pairs correspond to the EREW submodel. Unique destinations correspond to a further restriction of EREW to a single access per memory block, as discussed in Section 6.6.

3. *Random-access read* (RAR). This operation is similar to RAW and all of the considerations discussed above apply to it. A RAR operation can be decomposed into two RAW operations as follows. In the first RAW operation, the requesting processors write their read access requests, including their own IDs, into the target processors. In the second RAW operation, which is somewhat more complex than the simple version discussed in the preceding paragraph if concurrent reads from the same location/module are to be allowed, the target processors write the results of the read requests into the requesting processors.

We will discuss the implementation of these operations in Section 10.3 after dealing with some useful elementary or building-block computations in Section 10.2.

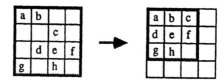

Figure 10.1. Example of data compaction or packing in a 2D mesh.

Processor addresses (also known as *node labels* or *node IDs*) can be specified by row–column numbers or according to their rank in a specified linear order such as those shown in Fig. 9.3. Such addresses are easily convertible to one another with a small, constant amount of computation. For example, a processor's rank k in row-major order can be obtained from its row number i and column number j based on the equation $k = i\sqrt{p} + j$. Conversely, the row and column numbers can be obtained from the processor's rank k in row-major order using $i = \lfloor k/\sqrt{p} \rfloor$ and $j = k \bmod \sqrt{p}$. Other ordering schemes are similar. For these reasons, in the remainder of our discussion of 2D mesh routing and various other algorithms, we switch freely between different addressing schemes, using each where it is most convenient.

10.2. USEFUL ELEMENTARY OPERATIONS

In performing data routing and many other operations on a 2D mesh, certain elementary operations arise quite frequently. It is convenient to review these operations before discussing routing algorithms.

Row or Column Rotation   (all-to-all broadcast within rows or columns).   In $\sqrt{p} - 1$ steps, data in one mesh row or column can be rotated once, such that each processor "sees" every data item. If each processor can send/receive data only to/from one neighbor at a time, $2\sqrt{p} - 2$ steps are needed, as right-moving and left-moving messages will be forced to alternate.

Sorting Records by a Key Field.   We presented and analyzed several sorting algorithms for 2D meshes in Chapter 9. In a permutation routing problem, routing the packets is equivalent to sorting them by the destination node address. In other situations, sorting is often used as one of several steps in designing the required routing algorithm.

Semigroup Computation.   A semigroup computation, such as summation or maximum finding, can be accomplished in $2\sqrt{p} - 2$ steps (optimal time) by using row rotations followed by column rotations with bidirectional communication. The time complexity increases to $4\sqrt{p} - 4$ if communication is restricted to one direction at a time. This simple algorithm was presented in Section 2.5. A recursive algorithm can be used that is particularly efficient in the second case above, but that requires commutativity as well as associativity. The mesh is divided into four quadrants and each quadrant recursively performs the semigroup computation in such a way that every processor in the quadrant knows the quadrant result. The quadrants then combine their results horizontally (Fig. 10.2); each processor in the center two columns exchanges values with its neighbor in the horizontally

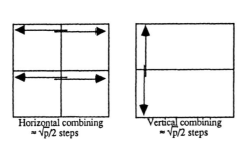

Horizontal combining   Vertical combining
≈ √p/2 steps   ≈ √p/2 steps

Figure 10.2. Recursive semigroup computation in a 2D mesh.

adjacent quadrant in one or two steps and then initiates a half-row broadcast. This phase thus requires $\sqrt{p}/2$ or $\sqrt{p}/2 + 1$ steps. Vertical combining in the next phase needs the same amount of time, leading to the recurrence $T(\sqrt{p}) = T(\sqrt{p}/2) + \sqrt{p} + 2\varepsilon$, where ε is 0 or 1. The solution to the above recurrence is $T(\sqrt{p}) = 2\sqrt{p} - 1 + \varepsilon\log_2 p$.

Parallel Prefix Computation.   A $(3\sqrt{p} - 3)$-step algorithm was given in Section 2.5. It was based on computing row prefixes, then doing a diminished prefix computation in the last column, and finally, broadcasting the results obtained in the last column within rows for final combining. As for semigroup computation, a more efficient recursive algorithm can be obtained if the binary operation is commutative. Quadrant prefixes are computed in row-major order, but in opposite directions in the left and right quadrants (Fig. 10.3). Vertical and horizontal combining take $\sqrt{p} + O(1)$ steps if the required data broadcasts, shown in the middle and right panels of Fig. 10.3, are pipelined. Supplying the details of the algorithm is left as an exercise.

Routing within a Row or Column.   Consider the problem of routing multiple packets on a linear array corresponding to a row or column of our square mesh. If the routing problem is a permutation, we simply apply $\sqrt{p}$ steps of odd–even transposition, using the destination addresses as the keys. Otherwise, we can proceed as follows (see Section 2.3). Each packet has an information part and a destination address part. It is more convenient to convert the destination addresses into a signed relative offset, with positive sign indicating movement to the right and negative sign corresponding to leftward movement. A processor's algorithm for dealing with a received packet is as follows. Figure 10.4 shows an example where right- and left-moving packets alternate.

Data routing on a linear array

        if *offset* = 0
        then remove the packet
        else if *offset* > 0
            then *offset* := *offset*–1; send to right neighbor
            else *offset* := *offset* + 1; send to left neighbor
            endif
        endif

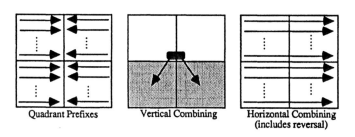

Quadrant Prefixes   Vertical Combining   Horizontal Combining
                                                   (includes reversal)

Figure 10.3. Recursive parallel prefix computation in a 2D mesh.

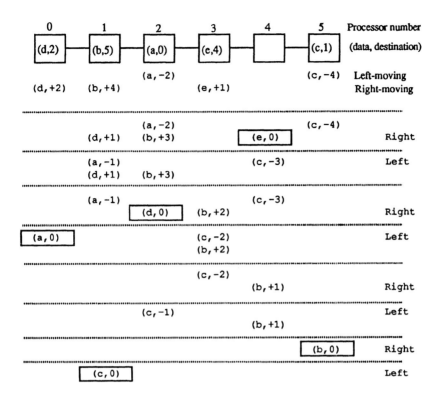

Figure 10.4. Example of routing multiple packets on a linear array.

In fact, the sign of the offset can be removed because each intermediate processor can recognize the direction in which the packet is moving from the port over which it was received. For example, in Fig. 9.4, a right-moving packet will enter through the R_3 port.

10.3 DATA ROUTING ON A 2D ARRAY

In this section, we discuss the three routing problems of data compaction (packing), random-access write (RAW), and random-access read (RAR) introduced in Section 10.1.

To pack a set of a values residing in active processors into the smallest possible square submesh in the upper left corner of the original mesh, we proceed as follows. First, each processor is assumed to hold a binary activity flag: 1 for active, 0 for inactive. A diminished parallel prefix sum on these activity flags yields the rank r of each active processor that is an integer in $[0, a - 1]$. This computation can be arranged such that, at the end, each active processor also knows the value of a. The dimension of the smallest square mesh that can hold a elements is $\lceil \sqrt{a} \rceil$. Thus, if the active processor holding the element with rank r sends it to the processor located in row $\lfloor r/\lceil \sqrt{a} \rceil \rfloor$, column $r \bmod \lceil \sqrt{a} \rceil$, the compaction or packing will be complete.

Considering the example shown in Fig. 10.1, the active processors holding the values "a" through "h" are ranked 0 through 7 as a result of the diminished parallel prefix computation (in row-major order), with $a = 8$ also becoming known to each active processor. The destination processor for the rank-r element is then determined to be in row $\lfloor r/3 \rfloor$, column r mod 3. The last step of the compaction or packing algorithm, which sends each element to its new location, is a RAW routing problem that we will describe next.

For RAW, we first consider the simple case where all destination processors are distinct, so that at most one write request will end up in each processor. If, in addition to the above constraint, every processor is required to participate, the routing problem is a permutation and we can easily solve it by simply sorting the packets by their destination addresses. For an incomplete, but exclusive RAW, where some processors do not have a write request, the following three-phase algorithm can be used.

Exclusive random-access write on a 2D mesh: *MeshRAW*

1. Sort the packets in column-major order by their destination column numbers, using the destination row numbers to break the ties.
2. Shift the packets to the right, so that each item is in the correct column. There will be no conflict because at most one element in each row is headed for a given column.
3. Route the packets within each column.

Figure 10.5 presents an example. At the left, we see the initial packet positions, with the destination row and column numbers given. In the second diagram from the left, the packets have been sorted in column-major order by their destination column numbers; packets headed for Column 0 appear first, followed by those headed for Column 1, and so forth. Next, the packets have been shifted to the right, if needed, so that each is in its destination column. Finally, the rightmost diagram in Fig. 10.5 depicts the state of the messages after the completion of routing within the columns.

Note that with the above algorithm, the packets do not necessarily take the shortest paths to their destinations. For example, in Fig. 10.5, the packet headed to Processor (3, 1) begins at Processor (2, 2), moves to Processor (0, 1) because of sorting, remains there in the row routing phase, and finally, moves down to its final location. This packet is forwarded at least six times (we cannot say for sure, as the sorting algorithm used is unspecified) to get to a destination that is only two hops away via a shortest path.

The above observation may lead to the concern that our RAW algorithm is inefficient. However, this is not the case. After the sorting phase, at most $p^{1/2} - 1$ row routing steps and

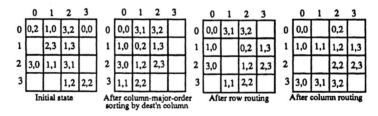

Figure 10.5. Example of random-access write on a 2D mesh.

$p^{1/2} - 1$ column routing steps are required. Row routing is always from left to right, so its time complexity does not change even if we allow only unidirectional communication. In the latter case, the time for the column routing phase may double to $2p^{1/2} - 2$. Assuming the use of the $(3p^{1/2} + o(p^{1/2}))$-step snakelike sorting algorithm of Section 9.6, suitably modified to do the sorting in column-major order and then reversing the order of odd-numbered columns, the total running time of the RAW algorithm is $6p^{1/2} + o(p^{1/2})$. With unidirectional communication, the constant 6 in the above expression will increase to 11 (why?).

In the following sections of this chapter, we will study some methods for, and the implication of, improving the running time of RAW in order to bring it closer to the absolute $2p^{1/2} - 2$ lower bound imposed by the diameter. Before that, however, we need to consider the problem of concurrent writes into the same processor.

If multiple write requests to the same processor are allowed, then routing can no longer be assumed to be conflict-free. In the worst case, all p write requests are addressed to the same processor. As, independent of the routing algorithm used, a processor cannot receive more than four packets in any one step, the worst-case running time is lower-bounded by $p/4$ (p, if only one communication is allowed per cycle). Because of this large speed penalty for concurrent RAWs, hot spots should be avoided to the extent possible. On the positive side, the processor to which multiple write requests are directed can use any priority or combining scheme to decide on the value to be written into a given memory location. So, even very complex selection or combining rules do not slow down the processor further.

An exclusive RAR operation, with each processor reading from a unique processor, can be implemented as two RAW operations. Concurrent reads can be handled with a slightly more complicated algorithm, as follows. If Processor i wants to read from Processor j, it constructs a record $< i, j >$. These records are sorted according to the key j. At this point, all read requests addressed to Processor j will reside in consecutive processors (say, k, $k+1$, . . . , $k + l - 1$). One of these processors (say k) will do the reading from j and broadcasts the value to the others. Finally, each read result is routed back to the requesting processor (i).

10.4. GREEDY ROUTING ALGORITHMS

A greedy routing algorithm is one that tries to reduce the distance of a packet from its destination with every routing step. The term *greedy* refers to the fact that such an algorithm only considers local short-term gains as opposed to the global or long-term effects of each routing decision. The simplest greedy algorithm is *dimension-ordered routing* or *e-cube* routing. The row-first version of the dimension-ordered routing algorithm is as follows.

Greedy row-first routing on a 2D mesh

> if the packet is not in the destination column
> then route it along the row toward the destination column
>> {processors have buffers to hold the incoming messages.}
> else route it along the column toward the destination node
>> {of the messages that need to use an upward or downward link,
>> the one that needs to go farthest along the column goes first.}
> endif

If the buffer space in each processor is unlimited, the greedy row-first algorithm is optimal and terminates in no more than $2p^{1/2} - 2$ steps for exclusive RAW. Clearly, the row routing phase needs at most $p^{1/2} - 1$ steps, provided that the processors can accept incoming messages from left and right simultaneously. If two messages destined for Column j arrive into the same processor, they can leave in the next step if they need to travel in different directions along the column. However, if both messages want to go in the same direction along the column, or if higher-priority messages exist among those waiting in the node's buffers, then one or both messages will be delayed for at least an extra cycle. Giving priority to messages that need to go farther along the column ensures that this phase takes no more than $p^{1/2}-1$ steps in all; this is easy to prove by noting that a message delayed by δ cycles does not need to move more than $p^{1/2} - 1 - \delta$ steps.

Figure 10.6 depicts the use of row-first algorithm for an exclusive RAW operation. In the initial state, all packets, except the one in Row 2, Column 0, have to move to a different column. Thus, they are routed horizontally toward their destination columns. The packet destined for Processor (0, 0) starts its column routing phase right away, moving to Row 1, Column 0, in the first step. Similarly, other packets begin their column routing phases as soon as each arrives into its destination column. In this particular example, no routing conflict is encountered and each packet gets to its destination in the shortest possible time. The maximum number of packets residing at any one node at a given time is two. This situation (dearth of conflicts and small buffer space requirements) is typical for random routing problems.

In the worst case, however, greedy routing suffers from degraded performance. Even assuming distinct destinations, the required node buffer size is $O(p^{1/2})$ in the worst case. For example, in Fig. 10.7, Node (i, j) receives two messages per cycle that are headed to nodes below it in the same column. Because only one message can be sent downward in each cycle, the node requires up to $p^{1/2}/2$ message buffers to keep the rest. In fact, once the messages arriving from above are also taken into account, the situation becomes worse and the buffer requirement increases to $2p^{1/2}/3$. However, with randomly distributed destinations, both the buffer requirements and the added delay related to conflicts will be $O(1)$ with high probability.

Based on our discussions of routing methods for a 2D mesh thus far, we are faced with a trade-off; i.e., a choice between the fast $(2p^{1/2}-2)$-step greedy routing scheme presented above, which requires fairly expensive buffers in each node to guarantee that buffer overflow will not occur, or the slower $6p^{1/2}$-step algorithm of Section 10.3, which avoids conflicts altogether and thus requires a single buffer per node. Ideally, we would like to have the

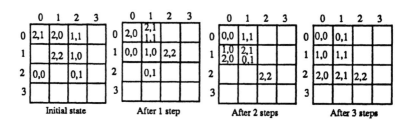

Figure 10.6. Example of greedy row-first routing on a 2D mesh.

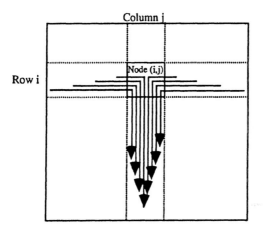

Figure 10.7. Demonstrating the worst-case buffer requirement with row-first routing.

highest speed with a constant buffer space per node. This, while possible, leads to a very complicated algorithm with fairly large buffers. So, from a practical standpoint, it makes sense to look for intermediate solutions with running times between $2p^{1/2}$ and $6p^{1/2}$ and buffer requirements between 0 and $O(p^{1/2})$.

The following algorithm is one such intermediate solution that needs $(2 + 4/q)p^{1/2} + o(p^{1/2}/q)$ routing steps with $2q - 1$ buffers per node. For $q = 1$, this algorithm degenerates into the one described in Section 10.3, while for very large q, it yields near-optimal speed. As an example of speed–cost trade-offs, the algorithm turns into a $3p^{1/2}$-step algorithm requiring seven message buffers per node if we pick $q = 4$.

The intermediate exclusive RAW routing algorithm is as follows. We view the p-processor mesh as q^2 square blocks of size $p^{1/2}/q$ (Fig. 10.8). We sort the packets in each block in column-major order according to their destination columns and then use the greedy routing algorithm discussed above to complete the routing. Using the optimal snakelike sorting algorithm of Section 9.6 and then reversing the order of elements in alternate columns allows us to complete the sorting phase in $4p^{1/2}/q + o(p^{1/2}/q)$ steps. The greedy routing phase takes $2p^{1/2} - 2$ steps. So, the correctness of the claimed running time is established. It only remains to be shown that $2q - 1$ message buffers are adequate.

Consider Row i and call the blocks containing it $B_0, B_1, B_2, ..., B_{q-1}$. Let r_k be the number of packets in B_k $(0 \le k < q)$ that are headed for Column j. Clearly, $\Sigma_{k=0}^{q-1} r_k \le p^{1/2}$, because at most $p^{1/2}$ packets go to Column j; given the assumption of distinct destinations (exclusive RAW). After sorting the blocks in column-major order, the packets in each block that are headed for Column j will be evenly divided between the $p^{1/2}/q$ rows. Thus, the total number of packets in Row i that are headed to Column j will be upper bounded by

$$\sum_{k=0}^{q-1} \left\lceil \frac{r_k}{p^{1/2}/q} \right\rceil < \sum_{k=0}^{q-1} \left(1 + \frac{r_k}{p^{1/2}/q} \right) \le q + (q/p^{1/2}) \sum_{k=0}^{q-1} r_k \le 2q$$

Note that in the above derivation, we have made use of the strict inequality $\lceil x \rceil < 1 + x$ to show that the number of message buffers needed is strictly less than $2q$ or at most $2q - 1$.

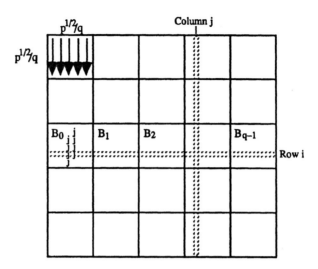

Figure 10.8. Illustrating the structure of the intermediate routing algorithm.

The design of a $(2p^{1/2} + o(p^{1/2}))$-step routing algorithm with constant queue size per node has been addressed by many researchers. Initial solutions [Leig89] involved large constant-size queues (i.e., independent of p). Even though subsequent refinements have reduced the queue size, these algorithms are still not quite practical. For example, the work of Gu and Gu [Gu95] has reduced the number of buffers to the constant 28 for a $(2p^{1/2} + O(1))$-step algorithm and to $12t_s/s$ for an optimal $(2p^{1/2} - 2)$-step algorithm, where t_s is the sorting time on an $s \times s$ mesh. The design of an asymptotically optimal $(2p^{1/2} + o(p^{1/2}))$-step routing algorithm with a small number of buffers (say 3 or 4) per node is still an open problem.

10.5. OTHER CLASSES OF ROUTING ALGORITHMS

Our inability to design fast deterministic routing algorithms with small buffers has led to an interest in randomized or probabilistic algorithms. One can prove that if the destination nodes are randomly distributed in the 2D array, the probability that a given packet is delayed by Δ additional steps because of conflicts in the row-first greedy algorithm is $O(e^{-\Delta/6})$. In view of the exponentially decreasing probabilities for larger delays, the expected delay related to conflicts is $O(1)$ and any packet needing to travel d hops reaches its destination in $d + O(\log p)$ steps with probability $1 - O(1/p)$. Furthermore, with a probability very close to 1, no more than four packets ever wait for transmission over the same link. Proofs of the above claims and related results have been given by Leighton ([Leig92], pp. 163–173).

In view of the very good average-case performance of the row-first greedy routing algorithm (on a randomized instance of the routing problem), it may be beneficial to convert an arbitrary (nonrandom) routing problem into two randomized instances by selecting a random intermediate destination for each packet and then doing the routing in two phases: from the source nodes to the randomly selected intermediate nodes and from these nodes to the desired destinations.

Independent of the routing algorithm used, concurrent writes can degrade the time complexity to $\Theta(p)$. However, it might be possible to reduce this time complexity to $O(p^{1/2})$ by allowing intermediate nodes to combine multiple write requests that are headed to the same destination node. Combining means applying the concurrent write rules to multiple writes destined for the same processor. This is possible if each processor has but one memory location (or a single location that may be accessed concurrently by multiple processors). Figure 10.9 shows an example where five write requests headed to the same destination node are combined into two requests by intermediate nodes.

The routing algorithms discussed thus far belong to the class of *oblivious* routing algorithms. A routing algorithm is oblivious if the path selected for the message going from Processor i to Processor j is dependent only on i and j and is in no way affected by other messages that may exist in the system. A *nonoblivious* or *adaptive* routing algorithm, on the other hand, allows the path to change as a result of link/processor congestion or failure.

Consider, for example, an algorithm that allows a packet to interlace horizontal and vertical movements, without any restriction, until it gets to the destination row or column, at which point it is restricted to move only along the row or column on its way to the destination node. Such a packet will still travel along a shortest path, but can avoid congested paths by taking alternate routes. A packet on its way from node (0, 0) to node (3, 2), on entering node (0, 1), can exit vertically to node (1, 1) if the vertical link is available but the horizontal link to node (0, 2) is not. Of course, there is no guarantee that the packet will get to its destination faster via this alternate path, as it may encounter congestion or faulty links/nodes farther ahead. But probabilistically, the availability of alternate paths helps reduce the routing time and provides some degree of resilience to permanent and/or transient node/link malfunctions.

As a second example of adaptive algorithms, consider the class of algorithms that provide one buffer per port in each processor and always send out the received messages (up to four) to neighboring processors if they are not addressed to the local processor. This class of algorithms is sometimes referred to as *hot-potato routing* because each processor immediately gets rid of any incoming message. As messages may be deflected away from the shortest path to their destinations, a control mechanism is needed to ensure that they do not wander about in the mesh without ever reaching their destinations. For example, a priority scheme based on the message age (time steps since its origination) may be used to choose which of several messages contending for the same outgoing edge should be allowed to use

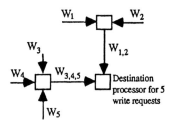

Figure 10.9. Combining of write requests headed for the same destination.

it and which are to be deflected to other nodes that may not be on their respective shortest paths.

Methods to introduce adaptivity into routing algorithms via proper organization of the information available about the network and the state of packet traffic as well as heuristics for making the "right" path selection with high probability constitute active areas of research in parallel processing.

Let us now say a few words about collective communication on 2D meshes using packet routing. Broadcasting can be simply achieved in two phases: row broadcast followed by column broadcast, or vice versa. All-to-all broadcasting can be performed in optimal $O(p)$ time using row and column rotations. Multicasting is very similar to broadcasting, except that each packet must contain information about its destinations. If the set of destinations is a submesh, or one of a previously agreed upon groups of processors, this information can be encoded compactly within the message. For many-to-many communication, routing can be performed in rounds. For example, if we have $k–k$ routing where each processor sends exactly k messages and receives exactly k messages, the problem can be decomposed into k $1–1$ routing problems that are then solved one at a time. Of course, all-to-all scatter-gather is a $p–p$ routing problem that can be solved in p rounds, or $O(p\sqrt{p})$ steps. This is asymptotically optimal because of the $p^2/4$ messages that have to pass through the $\sqrt{p}$ bisection of the 2D mesh.

Thus far, we have focused on routing problems in which all of the packets to be routed to their respective destinations initially reside in the mesh. These are known as *static routing* problems. In *dynamic routing* problems, messages are created by the various processors at regular intervals or at random (perhaps with a known distribution). The performance of routing algorithms for such dynamically created messages can be analyzed using methods from queuing theory, via simulation on a software model of the mesh architecture, or through actual programming and observation of a real machine. Analytical evaluation of routing algorithms often requires simplifying assumptions that may or may not hold in practice. Thus, even in such cases, experimental verification of the results may be required.

As an example of theoretical results for dynamic routing, consider the case of a synchronous array where, in any given cycle, a new packet is introduced at each node with a constant probability λ, where $\lambda < 4/\sqrt{p}$. The reason for restricting λ as above is that for $\lambda \geq 4/\sqrt{p}$, the expected number of packets crossing the bisection would be $\lambda(p/2(1/2)) \geq \sqrt{p}$, which can result in unbounded delays. One can prove that with greedy row-first routing, the probability that any particular packet is delayed by Δ steps beyond the length of the shortest path is an exponentially decreasing function of Δ, provided that the arrival rate of the packets is below (say at 99% of) the network capacity. Also, in any window of w steps, the maximum delay incurred by one packet is $O(\log w + \log p)$ and the maximum observed queue size is $O(1 + \log w / \log p)$. Thus, simple greedy routing can be expected to perform reasonably well under dynamic routing with the above conditions. Details have been given by Leighton ([Leig92], pp. 173–178).

10.6. WORMHOLE ROUTING

We have thus far discussed routing schemes in which a packet moves from node to node in its entirety. Because each packet is stored in an intermediate node before being forwarded to the next node on its path to the destination, this method is referred to as *store-and-forward routing* or *packet switching*. At the other extreme, we can use *circuit switching* where a dedicated path is established between the source and destination nodes (e.g., through link and node reservations) before the message is actually sent. This may be advantageous for very long messages, which would otherwise experience significant delays because of multiple storage and forwarding times and conflict-induced waits. However, the path setup and teardown times nullify some of this gain. *Wormhole switching or routing* is an intermediate solution that has become quite popular.

In wormhole routing, each packet is viewed as consisting of a sequence of *flits* (flow-control digits, typically 1–2 bytes). Flits, rather than complete packets, are forwarded between nodes, with all flits of a packet following its *head flit* like a worm (Fig. 10.10). At any given time, the flits of a packet occupy a set of nodes on the selected path from the source to the destination. However, links become available for use by other worms as soon as the tail of a worm has passed through. Therefore, links are used more efficiently compared with circuit switching. The down side of not reserving the entire path before transmitting a message is that deadlocks may arise when multiple worms block each other in a circular fashion (Fig. 10.10).

Theoretically speaking, any routing algorithm can be used to select the path of a worm. However, a simple algorithm is preferable as it can minimize the decision time, and thus the node-to-node delay, allowing the worm to travel faster. If we choose the row-first greedy algorithm, a possible format for the worm is as follows. The first flit indicates relative movement in the row direction (0 to 255 with 1 byte, e.g.). Sign or direction of movement is not needed as it is implicit in the incoming channel. The second flit indicates relative movement in the column direction (sign is needed here). The worm starts in the horizontal direction. Each intermediate processor decrements the head flit and forwards the head in the same direction as received. When the head flit becomes 0, the processor discards it and turns the worm in the vertical direction. A worm received in the vertical direction with its head flit containing 0 is at its destination.

Figure 10.11 shows some of the ways of handling conflicts in wormhole routing. One option is to buffer or store the worm until its needed outgoing channel becomes available. This option, which is intermediate between circuit switching and store-and-forward routing, is sometimes referred to as *virtual cut-through* routing. Its disadvantage is that it leads to excessive node complexity if buffer space is to be provided for the worst case. This complexity adversely affects the cost of the node as well as its speed.

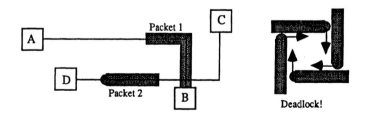

Figure 10.10. The notions of worms and deadlock in wormhole routing.

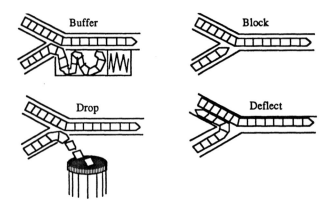

Figure 10.11. Various ways of dealing with conflicts in wormhole routing.

A second option is to block all but one of the conflicting worms, allowing a selected worm (based on some priority scheme) to advance toward its destination. The blocked worms will eventually start advancing, provided there is no deadlock.

A third option is to simply discard all but one of the conflicting worms, again based on some sort of priority. This scheme assumes the use of an acknowledgment mechanism between the receiver and the sender. For example, if the worms carry memory read requests, the acknowledgment takes the form of the returned memory value. The requesting processor can send a duplicate request if it has not received a reply to the original one within a reasonable amount of time. With this method, the nodes become quite simple because they do not need to store anything. However, message delay and network load increase as a result of the retransmissions. Under heavy load, the bulk of network capacity will be taken up by retransmissions, leading to poor efficiency and excessive delay.

Finally, some of the conflicting worms can be deflected to nodes other than the ones on the designated path (*hot-potato* routing). This may take the worm farther away from its destination but has the advantage of requiring no intermediate storage for the worms and no dropped worms. Of course, care must be taken to prevent a worm from going in circles, thus wasting communication bandwidth and never reaching its destination.

Various deadlock avoidance strategies are available. To determine if deadlock is possible, draw a graph with one node for each link in the original graph and an edge from Node i to j if the routing algorithm allows the use of j immediately after i. A sufficient condition for deadlock-freedom is that this *dependence graph* be cycle-free. This is in fact too strong a condition in that there exist routing algorithms that are free from deadlock but that their corresponding dependence graphs have cycles. Much research has dealt with determining the minimum restrictions needed for the routing algorithm to guarantee freedom from deadlock.

An example is shown in Fig. 10.12. A 3×3 mesh, with its associated edge labels, is shown at the top. With unrestricted or adaptive shortest-path routing, the dependence graph is as shown at the bottom left. In this case, after routing along Edge 7, any of Edges 11, 14, or 17 can be used. This directed graph has many cycles, thus the corresponding algorithm can lead to deadlocks. The row-first greedy algorithm, characterized by the dependence graph on the lower right, has no cycles, leading us to the conclusion that it must be deadlock-free.

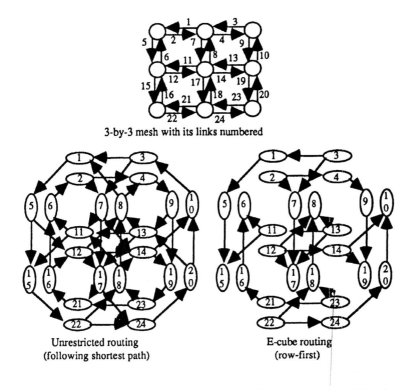

3-by-3 mesh with its links numbered

Unrestricted routing
(following shortest path)

E-cube routing
(row-first)

Figure 10.12. Use of dependence graph to check for the possibility of deadlock.

One way to avoid deadlocks is through the use of virtual channels; i.e., sharing a physical link by multiple virtual channels, each with its own flit buffer and a chance to be used according to a round-robin schedule. For example, Fig. 10.13 shows the use of two virtual channels on a northbound link, one each for westward-moving and eastward-moving worms. Deadlocks can always be avoided through the use of a sufficient number of virtual channels.

We have discussed wormhole routing only in connection with point-to-point messages. Collective communication can also be done through wormhole routing. A rich theory for such data communication problems has emerged in recent years [McKi95].

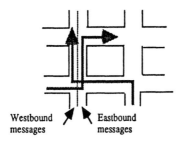

Westbound
messages

Eastbound
messages

Figure 10.13. Use of virtual channels for avoiding deadlocks.

PROBLEMS

10.1. Recursive parallel prefix computation
Specify the details of the parallel prefix computation algorithm given in Fig. 10.3. Present an analysis of your algorithm and determine an exact value for the $O(1)$ term in its performance.

10.2. Data routing on a linear array
a. Show that any k-to-1 routing problem can be solved in $p + k - 1$ steps on a p-processor linear array, provided that each processor starts with at most one packet.
b. How does the time complexity of the k-to-1 routing problem change if each processor can start with up to k packets and there are at most p packets overall?

10.3. Sorting-based routing on a 2D mesh
Consider the routing algorithm for 2D meshes in Section 10.3 with the added assumption that up to k packets can have the same destination.
a. Determine the worst-case running time of the algorithm with unlimited node buffers.
b. Determine the worst-case buffer space requirement per node.

10.4. Greedy row-first routing on a 2D mesh
a. Show that $2\sqrt{p}/3$ message buffers per node are adequate to ensure that the greedy row-first algorithm can run at full speed on a p-processor square mesh.
b. Show that the row-first greedy routing algorithm takes $\Theta(p)$ steps in the worst case if each node is constrained to have a constant number of message buffers (say 4).

10.5. Greedy routing on a 2D mesh
If data are to be routed on a nonsquare $r \times (p/r)$ mesh, which of the two greedy routing algorithms, row-first or column-first, would minimize the required buffer space per node? First assume distinct destinations, then relax this assumption.

10.6. Data compaction or packing
a. Analyze the data compaction or packing problem, described in Section 10.3, with regard to conflicts and buffer requirements when an adaptive packet routing algorithm is used.
b. Repeat part (a) for wormhole routing, focusing on the possibility of deadlock.

10.7. Greedy row-first routing on a 2D mesh
a. For a 4×4 mesh, determine the relative message load of each of the 24 links if row-first greedy routing is used and each node sends the same number of messages to every other node on the average.
b. How will the distribution change if messages sent by the same processor alternate between row-first and column-first routing?
c. Repeat part (a) for a 4×4 torus.
d. Repeat part (b) for a 4×4 torus.

10.8. Greedy row-first routing on a 2D mesh
Consider a scenario where node (i, j) in a square 2D mesh begins with x_{ij} packets to be routed, where the x_{ij} are independent Poisson random variables with mean λ, that is, $\text{prob}[x_{ij} = k] = \lambda^k e^{-\lambda}/k!$. Prove the following results.
a. The greedy row-first algorithm routes each packet with constant expected delay iff $\lambda < 1$.
b. The expected maximum queue size is constant iff $\lambda < 2$.

c. The condition of part (a) becomes "iff $\lambda < 2$" if the mesh is replaced with a torus.

d. The condition of part (b) becomes "iff $\lambda < 4$" if the mesh is replaced with a torus.

10.9. Greedy routing on a 2D mesh

Analyze the behavior of greedy row-first routing on a 2D mesh if it is known that no packet is more than d hops away from its intended destination, where d is a known constant independent of p.

10.10. Greedy routing on a complete binary tree

Analyze the behavior of a greedy routing algorithm on a complete binary tree with respect to running time and maximum number of message buffers per node. Specify your protocol for conflict resolution.

10.11. Wormhole routing

Analyze the following algorithm for broadcasting on a 2D mesh using point-to-point wormhole routing. The source node sends four messages to the four processors located at the lower left corner of each of the four quadrants of the mesh. Each of these four processors then uses the same method to broadcast the message within its own quadrant.

10.12. Wormhole routing

Consider wormhole routing with very short messages consisting of one header flit (holding the destination row and column offsets) and a single information flit.

a. Does wormhole routing still have advantages over packet routing in this case?

b. Is deadlock possible with such short messages?

c. Suppose that the single information flit holds the ID number of the sending processor. Can a message that carries only the destination and source addresses serve any useful purpose?

d. Going a step further, does it make sense for a message to hold only the destination address?

10.13. The turn model for adaptive wormhole routing

When routing on a 2D mesh, eight types of turns (four clockwise and four counterclockwise) are possible in switching from row/column movement to column/row movement. Show how by disallowing two of these turns, one from each set, an adaptive deadlock-free routing algorithm can be constructed that uses the remaining six turns without any restriction and does not need virtual channels [Glas92].

10.14. Interval routing

Interval routing is a routing scheme in which one or more intervals of nodes are associated with each outgoing link of a node, with a message sent out over a link if the destination node number is contained in one of the intervals associated with that link. In the simplest case, exemplified by the seven-node X-tree architecture shown below, a single interval is associated with each link and the intervals for different outgoing links do not overlap, leading to unique paths.

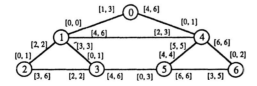

a. For the seven-node X-tree architecture shown above, determine the relative message load on each link if, on the average, each node sends the same number of messages to every other node.

b. Draw a link dependence graph and prove that deadlock is impossible with wormhole routing.

c. Replacing each bidirectional link with two unidirectional ones, divide the network into two subnetworks: the down/right subnetwork consisting of links that point downward or to the right, and the up/left subnetwork with upward and leftward links. Show that any assignment of intervals (or any routing scheme, for that matter) that causes a path to begin in the first subnetwork and either end in the same subnetwork or move to the second subnetwork after 0 or more hops and stay there until getting to the destination, is guaranteed to be deadlock-free.

d. Devise an interval routing scheme for a 4×4 mesh, with one interval attached to each link, that divides the load as equally as possible between the 24 links and is also deadlock-free. You are free to choose the node indexing scheme. *Hint:* The result of part (c) may help.

REFERENCES AND SUGGESTED READING

[Felp96]   Felperin, S., P. Raghavan, and E. Upfal, "A Theory of Wormhole Routing in Parallel Computers," *IEEE Trans. Computers*, Vol. 45, No. 6, pp. 704–713, June 1996.

[Glas92]   Glass, C. J. and L. M. Ni, "The Turn Model for Adaptive Routing," *Proc. 19th Int. Symp. Computer Architecture*, 1992, pp. 278–287.

[Gu95]   Gu, Q.-P., and J. Gu, "Two Packet Routing Algorithms on a Mesh-Connected Computer," *IEEE Trans. Parallel Distributed Systems*, Vol. 6, No. 4, pp. 436–440, April 1995.

[Leig89]   Leighton, T., F. Makedon, and I. G. Tollis, "A $2n–2$ Step Algorithm for Routing in an $n \times n$ Array with Constant Size Queues," *Proc. 1st ACM Symp. Parallel Algorithms and Architectures*, 1989, pp. 328–335.

[Leig92]   Leighton, F. T., *Introduction to Parallel Algorithms and Architectures: Arrays, Trees, Hypercubes*, Morgan Kaufmann, 1992.

[McKi95]   McKinley, P. K., Y.-J. Tsai, and D. F. Robinson, "Collective Communication in Wormhole-Routed Massively Parallel Computers," *IEEE Computer*, Vol. 28, No. 12, pp. 39–50, December 1995.

[MPIF94]   Message-Passing Interface Forum, "MPI: A Message-Passing Interface Standard," Version 1.0, University of Tennessee, Knoxville, 1994.

[Pink97]   Pinkston, T. M., and S. Warnakulasuriya, "On Deadlocks in Interconnection Networks," *Proc. Int. Symp. Computer Architecture*, 1997, pp. 38–49.

11

Numerical 2D Mesh Algorithms

In Chapters 9 and 10, we discussed 2D-mesh sorting and routing algorithms that are important in themselves and also form useful tools for synthesizing other parallel algorithms of interest. In this chapter, we cover a sample of numerical and seminumerical algorithms for 2D meshes. Even though the problems covered here do not exhaust all interesting or practically important algorithms, they do expose us to a variety of techniques and problems in parallel algorithm design for 2D mesh-connected computers. We should then be able to handle other applications with the knowledge gained from this chapter and the previous two. Chapter topics are

- 11.1. Matrix multiplication
- 11.2. Triangular system of equations
- 11.3. Tridiagonal system of linear equations
- 11.4. Arbitrary system of linear equations
- 11.5. Graph algorithms
- 11.6. Image-processing algorithms

11.1. MATRIX MULTIPLICATION

The matrix multiplication problem was defined in Section 5.6, where several PRAM algorithms were developed for solving the problem. To facilitate the development of a 2D mesh algorithm for matrix multiplication, we first consider matrix–vector multiplication on a linear array. Let A be an $m \times m$ matrix and x an m-vector. The product $y = Ax$ is an m-vector such that

$$y_i = \sum_{j=0}^{m-1} a_{ij} x_j$$

Figure 11.1 shows how the computation for $m = 4$ (including the presentation of the inputs A and x and the extraction of the output y) can be organized on a four-processor linear array. In the first computation step, a_{00} and x_0 are presented to Processor P_0, which computes their product $a_{00}x_0$, keeping the result in an internal register. P_0 then adds the products $a_{01}x_1$, $a_{02}x_2$, and $a_{03}x_3$ to its running sum in the next three computation cycles, obtaining its final result y_0 at the end of the fourth computation cycle. Similarly, P_1 computes and adds the terms $a_{10}x_0$, $a_{11}x_1$, $a_{12}x_2$, and $a_{13}x_3$, beginning with the second computation cycle and finishing in the fifth cycle. The x_j inputs are shifted from left to right after one cycle of delay in each processor. The last result, y_3, becomes available at the end of the seventh cycle.

With inputs of dimension m and $p = m$ processors, the computation takes $2m - 1 = 2p - 1$ cycles, each cycle corresponding to a processor performing a multiplication and an addition.

Because multiplying two $m \times m$ matrices can be viewed as m separate matrix–vector multiplications, the computation structure of Fig. 11.1 can be readily extended to an $m \times m$ processor array multiplying two $m \times m$ matrices (Fig. 11.2). The first row of processors is essentially identical to Fig. 11.1, receiving matrix A from above and Column 0 of matrix B from the left and computing Column 0 of the result matrix C. In general, Row j of the array will compute Column j of the result matrix, using all elements of A and only Column j of B, according to the equation

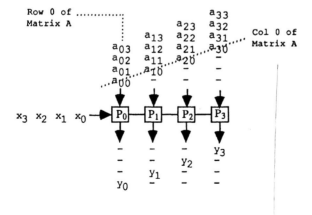

Figure 11.1. Matrix–vector multiplication on a linear array.

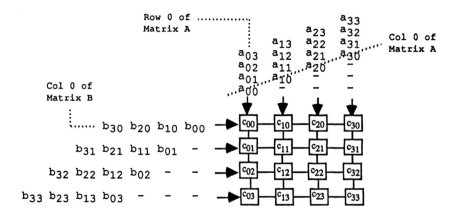

Figure 11.2. Matrix–matrix multiplication on a 2D mesh.

$$C_{ij} = \sum_{k=0}^{m-1} a_{ik}b_{kj}$$

Because elements of A are delayed by one cycle for each row of processors, columns of B must be similarly delayed at input in order for relative timings to be preserved in each row. The total computation time is $3m - 2 = 3\sqrt{p} - 2$ steps (there are $p = m^2$ processors).

Adding a wraparound link to Fig. 11.1 converts the architecture into a ring and allows us to rotate the elements of x, initially stored as shown in the example of Fig. 11.3, among the processors. Elements of A can be input from above or stored in the local memories of the processors, with P_j holding Row j of A. Figure 11.3 shows a snapshot of the computation when P_0 is reading or receiving x_0 from P_3 and a_{00} from above (or reading it from its local memory). This corresponds exactly to P_0's status in Fig. 11.1. However, whereas all other processors are idle in the snapshot shown in Fig. 11.1, no idle cycle is ever encountered here. Elimination of idle processor cycles reduces the computation time to the optimal $m = p$ steps (p^2 multiply–add operations done by p processors in p cycles).

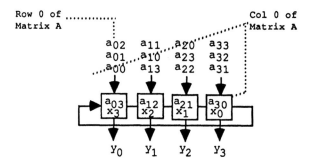

Figure 11.3. Matrix–vector multiplication on a ring.

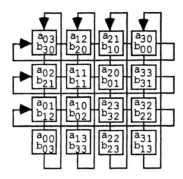

Figure 11.4. Matrix–matrix multiplication on a torus.

Adding wraparound links to Fig. 11.2 converts the architecture into a torus. Elements of A and B can now be stored into the processors as shown in Fig. 11.4. Elements of A are rotated vertically in the columns, while those of B undergo horizontal rotation in the rows. In the snapshot shown in Fig. 11.4, Processor P_{00} is reading or receiving a_{00} from P_{30} and b_{00} from P_{03}. This corresponds exactly to P_{00}'s status in Fig. 11.2. Again, no processor is ever idle. The computation time is reduced from $3\sqrt{p} - 2$ steps to the optimal $\sqrt{p}$ steps ($p^{3/2}$ multiply–add operations done by p processors in $p^{1/2}$ cycles).

The arrangement shown in Fig. 11.4 is easily extended to the practical situation when large $m \times m$ matrices must be multiplied on a small p-processor mesh ($p \ll m^2$). In this case, the elements a_{ij} and b_{ij} shown in the figure actually represent $(m/p^{1/2}) \times (m/p^{1/2})$ blocks of the two matrices, with regular multiplication/addition operations replaced by matrix multiplication/addition. Despite the fact that large matrix blocks cannot be passed between processors in a single cycle, arrangements can be made such that data transfers and computations overlap. As a processor works on multiplying its current blocks, the next A and B blocks needed will be loaded into its memory. In multiplying matrix blocks, the processor performs $(m/p^{1/2})^3$ multiply–add operations on $2(m/p^{1/2})^2$ data elements. Thus, there will be ample time for performing the required data transfers when $m/p^{1/2}$ is fairly large.

11.2. TRIANGULAR SYSTEM OF EQUATIONS

A (*lower/upper*) *triangular* square matrix is one in which all elements above the main diagonal or all elements below it are 0s, respectively (Fig. 11.5). If, additionally, all of the elements on the main diagonal are also 0s, the triangular matrix is called *strictly lower/upper triangular*. The determinant of an $m \times m$ triangular matrix A is $\Pi_{i=0}^{m-1} a_{ii}$. We will deal with lower triangular matrices only, but the techniques discussed can be applied to upper triangular matrices as well.

A triangular system of linear equations, written in matrix form as $Ax = b$, is one in which the matrix A is (lower) triangular. The $Ax = b$ matrix form is shorthand for

$$a_{00}x_0 \qquad\qquad\qquad\qquad = b_0$$

$$a_{10}x_0 + a_{11}x_1 \qquad\qquad\qquad = b_1$$

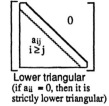 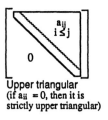

Lower triangular
(if $a_{ii} = 0$, then it is
strictly lower triangular)

Upper triangular
(if $a_{ii} = 0$, then it is
strictly upper triangular)

Figure 11.5. Lower/upper triangular square matrix.

$$a_{20}x_0 + a_{21}x_1 + a_{22}x_2 \qquad\qquad\qquad = b_2$$

$$\vdots$$

$$a_{m-1,0}x_0 + a_{m-1,1}x_1 + \ldots + a_{m-1,m-1}x_{m-1} \quad = b_{m-1}$$

Such a triangular system of linear equations can be easily solved by *back substitution*. Compute x_0 from the top equation, substitute into the next equation to find x_1, and so forth. In the ith step, when Equation i is being dealt with, we need i multiplications to compute the terms containing the already known variables, i subtractions to compute the new right-hand side, and one division by a_{ii} to compute the value of x_i. Thus, the total number of arithmetic operations is

$$\sum_{i=0}^{m-1} (2i + 1) = m^2$$

For comparison purposes, and to demonstrate that the algorithm contains a significant amount of parallelism, we first implement the back substitution algorithm on PRAM with $p = m$ processors:

Back substitution on an m-processor PRAM

> Processor i, $0 \le i < m$, do $t_i := b_i$
> for $j = 0$ to $m - 1$ do
>   Processor j compute $x_j := t_j/a_{jj}$
>   Processor j broadcast x_j to all other processors
>   Processor i, $j < i < m$, do $t_i := t_i - a_{ij}x_j$
> endfor

On a CREW PRAM, the broadcasting step is simply a concurrent memory access operation. Thus, each iteration of the algorithm involves three arithmetic operations, yielding a total running time of $3p$ steps and a speed-up of $p/3$.

Performing back substitution for m lower-triangular equations on a linear array of m processors is straightforward. As shown in Fig. 11.6, the lower triangular matrix A is input to the array from above and the b vector from the right (this represents the t vector being initialized to b). If the computation begins from the initial state depicted in Fig. 11.6, with $t_0 = b_0$ being available to the leftmost processor, then $2m - 1$ steps are needed (the first output

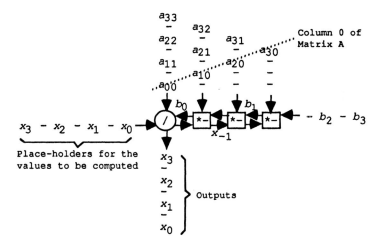

Figure 11.6. Solving a triangular system of linear equations on a linear array.

appears immediately, with one output emerging every two cycles afterwards). If the time for shifting in of b is also included, the time required will be $3m - 2$.

Figure 11.7 shows how the problem of inverting an $m \times m$ lower triangular matrix A can be viewed as m instances of solving a system of m lower triangular linear equations. This method of inverting a lower triangular matrix can be easily mapped onto an $m \times m$ mesh (Fig. 11.8), where each row of the mesh computes one column of A^{-1} and outputs it from the right. Because multiplication is usually faster than division, the top left processor in the mesh can be made to compute $1/a_{ii}$ and pass the result downward so that each of the other processors in Column 0 needs to perform one multiplication.

Inverting an $m \times m$ lower triangular matrix using the computation scheme depicted in Fig. 11.8, with $p = m^2$ processors, takes $3m - 2$ steps. If a second $m \times m$ lower triangular

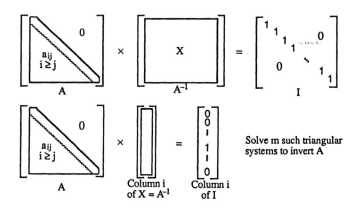

Figure 11.7. Inverting a triangular matrix by solving triangular systems of linear equations.

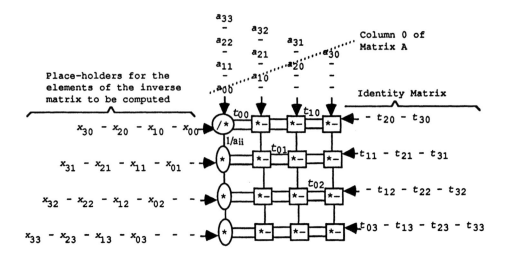

Figure 11.8. Inverting a lower triangular matrix on a 2D mesh.

matrix A' is supplied to the array in the alternate cycles where no element of A or X is present, both matrices can be inverted in $3m - 1$ steps.

11.3. TRIDIAGONAL SYSTEM OF LINEAR EQUATIONS

A *tridiagonal* square matrix is one in which all elements, except possibly those on the main diagonal, and the ones just above or below it, are 0s (Fig. 11.9). Instead of the usual notation a_{ij} for the element in Row i, Column j, of A, we use d_i to represent the main diagonal element a_{ii}, u_i for the upper diagonal element $a_{i,i+1}$, and l_i for the lower diagonal element $a_{i,i-1}$. For the sake of uniformity, we define $l_0 = u_{m-1} = 0$.

With the notation defined above, a tridiagonal system of linear equations can be written as follows, where $x_{-1} = x_m = 0$ are dummy variables that are introduced for uniformity:

$$
\begin{array}{c}
l_0 \\
l_1 \\
\\
\\
\\
\\
\\
\end{array}
\begin{bmatrix}
d_0 & u_0 & & & & & \\
l_1 & d_1 & u_1 & & & 0 & \\
 & l_2 & d_2 & u_2 & & & \\
 & & l_3 & \cdot & \cdot & & \\
 & & & \cdot & \cdot & \cdot & \\
 & 0 & & & \cdot & \cdot & u_{m-2} \\
 & & & & & l_{m-1} & d_{m-1} & u_{m-1}
\end{bmatrix}
\times
\begin{bmatrix}
x_0 \\
x_1 \\
x_2 \\
\cdot \\
\cdot \\
\cdot \\
x_{m-1}
\end{bmatrix}
=
\begin{bmatrix}
b_0 \\
b_1 \\
b_2 \\
\cdot \\
\cdot \\
\cdot \\
b_{m-1}
\end{bmatrix}
$$

Figure 11.9. A tridiagonal system of linear equations.

$$l_0 x_{-1} + d_0 x_0 + u_0 x_1 = b_0$$

$$l_1 x_0 + d_1 x_1 + u_1 x_2 = b_1$$

$$l_2 x_1 + d_2 x_2 + u_2 x_3 = b_2$$

$$\vdots$$

$$l_{m-1} x_{m-2} + d_{m-1} x_{m-1} + u_{m-1} x_m = b_{m-1}$$

One method to solve the above tridiagonal system of linear equations is to use *odd–even reduction*. Observe that the *i*th equation can be rewritten as

$$x_i = (1/d_i)(b_i - l_i x_{i-1} - u_i x_{i+1})$$

Taking the above equation for each odd *i* and substituting into the even-numbered equations (the ones with even indices for *l, d, u,* and *b*), we obtain for each even *i* $(0 \le i < m)$ an equation of the form

$$-\frac{l_{i-1}l_i}{d_{i-1}} x_{i-2} + \left(d_i - \frac{l_i u_{i-1}}{d_{i-1}} - \frac{u_i l_{i+1}}{d_{i+1}} \right) x_i - \frac{u_i u_{i+1}}{d_{i+1}} x_{i+2} = b_i - \frac{l_i b_{i-1}}{d_{i-1}} - \frac{u_i b_{i+1}}{d_{i+1}}$$

In this way, the *m* equations are reduced to $\lceil m/2 \rceil$ tridiagonal linear equations in the even-indexed variables. Applying the same method recursively, leads to *m*/4 equations, then *m*/8 equations, and, eventually, a single equation in x_0. Solving this last equation to obtain the value of x_0, and substituting backwards, allows us to compute the value of each of the *m* variables. Figure 11.10 shows the structure of the odd–even reduction method.

Forming each new equation requires six multiplications, six divisions, and four additions, but these can all be done in parallel using $p = m/2$ processors. Assuming unit-time arithmetic operations, we obtain the recurrence $T(m) = T(m/2) + 8 \approx 8 \log_2 m$ for the total number of computational steps. The six division operations can be replaced with one reciprocation per new equation, to find $1/d_j$ for each odd *j*, plus six multiplications. Obviously, the above odd–even reduction method is applicable only if none of the d_j values obtained in the course of the computation is 0.

In the above analysis, interprocessor communication time was not taken into account. The analysis is thus valid only for the PRAM or for an architecture whose topology matches the communication structure shown in Fig. 11.10. Figure 11.11 shows a binary X-tree architecture whose communication structure closely matches the needs of the above computation.

Comparing Figs. 11.10 and 11.11, we note that each of the required data transfers can be performed in no more than two steps on the X-tree. In fact, if we remove all of the dotted "left child" links in Fig. 11.11, leading to what is known as a 1D multigrid architecture, we can still perform odd–even reduction quite efficiently.

To perform odd–even reduction on a linear array of $p = m$ processors, we can assume that each processor initially holds one of the *m* equations. Direct one-step communication between neighboring processors leads to the even-numbered processors obtaining the reduced set of *m*/2 equations with a few arithmetic operations as discussed above. The next reduction phase requires two-step communication, then four-step, and eventually (*m*/2)-step,

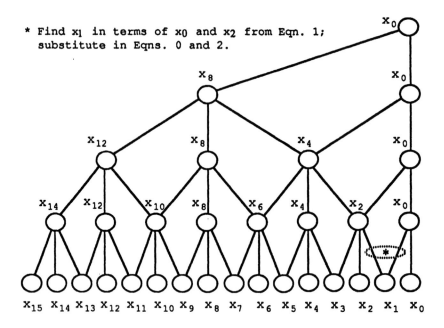

* Find x_1 in terms of x_0 and x_2 from Eqn. 1;
  substitute in Eqns. 0 and 2.

Figure 11.10. The structure of odd–even reduction for solving a tridiagonal system of linear equations.

leading to linear running time (of the same order as sequential time). On an m-processor 2D mesh, odd–even reduction can be easily organized to require $\Theta(\sqrt{p})$ time. Specifying the details is left as an exercise.

It is worth noting that solving a tridiagonal system of linear equations can be converted to a parallel prefix problem as follows. Define the 3×3 matrix G_i as

$$G_i = \begin{bmatrix} -d_i/u_i & -l_i/u_i & b_i/u_i \\ 1 & 0 & 0 \\ 0 & 0 & 1 \end{bmatrix}$$

Then, the ith equation can be written in matrix form as

$$\begin{bmatrix} x_{i+1} \\ x_i \\ 1 \end{bmatrix} = \begin{bmatrix} -d_i/u_i & -l_i/u_i & b_i/u_i \\ 1 & 0 & 0 \\ 0 & 0 & 1 \end{bmatrix} \times \begin{bmatrix} x_i \\ x_{i-1} \\ 1 \end{bmatrix} = G_i \times G_{i-1} \times \cdots \times G_0 \times \begin{bmatrix} x_0 \\ 0 \\ 1 \end{bmatrix}$$

In particular, we have

$$\begin{bmatrix} x_m \\ x_{m-1} \\ 1 \end{bmatrix} = G_{m-1} \times G_{m-2} \times \cdots \times G_0 \times \begin{bmatrix} x_0 \\ 0 \\ 1 \end{bmatrix}$$

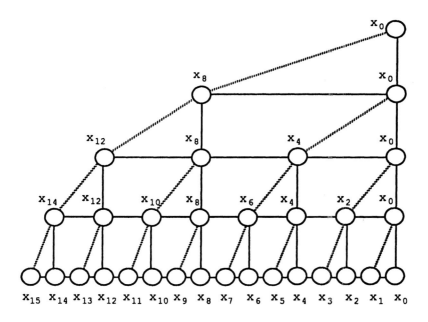

Figure 11.11. Binary X-tree (with dotted links) and multigrid architectures.

Solving this last set of three equations provides the value of x_0, which can then be used to determine the values of all other variables, given the prefix results $G_i \times G_{i-1} \times \cdots \times G_0$ for odd i.

11.4. ARBITRARY SYSTEM OF LINEAR EQUATIONS

Given a set of m linear equations $Ax = b$, Gaussian elimination consists of applying a sequence of row transformation to A and b (multiplying a row by a constant, interchanging rows, adding a multiple of one row to another). For a nonsingular matrix A, this is done until A turns into the identity matrix. At that point, $x = b$. If A is singular, it is turned into an upper triangular matrix U (we will not consider this case here). Because the same row transformations are applied to both A and b, it is convenient to construct an extended matrix A' that has A in its first m columns and b in the last column. The row transformations that convert the first m columns into the identity matrix will yield the solution in the last column. In fact, k systems of equations with the same A matrix and different b vectors can be solved simultaneously by simply appending each of the b vectors as a column of A'.

To illustrate the method, we apply it to the solution of two systems of three linear equations (sharing the same 3×3 matrix of coefficients) as follows:

$$2x_0 + 4x_1 - 7x_2 = 3 \qquad\qquad 2x_0 + 4x_1 - 7x_2 = 7$$

$$3x_0 + 6x_1 - 10x_2 = 4 \qquad\qquad 3x_0 + 6x_1 - 10x_2 = 8$$

$$-x_0 + 3x_1 - 4x_2 = 6 \qquad\qquad -x_0 + 3x_1 - 4x_2 = -1$$

The extended A' matrix for these two sets of equations has $m + k = 5$ columns:

$$A' = \begin{bmatrix} 2 & 4 & -7 & 3 & 7 \\ 3 & 6 & -10 & 4 & 8 \\ -1 & 3 & -4 & 6 & -1 \end{bmatrix}$$

Divide Row 0 by 2; then, add -3 times Row 0 to Row 1 and add 1 times Row 0 to Row 2 to get

$$A'^{(0)} = \begin{bmatrix} 1 & 2 & -7/2 & 3/2 & 7/2 \\ 0 & 0 & 3/2 & -1/2 & -5/2 \\ 0 & 5 & -15/2 & 15/2 & 5/2 \end{bmatrix}$$

Now exchange Rows 1 and 2 to make the next diagonal element nonzero:

$$A''^{(0)} = \begin{bmatrix} 1 & 2 & -7/2 & 3/2 & 7/2 \\ 0 & 5 & -15/2 & 15/2 & 5/2 \\ 0 & 0 & 1/2 & -1/2 & -5/2 \end{bmatrix}$$

Divide Row 1 by 5; then, add -2 times Row 1 to Row 0 and 0 times Row 1 to Row 2 to get

$$A'^{(1)} = \begin{bmatrix} 1 & 0 & -1/2 & -3/2 & 5/2 \\ 0 & 1 & -3/2 & 3/2 & 1/2 \\ 0 & 0 & 1/2 & -1/2 & -5/2 \end{bmatrix}$$

Finally, divide Row 2 by 1/2; then, add 1/2 times Row 2 to Row 0 and 3/2 times Row 2 to Row 1 to get

$$A'^{(2)} = \begin{bmatrix} 1 & 0 & 0 & -2 & 0 \\ 0 & 1 & 0 & 0 & -7 \\ 0 & 0 & 1 & -1 & -5 \end{bmatrix}$$

The solutions to the two sets of equations are thus $x_0 = -2$, $x_1 = 0$, $x_2 = -1$, and $x_0 = 0$, $x_1 = -7$, $x_2 = -5$, which are directly read out from the last two columns of $A'^{(2)}$.

A linear array with $p = m + k$ processors can easily perform one phase of Gaussian elimination. Take the first phase, e.g., that leads from A' to $A'^{(0)}$. The transformation involves dividing Row 0 by a_{00} and then subtracting a_{i0} times the new Row 0 from every Row i for $i \geq 1$. As depicted in Fig. 11.12, this can be done by computing the reciprocal of a_{00} in the circular node, passing this value to the right so that it can be multiplied by each of the other elements of Row 0 and the results stored in the corresponding square nodes (node variable z).

In subsequent steps, the circular node simply passes the values it receives from above to the right with no change. Denoting the left and top inputs to a square node by x and y, respectively, a cell must compute and output $y - xz = a_{ij} - a_{i0}(a_{0j}/a_{00})$ as each subsequent row passes over it. Elements of $A'^{(0)}$ emerge from the bottom of the linear array in the same staggered format as the inputs coming from above, with Rows 1 through $m - 1$ appearing in

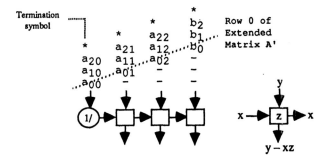

Figure 11.12. A linear array performing the first phase of Gaussian elimination.

order, followed by Row 0 which is output when the special termination symbol * is received as input.

Figure 11.13 shows a 2D architecture for Gaussian elimination. Circular nodes, on receiving the first nonzero value from above, reciprocate it (i.e., compute $1/a_{ii}$) and pass the reciprocal value to the right. Processors in Row i are responsible for computing and storing the ith row of $A'^{(i)}$, producing at their outputs the rows of $A'^{(i)}$ in order from $i + 1$ to $m - 1$, followed by Rows 0 through i. The total computation time is $4m - 1$: $2m$ steps for b_{m-1} to arrive into the top row of the array, $m - 1$ steps for it to move to the bottom row, and m steps for output.

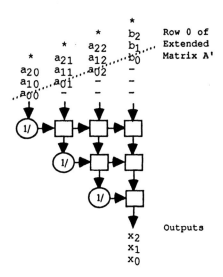

Figure 11.13. Implementation of Gaussian elimination on a 2D array.

Note that, because the inversion of an $m \times m$ matrix A is equivalent to solving m systems of linear equations with the same A matrix (one for each column of the unknown inverse matrix), the scheme of Fig. 11.13 can be easily extended to perform matrix inversion using Gaussian elimination. Figure 11.14 shows the resulting arrangement where the $m \times 2m$ extended matrix A', with the identity matrix in its last m columns, is input at the top and the inverse matrix X emerges from the bottom of the array.

An alternative to Gaussian elimination for solving systems of linear equations is the use of Jacobi relaxation. Assuming that each a_{ii} is nonzero, the ith equation can be solved for x_i, yielding m equations from which new better approximations to the answers can be obtained from already available approximations $x_j^{(t)}$:

$$x_i^{(t+1)} = (1/a_{ii})[b_i - \sum_{j \neq i} a_{ij}x_j^{(t)}]; \ x_i^{(0)} \text{ is an initial approximation for } x_i$$

On an m-processor linear array, each iteration of Jacobi relaxation takes O(m) steps, because essentially the values held by the m processors need to be rotated to allow each processor to compute its next approximation. The number of iterations needed is O(log m) in most cases, leading to the overall time complexity O(m log m).

A variant of the above, known as Jacobi overrelaxation, uses the iterative formula

$$x_i^{(t+1)} = (1 - \gamma)x_i^{(t)} + (\gamma/a_{ii})[b_i - \Sigma_{j \neq i} a_{ij}x_j^{(t)}]$$

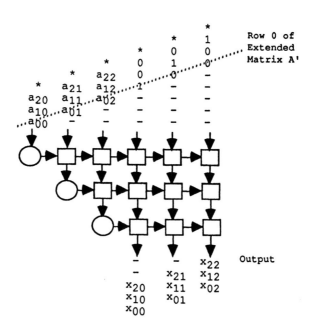

Figure 11.14. Matrix inversion by Gaussian elimination.

Here, γ $(0 < \gamma \le 1)$ is a parameter of the method. For $\gamma = 1$, the method is the same as Jacobi relaxation. For smaller values of γ, the overrelaxation method may lead to better performance because it tends to keep the new values closer to the old values.

11.5. GRAPH ALGORITHMS

An n-node graph can be represented by an n-by-n adjacency matrix A. Nodes are numbered from 0 to $n - 1$ with $a_{ij} = 1$ if there is an edge from Node i to Node j and 0 otherwise. This matrix representation is quite suitable for use on a mesh-connected computer, as each matrix entry can be assigned to a processor on an n-by-n mesh. If there are fewer than n^2 processors for dealing with an n-node graph, then blocks of A can be assigned to processors.

In some applications, weights are associated with the edges (representing, e.g., travel times on roads, road tolls, or pipeline capacities). In these cases, a weight matrix can be used in lieu of the adjacency matrix. Lack of an edge from Node i to Node j is represented by assigning a suitable value to the corresponding ij element in the weight matrix. For example, if minimum-weight paths are to be found, assigning the value "∞" to missing edges ensures proper selection. Note that weights can be negative in the general case.

To obtain the transitive closure of a graph, defined as a graph with the same number of nodes but with an edge between two nodes if there is a path of any length between them in the original graph, we begin with the adjacency matrix A and define

$A^0 = I$ Paths of length 0   (the identity matrix)

$A^1 = A$ Paths of length 1

and compute higher "powers" of A using matrix multiplication, except that in our matrix multiplication algorithm, AND is used instead of multiplication and OR in lieu of addition.

$A^2 = A \times A$ Paths of length 2

$A^3 = A^2 \times A$ Paths of length 3

$\vdots$

$A^* = A^0 + A^1 + A^2 + \ldots$ ($A_{ij}^* = 1$ iff Node j is reachable from Node i)

The matrix A^* is the transitive closure of A.

To compute A^*, we need only proceed up to the term A^{n-1}, because if there is a path from i to j, there must be a path of length less than n. Rather than base the derivation of A^* on computing the various powers of the Boolean matrix A, we can use the following simpler algorithm.

Transitive closure algorithm

Phase 0: Insert the edge (i, j) into the graph if $(i, 0)$ and $(0, j)$ are in the graph.
Phase 1: Insert the edge (i, j) into the graph if $(i, 1)$ and $(1, j)$ are in the graph.
$\vdots$

Phase k: Insert the edge (i, j) into the graph if (i, k) and (k, j) are in the graph.
The graph $A^{(k)}$ at the end of Phase k has an edge (i, j) iff there is a path

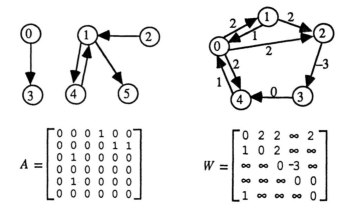

$$A = \begin{bmatrix} 0 & 0 & 0 & 1 & 0 & 0 \\ 0 & 0 & 0 & 0 & 1 & 1 \\ 0 & 1 & 0 & 0 & 0 & 0 \\ 0 & 0 & 0 & 0 & 0 & 0 \\ 0 & 1 & 0 & 0 & 0 & 0 \\ 0 & 0 & 0 & 0 & 0 & 0 \end{bmatrix} \qquad W = \begin{bmatrix} 0 & 2 & 2 & \infty & 2 \\ 1 & 0 & 2 & \infty & \infty \\ \infty & \infty & 0 & -3 & \infty \\ \infty & \infty & \infty & 0 & 0 \\ 1 & \infty & \infty & \infty & 0 \end{bmatrix}$$

Figure 11.15. Matrix representation of directed graphs.

from i to j that goes only through nodes $\{1, 2, \ldots, k\}$ as intermediate hops.

Phase $n-1$: The graph $A^{(n-1)}$ is the required answer A^*.

A key question is how to proceed so that each phase takes $O(1)$ time for an overall $O(n)$ time on an $n \times n$ mesh. The $O(n)$ running time would be optimal in view of the $O(n^3)$ sequential complexity of the transitive closure problem. Assume for now that each processor located on the main diagonal can broadcast a value to all processors in its row. Then the input, output, and computation can be arranged as shown in Fig. 11.16.

Phase 0 of the algorithm is carried out as Rows $1, 2, \ldots, n-1$ of A pass over Row 0 of A which is stored in the 0th row of the mesh. As Row i passes over Row 0, Processor $(0, 0)$ broadcasts the value of a_{i0} to all of the processors in the 0th row. Because the jth processor has already saved the value of a_{0j}, it can set the value of a_{ij} that is passing through to 1 if $a_{i0} = a_{0j} = 1$. By the time the kth row of A reaches Row k of the mesh, it has been updated to

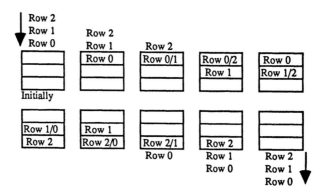

Figure 11.16. Transitive closure algorithm on a 2D mesh.

become the kth row of $A^{(k-1)}$, i.e., it has passed through the first $k - 1$ phases. Thus, the total number of steps for computing the transitive closure of an n-node graph, represented by an $n \times n$ adjacency matrix, is $3n$ steps.

The need for broadcasting can be eliminated through a technique known as *systolic retiming*, defined as inserting delays on some of the edges (and perhaps removing delays from some others) in such a way that each node still receives its input data in the same order/combination as before. Figure 11.17 shows the application of systolic retiming to the above transitive closure algorithm. The algorithm before retiming is shown on the left side of Fig. 11.17, where the 0-delay row edges represent the broadcasting of a_{kl}, for all $k > l$, by Processor P_{ll}.

In systolic retiming, we can multiply all edge delays by a constant factor (slowing down the computation by that factor) or add the same delay to the edges in a cut in which all edges go in the same direction. Also, for any node, we can add/subtract δ to/from each input edge delay and subtract/add δ from/to each output edge delay, as delaying/advancing all inputs by δ while advancing/delaying all outputs by δ cancel each other out as far as interactions with other nodes are concerned. Our goal here is to eliminate the broadcasting (making all edge delays nonzero).

In the case of Fig. 11.17, we can add 6 (more generally, $2n - 2$) units of delay to all edges crossing Cut 1. This is allowed because all of the edges involved cross the cut in the same direction. Now, we subtract 6 units of delay from the input to Node (0, 0) and add 6 units to each of its two outputs. Node (0, 1) now has its top and side inputs with 7 and 6 units of delay, respectively. In the next step, we reduce these by 5 (to 2 and 1) and increase the output delays by 5 (to 6 and 5). Continuing in this manner, we get the retimed version shown

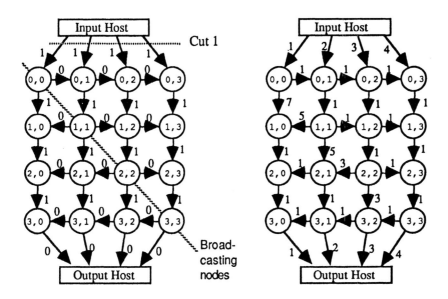

Figure 11.17. Systolic retiming to eliminate broadcasting.

on the right side of Fig. 11.17, which contains only nonzero edge delays. The retiming increases the total delay to $5n - 2$ steps, which is still asymptotically optimal.

The transitive closure algorithm is useful, e.g., for finding the connected components of a graph defined as a partitioning of the nodes such that each pair of nodes in a partition are connected. Clearly, once the transitive closure A^* of the adjacency matrix A is found, information about the graph's connected components can be easily read out from the rows of A^*. Assigning a unique component ID to each node is straightforward. One can use, e.g., the label of the node with the smallest ID to label all nodes in the same component.

Let us now consider briefly another example of graph problems. The *all-pairs shortest path* problem is defined as the problem of determining, simultaneously for all node pairs, the length of the shortest path between them. Taking the weight matrix W shown in Fig. 11.15 as input, the algorithm is quite similar to that for finding the transitive closure of an adjacency matrix A. There are n phases. In Phase 0, we replace the edge from i to j with the length of the shortest path that is allowed to pass only through Node 0 as an intermediate node. To do this, we compare w_{ij} with $w_{i0} + w_{0j}$ and choose the smaller of the two. This leads to $W^{(0)}$. Continuing in this way, $W^{(k)}$ will contain the length of the shortest path from i to j that passes only through nodes $\{1, 2, \ldots, k\}$ as intermediate nodes. With some additional work, we can also keep track of the shortest path, rather than just its length, if desired.

11.6. IMAGE-PROCESSING ALGORITHMS

In this section, we deal with example algorithms used in image analysis and computational geometry applications. Let an image be represented as an array of binary (black/white) pixels. By *labeling the (connected) components* of such a binary image (or *component labeling* for short), we mean grouping the 1 elements that can be reached from each other via horizontal, vertical, or diagonal steps into components. Figure 11.18 shows an example binary image that contains four connected components. Here, row-major indexing of the

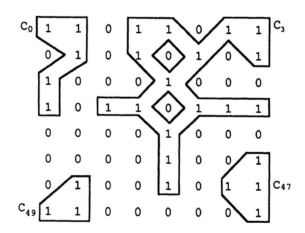

Figure 11.18. Connected components in an 8 × 8 binary image.

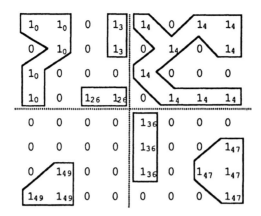

Figure 11.19. Finding the connected components via divide and conquer.

elements is assumed and each component is given the index of its lowest pixel as its unique identifying number.

Assuming that each pixel of the p-pixel image is assigned to one processor on a $\sqrt{n} \times \sqrt{n}$ mesh with $p = n$ processors, the following naive algorithm immediately suggests itself. Initially, the component ID of each processor holding a 1 is set to the processor's own ID. So, we designate each pixel as a separate component at the outset and then try to merge the components that are connected. Each processor holding a 1 reads the pixel values and component IDs of its eight neighbors (the diagonally adjacent values are read in two steps). Now, each processor holding a 1 adjusts its component ID to the lowest ID among the neighbors holding 1s if any of those IDs is smaller. The problem with this algorithm is that, in the worst case, it requires $\Theta(n)$ running time, e.g., when there is a single snakelike component that winds through even-numbered rows.

A recursive $O(\sqrt{n})$-step algorithm is described next.

Recursive component-labeling algorithm on a 2D mesh

Phase 1: Label the components in each quadrant.
Phase 2: Merge components horizontally in the upper and lower halves.
Phase 3: Merge component vertically.

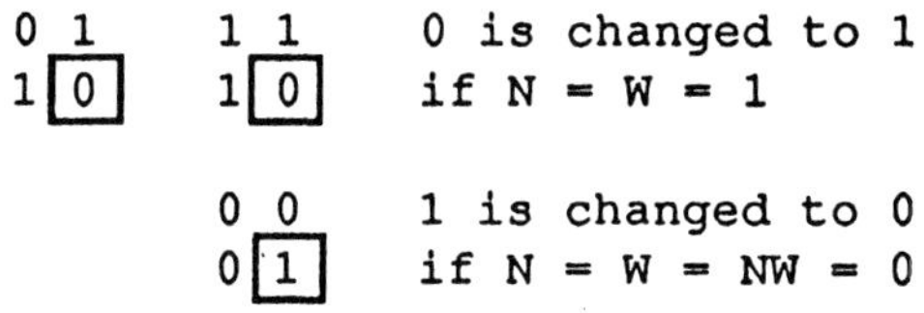

```
0 1     1 1     0 is changed to 1
1 0     1 0     if N = W = 1

        0 0     1 is changed to 0
        0 1     if N = W = NW = 0
```

Figure 11.20. Transformation or rewriting rules for Lavialdi's algorithm (no other pixel value changes).

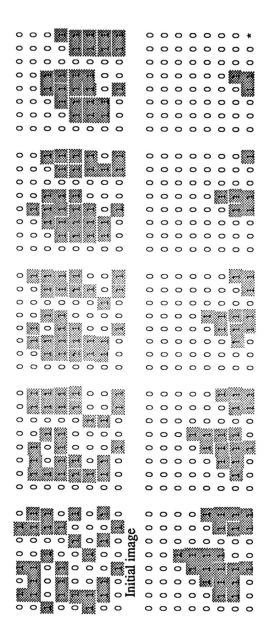

Figure 11.21. Example of the shrinkage phase of Lavialdi's algorithm.

If each of the two merge phases can be done in $O(\sqrt{n})$ steps, then the running time of the algorithm will be $T(n) = T(n/4) + O(\sqrt{n}) = O(\sqrt{n})$. Take the horizontal merge phase in the upper half of the mesh. There are at most $\sqrt{n}/2$ components that need to be merged ($\sqrt{n}/4$ on each side). Adjacency information for these components is readily available at the vertical boundary. A column rotate at this boundary will yield the new label for each merged component. Because there are no more than $\sqrt{n}/2$ such components, information on their new labels can be broadcast to all processors in the quadrant in $O(\sqrt{n})$ steps using pipelined communication.

Lavialdi's algorithm for component labeling is somewhat more efficient. Using the locally applied rules depicted in Fig. 11.20, components are shrunk to single pixels in $2\sqrt{n} - 1$ steps (this shrinkage phase does not disconnect components or merge them). Then, in a $(2\sqrt{n} - 1)$-step expansion phase, the process is reversed and the label of the single remaining pixel of each component becomes the component label for all of its pixels.

To see why components will not merge in the shrinkage phase, consider a 0 that is about to become 1 in the pattern

$$
\begin{array}{ccc}
x & 1 & y \\
1 & 0 & y. \\
y & y & z
\end{array}
$$

If any of the y pixels is 1, then the associated component is already connected to this component and no new connection will be created. If all of the y pixels are 0s, then even if the z pixel is 1, it will be converted to 0, again avoiding any new connection. Figure 11.21 shows 9 steps of Lavialdi's algorithm applied to an 8×8 binary image containing two components. In this example, complete shrinkage of components to single pixels occurs in 10 steps (the worst case would be 15 steps).

PROBLEMS

11.1. Multiplication of nonsquare matrices

    a. Explain the effect of a nonsquare matrix on Figs. 11.1 and 11.3.

    b. Modify Figs. 11.2 and 11.4 for multiplying an $m' \times m$ matrix A by an $m \times m''$ matrix B.

    c. How is the block matrix multiplication scheme described at the end of Section 11.1 affected if the matrices are nonsquare but the mesh is square?

11.2. Matrix multiplication

Figures 11.2 and 11.4 correspond to matrix multiplication with both inputs supplied from outside the array and both inputs prestored in the array. Show a suitable data organization on a p-processor array ($p = m^2$) to multiply a fixed prestored matrix A by several B matrices supplied as inputs.

11.3. Matrix multiplication

Consider the vector–matrix and matrix–matrix multiplication schemes depicted in Figs. 11.3 and 11.4 but assume that the architecture is a linear array or mesh (without the wraparound links).

    a. Discuss the effects of removing the wraparound links on algorithm execution and running time in Fig. 11.3.

    b. Repeat part (a) for the matrix–matrix multiplication algorithm of Fig. 11.4.

   c.   Would it be helpful if we could store four elements (matrix blocks) in each processor rather
        than just two in the course of executing the algorithm?

11.4.   Back substitution
        In the back substitution scheme depicted in Fig. 11.6, half of the processors are idle at any
        given time.

   a.   Show how we can take advantage of the idle processors to overlap the solution of two
        separate triangular systems of linear equations.
   b.   Show how we can merge pairs of adjacent processors into single processors, each less than
        twice as complex as the existing processors, without affecting the running time.
   c.   Can similar techniques be applied to the inversion of a triangular matrix (Fig. 11.8)?

11.5.   Bidiagonal systems of linear equations
        Any algorithm for solving tridiagonal systems of linear equations can obviously be applied to
        solving a bidiagonal system of linear equations where all of the nonzero elements of A are on
        the main and lower (upper) diagonals. Devise a more efficient algorithm for this special case.

11.6.   Gaussian elimination
        For one of the systems of three linear equations at the beginning of Section 11.4, show all of
        the intermediate computation steps, including values held by or passed between processors, on
        the diagram of Fig. 11.13.

11.7.   Jacobi relaxation

   a.   Solve one of the systems of three linear equations given near the beginning of Section 11.4
        using Jacobi relaxation, beginning with the initial value of 0 for each variable.
   b.   Show the computation steps, including values held by or passed between processors, as
        the solution of Part (a) is obtained by a linear array of three processors.
   c.   Repeat part (a) using Jacobi overrelaxation with $\gamma = 1/2$ and discuss the results.

11.8.   Systolic retiming

   a.   In Fig. 11.17, what happens if we make the delays associated with all edges leading to the
        output host in the retimed version of the graph equal to 1? Discuss the practical implications
        of this change.
   b.   Retime a modified form of Fig. 11.17 (left) in which broadcasting by each diagonal node
        proceeds to its right and then wraps around to cover the nodes to the left.

11.9.   Transitive closure algorithm
        Define the single-node-fault version $A^{*(1)}$ of the transitive closure of A as having $a_{ij}^{*(1)} = 1$ iff
        Nodes i and j are connected and remain connected if we remove any single node in the graph.
        Propose an algorithm for efficiently computing $A^{*(1)}$. *Hint:* In each phase of the algorithm, you
        need to figure out if a pair of nodes are connected with or without a worst-case single node
        fault.

11.10. All-pairs shortest path problem
        Describe the complete algorithm for the all-pairs shortest path problem (end of Section 11.5)
        that provides the shortest paths rather than only their lengths. *Hint:* When $w_{ik} + w_{kj}$ is less than
        w_{ij}, a new shortest path between Nodes i and j has been identified. This path is the concatenation
        of two previously stored paths, one from i to k and the other from k to j.

11.11. Component labeling on a 2D mesh
    Analyze the recursive component-labeling algorithm of Section 11.6 in more detail to find its
    exact worst-case step count and compare the result with Lavialdi's algorithm.

11.12. Component labeling on a 2D mesh
    Devise a component labeling algorithm that also yields the number of pixels in (area of) each
    component.

11.13. Lavialdi's component-labeling algorithm
    a. Specify the operations that need to be performed in the expansion phase of Lavialdi's
       algorithm.
    b. Complete the steps of the example depicted in Fig. 11.21 all of the way to the end of
       labeling.
    c. How many steps does Lavialdi's algorithm need to label the components in Fig. 11.18?
    d. Construct an 8×8 binary image such that the shrinkage phase of Lavialdi's algorithm
       requires the worst-case $2\sqrt{n} - 1 = 17$ steps.

REFERENCES AND SUGGESTED READING

[Bert89]   Bertsekas, D. P., and J. N. Tsitsiklis, *Parallel and Distributed Computation: Numerical Methods*,
            Prentice–Hall, 1989.
[Kung88]   Kung, S. Y., *VLSI Array Processors*, Prentice–Hall, 1988.
[Laks90]   Lakshmivarahan, S., and S. K. Dhall, *Analysis and Design of Parallel Algorithms: Arithmetic and
            Matrix Problems*, McGraw-Hill, 1990.
[Lavi72]   Lavialdi, S., "On Shrinking Binary Picture Patterns," *Communications of the ACM*, Vol. 15, No. 1,
            pp. 7–10, January 1972.
[Leig92]   Leighton, F. T., *Introduction to Parallel Algorithms and Architectures: Arrays, Trees, Hypercubes*,
            Morgan Kaufmann, 1992.
[Leis83]   Leiserson, C., and J. Saxe, "Optimizing Synchronous Systems," *J. VLSI & Computer Systems*, Vol.
            1, No. 1, pp. 41–67, Spring 1983.
[Mill85]   Miller, R., and Q. Stout, "Geometric Algorithms for Digitized Pictures on a Mesh-Connected
            Computer," *IEEE Trans. Pattern Analysis and Machine Intelligence*, Vol. 7, No. 2, pp. 216–228,
            March 1985.

12

Other Mesh-Related Architectures

In this chapter, we consider variations in mesh architectures that can lead to higher performance or greater cost-effectiveness in certain applications. The variations include higher dimensions, stronger and weaker connectivities, inclusion of buses, introduction of express channels, triangular or hexagonal shapes, different types of wraparound links, and reconfigurable connectivity. Also, extensions to pyramid networks, meshes of trees, and certain 2D product networks will be discussed. Chapter topics are

- 12.1. Three or more dimensions
- 12.2. Stronger and weaker connectivities
- 12.3. Meshes augmented with nonlocal links
- 12.4. Meshes with dynamic links
- 12.5. Pyramid and multigrid systems
- 12.6. Meshes of trees

12.1. THREE OR MORE DIMENSIONS

Our discussions of algorithms in Chapters 9–11 (as well as in Sections 2.3 and 2.5) have been in terms of 1D and 2D processor arrays. These are the most practical in terms of physical realization in view of the 2D nature of implementation technologies such as VLSI chips and printed-circuit boards. Recently, 3D mesh and torus architectures have become viable alternatives for parallel machine design (we will see why shortly), but higher-dimensional meshes are currently only of theoretical interest. In this section, we briefly review q-D meshes, focusing on their differences with 1D and 2D arrays in terms of hardware realization and algorithm design.

Theoretically, it should be possible to implement a 3D mesh or torus in the 3D physical space. The processors can be visualized as occupying grid points on a 3D grid (Fig. 12.1), with all six communication ports of each processor connected to neighboring processors by short local wires. Even though such 3D structures have been and are being considered by parallel processing researchers, numerous practical hurdles must be overcome before large-scale implementations become cost-effective or even feasible.

The prevailing hardware implementation technology for digital systems that do not fit on a single *printed-circuit* (PC) *board* is to mount multiple PC boards on a *backplane* that supports the boards mechanically and also provides the needed electrical connectivity between them (Fig. 12.1). This allows the boards to be easily replaced for repair or upgrade and the system to be expanded by inserting extra boards, up to the maximum capacity offered by the backplane. This method can be viewed as a 2.5D arrangement, with full 2D connectivity on the circuit boards and limited connectivity along the third dimension via the backplane.

Consider the example of implementing an $8 \times 8 \times 8$ mesh on eight boards, each holding an 8×8 mesh. Implementing an 8×8 2D mesh on a PC board is straightforward and can be done with only short local links. However, at least some of the 64 links that need to go from one PC board to the next involve long wires (from one processor to the backplane, a short distance on the backplane, and from the backplane to the other processor on the next board). With multiple lines per communication channel, a significant area on each PC board must be devoted to routing these interboard links. This nullifies some of the advantages of a mesh in terms of regularity and locality of connections. What we gain in return for the higher complexity/cost are a smaller network diameter ($3p^{1/3} - 3$ instead of $2p^{1/2} - 2$) and wider

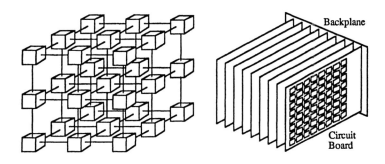

Figure 12.1. 3D and 2.5D physical realizations of a 3D mesh.

bisection ($p^{2/3}$ rather than $p^{1/2}$). Our example mesh above has a diameter of 21 and bisection width of 64. A comparably sized 22×23 2D mesh has a diameter of 43 and bisection width of 23.

You can now imagine how much harder the implementation of a 4D or 5D mesh would be with current technology. There is some speculation that using optical communication links may solve these problems for 3D, and perhaps even higher-dimensional, meshes. However, optical interconnections are not yet cost-effective, because of both technological factors and the added delay/cost of electronic/optical conversions.

Regardless of how 3D and higher-dimensional meshes are physically realized, their algorithms are quite similar to, or easily derivable from, those for 2D meshes discussed in the preceding chapters. The following paragraphs contain brief discussions of 3D mesh algorithms, with hints on how a 3D torus architecture, or higher-dimensional meshes/tori, can be handled. A q-D mesh with m processors along each of its q dimensions ($p = m^q$) has a node degree of $d = 2q$, a diameter of $D = q(m - 1) = q(p^{1/q} - 1)$, and a bisection width of $p^{1-1/q}$ when $p^{1/q}$ is even. A q-D torus with m processors along each of its q dimensions is sometimes referred to as an m-ary q-cube.

Sorting.   One may guess that just as it was possible to sort a 2D array using alternating row and column sorts (shearsort), it might be possible to sort a 3D array by suitably alternating between sorts along the various dimensions. Such a generalized form of shearsort for three and higher dimensions is indeed feasible [Corb92]. However, the following algorithm for sorting a 3D array is both faster and simpler (a rarity in algorithm design!); the algorithm is even simpler to describe than its 2D counterparts. Let Processor (i, j, k) in an $m×m×m$ mesh be in Row i (x dimension), Column j (y dimension), and Layer k (z dimension). Define the sorted order to correspond to the lexicographic ordering of reversed node indices: $(0,0,0), (1,0,0), \ldots, (m-1,0,0), (0,1,0), (1,1,0), \ldots, (m-1,1,0), (0,2,0)$, and so on. In this zyx order, the smallest m^2 elements end up on Layer 0 in column-major order, the next smallest m^2 elements on Layer 1, and so on (the yx order on a slice is the same as column-major order and the xy order corresponds to row-major order). The following five-phase algorithm sorts the elements of the 3D array into the zyx order [Kund86].

Sorting on a 3D mesh

Phase 1: Sort the elements on each zx plane into zx order.
Phase 2: Sort the elements on each yz plane into zy order.
Phase 3: Sort the elements on each xy layer into yx order (odd layers in reverse order).
Phase 4: Apply two steps of odd–even transposition along the z direction.
Phase 5: Sort the elements on each xy layer into yx order.

In Phase 4 of the algorithm, the m^3 processors are viewed as m^2 linear arrays of length m, aligned along the z direction, and two steps of odd–even transposition are applied to each of these arrays. The 2D sorts can be performed using any 2D sorting algorithm. If the 2D sorting algorithm needs $T(m×m)$ time, the time for our 3D algorithm will be $T(m×m×m) = 4T(m×m) + 2$. In particular, any $O(m)$-time 2D sorting algorithm will lead to a running time of $O(m) = O(p^{1/3})$ for the 3D algorithm. As usual, the proof is done using the zero–one principle.

Data Routing. A greedy zyx (layer-first) routing algorithm would route the packets along the z dimension until they are in the destination layers and then use a greedy yx (row-first) algorithm in each xy layer. Considerations with regard to buffer space in intermediate nodes and the delays introduced by conflicts are quite similar to those of 2D mesh algorithms. To reduce the node storage requirement to a single message buffer, a sorting-based routing algorithm can be used.

Data routing on a 3D mesh

Phase 1: Sort the packets by their destination addresses into zyx order.
Phase 2: Route each packet along the z dimension to the correct xy layer.
Phase 3: Route each packet along the y dimension to the correct column.
Phase 4: Route each packet along the x dimension to the correct row.

Each of the Phases 2–4 takes $m - 1$ routing steps, with no conflict ever arising ([Leig92], pp. 232–233). Thus, given that sorting in Phase 1 also takes $O(m)$ compare–exchange steps, the overall running time is $O(m)$. Adaptive and wormhole routing schemes can similarly be generalized to 3D and higher-dimensional meshes.

Matrix Multiplication. In Section 11.1, we saw that two $m \times m$ matrices can be multiplied on an $m \times m$ torus in m multiply–add steps. A 2D mesh requires longer, but still $O(m)$, running time, which is optimal. To devise a faster matrix multiplication algorithm on a 3D mesh, we divide each $m \times m$ matrix into an $m^{1/4} \times m^{1/4}$ array of $m^{3/4} \times m^{3/4}$ blocks. A total of $(m^{1/4})^3 = m^{3/4}$ block multiplications are needed. Let us assume that the algorithm is to be performed on an $m^{3/4} \times m^{3/4} \times m^{3/4}$ mesh with $p = m^{9/4}$ processors. Then each $m^{3/4} \times m^{3/4}$ layer of the mesh can be assigned to one of the $m^{3/4} \times m^{3/4}$ matrix multiplications, performing its computation in $m^{3/4}$ multiply–add steps. Finally, the addition of $m^{1/4}$ blocks to form each block of the product matrix can be accomplished in $m^{1/4}$ addition steps with proper distribution of elements to processors. The total running time is thus $O(m^{3/4}) = O(p^{1/3})$ steps, which is optimal from the point of view of both the computational work and network diameter. A more detailed description of the algorithm and its required data distribution is given by Leighton ([Leig92], pp. 226–228).

Physical Systems. Intuitively, a 3D mesh seems to be the ideal architecture for performing simulations of 3D physical systems. The ocean modeling and similar applications described in Section 1.1, e.g., map nicely onto a 3D mesh, with each processor holding a 3D block of the large model. Because in each update stage only adjacent data points interact, the 3D mesh is well equipped to perform the required interprocessor transfers rapidly and efficiently. In image processing, a 3D mesh can deal with 3D images in much the same way that a 2D mesh accommodates 2D digital images.

Low- versus High-Dimensional Meshes. A low-dimensional mesh, which can be implemented at much lower cost compared with a high-dimensional mesh with the same number of processors, can simulate the latter quite efficiently ([Leig92], pp. 234–236). It is thus natural to ask the following question: Is it more cost-effective, e.g., to have four-port processors in a 2D mesh architecture or six-port processors in a 3D mesh, given the fact that for the four-port processors, the economy in number of ports and ease of layout allows us to make each channel wider? This and similar questions have been studied by several researchers ([Agar91], [Ande97], [Dall90]). Despite a lack of consensus, there are indications that lower-dimensional arrays may be more cost-effective.

12.2. STRONGER AND WEAKER CONNECTIVITIES

One problem with a 2D mesh is its relatively large diameter. Higher-dimensional meshes, on the other hand, present difficult implementation problems. These considerations have resulted in a wide variety of architectures that are obtained by considering different (nonrectangular) grids or by inserting/removing links into/from an ordinary mesh. These and other variations are discussed in this section.

Figure 12.2 shows eight-neighbor and hexagonal meshes as examples of 2D meshes with stronger connectivities than standard 2D meshes. The eight-neighbor mesh allows direct communication between diagonally adjacent processors, which may be helpful for some image-processing applications (e.g., see Section 11.6). An eight-neighbor mesh has smaller diameter and wider bisection than an ordinary 2D mesh. However, these advantages are offset by its higher implementation cost. The node degree of 6 in a hex mesh is intermediate between those of ordinary 2D meshes/tori and the eight-neighbor mesh. However, the nonrectangular shape of a hex mesh makes it difficult to implement applications involving regular data structures such as matrices. Both eight-neighbor and hex meshes can have wraparound links. Such links can be defined in a variety of ways, some of which will be explored in the end-of-chapter problems.

Removing links from meshes and tori can result in simpler networks with correspondingly lower performance, offering interesting design trade-offs. For example, if an interprocessor link in a 2D torus is viewed as two unidirectional links, with links going in one direction removed in alternating rows/columns, a *Manhattan street network* results (the unidirectional links going in opposite directions in odd- and even-numbered rows/columns resemble the one-way streets of Manhattan in New York). Figure 12.3 shows a 4×4 example. Manhattan street networks offer the advantages of low diameter and simple node structure. Each node only has two input and two output ports. The down side is that routing and other algorithms become more complicated.

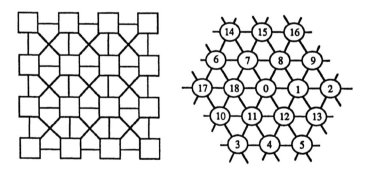

Figure 12.2. Eight-neighbor and hexagonal (hex) meshes.

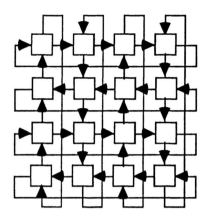

Figure 12.3. A 4×4 Manhattan street network.

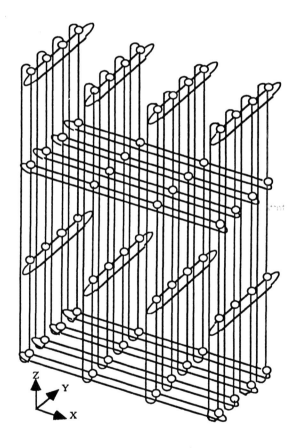

Figure 12.4. A pruned $4 \times 4 \times 4$ torus with nodes of degree 4 [Kwai97].

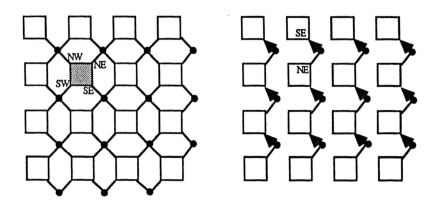

Figure 12.5. Eight-neighbor mesh with shared links and example data paths.

Another strategy that allows us to combine the advantages of low diameter and simple nodes is to prune a high-dimensional mesh/torus by selectively removing some of its links. Figure 12.4 shows a pruned 3D torus in which all of the z links have been kept, while the x or y links are removed in alternate layers [Kwai97].

Yet another way to reduce the node degree of a mesh is to share the links that are never/seldom used at the same time. Many mesh algorithms utilize communications along the same direction in each step (weak SIMD model) or can be easily modified to honor this constraint without a significant performance penalty. Algorithms of this type allow us to use the 2D mesh depicted in Fig. 12.5, which combines the advantages of the eight-neighbor mesh with the low node degree of a standard mesh. Using the natural designations NE, NW, SE, and SW for the four ports of each processor, the instruction "send to NE, receive from SE" corresponds to northward data movement as shown on the right side of Fig. 12.5. Similarly, "send to NE, receive from SW" would implement a diagonal data transfer operation.

12.3. MESHES AUGMENTED WITH NONLOCAL LINKS

Because one of the major drawbacks of low-dimensional meshes and tori is their rapidly increasing diameters when the number of processors becomes large, it has been suggested that mechanisms be provided in order to speed up long-distance communications among nodes. One example is the provision of *bypass links* or *express channels*, as shown in Fig. 12.6 for one row of a 2D mesh. In the top example, the worst-case distance along the nine-processor row has been reduced from 8 to 4. Such bypass links destroy the locality and regularity of connections, leading to both algorithmic complexity and hardware implementation problems. For example, routing becomes more difficult, particularly if a deadlock-free wormhole routing algorithm is to be devised that takes advantage of the shorter graph-theoretic distances for faster data transfers. However, they may prove worthwhile in some applications.

A wide variety of mesh architectures have been proposed in which the local links have been augmented with one or more shared buses to facilitate occasional long-distance

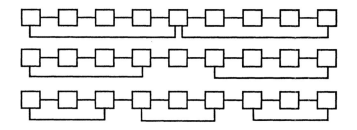

Figure 12.6. Three examples of bypass links along the rows of a 2D mesh.

communications. Figure 12.7 shows a 2D mesh augmented with a single global bus to which all processors are connected. For a large number p of processors, this organization is of theoretical interest only because buses cannot connect thousands of processors. Adding the global bus increases the node degree from 4 to 5 but has a significant effect on the speed of some computations. The bus does not help much in computations (such as sorting) that involve a large amount of data movements as it only increases the bisection width of the network by 1. However, in other applications, with sparse long-distance communications, the performance effect of the global bus might become significant.

Consider a semigroup computation such as max-finding, with one item per processor in a square $\sqrt{p} \times \sqrt{p}$ mesh. With a single global bus, this computation can be performed in $O(p^{1/3})$ rather than $O(p^{1/2})$ steps as follows. We assume that the semigroup operation $\otimes$ is commutative.

Semigroup computation on 2D mesh with a global bus

Phase 1: Find the partial results in $p^{1/3} \times p^{1/3}$ submeshes in $O(p^{1/3})$ steps, with the results stored in the upper left corner processor of each submesh (Fig. 12.7).

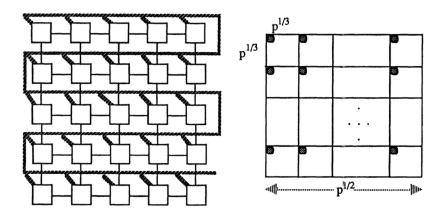

Figure 12.7. Mesh with a global bus and semigroup computation on it.

Phase 2: Combine the $p^{1/3}$ partial results in $O(p^{1/3})$ steps, using a sequential algorithm in one processor and the global bus for data transfers.

Phase 3: Broadcast the final result to all processors in one step.

In part because of the impracticality of connecting a large number of processors to a single global bus and partly to allow a larger number of long-distance data transfers to take place concurrently, meshes with row and column buses have been proposed. As shown in Fig. 12.8, each row/column has a separate bus that allows single-step data transfers from any processor to another processor in the same row/column (but only one such transfer per row or column in a given cycle). Any processor can be reached from any other in at most two steps. Again, algorithms like sorting are not significantly affected by the added buses as the bisection width has only doubled. However, semigroup computation now becomes much faster, requiring $O(p^{1/6})$ steps.

Semigroup computation on 2D mesh with row and column buses

Phase 1: Find the partial results in $p^{1/6} \times p^{1/6}$ submeshes in $O(p^{1/6})$ steps, with the results stored in the upper left corner of each submesh (Fig. 12.8).

Phase 2: Distribute the $p^{1/3}$ values left on some of the rows among the $p^{1/6}$ rows in the same slice so that each row only has $p^{1/6}$ values ($p^{1/6}$ steps).

Phase 3: Use the row buses to combine row values in $p^{1/6}$ steps; at this stage, there are $p^{1/2}$ values in Column 0 that must be combined.

Phase 4: Distribute the $p^{1/2}$ values in Column 0 among $p^{1/3}$ columns such that each column has $p^{1/6}$ values; constant time, using the row buses.

Phase 5: Use the column buses to combine column values in $p^{1/6}$ steps; at this stage, there are $p^{1/3}$ values in Row 0 that must be combined.

Phase 6: Distribute the $p^{1/3}$ values on Row 0 among the $p^{1/6}$ rows in Row Slice 0 in constant time, using the column buses.

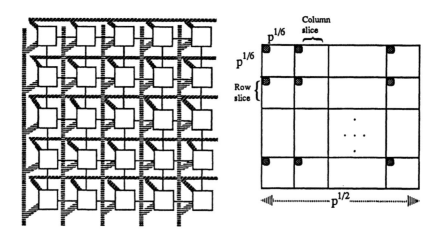

Figure 12.8. Mesh with row/column buses and semigroup computation on it.

Phase 7:   Combine the row values in $p^{1/6}$ steps using the row buses.
Phase 8:   Broadcast the final result to all processors in two steps.

Note that when row/column buses are added to a 2D mesh, a square mesh is no longer the best topology from the viewpoint of the above algorithm. It is relatively easy to show that if a $p^{5/8} \times p^{3/8}$ mesh is augmented with row/column buses, the above algorithm can be modified to run in $O(p^{1/8})$ steps, compared with $O(p^{1/6})$ in the square mesh. Supplying the details is left as an exercise.

12.4. MESHES WITH DYNAMIC LINKS

There are various ways of designing meshes so that node connectivities can change dynamically. For example, if buses are segmented through the insertion of switches that can be opened and closed under the control of a nearby processor, a powerful architecture results. When all switches on such a *separable bus* are closed, it becomes a single bus (e.g., row or column bus). At the other extreme, when all switches are open, multiple data transfers can be accommodated by using each bus segment independently. Figure 12.9 shows how a separable bus can be connected to, and its switches controlled by, the processors in a linear array.

A semigroup or fan-in computation can be performed on a p-processor linear array with a separable bus by first combining pairs of elements in even-numbered and the following odd-numbered processors and then successively dividing the bus into $p/4$, $p/8$, . . . , 2, 1 segments and allowing the processors connected to each segment to exchange their partial results in two bus transfer steps. This leads to an $O(\log p)$-step algorithm. The 2D mesh version of the algorithm is similar, with row combining and column combining done using row and column segmented buses as above.

Meshes with separable row/column buses have been studied in depth (see, e.g., [Serr93] and the references therein). One problem with such meshes is that the switches add to the data transmission delay over the bus, so that the bus cycle will become longer than that of a simple row/column bus. An advantage is that the buses provide a convenient mechanism for bypassing faulty processors so that certain fault tolerance schemes can be implemented with little effort (see, e.g., [Parh93]).

The additional power and flexibility provided by separable buses may allow us to use fewer buses for the same or higher performance. For example, if one separable row/column bus is provided for every $p^{1/6}$ rows or columns in a square mesh (say those whose row/column indices are multiples of $p^{1/6}$), then the semigroup computation of Fig. 12.8 can still be performed in $O(p^{1/6})$ steps. Once the submesh results are obtained, they can be combined in logarithmic time using the separable row buses to yield $p^{1/3}$ values in Column 0. A

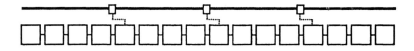

Figure 12.9. Linear array with a separable bus using reconfiguration switches.

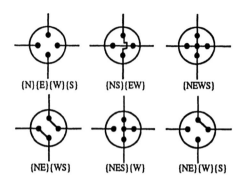

Figure 12.10. Some processor states in a reconfigurable mesh.

logarithmic time combining phase in Column 0 then yields the final result. In fact, we can do better than this by using more (but still fewer than $2p^{1/2}$) row and column buses or by utilizing an optimal nonsquare topology [Serr93].

It is also possible to provide reconfiguration capability within the processors as opposed to putting switches on the buses. One popular scheme, which has been investigated in great depth, is known as the *reconfigurable mesh* architecture. The processors have four ports and are connected to the ports of their four nearest neighbors as in a conventional mesh. However, internally each processor can tie together a subset of its ports to allow data to go through it and get from one neighbor to one or more other neighbors (Fig. 12.10). By proper setting of processor states, buses can be established: from a global bus linking all processors to a variety of complex patterns of connectivity. Row and column buses can also be formed as a special case if desired. The switch delay is still a problem in such architectures, particularly if a signal has to propagate through many switches.

12.5. PYRAMID AND MULTIGRID SYSTEMS

The pyramid architecture combines 2D mesh and tree connectivities in order to gain advantages from both schemes. Topologically, the pyramid inherits low logarithmic diameter from the tree and relatively wide bisection from the mesh. Algorithmically, features of each network can be utilized when convenient (e.g., fast semigroup or prefix computation on the tree and efficient sorting or data permutation on the mesh).

A pyramid network can be defined recursively. A single node is a one-level pyramid. The single node doubles as the pyramid's *apex* and its 1×1 *base*. An l-level pyramid consists of a $2^{l-1} \times 2^{l-1}$ base mesh, with groups of four nodes, forming 2×2 submeshes on the base, connected to each node of the base of an $(l-1)$-level pyramid (Fig. 12.11). The number of processors in an l-level pyramid is $p = (2^{2l} - 1)/3$. From this expression, it is evident that roughly three-fourths of the processors belong to the base. It is thus not very wasteful of processors if we assume that only the base processors contain data and other processors are only used for data routing and various combining operations. This is similar to our assumption in Section 2.4 that only leaf nodes of a tree architecture hold data elements. The diameter of an l-level pyramid is $2l-2$ and its maximum node degree is 9 for $l \geq 4$.

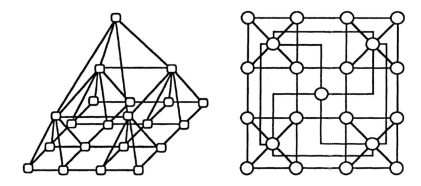

Figure 12.11. Pyramid with three levels and 4×4 base along with its 2D layout.

A pyramid can perform a semigroup computation in $O(\log p)$ steps when each processor on the base holds a single data item and the items are indexed in shuffled row-major order (see Fig. 9.3). Each processor combines the values from its four children until the final result is found at the apex. Then, the result is broadcast to all nodes. Parallel prefix computation is similarly quite simple with the same assumptions. Semigroup computation under other indexing schemes on the base is no different, provided that the semigroup operation ⊗ is commutative. Semigroup computation algorithm with other indexing schemes and a non-commutative operator becomes more complex, as does parallel prefix computation under similar conditions.

Sorting on a pyramid cannot be significantly faster than on a 2D mesh. The 2^l-link bisection width of an l-level pyramid ($l > 1$) establishes an $\Omega(\sqrt{p})$ lower bound on the worst-case running time of any sorting algorithm. Data routing, on the other hand, can be speeded up by the added links compared with a 2D mesh. To route from any node to any other node on the base mesh, one can simply route upward to the apex and then downward to the destination node. This algorithm works fine as long as the number of messages is small. Otherwise, congestion at and near the apex increases the routing delays and buffer requirements. The bisection-width argument can again be invoked to show that an arbitrary $O(p)$-packet routing problem would take at least $\Omega(\sqrt{p})$ steps to solve on a p-processor pyramid.

The 2D multigrid architecture can be derived from the pyramid by removing all but one of the downward links of each processor (Fig. 12.12). This reduces the maximum node degree (from 9 to 6) and thus the processor complexity, but otherwise preserves most of the properties of the pyramid, including its bisection width and logarithmic diameter. It is easy to see that the diameter of the l-level 2D multigrid architecture satisfies the recurrence $D(l) \leq D(l-1) + 6$, with $D(2) = 2$. Actually the diameter of the two-level 2D multigrid is 3, but for $l \geq 3$, we can take it to be 2 as far as the recurrence is concerned.

The 2D multigrid is to the pyramid what the 1D multigrid is to the binary X-tree (Fig. 11.11). In fact, each of the side views of the pyramid (2D multigrid) is a binary X-tree (1D multigrid).

Both the pyramid and 2D multigrid architectures are suitable for image-processing applications where the base holds the image data (one pixel or block of pixels per processor)

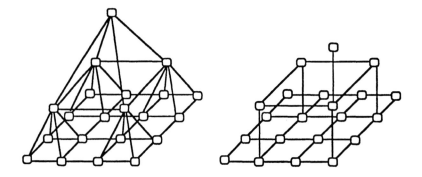

Figure 12.12. The relationship between pyramid and 2D multigrid architectures.

and performs low-level image operations that involve communication between nearby pixels. Processors in the upper layers of the pyramid or multigrid deal with higher-level features and processes involving successively larger parts of the image.

12.6. MESHES OF TREES

The mesh of trees architecture represents another attempt at combining the advantages of tree and mesh structures. Like the pyramid, an l-level mesh of trees architecture has a $2^{l-1} \times 2^{l-1}$ base whose processors are the leaves of 2^{l-1} row trees and 2^{l-1} column trees. The number of processors in an l-level mesh of trees is $p = 2^l(3 \times 2^{2l-2} - 1)$. From this expression, it is evident that roughly one-third of the processors belong to the base. The diameter of an l-level mesh of trees is $4l - 4$, its bisection width is 2^{l-1}, and its maximum node degree is 3.

Several variations to the basic mesh of trees architecture of Fig. 12.13 are possible. If the base processors are connected as a 2D mesh, the maximum node degree increases to 6. The ith row and ith column root nodes may be merged into a single node (increasing the node degree to 4) or interconnected by an extra link (preserving the maximum node degree of 3). Either modification increases the efficiency of some algorithms. One can also construct trees diagonally, in lieu of or in addition to row and/or column trees.

The mesh of trees architecture has a recursive structure in the sense that removing the row and column root nodes, along with their associated links, yields four smaller mesh of trees networks. This property is useful in the design of recursive algorithms. A mesh of trees network with an $m \times m$ base can be viewed as a switching network between m processors located at the row roots and m memory modules at the column roots (right side of Fig. 12.14). Note that P_i and M_j are connected to one and only one of the switches in the middle column. Hence, there is a unique path from each P_i to each M_j and the paths are node-disjoint. Thus, effectively a crossbar switch with full permutation capability and O(log m) switching delay is implemented. If row and column root nodes are merged, then a processor-to-processor interconnection network is obtained.

Semigroup and parallel prefix computations can be performed in $4l - 4$ and $6l - 6$ steps, respectively, on an l-level mesh of trees using row/column combining and prefix computations on the respective trees. The latter can be reduced to $4l - 3$ steps by doing row semigroup

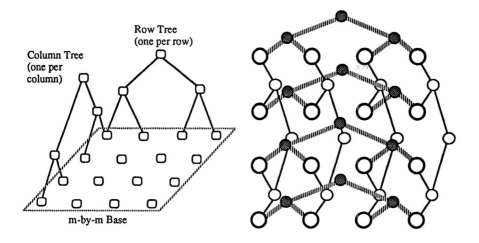

Figure 12.13. Mesh of trees architecture with three levels and a 4×4 base.

computations concurrently with row prefix computations (pipelining the two will add only one time step to the running time of one of them).

To route m^2 packets stored one per processor on the $m\times m$ base, one can use a variant of the row-first routing algorithm. Row trees are used to send each packet to its destination column. Then, column trees are utilized to route the packets to their destination rows. However, because the m^2 packets must all go through the $2m$ root nodes, the worst-case running time of this algorithm is $\Omega(m) = \Omega(\sqrt{p})$. If we take the view shown in Fig. 12.14, with only m packets to be routed from one side of the network to the other, only $2\log_2 m$ routing steps are required, provided that the destination nodes are all distinct.

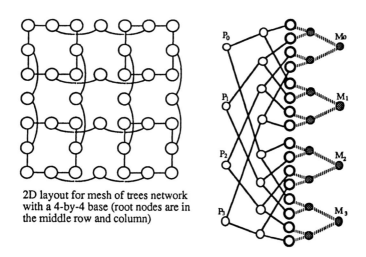

2D layout for mesh of trees network with a 4-by-4 base (root nodes are in the middle row and column)

Figure 12.14. Alternate views of the mesh of trees architecture with a 4×4 base.

To sort m^2 keys, stored one per processor on the $m \times m$ base, one can devise an algorithm based on shearsort, where row and column sorts are done on the respective trees rather than on linear arrays. Supplying the details of the algorithm is left as an exercise. Because an m-node binary tree can sort m items in $O(m)$ time, the running time of this algorithm is asymptotically the same as that of shearsort on a 2D mesh. If we take the view shown in Fig. 12.14, with only m keys to be sorted, then the following algorithm can be used (we assume that the row and column root nodes have been merged and each holds one of the keys).

Sorting m keys on a mesh of trees with an $m \times m$ base
_____

    Phase 1: Broadcast the keys to the leaves within both trees (Leaf i,j gets x_i and x_j)
    Phase 2: At a base processor: if $x_j > x_i$ or $x_j = x_i$ and $j > i$ then $flag := 1$ else $flag := 0$
    Phase 3: Add the $flag$ values in column trees (Root i obtains the rank of x_i)
    Phase 4: Route x_i from Root i to Root $rank[i]$

Matrix–vector multiplication $Ax = y$ can be done quite efficiently if the matrix A is stored on the base and the vector x in the column roots, say. Then, the result vector y is obtained in the row roots as follows.

Multiplying an $m \times m$ matrix by an m-vector on a mesh of trees
_____

    Phase 1: Broadcast x_j through the ith column tree (Leaf i,j has a_{ij} and x_j)
    Phase 2: At each base processor compute $a_{ij}x_j$
    Phase 3: Sum over row trees (Row root i obtains $\sum_{i=0}^{m-1} a_{ij}x_j = y_i$)

One can use pipelining to multiply r matrix–vector pairs in $2l - 2 + r$ steps.

    The convolution of two vectors can be easily computed if the mesh of trees with an $m \times (2m - 1)$ base contains m diagonal trees in addition to the row and column trees, as shown in Fig. 12.15. Assume that the ith element of the vector x is in ith row root and that the jth element of the vector y is in the $(m - 1 - j)$th diagonal root. The following algorithm yields the kth element of the convolution z, defined as $z_k = a_k b_0 + a_{k-1} b_1 + \cdots + a_0 b_k$, in the kth column root.

Convolution of two m-vectors on a mesh of trees with an $m \times (2m-1)$ base
_____

    Phase 1: Broadcast x_j from the ith row root to all row nodes on the base
    Phase 2: Broadcast y_{m-1-j} from the $(m - 1 - j)$th diagonal root to the base diagonal
    Phase 3: Leaf i,j, which has x_i and $y_{2m-2-i-j}$, multiplies them to get $x_i y_{2m-2-i-j}$
    Phase 4: Sum over columns to get $z_{2m-2-j} = \sum_{i=0}^{m-1} x_i y_{2m-2-i-j}$ in column root j

Note that Phases 1 and 2 of this algorithm can be overlapped to speed up the computation.

    The final algorithm described in this section deals with the construction of a minimal-weight spanning tree for an undirected graph with edge weights. A *spanning tree* of a connected graph is a subset of its edges that preserves the connectivity of all nodes in the graph but does not contain any cycle. A *minimal-weight spanning tree* (MWST) is a subset of edges that has the minimum total weight among all spanning trees. This is a very important problem. For example, if the graph under consideration represents a communication (trans-

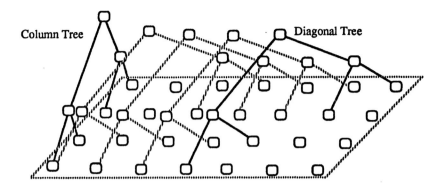

Figure 12.15. Mesh of trees variant with row, column, and diagonal trees.

portation) network, an MWST tree might correspond to the best way to broadcast a message to all nodes (deliver products to the branches of a chain store from a central warehouse).

The MWST problem can be solved by a simple greedy algorithm. Assume for simplicity that all edge weights are unique so that there is always a single minimum-weight edge among any subset of edges. At each step, we have a set of connected components or "supernodes" (initially n single-node components). We connect each component to its "nearest" neighbor, i.e., we find the minimum-weight edge that connects the component to another component. Any such minimum-weight outgoing edge from a component must be in the MWST. Assume that it is not; thus, the component is connected to the rest of the MWST by means of one or more other edges with larger weights. Remove any of these edges and replace it with the minimum-weight edge. This yields a spanning tree with smaller total weight than the MWST; clearly a contradiction.

An example is shown in Fig. 12.16. We begin with nine components and identify the minimal-weight outgoing edge from each. These are shown as heavy lines in the upper right diagram. Inclusion of these edges in the MWST reduces the problem to that of identifying the MWST of the four-node graph shown at the lower left, where each node corresponds to a subset of two or three nodes in the original nine-node graph. Again, the minimal-weight outgoing edge from each node is identified (heavy lines) and included in the MWST. This leaves us with two supernodes and their minimal-weight connecting edge with weight 25 completes the MWST as shown in the lower right diagram.

The proof of convergence for the greedy algorithm is simple. The spanning tree has $n - 1$ edges. The first phase of the greedy algorithm selects at least $n/2$ edges of the tree. Each subsequent phase cuts in half the number of unidentified edges. Thus, there will be $\log_2 n$ phases. If the graph's weight matrix W (see Fig. 11.15) is stored in the leaves of a mesh of trees architecture, each phase requires $O(\log^2 n)$ steps with a simple algorithm (to be shown) and $O(\log n)$ steps with a more sophisticated algorithm. The total running time is thus $O(\log^3 n)$ or $O(\log^2 n)$. For comparison purposes, sequential algorithms for this problem have the following complexities, where n is the number of nodes and e the number of edges in the graph:

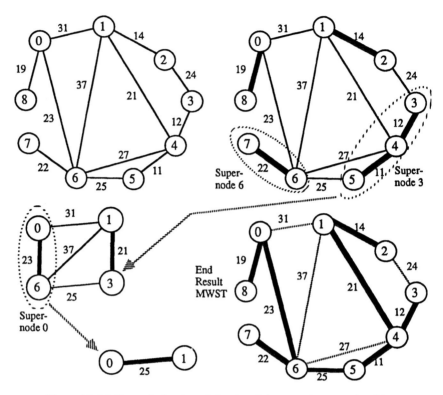

Figure 12.16. Example for the minimal-weight spanning tree algorithm.

Kruskal's algorithm: $O(e \log e)$ steps $\Rightarrow O(n^2 \log n)$ for dense
graphs with $e = O(n^2)$

Prim's algorithm with binary heap: $O((e + n) \log n) \Rightarrow O(n^2 \log n)$

Prim's algorithm with Fibonacci heap: $O(e + n \log n) \Rightarrow O(n^2)$

Thus, our best parallel solution offers a speed-up of $O(n^2/\log^2 n)$ which is sublinear in the number $p = O(n^2)$ of processors used.

The key part of the simple parallel version of the greedy algorithm is showing that each phase can be done in $O(\log^2 n)$ steps. Because weights are assumed to be unique, they can double as edge IDs. Edge weights are stored in leaves, with Leaf (i, j) holding the weight $w(i, j)$ of Edge (i, j). The roots of Row i and Column i are merged into a single degree-4 node representing Node i of the graph. A label $L(i)$ associated with each node i gives its supernode identity. $L(i)$ is initialized to i, i.e., there are n supernodes initially. If $L(i) = i$, Node i is the supernode *leader*. At the start of each of the $\log_2 n$ phases, Leaf (i, j) knows if Edge (i, j) is in the spanning tree and, if so, to which supernode it belongs. The algorithm for each phase consists of two subphases:

a. Find the minimum-weight edge incident to each supernode.
b. Merge the supernodes for the next phase.

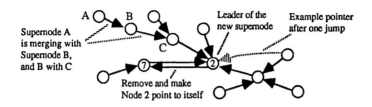

Figure 12.17. Finding the new supernode ID when several supernodes merge.

Subphase (a) can be done in $4 \log_2 n$ steps in the following way. Each member node of a supernode finds its minimum-weight outgoing edge in $2 \log_2 n$ steps (the minimum value in Column i). Then, the minimum among these minimums is found in $2 \log_2 n$ steps. Subphase (b) can be done in $O(\log^2 n)$ steps in the following way. Each supernode leader knows the "closest" supernode with which it must merge. The only remaining problems are to determine the identity of the new supernode and to disperse this identity to all nodes within the supernode. If Supernode A is merging with Supernode B, which is in turn merging with Supernode C, and so forth, a chain reaction occurs that might slow down the identification process. If we view the merging information in each Supernode X as a pointer to another supernode Y (Fig. 12.17), then there will always be a pair of supernodes that point to each other. Of these two nodes, the one with the smaller supernode ID can be designated as the new leader. Nodes can become aware of the new leader's ID by a pointer-jumping process (see Section 5.5) in $\log_2 n$ iterations, each requiring $O(\log n)$ steps. For details and improvements, consult Leighton ([Leig92], pp. 325–338).

PROBLEMS

12.1. Sorting on q-dimensional mesh and torus networks

   a. Justify the bisection-based lower bound $p^{1/q}/2$ for sorting on a q-D mesh.

   b. Show that if interprocessor communication is restricted to be in one direction in each step, then a corresponding *multisection lower bound* of $qp^{1/q}/2$ applies.

   c. How are the lower bounds of parts (a) and (b) affected in k–k sorting, where each processor begins and ends up with k records?

   d. Derive lower bounds similar to those of parts (a)–(c) in the case of a q-D torus.

12.2. q-dimensional torus networks

This problem deals with m-ary q-cubes, i.e., q-dimensional torus networks with sides of length m.

   a. Show that an m-ary q-cube is node-symmetric in the sense that the network looks exactly the same when viewed from any of its nodes.

   b. Show that the sum of distances from any node of a 2D torus to all other nodes is $m(m^2 - 1)/2$ if m is odd and $m^3/2$ if m is even. These lead to simple closed-form expressions for the average internode distance in the two cases.

   c. Show that the generalized forms for the expressions of part (b) in the case of an m-ary q-cube are $q(m^2 - 1)m^{q-1}/4$ and $qm^{q+1}/4$, respectively.

12.3. Hexagonal mesh

The node indexing scheme in the hexagonal mesh of Fig. 12.2 is such that each Node i is connected to Nodes $i \pm 1$, $i \pm 7$, and $i \pm 8$ (mod 19). Even though wraparound links are not shown in Fig. 12.2, assume that the same rules apply to them as well.

   a. Determine the number of nodes in a hex mesh with each outside edge having m processors.

   b. Generalize the above node indexing scheme for a hex mesh with sides of length m.

   c. Draw the hex mesh of Fig. 12.2, with the connectivity rules given above, as a chordal ring.

   d. Show that the general hex mesh, as defined in part (b), consists of three edge-disjoint rings.

12.4. Manhattan street networks

Consider a Manhattan street network with an even number r of rows and an even number p/r of columns.

   a. Find the exact network diameter in terms of p and r and for the special case of $r = \sqrt{p}$.

   b. Devise an efficient routing algorithm for the network and analyze its delay and buffer needs.

   c. Analyze the complexity of the shearsort algorithm on this network. *Hint:* Let pairs of rows and columns cooperate on row and column sorts.

   d. Describe a matrix multiplication algorithm with its associated data layout for this network.

12.5. Honeycomb mesh

Extend the hex mesh of Fig. 12.2 by adding two layers of nodes around its periphery. Then remove the nodes currently numbered 0, 2, 3, 5, 14, 16, 17, and so on (the resulting network resembles a honeycomb). Show that a honeycomb mesh with a rectangular boundary is in fact a pruned 2D mesh. Use this knowledge to derive its diameter and bisection width.

12.6. Pruned 3D torus

Consider a pruned 3D torus network, similar to that in Fig. 12.4, with an even number l of layers, r rows, and $p/(lr)$ columns.

   a. Find the exact network diameter in terms of p, l, and r and for the special case of $l = r = \sqrt[3]{p}$.

   b. Devise an efficient routing algorithm for the network and analyze its delay and buffer needs.

   c. Analyze the complexity of the 3D mesh sorting algorithm (Section 12.1) for this network. *Hint:* Let pairs of layers cooperate on the 2D sorts.

   d. How would you partition an $8 \times 8 \times 8$ pruned torus for implementation on eight circuit boards each holding 64 processors (see Fig. 12.1)?

12.7. Mesh with row/column buses

   a. Show that the optimal aspect ratio (number of rows divided by number of columns) in a mesh with row/column buses is $p^{1/4}$ for the semigroup computation; i.e., the optimal mesh is $p^{5/8} \times p^{3/8}$. *Hint:* The running time of the algorithm becomes $O(p^{1/8})$.

   b. Show that if multiple items can be stored in each processor, then a mesh with row/column buses can perform a semigroup computation in $O(n^{1/9})$ steps using $p = n^{8/9}$ processors in an $n^{5/9} \times n^{3/9}$ mesh.

12.8. Mesh with separable row/column buses

   a. In Fig. 12.9, why is a bus switch provided after every four processors rather than after every two?

   b. Can we remove the local interprocessor links and use the separable buses for all data transfers, thereby reducing the node degree to 2? Would this involve a speed penalty?

12.9. Mesh with fixed segmented row/column buses
Suppose that an $r \times (p/r)$ mesh is equipped with fixed segmented buses. In each column (row), groups of x (y) processors are connected to the same bus segment, with r/x ($p/(ry)$) bus segments in a column (row).

    a. Determine the optimal number of bus segments in each row and column, x^{opt} and y^{opt}, in order to maximize the speed of semigroup computation.

    b. Determine the optimal aspect ratio $r/(p/r)$ for a p-processor mesh performing semigroup computation.

12.10. Linear array with a separable bus
Consider a linear array having a single bus that spans the entire array, with a bus switch inserted after every g processors. Assume that each switch is immediately before, and controlled by, a processor whose index is a multiple of g. Figure 12.9 shows an example with $p = 16$ and $g = 4$.

    a. Develop algorithms for semigroup and parallel prefix computation on this architecture.

    b. Show how this architecture can efficiently execute the odd–even reduction of Section 11.3.

12.11. Pyramid architecture

    a. Derive and prove a formula for the bisection width of an l-level pyramid.

    b. Supply the details of parallel prefix computation on a pyramid and find its exact running time.

    c. Each row on the base of a pyramid can be viewed as forming the leaves of a complete binary tree rooted at the apex. Can we use this observation to develop a fast semigroup or parallel prefix computation algorithm for data elements stored on the base with row-major indexing?

12.12. Pyramid architecture
Can a pyramid with an $m \times m$ base efficiently simulate:

    a. A larger pyramid with a $2m \times 2m$ base?

    b. A mesh of trees architecture with an $m \times m$ base?

    c. An $m \times m$ mesh with a single global bus?

    d. An $m \times m$ mesh with row and column buses?

12.13. 2D multigrid architecture

    a. Derive and prove a formula for the bisection width of an l-level 2D multigrid architecture.

    b. Show that the recurrence $D(l) = D(l-1) + 6$ with $D(2) = 2$ provides a tight bound for the diameter of a 2D multigrid architecture when l is sufficiently large.

    c. How large does l need to be for the result of part (b) to hold? Find the exact value of the diameter for all smaller values of l.

    d. Describe and analyze a semigroup computation algorithm on a 2D multigrid.

    e. Describe and analyze a parallel prefix computation algorithm on a 2D multigrid.

12.14. Mesh of trees architecture

    a. Show that routing g packets between processors on the base of a mesh of trees networks requires $\Omega(\sqrt{g})$ routing steps in the worst case, even if no two destinations are the same.

    b. Show how to find the minimum of m numbers, each m bits wide, in $O(\log^2 m)$ steps on an $m \times m$ mesh of trees network.

12.15. *k*D meshes

Show that a *k*D *p*-processor mesh with equal sides along each of the *k* dimensions has a bisection width no smaller than $p^{1-1/k}$. Note that it is not adequate to observe that slicing the *k*D mesh down the middle along one of the dimensions will cut exactly $p^{1-1/k}$ links if $p^{1/k}$ is even and slightly more if $p^{1/k}$ is odd; this only establishes an upper bound on the bisection width. *Hint:* Show how to connect every pair of nodes in the array by a pair of directed paths, one in each direction, such that no edge of the array is contained in more than $p^{1+1/k}/2$ such paths, thereby establishing a correspondence between the *k*D mesh and a *p*-node directed complete graph whose bisection width is known.

REFERENCES AND SUGGESTED READING

[Agar91]   Agarwal, A., "Limits on Interconnection Network Performance," *IEEE Trans. Parallel and Distributed Systems*, Vol. 2, No. 4, pp. 398–412, October 1991.

[Ande97]   Anderson, J. R., and S. Abraham, "Multidimensional Network Performance with Unidirectional Links," *Proc. Int. Conf. Parallel Processing*, 1997, pp. 26–33.

[Corb92]   Corbett, P. F., and I. D. Scherson, "Sorting in Mesh-Connected Multiprocessors," *IEEE Trans. Parallel and Distributed Systems*, Vol. 3, No. 5, pp. 626–632, September 1992.

[Dall90]   Dally, W. J., "Performance Analysis of *k*-ary *n*-cube Interconnection Networks," *IEEE Trans. Computers*, Vol. 39, No. 6, pp. 775–785, 1990.

[Kund86]   Kunde, M., "A General Approach to Sorting on 3-Dimensionally Mesh-Connected Arrays," *Proc. CONPAR*, 1986, pp. 329–337.

[Kund91]   Kunde, M., "Concentrated Regular Data Streams on Grids: Sorting and Routing Near to the Bisection Bound," *Proc. Symp. Foundations of Computer Science*, 1991, pp. 141–150.

[Kwai97]   Kwai, D.-M., and B. Parhami, "A Class of Fixed-Degree Cayley-Graph Interconnection Networks Derived by Pruning *k*-ary *n*-cubes," *Proc. Int. Conf. Parallel Processing*, 1997, pp. 92–95.

[Leig92]   Leighton, F. T., *Introduction to Parallel Algorithms and Architectures: Arrays, Trees, Hypercubes*, Morgan Kaufmann, 1992.

[Parh93]   Parhami, B., "Fault Tolerance Properties of Mesh-Connected Parallel Computers with Separable Row/Column Buses," *Proc. 36th Midwest Symp. Circuits and Systems*, August 1993, pp. 1128–1131.

[Raja96]   Rajasekaran, S., "Mesh Connected Computers with Fixed and Reconfigurable Buses: Packet Routing and Sorting," *IEEE Trans. Computers*, Vol. 45, No. 5, pp. 529–539, May 1996.

[Serr93]   Serrano, M. J., and B. Parhami, "Optimal Architectures and Algorithms for Mesh-Connected Parallel Computers with Separable Row/Column Buses," *IEEE Trans. Parallel and Distributed Systems*, Vol. 4, No. 10, pp. 1073–1080, October 1993.

IV

Low-Diameter Architectures

The bulk of this part deals with the (binary) hypercube architecture and its many derivatives and variants, collectively referred to as *hypercubic networks*. However, we will also consider a variety of other interconnection structures that offer advantages over hypercubic networks under certain valuation criteria, work loads, or technological constraints. A common property that links all of these architectures is that their diameters are (or can be, with proper choice of their structural parameters) much lower than those of meshes and tori. Specifically, whereas a q-D p-node mesh or torus has a diameter of $\Theta(p^{1/q})$ with a node degree of $\Theta(q)$, these networks offer logarithmic or sublogarithmic diameters with maximum node degrees ranging from 3 to $\log_2 p$. By the end of this part, which is composed of the following four chapters, we will have a more or less complete picture of the sea of interconnection networks partially visible in Fig. 4.8.

- Chapter 13: Hypercubes and Their Algorithms
- Chapter 14: Sorting and Routing on Hypercubes
- Chapter 15: Other Hypercubic Architectures
- Chapter 16: A Sampler of Other Networks

13

Hypercubes and Their Algorithms

The hypercube architecture has played an important role in the development of parallel processing and is still quite popular and influential. The logarithmic diameter, linear bisection, and highly symmetric recursive structure of the hypercube support a variety of elegant and efficient parallel algorithms that often serve as starting points for developing, or benchmarks for evaluating, algorithms on other architectures. The hypercube's symmetry and recursive structure also lead to rich theoretical underpinnings that bring forth a wide array of theoretical results about its performance, layout in physical space, and robustness. In this chapter, we introduce the hypercube, study its topological and embedding properties, and present a number of simple algorithms. Sorting and routing algorithms will be covered in Chapter 14. Chapter topics are

- 13.1. Definition and main properties
- 13.2. Embeddings and their usefulness
- 13.3. Embedding of arrays and trees
- 13.4. A few simple algorithms
- 13.5. Matrix multiplication
- 13.6. Inverting a lower triangular matrix

13.1. DEFINITION AND MAIN PROPERTIES

The origins of the hypercube architecture can be traced back to the early 1960s [Squi63]. Subsequently, both the direct (single-stage) version, discussed in this chapter, and the indirect or multistage version, to be covered in Sections 14.4 and 15.2, were proposed as interconnection networks for parallel processing [Peas77], [Sull77]. None of these early proposals led to a hardware implementation, primarily because of high hardware cost [Haye89]. The development of routing algorithms and application programs for the Cosmic Cube, a 64-processor hypercube system built at the California Institute of Technology in the early 1980s [Seit85], was instrumental in the introduction of several hypercube-based commercial parallel computers in the late 1980s. One example of such machines is discussed in Section 22.3.

As special cases of m-ary q-cubes, hypercubes are also called *binary q-cubes*, or simply *q-cubes*, where q indicates the number of dimensions. We will use the term *hypercube* to refer to a generic architecture of this type and q-cube (particularly, 3-cube, 4-cube, and so forth) when the number of dimensions is relevant to the discussion.

A q-dimensional *binary hypercube* (q-cube) is defined recursively as follows:

- A 1-cube consists of two nodes, labeled 0 and 1, with a link connecting them.
- A q-cube consists of two $(q-1)$-cubes, with the nodes labeled by preceding the original node labels of the two *subcubes* with 0 and 1, respectively, and connecting each node with the label $0x$ to the node with the label $1x$. The two $(q-1)$-cubes forming the q-cube are known as its 0 and 1 subcubes.

Figure 13.1 shows the recursive construction of q-cubes for $q = 1, 2, 3,$ and 4. The same process is used to construct q-cubes for larger values of q, although it becomes increasingly difficult to represent the resulting structures in 2D drawings.

Because a 1-cube has two nodes and each recursive step in the above definition doubles the number of nodes, a q-cube has $p = 2^q$ nodes or processors. Similarly, because a 1-cube has nodes of degree 1 and each recursive step increases the node degree by 1, a q-cube consists of nodes with degree $d = q = \log_2 p$. The node structure of a hypercube (number of its interprocessor communication ports) changes as the system expands in size; thus, a hypercube architecture is not scalable.

If the label of a node x (its binary ID) is $x_{q-1}x_{q-2} \cdots x_2x_1x_0$, then its q neighbors are

$$x_{q-1}x_{q-2} \cdots x_2x_1x_0' \text{ neighbor along Dimension 0; denoted by } N_0(x)$$

$$x_{q-1}x_{q-2} \cdots x_2x_1'x_0 \text{ neighbor along Dimension 1 or } N_1(x)$$

$$\vdots$$

$$x_{q-1}'x_{q-2} \cdots x_2x_1x_0 \text{ neighbor along Dimension } q-1 \text{ or } N_{q-1}(x)$$

In other words, the labels of any two neighboring nodes differ in exactly 1 bit. Two nodes whose labels differ in k bits (have a *Hamming distance* of k) are connected by a shortest path of length k. For example, in the 4-cube of Fig. 13.1, a shortest path from Node $x = 0010$ to $y = 1001$ goes through the intermediate nodes $N_3(0010) = 1010$ and $N_1(1010) = 1000$, and

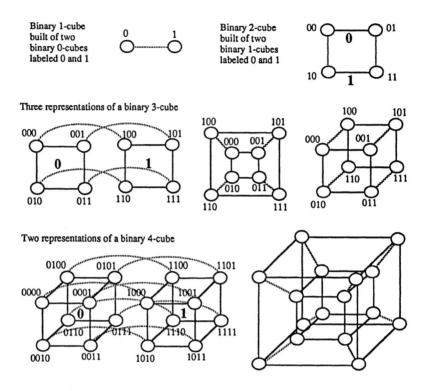

Figure 13.1. The recursive structure of binary hypercubes.

thus has a length of 3, which is equal to the Hamming distance between x and y. Consequently, it is easy to see that the diameter of a q-cube is $D = q = \log_2 p$. The bisection width of a q-cube is $B = p/2 = 2^{q-1}$. The logarithmic diameter and the linear bisection width of a hypercube are two reasons for its ability to perform many computations at high speed.

Hypercubes are both node- and edge-symmetric, meaning that the roles of any two nodes (edges) can be interchanged with proper relabeling of the nodes. Swapping the leftmost 2 bits in every node label of a q-cube interchanges the roles of dimensions $q - 1$ and $q - 2$. As a result, 0 and 1 subcubes can be defined for each of the q dimensions of a q-cube. Complementing a particular bit position in all node labels results in a relabeling of the nodes that switches the roles of the 0 and 1 subcubes associated with that dimension. A node label x can be transformed to a different node label y with k such complementation steps, where k is the Hamming distance between x and y. Similarly, swapping bit positions i and j in all node labels interchanges the roles of Dimension-i and Dimension-j links. Thus, the designations "Dimension 0," "Dimension 1," and so forth are arbitrary and no inherent order exists among the various dimensions.

Hypercubes have many interesting topological properties, some of which will be explored in the remainder of this chapter and the end-of-chapter problems. The recursive structure of hypercubes makes them ideal for running recursive or divide-and-conquer type algorithms. The results of subproblems solved on the two $(q-1)$-dimensional subcubes of a

q-cube can often be merged quickly in view of the one-to-one connectivity (*matching*) between the two subcubes. Multiple node-disjoint and edge-disjoint paths exist between many pairs of nodes in a hypercube, making it relatively easy to develop routing and other parallel algorithms that are tolerant of node or edge failures. A large MIMD-type hypercube machine can be shared by multiple applications, each of which uses a suitably sized subcube or partition.

13.2. EMBEDDINGS AND THEIR USEFULNESS

Given the architectures A and A' we *embed* A into A' by specifying

- A node mapping (indicating that Node v of A is mapped onto Node v' of A'); the node mapping can be many-to-one.
- An edge mapping (indicating that Edge uv of A is mapped onto a path from Node u' to node v' in A', where u' and v' are given by the node mapping).

Example embeddings of a seven-node complete binary tree into 3×3, 2×4, or 2×2 meshes are shown in Fig. 13.2. For the 3×3 and 2×4 meshes, each tree node is mapped onto a different mesh node, whereas for the 2×2 mesh, pairs of tree nodes are mapped onto all but one of the mesh nodes. Generally, edges of the tree are mapped onto single-edge paths in the meshes, the only exceptions being in the 2×4 mesh, where Edge d of the tree has been mapped onto the path between Nodes 1 and 4 that goes through Node 3, and in the 2×2 mesh, where Edges a and e of the tree have been mapped onto paths of length 0 (from a node to itself).

Embeddings are useful because they allow us to use an algorithm developed for an existing architecture on a new or different one by simply letting the new/different architecture follow the same steps as in the old architecture (we say that the new architecture *emulates* the old one). Hence, e.g., the embeddings shown in Fig. 13.2 allow each of the meshes to run tree-based algorithms, albeit with some slowdown in general. However, algorithms

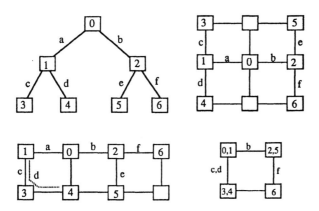

Figure 13.2. Embedding a seven-node binary tree into 2D meshes of various sizes.

developed directly for a given architecture tend to be more efficient as they take advantage of unique features or strengths of that architecture.

In order to gauge the effectiveness of an embedding with regard to algorithm performance, various measures or parameters have been defined. The most important ones are listed below. For these measures, the numerical values of the parameters for the three example embeddings of Fig. 13.2 are also provided as examples.

	Examples of Fig. 13.2 →	3×3	2×4	2×2
Dilation	Longest path onto which any given edge is mapped	1	2	1
Congestion	Maximum number of edges mapped onto one edge	1	2	2
Load factor	Maximum number of nodes mapped onto one node	1	1	2
Expansion	Ratio of the number of nodes in the two graphs	9/7	8/7	4/7

The *dilation* of an embedding is an indicator of the slowdown in the new architecture as a result of indirect data communications. In other words, if congestion is 1, a dilation of 2, e.g., means that one communication step in the old architecture may require two time steps in the emulating one in the worst case.

The *congestion* of an embedding represents potential slowdown when certain edges in the old architecture must carry messages at the same time. "Potential" is used because we may be able to schedule the communication steps on the emulating architecture to reduce, or even totally eliminate, this slowdown. For example, if Node 1 of the tree were to send messages to Nodes 3 and 4 at the same time over links c and d, the 4×2 mesh emulating these communications can avoid any slowdown related to congestion by pipelining the two messages between Nodes 1 and 3, with the message going to Node 4 sent first. In view of the above, one might say that the congestion of the embedding associated with the 2×4 mesh in Fig. 13.2 is 1.5 rather than 2, as there are two different paths of length 2 that can be used for routing messages between Nodes 1 and 4.

The *load factor* of an embedding is an indicator of the potential slowdown in the new architecture as a result of one processor having to perform the job of several processors. Again, the actual slowdown may be smaller if computation and communication are overlapped, because a processor may have extra cycles to complete its computations as it waits for *dilated* or *congested* communications to take place.

The *expansion* of an embedding is related to the other parameters in that, e.g., one can reduce the expansion by increasing the load factor. Occasionally, we are interested in embeddings that keep the dilation and/or congestion and/or load factor at 1, or some other small constant, in an effort to have an efficient emulation. In such cases, the expansion of the embedding is an indicator of the cost of achieving the desired efficiency. Often an expansion factor that is greater than 1 results from the fact that many architectures come in specific sizes (e.g., perfect square for a square 2D mesh and power of 2 for a binary hypercube).

13.3. EMBEDDING OF ARRAYS AND TREES

In this section, we show how meshes, tori, and binary trees can be embedded into hypercubes in such a way as to allow a hypercube to run mesh, torus, and tree algorithms efficiently, i.e., with very small dilation and congestion. We will see later in this chapter, and in Chapter 14, that there exist several hypercube algorithms that are significantly faster than their counterparts on meshes/tori and binary trees. These observations together establish the hypercube architecture as "more powerful" than mesh, torus, or tree architecture.

We begin by showing an embedding of a 2^q-node ring in a q-cube for $q > 1$. Any p-node graph that can embed a p-node ring with dilation and load factor of 1 is said to be *Hamiltonian*. Such an embedding defines a ring subgraph containing all of the nodes of the graph, or a *Hamiltonian cycle* of the graph. Not all graphs have Hamiltonian cycles. For example, a 3×3 mesh is not a Hamiltonian graph, nor is a binary tree (or, more generally, an acyclic graph) of any size. Possession of a Hamiltonian cycle allows an architecture to emulate a ring or linear-array algorithm efficiently and is viewed as a desirable property.

We now prove that any q-cube is Hamiltonian for $q \geq 2$. The proof is by induction, starting with the basis that a 2-cube is Hamiltonian and proceeding with the induction step that if the $(q-1)$-cube is Hamiltonian, then so is the q-cube.

Consider the q-cube as two $(q-1)$-cubes obtained by removing all Dimension $q-1$ links. Take an arbitrary Hamiltonian path in the 0-subcube. Consider the edge linking a Node x with its Dimension-k neighbor $N_k(x)$ on this path, where $0 \leq k \leq q-2$. Now consider a Hamiltonian path in the 1-subcube that contains the edge linking $N_{q-1}(x)$ with $N_{q-1}(N_k(x))$ $= N_k(N_{q-1}(x))$. Because of edge symmetry, such a Hamiltonian path must exist. Now an embedded ring results if the two edges linking x with $N_k(x)$ and $N_{q-1}(x)$ with $N_k(N_{q-1}(x))$ (dotted lines in Fig. 13.3) are removed from the two rings and instead the two Dimension-$(q-1)$ edges linking x with $N_{q-1}(x)$ and $N_k(x)$ with $N_{q-1}(N_k(x))$ (heavy lines in Fig. 13.3) are inserted.

Another way to prove that the q-cube is Hamiltonian is to show that a q-bit Gray code (a sequence of q-bit codewords such that any two consecutive codewords, including the last and the first one, differ in a single bit position) can be constructed. Because of the unit Hamming distance between the binary labels of neighboring nodes in a q-cube, the q-bit Gray code defines a Hamiltonian cycle in the q-cube.

A q-bit Gray code can be built by induction. Clearly $\{0, 1\}$ is a 1-bit Gray code. Given a $(q-1)$-bit Gray code that begins with 0^{q-1} and ends with 10^{q-2}, where the superscripts denote the number of times that a symbol is repeated, a q-bit Gray code can be constructed as follows:

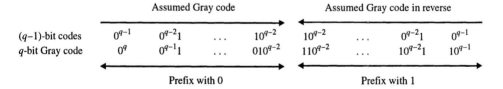

	Assumed Gray code			Assumed Gray code in reverse			
$(q-1)$-bit codes	0^{q-1}	$0^{q-2}1$	$\ldots$ 10^{q-2}	10^{q-2}	$\ldots$	$0^{q-2}1$	0^{q-1}
q-bit Gray code	0^q	$0^{q-1}1$	$\ldots$ 010^{q-2}	110^{q-2}	$\ldots$	$10^{q-2}1$	10^{q-1}
	Prefix with 0			Prefix with 1			

We next prove a more general result that a $2^{m_0} \times 2^{m_1} \times \cdots \times 2^{m_{h-1}}$ h-D mesh/torus is a subgraph of the q-cube, where $q = m_0 + m_1 + \cdots + m_{h-1}$; this is equivalent to the former being embedded in the latter with dilation 1, congestion 1, load factor 1, and expansion 1.

The proof is based on the notion of *cross-product graphs*, which we first define. Given k graphs $G_i = (V_i, E_i)$, $1 \leq i \leq k$, their (cross-)product graph $G = G_1 \times G_2 \times \cdots \times G_k$ is defined as the graph $G = (V, E)$, where

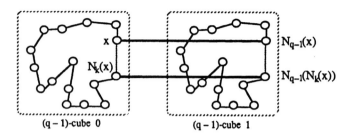

Figure 13.3. Hamiltonian cycle in the q-cube.

$$V = \{(v_1, v_2, \ldots, v_k) \mid v_i \in V_i, 1 \leq i \leq k\}$$

$$E = \{[(u_1, u_2, \ldots, u_k), (v_1, v_2, \ldots, v_k)] \mid \text{for some } j, (u_j, v_j) \in E_j \text{ and for } i \neq j, u_i = v_i\}$$

In other words, the nodes of the (cross-)product graph G are labeled with k-tuples, where the ith element of the k-tuple is chosen from the node set of the ith *component graph*. The edges of the product graph connect pairs of nodes whose labels are identical in all but the jth elements, say, and the two nodes corresponding to the jth elements in the jth component graph are connected by an edge. Figure 13.4 depicts three examples of product graphs. Note that the product graph $G = G_1 \times G_2$ can be viewed as being constructed from $|V_1|$ copies of G_2 or $|V_2|$ copies of G_1. It is easy to see that a 2D mesh is the product of two linear arrays and that a torus is the product of two rings.

If $G = G_1 \times G_2 \times \cdots \times G_k$ and $G' = G'_1 \times G'_2 \times \cdots \times G'_k$, where G_i is a subgraph of G'_i ($1 \leq i \leq k$), then G is clearly a subgraph of G'. The proof that a $2^{m_0} \times 2^{m_1} \times \cdots \times 2^{m_{h-1}}$ h-D mesh/torus is a subgraph of the $(m_0 + m_1 + \cdots + m_{h-1})$-cube now becomes easy:

1. The $2^{m_0} \times 2^{m_1} \times \cdots \times 2^{m_{h-1}}$ torus is the product of h rings of sizes $(2^{m_0}, 2^{m_1}, \ldots, 2^{m_{h-1}})$

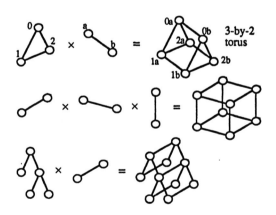

Figure 13.4. Examples of product graphs.

2. The $(m_0 + m_1 + \cdots + m_{h-1})$-cube is the product of an m_0-cube, an m_1-cube, $\ldots$, an m_{h-1}-cube.

3. The 2^{m_i}-node ring is a subgraph of the m_i-cube.

Part (2) above, which is the only part not yet proven, becomes obvious if we note that the q-cube is the product of q linear arrays of size 2 (see, e.g., the middle example in Fig. 13.4).

It is interesting to note that a 4-cube can be reduced to a 4×4 mesh by removing half of the Dimension-1 and Dimension-2 links (Fig. 13.5). Note that the links whose removal converts the 4-cube into a 4×4 mesh are exactly those that turn the 4×4 mesh into a 4×4 torus. Thus, the 16-node hypercube (2-ary 4-cube) is isomorphic to the 4×4 torus (4-ary 2-cube).

Note that for a mesh to be a subgraph of the hypercube, its sides must be powers of 2. The 3×5 mesh, e.g., is not a subgraph of the 16-node hypercube. However, because the 3×5 mesh is a subgraph of the 4×8 mesh/torus, it is a subgraph of the 5-cube.

We next examine the possibility of embedding the (2^q-1)-node complete binary tree in the q-cube. A simple argument shows that straight one-to-one embedding is impossible. Divide the hypercube nodes into those with odd and even weights, where the weight of a node is the number of 1s in its binary label. Exactly half of the nodes, i.e., 2^{q-1} nodes, fall into each category. If the node onto which the root of the binary tree is mapped has odd (even) weight, then the children of the root must be mapped onto even-weight (odd-weight) nodes. Proceeding in this manner, we see that about three-fourths of the nodes of the binary tree must be mapped onto hypercube nodes with odd or even weight. This is impossible because only half of the nodes have each type of weight.

The above negative result can be turned into a positive one by a slight modification in the graph to be embedded into the q-cube. The 2^q-node *double-rooted complete binary tree*, which is obtained from the (2^q-1)-node complete binary tree by inserting a node between the root and its right/left child, is in fact a subgraph of the q-cube (Fig. 13.6). Proving this result is equivalent to showing that the (2^q-1)-node complete binary tree can be embedded into a q-cube with dilation 2, congestion 1, load factor 1, and expansion $2^q/(2^q - 1)$.

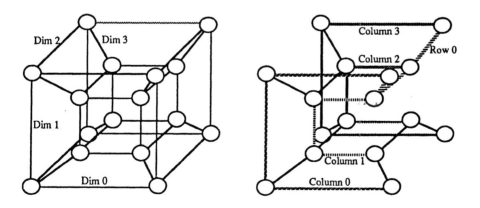

Figure 13.5. The 4×4 mesh/torus is a subgraph of the 4-cube.

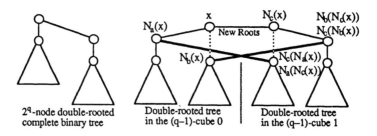

Figure 13.6. The 2^q-node double-rooted complete binary tree is a subgraph of the q-cube.

The proof is by induction. The 2-node double-rooted complete binary tree (with empty left and right subtrees) is a subgraph of the 1-cube. This forms our basis. Let the 2^{q-1}-node double-rooted complete binary tree be a subgraph of the $(q-1)$-cube. Figure 13.6 shows how the embedding in the q-cube can be obtained by taking two embedded trees in the 0 and 1 subcubes along Dimension c, removing one link from each (dotted lines in Fig. 13.6), and inserting two new links instead (heavy lines). Note that the roles of the a and b dimensions are interchanged in the embedded double-rooted complete binary tree within the $(q-1)$-cube 1 compared with that in the $(q-1)$-cube 0. But we know that this can be done in view of the complete symmetry of the hypercube with respect to its dimensions.

Embeddings do not have to be 1-to-1 to be efficient or useful. For example, an embedding of the 2^q-leaf, or $(2^{q+1}-1)$-node, complete binary tree in the q-cube is shown in Fig. 13.7. Here, each node and all of its left descendants (those that can be reached by only moving leftward) are mapped onto the same hypercube node. This embedding has dilation 1, congestion q, load factor $q+1$, and expansion of about 1/2. Even though large congestions and load factors are generally undesirable, this particular embedding is quite efficient if the hypercube is to emulate a tree algorithm in which only nodes at a single level of the tree are active at any given time.

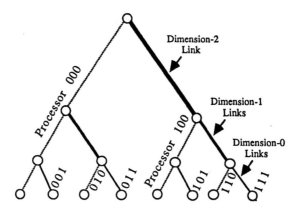

Figure 13.7. Embedding a 15-node complete binary tree into the 3-cube.

In Section 2.4, we saw examples of tree algorithms in which activity shifts from one tree level to the one above or below it. The embedding of Fig. 13.7 is ideally suited for emulating such tree algorithms on a hypercube.

In the semigroup computation algorithm for the binary tree, presented in Section 2.4, only the leaves were assumed to hold data elements. The nonleaf nodes served to combine data elements, send the partial results upward, and eventually direct the final result of the semigroup computation toward the leaves if needed. A hypercube emulating this algorithm with the embedding shown in Fig. 13.7 will have one node per tree leaf and thus one data element per node. As activity shifts from the leaves toward the root, successively fewer hypercube nodes will be doing useful work; the active nodes constitute a smaller and smaller subcube. In the broadcasting phase of the algorithm, activity shifts back from the root node toward the leaves, with more and more nodes (larger subcubes) becoming active in each successive step.

Similarly, for the parallel prefix computation, the activity shifts toward the root and from there, back toward the leaves. Again, the embedding of Fig. 13.7 leads to efficient emulation of the algorithm on a hypercube with roughly half as many nodes as the original binary tree.

13.4. A FEW SIMPLE ALGORITHMS

In this section, we present hypercube algorithms for semigroup computation, parallel prefix computation, and sequence reversal.

The following is an optimal algorithm involving q communication steps for semigroup computation on the q-cube, assuming that each Processor x holds one value $v[x]$. Recall that $N_k(x)$ denotes the neighbor of Node x along Dimension k; i.e., the node whose binary label differs from that of x only in bit position k.

Semigroup computation on the q-cube

```
Processor x, 0 ≤ x < p do t[x] := v[x] {initialize subcube "total" to own value}
for k = 0 to q – 1 Processor x, 0 ≤ x < p, do
    get y := t[Nₖ(x)]
    set t[x] := t[x] ⊗ y
endfor
```

The communication steps of the above semigroup computation algorithm for a 3-cube are depicted in Fig. 13.8. In the first step, pairs of elements are combined across Dimension 0, yielding partial results such as $v[0] \otimes v[1]$ and $v[2] \otimes v[3]$ (these are denoted by 0-1, 2-3, and so on in Fig. 13.8). Then, pairs of partial results are combined across Dimension 1 to yield $v[0] \otimes v[1] \otimes v[2] \otimes v[3]$ and $v[4] \otimes v[5] \otimes v[6] \otimes v[7]$. In general, this doubling of the scope of the partial results continues until the single final result is simultaneously obtained in all of the nodes.

The above algorithm is an instance of an *ascend* algorithm. Each node successively communicates with its neighbors in dimension order from 0 to $q-1$. Thus communication takes place between nodes that are $1, 2, 4, \ldots, 2^{q-1}$ apart in terms of numerical node labels. A *descend* algorithm is similar, except that the dimension order is $q-1$ to 0. The structure of

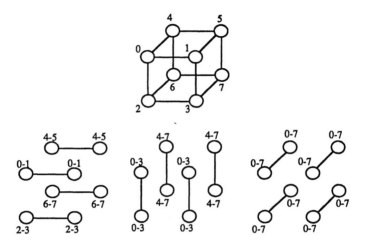

Figure 13.8. Semigroup computation on a 3-cube.

the hypercube is ideally suited to this type of ascend/descend algorithms that double the scope or coverage of the result with each step.

Parallel prefix computation is similar. Each node x performs the following steps.

Parallel prefix computation on the q-cube

    Processor x, $0 \leq x < p$, do $t[x] := u[x] := v[x]$
      {initialize subcube "total" and partial prefix to own value}
    for $k = 0$ to $q - 1$ Processor x, $0 \leq x < p$, do
      get $y := t[N_k(x)]$
      set $t[x] := t[x] \otimes y$
      if $x > N_k(x)$ then $u[x] := u[x] \otimes y$
    endfor

The above parallel prefix computation is also an ascend algorithm. Each node deals with two variables: a subcube "total" t that corresponds to the result of semigroup computation in the current subcube and a subcube partial prefix result u that gives the result of parallel prefix computation in the same subcube. Eventually, t becomes the semigroup computation result and u the required prefix within the entire q-cube. Figure 13.9 depicts the communication steps, and the partial results obtained, in a 3-cube. Again i-j stands for the partial combining result $v[i] \otimes v[i+1] \otimes \cdots \otimes v[j]$.

Figure 13.10 depicts another algorithm for parallel prefix computation on the hypercube using a recursive formulation. The hypercube is divided into two halves consisting of the even- and odd-numbered nodes (across the 0th dimension). Parallel prefix computation is performed recursively in each half, with the odd subcube doing a diminished version of the prefix computation in which the processor's own value is excluded. Then, the results are combined across Dimension-0 links. All that is left to do after this step is for the odd-numbered nodes to combine their own values with the results thus obtained. The running

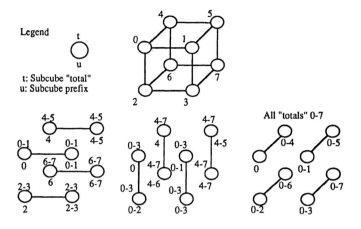

Figure 13.9. Parallel prefix computation on a 3-cube.

time of this algorithm on a q-cube is characterized by the recurrence $T(q) = T(q - 1) + 2 = 2q = 2 \log_2 p$.

Our final simple algorithm deals with reversing a sequence, stored one element per processor. By reversing a sequence $v[0]$, $v[1]$, . . . we mean that the element originally in Processor x must end up in Processor $p - 1 - x$; $v[0]$ in Processor $p-1$, $v[1]$ in Processor $p - 2$, and so forth.

Reversing a sequence on the q-cube

for $k = 0$ to $q - 1$ Processor x, $0 \leq x < p$, do

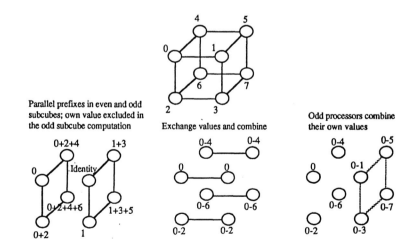

Figure 13.10. A second algorithm for parallel prefix computation on a 3-cube.

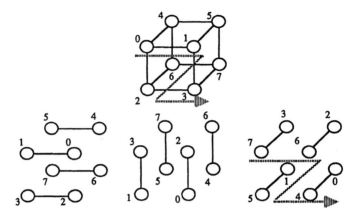

Figure 13.11. Sequence reversal on a 3-cube.

```
    get y := v[N_k(x)]
    set v[x] := y
endfor
```

Figure 13.11 shows the steps of the sequence reversal algorithm on a 3-cube. Sequence reversal is yet another example of an ascend-type algorithm.

13.5. MATRIX MULTIPLICATION

Consider now the problem of multiplying $m \times m$ matrices A and B on a q-cube to obtain the product matrix C, where $m = 2^{q/3}$ and $p = m^3 = 2^q$ processors are used. Note that the number q of dimensions in the hypercube is assumed to be a multiple of 3. Each processor has three registers R_A, R_B, and R_C. For the sake of algorithm description, it is convenient to label the hypercube processors by three indices i, j, k, where each index is a $(q/3)$-bit binary number. Initially, Processor $(0, j, k)$ holds A_{jk} and B_{jk} in its R_A and R_B registers, respectively. All other processor registers are initialized to 0. At the end of the computation, Register R_C of Processor $(0, j, k)$ will hold element C_{jk} of the product matrix C.

The algorithm performs all m^3 multiplications needed for multiplying two $m \times m$ matrices concurrently, one in each of the m^3 processors. The remainder of the process is to ensure that each processor holds the two elements of A and B that it multiplies and to add the requisite terms that form each element C_{jk} of the result matrix.

Multiplying $m \times m$ matrices on a q-cube, with $q = 3 \log_2 m$

```
for l = q/3 - 1 downto 0 Processor x = ijk, 0 ≤ i, j, k < m, do
    if bit l of i is 1
    then get y := R_A[N_{l+2q/3}(x)] and z := R_B[N_{l+2q/3}(x)]
        set R_A[x] : = y; R_B[x] := z
    endif
```

endfor
for $l = q/3 - 1$ downto 0 Processor $x = ijk$, $0 \le i, j, k < m$, do
   if bit l of i and k are different
   then get $y := R_A[N_l(x)]$
     set $R_A[x] := y$
   endif
endfor
for $l = q/3 - 1$ downto 0 Processor $x = ijk$, $0 \le i, j, k < m$, do
   if bit l of i and j are different
   then get $y := R_B[N_{l+q/3}(x)]$
     set $R_B[x] := y$
   endif
endfor
Processor x, $0 \le x < p$, do $R_C := R_A \times R_B$
   $\{p = m^3 = 2^q$ parallel multiplications in one step$\}$
for $l = 0$ to $q/3 - 1$ Processor $x = ijk$, $0 \le i, j, k < m$, do
   if bit l of i is 0
   then get $y := R_C[N_{l+2q/3}(x)]$
     set $R_C[x] := R_C[x] + y$
   endif
endfor

The above matrix multiplication algorithm appears complicated. However, the ideas behind it are quite simple. The first three "for" loops copy the elements of A and B into all other processors that need them to perform the m^3 parallel multiplications. Because $m = 2^{q/3}$ copies of each element must be made, a recursive doubling scheme is used to make the required copies in $O(q)$ communication steps. The final "for" loop, after the multiplications, computes the sum of the m terms that form each of the elements of C, again using recursive doubling within $(q/3)$-dimensional subcubes of the original q-cube. It should be clear that the total running time of this matrix multiplication algorithm is $O(q) = O(\log p)$.

An example for multiplying two 2×2 matrices on a 3-cube is shown in Fig. 13.12. For this simple example, $q/3 = 1$, so each of the "for" loops degenerates into a single communication step. In the first "for" loop, processors with 1 in bit position 2 of their node labels (i.e., Processors 4, 5, 6, and 7) receive and store R_A and R_B values from their Dimension-2 neighbors, as shown in the middle top diagram of Fig. 13.12. In the second "for" loop, Processors 1, 3, 4, and 6, i.e., those with different i and k components in their node labels, receive and store R_A values from their Dimension-0 neighbors. The third "for" loop updates the R_B values in those processors whose node labels have different i and j components (i.e., Processors 2, 3, 4, and 5). At this point, shown in the bottom left diagram of Fig. 13.12, data distribution is complete. The eight processors then independently multiply their R_A and R_B values, storing the results in R_C. The final "for" loop adds pairs of values across Dimension 2 in order to obtain elements of the result matrix C in Processors 0, 1, 2, and 3 (bottom right of Fig. 13.12).

The above algorithm, requiring m^3 processors to multiply $m \times m$ matrices, is obviously impractical for large matrices, which are the primary candidates for the application of parallel processing. However, the standard block matrix multiplication scheme can be used to reduce

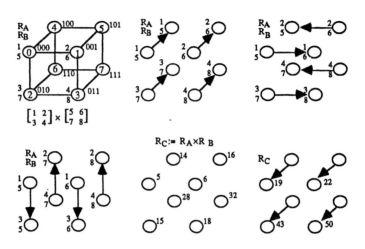

Figure 13.12. Multiplying two 2×2 matrices on a 3-cube.

the number of processors required. With the block scheme, one can multiply $m \times m$ matrices on a p-processor hypercube by simply viewing each data movement or multiplication in the above algorithm as being applied to $(m/p^{1/3}) \times (m/p^{1/3})$ matrix blocks rather than to single matrix elements. When $p^{1/3}$ is not an integer or does not divide m, the algorithm becomes slightly more complex.

An analysis of the above algorithm in the case of block matrix multiplication follows. Let the $m \times m$ matrices be partitioned into $p^{1/3} \times p^{1/3}$ blocks, each of size $(m/p^{1/3}) \times (m/p^{1/3})$. Then, each data communication step involves transferring the $m^2/p^{2/3}$ elements of a block and each multiplication corresponds to $2m^3/p$ arithmetic operations required to multiply two such blocks. Assuming unit-time data transfers and arithmetic operations, the total running time becomes

$$T_{\text{mul}}(m, p) = m^2/p^{2/3} \times O(\log p) + 2m^3/p$$

For $m = \Theta(p^{1/3} \log p)$ or $p = \Theta(m^3/\log^3 m)$, communication and computation times are asymptotically of the same order and $T_{\text{mul}}(m, p)$ becomes $O(\log^3 p)$ or $O(\log^3 m)$. For smaller values of m, the communication time $m^2/p^{2/3} \times O(\log p)$ is dominant. On the other hand, when very large matrices are multiplied on a relatively small number of processors, the $2m^3/p$ term dominates the running time and linear speed-up is obtained.

13.6. INVERTING A LOWER TRIANGULAR MATRIX

A lower triangular matrix A is a square $m \times m$ matrix in which every element above the main diagonal is 0 (see Section 11.2, particularly Fig. 11.5). The inverse of A, denoted by A^{-1}, is another square $m \times m$ matrix such that $A \times A^{-1} = A^{-1} \times A = I_m$, where I_m is the $m \times m$ identity matrix having 1 for each diagonal element and 0 elsewhere. Inversion of lower triangular matrices is of practical importance in itself and also forms a building block for inverting arbitrary matrices.

A recursive algorithm for inverting $m \times m$ lower triangular matrices on a q-cube with $2^q = m^3$ processors can be developed based on the following result from linear algebra:

$$\text{if } A = \begin{bmatrix} B & 0 \\ C & D \end{bmatrix} \text{ then } A^{-1} = \begin{bmatrix} B^{-1} & 0 \\ -D^{-1}CB^{-1} & D^{-1} \end{bmatrix}$$

where C is an $(m/2) \times (m/2)$ matrix and B and D are $(m/2) \times (m/2)$ lower triangular matrices. This statement can be easily verified through multiplication, noting the simplification $CB^{-1} - DD^{-1}CB^{-1} = CB^{-1} - I_{m/2}CB^{-1} = 0$.

$$\begin{bmatrix} B & 0 \\ C & D \end{bmatrix} \times \begin{bmatrix} B^{-1} & 0 \\ -D^{-1}CB^{-1} & D^{-1} \end{bmatrix} = \begin{bmatrix} I_{m/2} & 0 \\ 0 & I_{m/2} \end{bmatrix} = I_m$$

Thus, if B and D can be inverted in parallel within independent subcubes, the running time of the algorithm is characterized by the recurrence

$$T_{inv}(m) = T_{inv}(m/2) + 2T_{mul}(m/2)$$

where the last term represents the time of two matrix multiplications for computing $-D^{-1}CB^{-1}$. Because, using the algorithm of Section 13.5, matrix multiplication can be performed in logarithmic time, the running time of this matrix inversion algorithm is $O(\log^2 m)$. The only remaining problem is to show that the two $(m/2) \times (m/2)$ matrices B and D can in fact be inverted in parallel, with each using no more than half of the available processors. Specifying the details is left as an exercise.

PROBLEMS

13.1. Properties of the hypercube
   The bisection width of a q-cube is $2^{q-1} = \Theta(p)$. Let us call this the *link bisection width* of the q-cube to distinguish it from the *node bisection width* defined as the least number of nodes whose removal would bisect the network. Show that the node bisection width of a q-cube is much smaller and consists of $\Theta(p/\sqrt{\log p})$ nodes. *Hint*: Consider every hypercube node whose weight, or the number of 1s in its binary label, is $\lfloor q/2 \rfloor$ or $\lceil q/2 \rceil$.

13.2. Embedding meshes into hypercubes
   a. Show that the 3×3 mesh is a subgraph of the 4-cube.
   b. Show that the 3×3 torus is not a subgraph of the 4-cube.
   c. Show that the 3×5 mesh, and thus the 3×5 torus, is not a subgraph of the 4-cube.
   d. Generalize the result of part (b) to any h-D torus with at least one odd side.
   e. Prove or disprove: Any $m_0 \times m_1 \times \cdots \times m_{h-1}$ torus, with all of its sides even, is a subgraph of the q-cube, where $q = \sum_{i=0}^{h-1} \lceil \log_2 m_i \rceil$.

13.3. Embedding meshes into hypercubes
   Show an embedding of the $8 \times 8 \times 8$ torus into the 9-cube. Identify explicitly the hypercube node onto which the node (i, j, k) of the torus is mapped.

13.4. Embedding meshes into hypercubes
   a. Show that any p-node 2D mesh is a subgraph of the $(\lceil \log_2 p \rceil + 1)$-cube.

b. Extend the result of part (a) by showing that any p-node h-D mesh is a subgraph of the $(\lceil \log_2 p \rceil + h - 1)$-cube.

c. Show that the result of part (b) is in general the best possible by providing an example of a p-node h-D mesh that is not a subgraph of the $(\lceil \log_2 p \rceil + h - 2)$-cube.

13.5. Embedding trees into hypercubes

a. We have seen that the $(2^q - 1)$-node complete binary tree is not a subgraph of the q-cube. Show that it is a subgraph of the $(q+1)$-cube.

b. Show that the $(3 \times 2^{q-1} - 2)$-node back-to-back complete binary tree, composed of two $(2^q - 1)$-node complete binary trees whose leaves have been merged, is a subgraph of the $(q+1)$-cube.

13.6. Embedding trees into hypercubes
Show that the "in-order" labeling of the nodes of a $(2^q - 1)$-node complete binary tree corresponds to a dilation-2 embedding in the q-cube. The *in-order* labeling of a binary tree requires that each node be labeled after all of its left descendants and before any of its right descendants, with node labels beginning from 0 and ending with $2^q - 2$.

13.7. Embedding trees into hypercubes
Using the embedding of the eight-leaf complete binary tree into the 3-cube depicted in Fig. 13.7:

a. Draw a sequence of snapshots showing how the hypercube would emulate the tree algorithm for semigroup computation with data items stored at the leaves (see Section 2.4).

b. Compare the emulation of part (a) with the direct hypercube algorithm given in Section 13.4.

c. Repeat part (a) for the parallel prefix computation.

d. Repeat part (b) for the parallel prefix computation.

13.8. Simple algorithms on hypercubes

a. Extend the semigroup computation algorithm given in Section 13.4 and its analysis to the case where each of the p processors holds n/p data items.

b. Repeat part (a) for the parallel prefix computation.

c. Repeat part (a) for the sequence reversal algorithm.

13.9. Unidirectional hypercubes
In Section 12.2, Manhattan street networks were introduced as unidirectional mesh networks. Show how to construct a *unidirectional* q-cube (q even) with node in-degree and out degree of $q/2$ and a diameter of q. Provide the connectivity rule for each Node x.

13.10. Pruned hypercubes
Consider a q-cube, with q even, in which each link is replaced by two unidirectional links going in opposite directions and then outgoing links along odd (even) dimensions have been removed for nodes with odd (even) weights. This leads to a unidirectional network with node in-degree and out-degree of $q/2$.

a. Find the diameter of such a pruned q-cube.

b. Find the bisection width of such a pruned q-cube.

c. Devise an embedding of the complete q-cube into the pruned q-cube such that the dilation and congestion of the embedding are as small as possible.

13.11. Embedding large hypercubes into smaller ones

   a. Devise a dilation-1 embedding for a $(q+c)$-cube into a q-cube, where $c > 0$.

   b. What are the congestion and load factor of the embedding proposed in part (a)?

   c. Is the proposed embedding useful in performing semigroup computation, parallel prefix computation, or sequence reversal with n data elements $(n > p)$ through the emulation of an n-node hypercube on a p-node hypercube?

13.12. Matrix multiplication on a hypercube

   a. Modify the matrix multiplication algorithm of Section 13.5 such that $2^{q/2} \times 2^{q/2}$ matrices are multiplied on a q-cube (q even).

   b. Analyze the complexity of the algorithm proposed in part (a).

   c. Modify the matrix multiplication algorithm of Section 13.5 such that $2^q \times 2^q$ matrices are multiplied on a q-cube.

   d. Analyze the complexity of the algorithm proposed in part (c).

13.13. Solving numerical problems on a hypercube
Develop hypercube algorithms for the following problems:

   a. Solving a triangular system of linear equations via back substitution (see Section 11.2).

   b. Solving a tridiagonal system of linear equations (see Section 11.3).

   c. Solving an arbitrary system of linear equations by Gaussian elimination (see Section 11.4).

   d. Solving an arbitrary system of linear equations by Jacobi relaxation (see Section 11.4).

   e. Finding the transitive closure of a graph, given its adjacency matrix (see Section 11.5).

   f. Labeling the connected components of a binary image (see Section 11.6).

13.14. Mystery hypercube algorithm
Consider the following hypercube algorithm that deals with an $m \times m$ matrix A. Each of the $p = 2^q = m^2$ processors has a Register R_A that holds some element of A at any given time and a Register R_B used for temporary storage. Initially, a_{ij} is stored in the processor whose ID is $mi + j$, i.e., in row-major order.

Mystery algorithm operating on an $m \times m$ matrix A on a q-cube, with $q = 2 \log_2 m$
___

for $l = q - 1$ downto $q/2$ Processor x, $0 \le x < p$, do
   if $x_l = x_{l-q/2}$ {Compare bits l and $l - q/2$ of the processor's binary node label}
   then get $y := R_A[N_l(x)]$ {Get neighbor's A value}
      set $R_B[x] := y$ {and store it in the B register}
   endif
   if $x_l \ne x_{l-q/2}$ {Compare bits l and $l - q/2$ of the processor's binary node label}
   then   get $y := R_B[N_{l-q/2}(x)]$ {Get neighbor's B value}
      set $R_A[x] := y$ {and store it in the A register}
   endif
endfor

   a. What does the above algorithm accomplish?

   b. What is the algorithm's running time?

13.15. Pruned hypercubes
Consider a q-cube that is thinned by removing a fraction $1-f$ of the 2^{q-1} links between the two $(q-1)$-cubes, say one-half or three-fourths of them. This is recursively applied from the highest dimension down to some Dimension c (we cannot do this all the way down to Dimension 0,

because the network will become disconnected). The total number of links, and thus the network cost, is about f times that of the original q-cube. Suggest a rule for removing half of the links such that the resulting network possesses desirable properties [Hsu96].

REFERENCES AND SUGGESTED READING

[Akl97]   Akl, S. G., *Parallel Computation: Models and Methods*, Prentice–Hall, 1997.

[Haye89]   Hayes, J. P., and T. Mudge, "Hypercube Supercomputers," *Proceedings of the IEEE*, Vol. 77, No. 12, pp. 1829–1841, December 1989.

[Hsu96]   Hsu, W. -J., M. J. Chung, and Z. Hu, "Gaussian Networks for Scalable Distributed Systems," *The Computer Journal*, Vol. 39, No. 5, pp. 417–426, 1996.

[Peas77]   Pease, M. C., III, "The Indirect Binary n-cube Microprocessor Array," *IEEE Trans. Computers*, Vol. C-26, No. 5, pp. 458–473, May 1977.

[Seit85]   Seitz, C. L., "The Cosmic Cube," *Communications of the ACM*, Vol. 28, No. 1, pp. 22–33, January 1985.

[Squi63]   Squire, J. S., and S. M. Palais, "Programming and Design Considerations for a Highly Parallel Computer," *Proc. Spring Joint Computer Conf.*, 1963, pp. 395–400.

[Sull77]   Sullivan, H., T. R. Bashkow, and K. Klappholz, "A Large-Scale Homogeneous, Fully Distributed Parallel Machine," *Proc. 4th Symp. Computer Architecture*, March 1977, pp. 105–124.

14

Sorting and Routing on Hypercubes

In Chapters 9 and 10, we discussed the importance of sorting and data routing problems in parallel processing and presented several algorithms of varying complexities and efficiencies to solve these problems on 2D meshes and tori. This chapter is devoted to solving the same problems on the hypercube architecture. A single chapter is adequate here as we are already familiar with the fundamental notions and tools used in developing efficient sorting and routing algorithms. We will see that the smaller diameter and wider bisection of the hypercube allow us to develop more efficient algorithms, while the recursive structure of the hypercube makes the solutions easier to develop, describe, and understand. Chapter topics are

- 14.1. Defining the sorting problem
- 14.2. Bitonic sorting on a hypercube
- 14.3. Routing problems on a hypercube
- 14.4. Dimension-order routing
- 14.5. Broadcasting on a hypercube
- 14.6. Adaptive and fault-tolerant routing

14.1. DEFINING THE SORTING PROBLEM

The general problem of sorting on a hypercube is as follows: Given n records distributed evenly among the $p = 2^q$ processors of a q-cube (with each processor holding n/p records), rearrange the records so that the key values are in the same order as the processor node labels. Ideally, the product of the number p of processors used and the running time T of the sorting algorithm will be $pT = \Theta(n \log n)$, which is optimal. This implies a running time of $T = \Theta((n \log n)/p)$ and linear speed-up. Currently we cannot achieve this optimal running time for all values of n and p.

For the special case of $n = p$, i.e., each processor holding a single record before and after sorting, the most practical hypercube sorting algorithms are based on Batcher's odd–even merge or bitonic sort, which we will study in the following sections. Batcher's sorting algorithms (see Section 7.4) achieve asymptotically suboptimal $O(\log^2 n) = O(\log^2 p)$ running time. An $O(\log n)$-time deterministic sorting algorithm, which would be optimal in view of both the $O(n \log n)$ sequential-time lower bound and the $O(\log p)$ diameter of the hypercube, is not currently known. However, slightly relaxing the assumption $n = p$ or the requirement for determinism or worst-case bound, makes the problem manageable.

If we have fewer than p records to sort ($n \le p/4$), then a hypercube sorting algorithm exists that allows us to do the job in $O(\log p \log n/\log(p/n))$ time [Nass82]. When $n = p^{1-\varepsilon}$, for some $\varepsilon > 0$, the above algorithm runs in optimal logarithmic time, as in this case

$$\log p \log n/\log(p/n) = \frac{1 - \varepsilon}{\varepsilon} \log p = \frac{1}{\varepsilon} \log n$$

If we have many more than p records to sort ($n \gg p$), then hypercube algorithms exist that allow us to do the job in $O(n \log n /p)$ time, i.e., with linear speed-up [Plax89].

The best known deterministic sorting algorithm for the case $p = n$ was published in 1990 and requires $O(\log p \log \log p)$ or $O(\log p (\log \log p)^2)$ running time in the worst case, depending on assumptions [Cyph90].

From a practical standpoint, randomized algorithms that sort p records in $O(\log p)$ time on the average, but may have higher complexities in the worst case, are quite satisfactory. Since the late 1980s, several randomized sorting algorithms have been proposed [Reif87]. The proof of the $O(\log p) = O(\log n)$ average time complexity of such algorithms is based on demonstrating that for all but a minute fraction of possible input permutations, sorted order prevails in logarithmic time.

In Section 14.2, we will study a sorting algorithm for the hypercube that is based on Batcher's bitonic sorting method. For this reason, we review the definition of bitonic sequences and Batcher's bitonic sorting method in the remainder of this section.

A *bitonic sequence* is one that "rises then falls" ($x_0 \le x_1 \le \ldots \le x_i \ge x_{i+1} \ge x_{i+2} \ge \ldots \ge x_{n-1}$), "falls then rises" ($x_0 \ge x_1 \ge \ldots \ge x_i \le x_{i+1} \le x_{i+2} \le \ldots \le x_{n-1}$), or is obtained from the above two types of sequences through cyclic shifts or rotations (see the discussion of Batcher's bitonic sorting network at the end of Section 7.4). Figure 14.1 depicts four examples of bitonic sequences. The examples on the left are of the "rise-then-fall" and "fall-then-rise" types. Such sequences "change direction" at most once; contrast this to *monotonic sequences* that do not change direction. The examples on the right are obtained

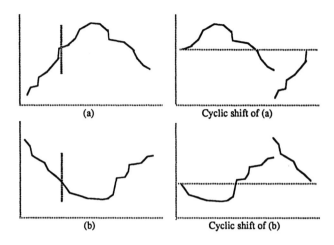

Figure 14.1. Examples of bitonic sequences.

by cutting a portion of the corresponding sequence and attaching it to the right/left of the remaining portion. This amounts to left/right rotation or cyclic shift of the sequence.

A bitonic sequence, stored one element per processor on a p-processor linear array, can be sorted in the following way (see Fig. 14.2). The right half of the sequence is shifted left by $p/2$ steps. Then, each processor in the left half of the array compares the two values that

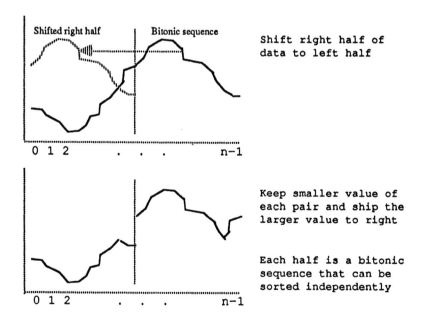

Figure 14.2. Sorting a bitonic sequence on a linear array.

it holds, keeps the smaller value, and sends the larger value to the right by $p/2$ steps. Each half of the array now holds a bitonic sequence. Furthermore, each element in the right half of the array is no smaller than any element in the left half. Thus, the bitonic sequence sorting problem has been reduced to solving two smaller problems of the same type independently on the two halves of the array. Because the shifting of the right half to the left half and shifting back of the larger values to the right half take a total of p steps, the running time of the above sorting algorithm for bitonic sequences is characterized by the recurrence $B(p) = B(p/2) + p = 2p - 2$, given that $B(1) = 0$.

An arbitrary input sequence on a p-processor linear array can be sorted recursively as follows. First sort the two halves of the array in the opposite directions so that the resulting sequence is bitonic (say, rising then falling). Then sort the bitonic sequence using the method presented above. The running time of this bitonic sorting algorithm is characterized by the recurrence

$$T(p) = T(p/2) + B(p)$$

$$= T(p/2) + 2p - 2$$

$$= 4p - 4 - 2 \log_2 p$$

What actually happens as this bitonic sorting algorithm is executed can be seen in the example of Fig. 14.3. First, subsequences of length 2 are sorted in opposite directions in $B(2)$ steps. Then, pairs of such sequences, which form bitonic sequences of length 4, are sorted (merged) in $B(4)$ steps, and so on. Thus, the following is an alternate formulation for the running time of the algorithm, proceeding in a bottom-to-top order:

$$T(p) = B(2) + B(4) + \cdots + B(p)$$

$$= 2 + 6 + 14 + \cdots + (2p - 2)$$

$$= 4p - 4 - 2 \log_2 p$$

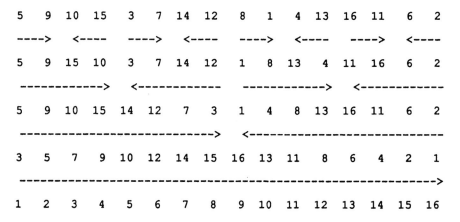

Figure 14.3. Sorting an arbitrary sequence on a linear array through recursive application of bitonic sorting.

For a linear array of processors, the bitonic sorting algorithm is clearly inferior to the simpler odd–even transposition sort, which requires only p compare–exchange steps or $2p$ unidirectional communication steps. However, the situation is quite different for a hypercube.

14.2. BITONIC SORTING ON A HYPERCUBE

If we sort the records in the lower ($x_{q-1} = 0$) and upper ($x_{q-1} = 1$) subcubes in opposite directions, the resulting sequence in the entire cube will be bitonic. Now the shifting of the upper half of the sequence to the lower half and shifting back of the larger values to the upper half can each be done in a single unidirectional communication step. These two routing steps, along with the comparison performed between them, constitute a parallel compare–exchange step. The complexity of the algorithm in terms of the number of compare–exchange steps is thus characterized by the recurrence $T(q) = T(q-1) + B(q)$, where $B(q)$ is the time needed for sorting a bitonic sequence. $B(q)$ in turn satisfies $B(q) = B(q-1) + 1 = q$, leading to

$$T(q) = T(q-1) + q = q(q+1)/2 = \log_2 p \, (\log_2 p + 1)/2$$

Here is the complete algorithm for sorting a bitonic sequence, stored one element per processor in a q-cube, with the element in Processor x denoted by $v[x]$.

Sorting a bitonic sequence of size n on the q-cube, where $q = \log_2 n$

```
for l = q − 1 downto 0 Processor x, 0 ≤ x < p, do
    if x_l = 0
    then get y := v[N_l(x)]; keep min(v(x), y); send max(v(x), y) to N_l(x)
    endif
endfor
```

The above algorithm is yet another instance of the ascend class of algorithms. An example for the algorithm is depicted in Fig. 14.4. The bitonic sequence 1, 3, 5, 8, 9, 6, 3, 2 is initially stored in the eight nodes of the 3-cube. After the compare–exchange step along Dimension 2, we have two size-4 bitonic sequences: 1, 3, 3, 2 in the lower cube and 9, 6, 5, 8 in the upper cube. Another compare–exchange step along Dimension 1 gives us four bitonic sequences of size 2, which are then sorted by the final compare–exchange step along Dimension 0.

Batcher's odd–even merge sort is similar to bitonic sort and takes the same amount of time (see Section 7.4). Details of its implementation are thus left as an exercise.

Batcher's $O(\log^2 p)$-time bitonic and odd–even merge sorting algorithms for ordering p elements on a p-processor hypercube are presently the fastest practical deterministic sorting algorithms available. The more complicated $O(\log p \log \log p)$-time algorithms (see, e.g., [Leig92], pp. 642–657) are not competitive for $p \leq 2^{20}$. Randomized algorithms, on the other hand, usually sort in $O(\log p)$ steps, so they are quite efficient on the average. However, they do not provide guaranteed speed-up. This is usually not a problem in practice in the same sense that the worst-case $O(n^2)$ running time of sequential quicksort for sorting a sequence of length n is not problematic.

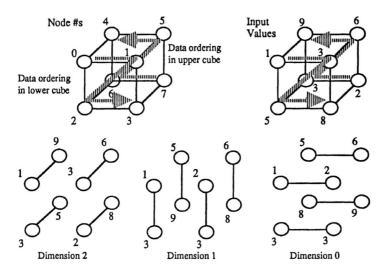

Figure 14.4. Sorting a bitonic sequence of size 8 on the 3-cube.

14.3.   ROUTING PROBLEMS ON A HYPERCUBE

Intuitively, hypercubes should perform better in dealing with routing problems than 2D meshes, because their larger node degree translates to the availability of more alternate (shortest) paths between processors, its logarithmic diameter leads to shorter routes, and its large bisection width allows many concurrent data transfers to take place between distant nodes. We will see shortly that this is usually the case. The improved performance is achieved for certain classes of routing problems unconditionally and for others on the average; the worst-case performance for a general one-to-one routing problem, however, is not much improved compared with 2D meshes. We will use an interesting lower-bound method to prove this latter result.

The types of routing problems that we will discuss in this and the following sections are essentially the same as those introduced in Section 10.1 in connection with 2D meshes and tori. In particular, we deal with one-to-one and one-to-many routing problems, which include packing and broadcasting as special cases, respectively. The simplicity of path selection strategies in most hypercube routing algorithms makes them suitable for both packet and wormhole routing. As usual, if the routing problem is a permutation, with each of the p processors having a packet to send and each node being the destination of exactly one packet, sorting the packets by their destination node address will solve the routing problem.

Recall, also, that routing algorithms can be divided into the two classes of *oblivious*, with the routing path uniquely determined by source and destination node addresses, and *nonoblivious* or *adaptive*, where the path taken by a message may also depend on other messages in the network. Finally, based on how the computations needed to determine the path of a message are performed, we have the following dichotomy.

- *On-line routing algorithms* make the routing decisions on the fly in the course of routing: Route selections are made by a parallel/distributed algorithm that runs on the same system for which routing is being performed.
- *Off-line routing algorithms* are applied to routing problems that are known a priori: Route selections are precomputed for each problem of interest and stored, usually in the form of routing tables, within the nodes.

An on-line routing algorithm is often preferred, not only because routing problems may develop dynamically and in unpredictable data-dependent ways, but also in view of the preprocessing overhead and storage requirements of an off-line algorithm.

Frequently, we restrict our routing algorithm to send each message along a shortest (or close to shortest) path. Because most pairs of nodes in a hypercube are connected via multiple shortest paths, a *shortest-path routing algorithm* can maintain a high degree of adaptivity and flexibility despite the restriction.

Though not an absolute requirement, on-line routing algorithms are often oblivious, or only locally adaptive, while off-line algorithms take advantage of available information to find routes that are (close to) globally optimal. Oblivious on-line routing algorithms may suffer from inefficiencies that lead to poor performance, particularly in the worst case. Routing decisions in on-line algorithms are necessarily local, potentially leading to heavy data traffic in some areas of the network, while available alternative paths are being underutilized.

Consider, for example, the following positive result: Any routing problem with p or fewer packets, having distinct sources and destinations, can be solved on a p-processor hypercube in $O(\log p)$ steps, using an off-line algorithm to precompute the paths. The off-line algorithm chooses the routes in such a way that the route taken by one message does not significantly overlap or conflict with those of other messages, leading to optimal time.

In the remainder of this section, we discuss some negative or lower-bound results whose scopes extend beyond the hypercube architecture. An oblivious routing algorithm can be characterized by its *dilation*, defined as the length of the longest path between a pair of nodes (which may be larger than the network diameter for some algorithms), and *congestion*, defined as the maximum number of paths going through the same link for the worst-case routing problem when that algorithm is used. It is obvious that such a routing algorithm requires $\Omega(\text{dilation} + \text{congestion})$ routing steps in the worst case. Randomized routing algorithms can be devised that asymptotically match the above lower bound in terms of performance [Leig94].

The effect of signal propagation delays on long wires can be taken into account in the above lower bound by defining *generalized dilation* as the sum of edge delays on the longest path and *generalized congestion* as the maximum over all edges of the number of packets that traverse that edge multiplied by the delay of the edge. In this case, efficient randomized routing algorithms can still be constructed [Gree95], though the performance of such algorithms does not quite match the above lower bound.

With unit-time edge delays, the network diameter can be used as a lower bound for maximum dilation. The maximum congestion, however, is harder to characterize. The following theorem allows us to establish a lower bound for maximum congestion, and thus for worst-case delay, of any oblivious routing algorithm on an arbitrary network. Hence, the theorem provides insight into the nature and intrinsic limitations of oblivious routing. When applied to the p-node hypercube, this general result implies that any oblivious routing algorithm requires $\Omega(\sqrt{p}/\log p)$ time in the worst case. Thus, the worst-case performance of an oblivious routing algorithm for the hypercube is only slightly better than the $\Omega(\sqrt{p})$ time required on a much simpler square mesh. However, in most instances, the actual routing performance is much closer to the logarithmic-time best case than to the above worst case.

THEOREM 14.1. *Let $G = (V, E)$ represent a p-node, degree-d network. Any oblivious routing algorithm for routing p packets in G needs $\Omega(\sqrt{p}/d)$ time in the worst case.*

PROOF.   There are $p(p-1)$ paths $P_{u,v}$ for routing among all node pairs. These paths are predetermined and independent of other traffic within the network. Our strategy will be to find k pairs of Nodes u_i, v_i $(1 \le i \le k)$ such that $u_i \ne u_j$ and $v_i \ne v_j$ for $i \ne j$, and P_{u_i,v_i} all pass through the same Edge e. Because at most two packets can go through a bidirectional link in each step, $\Omega(k)$ steps will be needed for some 1–1 routing problem. The main part of the proof consists of showing that k can be as large as $\sqrt{p}/d$. Consider the $p-1$ different paths $P_{u,v}$ ending in some Node v and let $E(v, k)$ denote the set of edges such that at least k of these paths pass through them. Let $V(v, k)$ be the set of nodes that are incident to the edges in $E(v, k)$. Clearly,

$$|V(v, k)| \le 2|E(v, k)|$$

If $k \le (p-1)/d$, then $v \in V(v, k)$, as no more than d edges enter v and at least one of them should be on $(p-1)/d$ or more of the $p-1$ paths. Let $k \le (p-1)/d$ and consider the $|V - V(v, k)|$ nodes that are not in $V(v, k)$. Because $v \in V(v, k)$, a path leading from such a node to v must, at some point, enter a node in $V(v, k)$. Let (w, w') be the edge leading the path under consideration to a node in $V(v, k)$; i.e., $w \notin V(v, k)$, $w' \in V(v, k)$. Given that $w \notin V(v, k)$, at most $k-1$ such paths can enter $V(v, k)$ via the Edge (w, w'). Additionally, because the degree of w' is at most d, no more than $d-1$ choices for w exist. Thus,

$$|V - V(v, k)| \le (k-1)(d-1)|V(v, k)|$$

In other words, for any k satisfying $k \le (p-1)/d$, we have

$$p = |V - V(v, k)| + |V(v, k)|$$

$$\le [1 + (k-1)(d-1)]|V(v, k)|$$

$$\le 2[1 + (k-1)(d-1)]|E(v, k)|$$

$$\le 2kd|E(v, k)|$$

In particular, for $k = \sqrt{p}/d$, we have $|E(v, k)| \ge p/(2kd)$. Summing over all nodes v, we get

$$\Sigma_{v \in V} |E(v, k)| \ge p^2/(2kd) = p\sqrt{p}/2$$

Because there are no more than $pd/2$ edges in G, there must be an Edge e such that $e \in V(v, k)$ for at least $k = (p\sqrt{p}/2)/(pd/2) = \sqrt{p}/d$ different choices of v. Select e and $v_1, v_2, \ldots, v_k$ such that $e \in E(v_i, k)$ for $1 \le i \le k$. It is easy to see that one can select the k nodes $u_1, u_2, \ldots, u_k$, such that P_{u_i,v_i} passes through e for $1 \le i \le k$. Node u_i is picked from among the previously unselected members of $E(v_i, k)$; because each such set has k or more members, one can always find an as yet unselected member. This completes the proof of Theorem 14.1. □

14.4. DIMENSION-ORDER ROUTING

Dimension-order routing on the hypercube is essentially a generalized version of the greedy row-first routing on the 2D mesh. In row-first routing, we "adjust" the column number or Dimension 1 of the message until it is aligned with the column number of the destination node. Then we adjust the row number or Dimension 0.

In a hypercube, we can do the adjustment of the q dimensions in any order. However, adjusting in ascending (descending) order of the dimensions is usually chosen in view of its correspondence with ascend (descend) class of algorithms. Here is an example:

Source node label	01011011
Destination node label	11010110
Dimensions that differ	↑　↑↑↑
Route	01011011
	$\overline{1}$1011011
	1101$\overline{0}$011
	11010$\overline{1}$11
	1101011$\overline{0}$

Discussion and analysis of routing algorithms on hypercube architectures is facilitated if we consider a derivative network that is obtained by "unfolding" the hypercube. An unfolded q-cube consists of $2^q(q + 1)$ nodes arranged into 2^q rows, numbered 0 through $2^q - 1$, and $q + 1$ columns, labeled 0 through q. Nodes in Columns i and $i + 1$ are connected by straight or horizontal links as well as "cross" links that correspond to Dimension-i links of the hypercube. The network obtained in this way (Fig. 14.5) is known as an *unfolded hypercube*, *indirect cube*, or *butterfly* network. Squeezing the network horizontally until all columns overlap will result in the hypercube network shown on the right side of Fig. 14.5.

Dimension-order routing between Nodes i and j in a hypercube can be viewed as routing from Node i in Column 0 (q) to Node j in Column q (0) of the butterfly network. This makes it easy to derive routing algorithms, visualize message paths, and analyze the delays resulting from link or node congestion.

Consider, for example, routing a message from Node 3 to Node 6 of a 3-cube. The heavy lines in Fig. 14.6 show that the message can be routed via a path of length 2 that goes through the intermediate node 2. The unique path of the message from Node i to Node j can be easily determined on the fly (on-line routing) if we XOR the labels of the source and destination nodes and append the result to the head of the message as a routing tag (LSB-first for ascend, MSB-first for descend). Then, in Column 0 of the butterfly network, the 0th bit of the routing tag is used to decide if the straight link (tag = 0) or the cross link (tag = 1) should be taken, in Column 1 the 1st bit is used, and in Column 2 the 2nd bit controls the path selection.

In the example of routing from Node 3 to Node 6, the routing tag is $011 \oplus 110 = 101$. This indicates the "cross–straight–cross" path consisting of the heavy solid lines in Fig. 14.6.

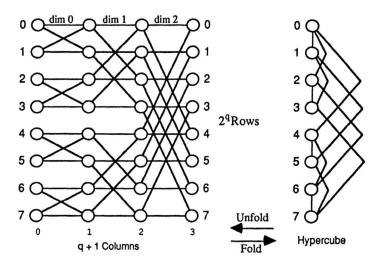

Figure 14.5. Unfolded 3-cube or the 32-node butterfly network.

A second example path is represented by the heavy dotted lines in Fig. 14.6. This path goes from Node 6 to Node 1 and corresponds to the routing tag $110 \oplus 001 = 111$. This represents a "cross–cross–cross" path, which is a diametral path in the original hypercube. It should be clear that the number of cross links taken, or the number of 1s in the routing tag, equals the length of path between the source and destination nodes.

The node using a particular bit of the routing tag to make its routing decision can either discard the bit or cyclically shift the tag by 1 bit. In the former case, the message arrives at its destination with the routing tag completely removed. With the latter option, the routing

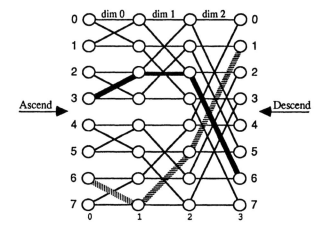

Figure 14.6. Example dimension-order routing paths.

tag returns to its original form by the time the message arrives at its destination and thus can be used by the receiving node to identify the sender.

The two messages shown in Fig. 14.6 are routed via disjoint nodes and links. Thus, they do not give rise to delays related to queuing or congestion. We can add still other paths, say from Node 4 to Node 7, without increasing the routing delay. Multiple messages that use distinct intermediate nodes and links can be routed simultaneously in q steps on the q-cube. On the other hand, message paths that "meet" in a particular node of the butterfly, or go through the same edge, may cause additional delays.

The question, now, is to determine the extent of these additional delays when dimension-order routing is used in the hypercube. First, observe that the butterfly network cannot route all permutations without node or edge conflicts. For example, any permutation involving the routes (1, 7) and (0, 3) leads to a conflict in the dimension-1 edge going from Row 1 to Row 3. Therefore, the extent of conflicts depends on the particular routing problem. There exist "good" routing problems for which conflicts are nonexistent or rare. There are also "bad" routing problems that lead to maximum conflicts and thus the worst-case running time predicted by Theorem 14.1.

The packing problem is an example of a good routing problem. Here, a subset of k nodes ($k \leq p$) in Column 0 of the butterfly network have messages or values and we want to "pack" these values into consecutive processors in Column q, beginning with Row 0. The hypercube counterpart of this problem is to pack a set of values, held by a subset of processors, into the smallest possible subcube that contains Processor 0. Figure 14.7 shows an instance of this problem with $k = 4$ values (A, B, C, D) routed to Rows 0–3 in Column 3. The destination node address for each value is easily obtained by a diminished parallel prefix computation yielding the rank of each value (a number between 0 and $k - 1$). It is fairly easy to show that such a packing problem always leads to node-disjoint and edge-disjoint paths and, thus, $O(q)$ routing time, regardless of the number k of the input packets.

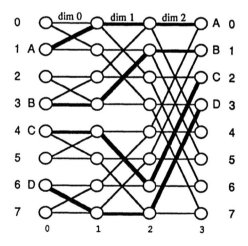

Figure 14.7. Packing is a "good" routing problem on the hypercube.

The bit-reversal permutation is an example of a bad routing problem for dimension-order routing. Bit-reversal permutation routing is when each Node $x = x_{q-1} x_{q-2} \ldots x_1 x_0$ needs to send a value to the node whose binary label is the reverse of that for x, i.e., to Node $x_0 x_1 \cdots x_{q-2} x_{q-1}$. It is easy to show that this routing problem requires $\Theta(\sqrt{p})$ time in the worst case. This is even worse than what is predicted by Theorem 14.1.

Let $q = 2a + 1$ and consider the source–destination pairs $0\,0\,0 \ldots 0\,0\, x_1 \ldots x_{a-1} x_a$ and $x_a x_{a-1} \ldots x_1\, 0\,0\,0 \ldots 0\,0$ (i.e., source/destination nodes whose labels begin/end with $a + 1$ zeros, with the rest of the bits being identical but in reverse order). All such packets must go through node $0\,0\,0 \ldots 0\,0$ when routed in dimension order. The number of packets of this type is $2^a = 2^{(\log_2 p - 1)/2} = \sqrt{p/2}$. This example shows us that there exist permutation routing problems of practical interest for which $\Theta(\sqrt{p})$ routing steps and roughly the same number of message buffers (per node) are needed.

Figure 14.8 depicts an example of the above worst-case routing problem for $a = 1$. Our aim is to route $2^a = 2$ packets from Node $00x_1$ to Node $x_1 00$, $x_1 \in \{0, 1\}$. We see that halfway through their routes, the two packets converge into Node 000 and then diverge on separate paths to their respective destinations. In this small example, we have $p = 8$ and thus only $\sqrt{p/2} = 2$ packets converge into Node 0. However, the problem would be much worse on a larger hypercube, as suggested by the above analysis.

The final item of concern here is to deal with the message buffer requirements of the dimension-order routing algorithm. One may think that if we limit each node to a small, constant number of message buffers, then the above bound still holds, except that messages will be queued at several levels before reaching Node 0, i.e., a message is not allowed to advance to the next column of the butterfly until the next node is ready to accept it. However, queuing the messages at multiple intermediate nodes may introduce additional delays that we have not accounted for, so that even the $\Theta(\sqrt{p})$ running time can no longer be guaranteed. In fact, one can prove that if each node of the hypercube is limited to $O(1)$ message buffers,

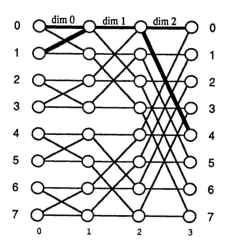

Figure 14.8. Bit-reversal permutation is a "bad" routing problem on the hypercube.

there exist permutation routing problems that require O(p) time, i.e., as bad as on a linear array!

Despite the poor performance of dimension-order routing in some cases, one should not be unduly alarmed by the above negative results. First, the performance is usually much better, i.e., $\log_2 p$ + o(log p) for most permutations. Hence, the average running time of the dimension-order routing algorithm is very close to its best case and its message buffer requirements are quite modest.

Second, if we anticipate any (near) worst-case routing pattern to occur in a given application, two options are available to us. In the first option, the routing paths for these worst-case patterns are precomputed, using an off-line routing algorithm, and stored within the nodes. With the second option, the algorithm is made to behave close to its average case by doing randomized routing: Each packet is first sent to a randomly chosen intermediate destination and from there to its final destination. In this way, any worst-case routing problem is converted to two average-case routing problems. The probabilistic analyses required to show the good average-case performance of dimension-order routing are quite complicated.

For wormhole routing, some of the above results are directly applicable. Obviously, any good routing problem, yielding node- and edge-disjoint paths, will remain good for wormhole routing. As an example, in Fig. 14.7, the four worms corresponding to the messages A, B, C, D will move in the network with no conflict among them. Each message is thus delivered to its destination in the shortest possible time, regardless of the length of the worms. For bad routing problems, on the other hand, wormhole routing aggravates the difficulties, as each message can now tie up a number of nodes and links.

In the case of wormhole routing, one also needs to be concerned with deadlocks resulting from circular waiting of messages for one another. Fortunately, dimension-order routing is guaranteed to be deadlock-free. With hot-potato or deflection routing, which is attractive for reducing the message buffering requirements within nodes, dimension orders are occasionally modified or more than one routing step along some dimensions may be allowed. Deadlock considerations in this case are similar to those of other adaptive routing schemes discussed in Section 14.6.

14.5. BROADCASTING ON A HYPERCUBE

A simple "flooding" scheme can be used for broadcasting a message from one node to all nodes in a q-cube in q steps, provided that each node can send a message simultaneously to all q neighbors (the *all-port communication* model). The source node sends the broadcast message to all of its neighbors. Each node, on receiving a broadcast message for the first time, relays it to all of its neighbors, except the one from which the message was received. Thus, in a 5-cube, the knowledge about the broadcast message spreads in the following pattern:

00000	Source node
00001, 00010, 00100, 01000, 10000	Neighbors of source
00011, 00101, 01001, 10001, 00110, 01010, 10010, 01100, 10100, 11000	
	Distance-2 nodes

00111, 01011, 10011, 01101, 10101, 11001, 01110, 10110, 11010, 11100

Distance-3 nodes

01111, 10111, 11011, 11101, 11110   Distance-4 nodes

11111   Distance-5 node

The *single-port communication* model is more reasonable and is the one usually implemented in practice. In this model, each processor (or actually the *router* associated with it) can send or receive only one message in each communication cycle. A simple recursive algorithm allows us to broadcast a message in the same q steps with this more restricted model. Suppose that in the first communication cycle, the source node sends the broadcast message to its Dimension-$(q-1)$ neighbor. The source node x and its Dimension-$(q-1)$ neighbor $N_{q-1}(x)$ now independently broadcast the message in their respective subcubes. Broadcasting time is characterized by the recurrence $T(q) = 1 + T(q - 1) = q$. Figure 14.9 shows the resulting broadcast pattern which is known as a *binomial tree*.

For long messages consisting of multiple smaller packets, or in wormhole routing, transmission of packets or flits can be pipelined. The top set of diagrams in Fig. 14.10 show a message composed of four parts A, B, C, D being broadcast in the 4-cube using the binomial tree scheme of Fig. 14.9. The message is sent in its entirety to a neighbor of the source node before being forwarded to other nodes on the path to various destinations.

The pipelined version of the binomial-tree routing algorithm is depicted in the middle set of diagrams in Fig. 14.10. Here the flit or packet A is forwarded by the neighbor as soon as it is received from the source node. Of course, we are assuming that each node can send/receive messages over all of its ports simultaneously. For example, in the rightmost snapshot shown for the pipelined binomial-tree scheme in Fig. 14.10, the node that is receiving D from the source node also has its other three ports active.

The last broadcasting scheme shown in Fig. 14.10, known as Johnsson and Ho's method [John89], is faster than the pipelined binomial-tree scheme but involves out-of-sequence transmission of the messages. For example, the neighbor to the right of the source node in Fig. 14.10 receives the C part of the message first, followed in turn by B, A, and finally D. This property creates additional storage and transmission overheads because of the need for supplying a sequence number on each part of the message.

When used with wormhole routing, all tree-based broadcasting schemes have the undesirable property that a path blockage in any branch propagates toward the source (root) node and eventually blocks the entire tree. No further progress can be made until the blocked

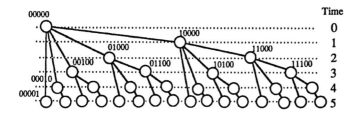

Figure 14.9. The binomial broadcast tree for a 5-cube.

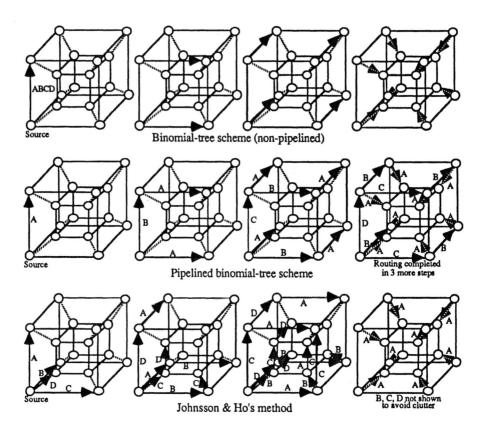

Figure 14.10. Three hypercube broadcasting schemes as performed on a 4-cube.

branch is freed; however, blockage may again occur by some other branch becoming congested. In the worst case, this may result in indefinite blockage or deadlock.

A variety of path-based broadcasting or multicasting schemes have been proposed to alleviate the above problems. In *path-based multicasting*, the destination nodes of a multicast message are divided into subsets, with the ith subset forming a list or path that begins at the source node and ends at a destination node D_i within the subset. Multicasting is then accomplished by sending a separate message from the source node to each D_i along the designated path. The message headed for D_i is picked up (copied) by all of the intermediate destination nodes along the path. A detailed discussion of path-based multicasting is given by Duato et al. ([Duat97], pp. 199–219).

14.6. ADAPTIVE AND FAULT-TOLERANT ROUTING

Because there are up to q node-disjoint and edge-disjoint shortest paths between any node pairs in a q-cube, it is possible to route messages around congested nodes/links or in spite of node and/or link faults. Such adaptive routing algorithms have been extensively studied for hypercube networks and the following discussion should be viewed only as an

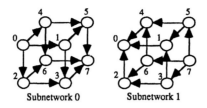

Figure 14.11. Partitioning a 3-cube into subnetworks for deadlock-free routing.

introduction to the issues and methods involved in designing such algorithms. Published research papers in this area consider one-to-one and collective communications for both packet and wormhole routing schemes.

A useful notion for designing adaptive wormhole routing algorithms is that of virtual communication networks. For example, if in a hypercube we replace each bidirectional link with two unidirectional ones going in opposite directions, we can divide the hypercube's communication links into two subsets, defining two subnetworks or virtual networks. Let Subnetwork 0 (1) consist of all of the links that connect a node to another node with larger (smaller) node label. Figure 14.11 depicts these subnetworks for a 3-cube.

Because each of the two subnetworks shown in Fig. 14.11 is acyclic, any routing scheme that begins by using the links in Subnetwork 0, at some point switches the routing path to Subnetwork 1, and from then on uses the links in Subnetwork 1 exclusively, is guaranteed to be deadlock-free. Such a routing scheme first adjusts all of the dimensions that need to be changed from 0 to 1, in Phase 0, before dealing with the dimensions that must change from 1 to 0, in Phase 1. Within each phase, the dimensions can be handled in any order, thus providing added flexibility in case a node/link becomes congested or fails.

The above scheme solves the problem of deadlock in adaptive wormhole routing for hypercubes but it has some drawbacks. A message from Node x to Node y is first sent from x to the node whose ID is $x \lor y$ (logical OR of x and y) and from there to y. Because of this, some nodes/links may become more congested than others, leading to performance degradation. Such problems can be avoided by more complicated schemes for partitioning the hypercube network into virtual networks. The methods used may involve dividing each unidirectional physical channel into multiple virtual channels that time-share the physical link.

Fault-tolerant routing on hypercubes and other networks constitutes a fascinating and active research area in parallel processing. We will revisit this problem in Chapter 19. For now, it suffices to note that the *fault diameter* of a hypercube (the diameter of the surviving part when faulty nodes/links are removed) grows slowly with an increase in the number of faulty elements. For example, the fault diameter of a q-cube is upper bounded by $q + 1$ with at most $q - 1$ faults and by $q + 2$ with $2q - 3$ or fewer faults [Lati93].

PROBLEMS

14.1. Bitonic sorting on a linear array
Unfold the four phases of the sorting example depicted in Fig. 14.3, showing all shifting and compare–exchange steps and verifying that the total number of steps is $T(16) = 4 \times 16 - 4 - 2 \log_2 16 = 52$.

14.2. Bitonic sorting on a ring
Does changing the linear array into a ring speed up the bitonic sorting algorithm? How or why not?

14.3. Batcher's odd–even merge sort

   a. Describe Batcher's odd–even merge sort (presented in Section 14.2) in the form of an algorithm for the q-cube.
   b. Draw a set of diagrams, similar to those in Fig. 14.4, that show how the algorithm works.
   c. Analyze the complexity of the algorithm and show that it requires $O(q^2)$ running time.

14.4. Batcher's bitonic sorting algorithm

   a. Analyze the complexity of Batcher's bitonic sorting algorithm when it is adapted to run with n/p elements in each of the $p = 2^q$ processors on a q-cube.
   b. Using the bitonic sorting algorithm (as depicted in the example of Fig. 14.4), show that any *shift permutation*, where the packet in each Node i needs to go to Node $i + k$ mod 2^q, can be routed on a q-cube in q steps, i.e., with no conflict.

14.5. Sorting by multiway merging
Suppose that you are given an algorithm to merge $\sqrt{p}$ sorted lists, each of size $\sqrt{p}$, on a p-processor hypercube in $O(\log p \log \log^2 p)$ time. Show how the p-processor hypercube can sort a list of size p in $O(\log p \log \log^2 p)$ time.

14.6. Alternative sorting algorithms
Show how the sorting algorithms discussed in Section 6.4 in connection with the PRAM abstract shared-memory model can be implemented on the hypercube.

14.7. Lower bounds for routing
Justify Ω(generalized dilation + generalized congestion) as a lower bound for oblivious routing on an arbitrary network.

14.8. Generalized packing
The generalized packing problem on a q-cube is defined as that of sending k packets, stored one per processor ($k \leq p$), to a sequence of k consecutive nodes, beginning with a given Node b. The packing problem exemplified by Fig. 14.7 corresponds to the special case of $b = 0$ in this generalized version.

   a. Show that the generalized packing problem is a good problem for dimension-order routing.
   b. Using the result of part (a), show that any *shift routing* problem, where a packet initially residing in Node i needs to go to Node $i + k$ mod 2^q, can be routed on a q-cube in q steps with no conflict.
   c. Can the order of traversing the q dimensions be reversed for packing or generalized packing?

14.9. Matrix transposition
The elements of an $m \times m$ matrix are stored, in row-major order, on the $p = 2^q = m^2$ processors of a q-cube. The *matrix transposition* routing problem is defined as rearranging the elements into column-major order. This requires the element in Row i, Column j to move to the processor currently holding the element in Row j, Column i.

   a. Show the paths needed to transpose a 4×4 matrix on a 16×5 butterfly network.
   b. Is matrix transposition a good or bad problem for dimension-order routing on a q-cube?
   c. Develop an efficient hypercube algorithm for matrix transposition as defined above.

14.10. Hypercube with diametral links

It is possible to augment the hypercube architecture by adding a link between each node and its diametrically opposite node. This increases the node degree from q to $q + 1$. In the augmented architecture, two nodes are connected iff the Hamming distance between their binary labels is either 1 or q.

    a. What is the effect of this change on the diameter of the hypercube?

    b. How does the change affect the bisection width of the hypercube?

    c. Devise a dimension-order routing algorithm for the q-cube augmented with diametral links.

14.11. Broadcasting on a hypercube

Consider the q-cube broadcasting schemes of Fig. 14.10.

    a. Analyze the communication time of the algorithms assuming long messages of length L (so that the message transfer time dominates message startup time).

    b. What is the average number of communication links in use during the algorithm?

    c. Experimental measurements on a particular hypercube multicomputer reveal a message latency of 50 µs and a transfer rate of 100 MB/s. Plot the estimated time needed for the three algorithms to broadcast k bytes ($10^3 \le k \le 10^6$) on a 1024-processor system. Use a log–log scale for your graph. Assume all-port communication where needed.

14.12. Broadcasting on a hypercube

The binomial-tree broadcasting algorithm was derived recursively: send to one node in the other half-cube, then broadcast in parallel in each half-cube. Discuss the algorithm obtained by reversing the order of the two steps: broadcast in the 0 half-cube, then send the message from each node in the 0 half-cube to its neighbor in the 1 half-cube.

14.13. Adaptive routing algorithms

Consider the routing scheme represented by Fig. 14.11 and assume uniform message traffic between all node pairs.

    a. Which hypercube node will be least congested and why?

    b. Which hypercube node will be most congested and why?

14.14. Architecture-independent routing models

The hypercube architecture has a rich connectivity, short diameter, and wide bisection. In many hypercube parallel systems utilizing message passing, the message transmission delay is dominated by the operating system overhead for the initiation or reception of a message, so that the actual source and destination addresses and the effects of possible congestion on the routing paths can be ignored for all practical purposes. An abstract model of the above situation consists of each node being able to send k messages and receive k messages in unit time, where k is a limit that is imposed by the system's aggregate communication bandwidth. Suppose that one processor needs to broadcast m different messages to all other $2^q - 1$ processors in a q-cube. Determine the minimum time needed to perform this task in each of the following cases:

    a. $m = 1, k = 1$.

    b. Arbitrary m, with $k = 1$.

    c. $m = 1, k = 2$.

14.15. The postal communication model

The postal communication model is a topology-independent model that associates an integer number λ of cycles of delay with each message transmission, independent of the source and destination node addresses. Each node can transmit one message per cycle, but the message transmitted in cycle i will not be received at the destination node until cycle $i + \lambda$. The name of this model derives from the following analogy. Suppose you are allowed to write one letter per day and that it takes the letter 2 days to reach its destination. Then the right-hand diagram below shows that you can broadcast a message to eight people in 5 days whereas the binomial-tree broadcasting algorithm on the left requires 6 days to complete the task. The numbers on multiple edges leaving a node correspond to the cycle number (day) in which the message is sent.

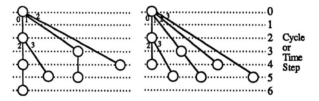

a. Show that the number of nodes that have received a broadcast message after t cycles satisfies the recurrence $N_\lambda(t) = N_\lambda(t-1) + N_\lambda(t-\lambda)$ for $t \geq \lambda$; for $t < \lambda$, we clearly have $N_\lambda(t) = 1$, as none of the messages has reached its destination yet.

b. Discuss the solution to the above recurrence for $\lambda = 2$.

14.16. Many-to-many routing on a hypercube

Consider a routing problem in which each node of a q-cube has up to k messages to send and no more than k of the messages in the entire q-cube are addressed to the same node. Let us call this a k–k routing problem. Show that any k–k routing problem can be decomposed into k 1–1 routing problems by an off-line algorithm. Given the above decomposition, how much time does the routing require with the all-port communication model?

REFERENCES AND SUGGESTED READING

[Batc68]   Batcher, K., "Sorting Networks and Their Applications," *Proc. AFIPS Spring Joint Computer Conf.*, 1968, Vol. 32, pp. 307–314.

[Cyph90]   Cypher, R., and G. Plaxton, "Deterministic Sorting in Nearly Logarithmic Time on the Hypercube and Related Computers," *Proc. 22nd ACM Symp. Theory of Computing*, 1990, pp. 193–203.

[Duat97]   Duato, J., S. Yalamanchili, and L. Ni, *Interconnection Networks: An Engineering Approach*, IEEE Computer Society Press, 1997.

[Ferr96]   Ferreira, A., "Parallel and Communication Algorithms on Hypercube Multiprocessors," Chapter 19 in *Parallel and Distributed Computing Handbook*, edited by A.Y. Zomaya, McGraw-Hill, 1996, pp. 568–589.

[Gree95]   Greenberg, R. I., and H.-C. Oh, "Packet Routing in Networks with Long Wires," *J. Parallel and Distributed Computing*, Vol. 31, pp. 153–158, 1995.

[John89]   Johnsson, S. L., and C. -T. Ho, "Optimum Broadcasting and Personalized Communication in Hypercubes," *IEEE Trans. Computers*, Vol. 38, No. 9, pp. 1249–1268, September 1989.

[Lati93]   Latifi, S., "Combinatorial Analysis of the Fault Diameter of the n-Cube," *IEEE Trans. Computers*, Vol. 42, No. 1, pp. 27–33, January 1993.

[Leig92]   Leighton, F. T., *Introduction to Parallel Algorithms and Architectures: Arrays, Trees, Hypercubes*, Morgan Kaufmann, 1992.

[Leig94]   Leighton, F. T., B. M. Maggs, and S. B. Rao, "Packet Routing and Job-Shop Scheduling in O(Congestion + Dilation) Steps," *Combinatorica*, Vol. 14, No. 2, pp. 167–180, 1994.

[McKi95]   McKinley, P. K., Y. -J. Tsai, and D. F. Robinson, "Collective Communication in Wormhole-Routed Massively Parallel Computers," *IEEE Computer*, Vol. 28, No. 12, pp. 39–50, December 1995.

[Nass82]   Nassimi, D., and S. Sahni, "Parallel Permutation and Sorting Algorithms and a New Generalized
            Connection Network," *J. ACM*, Vol. 29, No. 3, pp. 642–667, July 1982.
[Plax89]   Plaxton, G., "Load Balancing, Selection and Sorting on the Hypercube," *Proc. ACM Symp. Parallel
            Algorithms and Architectures*, 1989, pp. 64–73.
[Reif87]   Reif, J., and L. Valiant, "A Logarithmic Time Sort for Linear Size Networks," *J. ACM*, Vol. 34, No.
            1, pp. 60–76, January 1987.

15

Other Hypercubic Architectures

In this chapter, we discuss a number of modified and generalized hypercube-based architectures that can provide certain benefits over standard hypercubes. More importantly, we study several constant-degree parallel architectures that are derivable from, or intimately related to, the logarithmic-degree hypercube. These constant-degree derivatives share many properties of the hypercube and can emulate it quite efficiently, but are both realizable at lower cost and more readily scalable. Hence, one can use the rich structure of the hypercube, and the wide array of algorithms and theoretical results available for it, to develop efficient algorithms and then resort to the emulation results presented here to implement those algorithms or prove desired results for practically realizable parallel systems. Chapter topics are

- 15.1. Modified and generalized hypercubes
- 15.2. Butterfly and permutation networks
- 15.3. Plus-or-minus-2^i network
- 15.4. The cube-connected cycles network
- 15.5. Shuffle and shuffle–exchange networks
- 15.6. That's not all, folks!

15.1. MODIFIED AND GENERALIZED HYPERCUBES

The versatility and rich algorithmic and theoretical properties of the hypercube have led researchers to define modified, augmented, generalized, or hierarchical versions of the network. We postpone a discussion of hierarchical hypercubic networks to Section 16.5 where a general framework for multilevel or hierarchical interconnection networks is presented and several example networks are studied. In this section, we study a few variants of the standard binary hypercube that are obtained by redirecting some of the links, adding links/nodes, and changing the basis or "seed" network.

An example of the first category (i.e., redirecting some links) is the *twisted hypercube* obtained by redirecting two edges in any 4-cycle, as shown in Fig. 15.1. In general, any 4-cycle *uvxy* can be chosen in the *q*-cube, its *uv* and *xy* edges removed, and new edges *ux*, *vy* inserted to obtain a twisted *q*-cube. Let the edges in the 4-cycle be along Dimensions *k* and *l*. Then, each of the Nodes *u*, *v*, *x*, and *y* of the original 4-cycle will have a neighbor N_{kl} in the twisted version of the network whose node label differs from it in both bits *k* and *l*. It is easy to show that the diameter of a twisted *q*-cube is *q* − 1, i.e., one less than that of the *q*-cube. Additionally, rings of any odd length and the (2^q-1)-node complete binary tree are subgraphs of a twisted *q*-cube; properties that are not possessed by the ordinary *q*-cube [Esfa91].

An example of the second category (i.e., adding some links) is the *folded hypercube*, which is obtained from the hypercube by linking all pairs of diametrically opposite nodes. For example, in the 3-cube depicted in Fig. 15.2, Nodes 0 and 7 are diametrically opposite, as are three other node pairs (1, 6), (2, 5), and (3, 4). Thus, adding the four links shown in bold in the right-hand diagram of Fig. 15.2 yields a folded 3-cube. It is easy to see that the diameter of a folded hypercube is about half that of a regular hypercube. Let us designate the added diametral links as Dimension-*q* links. Then, a dimension-order routing algorithm can be devised that routes each message in $\lceil q/2 \rceil$ steps. Details of this algorithm, as well as deriving other topological properties of folded hypercubes are left as an exercise.

An important property of folded hypercubes is their improved robustness or fault tolerance. If one or several Dimension-*i* links fail, where $0 \le i < q$, Dimension-*q* links can be used in their stead. Figure 15.3 depicts an example where all Dimension-0 links are removed from a 3-cube and an intact 3-cube is recovered by conceptually rotating the right subcube, consisting of Nodes 1, 3, 5, and 7, counterclockwise until Nodes 3 and 5 (also, 1 and 7) switch places. In this way, an intact *q*-cube can be obtained by simply renaming half

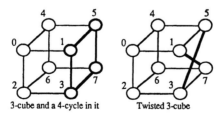

3-cube and a 4-cycle in it   Twisted 3-cube

Figure 15.1. Deriving a twisted 3-cube by redirecting two links in a 4-cycle

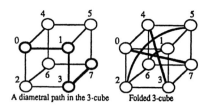

Figure 15.2. Deriving a folded 3-cube by adding four diametral links.

of the nodes. For other interesting properties of folded hypercubes, see El-Amawy and Latifi: [ElAm91].

A hypercube, as defined and analyzed in the previous two chapters, is the qth power of a two-node linear array. Thus, a hypercube can be viewed as a *power network* or *homogeneous product network* (a product network formed by "multiplying" identical component networks).

If we view the two-node linear array as a complete graph of size 2, a generalization of the hypercube immediately suggests itself. The r-node complete graph, K_r, is a graph in which every pair of nodes is directly connected by an edge. The qth power of K_r is a *generalized hypercube*. Node labels in a generalized hypercube can be viewed as q-digit radix r numbers, with each node connected to all of the $q(r-1)$ nodes whose labels differ from it in a single digit. Actually, as defined by Bhuyan and Agrawal [Bhuy84], a generalized hypercube is the product of complete graphs which may be of different sizes. The node labels in this more general case can be viewed as mixed-radix numbers, with each node connected to $\sum_{i=0}^{q-1}(r_i - 1)$ other nodes, where r_i is the radix in digit position i.

Another generalization of the hypercube results from using a ring of size m (instead of 2) as the basis or "seed" network. The qth power of the m-node ring is known as the m-ary q-cube interconnection network, which is the same as q-D torus of equal dimensions m. The hypercube is then a 2-ary (or binary) q-cube according to this terminology. Again multiplying rings of different sizes yields a more general structure. Note that hypercubes and 2D tori represent the two extremes of m-ary q-cubes. Fix q at 2 and you get 2D tori with $\Theta(\sqrt{p})$ diameter; fix m at 2 and you get the hypercube with logarithmic diameter.

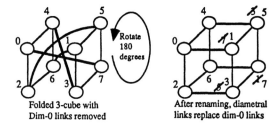

Figure 15.3. Folded 3-cube viewed as 3-cube with a redundant dimension.

15.2. BUTTERFLY AND PERMUTATION NETWORKS

In Section 14.4, we defined the butterfly network with 2^q nodes and $q + 1$ columns as an unfolded q-cube in order to facilitate the discussion, visualization, and analysis of hypercube routing algorithms. However, a butterfly network can be viewed as a parallel processing architecture in its own right. A butterfly architecture (Fig. 15.4, left) has $p = 2^q(q + 1)$ processors of maximum degree $d = 4$, a diameter of $2q = \Theta(\log p)$, and a bisection width of $(\sqrt{2} - 1)2^{q+1} + 0(2^q) = \Theta(p/\log p)$ [Born 98]. A *wrapped butterfly* architecture is obtained if we superimpose or merge the nodes in Columns 0 and q of an ordinary butterfly. The resulting network has $p = 2^q q$ processors, a uniform node degree of 4, a diameter of roughly $1.5q$, and a bisection width of 2^q.

Each node in a (wrapped) butterfly can be identified by its row and column numbers (x, y), where $0 \le x < 2^q - 1$ and $0 \le y \le q$ ($q - 1$ for wrapped butterfly). Node (x, y) of a butterfly is connected to the four nodes $(x, y - 1)$, $(x, y + 1)$, $(N_{y-1}(x), y - 1)$, and $(N_y(x), y + 1)$, if they exist. In the case of wrapped butterfly, the expressions $y \pm 1$ for the column numbers are evaluated modulo q.

If you shift the columns of a butterfly network cyclically, or permute them in any way, you can redraw the figure (by exchanging rows) such that it looks exactly the same as before. Figure 15.5 shows an example in which the connection pattern between Columns 0 and 1 has been interchanged with that between Columns 1 and 2. It is easily seen that if we redraw the network by interchanging the places of Rows 1 and 2 as well as Rows 5 and 6, the resulting diagram will look exactly like the left-hand diagram in Fig. 15.4.

The butterfly network is quite versatile. Many other independently developed networks are in fact butterfly networks in disguise. Take a fat tree, for example. Recall that a major disadvantage of a binary tree architecture is its small bisection width, making the root node a bottleneck when a large number of long-distance communications must be performed. A

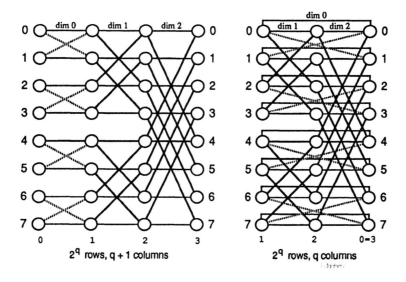

Figure 15.4. Butterfly and wrapped butterfly networks.

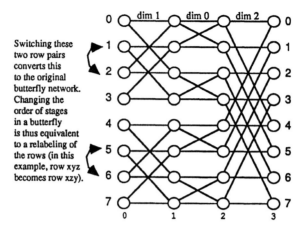

Switching these two row pairs converts this to the original butterfly network. Changing the order of stages in a butterfly is thus equivalent to a relabeling of the rows (in this example, row xyz becomes row xzy).

Figure 15.5. Butterfly network with permuted dimensions.

fat tree is a treelike network specifically designed to remedy this problem. In a fat tree, the link multiplicity or capacity increases as we approach the root node (Fig. 15.6). Of course, taking advantage of the added links or link capacities would require that the nodes near the root be different (have higher communication performance). To avoid this heterogeneity, one might divide each such node into a number of simpler, lower-performance nodes. The resulting architecture, shown in Fig. 15.7, is a butterfly network. We see that even if each of the eight leaf nodes wants to send a message to another leaf node, the messages can be routed through the eight root nodes with little or no conflict.

Anecdote. It has been suggested that because trees in nature are thicker near the root and thinner near the leaves, we should call the networks shown in Fig. 15.6 *trees* and refer to regular binary trees as *skinny trees*.

The structure of the fat tree, as drawn in Fig. 15.7, is such that the communication bandwidth between Level-i and Level-($i+1$) nodes is the same for all i (16 wires or channels in our example). This is based on the worst-case assumption that all messages entering a node from below must be directed to its parent. Real communication patterns are more local so that only a fraction of the messages entering a node from below must be routed up to the

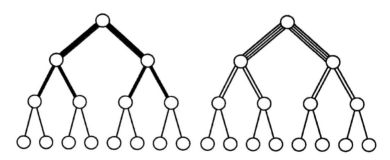

Figure 15.6. Two representations of a fat tree.

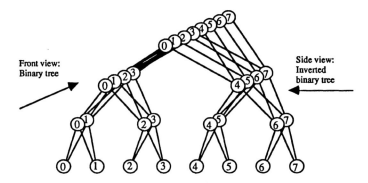

Front view:
Binary tree

Side view:
Inverted
binary tree

Figure 15.7. Butterfly network redrawn as a fat tree.

parent; most are addressed to nodes within the same subtree. This locality property allows us to put the fat tree on a diet, making it skinnier near the root. Such a "plump tree" is the interconnection network used in the CM-5 parallel computer built by Thinking Machines Corporation (see Section 22.4).

There are many variations of the butterfly network. First, the butterfly network may be viewed as a multilevel interconnection network connecting processors on one side to memory modules on the other side. In this type of usage, a $2^q \times (q+1)$ butterfly network built of 2×2 routing switches can interconnect 2^{q+1} modules on each side, when the nodes in Columns 0 and q are provided with two input and two output links, respectively (see Fig. 6.9). Replacing the memory modules by processors would yield an interprocessor interconnection network. Alternatively, a $2^q \times 2^q$ interconnection network results if all modules are connected to one side of the butterfly network, as shown in Fig. 15.8.

If we unfold Fig. 15.8, so that the processors remain on the left but the memory modules move to the right, and then merge the middle four nodes in each row which perform no useful

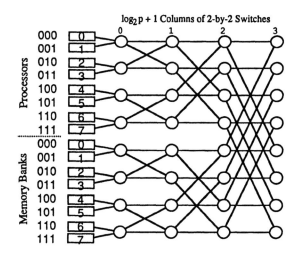

Figure 15.8. Butterfly network used to connect modules that are on the same side.

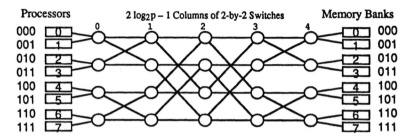

Figure 15.9. Beneš network formed from two back-to-back butterflies.

routing function, a Beneš network results. Figure 15.9 shows the resulting network for connecting eight processors to eight memory modules. In general, the q-dimensional Beneš network is obtained from two back-to-back q-dimensional butterflies, with the Column q of one superimposed on the Column 0 of the second one. Thus, a q-dimensional Beneš network has 2^q rows and $2q + 1$ columns.

An important property of a Beneš network is that it can route any permutation with no conflict. This is in part related to the availability of multiple edge-disjoint paths between any pair of input and output nodes. For example, in Fig. 15.10, we see Processors 0, 1, 2, 3, 5, 6, and 9 connected to Banks 6, 14, 0, 15, 11, 4, and 3, respectively. With the connections already established, Processor 4 can be connected to Bank 7 or 10 but not to other currently unused memory banks. However, if Processor 4 were to be connected to Bank 8, say, it is possible to re-route or rearrange the other connections such that the new connection can also be accommodated. For this reason, the Beneš network is called *rearrangeable*, meaning that it can route any permutation if rearranging previously established connections is allowed.

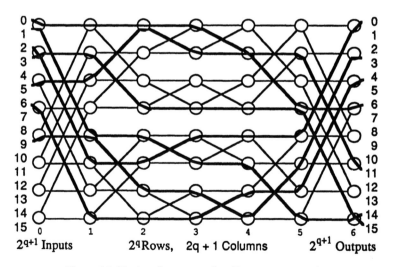

Figure 15.10. Another example of a Beneš network.

Finally, we note that a butterfly network can be generalized to a high-radix butterfly (or
m-ary butterfly) composed of nodes with degree $2m$ (or $m \times m$ switches). There are m^q rows
and $q + 1$ columns in an m-ary butterfly network.

15.3. PLUS-OR-MINUS-2^i NETWORK

Figure 15.11 shows a plus-or-minus-2^i (PM2I) network with eight nodes ($p = 2^q$ nodes
in general) in which each Node x is connected to every node whose label is $x \pm 2^i$ mod p for
some i. It is easy to see that the PM2I network is a supergraph of the hypercube. The heavy
lines in Fig. 15.11 show the hypercube subgraph of the eight-node PM2I network.

Just as an unfolded hypercube is isomorphic to the butterfly network, an unfolded PM2I
network yields a useful (multistage) interconnection network known as an *augmented data
manipulator* (ADM) network. Here, *augmented* means that the network is derived from a
data manipulator network which, as originally defined, restricted all switches in the same
column to be in identical states (provide exactly the same connectivity pattern between their
inputs and outputs). The data manipulator network was proposed as a multistage interconnection network and the common state for switches in the same column was needed to
simplify its control structure.

The dangling lines at the top and bottom of Fig. 15.12 represent wraparound links in
view of the $\pm 2^i$ mod 2^q connectivity rule. So, for example, the lines labeled "a" and "b" at
the top are connected to the lines with the same designations at the bottom.

Paths from one side to the other side of an ADM network are nonunique. For example,
there are two paths between Node 2 in Column 0 and Node 4 in Column 3 (heavy lines in
Fig. 15.12). Each link selected corresponds to adding or subtracting a power of 2. The paths
highlighted in Fig. 15.12 correspond to obtaining 4 from 2 by adding 2 to it or by subtracting
2 from it and then adding 4. Routing in ADM network corresponds to decomposing the
difference $y - x$ mod 2^q of source and destination rows into powers of 2. A binary routing
tag can be used to achieve self-routing, with the ith bit of the tag used to select the straight
output (0) or the lower output (1) in Column i. If the routing tag is represented as a binary
signed-digit number, with digit values in $\{-1, 0, 1\}$, then a digit -1 would correspond to
taking the upper output channel. For example, the routing tags corresponding to the two paths
highlighted in Fig. 15.12 are 0 1 0 and 1̄ 1 0, where ¯1 represents the signed digit or tag
value -1.

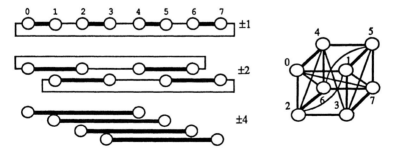

Figure 15.11. Two representations of the eight-node plus-or-minus-2^i network.

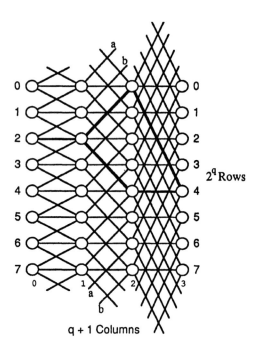

Figure 15.12. Augmented data manipulator network.

Having multiple paths is desirable both for improved performance (network bandwidth) and for fault tolerance. Thus, the ADM network is more resilient to node and link failure than a butterfly network of the same size. The hardware cost paid for this added resilience is a larger node degree and denser interconnections. The software cost is a more complex routing algorithm that is capable of distributing the traffic evenly among the multiple paths that are available.

15.4. THE CUBE-CONNECTED CYCLES NETWORK

The cube-connected cycles (CCC) network can be derived from a wrapped butterfly as follows. Remove the pair of cross links that connect a pair of nodes in Column $i - 1$ to the same two nodes in Column i and instead connect the two nodes in Column i (Fig. 15.13). The resulting network has node degree of 3 but is otherwise quite similar to the butterfly network. In particular, CCC can emulate any algorithm for a butterfly of the same size with only a constant factor slowdown.

The original definition of CCC was based on a q-cube in which each node has been replaced with a cycle of length q, with the aim of reducing the node degree without significantly affecting the diameter. Figure 15.14 shows how a 3-cube is converted to a 24-node CCC. Each node is replaced with a 3-cycle, with the original hypercube links distributed one per node in the cycle. Each node also has two cycle edges. The three edges of a node in CCC can be denoted as

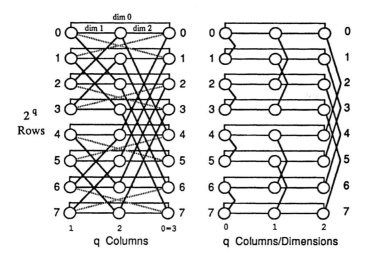

Figure 15.13. A wrapped butterfly (left) converted into cube-connected cycles.

F   Forward link in the cycle
B   Backward link in the cycle
C   Intercycle or cube link

Each node can be identified by a pair (x, y) of integers, where x is the cycle number (the node number in the original hypercube) and y is the node number within the cycle. This same numbering scheme is applicable to the representation of Fig. 15.13 where x and y correspond to row and column numbers. Two nodes (x_0, y_0) and (x_1, y_1) are adjacent iff

$$x_0 = x_1 \text{ and } y_0 = y_1 \pm 1 \text{ or } y_0 = y_1 \text{ and } x_0 \text{ differs from } x_1 \text{ in bit position } y_0$$

The number of processors in a CCC derived from a q-cube is $p = 2^q q$.

A simple argument can be used to establish the following bound on the diameter of CCC:

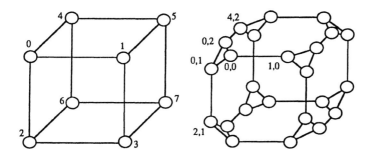

Figure 15.14. Alternate derivation of CCC from a hypercube.

$$D < 2.5q = \Theta(\log p)$$

The argument goes as follows. Simple dimension-order routing leads to a message taking up to $q/2$ steps in the source ring to gain access to a Dimension-$(q-1)$ link, $2q - 1$ steps in intermediate rings (cube edge, ring edge, cube edge, ring edge, . . . , ring edge, cube edge), and finally up to $q/2$ steps in the destination ring. These add up to $3q - 1$ steps. If we route the dimensions in arbitrary order, the first $q/2$ steps can be eliminated; we simply begin the routing path with whatever dimension that is accessible from the source node.

The CCC network can be somewhat generalized if the number of nodes in each cycle is specified to be at least q rather than exactly q. If there are k nodes in each cycle, with $k \geq q$, then the first q nodes will have cube links as before and the remaining $k - q$ nodes will have only F and B links in the cycle. This allows us, e.g., to make the number of nodes in a cycle a power of 2 (four nodes per cycle in the example of Fig. 15.14), leading to simpler and cleaner algorithms. In addition, increasing the parameter k provides a performance–cost trade-off mechanism in the sense that with larger values of k, the network diameter grows and its bisection width is reduced. In return, the network becomes less complex (e.g., easier to lay out in VLSI).

The exact diameter of CCC with 2^q cycles of size $k \geq q$ is as follows [Meli93]:

$$6 \qquad\qquad \text{if } k = q = 3$$

$$2q + \lfloor q/2 \rfloor - 2 \qquad \text{if } k = q > 3$$

$$2q + \lfloor k/2 \rfloor - 1 \qquad \text{if } q < k < 2q - 1$$

$$q + k \qquad\qquad \text{if } k \geq 2q - 1$$

CCC can emulate any hypercube algorithm with $O(q) = O(\log p)$ slowdown. However, for a class of hypercube algorithms known as *normal algorithms*, the slowdown is only a constant. Thus, for this class of algorithms, which includes the ascend/descend class of algorithms as special cases, CCC performs almost as well as the hypercube while having a much lower implementation cost. Recall that in ascend (descend) class of hypercube algorithms, each node communicates along all possible dimensions in order, beginning with 0 $(q-1)$ and ending with $q-1$ (0). More generally, when each communication activity is along a dimension that differs from the previous one by ± 1 mod q, the hypercube algorithm is called *normal*.

Assume, for clarity, that $q = 2^m$. The number of processors in our CCC network is then $p = 2^q q = 2^{2^m} 2^m = 2^{2^m + m}$. The hypercube to be simulated has $2^m + m$ dimensions. Communication along the first m dimensions is carried out by data rotation within cycles. The remaining 2^m dimensions are handled as follows. Suppose communication along Dimension j has just taken place between the values in Nodes (x, j) and $(N_j(x), j)$ (see Fig. 15.15). The next communication is along Dimension $j - 1$ or $j + 1$. Assume that it is to be along Dimension $j + 1$. Rotating the data values in the nodes in the direction of the arrows will align the values for Dimension-$(j+1)$ communication, as the value in Node (x, j) goes to Node $(x, j+1)$. Similarly, rotating in the opposite direction will allow communication along Dimension $j-1$ to take place. As the data originally in Node (x, j) perform their Dimension-$(j+1)$ communi-

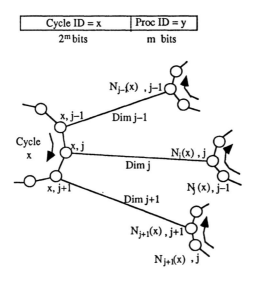

Figure 15.15. CCC emulating a normal hypercube algorithm.

cation through Node $(x, j+1)$, the data originally in Node $(x, j-1)$ are properly aligned for Dimension-j communication through Node (x, j).

15.5. SHUFFLE AND SHUFFLE–EXCHANGE NETWORKS

A *perfect shuffle*, or simply *shuffle*, connectivity is one that interlaces the nodes in a way that is similar to a perfect shuffle of a deck of cards. That is, Node 0 is connected to 0, Node 1 to 2, Node 2 to 4, . . . , Node $2^{q-1} - 1$ to $2^q - 2$, Node 2^{q-1} to 1, . . . , Node $2^q - 1$ to $2^q - 1$, as depicted in the leftmost diagram of Fig. 15.16. The reverse connectivity is sometimes referred to as *unshuffle*. The "exchange" connectivity, which links each even-numbered node with the next odd-numbered node, is also shown in Fig. 15.16.

Combining the shuffle and exchange connectivities, we get the connectivity of a shuffle–exchange network. By combining the two, we either mean that both "shuffle" connection as well as "shuffle-then-exchange" connections are provided or that both shuffle and exchange connections are provided as separate links. This latter interpretation corresponds to the rightmost diagram in Fig. 15.16 (throughout this figure, two copies of each node are drawn to show the connectivity rules more clearly). Figure 15.17 shows the eight-node shuffle–exchange interconnection network in the standard undirected graph form.

In a 2^q-node shuffle network, Node $x = x_{q-1}x_{q-2} \cdots x_2x_1x_0$ is connected to $x_{q-2} \cdots x_2x_1x_0x_{q-1}$, i.e., to the node whose label is the cyclically left-shifted version of x. The unshuffle connection is just the opposite and corresponds to a right cyclic shift in the node label. With undirected links, both the shuffle and unshuffle connectivities are obviously present, but the unidirectional version of such networks may have only shuffle or only unshuffle links. In

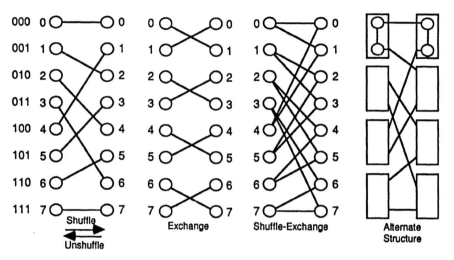

Figure 15.16. Shuffle, exchange, and shuffle–exchange connectivities.

the shuffle–exchange network, Node x is additionally connected to $x_{q-2} \cdots x_2 x_1 x_0 x'_{q-1}$, where x'_{q-1} is the complement of x_{q-1}.

Routing in a shuffle–exchange network is quite simple. A shuffle, and possibly an exchange, is needed for "adjusting" each address bit. This corresponds to one or two routing steps per address bit, depending on which of the two right-hand networks in Fig. 15.16 is implemented.

As an example, consider routing a message from the source node $x = 01011011$ to the destination node $y = 11010110$. The routing is done as follows:

Source	01011011
Destination	11010110
Positions that differ	↑ ↑↑ ↑

Route
    011011   Shuffle to 10110110 Exchange to 10110111
    10110111 Shuffle to 01101111

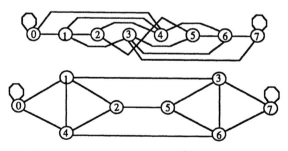

Figure 15.17. Alternate views of an eight-node shuffle–exchange network.

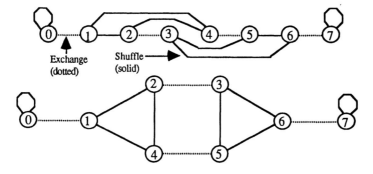

Figure 15.18. Eight-node network with separate shuffle and exchange links.

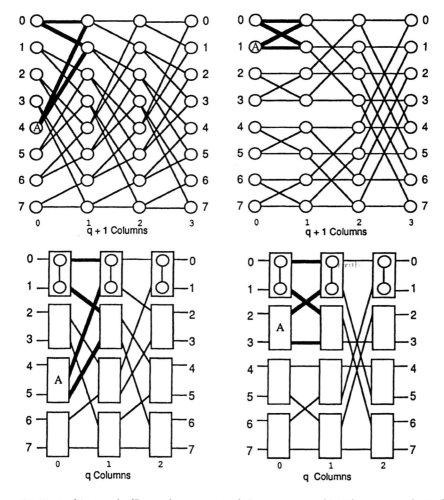

Figure 15.19. Multistage shuffle–exchange network (omega network) is the same as butterfly network.

01101111 Shuffle to 11011110
11011110 Shuffle to 10111101
10111101 Shuffle to 01111011   Exchange to 01111010
01111010 Shuffle to 11110100   Exchange to 11110101
11110101 Shuffle to 11101011
11101011 Shuffle to 11010111   Exchange to 11010110

Based on the routing algorithm implicitly defined in the above example, it should be obvious that the diameter of a 2^q-node shuffle–exchange network is $q = \log_2 p$ (the node degree is 4). With shuffle and exchange links provided separately, as shown in Fig. 15.18, the diameter increases to $2q - 1$ and node degree reduces to 3.

Cascading the two shuffle–exchange structures shown on the right side of Fig. 15.16 results in a multistage interconnection network, as shown on the left side of Fig. 15.19. By repositioning or renaming the nodes, these *omega networks* can be redrawn to look like butterfly networks (right side of Fig. 15.18). Note, for example, the repositioning of the node labeled "A" in each diagram. Drawing a butterfly network as a multistage shuffle–exchange network reveals a hardware saving scheme: Only one stage of a shuffle–exchange network might be implemented and routing done by multiple "passes" through this hardware; this is similar to periodic sorting networks that allowed us to sort by multiple passes through hardware corresponding to a single period (see Section 7.5).

15.6. THAT'S NOT ALL, FOLKS!

Thus far in this chapter, we have examined various interconnection architectures that are derived by changing, generalizing, or unfolding the hypercube. Other modifications and extensions are also possible. We cannot possibly examine all of them here, but offer only two examples of the wide array of possibilities.

We note that when q is a power of 2, the $2^q q$-node cube-connected cycles network derived from the q-cube, by replacing each of its nodes with a q-cycle, is a subgraph of the $(q + \log_2 q)$-cube. Thus, CCC can be viewed as a *pruned hypercube*. The hypercube itself is a pruned PM2I network in which roughly half of the links have been removed. Other pruning strategies are possible, leading to interesting performance–cost trade-offs.

For example, if the number q of dimensions in a q-cube is odd, the following pruning strategy can be applied to the q-cube to reduce its node degree from q to $(q + 1)/2$. All

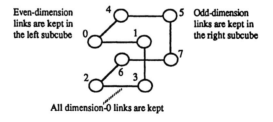

Figure 15.20. Example of a pruned hypercube.

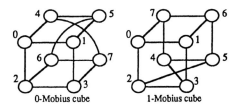

Figure 15.21. Two 8-node Möbius cubes.

Dimension-0 links remain intact, but within the subcube composed of nodes whose labels end in 0 (1), only even- (odd-) dimension links are kept and the rest are removed. The resulting pruned hypercube is much simpler than the unpruned version, yet it has a diameter that is only one unit more. Figure 15.20 shows a pruned 3-cube, with Dimension-0 links connecting the left and right 2-cubes each having only half of its original links.

Möbius cubes [Cull95] are similar to hypercubes, except that the Dimension-i neighbor of Node $x = x_{q-1}x_{q-2} \cdots x_{i+1}x_i \cdots x_1x_0$ is $x_{q-1}x_{q-2} \cdots 0x_i' \cdots x_1x_0$ if $x_{i+1} = 0$ (i.e., as in the hypercube, x_i is complemented to obtain the neighbor's node label) and $x_{q-1}x_{q-2} \cdots 1x_i' \cdots x_1'x_0'$ if $x_{i+1} = 1$ (i.e., x_i and all of the bits to its right are complemented to obtain the neighbor's node label). For Dimension $q - 1$, because there is no x_q, the neighbor can be defined in two ways, leading to 0-Möbius cubes (assume $x_q = 0$) and 1-Möbius cubes (assume $x_q = 1$). Figure 15.21 shows the 0- and 1-Möbius cubes for $q = 3$. For $q = 3$, Möbius cubes are identical to twisted cubes defined in Section 15.1. However, the two are different for larger values of q. For this reason, Möbius cubes have also been called *generalized twisted cubes*. A Möbius cube has a diameter of about one-half and an average internode distance of about two-thirds of that of a hypercube.

PROBLEMS

15.1. Twisted hypercubes

    a. Prove that the diameter of a twisted q-cube, defined in Section 15.1, is $q - 1$.

    b. Devise a routing algorithm for a *canonically twisted* q-cube, in which the twisted 4-cycle consists of Nodes 0, 1, 2, and 3, with links 01 and 23 replaced by 03 and 12.

    c. What is the bisection width of a twisted q-cube?

    d. Prove that a cycle of any length, up to 2^q, is a subgraph of a twisted q-cube.

    e. Prove that the 2^q-node double-rooted complete binary tree is a subgraph of a twisted q-cube.

    f. Prove that the (2^q-1)-node complete binary tree is a subgraph of a twisted q-cube. *Hint:* Begin by assuming that a 2^{q-1}-node double-rooted complete binary tree has been embedded in each half-cube.

15.2. Folded hypercubes

    a. Prove that the diameter of a folded q-cube, defined in Section 15.1, is $\lceil q/2 \rceil$.

    b. Devise a routing algorithm for a folded q-cube.

    c. What is the bisection width of a folded q-cube?

    d. What is the fault diameter of a folded q-cube? (See Section 14.6.)

15.3. The flip network

The flip network, which was used in some early parallel machines, is a multistage interconnection network with 2^q rows and $q + 1$ columns of 2×2 switches (nodes). Nodes (r, c), in Row r and Column c, and $(r', c + 1)$ are connected by an edge iff r' is obtainable by a 1-bit right cyclic shift of r or if r' is formed by inverting the LSB of r and then taking the right cyclic shift of the result. Show that the flip network is isomorphic to the butterfly network.

15.4. The baseline network

The baseline network is a multistage interconnection network with 2^q rows and $q + 1$ columns of 2×2 switches (nodes). Node (r, c), in Row r and Column c, is connected to Node $(r', c + 1)$ iff r' is obtainable by cyclically shifting the $q-c$ LSBs of r or if r' is formed by inverting the LSB of r and then cyclically shifting the $q-c$ LSBs of the result. Show that the baseline network is isomorphic to the butterfly.

15.5. Butterfly network with an extra stage

Study the implications of adding an extra column of nodes at the right end of the $2^q \times (q + 1)$ butterfly network in the following two ways:

a. Columns q and $q + 1$ are linked exactly as Columns 0 and 1.
b. Connections between Columns q and $q + 1$ correspond to the diametral (Dimension-q) links in a folded hypercube, as defined in Section 15.1.

15.6. PM2I network

a. Determine the node degree and the diameter of a 2^q-node PM2I network.
b. What is the diameter of a data manipulator (unfolded PM2I) network if each node represents a processor rather than a switch?
c. Describe an efficient routing algorithm for the network of part (b).

15.7. Cube-connected cycles

a. Complete the labeling of the CCC nodes in Fig. 15.14.
b. Modify the CCC in Fig. 15.14 such that each cycle has four nodes (i.e., show the placement of Node 3 in each cycle).
c. Show that the diameter of the CCC in Fig. 15.14 is 6.

15.8. Cube-connected cycles

Consider the $2^q q$-node CCC derived from the q-cube, where q is a power of 2.

a. Show that such a CCC is a subgraph of the $(q + \log_2 q)$-cube.
b. Show that the diameter of such a CCC is $D = 2.5q - 2$. How does this diameter compare with that of a hypercube of the same size?
c. Find the bisection width of the above CCC and compare it with that of a hypercube of the same size.

15.9. Layout for cube-connected cycles

Lower-degree networks generally have more efficient VLSI layouts than higher-degree ones. For example, the cube-connected cycles networks can be laid out in a much smaller area than a hypercube of the same size. Because the bisection width of a p-node hypercube is p, its required area is $\Omega(p^2)$.

a. Ignoring the area required for nodes and focusing only on the wires that must be routed on the lines of a uniform 2D grid, show that a p-node CCC can be laid out in $O(p^2/\log^2 p)$ area. *Hint:* By separating the nodes in Columns 1 and 2 of the CCC shown in Fig. 15.13

into two and four columns, respectively, so that all column connections can be established using straight vertical lines, the 24-node CCC can be laid out in $16(1 + 2 + 4) = 112$ units of space.

b. Show that the area derived in part (a) is asymptotically optimal, given the bisection width of the p-node CCC.

c. It has been shown that any VLSI circuit that can compute the product of two k-bit integers in T time steps must have a layout area A satisfying $AT^2 = \Omega(k^2)$ and $AT = \Omega(k^{3/2})$. Based on the above, what is a lower bound on the time required to multiply two p-bit integers, stored 1 bit per processor, on a p-node CCC?

15.10. VLSI layout of various networks
Ignoring the area required for nodes and focusing only on the wires that must be routed on the lines of a uniform 2D grid, as in the previous problem:

a. Produce a layout for the p-node butterfly network and express its area as a function of p.
b. Repeat part (a) for the p-node plus-or-minus-2^i network.
c. Repeat part (a) for the p-node shuffle–exchange network.

15.11. de Bruijn network
The de Bruijn network is defined as follows. There are 2^q nodes and 2^{q+1} directed edges. Each node $x = x_{q-1}x_{q-2}\ldots x_1x_0$ is connected, via directed edges, to the two nodes $x_{q-2}\ldots x_1x_00$ and $x_{q-2}\ldots x_1x_01$. The edges leading to the first (second) node are referred to as type 0 (type 1) edges.

a. What is the diameter of the de Bruijn graph?
b. What is the bisection width of the de Bruijn graph?
c. Propose an efficient routing algorithm for the de Bruijn graph.
d. Show that the 2^q-node de Bruijn graph is a subgraph of the graph obtained from the 2^{q+1}-node shuffle–exchange graph, with separate shuffle and exchange links (Fig. 15.18), if we merge the nodes $x_qx_{q-1}\ldots x_10$ and $x_qx_{q-1}\ldots x_11$.

15.12. Pruned hypercubes
Consider a pruned q-cube, with q odd, as exemplified by Fig. 15.20.

a. Show that the diameter of such a pruned q-cube is $q + 1$.
b. What is the bisection width of such a pruned q-cube?
c. Describe an efficient routing algorithm for such pruned hypercubes.
d. Show how to emulate a complete q-cube on a pruned one with constant slowdown, trying to make the constant as small as possible.

15.13. Pruned hypercubes
Consider a pruned q-cube, with q odd, as exemplified by Fig. 15.20. Show that such a hypercube essentially consists of $2^{(q+1)/2}$ clusters, each of which is a $2^{(q-1)/2}$-node hypercube. If we view each of these clusters as a supernode, we can divide the supernodes into two equal subsets of size $2^{(q-1)/2}$ that are interconnected as a complete bipartite graph.

15.14. Pruned folded hypercubes
Consider a folded q-cube with q even. Retain all diametral links and remove half of the other links, say those corresponding to Dimensions $q/2$ through $q-1$.

a. What is the diameter of such a pruned folded q-cube?
b. What is its bisection width?
c. Describe a shortest-path routing algorithm for this architecture.

    d. Devise an efficient scheme for emulating a complete q-cube on this architecture.

    e. How do the above change if a fraction h/q ($0 < h < q/2$), rather than 1/2, of the other links are pruned?

15.15. Möbius cubes

    a. Find the exact diameter of a q-dimensional Möbius cube, as defined in Section 15.6. Is the diameter different for 0- and 1-Möbius cubes?

    b. Define a Möbius-cube-connected cycles architecture in a manner similar to CCC. Does this architecture offer any advantage over CCC?

REFERENCES AND SUGGESTED READING

[Bhuy84]   Bhuyan, L., and D. P. Agrawal, "Generalized Hypercube and Hyperbus Structures for a Computer Network," *IEEE Trans. Computers*, Vol. 33, No. 4, pp. 323–333, April 1984.

[Born98]   Bornstein, C. et al., "On the Bisection Width and Expansion of Butterfly Networks," *Proc. Joint Int. Conf. Parallel Processing & Symp. Parallel Distributed Systems*, 1998, pp. 144–150.

[Cull95]   Cull, P., and S. M. Larson, "The Möbius Cubes," *IEEE Trans. Computers*, Vol. 44, No. 5, pp. 647–659, May 1995.

[ElAm91]   El-Amawy, A., and S. Latifi, "Properties and Performance of Folded Hypercubes," *IEEE Trans. Parallel Distributed Systems*, Vol. 2, No. 1, pp. 31–42, January 1991.

[Esfa91]   Esfahanian, A. -H., L. M. Ni, and B. E. Sagan, "The Twisted N-Cube with Application to Multiprocessing," *IEEE Trans. Computers*, Vol. 40, No. 1, pp. 88–93, January 1991.

[Kwai96]   Kwai, D. -M., and B. Parhami, "A Generalization of Hypercubic Networks Based on Their Chordal Ring Structures," *Information Processing Letters*, Vol. 6, No. 4, pp. 469–477, 1996.

[Kwai97]   Kwai, D. -M., and B. Parhami, "A Class of Fixed-Degree Cayley-Graph Interconnection Networks Derived by Pruning k-ary n-cubes," *Proc. Int. Conf. Parallel Processing*, 1997, pp. 92–95.

[Leig92]   Leighton, F. T., *Introduction to Parallel Algorithms and Architectures: Arrays, Trees, Hypercubes*, Morgan Kaufmann, 1992.

[Meli93]   Meliksetian, D. S., and C. Y. R. Chen, "Optimal Routing Algorithm and the Diameter of the Cube-Connected Cycles," *IEEE Trans. Parallel Distributed Systems*, Vol. 4, No. 10, pp. 1172–1178, October 1993.

[Ohri95]   Ohring, S. R., M. Ibel, S. K. Das, and M. J. Kumar, "On Generalized Fat Trees," *Proc. 9th Int. Parallel Processing Symp.*, 1995, pp. 37–44.

16

A Sampler of Other
Networks

In this chapter, we study several other classes of interconnection architectures, focusing in particular on hybrid or hierarchical schemes that combine features from two or more different architectures or are based on multilevel application of the same connectivity. The interconnection networks listed in this chapter by no means exhaust the space of possibilities. As this chapter is being written, new types of networks continue to appear in technical journals and conference proceedings at an astonishing rate. The novelty, usefulness, and impact of these interconnection architectures are often not immediately discernible but rather need time to be recognized or disputed. Chapter topics are

- 16.1. Performance parameters for networks
- 16.2. Star and pancake networks
- 16.3. Ring-based networks
- 16.4. Composite or hybrid networks
- 16.5. Hierarchical (multilevel) networks
- 16.6. Multistage interconnection networks

16.1. PERFORMANCE PARAMETERS FOR NETWORKS

In our discussions of various architectures thus far, we have taken the network diameter as an indicator of its communication latency. However, network diameter, though important, does not always provide an accurate measure of communication performance. Under light loads (so that congestion and the resulting queuing delays can be ignored) and with shortest-path routing, network diameter might be considered an accurate indicator of communication delay. However, even in such cases, the *average internode distance* is a better measure. In other contexts, such as with wormhole routing or when the network operates close to saturation, the diameter or average internode distance have at best secondary roles.

The *bisection width* of a network, or more generally its *bisection bandwidth*, which incorporates link capacities as well as their number, provides a rough measure of its capability in handling random message traffic. But bisection (band)width, like network diameter, is incomplete in itself.

The main reason for the introduction of so many different interconnection networks is that no single network provides optimal performance under all conditions. Each network has its advantages and drawbacks in terms of cost, latency, and bandwidth. We thus need to understand the interplay of these parameters in order to select a suitable interconnection architecture or to evaluate the relative merits of two or more networks (or parallel architectures). In the rest of this section, we introduce some concepts that are important in this regard.

Let us begin by examining the interplay between the node degree d and the network diameter D. Given a certain number p of processors with very simple computational capabilities, the node degree might be viewed as an indicator of system cost. For a first-order approximation of cost, we can assume that node cost grows linearly with its degree. In other words, the cost of a network with uniform degree-d nodes is proportional to the total number $pd/2$ of links. Given p nodes of known degree d, we can interconnect them in different ways, leading to networks of varying diameters. An age-old question in graph theory is determining the best way to interconnect p nodes of degree d in order to minimize the diameter of the resulting graph. This question is obviously important for parallel processing as well, although from our viewpoint, the interconnection complexity, as measured, e.g., by the area required for VLSI layout, is also important.

Let us ignore the interconnection complexity and focus only on minimizing the diameter for now. The problem of constructing a network of minimal diameter, given p nodes of degree d, or alternatively, building a network with the largest possible number of nodes for a given node degree d and diameter D, is quite difficult and no general method is available for its solution. However, some useful bounds can be established that can serve as benchmarks for determining how close a given network comes to being the absolute best in terms of diameter.

A diameter-D regular *digraph* (directed graph having the same in-degree and out-degree d for all nodes) can have no more than $1 + d + d^2 + \cdots + d^D$ nodes, where d^i is the maximum number of new nodes that can be placed at distance i from a given node. This yields a lower bound on the diameter of a p-node digraph of degree d, which is known as Moore's bound:

$$p \leq 1 + d + d^2 + \cdots + d^D = \frac{d^{D+1} - 1}{d - 1}$$

$$D \geq \log_d[p(d-1) + 1] - 1$$

A Moore digraph is a digraph for which D is equal to the above bound. It is known that the only possible Moore digraphs are rings ($d = 1$, $D = p-1$) and complete graphs ($d = p - 1$, $D = 1$); but there are near-optimal graphs that come close to Moore's bound and are good enough in practice.

A similar bound can be derived for undirected graphs. The largest possible undirected graph of diameter D and node degree d has no more than $1 + d + d(d - 1) + d(d - 1)^2 + \cdots + d(d - 1)^{D-1}$ nodes. This expression is obtained by noting that any given node can have d neighbors, each of which can in turn have $d - 1$ other neighbors, and so on. This leads to Moore's bound on the diameter of a p-node undirected graph of degree d:

$$p \leq 1 + d[1 + (d - 1) + (d - 1)^2 + \cdots + (d - 1)^{D-1}] = 1 + d \frac{(d - 1)^D - 1}{d - 2}$$

$$D \geq \log_{d-1}\left\lceil \frac{(p - 1)(d - 2)}{d} + 1 \right\rceil$$

For $d = 2$, the number p of nodes satisfies $p \leq 1 + 2D$ or $D \geq (p - 1)/2$. This diameter lower bound is achieved by the ring network with an odd number of nodes.

For $d = 3$, we have $D \geq \log_2[(p + 2)/3]$ or $p \leq 3 \times 2^D - 2$. A diameter of $D = 1$ allows us to have 4 nodes and leads to the complete graph K_4. The first interesting or nontrivial case is for $D = 2$, which allows at most $p = 10$ nodes. The 10-node Petersen graph, depicted in Fig. 16.1, matches this lower bound with its diameter of $D = 2$. Again, even though for larger networks, Moore's bound cannot be matched, there exist networks whose diameters come very close to this bound. For example, both the shuffle–exchange and CCC networks, composed of degree-3 nodes, have asymptotically optimal diameters within constant factors.

For $d = 4$, Moore's diameter lower bound is $\log_3[(p + 1)/2]$. Thus, mesh and torus networks are far from optimal in terms of their diameters, whereas the butterfly network is asymptotically optimal within a constant factor.

Finally, for a q-cube with $p = 2^q$ and $d = q$, Moore's lower bound yields $D = \Omega(q/\log q)$. The diameter $D = q$ of a q-cube is thus asymptotically a factor of $\log q$ worse than the optimal.

To summarize, for a given node degree, Moore's bound establishes the lowest possible diameter that we can hope to achieve. Coming within a constant factor of this lower bound is usually good enough in practice; the smaller the constant factor, the better.

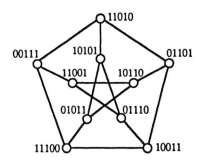

Figure 16.1. The 10-node Petersen graph.

As stated earlier, the average internode distance, Δ, defined as the average of the path lengths between all of the $p(p - 1)$ possible source–destination pairs, is perhaps more important than the diameter D. The distance between two nodes can be defined in different ways, leading to various definitions for Δ (e.g., shortest distance, shortest distance in the presence of certain faults, distance according to some routing algorithm). Even though it is possible to construct graphs for which Δ and D are quite different, for most networks of practical interest, Δ and D are intimately related, e.g., Δ is a constant factor smaller than D. In these cases, using the diameter D in lieu of the average distance Δ for comparing various networks would not be problematic.

Another important parameter for an interconnection network is its bisection width, which is a measure of the available network bandwidth for communication-intensive applications with random data exchange patterns. For example, in sorting, it is possible to initially arrange the data such that all data items must cross the bisection in order to appear in sorted order. Hence, the bisection width of a network establishes a lower bound on how fast sorting can be done in the worst case.

Unlike network diameter, which is related to the number of nodes and node degree through Moore bounds, the number of nodes or links in a network has no relation to its bisection width. It is fairly easy to construct large, dense networks with very small bisections.

Thus, determining the bisection width of a network is not always a simple matter. Consider, for example, the chordal ring network in Fig. 16.2 in which each Node i is connected to Nodes $i \pm 1$ and $i \pm 11$ (mod 32). At first glance, it appears that the bisection produced by drawing a straight line leads to the fewest number of links being cut. The heavy dotted line, shown in Fig. 16.2, is one such bisection that cuts through 24 links. Hence, it is tempting to conclude that the bisection width of this network is 24. However, one can bisect this particular network by cutting only 8 links. Supplying the details is left as an exercise. Showing that a network can be bisected by cutting through l links only establishes an upper bound on, rather than the exact value of, the bisection width. Finding the exact bisection width may require much more work.

The VLSI layout area required by an interconnection network is intimately related to its bisection width B. If B wires must cross the bisection in a 2D layout and wire separation is to be 1 unit, then the smallest dimension of the VLSI chip will be at least B units. The chip area will therefore be $\Omega(B^2)$ units. Networks with larger bisections are thus more likely to consume greater chip area in their VLSI realizations. Hence, whereas p-node 2D mesh or torus networks can be laid out in linear space in terms of p, the best layout of a p-node hypercube requires quadratic space.

As suggested earlier, the total number $pd/2$ of links (edges) is a very crude measure of interconnection network cost. With this measure, constant-degree networks have linear or $O(p)$ cost and the p-node hypercube has $O(p \log p)$ cost. For VLSI implementation, the hardware cost depends not just on the number of links but also on their lengths when the architecture is laid out in two dimensions. In general, there is no simple way to predict the VLSI area cost of an interconnection network short of devising an optimal layout for it.

The longest wire required in VLSI layout also affects the performance of the network in terms of speed. For example, it can be shown that any 2D layout of a p-node hypercube requires wires of length $\Omega(\sqrt{p}/\log p)$. Because the length of the longest wire grows with the system size, the per-node performance is bound to degrade for larger systems. This implies that speed-up will be sublinear as we scale to larger systems.

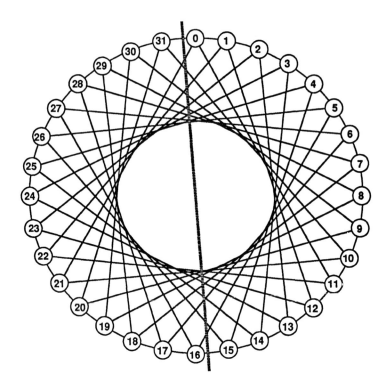

Figure 16.2. A network whose bisection width is not as large at it appears.

Composite figures of merit can be used to compare different interconnection networks. For example, it has been suggested that dD, the product of node degree and network diameter, is a good measure for comparing networks of the same size, as it is a rough indicator of the cost of unit performance (d is proportional to cost, $1/D$ represents performance). This measure has its limitations, particularly when applied to bus-based systems. If the p processors in a parallel system are interconnected by a shared bus, then $d = D = \Delta = 1$, leading to the best possible value for dD. However, such a system is clearly not the best under all conditions.

Other network parameters can be defined with regard to robustness or fault tolerance, which is particularly desirable for large networks in view of the inevitability of faults in some network components. For example, if there are at least k node-disjoint (edge-disjoint) paths between any pair of nodes, then $k - 1$ node (edge) failures can be tolerated. Such a system is called *k-fault-tolerant*. The *fault diameter* of a network, defined as its diameter in the presence of certain types of faults, is also a useful indicator of its resilience.

16.2. STAR AND PANCAKE NETWORKS

A hypercube has logarithmic diameter, which is suboptimal, given its logarithmic node degree. Butterfly, CCC, and other hypercubic networks, discussed in the previous chapter, have optimal diameters (to within a constant factor), given their fixed node degrees. However, the latter networks do not have large bisections and, thus, may have a poorer performance than the hypercube in applications where very high network bandwidth is required. A possible compromise is to construct a network with sublogarithmic, but nonconstant, node degree. Such constructions may lead to a network whose node degree does not grow as fast as that of a hypercube, while still providing good network bandwidth.

Star networks provide a good example. In a q-dimensional star network, or q-star, there are $p = q!$ (q factorial) nodes. Each node is labeled with a string $x_1 x_2 \ldots x_q$, where $(x_1, x_2, \ldots, x_q)$ is a permutation of $\{1, 2, \ldots, q\}$. Node $x_1 x_2 \ldots x_i \ldots x_q$ is connected to $x_i x_2 \ldots x_1 \ldots x_q$ for each i (note that x_1 and x_i are interchanged). For example, in the 4-star depicted in Fig. 16.3, Node 1234 is connected to Nodes 2134, 3214, and 4231. Because there are $q - 1$ possible choices for i, the node degree of a q-star with $q!$ nodes is $q - 1$. When the ith symbol is switched with x_1, the corresponding link is referred to as a Dimension-i link. So the $q - 1$ dimensions of a q-star are labeled 2 through q, as indicated on some of the links in Fig. 16.3.

The diameter of a q-star can be easily upper bounded through the following routing algorithm. The routing algorithm resembles dimension-order routing on the hypercube in that the various symbols in the node label are adjusted in dimension order. Consider, for example, routing a message from the source node 154362 to the destination node 346215 in a 6-star:

$$
\begin{array}{ll}
1\ 5\ 4\ 3\ 6\ 2 & \text{Source node} \\
\text{Dimension-2 link to } 5\ 1\ 4\ 3\ 6\ 2 & \\
\text{Dimension-6 link to } 2\ 1\ 4\ 3\ 6\ \underline{5} & \text{Last symbol now adjusted} \\
\text{Dimension-2 link to } 1\ 2\ 4\ 3\ 6\ \underline{5} & \\
\text{Dimension-5 link to } 6\ 2\ 4\ 3\ \underline{1\ 5} & \text{Last two symbols now adjusted} \\
\text{Dimension-2 link to } 2\ 6\ 4\ 3\ \underline{1\ 5} & \\
\text{Dimension-4 link to } 3\ 6\ 4\ \underline{2\ 1\ 5} & \text{Last three symbols now adjusted}
\end{array}
$$

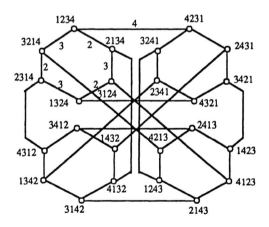

Figure 16.3. The four-dimensional star graph.

Dimension-2 link to 6 3 4 $\overline{2\ \ 1}$ 5

Dimension-3 link to 4 3 6 $\overline{2\ \ 1}$ 5 Last four symbols now adjusted

Dimension-2 link to $\overline{3\ \ 4}$ 6 2 1 5 Destination node

Based on the above routing algorithm, it is obvious that $D \leq 2q - 3$: We need two steps to adjust each of the last $q - 2$ symbols, plus possibly one final exchange of symbols 1 and 2. It is easily shown that the diameter is in fact exactly equal to $2q - 3$, making the above simple routing algorithm optimal with respect to the worst-case distance. Note, however, that the algorithm does not always route a message via a shortest path.

By Stirling's approximation, a q-star contains $p = q! \approx e^{-q}q^q\sqrt{2\pi q}$ processors. Thus,

$$\ln p \approx -q + (q + 1/2) \ln q + \ln(2\pi)/2 = \Theta(q \log q)$$

From the above, we find $q = \Theta(\log p/\log \log p)$. Thus, both the node degree and the diameter of the star graph are sublogarithmic in the number p of processors. In fact, the star graph is asymptotically optimal to within a constant factor with regard to Moore's diameter lower bound.

Routing on star graphs is simple and reasonably efficient. However, virtually all other algorithms are (much) more complex than the corresponding algorithms on a hypercube. This is in part related to the size and structure of a star graph. The number $q!$ of nodes is never a power of 2. The q-star does have a recursive structure in that it is composed of q copies of a $(q-1)$-star (the four 3-star subgraphs of the 4-star in Fig. 16.3 are easily identified). However, such a nonuniform recursion makes the development of recursive or divide-and-conquer algorithms somewhat more difficult.

Because the node degree of a star network grows with its size, making it nonscalable, a degree-3 version of it, known as *star-connected cycles* (SCC), has been proposed [Lati93]. Figure 16.4 depicts a four-dimensional SCC network where each node is labeled by a pair (x, y) denoting the cycle number x and the dimension number y $(2 \leq y \leq q)$. Of course, in this particular example, the node degree is not reduced relative to the original star graph, but this

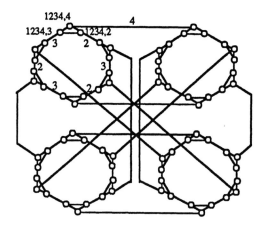

Figure 16.4. The four-dimensional star-connected cycles network.

is the largest example that one can draw without clutter rendering the diagram incomprehensible. The diameter of SCC is about the same as a comparably sized cube-connected cycles network [Lati93]. However, the routing algorithm for SCC is somewhat more complex. Also, whereas a CCC for which the cycle size is a power of 2 allows one-to-one node mapping in the emulation of a hypercube, the number $q!(q-1)$ of nodes in an SCC allows no such direct correspondence to a star graph.

Like the star graph, the *pancake network* also has $p = q!$ nodes that are labeled by the various permutations of the symbols $\{1, 2, \ldots, q\}$. In the q-pancake, Node $x_1x_2 \ldots x_{i-1}x_ix_{i+1} \ldots x_q$ is connected to Nodes $x_ix_{i-1} \ldots x_2x_1x_{i+1} \ldots x_q$ for each i ($x_1x_2 \ldots x_i$ is flipped, like a pancake). Routing in pancake networks is very similar to routing in star graphs. Denoting the connection that results from flipping the first i symbols ($2 \le i \le q$) as the dimension-i link, we have for example

	1	5 4 3 6 2	Source node
Dimension-2 link to		5 1 4 3 6 2	
Dimension-6 link to		2 6 3 4 1 5	Last two symbols now adjusted
Dimension-4 link to		4 3 6 2 1 5	Last four symbols now adjusted
Dimension-2 link to		3 4 6 2 1 5	Destination node

In the above example, we were lucky in that multiple symbols could be adjusted with some flips. Generally, however, we need two flips per symbol; one flip to bring the symbol to the front from its current position i, and another one to send it to its desired position j. Thus, like the star graph, the diameter of the q-pancake is $2q - 3$.

One can obviously define the connectivities of the $q!$ nodes labeled by the permutations of $\{1, 2, \ldots, q\}$ in other ways. In a *rotator graph* [Corb92], [Ponn94], Node $x_1x_2 \ldots x_ix_{i+1} \ldots x_q$ is connected to $x_2 \ldots x_ix_1x_{i+1} \ldots x_q$ (obtained by a left rotation of the first i symbols) for each i in the range $2 \le i \le q$. The node degree of a q-rotator is $q - 1$, as in star and pancake graphs, but its diameter and average internode distance are smaller.

Except for SCC, all of the networks introduced in this section represent special cases of a class of networks known as *Cayley graphs*. A Cayley graph is characterized by a set Λ of node labels and a set Γ of *generators*, each defining one neighbor of a Node x. The ith generator γ_i can be viewed as a rule for permuting the node label to get the label of its "Dimension-i" neighbor. For example, the star graph has $q - 1$ generators that correspond to interchanging the first and ith symbols in the node label. Cayley graphs are node-symmetric, a property that is important for developing simple and efficient parallel algorithms. *Index-permutation graphs*, a generalization of Cayley graphs in which the node labels are not restricted to consist of distinct symbols [Yeh98], can lead to other interesting and useful interconnection networks.

16.3. RING-BASED NETWORKS

The ring interconnection scheme has proven quite effective in certain distributed and small-scale parallel architectures [Berm95] in view of its low node degree and simple routing algorithm. However, the diameter of a simple ring would become too large for effective utilization in a large parallel system. As a result, multilevel and hybrid architectures, utilizing

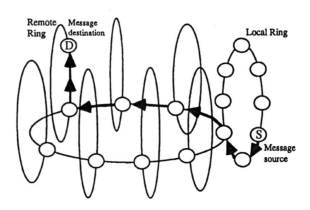

Figure 16.5. A 64-node ring-of-rings architecture composed of eight 8-node local rings and one second-level ring.

rings at various levels of a hierarchically structured network or as a basis for synthesizing richer interconnection schemes, have been proposed.

The multilevel ring structure of KSR1's (Kendall Square Research) interconnection network [Kend92] and the QuickRing Network of Apple Computer [Vale94] are good examples of the hierarchical approach. As shown in the two-level ring structure of Fig. 16.5, each node is a member of a *local ring* and communicates with *remote rings* via a second-level ring. Of course, there is no reason to limit the second-level ring to just one; in the extreme case of the ith node in each local ring being interconnected by a second-level ring, the architecture becomes a 2D torus. Similarly, the number of levels can be increased beyond 2. With 8-node rings connected into a three-level structure, e.g., we get an architecture with 8^3 = 512 nodes and a diameter of $4 + 4 + 4 = 12$.

The *chordal ring* architecture, in which each node is connected to its ring neighbors as well as to one or more distant nodes through *skip links* or *chords* (see, e.g., the references in [Mans94]), and optical multichannel ring networks with variable skip capability in connection with wormhole routing [Reic93] provide examples of the second approach. Such skip links, chords, or "express channels" reduce the network diameter at the expense of increased node degree. Because the basic ring structure is preserved, many nice features of a simple ring, including ease of routing and deadlock avoidance, carry over to these enhanced ring architectures.

Figure 16.6 shows a simple eight-node unidirectional ring as well as two eight-node chordal rings with chords, or forward skip links, of length 3 at the top right and of lengths 2 and 4 at the bottom left, added to each node. More generally, the node in- and out-degrees in a chordal ring may be $g + 1$, with g skip links of lengths $s_1, s_2, \ldots, s_g$ (satisfying $1 < s_1 < s_2 < \ldots < s_g < p$) originating from each of the p nodes. For our subsequent discussion, it is convenient to view 1 and p as the 0th and $(g+1)$th skip distances. Thus, s_0 corresponds to the ring edges and s_{g+1} to a node being connected to itself. We thus have a total of $g+2$ skips satisfying

$$1 = s_0 < s_1 < s_2 < \ldots < s_g < s_{g+1} = p$$

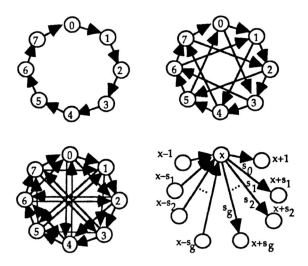

Figure 16.6. Unidirectional ring, two chordal rings, and node connectivity in general.

which connect a Node x to Nodes $x + s_i$ mod p, $0 \le i \le g + 1$. Because all node index expressions are evaluated modulo p, we will omit the mod-p designation in the following.

A simple greedy routing algorithm is applicable to chordal rings. A message going from Node x to Node y, which has to travel $y - x$ mod p nodes forward, takes the longest skip that will not lead past the destination node. To implement this scheme, the routing tag $y - x$ mod p is attached to the message by the source node. Each node then sends the message over the longest skip link that is smaller than the routing tag and decrements the routing tag by the length of that skip.

Based on the above greedy routing algorithm, an upper bound for the diameter of a chordal ring is easily obtained. Note that the skip s_i will be taken at most $\lceil s_{i+1}/s_i \rceil - 1$ times because of the greedy strategy of the routing algorithm. Thus, the diameter of a chordal ring satisfies

$$D \le \Sigma_{i=0}^g (\lceil s_{i+1}/s_i \rceil - 1) < \Sigma_{i=0}^g s_{i+1}/s_i$$

For example, in the case of the two chordal rings shown in Fig. 16.6, the above diameter upper bound yields

$$D \le \lceil 8/3 \rceil - 1 + \lceil 3/1 \rceil - 1 = 4$$

$$D \le \lceil 8/4 \rceil - 1 + \lceil 4/2 \rceil - 1 + \lceil 2/1 \rceil - 1 = 3$$

The diameter of either chordal ring is in fact 3.

Determining the exact diameter of chordal rings, or selecting skip distances in such a way that the diameter is minimized, are challenging combinatorial problems. Thus, we base the following analysis on the assumption that the diameter is the same as the upper bound

$\Sigma_{i=0}^{g} s_{i+1}/s_i$. Differentiating the upper-bound formula with respect to each skip distance s_i and equating the resulting expressions with zero leads to the optimal skip distances

$$dD/ds_i = -s_{i+1}/s_i^2 + 1/s_{i-1} = 0 \Rightarrow s_i^2 = s_{i+1}s_{i-1} \Rightarrow s_i = p^{i/(g+1)}$$

For example, with $p = 8$ nodes and $g = 1$ skip link per node, the above analysis suggests that the optimal skip distance is $8^{1/2} \approx 3$. With $p = 8$ and 2 skip links per node, the optimal distances are $8^{1/3} = 2$ and $8^{2/3} = 4$. Of course, such an analysis is at best approximate. It works nicely in some cases and gives optimal results. In other cases, the "optimal" results obtained as above are not even close to the best possible. This is related to the combinatorial nature of the problem and the restriction of the parameter values to whole numbers.

Note that the greedy routing algorithm presented above, though reasonable and near-optimal in many cases, does not route messages via shortest paths. In fact, the route selected by the algorithm may be far from the shortest one available. Take the skips $s_0 = 1$, $s_1 = 10$, and $s_2 = 12$ as an example. To route from Node x to Node $x + 20$, the greedy algorithm will choose a skip of 12 followed by 8 steps on the ring edges, while the shortest path has a length of just 2.

Chordal rings are node symmetric. The optimal chordal rings derived as above are very similar, though not isomorphic, to $(g+1)$-dimensional torus networks. Figure 16.7 shows the top eight-node chordal ring of Fig. 16.6, as well as a nine-node chordal ring with a skip of $s_1 = 3$, as toruslike structures. The toruslike network on the right side of Fig. 16.7, in which the row wraparound links are connected to the following row as opposed to the same row, are known as *twisted torus* networks. The ILLIAC IV computer, one of the earliest parallel machines built, used the 8×8 bidirectional version of this network.

The node-symmetric chordal ring architecture is wasteful in that it includes long-distance, medium-distance, and short-distance links for every node. In a manner similar to deriving the cube-connected cycles architecture from the hypercube, one can distribute the various skips among a sequence of nodes, each having only one skip link.

Assume that the p ring nodes are split into p/g groups of g consecutive nodes, where g divides p. The jth node in each group, $0 \le j \le g - 1$, has the skip link s_{g-j} in addition to the ring link s_0. We assume that each skip distance s_i, except for s_0, is a multiple of g. This will ensure that the network is regular with respect to the nodes' in-degrees as well as their out-degrees. Figure 16.8 shows the structure of the resulting network, called *periodically*

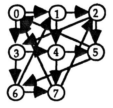
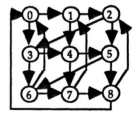

Figure 16.7. Chordal rings redrawn to show their similarity to torus networks.

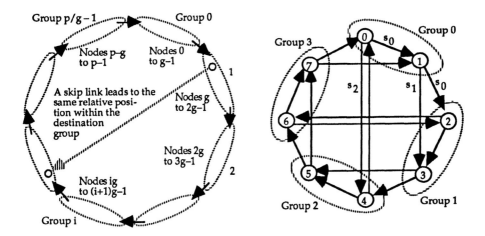

Figure 16.8. Periodically regular chordal ring.

regular chordal ring [Parh95], as well as an example with $g = 2$ and skip distances $s_1 = 2$ and $s_2 = 4$.

A variant of the greedy routing algorithm, in which we first route a packet to the head (first node) of a group via the ring edges, and then continue in a pure greedy fashion, works nicely for PRC rings and yields good results on the average. Routing from Node 1 to Node 7 in the example PRC ring of Fig. 16.8 would take the packet to Node 2 (the head node of Group 1), then to Node 6, and finally to Node 7. As another example, a packet sent from Node 1 to Node 5 goes through Nodes 2 and 3. The first example path above is a shortest path, while the second one is nonminimal.

Interesting optimality results have been obtained for PRC rings. For example, it is known that optimal logarithmic diameter is obtained for $g = \Theta(\log p)$.

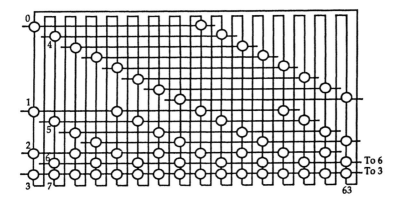

Figure 16.9. VLSI layout for a 64-node periodically regular chordal ring.

Area-efficient VLSI layouts are known for PRC rings, as exemplified by Fig. 16.9. Note that most of the wraparound links in the layout have been deleted to avoid clutter. These long links can be replaced by shorter ones through standard folding of the layout if desired.

Both chordal rings and PRC rings have bidirectional variants with similar properties to the unidirectional versions discussed in this section. As an example of bidirectional PRC rings, consider the 32-node PRC ring depicted in Fig. 16.10. Here, the group size or period is $g = 4$, with the skips $s_1 = $ nil, $s_2 = 2$, $s_3 = 4$, and $s_4 = 8$. In this example, the nil or nonexistent skips are necessitated by our desire to choose all skips to be powers of 2 and the fact that there are only three powers of 2 that are less than 32 and multiples of $g = 4$.

More generally, providing nil skips for some of the nodes in each group constitutes an important mechanism for performance–cost trade-offs that are identical in nature to those

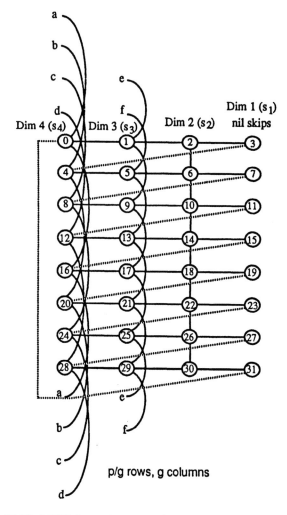

Figure 16.10. A PRC ring redrawn as a butterfly- or ADM-like network.

offered by the q-D CCC architecture when rings have more than q nodes. Note, for example, that removing the longest skips from the layout of Fig. 16.9 reduces its area requirement substantially, at the cost of increased network diameter.

Figure 16.10 has been drawn in such a way as to highlight the similarity of PRC rings built with power-of-2 skip distances to butterfly and augmented data manipulator networks. This similarity can be exploited for developing efficient algorithms for the practically important subclass of PRC ring networks with power-of-2 size, group length, and skip distances. For example, an ascend- or descend-type hypercube algorithm can be efficiently emulated on such a PRC ring. In the network of Fig. 16.10, nodes whose labels differ in either of the least-significant 2 bits communicate via ring edges, while those that are distance 4, 8, or 16 away communicate via skip links, either directly or through intermediate nodes. Details of the emulation method are very similar to those of the CCC emulating the hypercube (Section 15.4).

16.4. COMPOSITE OR HYBRID NETWORKS

Most of the networks that we have considered thus far can be classified as "pure" networks, meaning that a single set of connectivity rules governs the entire network. Composite or hybrid networks, on the other hand, combine the connectivity rules from two (or more) pure networks in order to achieve some advantages from each structure, derive network sizes that are unavailable with either pure architecture, or realize any number of performance/cost benefits.

Two or more networks can be combined in many different ways. In this section, we consider only network composition by Cartesian product operation, in view of its many interesting properties. The (Cartesian) product of networks or graphs was defined in Section 13.3, where it was used as a tool to prove that the hypercube network contains meshes and tori as subgraphs. Let us focus, for concreteness, on the product $G = (V, E)$ of two graphs/networks $G' = (V', E')$ and $G'' = (V'', E'')$, with its node and edge sets defined as

$$V = \{v'v'' \mid v' \in V', v'' \in V''\}, \text{ where } v'v'' \text{ is shorthand for } (v', v'')$$

$$E = \{(u'u'', v'v'') \mid u'v' \in E' \text{ and } u'' = v'' \text{ or } u''v'' \in E'' \text{ and } u' = v'\}$$

From the above definition, we see that there are two classes of edges in G, which we call G' edges ($u'v' \in E'$ and $u'' = v''$) and G'' edges ($u''v'' \in E''$ and $u' = v'$). Examples of product graphs were provided in Fig. 13.4. The product graph G defined as above has p nodes, where

$$p = |V| = |V'| \times |V''| = p'p''$$

The product operation on graphs is associative and commutative. Thus, the structure of a product graph is uniquely specified by specifying the component graphs. When the component graphs of a product graph are all identical, a *homogeneous product network* or a *power network* results.

Topological properties and many algorithms for product graphs are derivable from those of its component graphs. For example, the node degree, diameter, and average internode distance of G are the sums of the respective parameters for G' and G'' ($d = d' + d''$, $D = D' + D''$, $\Delta = \Delta' + \Delta''$). As a result of the above, if both G' and G'' have node degrees or diameters that are (sub)logarithmic in terms of their sizes p' and p', the product graph G will also have a (sub)logarithmic node degree or diameter in terms of its size p.

Given optimal or efficient routing algorithms for G' and G'', the following two-phase routing algorithm will be optimal or efficient for routing from $u'u''$ to $v'v''$ in the product graph G:

> Phase 1. Route from $u'u''$ to $v'u''$ via G' edges using the routing algorithm for G'
> Phase 2. Route from $v'u''$ to $v'v''$ via G'' edges using the routing algorithm for G''

The above algorithm, which may be called the G'-*first* routing algorithm, is a generalized version of row-first routing in 2D meshes. If the routing algorithms for the component graphs are deadlock-free, so is the above two-phase routing algorithm for G.

Similarly, broadcasting from a node $v'v''$ to all nodes in G can be done by first broadcasting to all nodes xv'', $x \in V'$, using a broadcasting algorithm for G' and then broadcasting from each node xv'' to all nodes xy, $y \in V''$, using a broadcasting algorithm for G''.

Semigroup and parallel prefix computations can be similarly performed by using the respective algorithms for the component networks. If the component graphs are Hamiltonian, then the $p' \times p''$ torus will be a subgraph of G. This allows us to use any torus algorithm to perform computations such as matrix multiplication, sorting, and the like. In the case of sorting, it is possible to emulate, e.g., the shearsort algorithm for a $p' \times p''$ mesh on the product network. The row and column sorts required in shearsort can be performed by using any available sorting algorithm for the component graphs G' and G''.

Note that product graphs allow us to synthesize networks of virtually any desired size. For example, the product of a 3-cube (8 nodes) and a 4-star (24 nodes) will have 192 nodes, whereas no pure hypercube or star network can match this size exactly or even approximately.

As an example of a product network that we have not examined previously, consider the product of two binary trees, yielding a network known as *mesh-connected trees* [Efe96]. Note that this network is different from, and higher-performing than, the mesh of trees network studied in Section 12.6. Examples of the two networks are shown side by side in Fig. 16.11. It is clear from Fig. 16.11 that a mesh of trees network with an $m \times m$ base ($3m^2$

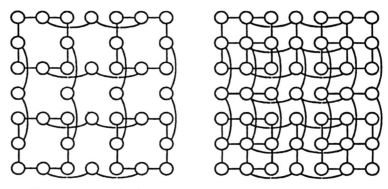

Figure 16.11. Mesh of trees compared with mesh-connected trees.

– $2m$ processors) is a subgraph of the mesh-connected trees network with $(2m - 1)^2$ processors; for large m, the latter network has roughly 4/3 as many processors as the former.

If instead of binary trees, we use X-trees as the component networks, the resulting product graph will contain the square torus of the same size as a subgraph. This is easily proven by showing that a complete X-tree network is Hamiltonian. Thus, the mesh of X-trees network can run any torus algorithm with no slowdown.

A layered network is one in which the nodes can be partitioned into numbered layers, with links connecting only nodes that belong to adjacent layers. Binary trees, butterfly networks, and mesh of trees networks are examples of layered networks. The *layered cross product* of two l-layer networks G' and G'' is another l-layer network G whose nodes in Layer i are labeled (u'_i, u''_i), where u'_i and u''_i are Layer-i nodes in G' and G'', respectively. A Layer-i node (u'_i, u''_i) is connected to a Layer-$(i+1)$ node (u'_{i+1}, u''_{i+1}) in G iff u'_i is connected to u'_{i+1} in G' and u''_i is connected to u''_{i+1} in G''. As an example, the butterfly network can be shown to be the layered cross product of two binary trees. The notion of layered cross product is helpful, among other things, for producing rectilinear planar layouts for interconnection networks [Even97].

16.5. HIERARCHICAL (MULTILEVEL) NETWORKS

Hierarchical or multilevel interconnection networks can be defined in a variety of ways. In this section, we consider hierarchical composition of networks through *recursive substitution*, i.e., replacing each node of a network with another network. Figure 16.12 shows an example, where a top-level 3×3 mesh network is expanded by replacing each of its nine nodes with a 3×3 mesh. In this particular example, the top- and bottom-level networks happen to be identical, but this does not have to be the case in general. The CCC network is an example of this more general type where the top-level network is a q-cube and the bottom-level network is a q-ring.

To fully characterize a hierarchical interconnection network derived by recursive substitution, we need to know the network size and topology at various levels of the hierarchy as well as the rules by which Level-i links are to be assigned to the nodes of Level-$(i–1)$ networks. In the example of Fig. 16.12, the Level-2 network is a 3×3 mesh, with each node

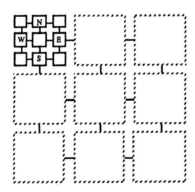

Figure 16.12. The mesh of meshes network exhibits greater modularity than a mesh.

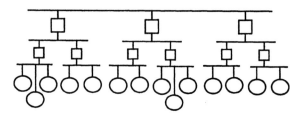

Figure 16.13. Hierarchical or multilevel bus network.

having two to four links. The assignment of the NEWS links of this Level-2 network to the nodes of the 3×3 Level-1 network is shown in the upper left corner of Fig. 16.12. If the size of the Level-$(i-1)$ network is greater than the node degree of the Level-i network, then increase in node degree can be limited to only 1 for each recursion level. This results in modular networks with fairly small node degrees.

Motivations for designing hierarchical interconnection networks include obtaining greater modularity, lower cost, finer scalability, and better fault tolerance. The particular hierarchical composition scheme and component networks used depend on the types of communications that are expected from target applications. For example, the hierarchical bus scheme, exemplified by Fig. 16.13, might be quite efficient when the bulk of interprocessor communications are within the same low-level cluster, with occasional remote communications to distant clusters through higher-level buses which introduce higher delays and have lower aggregate bandwidth. The same network, however, becomes hopelessly congested under heavy random traffic.

Numerous hierarchical combinations of known interconnection networks have been proposed over the past decade. Unifying theories that allow us to investigate such networks in classes, rather than as one-of-a-kind structures, are emerging [Yeh98].

16.6. MULTISTAGE INTERCONNECTION NETWORKS

Most of the networks that we have studied thus far belong to the class of *direct networks*, meaning that processors are directly connected to other processors via their communication links. *Multistage interconnection networks* (MINs), by contrast, connect the processors indirectly via multiple layers of intermediate nodes or switches. We have already seen several examples of multistage interconnection networks. In Section 6.6, we introduced the butterfly network as a mechanism for interconnecting processors and memory modules. Subsequently, in Chapter 15, we looked at butterfly and related networks in some depth. The butterfly, or the equivalent shuffle–exchange or omega network, is known as the *indirect cube (cubic) network* because it provides the hypercube connectivities between its input and output ports indirectly.

Beneš networks, composed of back-to-back butterflies, were introduced as examples of rearrangeable permutation networks near the end of Section 15.2. Even though any desired permutation can be routed through a Beneš network without any conflict, the required switch setups for each permutation must be computed off-line. In practice, we would like to be able to route messages using an on-line algorithm. A MIN that can determine the path of a message on the fly, using simple computational steps within the switches, is known as a *self-routing MIN*. The butterfly network is a self-routing MIN, but it is not a permutation network. The Beneš network can realize any permutation, but is not self-routing.

A natural question is whether there exist self-routing permutation networks. The answer to this question is positive. In what follows, we focus on realizing full permutations, meaning that every input port must be connected to a distinct output port.

A full permutation can be realized via sorting of the destination addresses. Thus, any p-sorter of the type discussed in Chapter 7, when suitably augmented to carry along the message bodies with the key headers, can be viewed as a self-routing MIN that is capable of routing any $p \times p$ permutation. For example, we saw that a Batcher p-sorter consists of $\Theta(p \log^2 p)$ comparators, arranged in $\Theta(\log^2 p)$ levels. Because the line labels in a p-sorter are $(\log_2 p)$-bit binary numbers, a *bit-level complexity analysis* is needed for complete fairness. At the bit level, these networks have $\Theta(p \log^3 p)$ cost and $\Theta(\log^3 p)$ delay, assuming that the $(\log_2 p)$-bit destination addresses are supplied in parallel to each cell, where they are compared by a simple ripple-type comparator having $\Theta(\log p)$ cost and $\Theta(\log p)$ delay. When the inputs are supplied bit-serially, the cost and delay drop to $\Theta(p \log^2 p)$ and $\Theta(\log^2 p)$, respectively.

These results have been improved by Batcher himself and others. For example, Al-Hajery and Batcher [AlHa93] have presented bitonic sorting networks that have $\Theta(p \log p)$ bit-level cost and $\Theta(\log^2 p)$ bit-level delay. Sorting by such networks requires that the items being sorted pass through a $(\log_2 p)$-stage bit-level network $\log_2 p$ times. Because each key is $\log_2 p$ bits long, successive passes are easily pipelined with no interference. Cheng and Chen [Chen96] have presented a design based on binary radix sort that uses $\log_2 p$ stages of single-bit sorters that require a delay of $\log_2 p$ levels and cost of $p \log_2 p$ (bit-parallel) or p (bit-serial). For parallel inputs, this design leads to $O(p \log^2 p)$ bit-level cost and $O(\log^2 p)$ bit-level delay. With serial inputs, the cost and delay become $O(p \log p)$ and $O(\log^2 p)$, respectively (Fig. 16.14).

Below is a partial listing of some of the important types of multistage interconnection networks, and associated terminology, for ready reference:

- *Augmented data manipulator* (ADM): Also known as *unfolded PM2I* (Fig. 15.12).
- *Banyan*: Any MIN with a unique path between any input and any output (e.g., butterfly).

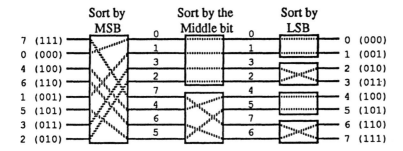

Figure 16.14. Example of sorting on a binary radix sort network.

- *Baseline*: Butterfly network with nodes labeled differently; see, e.g., [Leig92], p. 735.
- *Beneš*: Back-to-back butterfly networks, sharing one column (Figs. 15.9 and 15.10).
- *Bidelta*: A MIN that is a *delta network* in either direction.
- *Butterfly*: Also known as *unfolded hypercube* (Figs. 6.9, 15.4, and 15.5).
- *Data manipulator*: Same as ADM, but with switches in a column restricted to same state.
- *Delta*: Any MIN for which the outputs of each switch have distinct labels (say 0 and 1 for 2×2 switches) and the path label, composed of concatenating the switch output labels, leading from an arbitrary input to a given output depends only on the output.
- *Flip*: Reverse of the *omega network* (i.e., roles of inputs and outputs interchanged).
- *Indirect cube*: Same as *butterfly* or *omega*.
- *Omega*: Multistage shuffle–exchange network; isomorphic to *butterfly* (Fig. 15.19).
- *Permutation*: Any network that can realize all possible permutations (e.g., *Beneš*).
- *Rearrangeable*: Same as *permutation network*.
- *Reverse baseline*: *Baseline network*, with the roles of inputs and outputs interchanged.

PROBLEMS

16.1. Petersen graph

    a. Find the average internode distance in the 10-node Petersen graph of Fig. 16.1.

    b. Find the bisection width of the 10-node Petersen graph.

    c. Express the connectivity rules of the 10-node Petersen graph in terms of the 5-bit node IDs given in Fig. 16.1.

16.2. Swapped networks

    a. Consider a 100-node graph composed of 10 copies of the 10-node Petersen graph (clusters) in which each node has a two-digit decimal label xy ($0 \le x, y \le 9$), with Node xy, i.e., Node y of Cluster x, connected to Node yx by an additional link; thus, the node degree becomes 4. Node xx does not have an intercluster link. Determine the diameter of this network and compare it with Moore's bound.

    b. Compare the cost and performance of the network of part (a) to the product of two Petersen networks.

    c. We can generalize the construction of part (a) to any p-node graph to obtain a p^2-node graph. Devise semigroup computation, parallel prefix computation, and broadcasting algorithms for the resulting p^2-node network, given the corresponding algorithms for the original graph.

16.3. Topological parameters of a network
    Consider the chordal ring network of Fig. 16.2.

    a. Determine the diameter of the network.

    b. Suggest a shortest-path routing algorithm for the network.

    c. Find the average internode distance for the network. *Hint:* The network is node-symmetric.

    d. By renumbering Node i of the network as Node $3i$ mod 32 and redrawing the network as a ring in order of the new node numbers, show that the bisection width of the network is at most 8.

    e. Derive the exact bisection width of the network.

16.4. Odd networks

A q-dimensional odd graph/network is one in which each node is identified by a $(2q-1)$-bit binary number with exactly q 1s and $q - 1$ 0s. Thus, there are $\binom{2q-1}{q}$ nodes. Each Node x is connected to q neighbors whose labels are obtained by keeping one of the 1 bits unchanged and complementing the other $2q$ bits.

a. Show that the 10-node Petersen graph of Fig. 16.1 is in fact the 3D odd graph.
b. Derive the sizes of q-D odd graphs for $4 \le q \le 10$ and compare with those of the q-cube.
c. Devise an efficient routing algorithm for the q-D odd network.
d. Determine the diameter of the q-D odd graph and compare it with Moore's lower bound.

16.5. Star and pancake networks

a. Compare the sizes of q-D star graphs with those of odd graphs (defined in Problem 16.4) and hypercubes with the same node degrees.
b. Does the routing example from Node 154362 to Node 346215 for the star graph given in Section 16.2 correspond to a shortest path? If not, what is the shortest path?
c. Repeat part (b) for the routing example for the pancake network given in Section 16.2.
d. Give an example of a diametral path for the 4D star graph of Fig. 16.3. Is the diameter of this particular q-star equal to $2q - 3$?
e. Repeat part (d) for the 4D pancake network.

16.6. Unfolded star, pancake, and rotator networks

Unfolded star, pancake, and rotator networks can be defined in the same way as unfolded hypercubes.

a. Draw the unfolded 4-star, 4-pancake, and 4-rotator networks.
b. Determine the diameters of unfolded 4-star, 4-pancake, and 4-rotator networks.
c. Compare the diameters obtained in part (b) with Moore's lower bound.
d. Determine the bisection widths of unfolded 4-star, 4-pancake, and 4-rotator networks.

16.7. Ring of rings networks

a. Find the optimal number of nodes in each local ring if the diameter of a p-processor ring of rings network exemplified by Fig. 16.5 is to be minimized.
b. Find the optimal configuration of an h-level, p-processor ring of rings with respect to its diameter.
c. Determine the maximum number of nodes that can be incorporated in a multilevel ring of rings network using nodes of degree 4 for various desired diameters in the range $2 \le D \le 5$.
d. Devise an algorithm for multiplying $m \times m$ matrices on an m^2-processor ring of rings network with m processors in each local ring.

16.8. Ring of rings networks

Consider a three-level ring of rings network with 6 nodes in each ring. Each of the 216 nodes in this network can be identified by a three-digit radix-6 integer.

a. Devise a node indexing scheme that makes it easy to identify which nodes belong to rings at various levels.
b. Describe a shortest-path routing algorithm based on the indexing scheme of part (a).
c. Identify all of the diametral endpoints in the network (nodes that can be at the end of a diametral path).
d. How will the diameter of the network change if we connect the diametral endpoints identified in part (c) into a ring using their unused ports?

16.9. Product networks

    a. Prove that the diameter and average internode distance in a product network is the sum of the respective parameters for the two component networks. *Hint:* First prove that given a shortest path of length l' between u' and v' in G' and a shortest path of length l'' between u'' and v'' in G'', the length of the shortest path between $u'u''$ and $v'v''$ in G is $l = l' + l''$.

    b. Extend the result of part (a) to the product of k graphs.

    c. Find a formula for the number of edges in a product graph in terms of the parameters of its k component networks.

    d. Prove or disprove: The bisection width of a product graph $G = G' \times G''$ is lower bounded by $\min(p'B'', p''B')$, where p' and p'' are the numbers of nodes, and B' and B'' are the bisection widths of G' and G'', respectively.

16.10. Layered networks

    a. Show that a q-D mesh is a layered network.

    b. What can you say about the layered cross product of an l-layer graph G and the l-node linear array?

    c. A one-sided binary tree is a binary tree in which the left (right) child of every node is a leaf. What is the layered cross product of two one-sided binary trees of the same kind? Of opposite kinds?

16.11. Layered cross-product networks
Prove the following results:

    a. The butterfly network is the layered cross product of two binary trees. *Hint:* One is inverted.

    b. The mesh of trees network is the layered cross product of two binary trees with "paths" (linear array of nodes) "hanging from" their leaves, as shown in the following diagram.

16.12. Mesh-connected trees

    a. Show that a mesh-connected trees network (Fig. 16.11) has four copies of the next smaller mesh-connected trees network as its subgraphs.

    b. Show that the largest complete binary tree whose size does not exceed that of a mesh-connected trees network is a subgraph of the latter.

16.13. Waksman's permutation network
A $p \times p$ Waksman permutation network [Waks68] is recursively constructed using 2×2 switches. First, $p/2$ switches are used to switch the inputs 0 and 1, 2 and 3, ..., $p-1$ and p. The upper and lower outputs of the above switches are separately permuted using $p/2$-permuters. Finally, $p/2-1$ switches are used to switch the corresponding outputs of the $p/2$-permuters, except for their lowermost outputs.

    a. Show that Waksman's permutation network can in fact route all permutations.

    b. Determine the cost and delay of Waksman's permutation network in terms of p.

16.14. ADM and gamma networks
The augmented data manipulator network (Fig. 15.12), as originally defined, was a unidirectional multistage interconnection network with inputs on the right and outputs at the left. The

gamma network (also called *inverse ADM* or IADM) is an ADM in which the input and output sides have been switched.

a. Show that ADM and gamma networks are essentially the same network (they are isomorphic).

b. Show that, more generally, any permutation of the intercolumn connectivities of an ADM network leads to an isomorphic network.

c. Use the result of part (b) to determine the diameter of a wrapped ADM network with bidirectional links if the nodes are processors rather than switches.

16.15. Hierarchical hypercube networks
A hierarchical $(q+1)$-dimensional hypercube consists of 2^q copies of a q-cube (2^q clusters) with Node x in Cluster y connected to Node y in Cluster x via a Dimension-q link. Node x in Cluster x has no intercluster link.

a. Find the diameter of the hierarchical $(q+1)$D hypercube.

b. Compare the diameter obtained in part (a) with that of a $2q$-cube and with Moore's lower bound.

c. Devise an efficient routing algorithm for the hierarchical $(q+1)$D hypercube.

d. Show that an ascend- or descend-type algorithm for the $2q$-cube can be efficiently emulated by the hierarchical $(q+1)$D hypercube.

REFERENCES AND SUGGESTED READING

[AlHa93]   Al-Hajery, M. Z., and K. E. Batcher, "On the Bit-Level Complexity of Bitonic Sorting Networks," *Proc. Int. Parallel Processing Conf.*, 1993, Vol. III, pp. 209–213.

[Arde81]   Arden, B. W., and H. Lee, "Analysis of Chordal Ring Networks," *IEEE Trans. Computers*, Vol. 30, No. 4, pp. 291–295, April 1981.

[Berm95]   Bermond, J.-C., F. Comellas, and D. F. Du, "Distributed Loop Computer Networks: A Survey," *J. Parallel Distributed Computing*, Vol. 24, No. 1, pp. 2–10, January 1995.

[Chen96]   Cheng, W.-J., and W.-T. Chen, "A New Self-Routing Permutation Network," *IEEE Trans. Computers*, Vol. 45, No. 5, pp. 630–636, May 1996.

[Corb92]   Corbett, P. F., "Rotator Graphs: An Efficient Topology for Point-to-Point Multiprocessor Networks," *IEEE Trans. Parallel Distributed Systems*, Vol. 3, No. 5, pp. 622–626, September 1992.

[Day94]   Day, K., and A. Tripathi, "A Comparative Study of Topological Properties of Hypercubes and Star Graphs," *IEEE Trans. Parallel Distributed Systems*, Vol. 5, No. 1, pp. 31–38, January 1994.

[Day97]   Day, K., and A.-E. Al-Ayyoub, "The Cross Product of Interconnection Networks," *IEEE Trans. Parallel Distributed Systems*, Vol. 8, No. 2, pp. 109–118, February 1997.

[Efe96]   Efe, K., and A. Fernandez, "Mesh-Connected Trees: A Bridge Between Grids and Meshes of Trees," *IEEE Trans. Parallel Distributed Systems*, Vol. 7, No. 12, pp. 1281–1291, December 1996.

[Even97]   Even, G., and S. Even, "Embedding Interconnection Networks in Grids via the Layered Cross Product," *Proc. 3rd Italian Conf. Algorithms and Complexity*, Rome, March 1997, pp. 3–12.

[Kend92]   Kendall Square Research, "KSR1 Technology Background," 1992.

[Kwai96]   Kwai, D.-M., and B. Parhami, "A Generalization of Hypercubic Networks Based on Their Chordal Ring Structures," *Information Processing Letters*, Vol. 6, No. 4, pp. 469–477, 1996.

[Kwai97]   Kwai, D.-M., and B. Parhami, "A Class of Fixed-Degree Cayley-Graph Interconnection Networks Derived by Pruning k-ary n-cubes," *Proc. Int. Conf. Parallel Processing*, 1997, pp. 92–95.

[Lati93]   Latifi, S., M. M. de Azevedo, and N. Bagherzadeh, "The Star Connected Cycles: A Fixed-Degree Network for Parallel Processing," in *Proc. Int. Parallel Processing Conf.*, 1993, Vol. I, pp. 91–95.

[Leig92]   Leighton, F. T., *Introduction to Parallel Algorithms and Architectures: Arrays, Trees, Hypercubes*, Morgan Kaufmann, 1992.

[Mans94]   Mans, B., and N. Santoro, "Optimal Fault-Tolerant Leader Election in Chordal Rings," *Proc. 24th Int. Symp. Fault-Tolerant Computing*, June 1994, pp. 392–401.

[Parh95]   Parhami, B., "Periodically Regular Chordal Ring Networks for Massively Parallel Architectures,"
             Proc. 5th Symp. Frontiers Massively Parallel Computation, February 1995, pp. 315–322. [Extended
             version to appear in *IEEE Trans. Parallel Distributed Systems.*]
[Ponn94]   Ponnuswamy, S., and V. Chaudhary, "A Comparative Study of Star Graphs and Rotator Graphs," in
             Proc. Int. Parallel Processing Conf., 1994, Vol. I, pp. 46–50.
[Reic93]   Reichmeyer, F., S. Hariri, and K. Jabbour, "Wormhole Routing on Multichannel Ring Networks,"
             Proc. 36th Midwest Symp. Circuits and Systems, August 1993, pp. 625–628.
[Sche94]   Scherson, I. D., and A. S. Youssef, *Interconnection Networks for High-Performance Parallel Com-
             puters*, IEEE Computer Society Press, 1994.
[Vale94]   Valerio, M., L. E. Moser, P. M. Melliar-Smith, and P. Sweazey, "The QuickRing Network," *Proc.
             ACM Computer Science Conf.*, 1994.
[Waks68]   Waksman, A., "A Permutation Network," *J. ACM*, Vol. 15, No. 1, pp. 159–163, January 1968.
[Yeh98]   Yeh, C.-H., and B. Parhami, "A New Representation of Graphs and Its Applications to Parallel
             Processing," *Proc. Int. Conf. Parallel and Distributed Systems*, 1998, to appear.
[Yous95]   Youssef, A., "Design and Analysis of Product Networks," *Proc. 5th Symp. Frontiers Massively
             Parallel Computation*, February 1995, pp. 521–528.

V

Some Broad Topics

In this part, we consider several topics that influence the acceptance, efficiency, and quality of parallel computers. For example, coordination and resource management schemes for computations and data accesses have a direct bearing on the effectiveness of parallel computers. Likewise, to ensure a balanced design with no obvious performance bottleneck, any parallel system must be equipped with high-bandwidth input/output devices capable of supplying data to processors, and removing the computation results, at appropriate rates. The I/O capabilities of parallel computers are particularly important in data-intensive applications found in corporate database and network server environments. From another angle, the high component count of parallel systems makes them susceptible to hardware faults, thus necessitating fault tolerance provisions in their designs. Finally, coordination, programming, user views/interfaces, and system software are important for all types of parallel systems. The above broad topics are treated in this part, which consists of the following four chapters:

- Chapter 17: Emulation and Scheduling
- Chapter 18: Data Storage, Input, and Output
- Chapter 19: Reliable Parallel Processing
- Chapter 20: System and Software Issues

17

Emulation and Scheduling

We have previously used the notion of one parallel machine emulating another one in the development and evaluation of certain algorithms. We now take a closer look at emulation and, in particular, demonstrate how it is applicable to the provision of a shared-memory view in a distributed-memory environment. In a coarse-grained MIMD-type parallel computer, the multiple processors often work independently on different subproblems or subtasks of a large problem. The processing nodes may be homogeneous or heterogeneous and the subtasks often have varying complexities and data interdependencies. Once a parallel algorithm for solving a particular problem has been developed, its subtasks and their interdependencies must be specified and then assigned to the available computation and communication resources. Because subtask execution times can vary as a result of data-dependent conditions, dynamic scheduling or load balancing might be required to achieve good efficiency. Chapter topics are

- 17.1. Emulations among architectures
- 17.2. Distributed shared memory
- 17.3. The task scheduling problem
- 17.4. A class of scheduling algorithms
- 17.5. Some useful bounds for scheduling
- 17.6. Load balancing and dataflow systems

17.1. EMULATIONS AMONG ARCHITECTURES

Emulations are sometimes necessitated by our desire to quickly develop algorithms for a new architecture without expending the significant resources that would be required for native algorithm development. Another reason for our interest in emulations among parallel architectures is that they allow us to develop algorithms for architectures that are easier to program (e.g., shared-memory or PRAM) and then have them run on machines that are realizable, easily accessible, or affordable. The developed algorithm then serves as a "source code" that can be quickly "compiled" to run on any given architecture via emulation.

Emulation results are sometimes used for purposes other than practical porting of software. For example, we know that the hypercube is a powerful architecture and can execute many algorithms efficiently. Thus, one way to show that a new architecture is useful or efficient, without a need for developing a large set of algorithms for it, is to show that it can emulate the hypercube efficiently. We used this method, e.g., to prove the versatility of the cube-connected cycles architecture in Section 15.4. The results were that CCC can emulate a p-node hypercube with O(log p) slowdown and that in the special case of normal hypercube algorithms, which includes many of the algorithms of practical interest in the ascend/descend class, emulation is done with $\Theta(1)$ slowdown.

Results similar to the above between the hypercube and CCC have been obtained for many other pairs of parallel architectures. Interestingly, a form of transitivity can be used to derive new emulation results from existing ones. If architecture A emulates architecture B with O($f(p)$) slowdown and B in turn emulates C with O($g(p)$) slowdown (assuming, for simplicity, that they all contain p processors), then A can emulate C with O($f(p) \times g(p)$) slowdown. In this way, if an architecture is shown to emulate CCC with $\Theta(1)$ slowdown, then based on the results of CCC emulating the hypercube, we can deduce that the new architecture can emulate normal hypercube algorithms with $\Theta(1)$ slowdown.

The above are examples of emulation results that are specific to a target (emulated) architecture and a host (emulating) architecture. In the rest of this section, we introduce three fairly general emulation results involving classes of, rather than specific, architectures. We will follow these with a fourth, very important, emulation result in Section 17.2.

Our first result is based on embedding of an architecture or graph into another one. As discussed in Section 13.2, a graph embedding consists of a node mapping and an edge mapping. The cost of an embedding is reflected in

Expansion   Ratio of the number of nodes in the two graphs

whereas its performance characteristics are captured by

Dilation   Longest path onto which any given edge is mapped
Congestion   Maximum number of edges mapped onto the same edge
Load factor   Maximum number of nodes mapped onto the same node

Assuming communication is performed by packet routing, such a graph embedding can be the basis of an emulation with a slowdown factor that is upper bounded by

slowdown ≤ dilation × congestion × load factor

As a special case, any embedding with constant dilation, congestion, and load factor defines an emulation with constant-factor slowdown. The above bound is tight in the sense that slowdown may equal the right-hand side in some cases. As an example, embedding the p-node complete graph K_p into the two-node graph K_2 involves dilation of 1, congestion of $p^2/4$, load factor of $p/2$, and a worst-case slowdown of $p^3/8$. Despite the above worst-case example, it is often possible to schedule the communications over dilated and congested paths in such a way that the resulting slowdown is significantly less than the upper bound.

Our second general emulation result is that the PRAM can emulate any degree-d network with O(d) slowdown, where slowdown is measured in terms of computation steps rather than real time; i.e., each PRAM computation step, involving memory access by every processor, counts as one step. The proof is fairly simple. Each processor of the PRAM host emulates one degree-d node in the target architecture. In one computation step, the emulated node can send/receive up to d messages to/from its neighbors. In the PRAM emulation, each link buffer (there are two buffers per bidirectional link) corresponds to a location in shared memory. The sending of up to d messages by each node can be done in d steps, with the ith step being devoted to writing a message from the ith send buffer to the ith link buffer (assume that the neighbors of each node have been ordered). Similarly, the receiving part, which involves reading up to d messages from known locations in the shared memory, can be done in O(d) steps.

Because each link buffer is associated with a unique receiving node, the EREW PRAM submodel is adequate for this emulation. As a special case of the above general result, the PRAM can emulate any bounded-degree network with constant slowdown. Hence, the PRAM can be said to be more powerful than any bounded-degree network. As another special case, any network with logarithmic or sublogarithmic node degree can be emulated with at most logarithmic slowdown. With the CREW PRAM submodel, we can emulate a hyper-graph-based architecture (i.e., one including buses and multipoint links) with O(d) slowdown.

Our third and final general result, that the (wrapped) butterfly network can emulate any p-node degree-d network with O($d \log p$) slowdown, is somewhat more difficult to prove. Here is a proof sketch. The cornerstone of the proof is a result that shows the ability of a p-node (wrapped) butterfly network to route any permutation in O($\log p$) steps (see [Leig92], p. 457). Thus, if a communication step of an arbitrary p-node degree-d network can be translated into d permutation routing problems, the desired conclusion will be immediate. This latter property is a direct consequence of the following result from graph theory:

Consider a $2p$-node *bipartite graph* G with node set $U \cup V$, such that U and V each contain p nodes and every edge connects a node in U to a node in V. If all nodes in G have the same degree d, then G contains a *perfect matching*, i.e., a set of p edges that connect every node in U to every node in V.

If we remove the p edges corresponding to a perfect matching, which define a p-permutation, the remaining graph will have uniform node degree $d - 1$ and will again contain a perfect matching by the same result. Removal of this second perfect matching (p-permutation) leaves us with a bipartite graph with node degree $d - 2$. Continuing in this manner, we will eventually get a bipartite graph with node degree 1 that defines the dth and final permutation.

Consider, for example, the five-node graph, with maximum node degree 3, depicted in Fig. 17.1. We augment this graph with a link from Node 1 to Node 3, in order to make the

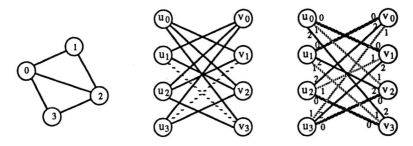

Figure 17.1. Converting a routing step in a degree-3 network to three permutations or perfect matchings.

node degree uniformly equal to 3, and represent the augmented graph by the bipartite graph, shown in the middle, which has Nodes u_i and v_i in its two parts corresponding to Node i in the original graph. We next identify a perfect matching in this bipartite graph, say, the heavy dotted edges on the right. This perfect matching, with its edges carrying the label 0 in the right-hand diagram of Fig. 17.1, defines the permutation $P_0 = \{1, 0, 3, 2\}$ of the node set $\{0, 1, 2, 3\}$. Removing these edges, we arrive at a bipartite graph having the uniform node degree 2 and the perfect matching defined by the light dotted edges labeled with 1. This time, we have identified the permutation $P_1 = \{2, 3, 1, 0\}$. Finally, the remaining edges, marked with the label 2 in Fig. 17.1, define the last perfect matching or permutation $P_2 = \{3, 2, 0, 1\}$.

A consequence of the above emulation result is that if a problem is efficiently parallelizable on any bounded-degree architecture, then it is efficiently parallelizable on the butterfly network, because emulating the bounded-degree network on the butterfly increases the running time by at most a factor of $O(\log p)$. In this sense, the butterfly network is a *universal*, or *universally efficient*, bounded-degree parallel architecture.

A fourth general emulation result, that of emulating the abstract PRAM architecture on feasible bounded-degree networks, is important enough to warrant separate discussion (next section).

17.2. DISTRIBUTED SHARED MEMORY

We mentioned, in the introduction to Chapter 5, that the shared-memory model of parallel computation, and PRAM in particular, facilitates the development of parallel algorithms using a variety of programming paradigms. This ease of algorithm development is practically useful only if the underlying model can be built directly in hardware, or at least lends itself to efficient emulation by feasible (bounded-degree) networks. In this section, we show that the butterfly network can indeed emulate the PRAM rather efficiently. Such an emulation, by butterfly or other networks, provides the illusion of shared memory to the users or programmers of a parallel system that in fact uses message passing for interprocessor communication. This illusion, or programming view, is sometimes referred to as *distributed* (or *virtual*) *shared memory*.

We discuss two types of PRAM emulations on the butterfly: (1) randomized or probabilistic emulation, which allows us to make statements about the average-case or expected slowdown, but provides no performance guarantee in the worst case, and (2) deterministic emulation, which involves greater overhead, and may thus be slower on the average, but in return guarantees good worst-case performance. The randomized emulation is good enough for most practical purposes. We thus treat deterministic PRAM emulation as a topic of theoretical interest.

Let us now discuss a randomized emulation of the p-processor PRAM on a butterfly distributed-memory machine. Assume, for simplicity, that $p = 2^q(q + 1)$ for some q. Thus, a p-node butterfly exists that can emulate the PRAM processors on a one-to-one basis (Fig. 17.2). The PRAM processors are arbitrarily mapped onto the butterfly processors. Each of the m PRAM memory locations is assigned to one of the processors using a hash function h (a function that maps a set of keys onto a set of integers such that roughly the same number of keys are mapped to each integer). Thus, a processor needing access to memory location x will evaluate $h(x)$ to determine which processor holds that particular memory location and then sends a message to that processor to read from or write into x. Because the hash function h is a random function, emulating one EREW PRAM step involves a randomized (average-case) routing problem that can be completed on the butterfly in O(log p) steps with high probability. One can use, e.g., the simple routing algorithm that sends each packet to Column 0 in the source row, then to Column q in the destination row, and finally to the destination node within the destination row.

Note that in the EREW PRAM, the processors are constrained to access different memory locations in each step. When we apply the hash function h in the above emulation scheme, the p different memory locations accessed by the PRAM processors may not be in distinct memory modules. However, at most O(log p) of the memory locations accessed will be in the same butterfly row with high probability. Thus, the O(log p) average slowdown factor of the emulation can be maintained by suitably pipelining these accesses. The same result holds for emulating the CRCW PRAM, provided that multiple accesses to the same memory location are combined.

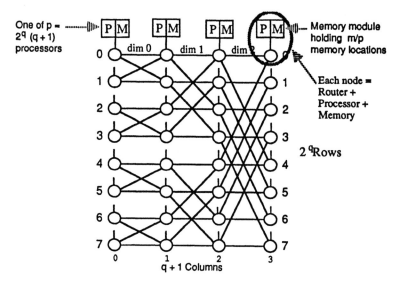

Figure 17.2. Butterfly distributed-memory machine emulating the PRAM.

Figure 17.3 depicts an alternative emulation of the p-processor PRAM using a butterfly MIN connecting $p = 2^q$ processors and memory modules on its two sides. Thus, nodes in the intermediate columns are not connected to processor or memory modules but merely act as switching nodes for routing messages back and forth between processors and memory modules. If we convert the butterfly network into a wrapped butterfly, the processors and memory modules can be merged to form a distributed-memory machine. The slowdown factor in this emulation is still O(log p).

The PRAM emulation scheme depicted in Fig. 17.3 is quite inefficient because it leads to roughly the same slowdown factor as that of Fig. 17.2, which uses a smaller butterfly. However, this inefficient scheme can become quite efficient if we use it to emulate a 2^q q-processor PRAM rather than one with 2^q processors. Each processor on the left now emulates q of the p PRAM processors instead of just one. Each memory module on the right holds $m/2^q = \Theta(m \log p/p)$ memory locations. The emulating processor simply cycles through the emulated processors in a round-robin fashion, issuing their respective memory read requests (which are pipelined through the butterfly network), then receiving the returned data from memory, then performing the corresponding computation steps, and finally issuing write requests for storing the results in shared memory. With pipelining of the read and write accesses through the network, the entire process of emulating one computation step of the q processors takes O(q) steps with high probability. Thus, the emulation has $\Theta(1)$ efficiency on the average.

Deterministic emulation is both more difficult and less efficient [Harr94]. Because conflicts in the routing of memory access requests may delay the completion of such requests, the main idea is to store multiple copies of each memory data word so that if access to one copy is delayed by routing conflicts, we can access another copy. The cost penalty is obviously the need for more memory locations. By storing $k = \log_2 m$ copies of each of the m data items, we can successfully access any p items in O(log m log p log log p) time in a

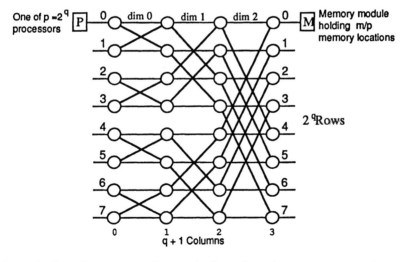

Figure 17.3. Distributed-memory machine, with a butterfly multistage interconnection network, emulating the PRAM.

p-node butterfly, provided that accesses belonging to a particular PRAM cycle are time-stamped with the cycle number.

Intuitively, the improved worst-case performance of the above method results from the fact that for each access, only $\lceil (k + 1)/2 \rceil$ of the k copies need to be read/updated. This ensures the condition

$$| \text{ read set} \cap \text{update set } | \geq 1$$

which in turn leads to any read set being guaranteed to have one up-to-date value with the latest time stamp. Requests are issued for reading/updating all k copies of the required data item but the request is considered satisfied once $\lceil (k + 1)/2 \rceil$ copies have been returned or updated. Thus, congestion on some of the access paths will not lead to significant slowdown. The detailed mechanism that allows groups of processors to cooperate in satisfying each round of memory access requests is fairly complicated [Upfa87].

In one sense, the replication factor log m of the preceding emulation is very close to the best possible; the lower bound on the replication factor to guarantee fast access to at least one up-to-date copy is $\Omega(\log m/\log \log m)$. However, this lower bound applies only if data items must be stored as atomic or indivisible objects. Using Rabin's information dispersal scheme [Rabi89], one can encode each data item z in $k = \log m$ pieces $z_1 z_2 \ldots z_k$, with each z_i of size $\approx 3|z|/k$, in such a way that any $k/3$ pieces can be used to reconstruct z (Fig. 17.4). Then, in each read or write access, we deal with $2k/3$ pieces, as this will guarantee that at least $k/3$ of the $2k/3$ pieces accessed will have the latest time stamp. If accessing each piece is $\Theta(k)$ times faster than accessing the entire data item (which is k times larger), then we need only $O(\log m \log p \log \log p/k) = O(\log p \log \log p)$ time with the above constant-factor redundancy scheme.

Thus far, our discussion of distributed shared memory has been in terms of emulating a synchronous PRAM. Because, in such an emulation, one set of memory accesses is completed before another set begins, the semantics of memory accesses is quite clear and

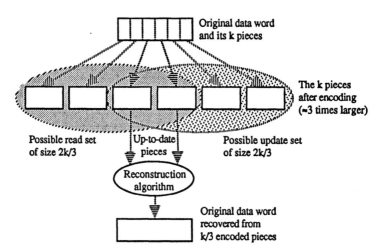

Figure 17.4. Illustrating the information dispersal approach to PRAM emulation with lower data redundancy.

corresponds to the emulated PRAM model. More generally, however, shared memory may be accessed by multiple asynchronous processes running on different processors (asynchronous PRAM). In such cases, a shared-memory consistency model [Adve96] must be defined in order to allow efficient and correct parallel programming. The actual shared-memory view can be provided to the programmer by software or hardware means [Prot96].

17.3. THE TASK SCHEDULING PROBLEM

Virtually all parallel algorithms that we developed in the previous chapters were such that the allocation of computations to processors was explicit in the algorithm. In other words, the algorithms explicitly specified what each processor should do in any given computation step. With coarse-grain parallel computations, it is possible to decouple the algorithm's specification from the assignment of tasks to processors. This is in fact required if the computation is to be executed on a variable number of processors to be determined at compile time or even run time. It is also necessary for dynamic load balancing (see Section 17.6).

The task scheduling problem is defined as follows: Given a task system characterizing a parallel computation, determine how the tasks can be assigned to processing resources (scheduled on them) to satisfy certain optimality criteria. The task system is usually defined in the form of a directed graph, with nodes specifying computational tasks and links corresponding to data dependencies or communications. Optimality criteria may include minimizing execution time, maximizing resource utilization, minimizing interprocessor communication, meeting deadlines, or a combination of these factors.

Associated with each task is a set of parameters, including one or more of the following:

1. *Execution or running time.* We may be given the worst case, average case, or the probability distribution of a task's execution time.
2. *Creation.* We may be faced with a fixed set of tasks, known at compile time, or a probability distribution for the task creation times.
3. *Relationship with other tasks.* This type of information may include criticality, priority order, and/or data dependencies.
4. *Start or end time.* A task's *release time* is the time before which the task should not be executed. Also, a hard or soft deadline may be associated with each task. A *hard deadline* is specified when the results of a task become practically worthless if not obtained by a certain time. A *soft deadline* may penalize late results but does not render them totally worthless.

Resources or processors on which tasks are to be scheduled are typically characterized by their ability to execute certain classes of tasks and by their performance or speed. Often uniform capabilities are assumed for all processors, either to make the scheduling problem tractable or because parallel systems of interest do in fact consist of identical processors. In this latter case, any task can be scheduled on any processor.

The scheduling algorithm or scheme is itself characterized by

1. *Preemption.* With *nonpreemptive* scheduling, a task must run to completion once started, whereas with *preemptive* scheduling, execution of a task may be suspended to accommodate a more critical or higher-priority task. In practice, preemption involves some overhead for storing the state of the partially completed task and for

continually checking the task queue for the arrival of higher-priority tasks. However, this overhead is ignored in most scheduling algorithms for reasons of tractability.

2. *Granularity*. Fine-grain, medium-grain, or coarse-grain scheduling problems deal with tasks of various complexities, from simple multiply–add calculations to large, complex program segments, perhaps consisting of thousands of instructions. Fine-grain scheduling is often incorporated into the algorithm, as otherwise the overhead would be prohibitive. Medium- and coarse-grain scheduling are not fundamentally different, except that with a larger number of medium-grain tasks to be scheduled, the computational complexity of the scheduling algorithm can become an issue, especially with *on-line* or *run-time* scheduling.

Unfortunately, most interesting task scheduling problems, some with as few as two processors, are NP-complete. This fundamental difficulty has given rise to research results on many special cases that lend themselves to analytical solutions and to a great many heuristic procedures that work fine under appropriate circumstances or with tuning of their decision parameters. Stankovic et al. [Stan95] present a good overview of basic scheduling results and the boundary between easy and hard problems. El-Rewini et al. [ElRe95] provide an overview of task scheduling in multiprocessors.

In what follows, we briefly review task scheduling problems of a very restricted type. A task system is represented by a directed acyclic graph $G = (V, E)$, where V is the set of vertices representing unit-time tasks or computations $v_1, v_2, \ldots, v_{T_1}$ and E is the set of edges representing precedence constraints:

$$E = \{(v_i, v_j) \mid v_i, v_j \in V \text{ and Task } v_i \text{ feeds data to Task } v_j\}$$

An example task system is depicted in Fig. 17.5.

Each task must be scheduled on one of p identical processors. There are no other resource constraints, such as I/O or memory requirements, and no timing restrictions, such as release times or deadlines. With these conditions, a schedule S is a set of triples (v_i, t_j, P_k) assigning a Task v_i to a Processor P_k for a particular time step t_j, and satisfying

a. $(x, y, z) \in S \Rightarrow (x', y, z) \notin S$ for $x' \neq x$
b. $(x, x') \in E, (x, y, z) \in S, (x', y', z') \in S \Rightarrow y' > y$

Condition (a) simply means that one processor can execute only one task at each time step, whereas Condition (b) requires that precedence relationships be honored.

An analogy might be helpful. Tasks can be likened to courses, each with a set of prerequisites. There are, say, T quarters or semesters over which courses needed to satisfy a degree requirement must be scheduled such that the number of courses in each academic term does not exceed the maximum allowed course load and the prerequisites for each course are all taken before the course. Here, the maximum course load corresponds to the number of processors available and the number T of terms is the analogue of the total execution time on the parallel machine. Of course, for constructing a study plan, we also have timing constraints in that not all courses are offered in every term. This analogy should be sufficient to convince any college student that the task scheduling problem is NP-hard!

Polynomial time optimal scheduling algorithms exist only for very limited classes of scheduling problems. Examples include scheduling tree-structured task graphs with any number of processors and scheduling arbitrary graphs of unit-time tasks on two processors [ElRe95]. Most practical scheduling problems are solved by applying heuristic algorithms. An important class of heuristic scheduling algorithms, known as *list scheduling*, is discussed next.

17.4. A CLASS OF SCHEDULING ALGORITHMS

In *list scheduling*, a priority level is assigned to each task. A task list is then constructed in which the tasks appear in priority order, with some tasks tagged as being ready for execution (initially, only tasks having no prerequisite are tagged). With each processor that becomes available for executing tasks, the highest-priority tagged task is removed from the list and assigned to the processor. If q processors become available simultaneously, then up to q tasks can be scheduled at once. As tasks complete their executions, thus satisfying the prerequisites of other tasks, such tasks are tagged and become ready for execution. When all processors are identical, the schedulers in this class differ only in their priority assignment schemes.

In the case of unit-time tasks, tagging of new tasks can be done right after scheduling is completed for the current step. With different, but deterministic, running times, tagging can be done by attaching a time stamp, rather than a binary indicator, with each task that will become ready in a known future time. In what follows, we will consider the simple case of unit-time tasks. Additionally, we will ignore scheduling and communication overheads. Thus, once a task is run to completion and its processor becomes available, the communication of results to subsequent tasks and the scheduling of a new task on the released processor are instantaneous.

Here is a possible priority assignment scheme for list scheduling. First the depth T_∞ of the task graph, which is an indicator of its minimum possible execution time, is determined. The depth of the graph is designated as T_∞ because it corresponds to the execution time of the task graph with an unlimited number of processors. As an example, the depth of the task graph in Fig. 17.5 is 8. We then take T_∞ as our goal for the total running time T_p with p processors and determine the latest possible time step in which each task can be scheduled if our goal is to be met. This is done by "layering" the nodes beginning with the output node. For the example in Fig. 17.5, the output node v_{13} is assigned with $T_\infty = 8$ as its latest possible time. The prerequisites of v_{13}, namely, v_{10}, v_{11}, and v_{12}, are assigned a latest time of 7, their prerequisites get 6, and so forth. If we have not made a mistake, some input node will be assigned 1 as its latest possible time. The results of layering for the task graph of Fig. 17.5 are as follows:

1	2	3	4	5	6	7	8	9	10	11	12	13	Tasks in numerical order
1	2	3	4	6	5	6	6	6	7	7	7	8	Latest possible times (layers)

The priority of tasks is then assigned in the order of the latest possible times. Ties can be broken in various ways. Let us give priority to a task with a larger number of descendants in case of equal values of the latest possible times. For our example, this secondary criterion is

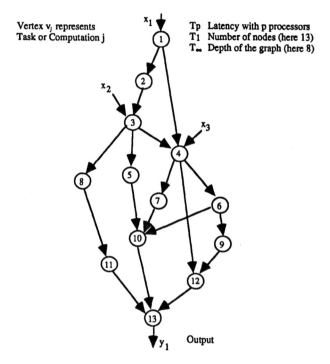

Vertex v_j represents
Task or Computation j

Tp Latency with p processors
T1 Number of nodes (here 13)
T∞ Depth of the graph (here 8)

Figure 17.5. Example task system showing communications or dependencies.

of no help, but generally, if a task with more descendants is executed first, the running time will likely be improved.

1*	2	3	4	6	5	7	8	9	10	11	12	13	Tasks in priority order
1	2	3	4	5	6	6	6	6	7	7	7	8	Latest possible times
2	1	3	3	2	1	1	1	1	1	1	1	0	Number of descendants

Now, to schedule our example task graph on $p = 2$ processors, we scan the constructed list from left to right, to select up to two tagged tasks for execution in each time step. Selection of each task in a time step may result in other tasks being tagged as ready for the next step.

Tasks listed in priority order

1*	2	3	4	6	5	7	8	9	10	11	12	13	$t = 1$	v_1 scheduled
2*	3	4	6	5	7	8	9	10	11	12	13		$t = 2$	v_2 scheduled
3*	4	6	5	7	8	9	10	11	12	13			$t = 3$	v_3 scheduled
4*	6	5*	7	8*	9	10	11	12	13				$t = 4$	v_4, v_5 scheduled
6*	7*	8*	9	10	11	12	13						$t = 5$	v_6, v_7 scheduled
8*	9*	10*	11	12	13								$t = 6$	v_8, v_9 scheduled
10*	11*	12*	13										$t = 7$	v_{10}, v_{11} scheduled
12*	13												$t = 8$	v_{12} scheduled
13*													$t = 9$	v_{13} scheduled (done)

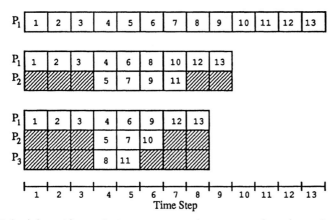

Figure 17.6. Schedules with p = 1, 2, 3 processors for an example task graph with unit-time tasks.

With $p = 3$ processors, the scheduling of our example task graph goes as follows:

Tasks listed in priority order

1*	2	3	4	6	5	7	8	9	10	11	12	13	$t = 1$	v_1 scheduled
2*	3	4	6	5	7	8	9	10	11	12	13		$t = 2$	v_2 scheduled
3*	4	6	5	7	8	9	10	11	12	13			$t = 3$	v_3 scheduled
4*	6	5*	7	8*	9	10	11	12	13				$t = 4$	v_4, v_5, v_8 scheduled
6*	7*	9	10	11*	12	13							$t = 5$	v_6, v_7, v_{11} scheduled
9*	10*	12	13										$t = 6$	v_9, v_{10} scheduled
12*	13												$t = 7$	v_{12} scheduled
13*													$t = 8$	v_{13} scheduled (done)

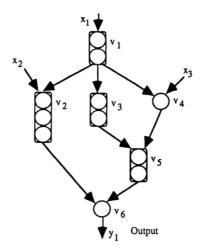

Figure 17.7. Example task system with task running times of 1, 2, or 3 units.

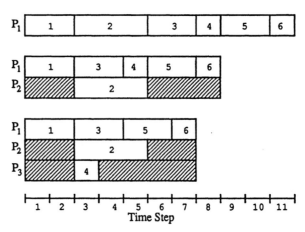

Figure 17.8. Schedules with $p = 1, 2, 3$ processors for an example task graph with nonuniform running times.

The schedules derived above for $p = 2$ and $p = 3$ processors are depicted in Fig. 17.6, along with a single-processor schedule for reference. Both schedules happen to be optimal, though list scheduling does not guarantee this outcome in all cases.

Figures 17.7 and 17.8 show a task graph with nonuniform running times and the resulting schedules for one, two, or three processors. Derivation of the schedules is left as an exercise.

More general versions of list scheduling, as well as other sophisticated scheduling algorithms may take communication delays, deadlines, release times, resource requirements, processor capabilities, and other factors into account. Because most scheduling algorithms do not guarantee optimal running times anyway, a balance must be struck between the complexity of the scheduler and its performance in terms of the total schedule length achieved. The simplicity of the scheduler is particularly important with on-line or run-time scheduling, where the scheduling algorithm must run on the parallel system itself, thus using time and other resources like the tasks being scheduled. With *off-line* or compile-time scheduling, the running time of the scheduler is less of an issue.

If timing parameters, such as task deadlines and release times, are considered in making scheduling decisions, we have a *real-time* scheduling problem or scheduler. Example scheduling strategies for real-time tasks include "nearest-deadline first" or "least-laxity first," where the *laxity* of a task with deadline d and execution time e at current time t is defined as $d - t - e$. When the possibility of failure for processors and other resources is considered in task assignment or reassignment, we have *fault-tolerant* scheduling.

17.5. SOME USEFUL BOUNDS FOR SCHEDULING

Section 17.4 reported the bad news that task scheduling is a difficult problem and that optimal scheduling algorithms are either nonexistent or hard to come by for most cases of practical interest. Now, it's time for some good news!

Let T_p be the execution time of a task graph, with unit-time nodes, when using p processors and a particular scheduling algorithm. T_1 is the number of nodes in the task graph and T_∞ is its depth. The following inequalities are easily derived, where c is an arbitrary integer constant, l is the number of input nodes, and f is the maximum node in-degree or fan-in:

$$\log_f l \leq T_\infty \leq T_p \leq T_1$$

$$T_p \leq cT_{cxp}$$

Less obvious is the following result, known as *Brent's scheduling theorem*:

$$T_p < T_\infty + T_1/p$$

The proof of this result is based on constructing a p-processor schedule whose running time is strictly less than $T_\infty + T_1/p$ in the worst case. First assume the availability of an unlimited number of processors and schedule each node at the earliest possible time. Let there be n_t nodes scheduled at time t. Clearly, $\Sigma_t \, n_t = T_1$. With only p processors, the tasks scheduled for time step t can be executed in $\lceil n_t/p \rceil$ steps by running them p at a time. Thus,

$$T_p \leq \Sigma_{t=1}^{T_\infty} \lceil n_t/p \rceil < \Sigma_{t=1}^{T_\infty} (n_t/p + 1)$$

Expanding the summation on the right-hand side above yields

$$T_p < (1/p)\Sigma_{t=1}^{T_\infty} n_t + T_\infty = T_1/p + T_\infty$$

Note that Brent's scheduling theorem offers the following upper bound for the speed-up:

$$\text{Speed-up} \leq \; = \frac{T_1}{T_\infty + T_1/p} = \frac{p}{1 + pT_\infty/T_1}$$

This can be viewed as a generalized form of Amdahl's law. A large value for T_∞/T_1 is an indication that the task has a great deal of sequential dependencies, which limits the speed-up to at most T_1/T_∞ with any number of processors. A small value for T_∞/T_1 allows us to approach the ideal speed-up of p with p processors.

The promised good news are derived as corollaries to Brent's scheduling theorem. The first "good-news" corollary is obtained by observing that for $p \geq T_1/T_\infty$, we have $T_1/p \leq T_\infty$. This inequality, along with $T_\infty \leq T_p$ and $T_p < T_1/p + T_\infty$, leads to

$$T_\infty \leq T_p < 2T_\infty \qquad \text{for } p \geq T_1/T_\infty$$

What the above inequalities suggest is that we can come within a factor of 2 of the best running time possible, even with a very simple scheduling algorithm, provided that a suitably large number of processors is available.

From Figs. 17.6 and 17.8, we observe that using too many processors to execute a task system that exhibits limited parallelism is wasteful in that processing resources may remain idle for extended periods. The second "good-news" corollary to Brent's scheduling theorem is obtained by observing that for $p \leq T_1/T_\infty$, we have $T_\infty \leq T_1/p$, leading to

$$T_1/p \leq T_p < 2T_1/p \qquad \text{for } p \leq T_1/T_\infty$$

Here, the interpretation is that we can come within a factor of 2 of the ideal speed-up if we do not use too many processors.

Combining the above two pieces of good news, we can achieve linear or $\Theta(p)$ speed-up, along with near-minimal $\Theta(T_\infty)$ running time and optimal $\Theta(1)$ efficiency, by using roughly T_1/T_∞ processors to execute a task system of depth T_∞ composed of T_1 unit-time tasks. Thus, as long as we can control the number of processors that are applied to a given parallel task system, we can obtain near-optimal results. The architectural implication of the above observations is that the user must be allowed to choose the number of processors that would run his or her application most efficiently; hence, the need for partitionable parallel computers that can run several tasks on different subsets of processors (e.g., subcubes, submeshes, subtrees).

17.6. LOAD BALANCING AND DATAFLOW SYSTEMS

One approach to scheduling a task graph is to initially distribute the tasks among the available processors, based on some criteria, and then let each processor do its own internal scheduling (ordering the execution of its set of tasks) according to interdependencies of tasks and the results received from other processors. The advantage of this approach is that most scheduling decisions are performed in a distributed manner. A possible drawback is that the results may be far from optimal. However, if such a scheme is combined with a method for redistributing the tasks when the initial distribution proves to be inappropriate, good results may be achieved.

Suppose the tasks are distributed to processors in such a way that the total expected running times of the tasks assigned to each processor are roughly the same. Because task running times are not constants, a processor may run out of things to do before other processors complete their assigned tasks. Also, some processors may remain idle for long periods of time as they wait for prerequisite tasks on other processors to be executed. In these cases, a *load balancing* policy may be applied in an attempt to make the load distribution more uniform. As we learn about the actual execution times and interdependencies of the tasks at run time, we may switch as yet unexecuted tasks from an overloaded processor to a less loaded one. Load balancing can be initiated by an idle or lightly loaded processor (receiver-initiated) or by an overburdened processor (sender-initiated).

Unfortunately, load balancing may involve a great deal of overhead that reduces the potential gains. If moving a task from one processor to another means copying a large program with huge amounts of data and then updating various status tables to indicate the new location of the task (for the benefit of other processors that may need the results of the moved task), then communication overhead is significant and load balancing may not be worth its cost. At the other extreme, if the tasks belong to a standard set of tasks, each of which is invoked with a small set of parameters (data) and with copies already available locally to every processor, then moving the tasks may involve only a small broadcast message to pass the parameters and update the system status tables. In this case, the load balancing overhead will be minimal.

In circuit-switched networks that use wormhole routing, the load balancing problem can be formulated as a network flow problem and thus solved using available methods and algorithms for the latter problem [Bokh93]. The excess (deficiency) of work load at some nodes may be viewed as flow sources (sinks) and the requirement is to allow the excess work load to "flow" from sources to sinks via paths that are, to the extent possible, disjoint and thus free from conflicts.

The ultimate in automatic load-balancing is a self-scheduling system that tries to keep all processing resources running at maximum efficiency. There may be a central location or authority to which processors refer for work and where they return their results. An idle processor requests that it be assigned new work by sending a message to this central supervisor and in return receives one or more tasks to perform. This works nicely for tasks with small contexts and/or relatively long running times. If the central location is consulted too often, or if it has to send (receive) large volumes of data to (from) processors, it can become a bottleneck.

A hardware-level implementation of such a self-scheduling scheme, known as *dataflow computing*, has a long history. A dataflow computation is characterized by a dataflow graph, which is very similar to the task graphs of Section 17.4, but may contain decision elements and loops. We will limit our discussion to decision-free and loop-free dataflow graphs. Figure 17.9 depicts an example that is very similar to the task graph of Fig. 17.7. Tokens, shown in the form of heavy dots, are used to keep track of the availability of data. Initially only the primary inputs carry tokens (data values). Once tokens appear on all inputs of a node, the node is enabled or "fired," resulting in tokens to be removed from its inputs and placed on each of its outputs. If an edge is restricted to carry no more than one token, we have a *static dataflow* system. If multiple tagged tokens can appear on the edges and are "consumed" after matching their tags, we have a *dynamic dataflow* system that allows computations to be pipelined but implies greater overhead as a result of the requirement for matching of the token tags.

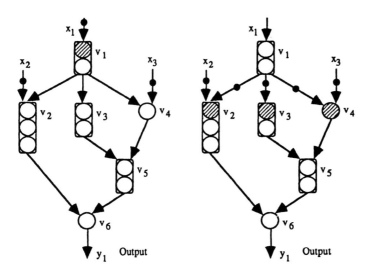

Figure 17.9. Example dataflow graph with token distribution at the outset (left) and after two time units (right).

Hardware implementation of dataflow systems with fine-grain computations (one or a few machine instructions per node), though feasible, has proven impractical [Lee94]. However, when each node or task is a computation thread consisting of longer sequences of machine instructions, then the activation overhead is less serious and the concept becomes quite practical. We will discuss the notion of *multithreading*, and its implications for tolerating or hiding the memory access latency in parallel computers, in Section 18.3.

PROBLEMS

17.1. Emulation through graph embedding
  In Section 17.1, we saw an example of embedding that led to emulation with the maximum slowdown of dilation × congestion × load factor. This example is extreme in that it involves an unrealistic parallel architecture being emulated by a very small (two-node) system.
  a. Show that the bound can be equaled or approached in more realistic examples as well.
  b. Consider embeddings of target systems into host systems with dilation 1. Under what conditions can the slowdown for the corresponding emulation become the larger of congestion and load factor rather than their product?
  c. Provide a complete example that exhibits the slowdown of part (b).

17.2. Emulation through graph embedding
  Suppose that an n_T-node, e_T-edge, degree-d_T target graph, with diameter D_T and bisection width B_T, is to be embedded into a host graph with corresponding parameters n_H, e_H, d_H, D_H, B_H. Can you derive bounds on the dilation, congestion, and load factor of the embedding, given only the above information?

17.3. Regular graphs
  Prove or disprove: If G is a regular degree-d, p-node undirected graph with no self-loop (edge from one node to itself), then either p or d must be even. What happens to the above result if G is a regular directed graph with in-degree and out-degree of d?

17.4. Graph embedding
  Which of the following embeddings is possible? Why (not)?
  a. Dilation-1 embedding of the hex-mesh of Fig. 12.2 into a hypercube of at most twice its size.
  b. Congestion-2 embedding of the eight-neighbor mesh (Fig. 12.2) into a mesh of the same size.
  c. Dilation-1 embedding of the 2^q-node shuffle–exchange network (Fig. 15.18) into the q-cube.
  d. Congestion-1 embedding of a 2^q-node Möbius cube (Fig. 15.21) into the q-cube.
  e. Dilation-1 embedding of a star graph (Fig. 16.3) into a hypercube of at most twice its size.
  f. Constant-dilation embedding of the mesh-connected trees into the mesh of trees (Fig. 16.11).

17.5. Graph embedding
  Scheduling of a task graph, with unit-time tasks, on a parallel system (specified in terms of a directed graph) can also be viewed as a graph embedding problem. Describe the significance of dilation, congestion, and load factor in this context.

17.6. PRAM emulation of a degree-d network

 a. The emulation of a degree-d network by PRAM suggested in Section 17.1 requires pd buffers in shared memory (two per bidirectional link). Can the perfect-matching result of Section 17.1 be used to reduce the number of buffers to p?
 b. A degree-d architecture is restricted to single-port communication, i.e., a processor can send/receive a message to/from at most one neighbor in each step. Can the PRAM emulation of this architecture be speeded up to require $O(1)$ rather than $O(d)$ slowdown?
 c. Suppose that we want to emulate a hypergraph with maximum node degree d (in a hypergraph, an edge can connect more than two nodes). What is the worst-case slowdown factor if the emulation is done by the EREW PRAM?
 d. Either prove, by constructing a worst-case example, that the upper bound of part (c) is tight or try to improve your bound.

17.7. Butterfly emulation of a degree-d network

 a. Prove the existence of a perfect matching in any $p \times p$ bipartite graph with uniform node degree d (Section 17.1).
 b. State and prove a more general result relating to the emulation of an architecture characterized by a directed graph with maximum node in- and out-degrees of d_{in} and d_{out}, respectively, on a butterfly network.

17.8. Distributed shared memory
 Show that in each of the following two cases, the butterfly network can emulate the PRAM with worst-case $O(\log p)$ slowdown and no data replication.

 a. The number m of shared-memory locations and the number p of processors satisfy $m = O(p)$.
 b. The m memory locations are divided into $O(p)$ banks. Shared data structures and memory accesses are organized so that no two processors ever need to access the same memory bank.

17.9. Optimal scheduling

 a. Show that the list scheduling algorithm of Section 17.4 yields an optimal schedule for $p = 1$.
 b. It was mentioned in Section 17.3 that a task graph with unit-time tasks can be optimally scheduled on two processors using a deterministic polynomial-time algorithm. Show that the list scheduling algorithm discussed in Section 17.4 is such an algorithm.
 c. Provide an example to show that the list scheduling algorithm of Section 17.4 is not optimal for three processors.
 d. Provide an example to show that the list scheduling algorithm of Section 17.4 is not optimal for two processors if task execution times are one or two units.
 e. It has been argued that replacing a task with running time of k units with a chain of k unit-time tasks converts the scheduling problem of part (d) to one with unit-time tasks that can be optimally solved by a list scheduler per the result of part (b). What is wrong with this argument?

17.10. List scheduling
 Let us call the task graph of Fig. 17.5 with unit-time tasks "version U" of the task graph. We saw that the list scheduling algorithm introduced in Section 17.4 is optimal for this version U. Define version E/O of the task graph as one in which all odd-numbered tasks are unit-time but even-numbered tasks take twice as long.

a. Is the list scheduling algorithm of Section 17.4 optimal for version E/O with $p = 2$?
b. Repeat part (a) with $p = 3$.

17.11. List scheduling
Modify the list scheduling algorithm of Section 17.4 so that the *slack* of each task, i.e., the difference between its latest possible execution time (to meet the minimum T_∞ running time) and its earliest possible execution time in view of task interdependencies, is used for assigning priorities. Apply the modified algorithm to both examples of Section 17.4 and discuss.

17.12. Amdahl's law
Consider a task graph that begins with one input node of running time $f/2$, then branches out into a very large number m of parallel nodes of running time $(1 - f)/m$ each, and finally converges into a single output node of running time $f/2$. Assume that $m \gg p$.

a. Show that Brent's scheduling theorem applied to this task graph yields Amdahl's law.
b. Formulate the "good-news" corollaries, discussed near the end of Section 17.5, for this case.

17.13. Brent's scheduling theorem

a. Show that the scheduling algorithm implicitly defined in the proof of Brent's scheduling theorem does not yield an optimal schedule for the task graph of Fig. 17.5 with $p = 2$.
b. Construct a T_1-node task graph, with unit-time tasks, that can be scheduled in $\lceil T_1/2 \rceil$ time steps with $p = 2$ but that leads to a $\lceil 3T_1/4 \rceil$-step schedule using the algorithm of part (a). *Hint:* The graph must contain many nodes that can be scheduled at virtually any time before the final node is to be executed but that are scheduled very early by the above algorithm.

17.14. Real-time scheduling
Real-time scheduling was very briefly discussed at the end of Section 17.4, where the "nearest-deadline first" (NDF) and "least-laxity first" (LLF) scheduling policies were introduced.

a. Show that with unit-time tasks, the NDF scheduling policy is optimal in that if the task graph can be scheduled to meet all deadlines, it can be scheduled using the NDF policy.
b. Show that the NDF scheduling policy is not optimal with non-unit-time tasks.
c. Show that the LLF scheduling policy is optimal with unit-time or non-unit-time tasks.

17.15. Load balancing by data redistribution
Load balancing may sometimes be required as a result of processor failures rather than unpredictable execution times. Study the implications of various data redistribution schemes in iterative matrix computations in which matrix elements are recomputed based on the values in a small neighborhood around them [Uyar88].

17.16. Dataflow computation

a. Draw a dataflow graph for computing the roots of the quadratic equation $ax^2 + bx + c = 0$.
b. Derive schedules for executing this computation with one, two, or three arithmetic units, assuming that each arithmetic operation is a unit-time task. Ignore the control overhead.
c. Repeat part (b), this time assuming that addition, multiplication/squaring, and division/square-rooting take one, three, and seven time units, respectively.
d. Modify your dataflow graph to yield minimal execution time with the assumptions of part (c).

REFERENCES AND SUGGESTED READING

[Adve96]   Adve, S. V., and K. Gharachorloo, "Shared Memory Consistency Models: A Tutorial," *IEEE Computer*, Vol. 29, No. 12, pp. 66–76, December 1996.

[Bert89]   Bertsekas, D. P., and J. N. Tsitsiklis, *Parallel and Distributed Computation: Numerical Methods*, Prentice–Hall, 1989.

[Bokh93]   Bokhari, S. H., "A Network Flow Model for Load Balancing in Circuit-Switched Multicomputers," *IEEE Trans. Parallel Distributed Systems*, Vol. 4, No. 6, pp. 649–657, June 1993.

[ElRe95]   El-Rewini, H., H. H. Ali, and T. Lewis, "Task Scheduling in Multiprocessing Systems," *IEEE Computer*, Vol. 28, No. 12, pp. 27–37, December 1995.

[Harr94]   Harris, T. J., "A Survey of PRAM Simulation Techniques," *ACM Computing Surveys*, Vol. 26, No. 2, pp. 187–206, June 1994.

[Lee94]   Lee, B., and A. R. Hurson, "Dataflow Architectures and Multithreading," *IEEE Computer*, Vol. 27, No. 8, pp. 27–39, August 1994.

[Leig92]   Leighton, F. T., *Introduction to Parallel Algorithms and Architectures: Arrays, Trees, Hypercubes*, Morgan Kaufmann, 1992.

[Prot96]   Protic, J., M. Tomacevic, and V. Milutinovic, "Distributed Shared Memory: Concepts and Systems," *IEEE Parallel & Distributed Technology*, Vol. 4, No. 2, pp. 63–79, Summer 1996.

[Rabi89]   Rabin, M., "Efficient Dispersal of Information for Security, Load Balancing, and Fault Tolerance," *J. ACM*, Vol. 36, No. 2, pp. 335–348, April 1989.

[Stan95]   Stankovic, J. A., M. Spuri, M. Di Natale, and G. C. Buttazzo, "Implications of Classical Scheduling Results for Real-Time Systems," *IEEE Computer*, Vol. 28, No. 6, pp. 16–25, June 1995.

[Upfa87]   Upfal, E., and A. Wigderson, "How to Share Memory in a Distributed System," *J. ACM*, Vol. 34, No. 1, pp. 116–127, January 1987.

[Uyar88]   Uyar, M. U., and A. P. Reeves, "Dynamic Fault Reconfiguration in a Mesh-Connected MIMD Environment," *IEEE Trans. Computers*, Vol. 37, pp. 1191–1205, October 1988.

18

Data Storage, Input, and Output

When discussing the implementation aspects of shared-memory machines in Section 6.6, we learned of the importance of proper data distribution within memory banks to allow conflict-free parallel access to required data elements by multiple processors. In this chapter, we elaborate further on the problem of data distribution in parallel systems, particularly of the distributed-memory variety. In particular, we study two complementary approaches to the memory latency problem: latency tolerance/hiding and data caching. Additionally, we deal with data input and output explicitly. Thus far, we have conveniently ignored the I/O problem, assuming, in effect, that the needed data fit in the local memories of participating processors or that the right data are recognized magically and made memory-resident before they are first accessed. Chapter topics are:

- 18.1. Data access problems and caching
- 18.2. Cache coherence protocols
- 18.3. Multithreading and latency hiding
- 18.4. Parallel I/O technology
- 18.5. Redundant disk arrays
- 18.6. Interfaces and standards

18.1. DATA ACCESS PROBLEMS AND CACHING

Memory access latency is a major performance hindrance in parallel systems. Even in sequential processors, the gap between processor and memory speeds has created difficult design issues for computer architects, necessitating pipelined memory access and multiple levels of cache memories to bridge the gap. In vector processors, the mismatch between processor and memory speeds is made tolerable through the provision of vector registers (that can be loaded/stored as computations continue with data in other registers) and pipeline chaining, allowing intermediate results to be forwarded between function units without first being stored in memory or even in registers.

Parallel processing aggravates this speed gap. In a shared-memory system, the memory access mechanism is much more complicated, and thus slower, than in uniprocessors. In distributed-memory machines, severe speed penalties are associated with access to nonlocal data. In both cases, three complementary approaches are available to mediate the problem:

1. Distributing the data so that each item is located where it is needed most. This involves an initial assignment and periodic redistribution as conditions change.
2. Automatically bringing the most useful, and thus most frequently accessed, data into local memory whenever possible. This is known as *data caching*.
3. Making the processors' computational throughput relatively insensitive to the memory access latency. This is referred to as *latency tolerance* or *latency hiding*.

These methods may be used in combination to achieve the best results. For example, with caching, we may still need latency tolerance in cases where the required data are not found in the cache. Option 1, or judicious distribution of data, is possible in applications where the data sets and their scopes of relevance are static or change rather slowly. Some of the issues discussed in Section 6.6 are relevant here. We will discuss Option 3, or latency tolerance/hiding methods, in Section 18.3. In the remainder of this section, we introduce some notions relating to Option 2 to facilitate our discussion of cache coherence protocols in Section 18.2. This review is by necessity brief. Interested readers can consult Patterson and Hennessy [Patt96], pp. 375–427, for an in-depth discussion.

A cache is any fast memory that is used to store useful or frequently used data. A *processor cache*, e.g., is a very fast (usually static RAM) memory unit holding the instructions and data that were recently accessed by the processor or that are likely to be needed in the near future. A *Level-2 cache* is somewhat slower than a processor cache, but still faster than the high-capacity dynamic RAM main memory. A *disk cache* or *file cache* is usually a portion of main memory that is set aside to hold blocks of data from the secondary memory. This allows multiple records or pages to be read and/or updated with a single disk access, which is extremely slow compared with processor or even main memory speeds.

To access a required data word, the cache is consulted first. Finding the required data in the cache is referred to as a *cache hit*; not finding it is a *cache miss*. An important parameter in evaluating the effectiveness of cache memories of any type is the *hit rate*, defined as the fraction of data accesses that can be satisfied from the cache as opposed to the slower memory that sits beyond it. A hit rate of 95%, e.g., means that only 1 in 20 accesses, on the average, will not find the required data in the cache. With a hit rate r, cache access cycle of C_{fast}, and slower memory access cycle of C_{slow}, the effective memory cycle time is

$$C_{eff} = C_{fast} + (1 - r)C_{slow}$$

This equation is derived with the assumption that when data are not found in the cache, they must first be brought into the cache (in C_{slow} time) and then accessed from the cache (in C_{fast} time). Simultaneous forwarding of data from the slow memory to both the processor and the cache reduces the effective delay somewhat, but the above simple formula is adequate for our purposes. We see that when r is close to 1, an effective memory cycle close to C_{fast} is achieved. Therefore, the cache provides the illusion that the entire memory space consists of fast memory.

In typical microprocessors, accessing the cache memory is part of the instruction execution cycle. As long as the required data are in the cache, instruction execution continues at full speed. When a cache miss occurs and the slower memory must be accessed, instruction execution is interrupted. The cache miss penalty is usually specified in terms of the number of clock cycles that will be wasted because the processor has to stall until the data become available. In a microprocessor that executes an average of one instruction per clock cycle when there is no cache miss, a cache miss penalty of four cycles means that four cycles of delay will be added to the instruction execution time. Given a hit rate of 95%, the effective instruction execution delay will be $1 + 0.05 \times 4 = 1.2$ cycles per instruction (CPI).

A cache memory is characterized by several design parameters that influence its implementation cost and performance (hit rate). In the following description, we limit our attention to a processor cache that is located between the central processor and main memory, i.e., we assume that there is no Level-2 cache. Similar considerations apply to other types of caches. The most important cache parameters are

1. *Cache size* in bytes or words. A larger cache can hold more of the program's useful data but is more costly and likely to be slower.

2. *Block* or *cache-line size*, defined as the unit of data transfer between the cache and main memory. With a larger cache line, more data are brought into the cache with each miss. This can improve the hit rate but also tends to tie up parts of the cache with data of lesser value.

3. *Placement policy* determining where an incoming cache line can be stored. More flexible policies imply higher hardware cost and may or may not have performance benefits in view of their more complex, and thus slower, process for locating the required data in the cache.

4. *Replacement policy* determining which of several existing cache blocks (into which a new cache line can be mapped) should be overwritten. Typical policies include choosing a random block or the least recently used block.

5. *Write policy* determining if updates to cache words are immediately forwarded to the main memory (*write-through* policy) or modified cache blocks are copied back to main memory in their entirety if and when they must be replaced in the cache (*write-back* or *copy-back* policy).

The most commonly used placement policy for processor caches is the *set-associative* method, which, at the extreme of single-block sets, degenerates into a *direct-mapped* cache. The read operation from a set-associative cache with a set size of $s = 2$ is depicted in Fig. 18.1. The memory address supplied by the processor is composed of tag and index parts.

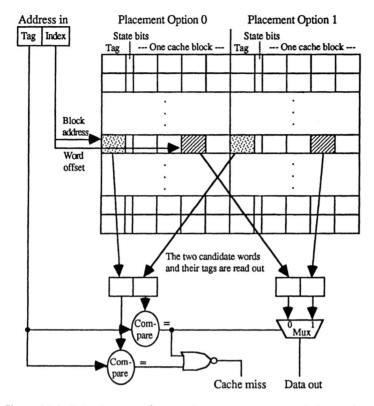

Figure 18.1. Data storage and access in a two-way set-associative cache.

The index part, itself consisting of a block address and word offset within the block, identifies a set of s cache words that can potentially hold the required data, while the tag specifies one of the many cache lines in the address space that map into the same set of s cache blocks by the set-associative placement policy. For each memory access, all s candidate words, along with the tags associated with their respective blocks, are read out. The s tags are then simultaneously compared with the desired tag, resulting in two possible outcomes:

1. None of the stored tags matches the desired tag. The data parts are ignored and a cache miss signal is asserted in order to initiate block transfer from main memory.
2. The ith stored tag, which corresponds to the placement option i ($0 \le i < s$), matches the desired tag. The word read out from the block corresponding to the ith placement option is chosen as the data output.

As a practical matter, each cache block may have a *valid bit* that indicates whether or not it holds valid data. This valid bit is also read out along with the tag and is ANDed with the comparison result to indicate a match with valid data. A block of a write-back cache may also have a *dirty bit* that is set to 1 with every write update to the block and is used at the time of block replacement to decide if a block to be overwritten needs to be copied back into main memory.

18.2. CACHE COHERENCE PROTOCOLS

As briefly discussed in Section 4.3, placement of shared data into the cache memories of multiple processors creates the possibility of the multiple copies becoming inconsistent. If caching of shared modifiable data is to be allowed, hardware provisions for enforcing cache coherence are needed. There exist many cache coherence protocols that share some fundamental properties but that differ in implementation details. The differences typically result from attempts to optimize the protocols for particular hardware platforms and/or application environments. In what follows, we will review two representative examples, one from the class of snoopy protocols and another from the class of directory-based schemes.

Figure 18.2 shows four data blocks w, x, y, and z in the shared memory of a parallel processor along with some copies in the processor caches. The primed values y' and z' represent modified or updated versions of blocks y and z, respectively. The state of a data block being cached can be one of the following:

- *Multiple-consistent.* Several caches contain copies of w; the cache copies are consistent with each other and with the copy of w in the main memory.
- *Single-consistent.* Only one cache contains a copy of x and that copy is consistent with the copy in the main memory.
- *Single-inconsistent.* Only one cache contains a copy of y which has been modified and is thus different from the copy in main memory.
- *Invalid.* A cache contains an invalid copy of z; the reason for this invalidity is that z has been modified in a different cache which is now holding a single consistent copy.

Clearly, we want to avoid having multiple inconsistent cache copies. For this reason, when there are multiple cache copies and one of the copies is updated, we must either invalidate all other cache copies (*write-invalidate* policy) or else modify all of these copies as well (*write-update* policy).

Snoopy cache coherence protocols are so named because they require that all caches "snoop" on the activities of other caches, typically by monitoring the transactions on a bus,

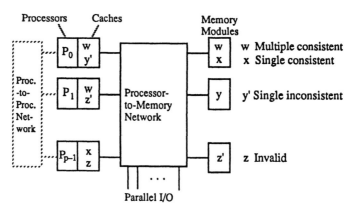

Figure 18.2. Various types of cached data blocks in a parallel processor with global memory and processor caches.

to determine if the data that they hold will be affected. Several implementations of snoopy protocols can be found in bus-based shared-memory multiprocessors, including machines in the Sequent Symmetry series which use two-way set-associative caches.

A bus-based write-invalidate write-back snoopy cache coherence protocol can be implemented by a simple finite-state control mechanism within each participating cache (Fig. 18.3). For simplicity, we do not distinguish between the single-consistent and multiple-consistent states discussed above and collectively refer to them as the *shared* state (top right of Fig. 18.3) where the processors can freely read data from the block but have to change the block's state to *exclusive* before they can write into it (top left of Fig. 18.3). The shared and exclusive states might have been called *valid clean* and *valid dirty*, respectively.

The state transitions in Fig. 18.3 are explained next. Each transition is labeled with the event that triggers it, followed by the action(s) that must be taken (if any). Possible events are CPU read/write requests, a cache hit or miss, and read/write miss notifications from other caches as observed on the bus. Possible actions are putting a read or write miss notification on the bus and writing back the block into main memory.

1. *CPU read hit.* A shared block remains shared; an exclusive block remains exclusive.
2. *CPU read miss.* A block is selected for replacement; if the block to be overwritten is invalid or shared, then "read miss" is put on the bus; if it is exclusive, it will have to be written back into main memory. In all cases, the new state of the block is "shared."
3. *CPU write hit.* An exclusive block remains exclusive; a shared block becomes exclusive and a "write miss" is put on the bus so that other copies of the block are invalidated.
4. *CPU write miss.* A block is selected for replacement; if the block to be overwritten is invalid or shared, then "write miss" is put on the bus; if it is exclusive, it will have to be written back into main memory. In all cases, the new state of the block is "exclusive."
5. *Bus read miss.* This is only relevant if the block is exclusive, in which case the block must be written back to main memory. The two copies of the block will then be

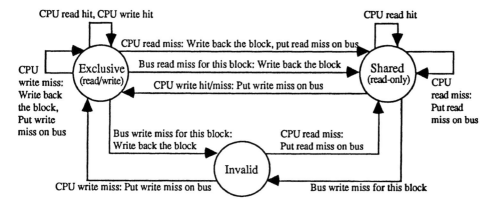

Figure 18.3. Finite-state control mechanism for a bus-based snoopy cache coherence protocol.

consistent with each other and with the copy in main memory; hence the new state will be "shared."

6. *Bus write miss.* If the block is exclusive, it must be written back into main memory; in any case, the new state of the block becomes "invalid."

In a directory-based coherence protocol, a centralized or distributed directory is used to maintain data on the whereabouts of the various cache line copies and on the relationship of those copies. There are two finite-state control mechanisms, one for the individual cache blocks and one for directory entry representing all of the copies of the cache block. The finite-state control for individual cache blocks is quite similar to that shown in Fig. 18.3, except that interaction with other caches is accomplished through messages sent to, and received from, the directory rather than by monitoring the bus. We leave the required modifications to the state diagram of Fig. 18.3 to make it correspond to a directory-based scheme as an exercise for the reader.

The directory entry corresponding to a cache block contains information on the current state of the block and its cache copies, as described below. The directory receives messages from various cache units regarding particular blocks and in response, updates the block's state and, if required by the protocol, sends messages to other caches that may hold copies of that block. Figure 18.4 depicts the state transition diagram for a directory entry. The three states of a data block, from the viewpoint of the directory, are *uncached* (no cache holds a copy), *shared* (read-only), and *exclusive* (read/write). When in the exclusive state, a data block is viewed as being "owned" by the single cache that holds a copy of the block. In this state, the main memory copy of the block is not up-to-date. Thus, to overwrite the block, the owner must perform a write-back operation.

The state transitions in Fig. 18.4 are explained next. Each transition is labeled with the type of message that triggers it, followed by the action(s) taken. Possible messages arriving at a directory are read miss, write miss, and data write-back. Possible actions are sending data to a requesting cache, fetching data from another cache, requesting invalidation in another cache, and updating the sharing set (list of caches that hold a copy of the block).

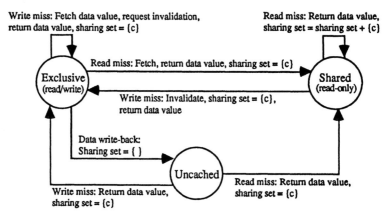

Figure 18.4. States and transitions for a directory entry in a directory-based coherence protocol (c denotes the cache sending the message).

1. *Read miss.* For a shared block, its data value is sent to the requesting cache unit, and the new cache is added to the sharing set. For an exclusive block, a fetch message is sent to the owner cache unit, the data are returned to the requesting cache, and the new cache is included in the sharing set. For an uncached block, the data value is returned to the requesting cache, which now forms the singleton sharing set. The block remains or becomes "shared."

2. *Write miss.* For a shared block, an invalidate message is sent to member caches of the sharing set, a new singleton sharing set consisting of the requesting cache is built, and the data value is returned to the requesting cache unit. For an exclusive block, a message is sent to the old owner to fetch the data and to invalidate the existing copy. The requesting cache becomes the new owner and thus the only member of the sharing set. For an uncached block, the data value is returned to the requesting cache which is now the block's owner. The block remains or becomes "exclusive."

3. *Data write-back.* This can only occur for an exclusive block. The sharing set is emptied and the block becomes "uncached."

The sharing set can be implemented in different ways. In the *full-map* approach, a bit-vector, containing 1 bit for each cache unit, indicates the cache that owns the block or all of the caches that hold read-only copies. This is quite efficient when the number of caches is small and fixed. A more flexible approach, typically used in distributed directories, is to use a singly or doubly linked list, with each directory holding a pointer to the next/previous directory that has a copy of the block. Notifications are then done by a chain of messages forwarded along the list from each directory to the next in sequence.

18.3. MULTITHREADING AND LATENCY HIDING

The emulation of a $2^q q$-processor PRAM on a 2^q-processor distributed-memory system, with its processors interconnected via a butterfly network (Section 17.2), is an example of methods for hiding the remote memory access latency in a NUMA parallel processor. The general idea of *latency hiding* methods is to provide each processor with some useful work to do as it waits for remote memory access requests to be satisfied. In the ideal extreme, latency hiding allows communications to be completely overlapped with computation, leading to high efficiency and hardware utilization.

Multithreading is a practical mechanism for latency hiding (Fig. 18.5). A multithreaded computation typically starts with a sequential thread, followed by some supervisory overhead to set up (schedule) various independent threads, followed by computation and communication (remote accesses) for individual threads, and concluded by a synchronization step to terminate the threads prior to starting the next unit of parallel work. Thread computations and remote accesses are separated in Fig. 18.5 for clarity, but they can be interleaved.

When in between the two shaded boxes in Fig. 18.5, a processor is working on a thread and the thread requires a remote memory access before it can continue, the processor places the thread in a wait queue and switches to a different thread. This switching of context in the processor involves some overhead which must be considerably less than the remote access latency for the scheme to be efficient. A processor for multithreaded computation is thus

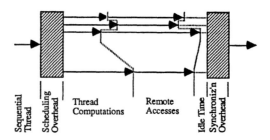

Figure 18.5. The concept of multithreaded parallel computation.

likely to have multiple register sets, one per active thread, in order to minimize the context switching overhead. The higher the remote memory access delay, the larger is the number of threads required to successfully hide the latency. At some point in its computation, the newly activated thread may require a remote memory access. Thus, another context switch occurs, and so on.

The access requests of the threads that are in the wait state may be completed out of order because, e.g., they involve accesses to memory modules at different network distances or are routed through paths with varying congestions. It is thus common to tag each access request with a unique thread identifier so that when the result is returned, the processor knows which of the waiting threads should be activated. Thread identifiers are sometimes called *continuations*. The Tera MTA parallel computer system (see Section 21.4) has hardware support for 10-bit continuations, thus allowing up to 1024 threads awaiting remote memory accesses.

Note that application of multithreading is not restricted to a parallel processing environment but offers advantages even on a uniprocessor. A uniprocessor that is provided with multiple independent threads to execute, can switch among them on each cache miss, on every load, after each instruction, or after each fixed-size block of instructions, for improved performance. The processor may need multiple register sets (to reduce the context switching overhead) and a larger cache memory (to hold recently referenced data for several threads), but the benefits can outweigh the costs. Hirata et al. [Hira92] report speed-ups of 2.0, 3.7, and 5.8 in a processor that has nine functional units and executes two, four, and eight independent threads, respectively.

It is interesting to note that a form of (redundant) parallel processing has been suggested, and shown to be beneficial, in closing the gap between computation speed and off-chip memory access latency. In data-scalar computation [Burg97], which is in a sense the opposite of data-parallel or SIMD-type parallel processing, multiple copies of the same program are run on several nodes, each of which holds a fraction of the program's address space. Each write is performed locally by one of the processors and thus involves no off-chip communication. When a processor needs to read data from a nonlocal memory address, it simply idles until the required data word arrives. When read access to local memory is performed, the data that are read out are also broadcast to all other processors that have already encountered the same access, or will do so shortly. The elimination of off-chip writes, as well as read requests, can lead to speed gains of up to 50% with two processors and up to 100% with four processors [Burg97].

18.4. PARALLEL I/O TECHNOLOGY

An important requirement for highly parallel systems is the provision of high-bandwidth I/O capability. For some data-intensive applications, the high processing power of a massively parallel system is not of much value unless the I/O subsystem can keep up with the processors. A problem that illustrates the need for high-speed I/O is that of detecting faint radio pulsars whose solution involves an FFT computation of 8 to 64 billion points. Solving this problem requires an I/O throughput of at least 1 billion bytes per second (1 GB/s) [Thak96].

Some architectures can be easily augmented to incorporate I/O capabilities. For example, the unused links at the boundary of a 2D or 3D mesh can be assigned for I/O functions. In our treatment of 2D mesh algorithms (Chapters 9–12), we specified I/O explicitly in some cases, while for others, we assumed implicit I/O by identifying which data are to be held by each processor as the algorithm is executed. In a hypercube, each node may be provided with an extra port for I/O, with these ports connected directly, via a smaller number of I/O buses, or through a more complex switching mechanism, to several high-speed I/O controllers. In addition to providing access paths to I/O, one needs high-bandwidth devices that can supply the parallel machine with huge amounts of data at the required rate. Over the years, various solutions to the parallel I/O problem have been proposed and studied.

Before discussing parallel I/O, it is instructive to review modern magnetic disk technology, which forms the cornerstone of fast I/O on most computers. Figure 18.6 shows a *multiple-platter* high-capacity magnetic disk. Each platter has two *recording surfaces* and a *read/write head* mounted on an *arm*. The access arms are attached to an *actuator* that can move the heads radially in order to align them with a desired *cylinder* (i.e., a set of *tracks*, one per recording surface). A *sector* or *disk block* is part of a track that forms the unit of data transfer to/from the disk. Access to a block of data on disk typically consists of three phases:

1. *Cylinder seek:* moving the heads to the desired cylinder (seek time)
2. *Sector alignment:* waiting until the desired sector is under the head (rotational latency)
3. *Data transfer:* reading the bytes out as they pass under the head (transfer time)

Of course, when accessing consecutive or nearby blocks because of data locality, the overhead of a random seek and average rotational latency of one-half disk revolution (each being on the order of several milliseconds) is not paid for each block.

Here are the density data for a vintage 1994 disk drive [Chen94]:

2627	×	21	×	99	×	512	≈	2.8 GB
Cylinders		Tracks/cylinder		Sectors/track		Bytes/sector		

The above disk uses 5.25-inch platters, with full rotation time of 11.1 ms, minimum (single-cylinder) seek time of 1.7 ms, maximum (full-stroke) seek time of 22.5 ms, and average (random cylinder-to-cylinder) seek time of 11.0 ms. It can transfer data at a rate of

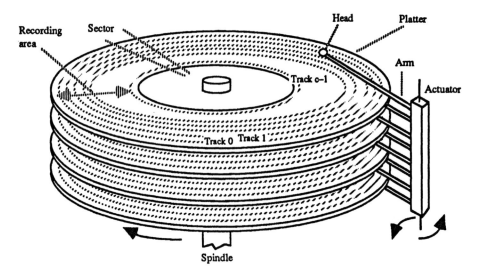

Figure 18.6. Moving-head magnetic disk elements.

4.6 MB/s. Even ignoring seek time and rotational latency, such a data transfer rate is inadequate for many parallel processing applications.

One of the earliest attempts at achieving high-throughput parallel I/O was the use of head-per-track disks (Fig. 18.7), with their multiple read/write heads capable of being activated at the same time. The seek (radial head movement) time of a disk can be approximately modeled by the equation

$$\text{Seek time} = a + b\sqrt{c - 1}$$

where c is the seek distance in cylinders. Typical values for the constants a and b are 2 and 0.4 ms, respectively. Head-per-track or fixed-head disks, as originally developed, were meant to eliminate seek time and were therefore designed to use a single head at any given time, with the active head selected electronically. Thus, they had to be modified and specially

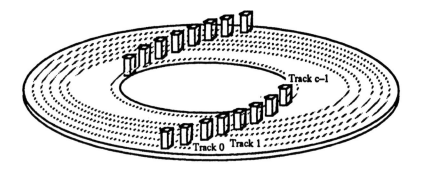

Figure 18.7. Head-per-track disk concept.

outfitted to allow high-bandwidth I/O using all heads concurrently, which made them even more expensive.

In fact, it was recognized early on that by adding a little extra logic to the already complex read–write electronics of a head-per-track disk, a massively parallel processor can be developed that searches the disk data on the fly. Such a device eliminates the need for reading massive amounts of data from the disk into a parallel processor, in effect allowing us to replace the parallel processor and its fast I/O system with an intelligent I/O filter and a high-performance sequential host computer [Parh72]. However, this only works for certain types of database and text-storage/retrieval applications.

A similar idea was the concurrent use of multiple heads provided on the same track in order to reduce the average rotational latency. If, for example, two diametrically opposite heads are provided to reduce the average rotational latency from one-half to one-fourth revolution (Fig. 18.7), then the heads, when activated simultaneously, can be used to read out or write two sectors on each track. This scheme is beneficial for both fixed- and moving-head disks, but again requires special disk units to be developed for parallel systems.

In the mid-1980s, with the personal computer market flourishing and the prices of hard disks for use with such PCs dropping at an astonishing rate, parallel machine designers realized that any long-term solution to parallel I/O must take advantage of such commodity products. Developing one-of-a-kind I/O subsystems, with their attendant design, maintenance, reliability, scalability, and obsolescence problems, no longer made economic sense. Thus, the use of *disk arrays* became dominant. Disk storage technology and price/performance continue to improve. Early disk drives cost in excess of U.S. $1000 per megabyte of capacity. Today the cost per megabyte is about 10^4 times lower, representing an average improvement factor of 10 per decade. With new techniques allowing the recording of several gigabytes of data on 1 cm^2 of disk surface, this downward trend shows no sign of slowing.

Provision of many disks that can be accessed concurrently is only part of the solution to the I/O problem in parallel systems. Development of suitable file structures and access strategies in order to reduce the I/O overhead is perhaps more important. A common technique of file organization in parallel systems is *declustering* or *striping* of the files in order to allow parallel access to different parts of a single file. A *striping unit* is a collection of data items stored contiguously on a disk, with round-robin placement of the units forming a file on multiple disks. Such a unit can range from a single bit to a complete file block depending on the application. However, if multiple processors independently read from or write into small portions of the file, the I/O access overhead might become excessive. The mechanical movement of disks and their read/write heads is extremely slow compared with processor speeds; thus, even reading an entire row or column of a matrix at once may not be enough to reduce the overhead to an acceptable level.

In general, knowledge of the collective I/O patterns for all processors is required to allow global optimization for higher I/O performance. In particular, it may be possible to devise a globally optimal I/O strategy in which processors access more data than they need, forwarding some of the data to other processors that may need them, and discarding the rest. This strategy allows us to replace many small I/O requests with fewer large I/O accesses, taking advantage of the relatively faster interprocessor transfers to route data to where they are needed [Thak96].

The problem of parallel I/O has received considerable attention in recent years. Processor speeds have improved by several orders of magnitude since parallel I/O became an issue, while disk speeds have remained virtually stagnant. The use of large *disk caches*, afforded by higher capacity and cheaper semiconductor memories, does not solve the entire I/O problem, just as ordinary caches only partially compensate for slow main memories. Various technologies for parallel I/O, along with tools and standardization issues, are under extensive scrutiny within the framework of annual workshops [IOPD].

18.5. REDUNDANT DISK ARRAYS

Compared with the large, expensive disks that were being developed for the high-performance computer market, PC-type hard disks are small, slow, and unreliable. Capacity is the least serious of these problems in view of steady improvements in disk technology (multi-gigabyte units are now commonplace and terabyte units will be available shortly) and the possibility of simply using more disks. Conceptually, both performance and reliability can be improved through redundancy: Storing multiple copies of a file, e.g., allows us to read the copy that is most readily accessible and to tolerate the loss of one or more copies related to disk crashes and other hardware problems. For these reasons, disk array technology began with the notion of redundancy built in. The acronym "RAID," for redundant array of inexpensive disks, reflects this view [Gang94]. Of course, nowadays, there is no such thing as an expensive disk; the "I" in RAID has thus been redesignated as "independent."

The reference point for RAID architectures is Level 0, or RAID0 for short, which involves the use of multiple disks for I/O performance improvement without any redundancy for fault tolerance. For example, if a file is declustered or striped across disks 0 and 1, then file data can be accessed at twice the speed, once they have been located on the two disks. The performance gain is significant only for large files, as otherwise the disk access delay dwarfs the readout or write time. In fact, striping degrades the performance for small files, unless the multiple disks are synchronized. This is because the data access time is now dictated by the larger of the two disk head movements and rotational latencies. Synchronization of multiple disks is again undesirable because it involves costly modifications to commercial off-the-shelf components.

RAID1 takes the above concept and introduces fault tolerance via mirrored disks (Fig. 18.8). For each data disk, there is a backup that holds exactly the same data. If the disks are truly inexpensive, then this doubling of size should not be a problem. However, there is a performance overhead to be paid whether or not striping is used. Each update operation on a file must also update the backup copy. If updating of the backup is done right away, then the larger of the two disk head movements will dictate the delay. If backup updates are queued and performed when convenient, then the probability of data loss from a disk crash increases.

An obvious way of reducing the factor-of-2 redundancy of mirrored disk arrays is to encode, rather than duplicate, the data. RAID2 used a single-error-correcting Hamming code, combined with striping, to allow for single-disk fault tolerance. This idea proved somewhat impractical because striping files across several disk in order to reduce the redundancy level leads to severe performance problems.

In RAID3, data are striped across multiple disks, with parity or checksum information stored on a separate redundant disk. For example, with parity, the file may be four-way striped at the bit or byte level and the XOR of 4 bits or bytes stored on a fifth disk. If a data disk fails, its data can be reconstructed as the XOR of the other three data disks and the parity

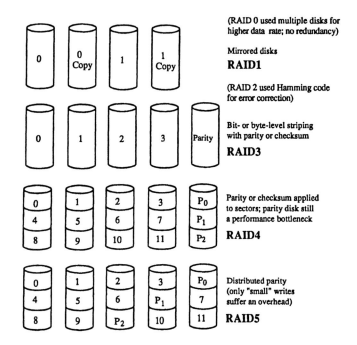

Figure 18.8. Alternative data organizations on redundant disk arrays.

disk. The reconstructed data may then be stored on a spare disk that is normally unused. Unfortunately, this scheme too has its performance problems. Using multiple parity groups helps as it allows multiple accesses to occur concurrently. However, the full benefits of multiple independent disks are not realized.

Because disk data are usually accessed in units of sectors rather than bits or bytes, RAID4 applies the parity or checksum to disk sectors. In this case, striping does not affect small files that fit entirely on one sector. However, even in these cases, multiple files cannot be modified simultaneously in view of the need to access the parity disk at the same time. When writing any new sector, the parity disk must be accessed to get the old parity for computing the new parity:

$$\text{New parity} = \text{New sector data} \oplus \text{Old sector data} \oplus \text{Old parity}$$

The new parity must then be written onto the parity disk. Accesses to the parity disk thus constitutes a serious performance bottleneck.

In RAID5, the above problem is solved by distributing the parity data on multiple disks instead of putting them on a dedicated disk. As seen in the example depicted in Fig. 18.8, the parity data for sectors 0 through 3 are stored on the rightmost disk, whereas sectors 4 through 7 have their parity data on a different disk. This scheme distributes the parity accesses and thus eases the performance bottleneck resulting from parity updates.

Note that in all RAID variants, reading from the disks can be performed independently, with no parity access conflict, assuming that the data are adequately protected by standard error-detecting coding schemes.

A new variant of RAID, sometimes referred to as RAID Level 6, combines the above ideas with a log-structured file system. In a log-structured file, sectors are not modified in place but rather a fresh copy is made, in a different location, with each update. This method requires special support for data mapping but allows the system to write data to whichever disk that is available. As an added benefit, data compression methods can be applied because file expansion creates no special problem. For example, in Storage Tek's 9200 Iceberg disk array system, 13 data disks, 2 parity disks, and a spare disk are used. Updates are held in nonvolatile cache memory (battery-backed) until there are enough data to fill an array cylinder. The data are then written onto an empty cylinder in compressed form. Contents of nearly empty cylinders are relocated by a background garbage collection mechanism to free up complete cylinders.

Other commercial RAID products include IBM's Ramac disk array, Hewlett-Packard's XLR1200 disk array, and Data General's Clariion disk array. IBM's product is a Level-5 system, while the latter two products offer some flexibility to the user in reconfiguring the data organization based on application needs.

Although disk arrays have gained acceptance as high-performance I/O subsystems, research is actively continuing into various problems and performance issues:

1. Data distribution patterns and their effects on performance under different work loads (e.g., on-line transaction processing, scientific benchmarks). Aspects of performance include read time, write time, and rebuild time, with the latter being less critical for systems composed of highly reliable components.
2. Combination of data organization with data caching schemes to improve efficiency.
3. Redundancy schemes to provide greater robustness (e.g., tolerance to double disk failures).
4. Coding schemes that imply lower storage overhead and/or simpler rebuilding.
5. Architectural designs that increase the available bandwidth.

In the past few decades, the demise of magnetic storage media, and their replacement by faster solid-state memories, has been predicted more than once. It appears, however, that with the continuing improvement in technology, magnetic disks and disk arrays may be here to stay.

18.6. INTERFACES AND STANDARDS

Data in parallel systems come from a variety of sources, including local/remote memory modules, secondary storage devices, and network interfaces. As is the case for uniprocessors, it is desirable that certain aspects of the mechanisms required to gain access to data be standardized to allow flexible and easily expandable designs. Adherence to standards could allow various parts of a parallel system to be modified or upgraded without affecting the rest of the design. Additionally, use of standard interfaces facilitates the integration of components and subsystems from different suppliers into efficient and usable parallel systems. In the remainder of this section, we present brief overviews of two such standards: the Scalable Coherent Interface and High-Performance Parallel Interface.

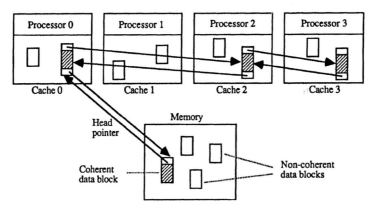

Figure 18.9. Two categories of data blocks and the structure of the sharing set in the Scalable Coherent Interface.

The *Scalable Coherent Interface* (SCI) standard was developed to facilitate the implementation of large-scale cache-coherent parallel systems using existing or future interconnection technologies. The interface, which is synchronously clocked, can interconnect a large number of nodes (each with a processor, attached memory, and possibly even I/O devices) using a ring or crossbar structure. A directory-based cache coherence protocol is part of the SCI standard. A doubly-linked list of shared data is maintained in each participating cache and forms a part of a shared, and concurrently accessible, data structure. This shared structure has no size limit, making the system totally scalable in theory. However, the overhead of maintaining and updating a large shared structure puts a practical limit on the system size.

The directory scheme of SCI is depicted in Fig. 18.9. Data blocks can be noncoherent or coherent. Noncoherent blocks essentially contain private data. Processors have the option of bypassing the coherence protocol when requesting data from main memory. Cache c can request a coherent copy of a data block from main memory as a result of a read miss, a write miss, or a write hit. We only describe the required actions in the case of a read miss; the reader should be able to supply the details for the other two cases. If the block is noncached, then the memory returns the data, changes the block's state to "cached," and sets the head pointer to point to c. For a cached block, the old head pointer is also sent to the requesting cache so that it can set its forward pointer accordingly. Also, the previous head block must set its backward pointer to point to c. In either case, the backward pointer of the block in Cache c is set to point to the data block in main memory.

The *High-Performance Parallel Interface* (HiPPI) is a point-to-point connection scheme between two devices (typically a supercomputer and a peripheral) at either 0.8 or 1.6 Gb/s over a (copper) cable that is no longer than 25 m. Packets in HiPPI are sent as a sequence of bursts, where each burst is a group of 1 to 256 words of 32 (0.8 Gb/s) or 64 bits (1.6 Gb/s). The HiPPI cables are very wide, so a clock rate of only 25 MHz is needed on the cable. Packet length can range from 2 B to 4 GB. In addition to data, each HiPPI packet contains a higher layer protocol identifier and up to 1016 B of control information.

HiPPI, which is an ANSI standard, includes electrical, signaling, and connector specifications as well as the definition of a connectionlike packet framing protocol. To send data, a device requests that it be connected to the destination device. If a connection cannot be established, because the destination is already connected to another system, HiPPI allows the requesting device to either wait for the destination to become available or be notified that a conflict exists so it can try again later. HiPPI does not allow multiple simultaneous connections to be multiplexed over a line. When a device is done sending, it asks that the connection be terminated.

When sending variable length packets through a switch, the usual procedure is to establish and tear down the connection after every packet, to allow maximum multiplexing of the switch. As a result, part of the packet overhead is the time required to get a connection request to the switch and get the answer back and for the sending device to handle the connection setup and teardown. The connection setup and teardown times depend on the length of the HiPPI cable.

PROBLEMS

18.1. Cache memories
A computer system has a 32-KB processor cache and a 256-KB Level-2 cache. The miss penalty in the processor cache is 3 cycles if the required data are found in the Level-2 cache and 10 cycles if the data have to be fetched from main memory. Without misses, the machine executes one instruction per clock cycle.

a. Determine the instruction execution rate as a function of the hit rates r_1 and r_2 for the two caches.
b. For $r_1 = 0.9$, what is the least value of r_2 if one instruction is to be executed per 1.5 cycles on the average?

18.2. Cache memories
A computer system has 4 GB of byte-addressable main memory and a 64 KB cache memory with 32B blocks.

a. Draw a diagram showing each of the components of the main memory address (i.e., how many bits for tag, set index, and byte offset within a block) for a four-way set-associative cache.
b. Draw a diagram similar to Fig. 18.1 to show how data are stored and accessed in the cache.
c. The performance of the computer system with four-way set-associative cache turns out to be unsatisfactory. The designers are considering two redesign options, each implying roughly the same additional cost. Option A is to increase the size of the cache to 128 KB. Option B is to increase the associativity of the 64-KB cache to 16-way. Which option do you think is more likely to result in higher overall system performance and why?

18.3. Separate instruction and data caches
Discuss the advantages and disadvantages of providing separate instruction and data caches. Which of these two caches must be larger and why? Which one would you make faster if you had to choose?

18.4. Direct-mapped versus set-associative caches
Sketch the structure of a program and its associated data such that it produces an intolerable amount of cache block swaps in a direct-mapped cache, performs quite well with a two-way set-associative cache, and experiences only minor improvement if the associativity is increased

to four-way. *Hint:* Consider a matrix of such a size that all elements in one row or one column map onto the same cache block when direct mapping is used.

18.5. Cache coherence
Show how Fig. 18.2 should be modified after each of the following events that occur in sequence.
a. Processor 0 generates a read miss for x.
b. Processor 0 overwrites y' with a new block u.
c. Processor 1 changes z' to z''.
d. Processor $p - 1$ generates a write miss for w.

18.6. Write-through snoopy caches
In a small-scale bus-based multiprocessor, implementation of a write-through snoopy cache protocol offers the advantage of simpler coherence enforcement. Modify the snoopy protocol depicted in Fig. 18.3 to correspond to a write-through scheme.

18.7. Snoopy caches
In Fig. 18.3, one can split the shared state into two states called *shared clean* and *private clean* and rename the "exclusive" state *private dirty*. Draw the new state diagram and explain if it offers any advantage over the original one.

18.8. Directory-based cache coherence
Draw a state diagram similar to Fig. 18.3 for cache blocks in a directory-based cache coherence protocol.

18.9. Multitasking or multithreading
Consider a master computation task that spawns a new subordinate task (subtask) after every time unit. The computation ends after five subtasks have been created and run to completion. Each subtask runs on a different processor.
a. What is the total running time of this computation if each subtask terminates in six time units?
b. Repeat part (a) with the running time of each subtask uniformly distributed in [2, 10].
c. Repeat part (a) for the case where each subtask has two time units of computation and two remote memory accesses, each taking one to three time units; assume uniform distribution in [1, 3].

18.10. Magnetic disks
For the example moving-head disk system whose parameters were given in Section 18.4, derive the rotation speed, approximate track density, recording density, and full disk copying time (e.g., for backup). Also, show that the data transfer rate can be derived from the other parameters given.

18.11. Magnetic disks
Consider the example moving-head disk system whose parameters were given in Section 18.4.
a. Derive the parameters a and b of the seek-time formula.
b. It has been suggested that for disks with a large number of cylinders, a better formula for seek time is $a + b\sqrt{c - 1} + \beta(c - 1)$. Derive the parameters a, b, and β if the average (random) seek time given is for one third of a full stroke.
c. Can you provide an intuitive justification for the added linear term in the formula of part (b)?

18.12. Head-per-track and multiple-arm disks

A 3.5-inch disk platter contains 256 tracks on each side and rotates at 3600 rpm. Data on the outermost track are recorded at a density of 50,000 b/inch and are read out from or written onto the disk in 512B sectors. Radial head movement takes 1 ms per 10 cylinders or fraction thereof (e.g., 3 ms for 27 cylinders).

a. With the head positioned on a random track, what is the average head movement in terms of tracks and the expected seek time (for moving the head to a randomly chosen track)?

b. With single sectors read out or written in each disk access, what is the expected improvement in disk access speed if we use a head-per-track disk?

c. What about the improvement resulting from using four equally spaced moving-head arms?

18.13. Disk arrays

Consider the example RAID4 and RAID5 data organizations in Fig. 18.8 for 12 data sectors and their associated three parity sectors, with P_i being the parity sector for data sectors $4i$, $4i + 1$, $4i + 2$, and $4i + 3$.

a. If each disk read access involves a single sector, which organization will lead to higher data bandwidth? Quantify the difference assuming random distribution of read addresses.

b. Repeat part (a) for write accesses.

c. Suppose that one of the disks fails and its data must be reconstructed on a spare disk. Which organization offers better performance for read requests during the reconstruction process?

d. Repeat part (c) for write requests.

18.14. Scalable Coherent Interface

Supply the missing details for the cache coherence protocol used in connection with the Scalable Coherent Interface discussed in Section 18.6. In particular, indicate the sequence of events on a write miss, write hit, and block overwrite in a cache.

18.15. Scalable Coherent Interface

Show how Fig. 18.9 should be modified after each of the following events that occur in sequence.

a. Processor 0 generates a write hit in the shared block shown.

b. Processor 1 generates a read miss for data in the shared block shown.

c. Processor 2 overwrites the shared block with a different shared block.

d. Processor 1 generates a write hit in the shared block shown.

REFERENCES AND SUGGESTED READING

[Burg97]   Burger, D., S. Kaxiras, and J. R. Goodman, "Data Scalar Architectures," *Proc. Int'l. Symp. Computer Architecture*, June 1997, pp. 338–349.

[Chen94]   Chen, P. M., E. K. Lee, G. A. Gibson, R. H. Katz, and D.A. Patterson, "RAID: High-Performance, Reliable Secondary Storage," *ACM Computing Surveys*, Vol. 26, No. 2, pp. 145–185, June 1994.

[Chen96]   Chen, S., and D. Towsley, "A Performance Evaluation of RAID Architectures," *IEEE Trans. Computers*, Vol. 45, No. 10, pp. 1116–1130, October 1996.

[Frie96]   Friedman, M. B., "RAID Keeps Going and Going and . . . ," *IEEE Spectrum*, Vol. 33, No. 4, pp. 73–79, April 1996.

[Gang94]   Ganger, G. R., B. R. Worthington, R. Y. Hou, and Y. N. Patt, "Disk Arrays: High-Performance, High-Reliability Storage Subsystems," *IEEE Computer*, Vol. 27, No. 3, pp. 30–36, March 1994.

[Hira92]   Hirata, H., et al., "An Elementary Processor Architecture with Simultaneous Instruction Issuing from Multiple Threads," *Proc. 19th Int. Symp. Computer Architecture*, pp. 136–145, May 1992.

[IOPD]   I/O in Parallel and Distributed Systems, Annual Workshops. The 5th workshop in this series was held during November 1997 in San Jose, CA.

[Parh72]   Parhami, B., "A Highly Parallel Computing System for Information Retrieval," *AFIPS Conf. Proc.*, Vol. 41 (1972 Fall Joint Computer Conf.), AFIPS Press, pp. 681–690.

[Patt96]   Patterson, D. A., and J. L. Hennessy, *Computer Architecture: A Quantitative Approach*, Morgan Kaufmann, 1996.

[SCI92]   *The Scalable Coherent Interface Standard*, IEEE Computer Society, 1992.

[Thak96]   Thakur, R., A. Choudhary, R. Bordawekar, S. More, and S. Kuditipudi, "Passion: Optimized I/O for Parallel Applications," *IEEE Computer*, Vol. 29, pp. 70–78, June 1996.

[Tolm94]   Tolmie, D., "High Performance Parallel Interface (HIPPI)," in *High Performance Networks— Technology and Protocols*, edited by A. Tantawy, Kluwer, 1994, pp. 131–156.

19

Reliable Parallel
Processing

Modern digital components and subsystems are remarkably robust, but when one puts a large number of them together to build a parallel computer with data being passed back and forth between them at extremely high rates, things can and do go wrong. In data communication, a bit error probability of 10^{-10} is considered quite good. However, at gigabyte per second data transmission or processing rate, such an error probability translates roughly into one bit-error per second. While coding methods can be used to protect against errors in data transmission or storage, the same cannot be said about data manipulations performed in a CPU. In this chapter, we examine some techniques that can be used to improve the robustness and reliability of parallel systems. Chapter topics are

- 19.1. Defects, faults, . . . , failures
- 19.2. Defect-level methods
- 19.3. Fault-level methods
- 19.4. Error-level methods
- 19.5. Malfunction-level methods
- 19.6. Degradation-level methods

19.1. DEFECTS, FAULTS, . . . , FAILURES

So far, we have assumed that the many components of a parallel machine always behave as expected: A processor instruction always yields the expected result, a router consistently makes the correct routing decision, and a wire remains permanently connected. Even though modern integrated circuits and electronic assemblies are extremely reliable, errors or malfunctions do occur in the course of lengthy computations, especially in systems that are highly complex, operate under harsh environmental conditions, deal with extreme/unpredictable loads, or are used during long missions where maintenance is impractical. The output of an AND gate in a processor or router may become permanently "stuck on 1," yielding an incorrect output when at least one input is 0. Or the AND gate may suffer a "transient fault" where its output becomes incorrect for only a few clock cycles as a result of cross talk or interference. A table entry may be corrupted by manufacturing imperfections in the memory cells or logic faults in the read/write circuitry. Wires may break, or short-circuit, because of overheating, VLSI manufacturing defects, or a combination of both.

Parallel processors are quite complex. A system with hundreds or thousands of components (processors, memory modules, routers, links, switches) is more likely to contain faulty or malfunctioning elements than a conventional uniprocessor. Thus, there is a need to explicitly address the testing, fault diagnosis, and reliability issues in parallel processors. The inherent redundancy of parallel systems is, in principle, good for fault tolerance; after all, a 1024-processor system remains highly parallel even after losing a dozen or so processors. However, numerous problems must be dealt with in order to take advantage of this built-in redundancy.

To see the difficulties, consider a $\sqrt{p} \times \sqrt{p}$ mesh-connected parallel computer. While it is true that the failure of one processor still leaves us $p - 1$ processors to work with, the structure of the faulty system is no longer a complete 2D mesh. Thus, any algorithm for routing, sorting, matrix multiplication, and the like, whose proper functioning depends on the complete 2D mesh structure, will no longer be valid for the surviving $(p - 1)$-processor configuration. Even if our algorithms are such that they can run on meshes of various sizes, a single worst-case processor or link failure can leave us with a nonsquare mesh of about one-half the original size or a square mesh of one-fourth the size. The same problem exists for a q-cube, where a single processor or link failure may leave us with a much smaller $(q - 1)$-cube.

To dispel any thought that the above difficulty is related to the rigid structure of a 2D mesh or a hypercube and will go away with a more flexible parallel architecture, consider p processors that are interconnected via b shared buses. For maximum flexibility and redundancy, assume that each processor is connected to every bus. Again, theoretically, the system should be able to continue functioning, albeit with degraded performance, despite processor or bus failures. However, this is only true with certain strong assumptions about the failures and their effects. For example, if processors fail in *fail-stop* mode, meaning that they simply quit all computation and communication, then the healthy processors will remain unaffected. However, an arbitrary or *Byzantine* failure may lead to a single faulty processor disabling the b buses by continually broadcasting bogus messages or by simply grounding all of them. While researchers have developed methods for ensuring that processors do in fact fail in fail-stop mode or that any maliciously faulty processor is quickly isolated from common resources, the design methods required, and their cost/performance overheads, are far from trivial.

Ensuring correct functioning of digital systems in the presence of (permanent and transient) faults is the subject of a discipline known as *fault-tolerant* (or *dependable*) *computing*. In this chapter, we review some ideas in the field of fault-tolerant computing that are particularly relevant to ensuring the reliable functioning of parallel systems.

For the sake of precision, we distinguish among various undesirable conditions, or *impairments*, that lead to unreliability in any digital system. The six views of impairments introduced below, along with the ideal system state, define a seven-level model for the study of dependable computing, depicted in Fig. 19.1 [Parh94]. In the literature, you may find all of the six italicized concepts below imprecisely referred to as "faults" or "failures":

- *Defect* level or component level, dealing with deviant atomic parts
- *Fault* level or logic level, dealing with deviant signal values or decisions
- *Error* level or information level, dealing with deviant data or internal states
- *Malfunction* level or system level, dealing with deviant functional behavior
- *Degradation* level or service level, dealing with deviant performance
- *Failure* level or result level, dealing with deviant outputs or actions

Note that a system can begin its life in any of the seven states depicted in Fig. 19.1 (sideways arrows), though we certainly hope that our testing and validation efforts will move the starting state to the highest possible of these levels. Briefly, a hardware or software component may be defective (hardware may also *become* defective by wear and aging). Certain system states will expose the defect, resulting in the development of faults defined as incorrect signal values or decisions within the system. If a fault is actually exercised, it may contaminate the data flowing within the system, causing errors. Erroneous information or states may or may not cause the affected subsystem to malfunction, depending on the subsystem's design and error tolerance. A subsystem malfunction does not necessarily have a catastrophic, unsafe, or even perceivable service-level effect. Finally, degradation of service could eventually lead to system failure (producing results or actions that are incorrect, incomplete, or too late to be useful).

The goal of this chapter is to review some of the methods that allow us to prevent a system from ever entering the failed state. For each of the five states between ideal and failed in Fig. 19.1, the complementary approaches of *prevention* (avoidance or removal) and *tolerance* can be used to inhibit a downward transition or to facilitate an upward transition. These methods are discussed in the following five sections of this chapter.

Figure 19.2 provides an interesting analogy for clarifying the states and state transitions in our model, using a system of six concentric water reservoirs. Pouring water from above corresponds to defects, faults, and other impairments, depending on the layer(s) being affected. These impairments can be avoided by controlling the flow of water through valves or tolerated by the provision of drains of acceptable capacities for the reservoirs. The system fails if water ever gets to the outermost reservoir. This may happen, for example, by a broken valve at some layer combined with inadequate drainage at the same and all outer layers. Wall heights between adjacent reservoirs represent the natural interlevel latencies in our model. Water overflowing from the outermost reservoir into the surrounding area corresponds to a computer failure adversely affecting the larger physical, corporate, or societal system.

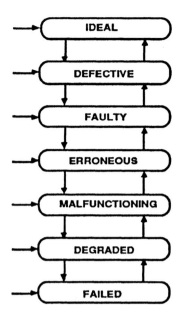

Figure 19.1. System states and state transitions in our multilevel model.

It is worth noting that even though we discuss each method in only one section, according to the abstraction level for which it is most suitable, or where it has been most successfully applied, many of these techniques are applicable to more than one level. For example, reconfiguration of processor arrays, introduced in Section 19.2 as a means for defect tolerance, can be applied to fault, or even malfunction, tolerance with the following additional provisions:

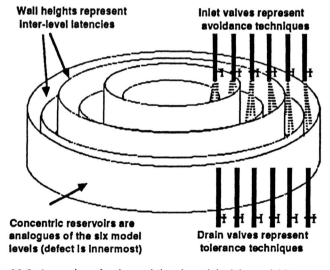

Figure 19.2. An analogy for the multilevel model of dependable computing.

- On-line fault or malfunction detection
- More flexible reconfiguration switching
- Data backup and recovery mechanisms

As a second example, circuit-level redundancy/replication methods, introduced for fault tolerance in Section 19.3, can be applied to malfunction or even degradation tolerance, albeit with some challenging problems in

- Synchronizing higher-level modules
- Sophisticated comparison or voting schemes
- Performance/reliability trade-off mechanisms

19.2. DEFECT-LEVEL METHODS

Defects are accepted occurrences in the process of integrated-circuit manufacturing and in software development; their complete avoidance or removal, where not technically impossible, tends to be cost-ineffective. Defects are caused in two ways, corresponding to the sideways and downward transitions into the *defective* state in Fig. 19.1: (1) physical design slips leading to defective system components, by improper design or inadequate screening, and (2) development of defects as a result of component wear and aging or operating conditions that are harsher than those originally envisaged. A defect may be *dormant* or *ineffective* long after its occurrence. During this dormancy period, external detection of the defect is impossible or, at the very least, extremely difficult. If, despite efforts to avoid or remove them, defects are nevertheless present in a product, nothing is normally done about them until they develop into faults. Replacement of sensitive components, as part of scheduled *periodic maintenance*, is one way of removing defects before they develop into faults. Similarly, *burn-in* of hardware components tends to remove most dormant defects. Component modifications and improvements, motivated by the analyses of degraded or failed systems, are other major ways of hardware and software defect removal.

Parallel systems are ideally suited to the application of *defect tolerance* methods, both as a way of improving the manufacturing yield [Cici95], and thus making the systems more cost-effective, and as a way for dynamically reconfiguring the system during its operation. As an example, consider the development of a VLSI or WSI (wafer-scale integration) component that houses a square mesh to be used as a building block for synthesizing larger mesh-connected computers. A large VLSI chip or a wafer is likely to have one or more defects that could affect the processors or links within the chip. Because a complete square mesh is needed, even a small defect will render the mesh unusable, thus lowering the manufacturing yield and increasing the component price.

Before reviewing some of the proposed methods for improving the manufacturing yield in the above context, let us consider the simpler case of a linear array. Figure 19.3 shows a four-processor linear array built by including a spare processor and a switching mechanism that allows any four of the five on-chip processors to be configured into a linear array of the desired size. Of course a single defective switch would still make the chip unusable. However, if one views each switch as a pair of multiplexers under common control, it is easy to deduce how redundancy can be incorporated in the switches to make them tolerant to defects that

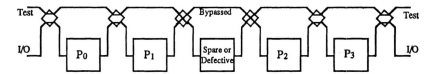

Figure 19.3. A linear array with a spare processor and reconfiguration switches.

affect one multiplexer. Alternatively, the multiplexers can be distributed to the processors, with each processor independently selecting its right/left neighbor from among two possibilities (Fig. 19.4).

Extension of the above ideas to 2D arrays is straightforward. Figure 19.5 shows two of the many schemes that are possible for reconfiguring 2D processor arrays in order to bypass defective elements. The scheme shown on the left is very similar to that of Fig. 19.3, except that it uses three-state switches (two "bent" states and one "crossed" state). We see, for example, that by putting two switches in the NW–SE bent state, Processor P_d becomes the south neighbor of Processor P_a, thus allowing a defective P_c to be bypassed. The scheme shown on the right side of Fig. 19.5 is the 2D analogue of Fig. 19.4 in that it integrates the multiplexers with the input ports of the processors. In this way, Processor P_d can pick any of the three processors above, to its upper left, or to its upper right as its logical north neighbor. The available choices can be extended to five or more processors for greater flexibility and defect tolerance level.

With the schemes shown in Fig. 19.5, if we have one row and one column of spare processors in the array, many defect patterns can be tolerated. Figure 19.6 shows a 6×6 processor array with defective components from which a 5 × 5 working mesh has been salvaged. The reconfiguration switching capability assumed here is slightly more complex than that shown in Fig. 19.5 (left) in that defective, or otherwise unused, processors (circular nodes) can be bypassed.

Clearly, reconfiguration switches are themselves subject to defects. Thus, a good reconfiguration switching scheme should allow the tolerance of switch, as well as processor and link, defects. The effectiveness of a reconfiguration switching scheme is measured by the extent of defect tolerance (e.g., random single/double defects, or a cluster of defective elements of a certain size). Ease of reconfiguration, which includes the determination of the new working configuration and its associated switch settings, is also an issue, particularly if reconfiguration is to be dynamic rather than just as a yield enhancement method at manufacturing time.

Consider, as an example, the reconfiguration switching scheme implicit in Fig. 19.6; i.e., provision of a *single track* of switches between rows and columns of processors in a

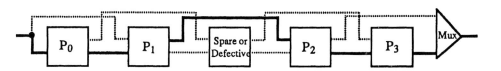

Figure 19.4. A linear array with a spare processor and embedded switching.

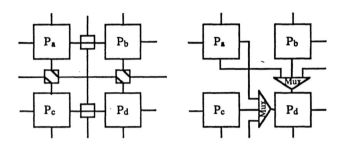

Figure 19.5. Two types of reconfiguration switching for 2D arrays.

manner similar to Fig. 19.5 (left), with processor bypass capability included, along with a spare row and spare column of processing nodes in the array. It is relatively easy to show that a particular pattern of defective processors can be tolerated (bypassed) using this scheme if one can draw straight nonintersecting *compensation paths* from the spare row or spare column to every defective processor [Kung88]. Figure 19.7 shows seven defective processors and a set of nonintersecting compensation paths for them. The derivation of switch states to bypass the seven defective processors is quite easy if we note the rightward/downward shifting of the horizontal/vertical connections along the compensation paths.

Based on the above, it is easy to see that the reconfiguration scheme of Figs. 19.6 and 19.7 is capable of tolerating any two defective processors. Most, but not all, triple defects are also tolerated; if a node and both of its east and south neighbors are defective, we cannot find three nonintersecting compensation paths for them.

A system makes the transition from the *defective* state to the *faulty* state when a dormant defect is *awakened* and gives rise to a fault. Designers try to impede this transition by providing adequate safety margins for the components and/or by using defect tolerance methods. Ironically, one may occasionally try to facilitate this transition for the purpose of

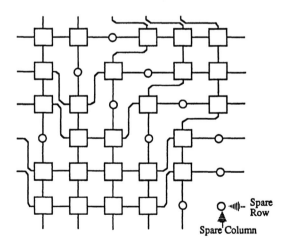

Figure 19.6. A 5 × 5 working array salvaged from a 6 × 6 redundant mesh through reconfiguration switching.

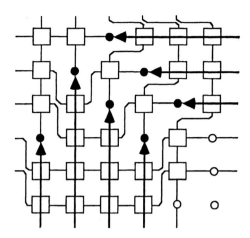

Figure 19.7. Seven faulty processors and their associated compensation paths.

exposing defects, as faults are more readily observable than defects. To do this, the components are usually subjected to loads and stresses that are much higher than those encountered during normal operation. This *burning in* or *torture testing* of components results in the development of faults in marginal components, which are then identified by *fault testing* methods. To be able to deduce the underlying defect from an observed fault, we need to establish a correspondence between various defect and fault classes. This is referred to as *fault modeling*.

19.3. FAULT-LEVEL METHODS

A hardware fault may be defined as any anomalous behavior of logic structures or substructures that can compromise the correct signal values within a logic circuit. The reference behavior is provided by some form of specification. If the anomalous behavior results from implementing the logic function g rather than the intended function f, then the fault is related to a logical design or implementation slip. The alternative cause of faults is the implementation of the correct logic functions with defective components. Defect-based faults can be classified according to duration (permanent, intermittent/recurring, or transient), extent (local or distributed/catastrophic), and effect (dormant or active). Only active faults produce incorrect logic signals. An example of a dormant fault is a line stuck on logic-value 1 that happens to carry a 1. If incorrect signals are produced as output or stored in memory elements, they cause errors in the system state.

One way to protect the computations against fault-induced errors is to use duplication with comparison of the two results (for single fault detection) or triplication with two-out-of-three voting on the three results (for single fault masking or tolerance). Figure 19.8 shows possible ways to implement these schemes.

In the top circuit of Fig. 19.8, the decoding logic is duplicated along with the computation part to ensure that a single fault in the decoder does not go undetected. The encoder, on the other hand, remains a critical element whose faulty behavior will lead to undetected

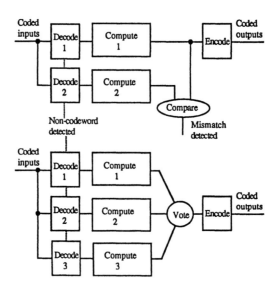

Figure 19.8. Fault detection or tolerance with replication.

errors. However, because the output of the encoder is redundant (coded), it is possible to design the encoding circuitry in such a way as to ensure the production of a non-codeword at its output if anything goes wrong. Such a design, referred to as *self-checking*, leads to error detection by the checker associated with the memory subsystem or later when the erroneous stored value is used as an input to some other computation. Thus, the duplicated design in Fig. 19.1 can detect any fault that is totally confined to one of the blocks shown. This includes a faulty "compare" block which may produce a "false alarm." An undetected mismatch would require at least two faults in separate blocks.

The design with triplicated computation in Fig. 19.8 is similar. Here, the voter is a critical element and must be designed with care. Self-checking design cannot be applied to the voter (as used in the diagram) because its output is nonredundant. However, by combining the voting and encoding functions, one may be able to design an efficient self-checking voter-encoder. This *three-channel* computation strategy can be generalized to m channels in order to tolerate more faults. However, the cost overhead of a higher degree of replication becomes prohibitive.

The above replication schemes are quite general and can be applied to any part of a parallel system for any type of fault. However, the cost of full replication is difficult to justify for most applications. Note that for faults in the two or three channels to be truly independent, the various channels must be packaged separately and be fed from independent power supplies in order to avoid catastrophic single-point faults. This aggravates the cost and complexity problems.

Researchers have thus devised various fault tolerance schemes for specific parallel systems or under restricted fault classes (*fault models*). For example, in Section 7.5, we noted that the periodic balanced sorting network can be made tolerant to certain types of faults by adding one (missed exchanges) or two (missed/incorrect exchanges) extra blocks to it. A 1024-input sorting network with 10 blocks thus requires a redundancy of 10 or 20%. We also noted that in the single-block version with multiple passes, an extra stage of comparators can provide tolerance to single faults; this again implies a redundancy of 10% for $n = 1024$ inputs.

A second interesting example is the design of fault-tolerant multistage interconnection networks. Consider the 8×8 butterfly network of Fig. 19.9 (left) and its extra-stage version (right). Because of the extra stage, there exist two paths between any input and any output. Thus, any single switch fault can be tolerated by using one of the two alternate paths. The circular nodes are multiplexers and demultiplexers that are required for the tolerance of faults in the leftmost and rightmost columns, respectively. On the extra-stage butterfly network of Fig. 19.9, two node- and edge-disjoint paths are shown from Input 4 to Output 3. Thus, any fault in a single switch, multiplexer, or demultiplexer can be tolerated.

Like the original butterfly network, the extra-stage butterfly network of Fig. 19.9 is self-routing. To see this, note that the connections between Columns $q - 1$ and q are identical to those between Columns 0 and 1. Thus, the two paths essentially correspond to taking the Dimension-0 link first (as in the regular butterfly) and bypassing Column q, or bypassing Column 0 and taking the Dimension-0 link last. Hence, a processor that is aware of the fault status of the network switches can append a suitable routing tag to the message and insert it into the network through one of its two available access ports. From that point onward, the message finds its way through the network and automatically avoids the faulty element(s). Of course, if more than one element is faulty, existence of a path is not guaranteed.

Transition from *faulty* to *erroneous* state occurs when a fault affects the state of some storage element or output. Designers try to impede this transition by using fault tolerance methods. Another approach is to control this transition so that it leads to an incorrect but safe state. An example is the provision of internal fault detection mechanisms (e.g., comparators, activity monitors, or consistency checkers) that can disable a given module or system, assuming of course that the *disabled* state is safe. Ironically, one may also try to facilitate this transition for the purpose of exposing system faults, as errors are more readily observable than faults. This is precisely the objective of all fault testing schemes. With off-line test application methods, special input patterns are applied to the circuit or system under test,

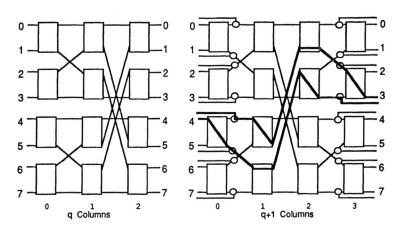

Figure 19.9. Regular butterfly and extra-stage butterfly networks.

while observing possible errors in its outputs or internal state. To deduce underlying faults from observed errors, we need to establish a correspondence between various fault and error classes. This is referred to as *error modeling*. With on-line or concurrent testing, faults must be exposed during normal system operation and without disrupting its operation. Such a *self-checked* mode of operation relies heavily on informational coding and deals with faults through detecting the errors that they produce.

19.4. ERROR-LEVEL METHODS

An error is *any deviation of a system's state from the reference state as defined by its specification*. Errors are either built into a system by improper initialization (e.g., incorrect ROM contents) or develop as a result of fault-induced deviations. Assuming that the system's state is encoded as a binary vector, an error consists of a set of 0→1 (read 0-to-1) and/or 1→0 *inversions*. With this view, errors can be classified according to the multiplicity of inversions (*single* versus *multiple*), their directions (*symmetric* if both 0→1 and 1→0 inversions are considered at the same time, *asymmetric* if for example the inversions can only be of the 1→0 type, and *unidirectional* if multiple inversions are of the same type), and their dispersion (*random* versus *correlated*). There are finer subdivisions in each category. For example, *byte* errors and *bursts* confined to a number of adjacent bit positions are important special cases of correlated multiple errors.

Methods of detecting or correcting data errors have their origins in the field of communications. Early communications channels were highly unreliable and extremely noisy. So signals sent from one end were often distorted or changed by the time they reached the receiving end. The remedy, thought up by communications engineers, was to encode the data in redundant formats known as *codes*. Examples of coding methods include adding a parity bit (an example of a single-error-detecting or SED code), checksums, and Hamming single-error-correcting double-error-detecting (SEC/DED) code. Today, error-detecting and error-correcting codes are still used extensively in communications, for even though the reliability of these systems and noise reduction/shielding methods have improved enormously, so have the data rates and data transmission volumes, making the error probability nonnegligible.

Codes originally developed for communications can be used to protect against storage errors. When the early integrated-circuit memories proved to be less reliable than the then common magnetic-core technology, IC designers were quick to incorporate SEC/DED codes into their designs. The data processing cycle in a system whose storage and memory-to-processor data transfers are protected by an error code can be represented as in Fig. 19.10. In this scheme, which is routinely used in modern digital systems, the data manipulation part is unprotected. Decoding/encoding is necessary because common codes are not closed under arithmetic and other operations of interest. For example, the sum of two even-parity numbers does not necessarily have even parity. As another example, when we change an element within a list that is protected by a checksum, we must recompute the checksum.

The above problem can be solved in two ways. One is the use of codes that are closed under data manipulation operations of interest. For example, *product codes* are closed under addition and subtraction. A product code with check modulus 15, say, represents the integers x and y as $15x$ and $15y$, respectively. Adding/subtracting the two values directly yields the

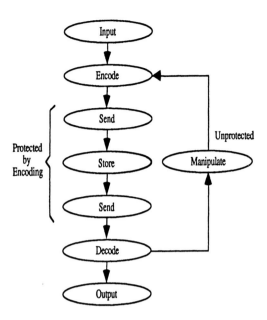

Figure 19.10. A common way of applying information coding techniques.

correct encoded form $15(x \pm y)$ of the sum/difference $x \pm y$. While product codes are not closed under multiplication, division, and square-rooting, it is possible to devise arithmetic algorithms for these operations that deal directly with the coded operands [Parh99].

A second approach, *algorithm-based error tolerance*, is based on the application of coding methods at the data-structure level as opposed to at the level of atomic data elements. The coding methods used, and the required modifications in the algorithms, are highly application-dependent. However, where applicable, this method yields good error coverage with a moderate amount of redundancy in data representation and computational steps.

As an example of this approach, consider the multiplication of matrices X and Y yielding the result matrix Z. The checksum of a list of numbers (a vector) is simply the algebraic sum of all of the numbers modulo some check constant A. For any $k \times l$ matrix M, we define the row-checksum matrix M_r as a $k \times (l{+}1)$ matrix that is identical to M in its Columns 0 through $l-1$ and has as its lth column the respective row checksums. Similarly, the column-checksum matrix M_c is a $(k{+}1) \times l$ matrix that is identical to M in its Rows 0 through $k-1$ and has as its kth row the respective column checksums. The full-checksum matrix M_f is defined as the $(k{+}1) \times (l{+}1)$ matrix $(M_r)_c$, i.e., the column-checksum matrix of the row-checksum matrix of M. For example, using modulo-A checksums with $A = 8$, we might have

$$M = \begin{bmatrix} 2 & 1 & 6 \\ 5 & 3 & 4 \\ 3 & 2 & 7 \end{bmatrix} \quad M_r = \begin{bmatrix} 2 & 1 & 6 & 1 \\ 5 & 3 & 4 & 4 \\ 3 & 2 & 7 & 4 \end{bmatrix} \quad M_c = \begin{bmatrix} 2 & 1 & 6 \\ 5 & 3 & 4 \\ 3 & 2 & 7 \\ 2 & 6 & 1 \end{bmatrix} \quad M_f = \begin{bmatrix} 2 & 1 & 6 & 1 \\ 5 & 3 & 4 & 4 \\ 3 & 2 & 7 & 4 \\ 2 & 6 & 1 & 1 \end{bmatrix}$$

If X, Y, and Z are matrices satisfying $Z = X \times Y$, we can prove that $Z_f = X_c \times Y_r$ [Huan84]. Based on this result, we can perform standard matrix multiplication on the encoded matrices X_c and

Y_r, and then compare the values in the last column and row of the product matrix with checksums that are computed based on the remaining elements to detect any error that may have occurred. If the matrix elements are floating-point numbers, then the equalities will hold approximately, leading to difficulties in selecting a suitable threshold for considering values equal. Some methods to resolve this problem are given by Dutt and Assaad [Dutt96].

One can easily prove that in the full-checksum matrix, any single erroneous element can be corrected and any three erroneous elements can be detected [Huan84]. Consider, for example, the matrix multiplication algorithm on a 2D mesh, where each processor is in charge of computing one element of the result matrix Z (Fig. 11.2). According to the above result, any fault-induced error in one processor leads to an erroneous, but correctable, result matrix Z. The error correction procedure can be incorporated as part of the error-tolerant matrix multiplication algorithm. In the arrangement of Fig. 11.2, processors are also involved in relaying data elements to other processors. Thus, we cannot say that the algorithm is completely tolerant to single-processor malfunctions. Alternatively, up to three erroneous elements in the result matrix can be detected. In this case, we might rely on redoing the computation right away (in the hope that the errors were related to transient faults) or after the system has been tested and reconfigured or repaired to remove faulty/malfunctioning elements.

The full-checksum matrix M_f is an example of a *robust data structure* with certain error detection/correction properties. Designing such robust data structures with given error detection or correction capabilities, such that they also lend themselves to direct manipulation by suitably modified algorithms, is still an art. However, steady progress is being made in this area.

A system moves from *erroneous* to *malfunctioning* state when an error affects the functional behavior of some component subsystem. This transition can be avoided by using error tolerance techniques. An alternative is to control the transition so that it leads to a *safe* malfunction. This latter technique has been extensively applied to the design of *malfunction-safe* (fail-safe) sequential circuits. The idea is to encode the states of the sequential circuit in some error code, specify the transitions between valid states (represented by codewords) in the normal way, and define the transitions for erroneous states in such a way that they never lead to a valid state. Thus, an invalid state persists and is eventually detected by an external observer or monitor. In the meantime, the output logic produces *safe* values when the circuit is in an invalid state. One may also try to facilitate this transition for the purpose of exposing latent system errors. For example, a memory unit containing incorrect data is in the erroneous state. It will operate correctly as long as the erroneous words are not read out. Systematic testing of memory can result in a memory malfunction that exposes the errors.

19.5. MALFUNCTION-LEVEL METHODS

A malfunction is *any deviation of a system's operation from its expected behavior according to the design specifications*. For example, an arithmetic/logic unit computing $2 + 2 = 5$ can be said to be malfunctioning, as is a processor executing an unconditional branch instead of a conditional one. Malfunctions (like defects, faults, and errors) may have no external symptoms, but they can be made externally observable with moderate effort. In fact, malfunction detection (complemented by a recovery mechanism) constitutes the main strategy in the design of today's dependable computer systems. Even though such systems are called *fault-tolerant* in the prevailing terminology, we will use the adjective *malfunction-tolerant* for consistency. Many such systems are built from standard off-the-shelf building blocks with little or no fault and error handling capabilities and use higher-level hardware and software techniques to achieve malfunction tolerance at the module or subsystem level.

In a parallel computer, multiple processing resources can be used for malfunction detection and diagnosis. This is sometimes referred to as *system-level fault diagnosis* in the literature. Consider the following strategy for malfunction diagnosis. Each processor is tested by one or more of its neighbors that send it test computations and in return receive the computation results for comparison with expected results. If the results match, then the tested processor is considered healthy; otherwise, it is considered to be malfunctioning. The test routine may be an internal program that exercises most parts of the processor's hardware. The testing processor simply supplies a seed value (one data word, say) that affects the final computation result(s). This seed value is needed to protect against a condition where a malfunctioning processor accidentally gets a correct result for its internally stored test program.

In a p-processor system, the diagnosis results can be viewed as a $p \times p$ matrix D, with three-valued elements: $D_{ij} = 1$ means that P_i thinks P_j is healthy; $D_{ij} = 0$ means that P_i thinks P_j is malfunctioning; an "x" entry means that P_i has not tested P_j, perhaps because of the fact that the two are not neighbors. Even though self-test routines usually do not provide complete coverage, let us assume, for simplicity, that a healthy processor always correctly diagnoses a malfunctioning one. Of course, a malfunctioning processor provides an unreliable diagnosis. Figure 19.11 shows an undirected-graph representation of the testing relationships among five processors and the resulting diagnosis matrix D.

Identifying the malfunctioning processors from the diagnosis matrix D is a challenging problem. Intuitively, the reason for the difficulty is that the trustworthy diagnoses from healthy processors are intermixed with unreliable diagnoses offered by malfunctioning processors. If we insist that all malfunctioning processors be directly identifiable from D, then correct diagnosis is possible only if we place an upper bound on the number of malfunctions. In the example of Fig. 19.11, the diagnosis matrix D is consistent with P_4 being the only malfunctioning unit. It is also consistent with P_4 being the only healthy unit. Thus, if we know that there is at most one malfunctioning processor, correct diagnosis is achieved. The upper bound on the number of malfunctions that are fully diagnosable depends on the testing graph.

We may be able to do somewhat better by relaxing the strong requirement for full diagnosis. The weakest diagnosis condition is to be able to correctly identify at least one

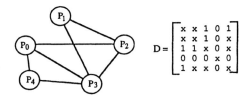

$$D = \begin{bmatrix} x & x & 1 & 0 & 1 \\ x & x & 1 & 0 & x \\ 1 & 1 & x & 0 & x \\ 0 & 0 & 0 & x & 0 \\ 1 & x & x & 0 & x \end{bmatrix}$$

Figure 19.11. A testing graph and the resulting diagnosis matrix.

malfunctioning unit. After such an identification, the known malfunctioning node can be repaired, replaced, or bypassed and another round of diagnosis conducted with fewer malfunctioning units. Also, it might be acceptable to identify a superset of the malfunctioning nodes, because the replacement of such a superset with healthy nodes will remove all malfunctioning units. Of course, for this method to be useful, the identified superset must be relatively small (clearly, the set of all p processors is always a valid, but useless, superset of the set of faulty nodes).

Once a malfunction has been diagnosed, the system must be reconfigured with all, or a subset of, the healthy units. This is relatively simple in a bus-based system; the malfunctioning processor, memory module, or I/O controller is simply isolated from the bus and subsequently removed for inspection and repair. In more rigid parallel architectures, the problem is more difficult. Reconfiguration methods similar to those discussed for defect tolerance in Section 19.2 can be used to reconfigure the system around faulty units. However, because each unit is fairly complex at this level, it is desirable to use lower-redundancy methods if possible.

As an example, consider a reconfigurable 2D mesh that utilizes only one spare processor, as shown in Fig. 19.12 [Bruc93]. Each processor still has a degree of 4; however, the normally unused links of the boundary processors are used to accommodate a spare processor in such a way that any single malfunctioning processor can be removed and the mesh reconfigured into its original topology by simply renaming the nodes. Of course, a full restart would be required to initialize the processors with their new node labels and data. In the example of Fig. 19.12, the processor originally numbered 5 has been removed and the remaining processors (including the spare) renumbered to form a complete 4 × 4 mesh. Similar methods can be used for meshes of higher dimensions, without increasing the node degree.

Similar low-redundancy schemes have been developed for other networks, such as tori and hypercubes, but they generally involve an increase in node degree and the provision of additional interconnection switches. A method that works for tolerating a single processor malfunction in any p-processor architecture involves the use of an extra port per processor. The p extra links, which are unused during normal operation, are interconnected via a $p \times d$ crossbar switch to a degree-d spare node, where d is the maximum node degree in the original network. When a processor malfunctions, the spare can be made to take its place by setting up the crossbar switch so that the p neighbors of the malfunctioning processor are linked to the spare processor. To avoid an excessively complex crossbar switch, various subsets of

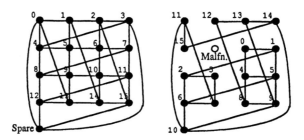

Figure 19.12. Reconfigurable 4 × 4 mesh with one spare.

processors can be provided with their own crossbar switch, all linked to the same spare processor or to different spares.

If a spare is not available, or after all spares have been used up, the malfunctioning unit can be isolated from the rest of the system. This reduces the amount of hardware resources (e.g., memory, processing power, I/O bandwidth) available, thus leading to a corresponding performance degradation. In fact, in the absence of special monitoring facilities, a degraded performance (e.g., delayed response) may be the first indication of the underlying impairments. Provision of backup resources can postpone this transition, as can the ability to replace or repair the malfunctioning modules without having to shut down or otherwise disturb the system. Whereas overall system performance may be degraded, individual users or processes need not experience the same level of service degradation (e.g., because of reassessment of priorities). In fact, when degradation is severe, only critical computations may be allowed to run.

19.6. DEGRADATION-LEVEL METHODS

A dependable computer system is often defined as one producing trustworthy and timely results. Actually, neither trustworthiness nor timeliness is a binary (all or none) attribute. The obtained results may be incomplete or inaccurate rather than totally missing or completely wrong and they may be tardy enough to cause some inconvenience, without being totally useless or obsolete. Thus, various levels of inaccuracy, incompleteness, and tardiness can be distinguished and those that fall below particular thresholds might be viewed as *degradations* rather than *failures*. A computer system that is organized such that module malfunctions usually lead to degradations rather than to failures is *gracefully degrading* or *fail-soft* and is usually a multiprocessor system.

Figure 19.13 depicts the performance variations in three types of parallel systems:

S_1:   A *fail-hard* system with performance P_{max} up to the failure time t_1 as well as after completion of *off-line repair* at time t_1'.

S_2:   A *fail-soft* system with gradually degrading performance level and *off-line repair* at time t_2.

S_3:   A *fail-soft* system with *on-line repair* which, from the viewpoint of an application that requires a performance level of at least P_{min}, postpones its failure time to t_3.

The traditional notion of reliability is clearly inadequate for systems such as S_2 and S_3. Such systems must be characterized by their *performability*, a measure that encompasses performance and reliability and that constitutes a proper generalization of both.

Malfunction detection/diagnosis and system reconfiguration are starting stages of graceful degradation but they are not adequate as they form only the system components of degradation tolerance. Equally important are the application components. Applications may be designed such that they tolerate temporary or permanent reductions in system resources or performance. Two fundamental notions that allow an application to be degradation-tolerant are those of scalable and robust algorithms.

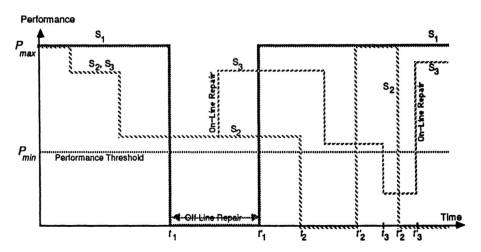

Figure 19.13. Performance variations in three example parallel computers.

A *scalable algorithm* is one that can be executed at various levels of resource availability, from the full *p*-processor parallel system down to a certain minimal configuration (ideally, all the way down to a single processor). Examples include the shared-memory parallel sorting algorithm described in Section 6.3 or any algorithm that is characterized by a task graph and run with the tasks dynamically scheduled on the available processors. In order to avoid the need for restarting an unfinished application program with each configuration change, a *checkpointing* scheme may be applied (Fig. 19.14). Saving of partial computation results in stable storage allows us to *roll back* the program to the last checkpoint instead of restarting it from the beginning. Checkpointing frequency is determined by cost–performance trade-offs in order to balance the overhead against the performance gain in the event of malfunctions.

Parallel systems offer special challenges for correct checkpointing and rollback. Figure 19.14 depicts a set of three communicating tasks, along with examples of consistent and inconsistent checkpoints. An arrow indicates a message, with the arrow's tail at the sending time and its head at the receiving time. The inconsistent checkpoint is so because if we roll back the three tasks to the points indicated, Task 0 would have received a message that is not yet sent by Task 2.

Like scalable algorithms, a *robust algorithm* is one that can be executed at various levels of resource availability. The difference is that with a robust algorithm, no assumption is made about the original architecture being preserved. The 2D mesh architecture provides a good example. A scalable algorithm for 2D mesh can run on various mesh sizes. A single malfunctioning processor can reduce the size of the available mesh to one-half, if a nonsquare mesh is acceptable, or to one-fourth, if the algorithm can only work on a square mesh. A robust algorithm, however, can run on an incomplete mesh that does not have all processors working [Parh98]. As long as it is known which processors are unavailable, the algorithm can work its way around them.

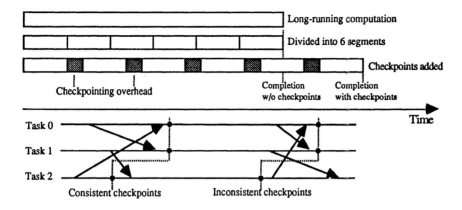

Figure 19.14. Checkpointing, its overhead, and pitfalls.

It is not difficult to envisage a routing algorithm that works on an incomplete mesh or hypercube. Other robust algorithms are harder to grasp, so let us provide an example for sorting on an incomplete mesh. If the mesh is designed in such a way that malfunctioning processors can be bypassed in their respective rows and columns (Fig. 19.15, left), then one can still use shearsort in an r-row, p-processor mesh. The only difference is that, after $\log_2 r$ iterations, there may be more than one dirty row, with the exact number being a function of the number of bypassed processors and their distribution in the various columns. If the maximum number of bypassed nodes in odd or even rows of any given column is b, then the number of dirty rows at the termination of the iterative part of *robust shearsort* is upper bounded by $4b + 1$ [Parh95]. Thus, if the final row-sort is replaced by the application of $(4b + 1)p/r$ steps of odd–even transposition along the overall snake, the sorted order will be achieved. The nice thing about the resulting robust algorithm is that with no malfunctioning processor, it sorts just as fast as standard shearsort, its performance degrades only slightly with scattered malfunctions (up to one per column, say), and it still works with even a large number of malfunctions, albeit at degraded performance.

Another robust sorting algorithm, which also works on an incomplete mesh with no node bypass capability and is thus more general, is based on identifying a submesh that has a significant number of complete rows and complete columns. In the example of Fig. 19.5 (right), the entire mesh has two complete rows and two complete columns, the submesh enclosed in the dotted box has three and two, and the submesh consisting of Processors 7–9 and 11–13 has two and three, respectively. The processors located at the intersections of these complete submesh rows and columns can be used to emulate any 2D mesh sorting algorithm. Thus, the sorting algorithm consists of three phases: (1) sending data items from all processors to the designated processors, (2) performing the emulation, and (3) redistributing the data to the original sources [Yeh97].

For example, taking Processors 1, 3, 7, 9, 11, and 13 as the processors designated to do the emulation in Fig. 19.15 (right), we first send all data elements to these processors, with each getting up to three elements. Then, we perform sorting on the 3×2 mesh with each processor holding three items, and finally we redistribute the three elements in each processor

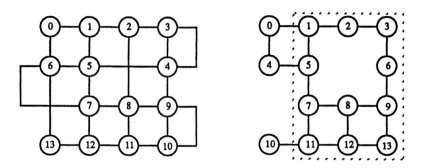

Figure 19.15. Two types of incomplete meshes, with and without bypass links.

to the original source processors. The sorting phase itself can be done using any mesh sorting algorithm.

A system fails when its degradation tolerance capacity is exhausted and, as a result, its performance falls below an acceptable threshold. As degradations are themselves consequences of malfunctions, it is interesting to skip a level and relate system failures directly to malfunctions. It has been noted that failures in a gracefully degrading system can be attributed to

1. Isolated malfunction of a critical subsystem.
2. Occurrence of catastrophic (multiple space-domain) malfunctions.
3. Accumulation of (multiple time-domain) malfunctions beyond detectability/tolerance.
4. Resource exhaustion causing inadequate performance or total shutdown.

Analysis of the PRIME gracefully degrading time-sharing system (developed at Berkeley in the early 1970s) showed that the first two items, i.e., intolerable malfunctions, are the most common causes of system failures; this conclusion has since been reinforced by other studies. In this context, a degradation is almost good news in that the mere fact of its occurrence means that the highest danger of failure has passed! Minimizing the number and size of critical subsystems (the *hard core*) and providing strong protection against catastrophic common-cause malfunctions are important requirements for recovery and continued operation in a degraded mode.

PROBLEMS

19.1. Defects, faults, . . . , failures

a. Consider the floating-point division flaw in early Pentium processors. Place this flaw and its consequences and remedies in the context of the seven-level model presented in Section 19.1.

b. Repeat part (a) for the Millennium bug, aka the Y2K (year-2000) problem, which will cause some programs using dates with two-digit year fields to fail when the year turns from 1999 to 2000.

19.2. Defects, faults, . . . , failures
Relate the following situations to the analogy of Fig. 19.2.

 a. A parallel system is designed to tolerate up to two malfunctioning processors. When a malfunction is diagnosed, the IC card that holds the malfunctioning processor is isolated, removed, and replaced with a good one, all in about 15 minutes.
 b. When the Pentium division flaw was uncovered, a software package was modified through "patches" to avoid operand values for which the flaw would lead to errors. On replacing the Pentium chip with a redesigned chip (without the flaw), the patched software was not modified.

19.3. Defect tolerance in a linear array
Consider the linear-array reconfiguration scheme depicted in Fig. 19.3, with switch defects being of a type that leaves them forever stuck in the cross or bent state.

 a. Show that the reconfiguration scheme in Fig. 19.3 is still single-defect-tolerant.
 b. Insert extra switches in the reconfiguration logic to make the scheme tolerant to single-switch plus single-processor defects. *Hint*: Data might pass through two switches in getting from one processor to the next, with the effect of one switch being stuck offset through proper setting of the other one.
 c. What can you say about the scheme in Fig. 19.4 in these regards?

19.4. Defect tolerance in 2D meshes

 a. In the scheme of Figs. 19.6 and 19.7, what fraction of triple processor defects are tolerable?
 b. How should the switching schemes of Fig. 19.5 be modified to accommodate the processor bypass capability assumed by the compensation path method?
 c. Generalize the compensation path method for defect tolerance to the case where a spare row/column is provided on each edge of the array (two spare rows, two spare columns).
 d. What is the smallest number of defective processors that can disable the scheme of part (c)?

19.5. Fault-tolerant MINs
The fault-tolerant extra-stage butterfly network of Fig. 19.9 essentially provides connectivity between 16 inputs and 16 outputs. Can a 16-input butterfly network provide the same function? How or why not?

19.6. Approximate voting
Suppose the three-input voter shown in Fig. 19.8 is to interpret its 32-bit unsigned inputs as fractional values that may contain small computational errors (possibly a different amount for each input).

 a. Provide a suitable definition of majority agreement in this case.
 b. Is a bit-serial voter, producing its output on the fly, feasible per the definition of part (a)?
 c. Design a bit-serial "median voter" that outputs the middle value among its three inexact inputs.
 d. Under what conditions is the output of a median voter the same as that of a majority voter?

19.7. Design of comparators
For the two-channel redundant scheme of Fig. 19.8, discuss the design of bit-serial comparators for integer (exact) and fractional (approximate) results in a manner similar to the voters of Problem 19.6.

19.8. Mean and median voting
One way to reconcile inexact values obtained from multiple computation channels is to take the mean of the values as the "correct" output.

a.   What are the advantages and drawbacks of mean voting?
b.   Consider a five-channel computation. Show that if the smallest and the largest of the five values are discarded and the mean of the remaining three values is taken as the "correct" output, better fault tolerance is obtained.
c.   Compare the voting scheme of part (b) to median voting, which chooses the middle value among the five results, with regard to advantages and disadvantages.

19.9. Algorithm-based error tolerance

a.   Verify that the product of the matrices M_c and M_r given in Section 19.4 yields the full checksum matrix $(M^2)_f$ if the additions are performed modulo 8.
b.   Prove the result in general.

19.10. Algorithm-based error tolerance

a.   Devise an algorithm-based error tolerance scheme for matrix–vector multiplication.
b.   Apply the scheme of part (a) to DFT computation (see Section 8.5).
c.   Given the special structure of the Fourier matrix, can you find a simplified error tolerance scheme for the DFT computation?

19.11. Malfunction diagnosis

a.   Is the matrix D in Fig. 19.11 consistent with some malfunctioning set of two or three processors?
b.   Prove or disprove: If the node degree of the testing graph is d and if there are at most $d - 1$ malfunctioning nodes, then at least one malfunctioning node can be identified with certainty.

19.12. Robust shearsort
Show that if there are x dirty rows when doing shearsort on an incomplete mesh with bypassed faulty processors, then one iteration (snakelike row sort followed by column sort) reduces the number of dirty rows to $x/2 + 2b$, where b is as defined in Section 19.6. Use this result to prove the $(4b + 1)p/r$ upper bound on the number of odd–even transposition steps needed at the end.

19.13. Malfunction-tolerant routing in hypercubes
A hypercube node is said to be k-capable if every nonfaulty node at distance k from it is reachable through a shortest path. Show that in an q-cube, the q-bit *capability vectors* of all nodes can be computed recursively through a simple algorithm and devise a fault-tolerant routing algorithm whereby each node makes its routing decisions solely on the basis of its own and its neighbors' capability vectors [Chiu97].

19.14. Fault diameter of q-D meshes and tori
The fault diameter of a network is defined as the diameter of its surviving part after faults have occurred.

a.   What is the fault diameter of a 2D mesh with a single faulty link? What about with a faulty node?
b.   Repeat part (a) for a 2D torus with two faults (node–node, link–link, link–node).

19.15. Reliability evaluation

Assume that nodes are perfectly reliable but that a link has reliability r. The terminal reliability of an interconnection network is defined as the minimal probability (over all node pairs) that a pair of nodes remain connected. Compute the terminal reliability of the following networks.

a. p-node linear array.
b. p-node ring.
c. q-cube.
d. q-star.

REFERENCES AND SUGGESTED READING

[Adam87]   Adams, G. B., III, D. P. Agrawal, and H. J. Siegel, "Fault-Tolerant Multistage Interconnection Networks," *IEEE Computer*, Vol. 20, No. 6, pp. 14–27, June 1987.

[Bruc93]   Bruck, J., R. Cypher, and C.-T. Ho, "Fault-Tolerant Meshes and Hypercubes with Minimal Numbers of Spares," *IEEE Trans. Computers*, Vol. 42, No. 9, pp. 1089–1104, September 1993.

[Chiu97]   Chiu, G.-M., and K.-S. Chen, "Use of Routing Capability for Fault-Tolerant Routing in Hypercube Multicomputers," *IEEE Trans. Computers*, Vol. 46, No. 8, pp. 953–958, August 1997.

[Cici95]   Ciciani, B., *Manufacturing Yield Evaluation of VLSI/WSI Systems*, IEEE Computer Society Press, 1995.

[Dutt96]   Dutt, S., and F. T. Assaad, "Mantissa-Preserving Operations and Robust Algorithm-Based Fault Tolerance for Matrix Computations," *IEEE Trans. Computers*, Vol. 45, No. 4, pp. 408–424, April 1996.

[Huan84]   Huang, K. H., and J. A. Abraham, "Algorithm-Based Fault Tolerance for Matrix Operations," *IEEE Trans. Computers*, Vol. 33, No. 6, pp. 518–528, June 1984.

[Kung88]   Kung, S. Y., *VLSI Array Processors*, Prentice–Hall, 1988.

[Parh94]   Parhami, B., "A Multi-Level View of Dependable Computing," *Computers & Electrical Engineering*, Vol. 20, No. 4, pp. 347–368, 1994.

[Parh95]   Parhami, B., and C. Y. Hung, "Robust Shearsort on Incomplete Bypass Meshes," *Proc. 9th Int. Parallel Processing Symp.*, April 1995, pp. 304–311.

[Parh98]   Parhami, B., and C.-H. Yeh, "The Robust-Algorithm Approach to Fault Tolerance on Processor Arrays: Fault Models, Fault Diameter, and Basic Algorithms," *Proc. Joint 12th Int. Parallel Processing Symp. and 9th Symp. Parallel and Distributed Processing*, 1998, pp. 742–746.

[Parh99]   Parhami, B., *Computer Arithmetic: Algorithms and Architectures*, to be published by Oxford University Press.

[Prad96]   Pradhan, D. K., and P. Banerjee, "Fault-Tolerant Multiprocessor and Distributed Systems: Principles," Chapter 3 in *Fault-Tolerant Computer System Design*, Prentice–Hall, 1996, pp. 135–235.

[Yeh97]   Yeh, C.-H., and B. Parhami, "Optimal Sorting Algorithms on Incomplete Meshes with Arbitrary Fault Patterns," *Proc. Int. Conf. Parallel Processing*, August 1997, pp. 4–11.

[Ziv96]   Ziv, A., and J. Bruck, "Checkpointing in Parallel and Distributed Systems," Chapter 10 in *Parallel and Distributed Computing Handbook*, edited by A. Y. Zomaya, McGraw-Hill, 1996, pp. 274–302.

20

System and Software Issues

This book is about algorithms and architectures for parallel processing. Therefore, I have chosen not to deal with questions such as how to build real parallel programs, what specification language or execution environment to use, how parallel system resources are managed, and how hardware and software interact from economic and application standpoints. So that there is not a complete void in these practically important areas, some system, software, and application aspects of parallel processing are reviewed in this chapter, with the goal of providing a broad picture and pointing the reader to key references for further study. Chapter topics are

- 20.1. Coordination and synchronization
- 20.2. Parallel programming
- 20.3. Software portability and standards
- 20.4. Parallel operating systems
- 20.5. Parallel file systems
- 20.6. Hardware/software interaction

20.1. COORDINATION AND SYNCHRONIZATION

Multiple processors working on pieces of a common problem require some form of coordination in order to ensure that they obtain meaningful and consistent results. The mechanism used for coordination may take various forms that involve the exchange of application data, state indicators, and timing information among the processors. Such activities are collectively referred to as *synchronization*, a term that is used even when the processors operate asynchronously.

In message-passing systems, synchronization is automatic. A task or process requiring data from another one typically executes a "receive" operation which either retrieves the data immediately from communication buffers or else will make the requesting process wait until the data source has executed a matching "send" operation. Figure 20.1 shows an example. At the top, the dependence of Task B on Task A is depicted by an arrow going from A to B. We used this notation, e.g., in the task graphs of Chapter 17. This is a coarse representation of the data dependence in that it does not specify where in the course of running A the required data are produced or where in B they are first needed. In a message-passing system, A and B are viewed as concurrent processes that can be initiated independently. Once B gets to the point where it needs the data from A (time t_1), it may have to wait until A prepares and sends the data (time t_2) and the communication network forwards the data from A to B (time t_3). Because the rate of progress in computations is in general load- and data-dependent, matching sends and receives can be encountered in either order in time. The semantics of send and receive automatically imposes the required waits, ensuring correct execution with no extra effort on our part.

In shared-memory systems, synchronization can be accomplished by accessing specially designated shared control variables. A popular way is through an atomic *fetch-and-add*

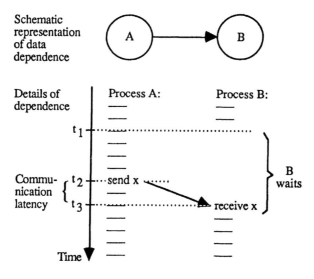

Figure 20.1. Automatic synchronization in message-passing systems.

instruction. The fetch-and-add instruction has two parameters: a shared variable x and an increment a. Suppose that the current value of x is c. On executing fetch-and-add(x, a) by a process, c is returned to the process and the new value $c + a$ replaces the old value of x in memory. A second process executing fetch-and-add(x, b) would then get the now current value $c + a$ and cause the value of x to be modified to $c + a + b$.

Based on the above description, multiple processes executing fetch-and-add with positive increments will always get different values in return. The actual values returned to the processes will depend on the particular order in which the memory "sees" the multiple fetch-and-add instructions. In this regard, the atomicity requirement is important to guarantee correct execution of concurrent or near-concurrent fetch-and-add instructions issued by several processes. As an example, consider the following timing of events if each of two processes were to execute fetch-and-add by reading the value of x from memory into an accumulator register, adding its increment to the accumulator, and storing the sum back into x. The three steps of fetch-and-add for the two processes may be interleaved in time as follows:

	Process A	Process B	Comments
Time step 1	read x		A's accumulator holds c
Time step 2		read x	B's accumulator holds c
Time step 3	add a		A's accumulator holds $c + a$
Time step 4		add b	B's accumulator holds $c + b$
Time step 5	store x		x holds $c + a$
Time step 6		store x	x holds $c + b$

This leads to incorrect semantics, as both processes will receive the same value c in return and the final value of x in memory will be $c + b$ rather than $c + a + b$.

Fetch-and-add is a powerful primitive that is useful in many different contexts. For example, if iterations of a loop with loop index i ranging from min to max are to be assigned to different processors for execution, the processors can execute fetch-and-add(x, 1) in order to get a value of the loop index to work on, where x is initialized to min. As another example, to verify that all of the h subtasks of a task have been completed, one can use a fetch-and-add(x, 1) at the end of each subtask. Assuming an initial value of 0 for x, all subtasks have been completed when the value of x becomes h.

Besides fetch-and-add, other atomic operations have been used for the purpose of coordination or synchronization. One example is "test-and-set," which causes a Boolean value to be read from location x and location x be set to 1 in one indivisible operation. One application is in implementing a lock that allows a single process to enter a critical section but stops all subsequent processes attempting to enter until the first process releases the lock by resetting the variable x to 0. Another example is "compare-and-swap" where a value provided by the process is compared against the value stored in the shared variable x and the values are swapped in one indivisible operation.

One problem with using fetch-and-add, test-and-set, compare-and-swap, or similar mechanisms for synchronization is that the shared memory locations corresponding to the control variables will be accessed by many processors, creating a condition known as *hot-spot contention*. When a multistage interconnection network is used for routing access requests from processors to memory banks (see, e.g., Fig. 6.9), special *combining switches*

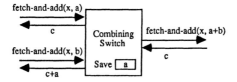

Figure 20.2. Combining of two fetch-and-add requests.

can be used to mediate the memory access conflicts. Figure 20.2 shows how combining of memory access requests can be used to reduce two memory access requests to just one.

A particularly useful synchronization scheme is *barrier synchronization* where a processor, in a designated set, must wait at a *barrier* until each of the other processors has arrived at the corresponding point in its respective computation. Basically, in MIMD computations, we prefer to let each processor proceed at its own speed for maximum efficiency. We try to keep synchronizations to a minimum, not only because synchronization itself has an overhead but also in view of the fact that some of the processors must remain idle until all other processors, which may have been slowed down by data-dependent conditions (e.g., more difficult subproblems, higher cache miss rates), have caught up. Figure 20.3 accentuates the performance benefit of less frequent synchronizations among a set of four processors.

Synchronous parallel computations are easier to visualize, and thus to develop and debug. Asynchronous computations are more efficient because they allow each processor to do its share of the work at full speed. Note that synchronization is required only when two or more processors must interact; no synchronization is needed during periods that are devoid of interprocessor communication. We can deal with the synchronization problem in two complementary ways. On the one hand, we can make synchronizations faster by providing hardware support. On the other hand, we can reduce the need for synchronization through suitable programming paradigms. Each of these alternatives will be briefly discussed in the following paragraphs. As usual, there is a trade-off in practice, with hybrid solutions that

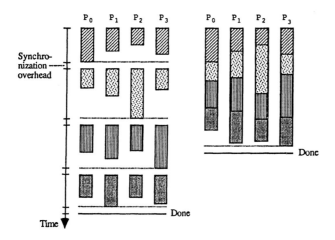

Figure 20.3. The performance benefit of less frequent synchronization.

borrow elements from each approach being the most cost-effective in a given application context.

A simpleminded approach to barrier synchronization is the use of an AND tree. Suppose that, on reaching a barrier, a processor raises a "barrier flag" and then checks to see if the AND tree output is 1. If it is, then the processor lowers its flag and proceeds past the barrier, because all other processors have reached the barrier. However, if it is possible for a processor to be randomly delayed between raising its flag and checking the AND tree output, then it is possible for some processors to go past the barrier and lower their flags before others have had a chance to examine the AND tree output.

Using two AND trees that are connected to the set and reset inputs of a flip-flop can solve the above problem [Hoar96]. Assume that the synchronization barriers are numbered consecutively. For each odd-indexed barrier, a processor sends a 1 into the set AND tree and a 0 into the reset AND tree (Fig. 20.4). Thus, when all processors have reached the barrier, the flip-flop will be set and checking for a 1 output from the flip-flop allows the processors to proceed past the odd-indexed barrier. For even-indexed barriers, the roles of the two trees are reversed, with each processor sending a 0 into the set AND tree and a 1 into the reset AND tree and checking for 0. Because the flip-flop will not be reset (set) until all of the processors have reached the next barrier, even a processor that has been significantly slowed down will detect the correct barrier signal and no processor ever goes into an infinite wait state.

Once we provide a mechanism like Fig. 20.4 to facilitate barrier synchronization, it is only a small step to generalize it to a more versatile "global combine" (semigroup computation) facility. Note that the AND tree essentially implements a semigroup computation using the binary AND operator. The generalization might involve the ability to do OR and XOR logical reductions as well.

An example for the second strategy, i.e., that of reducing the need for synchronizations, is the bulk-synchronous parallel (BSP) mode of parallel computation [Vali90], briefly discussed near the end of Section 4.5. In the BSP mode, synchronization of processors occurs once every L time steps, where L is a periodicity parameter. A parallel computation consists of a sequence of *supersteps*. In a given superstep, each processor performs a task consisting of local computation steps, message transmissions, and message receptions from other processors. Data received in messages will not be used in the current superstep but rather beginning with the next superstep. After each period of L time units, a global check is made to see if the current superstep has been completed. If so, then the processors move on to

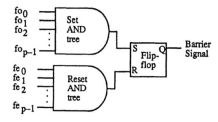

Figure 20.4. Example of hardware aid for fast barrier synchronization [Hoar96].

executing the next superstep. Otherwise, the next period of L time units is allocated to the unfinished superstep.

BSP is essentially a mechanism for ensuring overlap between computation and communication. If sufficient *parallel slack* is available (i.e., matrix multiplication, with each processor being responsible for computing a sizable block of the result matrix), then the processors will have more than enough local computations to perform in between data arrivals. We thus gain the benefits of synchronous communication (simple to visualize, easy to prove correct) and asynchronous computation (efficient use of processing resources).

Recall that in the LogP model of communication, also discussed near the end of Section 4.5, the aim was to characterize the communication performance of a parallel architecture in terms of a small number of parameters in order to facilitate the development of efficient parallel algorithms without a need for taking a great deal of machine-specific details into account. In BSP, we go a step further by squeezing all machine-dependent considerations into the periodicity parameter L. Note that the periodicity parameter L of BSP is different from the network latency parameter L of LogP. However, the two are not unrelated, as given a network with sufficient bandwidth, the periodicity in BSP can be chosen to be equal to, or a small multiple of, the latency in LogP.

20.2. PARALLEL PROGRAMMING

The preparation of programs for parallel execution is of immense practical importance. We have seen that the design of parallel processing hardware, particularly the interconnection architecture, and of parallel algorithms are full of challenging problems. As difficult as these problems are, the single most important reason for the lack of acceptance and limited application of parallel processing is neither hardware nor algorithms but rather obscure and cumbersome programming models. Since the early 1970s, we have witnessed moderate successes with parallelizing compilers, which automatically extract parallelism from essentially sequential specifications, and with array languages such as High-Performance Fortran. However, the goal of simple, efficient machine-independent parallel programming has remained elusive.

In this section, we briefly review five approaches to the development of parallel programs:

- Parallelizing compilers
- Data-parallel programming
- Shared-variable programming
- Communicating processes
- Functional programming

In the first approach, the parallelism is implicit in the program and is automatically extracted by the parallelizing compiler, while with the other four approaches, parallelism is explicitly specified by the programmer using appropriate constructs in a *parallel programming language*. There are two strategies for designing a parallel programming language: extending an existing popular language with capabilities for dealing with parallel constructs and building a new language from scratch. The former approach is easier and more likely to lead to adoption of the language.

A *parallelizing compiler* is one that takes a standard sequential program (written in Fortran, C, or other language) as input and produces a parallel program as output. *Vectorizing compilers* are similar and have been in use for many years in connection with pipelined vector processors. The idea in both cases is to deduce, through automatic *dependence analysis*, which computations lack interdependencies and can thus be executed concurrently.

The motivation behind the use of a parallelizing compiler is twofold. First, a parallelizing compiler allows us to utilize existing programs without the need to rewrite them for execution on each new parallel machine. Second, there is a great deal of expertise in most large organizations for writing and debugging sequential programs in standard languages, whereas the development of explicitly parallel programs requires retraining of programmers not only in the use of new parallel programming languages, but also in working with software aids for parallel program development and debugging.

As an example, consider the two nested "for" loops in the following program fragment:

for $i = 2$ to k do
    for $j = 2$ to k do
        $a_{i,j} := (a_{i,j-1} + a_{i,j+1})/2$
    endfor
endfor

In this example, each iteration of the i loop can be scheduled for execution on a different processor with complete asynchrony, because successive iterations are totally independent. Techniques similar to those used in vectorizing compilers, including reversal of nesting order, loop unrolling (or unfolding), and conversion of conditionals to reduction operations, are useful for deriving more efficient parallelized versions from a given sequential program.

It may seem ironic that forcing a naturally parallel computation into a sequential mold, and then applying the powers of an intelligent compiler to determine which of these artificially sequentialized computations can be performed concurrently, is a viable approach to parallel processing. But this is just one example of cultural inertia and economics dictating an approach that defies common sense.

Data-parallel programming is an approach with a long history. The APL programming language, with its array and reduction operations, was an early example of an explicit data-parallel programming scheme. For example, in APL, $C \leftarrow A + B$ meant that the matrix C is to be computed by the componentwise addition of the matrices A and B, $x \leftarrow +/V$ specified that x is the sum of all elements of the vector V, and $U \leftarrow +/V \times W$ represented the inner product of V and W (sum of all elements in the componentwise product of the two vectors). The "+/" operation, called *sum reduction*, was an instance of a generic reduction operation that could be used with any arithmetic, logic, selection, or comparison operator.

Although APL was devised primarily for making the specification of numerical computations mathematically elegant and more concise, its implications for data-parallel programming were also exploited in some parallel systems. The conciseness of APL specifications was at times a drawback because the ability of programmers to specify highly complex computations in one or two lines of code made the deciphering or understanding of the specifications, and thus their debugging and maintenance, very difficult, to the extent that APL was only half-jokingly referred to as a write-only language.

A much simpler version of the APL ideas are incorporated into an extension of the Fortran language known as High Performance Fortran (HPF), which was developed in 1992 to improve the performance and usability of Fortran-90 [Love93]. Fortran, though often criticized for its inelegance and lack of support for modular and structured programming, is extensively used in scientific computations, the primary application area for early parallel and vector supercomputers. Thus, prior to Fortran-90 and HPF, many Fortran extensions had been proposed for, and used on, various parallel machines. Examples include CFD Fortran of ILLIAC IV (an early 2D mesh parallel computer) and CFT or Vector Fortran developed for the Cray line of supercomputers. The introduction of HPF by a forum of researchers and industry representatives has been a major step for imposing uniformity and compatibility in the area of scientific parallel applications. HPF compilers are currently offered by several parallel computer vendors.

Fortran-90, a superset of Fortran-77, is an ISO and ANSI standard language, with extensions that include facilities for array operations. In Fortran-90, a statement such as

$$A = SQRT(A) + B ** 2$$

squares every element of array B, extracts the square root of every element of array A, and adds the corresponding elements of the two arrays, storing the results in array A. As a second example,

$$WHERE (B /= 0) \; A = A / B$$

performs a masked array assignment, resulting in each element of A being divided by the corresponding element of B, except in those cases where the B element is 0.

The semantics of Fortran-90 is independent of the underlying machine model. It simply provides a global name space and a single thread of control. However, array operations of the type presented above allow Fortran-90 programs to be efficiently executed on parallel machines. When run on a distributed-memory machine, some Fortran-90 constructs imply interprocessor communication. Assignment of a scalar value to an array

$$A = S/2$$

may imply multicasting or broadcasting (one-to-many communication). Use of "array section" notation or index vectors

$$A(I:J) = B(J:I:-1) \quad \{\text{a section of array B is assigned, in reverse order, to array A}\}$$
$$A(P) = B \quad \quad \quad \{\text{P is an integer index vector; means } A(P(I)) = B(I) \text{ for all } I\}$$

may require data permutation (many-to-many communication). Finally, reduction operations, such as summing all elements of an array

$$S = SUM(B)$$

may require a gather operation (many-to-one communication).

HPF extends Fortran-90 by adding new directives and language constructs. It also imposes some restrictions for efficiency reasons. HPF includes a number of compiler directives that assist the compiler in data distribution. These directives, which do not alter the semantics of the program, are presented as Fortran-90 comments (begin with the comment symbol "!"). Thus, if an HPF program is presented to a Fortran-90 compiler, it will be compiled, and subsequently executed, correctly. As an example, the HPF statement

!HPF ALIGN A(I) WITH B(I + 2)

is a hint to the compiler that it should distribute the elements of arrays A and B among processors or memory banks such that A(I) and B(I + 2) are stored together. If this statement is ignored, the program will still execute correctly, but perhaps less efficiently.

Data-parallel extensions have also been implemented for other popular programming languages. For example, the C* language was introduced in 1987 by Thinking Machines Corporation for use with its Connection Machine parallel computers. A key element in C* is the notion of "shape," which is defined, given a name, and then associated with the variables that are to have that particular shape (e.g., 20-element vector, 128 × 128 matrix). Parallel operations are specified using constructs such as the "with" statement, for componentwise or array reduction operations, and the "where" statement for conditional parallel operations such as

```
with (students) {
   where (credits > 0.0) {
      gpa = points / credits
   }
}
```

Like "if" statements, "where" statements in C* can have "else" clauses or be nested.

Another example of a data-parallel language is pC++, which is based on the popular sequential language C++ [Malo94]. A key notion in pC++ is that of "distributed collection," which is a structured set of objects distributed across multiple processors in a manner similar to what is done in HPF. The user can easily build collections from some base *element* class and also has access to a library of standard collection classes (e.g., vectors, arrays, matrices, grids, and trees). Profiling and performance analysis tools that are built into pC++ allow the user to establish the need for, and the resulting benefits of, various optimizations.

Shared-variable programming is exemplified by Concurrent Pascal and Modula-2. Concurrent Pascal is an extension of Pascal, with the addition of *processes*, *monitors*, and *classes*, along with three new statements (init, delay, continue) and a new data type (queue). Monitors can be viewed as mechanisms that allow us to put walls around a collection of shared resources in order to regulate multiple accesses to them. Concurrent Pascal also provides facilities for initiating, delaying, and continuing the execution of processes and a way of scheduling the various calls made by outside procedures in FIFO order. A class defines a data structure and its associated operations that can be performed by a single process or monitor (mutual exclusion). Modula-2 contains only primitive concurrency features that allow processes to interact through shared variables or via (synchronizing) signals.

In the Sequent C shared-variable programming language, developed for use with Sequent's shared-memory multiprocessors, the keyword *shared* placed before a global variable declaration forces all processors to share a single instance of that variable, whereas an ordinary declaration implies that each processor will have a private copy of that variable. A program begins execution as a single process, which may then fork into a number of parallel processes. Program execution alternates between sequential and parallel segments, with the transition from a parallel to a sequential segment delimited by a barrier synchronization. Even though Sequent C has no built-in support for monitors, they can be easily implemented by using its shared lock declaration and associated "lock" and "unlock" statements.

Communicating processes form the basis of several concurrent programming languages such as Ada and Occam. This approach, which involves passing of messages among concurrently executing processes, has four basic features: (1) process/task naming, (2) synchronization, (3) messaging scheme, and (4) failure handling. Process naming can be direct (explicit) or indirect (the sender names an intermediate object such as a channel, mailbox, or pipe). Synchronization can be nonexistent, complete (sender proceeds only after ensuring that its message has been delivered), or partial (e.g., remote procedure calls and use of acknowledgments). The messaging scheme can be quite flexible and general, as in Ada, or rigidly linked to an assumed hardware structure (such as channels in Occam). Finally, failure handling is needed for undesirable situations such as deadlocks (complete system lockup) or starvation (a particular process's messages not getting through).

Instead of building interprocess communication facilities into a programming language, it is possible to provide users with language-independent libraries. This approach, as embodied in the MPI standard, is now the dominant approach for programming distributed-memory machines (see Section 20.3). Though not as elegant as the above-mentioned languages, the use of libraries is practically much simpler. Compilers for powerful parallel languages are notoriously difficult and costly to develop. These factors, along with the limited acceptance of each such language by the user community, render the approach economically unviable. Libraries, on the other hand, are easier to develop and can be used in conjunction with the user's favorite language.

Functional programming is based on reduction and evaluation of expressions. There is no concept of storage, assignment, or branching in a functional program. Rather, results are obtained by applying functions to arguments, incorporating the results as arguments of still other functions, and so forth, until the final results are obtained. Alternatively, we can view a functional programming language as allowing only one assignment of value to each variable, with the assigned value maintained throughout the course of the computation. Thus, computations have the property of *referential transparency* or freedom from side effects, which makes their final results independent of the history of how, and in what order, various partial results were obtained. These appear to be ideal properties for parallel processing. However, because of the inefficiencies inherent in the single-assignment approach, the practical application of functional programming has thus far been limited to Lisp-based systems (e.g., MIT's Multilisp) and data-flow architectures (e.g., Manchester University's SISAL).

20.3. SOFTWARE PORTABILITY AND STANDARDS

During much of the history of parallel processing, parallel applications have been developed as machine-specific, and thus nonportable (often one-of-a-kind), programs. This has made parallel applications quite costly to develop, debug, and maintain. The reasons for this undesirable state of affairs are

- Proliferation of parallel architectures and lack of agreement on a common model
- Infeasibility of commercial software development based on the limited customer base
- Desire for efficient hardware utilization, given the high cost of parallel processors

Changes are afoot in all of these areas, making the prospects of truly portable parallel software brighter than ever. Ideally, a portable parallel program should run on a variety of hardware platforms with no modification whatsoever. In practice, minor modifications that do not involve program redesign or significant investments of time and effort are tolerated.

Program portability requires strict adherence to design and specification standards that provide machine-independent views or logical models. Programs are developed according to these logical models and are then adapted to specific hardware architectures by automatic tools (e.g., compilers). HPF is an example of a standard language that, if implemented correctly, should allow programs to be easily ported across platforms. In what follows, we briefly review two other logical models, or user-level views, that have been developed for parallel systems: MPI and PVM. These descriptions are necessarily oversimplified and incomplete. They are meant only as an annotated list of user-level implementation options and issues in parallel computing. The cited references should be consulted for details.

The *message-passing interface* (MPI) standard specifies a library of functions that implement the message-passing model of parallel computation [MPIF94] [Snir96]. MPI was developed by the MPI Forum, a consortium of parallel computer vendors and software development specialists. As a standard, MPI provides a common high-level view of a message-passing environment that can be mapped to various physical systems. Software implemented using MPI functions can be easily ported among machines that support the MPI model. MPI includes functions for

- Point-to-point communication (blocking and nonblocking send/receive, . . .)
- Collective communication (broadcast, gather, scatter, total exchange, . . .)
- Aggregate computation (barrier, reduction, and scan or parallel prefix)
- Group management (group construction, destruction, inquiry, . . .)
- Communicator specification (inter-/intracommunicator construction, destruction, . . .)
- Virtual topology specification (various topology definitions, . . .)

Most of the above functions are self-explanatory (refer to Section 10.1 for definitions of point-to-point and collective communications and to Section 20.1 for barrier synchronization).

Both blocking and nonblocking sends can start independent of whether or not a matching receive has been posted. A blocking send completes when the send buffer can be reused, whereas nonblocking send returns before the message has been copied out from the buffer. Thus, nonblocking send allows computation and communication to be overlapped, but requires a separate check for completion. Blocking receive and nonblocking receive are similarly related. A communicator is a *process group* (ordered set of processes) plus a *context*. Each communicator has a distinct context; a message sent in one context must be received in the same context. This feature allows multiple communications to coexist in the parallel system without interfering with one another. The *virtual topology* specification allows for hardware-independent program development. If a 2D-mesh virtual topology is specified, the implementation of MPI on any given machine maps the virtual topology to the target machine's real topology (e.g., 2D mesh, 3D torus, hypercube) in such a way that efficient communications can be performed.

MPI assumes the use of a reliable user-level transmission protocol with nonovertaking messages. Because message-passing programs often exhibit a great deal of temporal locality, in the sense that a process sending a message to another one is likely to send another message to the same process in the near future, MPI includes features for *persistent communication* that allow some of the overhead of sending and receiving messages to be shared across multiple transmissions.

Parallel virtual machine (PVM) is a software platform for developing and running parallel applications on a collection of independent, heterogeneous, computers that are interconnected in a variety of ways [Geis95]. PVM defines a suite of user-interface primitives that support both the shared-memory and the message-passing parallel programming paradigms. These primitives provide functions similar to those listed above for MPI and are embedded within a procedural host language (usually Fortran or C). A PVM support process or daemon (PVMD) runs independently on each host, performing message routing and control functions. PVMDs perform the following functions:

- Exchange network configuration information
- Allocate memory to packets that are in transit between distributed tasks
- Coordinate the execution of tasks on their associated hosts

The available pool of processors may change dynamically. Names can be associated with groups or processes. Group membership can change dynamically and one process can belong to many groups. Group-oriented functions, such as broadcast and barrier synchronization, take group names as their arguments.

20.4. PARALLEL OPERATING SYSTEMS

A parallel computer, like a sequential machine, needs system programs that manage its resources, provide various services to user processes, and enforce the required protection, performance monitoring, and accounting functions. From the viewpoint of how the available computational, storage, and communication resources are managed, we distinguish two classes of parallel processors: back-end/front-end and stand-alone.

In the *back-end* system subclass, the parallel processor is viewed as a resource that is attached to a conventional (sequential) host computer. The host computer has a standard operating system, like Unix, and manages the parallel processor essentially like a coprocessor or I/O device. Required data are provided to the parallel processor, and the computation results received from it, in much the same way as I/O data transfers. The host computer is also responsible for program compilation, diagnostic testing, access control, and interface with the users. The main advantage of this approach, which is particularly suited to computation-intensive applications where a great deal of manipulation is performed on a limited set of data, is that it avoids the high cost of developing and maintaining special system software. The *front-end* system subclass is similar, except that the parallel processor handles its own data (e.g., an array processor doing radar signal processing) and relies on the host computer for certain postprocessing functions, diagnostic testing, and interface with the users.

In the *stand-alone* system class, a special operating system is included that can run on one, several, or all of the processors in a floating or distributed (master–slave or symmetric) fashion. Because of the popularity of Unix, most parallel operating systems in use today are extensions of Unix (Unix-based) or have very similar structures to that of Unix (Unix-like). Note that a parallel operating system is not fundamentally different from a standard operating system such as Unix. Modern operating systems are all concurrent programs that deal with multiple hardware resources (e.g., processors, I/O channels), multiple asynchronous events (e.g., interrupts), and interdependent tasks or computation threads.

Parallel operating systems have a long history. In 1960, Burroughs introduced its AOSP (Automatic Operating and Scheduling Program) for a 4-processor shared-memory computer. Progress in small-scale shared-memory operating systems continued in the 1970s with TOPS-10 for the PDP-10 by Digital Equipment Corporation and OS/VS2 for the IBM System 370 Models 158 MP and 168 MP. The advent of low-cost minicomputers in the 1970s allowed experimentation with larger-scale parallel systems. Notable examples were the Hydra operating system for Carnegie-Mellon University's 16-processor C.mmp and the Medusa and StarOS systems for CMU's 50-processor Cm* system.

Beginning with the introduction of the MUNIX system for a dual PDP-11 configuration in the mid-1970s, numerous Unix-based and Unix-like parallel operating systems have been designed. Recent examples include the Dynix operating system for the Sequent Balance shared-memory MIMD computer with up to 30 processors, the OSF/1 operating system introduced by the nonprofit Open Software Foundation (now the Open Group) that runs the Intel Paragon, and IBM's AIX for its SP-2 line of parallel systems. The advent of parallel environments based on clusters of workstations has made the Unix-based approach even more attractive.

The Mach operating system developed at Carnegie-Mellon University is sometimes classified as a Unix-based system in view of its ability to run serial Unix applications as single-threaded tasks. Mach's capability-based object-oriented design supports multiple tasks and threads that can communicate with each other via messages or memory objects. Tasks and threads are conceptually the same in that they specify concurrently executable code segments. However, context switching between two threads executing the same task is much faster than that between two arbitrary threads. This is why threads are sometimes called *lightweight processes*, where lightness refers to the limited state information associated with a process or thread.

Figure 20.5 depicts the structure of the Mach operating system. The Mach kernel runs in the supervisor mode, performing functions relating to virtual memory management, port and message management, and task or thread scheduling. Everything else runs in the user mode. To make a compact, modular kernel possible, Mach designers have opted to define a small set of basic abstractions:

- *Task*: a "container" for resources like virtual address space and communication ports
- *Thread*: an executing program with little context; a task may contain many threads
- *Port*: a communication channel along with certain access rights
- *Message*: a basic unit of information exchange
- *Memory object*: a "handle" to part of a task's virtual memory

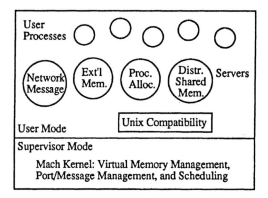

Figure 20.5. Functions of the supervisor and user modes in the Mach operating system.

Unlike Unix whose memory consists of contiguous areas, the virtual address space in Mach is composed of individual pages with separate protection and inheritance. This makes it possible to efficiently handle programs with large and/or sparse address spaces. Inheritance refers to what is in the page: shared, private, or invalid (absent) data.

Messages in Mach are communicated via ports. The messages are typed to indicate the data type they carry and can be communicated over a port only if the sending/receiving thread has the appropriate access rights. For efficiency purposes, messages that involve a large amount of data do not actually carry the data; instead a pointer to the actual data pages is transmitted. Copying of the data to the receiver's pages does not occur until the receiver accesses the data. So, even though a message may refer to an extensive data set, only the segments actually referenced by the receiver will ever be copied.

The Mach scheduler has some interesting features. Each thread is assigned a time quantum on starting its execution. When the time quantum expires, a context switch is made to a thread with highest priority, if such a thread is awaiting execution. To avoid starvation of low-priority threads, priorities are reduced based on "age"; the more CPU time a thread uses, the lower its priority becomes. This policy not only prevents starvation, but also tends to favor interactive tasks over computation-intensive ones.

A number of user-mode servers, some of which are shown in Fig. 20.5, perform user-defined functions or extend the kernel's capabilities. For example, interprocess communication over the network is not supported by the Mach kernel. Instead, messages are sent to a *network server*, which represents tasks running on remote nodes. The network server converts process names to physical addresses and sends the messages over the network. Similarly, at the destination, a network server receives the message, derives a local destination port from the information contained in the message, and forwards the message to its final destination. The various steps outlined above can be made transparent to the user who sends messages using process names rather than physical port numbers. In a similar vein, shared-memory accesses to remote pages are handled by a *distributed shared-memory server*.

20.5. PARALLEL FILE SYSTEMS

Considerations for I/O devices to support the high bandwidth requirements of parallel processors were discussed in Sections 18.4 and 18.5. Raw I/O bandwidth, however, is not sufficient to balance the I/O performance with the processing power. A *parallel file system*, which efficiently maps data access requests by processors to high-bandwidth data transfers between primary and secondary memory devices, is another important piece. In fact, as the focus of parallel processing applications shifts from number crunching to databases and data mining, parallel file systems cannot help but grow in importance.

If the parallel file system is not to become a performance bottleneck, it must itself be written as a highly parallel and scalable program that can efficiently deal with many access scenarios:

- Concurrent access to files by multiple independent processes
- Shared access to files by groups of cooperating processes
- Access to large amounts of data by a single process

Figure 20.6 shows some of the complexities involved in the third case above. A read request issued by a user process is sent to a dispatcher process which creates a server task or thread to effect the required transfer. The actual data needed may come in part from cache copies of various disk pages and in part satisfied by initiating disk read accesses. To achieve its goal, the READ server process might spawn multiple COPYRD threads, one for each fixed-size block of data to be transferred. These threads must be distributed throughout the system, not just to allow them to be executed in parallel but also to balance the memory load and network traffic resulting from the transfers. Hopefully, the file block allocation mechanism has declustered the data on the disk in such a way that the disk accesses required will also be performed in parallel.

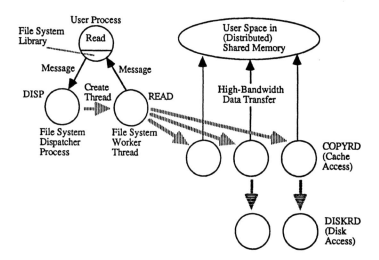

Figure 20.6. Handling of a large read request by a parallel file system [Hell93].

Examples of existing file systems for parallel machines include Sun's network file system, Intel's concurrent file system [Pier89], and nCUBE's I/O system software [DeBe92].

20.6. HARDWARE/SOFTWARE INTERACTION

Parallel processing has been and is being done on many different platforms. At one extreme lie homogeneous tightly coupled parallel processors, with custom, highly optimized interconnection structures. These machines are least flexible in terms of system scalability, program portability, and run-time performance fine tuning. At the other extreme lie heterogeneous loosely coupled distributed systems, usually composed of commodity processing and communication resources. The built-in management of heterogeneity and asynchrony in such systems often makes them more readily adaptable, scalable, and portable. Many parallel processing systems, particularly those with standard or hierarchical buses, fall between these two extremes. Parallel applications are often not portable between these various classes of parallel systems (sometimes not even between different machines in the same general class).

Given the programming models and user-level views discussed in the preceding sections of this chapter, it is possible, and highly desirable, to completely decouple the two issues of hardware configuration and algorithm or program development for parallel systems. A parallel application program should be executable, with little or no modification, on a variety of parallel hardware platforms that differ in architecture and scale. This is necessary from an economic standpoint, as very few users can afford the cost of developing parallel applications from scratch with each new generation of hardware or, worse, with each increment in system size. For example, it is fairly common for an organization to begin with a small (say 8-processor) parallel system and then upgrade to larger systems as its needs warrant. The changeover from the 8-processor to the 16-processor configuration, say, should not require modification in the system or application programs; ideally, the upgrade should be done by simply plugging in the new processors with associated interconnects and rebooting the system.

From the above viewpoints, workstation clusters are ideal platforms for parallel computation, as they are readily scalable both in time and in space. They are scalable in time, because the introduction of faster workstations and interconnects leads to a corresponding increase in system performance with little or no redesign. They are scalable in space, because their computational power can be increased by simply plugging in more processors. While it is true that increasing the number of processors may lead to an imbalance between the available computational power and communication bandwidth, compilers and operating systems can partially compensate for this imbalance by adjusting the task granularity and their partitioning, scheduling, and load-balancing strategies. Also, computation can be traded off for communication by using data compression methods or context-dependent messaging schemes.

Obviously, it is desirable to provide the same type of scalability enjoyed by loosely coupled workstation clusters for tightly coupled multiprocessors. Many of the commercially available parallel processors are in fact scalable in space within specific ranges (say 4–256 processors). Scalability in time is difficult at present but may be made possible in the future through the adoption of implementation and interfacing standards of the same types that have made personal computer modules compatible and readily interchangeable.

Besides hardware scalability, users are interested in software or application scalability. The notion of algorithm scalability (being able to run an algorithm at various levels of resource availability) was defined in Section 19.6. Algorithm or application scalability is useful not only for achieving degradation tolerance but also for portability. In the remainder of this section, we quantify the above notion and define the related measures of *scaled speed-up* and *isoefficiency*.

Recall the definition $T(1)/T(p)$ of speed-up introduced in Section 1.6 for a given (fixed-size) problem. As noted near the end of Section 1.1, we use parallel processing not just to speed up the solution of fixed problems but also to make the solution of larger problems feasible with realistic turnaround times. The equation for speed-up, with the problem size n explicitly included, is

$$S(n,p) = \frac{T(n, 1)}{T(n, p)}$$

The cumulative time $pT(n, p)$ spent by the processors can be divided into computation time $C(n,p)$ and overhead time $H(n, p) = pT(n, p) - C(n, p)$, where the latter incorporates everything besides computation, including communication time and processor idle time. Assuming for simplicity that we have no redundancy, $C(n, p) = T(n, 1)$ and we get $H(n, p) = pT(n, p) - T(n, 1)$ and

$$S(n, p) = \frac{p}{1 + H(n, p)/T(n, 1)}$$

Efficiency, defined as $E(n, p) = S(n, p)/p$, is then simply

$$E(n, p) = \frac{1}{1 + H(n, p)/T(n, 1)}$$

If the overhead per processor, $H(n, p)/p$, is a fixed fraction f of $T(n, 1)$, then speed-up and efficiency will become

$$S(n, p) = \frac{p}{1 + pf}$$

$$E(n, p) = \frac{1}{1 + pf}$$

The speed-up formula above is essentially an alternate form of Amdahl's law that establishes an upper bound of $1/f$ on speed-up.

In what follows, we assume that efficiency is to be kept above one-half, but the arguments apply to any fixed efficiency target. Based on the above formula, to have $E(n, p) > 1/2$, we need $pf < 1$ or

$$p < 1/f$$

implying that, for a fixed problem size and under the assumption of the per-processor overhead being a fixed fraction of the single-processor running time, there is an upper limit to the number of processors that can be applied cost-effectively.

Going back to our initial efficiency equation, we note that keeping $E(n, p)$ above one-half requires

$$T(n, 1) > H(n, p)$$

Generally, the cumulative overhead $H(n, p)$ is an increasing function of both n and p, whereas $T(n, 1)$ only depends on n. Recall that we are proceeding with the assumption $C(n, p) = T(n, 1)$, meaning that $T(n, 1)$ represents the amount of useful computation performed by the p processors. As we scale the machine size (increase p) with a fixed problem size, $H(n, p)$ grows but $T(n, 1)$ remains constant, thus leading to lower speedup and efficiency.

For many problems, good efficiency can be achieved provided that we sufficiently scale up the problem size. The amount of growth in problem size that can counteract the increase in machine size in order to achieve a fixed efficiency is referred to as the *isoefficiency* function $n(p)$, which can be obtained from the equation

$$T(n, 1) = H(n, p)$$

With the above provisions, a *scaled speed-up* of $p/2$ or more is achievable for problems of suitably large size. Note, however, that the parallel execution time

$$T(n, p) = \frac{T(n, 1) + H(n, p)}{p}$$

grows as we scale up the problem size to obtain good efficiency. Thus, there is a limit to the usefulness of scaled speed-up. In particular, when there is a fixed computation time available because of deadlines (as in daily or weekly weather forecasting), the ability to achieve very good scaled speed-up may be irrelevant.

PROBLEMS

20.1. Data dependence
Consider the data dependence diagram of Fig. 20.1 to which an arrow going from B to A has been added. If the resulting circular dependence does not make sense, say why; otherwise provide a detailed example.

20.2. Fetch-and-add versus test-and-set
a. Show how an atomic fetch-and-add capability can do the job of test-and-set.
b. Can test-and-set be used to provide an atomic fetch-and-add capability?
c. Fetch-and-op is a generalization of fetch-and-add with an arbitrary operator. Which operators besides "add" might be useful in this context?

20.3. Mutual exclusion
Several concurrent processes are to read and update the shared variables x, y, and z. The nature of the application is such that in each use, all three variables are read out but only one is updated.
a. How can access to these variables be restricted to one process at a time using a shared *lock* variable?

b.   Is there any advantage to using three shared variables *lockx*, *locky*, and *lockz* to regulate the accesses? What about drawbacks?

20.4. Mutual exclusion and deadlock
When resources are to be shared by multiple processes, a permission and release (lock/unlock) mechanism can be employed. A process obtains a lock to use a shared resource; when done, it returns the lock.

a.   Show that deadlock is possible with as few as two shared resources, even if processes never fail to return a lock when they are done using a resource (i.e., processes are correct and never hang up).
b.   Show that if shared resources are numbered and each process is restricted to request resources in ascending numerical order, then deadlock cannot occur.

20.5. Fetch-and-add operation
Draw a diagram similar to Fig. 20.2 to show how six concurrent fetch-and-adds might be combined in the switches of a multistage interconnection network.

20.6. Processor synchronization
Consider the Jacobi relaxation method, presented near the end of Section 11.4, for solving a linear system of equations. There are n equations and p processors, so that in each iteration, a processor must determine the new value for n/p variables based on the old values of all n variables.

a.   Assume that barrier synchronization is used so that processors move from one iteration to the next in lockstep. Discuss the running time of the algorithm in view of the synchronization overhead.
b.   Suppose that we use the asynchronous version of the algorithm by allowing each processor to proceed at its own speed, with no synchronization. Processors may drift apart, causing values from different iterations to be intermixed. Discuss the effects of this strategy on the convergence and running time of the algorithm ([Bert89], pp. 434–437).

20.7. Processor synchronization
A generalized synchronization network may consist of a *parallel counter* that receives p single-bit inputs and produces their $\lceil \log_2(p + 1) \rceil$-bit sum at the output.

a.   Show how such a generalized network can be used for barrier synchronization.
b.   Give examples where the above network is more useful than the AND-tree of Fig. 20.4.
c.   Using the above network, devise an algorithm that implements a global sum operation.

20.8. Parallelizing "for" loops
Consider a "for" loop with its index i ascending from 1 to k.

a.   The loop is said to have *forward dependence* if it contains statements such as $a_i := a_{i+1} + b$. Explain why such a forward dependence does not prevent parallelization.
b.   An example loop with *backward dependence* contains the statement $a_i := b_i + c_i$ followed by $b_{i+1} := \mathrm{sqrt}(d_i)$. Show how this particular loop can be parallelized.
c.   Can you parallelize the loop containing the single statement $a_{i+1} := a_i + b_i$?
d.   Can you parallelize the loop containing the conditional statement if $a_i \leq 0$ then $s := s + a_i \times b_i$?

20.9. HPF Fortran
Answer the following questions for High-Performance Fortran, where A, B, C are real vectors and P, Q are integer index vectors (permutations of the integers in [1, N]).

   a. Does the assignment $A(P) = B(P)$ make sense? What about $Q = N + 1 - P$ followed by $A(P)$ $= B(Q)$?

   b. Describe the effect of the assignment statement $A = B(P) + C(N:1:-1)$.

   c. Are the directives ALIGN A(I) with B(I + 2) and ALIGN B(I) WITH C(I − 2) conflicting or compatible?

20.10. Parallel programming

Sketch the designs of parallel programs corresponding to the sieve of Eratosthenes (see Section 1.2) in two parallel programming languages of your choice. Outline the differences in the two implementations and the application characteristics that led to them.

20.11. Functional programming

Study the functional programming approach to parallel program development, highlighting some of the key reasons for its lack of popularity despite clean semantics and freedom from side effects.

20.12. MPI and PVM

Study the Message-Passing Interface and Parallel Virtual Machine standards. Enumerate their similarities and differences and contrast their domains of applicability.

20.13. Parallel systems software

Study the Unix-based operating systems, and their associated file systems, for two real parallel machines of your choice. Explain the differences between the two in terms of interprocess communication, protection mechanisms, task/thread scheduling, synchronization support, and compatibility with Unix.

20.14. Isoefficiency and scaled speed-up

It can be shown that the cumulative overhead $H(n, p)$ for n-point FFT computation on a p-processor hypercube and 2D mesh is $O(n \log p + p \log p)$ and $O(\log p + n/\sqrt{p})$, respectively. The work required for an n-point FFT is $T(n, 1) = O(n \log n)$. Find the isoefficiency function and comment on the application scalability and speedup in each of the two cases.

20.15. Parallel computation speed-up and efficiency

Relate the discussion of scaled speed-up and isoefficiency in Section 20.6 to the "good-news" corollaries to Brent's scheduling theorem in Section 17.5.

20.16. Digital libraries

Briefly discuss how the material in each of the six sections in this chapter is relevant to the use of a highly parallel processor as a high-performance server for a digital library [CACM95].

REFERENCES AND SUGGESTED READING

[Bert89]   Bertsekas, D. P., and J. N. Tsitsiklis, *Parallel and Distributed Computation: Numerical Methods*, Prentice–Hall, 1989.

[Blel96]   Blelloch, G. E., "Programming Parallel Algorithms," *Communications of the ACM*, Vol. 39, No. 3, pp. 85–97, March 1996.

[CACM95]   *Communications of the ACM*, special issue on digital libraries, Vol. 38, No. 4, April 1995.

[DeBe92]   DeBenedictis, E., and J. M. del Rosario, "nCUBE Parallel I/O Software," *Proc. 11th IEEE Int. Phoenix Conf. on Computers and Communications*, 1992, pp. 117–124.

[Geis95]   Geist, A., et al., *PVM, Parallel Virtual Machine, A User's Guide and Tutorial for Networked Parallel Computing*, MIT Press, 1995.

[Gram93]   Grama, A. Y., A. Gupta, and V. Kumar, "Isoefficiency: Measuring the Scalability of Parallel Algorithms and Architectures," *IEEE Parallel & Distributed Technology*, Vol. 1, No. 3, pp. 12–21, August 1993.

[Hell93]   Hellwagner, H., "Design Considerations for Scalable Parallel File Systems," *The Computer Journal*, Vol. 36, No. 8, pp. 741–755, 1993.

[Hoar96]   Hoare, R., H. Dietz, T. Mattox, and S. Kim, "Bitwise Aggregate Networks," *Proc. 8th IEEE Symp. Parallel & Distributed Processing*, October, 1996, pp. 306–313.

[Love93]   Loveman, D. B., "High Performance Fortran," *IEEE Parallel & Distributed Technology*, Vol. 1, No. 1, pp. 25–42, February 1993.

[Malo94]   Malony, A., et al., "Performance Analysis of pC++: A Portable Data-Parallel Programming System for Scalable Parallel Computers," *Proc. 8th Int. Parallel Processing Symp.*, April 1994, pp. 75–84.

[MPIF94]   MPI Forum, "MPI: A Message-Passing Interface Standard," *Int. J. Supercomputer Applications*, Vol. 8, Nos. 3/4, pp. 169–414, 1994.

[Perr96]   Perrott, R. H., "Parallel Languages," Chapter 29 in *Parallel and Distributed Computing Handbook*, edited by A. Y. Zomaya, McGraw-Hill, 1996, pp. 843–864.

[Pier89]   Pierce, P., "A Concurrent File System for a Highly Parallel Mass Storage Subsystem," *Proc. 4th Conf. on Hypercube Concurrent Computers and Applications*, 1989, pp. 155–160.

[Snir96]   Snir, M., et al., *MPI: The Complete Reference*, MIT Press, 1996.

[Vali90]   Valiant, L. G., "A Bridging Model for Parallel Computation," *Communications of the ACM*, Vol. 33, No. 8, pp. 103–111, August 1990.

VI

Implementation Aspects

To learn how the theories and techniques covered in the previous chapters are applied to the design of real machines, in this part we review the architectures and other characteristics of several production and prototype parallel computers. The case studies have been chosen to represent the various architectural classes and to illustrate how implementation methods are used in the context of overall design goals, technological constraints, and application requirements. Within each class, we review key concepts related to the user view and then study a cross section of real designs that include historically significant computers, machines that have influenced the parallel processing industry, those that have contributed significantly to a better understanding of the field, and, of course, modern production machines that are still in use. In the final chapter, we present a roadmap of the past and current trends and review some of the promising and exciting research areas that are likely to shape the field of parallel processing in the next decade. This part consists of four chapters:

- Chapter 21: Shared-Memory MIMD Machines
- Chapter 22: Message-Passing MIMD Machines
- Chapter 23: Data-Parallel SIMD Machines
- Chapter 24: Past, Present, and Future

21

Shared-Memory MIMD Machines

The shared-memory view can be provided in different ways. In this chapter, following a survey of topics pertaining to the practical implementation and performance of shared memory, we review several parallel computer systems that use global or distributed shared memory. Two of the machines chosen are products of groundbreaking research (BBN Butterfly and Stanford DASH), one was developed in the private sector with extensive support from the U.S. government (Tera MTA), and two are production machines from different generations: Cray Y-MP, which is a cluster of several vector supercomputers, and Sequent NUMA-Q, which is a modern machine based on the SCI standard. Chapter topics are

- 21.1. Variations in shared memory
- 21.2. MIN-based BBN Butterfly
- 21.3. Vector-parallel Cray Y-MP
- 21.4. Latency-tolerant Tera MTA
- 21.5. CC-NUMA Stanford DASH
- 21.6. SCI-based Sequent NUMA-Q

21.1. VARIATIONS IN SHARED MEMORY

Shared-memory implementations vary greatly in the hardware architecture that they use and in the programming model (logical user view) that they support. In this section we review the most common hardware architectures for shared memory, and also discuss the various logical user views and their performance implications, to set the stage for the case studies that follow in Sections 21.2 through 21.6. Ideas and terminology introduced in Section 4.3 are relevant to our discussion here, as is the discussion of cache coherence in Section 18.2.

With respect to hardware architecture, shared-memory implementations can be classified according to the placement of the main memory modules within the system (central or distributed) and whether or not multiple copies of modifiable data are allowed to coexist (single- or multiple-copy). The resulting four-way classification is depicted in Fig. 21.1.

With a central main memory, access to all memory addresses takes the same amount of time, leading to the designation *uniform memory access* (UMA). In such machines, data distribution among the main memory modules is important only to the extent that it leads to more efficient conflict-free parallel access to data items that are likely to be needed in succession (see Section 6.6). If multiple copies of modifiable data are to be maintained within processor caches in a UMA system, then cache coherence becomes an issue and we have the class of CC-UMA systems. Simple UMA has been used more widely in practice. An early, and highly influential, system of this type was Carnegie-Mellon University's C.mmp system that was built of 16 PDP-11 minicomputers in the mid-1970s (Fig. 21.2). It had both a crossbar and a bus for interprocessor communication via shared variables or message passing. Here, we will study two example systems from this class: the pioneering BBN Butterfly in Section 21.2 and the vector-parallel Cray Y-MP in Section 21.3.

When memory is distributed among processing nodes, access to locations in the global address space will involve different delays depending on the current location of the data. The access delay may range from tens of nanoseconds for locally available data, somewhat higher for data in nearby nodes, and perhaps approaching several microseconds for data located in distant nodes. This variance of access delay has led to the designation *nonuniform memory access* (NUMA). One approach to softening the impact of slow remote accesses is through

	Single Copy of Modifiable Data	Multiple Copies of Modifiable Data
Central Main Memory	**UMA** BBN Butterfly Cray Y-MP	**CC-UMA**
Distributed Main Memory	**NUMA** Tera MTA	**COMA** **CC-NUMA** Stanford DASH Sequent NUMA-Q

Figure 21.1. Classification of shared-memory hardware architectures and example systems that will be studied in this chapter.

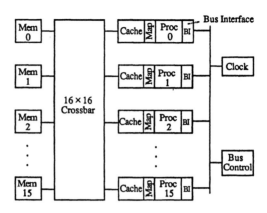

Figure 21.2. Organization of the C.mmp multiprocessor.

latency hiding or latency tolerance methods (see Section 18.3). In Section 21.4, we will study the Tera MTA as an example of machines in this class.

Another approach for dealing with slow remote accesses is to cache the needed data within individual processors (cache-coherent NUMA or CC-NUMA). We will study two examples of this most widely used approach: the Stanford DASH in Section 21.5 and the Sequent NUMA-Q in Section 21.6. Alternatively, one can allow data replication in multiple processors that have but one level of memory. This single level could be called the main memory (no cache) or it may be viewed as the cache. The second interpretation, leading to the designation *cache-only memory architecture* (COMA), is more suitable because the multiple copies must be kept consistent and thinking of the memories as caches highlights the connection with cache coherence protocols.

UMA machines typically use a high-performance crossbar or multistage interconnection network to allow many processors to access the central main memory simultaneously. In many data-parallel applications, it is possible to lay out the data in main memory in a way that access conflicts are minimized. Additionally, memory access requests can be pipelined through the interconnection network so that processor speed depends on the network's throughput rather than its end-to-end latency. In this case, the effect of the interconnection network is akin to a lengthening of the memory access pipeline. Computation can be overlapped with memory accesses by providing large register files (e.g., the vector registers of Cray Y-MP) that are loaded from, or stored into, main memory concurrently with processing functions on other registers.

Similar latency hiding techniques are applicable to NUMA machines lacking processor caches. Additionally, multithreading has been found to be quite effective for this purpose. In a multithreaded architecture capable of switching between threads with little overhead, the processor can be kept busy by executing portions of several other threads while waiting for a remote access request of one thread to be satisfied via the interconnection network. Again, it is the aggregate bandwidth of the interconnection network, rather than its end-to-end delay, that is most important. The only effect of lower network latency is to allow the processors to hide the memory access delay with fewer threads. This reduces the processor complexity in terms of control and needed register space (for highly parallel applications that have many threads readily available) and also leads to better performance in the processing of tasks with limited parallelism.

CC-NUMA machines typically enforce cache coherence via a directory-based scheme. The address placed on the memory bus of a processing node is locally translated into the identity of the home directory for the requested data. The node's local cache hierarchy holds copies of data from the local memory as well as from the memory of remote nodes. The penalty for accessing remote memory is paid only if the requested data are not found in the local node or if the enforcement of the coherence protocol (i.e., for writing to shared data) requires coordination with other nodes.

The local memory of a COMA machine must be outfitted with additional hardware, including tag and state storage for the coherence protocol (typically a directory-based write-invalidate scheme). The augmented memory unit is sometimes called *attraction memory*. The main advantage of COMA is its adaptivity, as data items are not permanently tied to specific homes. Another advantage is its natural support for reliable system design using backward error recovery (checkpointing). A simple extension of the coherence protocol used for COMA allows recovery data to be stored in other caches just like replicated data, except that recovery data cannot be used once their new versions have been modified [Mori96]. The main disadvantages are in more complex procedures for locating the required data and for enforcing the coherence of multiple data copies. As an example, note that the replacement of data in attraction memories must be done with care to ensure that the only copy of a data item is not permanently lost.

We next discuss the various logical views of shared memory and their design and performance implications. These are known as *shared-memory consistency models*.

1. *Sequential consistency* is the strictest, and most intuitive, shared-memory consistency model. It mandates that the interleaving of read and write operations be the same from the viewpoint of all processors. In effect, sequential consistency provides the illusion of a single-port memory system that services the read and write requests on a first-come first-served basis. Thus, memory access requests of one processor are always satisfied in program order and the accesses of multiple processors are serialized arbitrarily, but in the same way as judged by several observing processors.

2. *Processor consistency* is less strict because it only mandates that write operations be observed in the same order by multiple processors. This allows read operations to overtake write operations in memory service queues, providing better performance as a result of optimizations afforded by out-of-order executions.

3. *Weak consistency* separates ordinary memory accesses from synchronization accesses and only mandates that memory become consistent on synchronization accesses. Thus, a synchronization access must wait for the completion of all previous accesses, while ordinary read and write accesses can proceed as long as there is no pending synchronization access.

4. *Release consistency* is similar to weak consistency but recognizes two synchronization accesses, called *acquire* and *release*, with protected shared accesses sandwiched between them. In this model, ordinary read and write accesses can proceed only when there is no pending acquire access from the same processor and a release

access must wait for all reads and writes to be completed. Further relaxation of release consistency to improve the performance has also been suggested [Prot96].

The particular consistency model chosen affects the design and performance of the cache coherence protocol required to enforce it. Even though most distributed shared-memory systems are built with extensive hardware support for enforcing the chosen consistency model, this is not an absolute necessity. Software-based, operating-system-based, and language-based implementations have also been attempted [Prot96].

21.2. MIN-BASED BBN BUTTERFLY

The Butterfly parallel processor of Bolt, Beranek, and Newman became available in 1983. It is a general-purpose parallel computer that is particularly suitable for signal processing applications. The BBN Butterfly was built of 2–256 nodes (boards), each holding an MC68000 processor with up to 4 MB of memory, interconnected by a 4-ary wrapped butterfly network. Typical memory referencing instructions took 2 μs to execute when they accessed local memory, while remote accesses required 6 μs. The relatively small difference between the latencies of local and remote memory accesses leads us to classify the BBN Butterfly as a UMA machine.

The structure of each node is shown in Fig. 21.3. A microcoded processor node controller (PNC) is responsible for initiating all messages sent over the switch and for receiving messages from it. It also handles all memory access requests, using the memory management unit for translating virtual addresses to physical addresses. PNC also augments the functionality of the main processor in performing operations needed for parallel processing (such as test-and-set, queuing, and scheduling), easily enforcing the atomicity requirements in view of its sole control of memory.

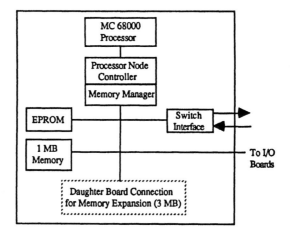

Figure 21.3. Structure of a processing node in the BBN Butterfly.

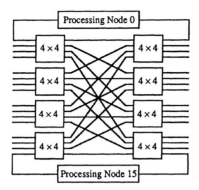

Figure 21.4. A small 16-node version of the multistage interconnection network of the BBN Butterfly.

The wrapped 4-ary butterfly network of the BBN Butterfly required four stages of 4×4 bit-serial switches, implemented as custom VLSI chips, to accommodate the largest 256-processor configuration. A small, 16-node version of the network is depicted in Fig. 21.4. Routing through the network was done by attaching the binary destination address as a routing tag to the head of a packet, with each switch using and discarding 2 bits of this tag. For example, to send a message to Node 9 = $(1001)_{two}$ in Fig. 21.4, the least-significant 2 bits would be used to select the second output of the switch at the first level and the most-significant 2 bits would indicate the choice of the third output in the second-level switch. In typical applications, message collision did not present any problem and the latency for remote memory accesses was dominated by the bit-serial transmission time through the network.

Because the probability of some switch failing increases with the network size, BBN Butterfly systems with more than 16 processing nodes were configured, through the inclusion of extra switches, to have redundant paths. Besides improving the reliability, these redundant paths also offered performance benefits by reducing message collisions.

Much of the programming for the BBN Butterfly was done in the C language, although Lisp and Fortran were also available. Applications were run under a specially developed operating system and a Unix-based front end computer was used for program compilation and loading.

A related machine, New York University's Ultracomputer [Gott83], built around the same time as the BBN Butterfly and using the butterfly network, merits a mention here. It used special switches for combining fetch-and-add operations. Several versions of the NYU Ultracomputer were built, with the largest having 16 processors.

21.3. VECTOR-PARALLEL CRAY Y-MP

The Cray Y-MP series of vector-parallel computers were introduced in the late 1980s, following several previous Cray vector supercomputers including Cray-1, Cray-2, and Cray X-MP. Subsequently, the Cray C-90 series of machines were introduced as enhanced and scaled-up versions of the Y-MP.

The Cray Y-MP consisted of a relatively small number (up to eight) of very powerful vector processors. A vector processor essentially executes one instruction on a large number of data items with a great deal of overlap. Such vector processors can thus be viewed as time-multiplexed implementations of SIMD parallel processing. With this view, the Cray Y-MP, and more generally vector-parallel machines, should be classified as hybrid SIMD/MIMD machines.

Figure 21.5 shows the Cray Y-MP processor and its links to the central memory and interprocessor communication network. Each processor has four ports to access central memory, with each port capable of delivering 128 bits per clock cycle (4 ns). Thus, a CPU can fetch two operands (a vector element and a scalar), store one value, and perform I/O simultaneously. The computation section of the CPU is divided into four subsystems as follows:

1. Vector integer operations are performed by separate function units for add/subtract, shift, logic, and bit-counting (e.g., determining the weight or parity of a word).

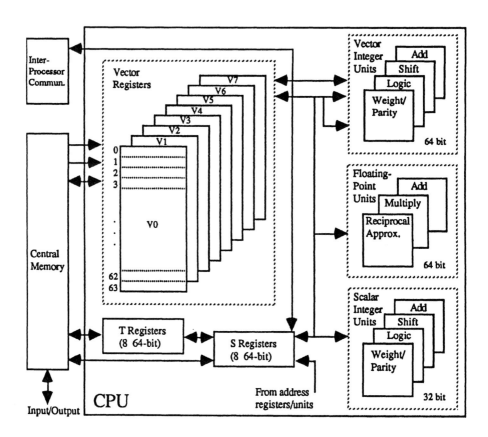

Figure 21.5. Key elements of the Cray Y-MP processor. Address registers, address function units, instruction buffers, and control not shown.

2. Vector floating-point operations are performed by separate function units for add/subtract, multiply, and reciprocal approximation. The latter function unit is used in the first step of a division operation x/y. The approximation to $1/y$ that is provided by this unit is refined in a few iterations to derive an accurate value for $1/y$, which is multiplied by x in the final step to complete the division operation.

3. Scalar integer operations are performed by separate integer function units for addition/subtraction, shift, logic, and bit-counting.

4. The add/subtract and multiply operations needed in address computations are performed by separate function units within an address subsystem that also has two sets of eight address registers (these 32–bit address registers and their associated function units are not shown in Fig. 21.5).

The eight vector registers, each holding a vector of length 64 or a segment of a longer vector, allow computation and memory accesses to be overlapped. As new data are being loaded into two registers and emptied from a third one, other vector registers can supply the operands and receive the results of vector instructions. Vector function units can be *chained* to allow the next data-dependent vector computation to begin before the current one has stored all of its results in a vector register. For example, a vector multiply–add operation can be done by chaining of the floating-point multiply and add units. This will cause the add unit to begin its vector operation as soon as the multiply unit has deposited its first result in a vector register.

A key component of Cray Y-MP is its processor-to-memory interconnection network depicted in Fig. 21.6 for an eight-processor configuration. This is a multistage crossbar network built of 4×4 and 8×8 crossbar switches and 1×8 demultiplexers. The network

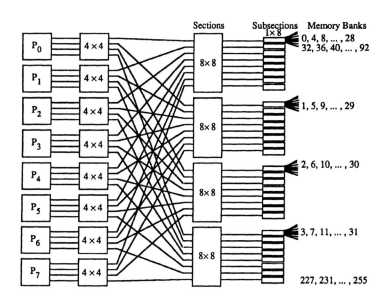

Figure 21.6. The processor-to-memory interconnection network of Cray Y-MP.

uses circuit switching and ensures that multiple access requests from the same port are satisfied in presentation order.

The enhanced Cray C-90 version of the Y-MP architecture increased the maximum number of processors to 16. In each cycle, up to four vector results can be produced by the C-90 processor's function units, leading to the peak performance of 1 GFLOPS per processor. The Cray C-90 has a peak I/O bandwidth of 13.6 GB/s and works under UNICOX, an extended Unix operating system. Vectorizing compilers for common scientific languages, such as Fortran and C, are available. Multiple Cray C-90s can be linked through gigabyte per second channels to a multigigabyte solid-state storage device (SSD) that acts as secondary main memory. By sharing access to the SSD, the multiple C-90s can be used to solve large-scale computational problems.

21.4. LATENCY-TOLERANT TERA MTA

The Tera MTA multithreaded parallel computer is unique in several ways [Tera97]. It uses a pruned 3D torus interconnection scheme for its routing nodes (see Fig. 12.4), along with extensive pipelining and multithreading to hide the memory access latency. It is designed to be truly general-purpose, with near-peak performance for a wide array of numerical and nonnumerical applications. Its clock period is 3 ns.

In its full configuration, Tera MTA has 4096 routing nodes interconnected as a $16 \times 16 \times 16$ pruned torus. Each routing node has a degree of 4 or 5, depending on the lack or presence of a resource connected to that node. Up to 256 processors, 512 memory modules, 256 I/O cache units, and 256 I/O processors are connected to a subset of the routing nodes. The network diameter is 24 and its average internode distance is about 12. The ratio of 16 between the numbers of routing nodes and processors (64 between routing-node ports and processors) allows each processor to have many memory access requests in transit without creating a communication bottleneck.

Each routing node can handle a 164-bit packet consisting of source and destination addresses, an operation, and 64 data bits in both directions on each link on every clock tick. Because the bisection width of the $16 \times 16 \times 16$ pruned torus is 256, and each link can transport two 8-byte data words per 3-ns clock period, the effective bisection bandwidth of the fully configured network is an impressive 1.4 TB/s. A packet spends two clock cycles in the routing node's logic and one cycle on the wire going to the next node. Routing nodes do not buffer messages other than in their pipeline registers. Each message is immediately routed to an output port, which may lead to derouting under heavy loads. However, because messages are assigned random priorities at each node, each message will eventually reach its destination.

As the MTA system is scaled up, it is envisaged that the number of routing nodes in the 3D pruned torus network grow in proportion to $p^{3/2}$, in contrast to p in other multicomputers with direct networks or $p \log p$ in machines with multistage networks. This is justified by the fact that the average routing distance of $O(p^{1/2})$ requires $O(p^{1/2})$ in-transit memory access messages from each of the p processors in order to hide the memory access latency. Because the degree of each routing node is a constant, $O(p^{3/2})$ such nodes are needed to route all of the in-transit messages without significant delays (ideally no delay at all). The above can also be justified from the viewpoint of the network's bisection bandwidth. An $O(p^{3/2})$-node 3D torus has a bisection of $O(p)$ that scales linearly with the number p of processors.

Processors of the Tera MTA are multithreaded. Each processor can have as many as 128 program counters active at once. On every clock tick, a thread that is ready for execution is selected and its next instruction placed into the execution pipeline. On the next clock tick, a different thread may execute. If a single instruction is issued from each thread, then roughly 70 threads would be required to completely hide the expected latency (processor pipeline, interconnection network, internal memory pipeline). However, because threads in general allow multiple independent instructions to be issued at once, fewer threads may suffice. The state of each thread, which consists of a 32-bit program counter, various mode/mask/condition bits, 8 branch target registers, and 32 general-purpose registers (all 64 bits wide), is held in dedicated hardware of which a processor has 128 copies.

As shown in Fig. 21.7, the three pipelines M (memory access operation), A (arithmetic operation), and C (control or simple arithmetic operation) can be used simultaneously. A 64-bit instruction can contain one operation of each type. With multithreaded execution, a processor can support over 1 billion operations per second, even though each thread may run at only 1/10 of this rate. Every processor has a clock register that is synchronized exactly with its counterparts in the other processors and counts up once per cycle. In addition, the processor counts the total number of unused instruction issue slots (degree of underutilization of the processor) and the time integral of the number of instruction streams ready to issue (degree of overutilization of the processor). All three counters are user-readable in a single unprivileged operation.

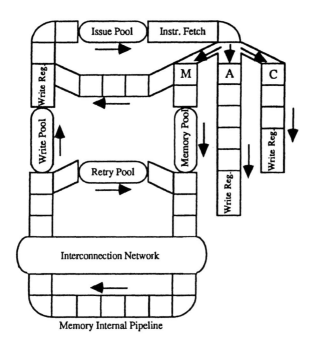

Figure 21.7. The instruction execution pipelines of Tera MTA.

The memory system of a p-processor Tera MTA consists of $2p$ or $4p$ memory modules distributed around the network. Each 0.5-GB module is 64-way interleaved and memory data references by the processors are randomly scattered among all banks of all memory modules. Memory accesses to fetch instructions are directed to two nearby memory modules. The peak performance of the Tera MTA is 1 GFLOPS per processor, yielding a maximum of about 0.25 TFLOPS in the full 256-processor configuration.

Input/output is carried out primarily via disk arrays that are connected to some routing nodes. One disk array (360 GB, 130 MB/s) for every 16 processors is the recommended minimum requirement. Data read out from disks are placed in I/O cache memories that are then directly mapped into the user's address space. Concurrent I/O arising from parallel loops or elsewhere is automatically parallelized by Tera's Fortran, C, and C++ compilers and libraries by letting each thread access the buffers for data.

The Tera MTA operating system is a distributed parallel version of Unix. Instruction streams are dynamically created or destroyed using a single instruction. Large and small tasks are run concurrently without a need for system partitioning or manual intervention. A two-tier scheduler is incorporated into the Tera microkernel; it provides better resource allocation to large tasks (those currently running on more than a single processor) via a bin-packing scheme, and schedules the smaller tasks using a traditional Unix approach.

21.5. CC-NUMA STANFORD DASH

Stanford University's directory architecture for shared memory (DASH) project of the early 1990s had the goal of building an experimental cache-coherent multiprocessor. The 64-processor prototype resulting from this project, along with the associated theoretical developments and performance evaluations, contributed insight and specific techniques to the design of scalable distributed shared-memory machines. According to the terminology introduced in Section 4.3, DASH can be classified as a cache-coherent NUMA (CC-NUMA) architecture.

DASH has a two-level processor-to-memory interconnection structure and a corresponding two-level cache coherence scheme (Fig. 21.8). Within a cluster of 4–16 processors, access to main memory occurs via a shared bus. Each processor in a cluster has a private instruction cache, a separate data cache, and a Level-2 cache. The instruction and data caches use the write-through policy, whereas write-back is the update policy of the Level-2 cache. The clusters are interconnected by a pair of wormhole-routed 2D mesh networks: a request mesh, which carries remote memory access requests, and a reply mesh, which routes data and acknowledgments back to the requesting cluster. Normally, a processor can access its own cache in one clock cycle, the caches of processors in the same cluster in a few tens of clock cycles, and remote data in hundreds of clock cycles. Thus, data access locality, which is the norm in most applications, leads to better performance.

Inside a cluster, cache coherence is enforced by a snoopy protocol, while across clusters, coherence is maintained by a write-invalidate directory protocol built on the release consistency model for improved efficiency. The unit of data sharing is a block or cache line. The directory entry for a block in the home cluster holds its state (uncached, shared, or dirty) and includes a bit-vector indicating the presence or absence of the cache line in each cache. Remote memory accesses, as well as exchanges required to maintain data coherence, are

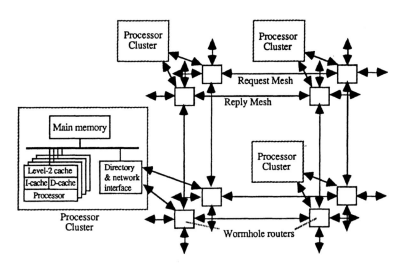

Figure 21.8. The architecture of Stanford DASH.

orchestrated via point-to-point wormhole-routed messages that are sent between cluster directories over 16-bit-wide channels.

When the required data are not found in the local cluster, an access request is sent to the cluster holding the home directory, which then initiates appropriate actions based on the type of request and the state of the requested data. In the case of a read request, the following will happen:

1. For a shared or uncached block, the data are sent to the requester from the home cluster and the directory entry is updated to include the new (only) sharer.
2. For a dirty block, a message is sent to the cluster holding the single up-to-date copy. This remote cluster then sends a shared copy of the block to the requesting cluster and also performs a sharing write-back to the home cluster.

A write (read-exclusive) request will trigger the following actions by the home directory, with the end result of supplying the requester with an exclusive copy of the block and invalidating all other copies, if any:

3. For a shared or uncached block, the data are sent to the requester and the directory entry is updated to indicate that the block is now dirty. Additionally, for a shared block, invalidation messages are sent to all caches that hold copies of the block, with the expectation that they will acknowledge the invalidation to the requester (new owner).
4. For a dirty block, the request is forwarded to the appropriate cluster. The latter then sends an exclusive copy of the block to the requesting cluster and also performs a sharing write-back to the home cluster.

Each of the 16 clusters in the DASH prototype is a four-processor Silicon Graphics 4D/340 Powerstation symmetric multiprocessor based on the MIPS R3000 chip. The 4D/340 clusters are modified in minor ways and augmented with two special boards that hold the directory and network interface subsystems. The processor board modifications consist of the addition of a bus retry signal and provision of masking capability for the bus arbiter. The retry signal is used when a request involves service from a remote node. The masking capability allows the directory to hold off a processor's retry (via the bus arbiter) until the requested remote access has been completed. Thus, effectively, a split-transaction bus protocol is used for performing remote accesses. The added boards contain memory for the directory entries, buffers, and a piece of the global interconnection network.

A follow-on project to DASH at Stanford aims to build flexible architectures for shared memory (FLASH) that also supports message passing [Kusk94]. One goal of FLASH is to integrate the SMP cache-coherent shared-memory model and the MPP software-based cache-coherent message-passing model into one architecture. To achieve the desired flexibility, the hard-wired controller has been replaced with a programmable engine and the directory data are placed in a portion of main memory rather than in a separate memory.

21.6. SCI-BASED SEQUENT NUMA-Q

NUMA-Q is the name given by Sequent to a series of CC-NUMA parallel computers that originated in 1992. These machines are aimed at the on-line transaction processing and database markets and have special provisions for improved availability, including redundant power supplies that can be inserted on-line, enhanced shielding, and a specially designed management and diagnostic processor (MDP). The SCI protocol has been slightly modified in some respects as a result of performance fine tuning.

The following description is based on the NUMA-Q 2000 model that can have up to 252 processors, in 63 clusters of 4 processors (quads), and was first shipped in 1996. The NUMA-Q 2000 cluster or quad is a modified Intel SHV server board containing 0.5–4 GB of memory along with four Intel Pentium Pro (P6) chips, each with 0.5 MB of on-chip Level-2 cache. A key element in the quad is a proprietary interquad (IQ) link that follows the SCI standard, holds and controls a Level-3 or "remote" cache, and is the glue that connects multiple quads into a large system. The 64-MB Level-3 cache uses 64-byte lines and is four-way set-associative in order to minimize conflict misses. It holds copies of cache lines from remote quads and, given its large size, can satisfy many of the remote access requests without any interquad communication.

The architecture of Sequent NUMA-Q 2000 is depicted in Fig. 21.10. The IQ-Link unit takes advantage of a "hook" provided by Intel to take control of the quad's local bus that is 64 bits wide and operates at 66 MHz. Other quad subsystems include two Intel Orion PCI bridges, a PCI fiber channel interface, a PCI local-area-network interface, and a management and diagnostic processor that is linked to a console via a private Ethernet. Quads are interconnected either by an optional IQ-Plus box, as shown in Fig. 21.10, or by simply connecting the IQ-Links into a ring using copper cables. The console is a PC running under the Windows NT operating system.

One of the goals of the design was to take advantage of commodity off-the-shelf (COTS) components to the extent possible. To this end, only a few of the components, including portions of IQ-Link and Bridge (between LAN and fiber channel), were custom designed by Sequent.

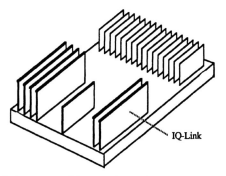

Figure 21.9. The physical placement of Sequent's quad components on a rackmount baseboard (not to scale).

Figure 21.11 depicts the internal organization of IQ-Link. The bus interface controller provides the needed interface to the P6 bus, manages the bus side of the directory, and provides the bus snooping logic. The bus controller and its associated snooping tags allow access to data held within the remote cache to be satisfied with a latency comparable to that of accesses to the local main memory. Within the directory controller, which manages the network-side tags, local memory blocks are represented by a 2-bit state field and a 6-bit

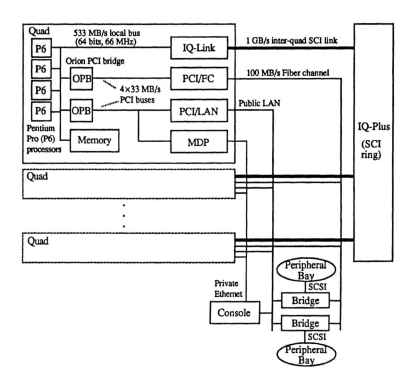

Figure 21.10. The architecture of Sequent NUMA-Q 2000.

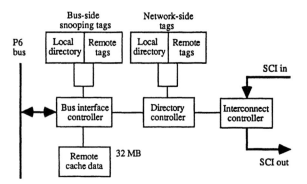

Figure 21.11. Block diagram of the IQ-Link board.

sharing list head pointer (the 6 bits are reduced from SCI's 16 bits for the sake of efficiency). For each block in the remote cache, the directory maintains a 7-bit state field, a 6-bit forward pointer, a 6-bit backward pointer, and a 13-bit address tag. An important part of the directory controller is a protocol engine that is implemented as programmable pipelined processor for flexibility and ease of fine tuning.

Details of the key interconnect controller component, which handles the SCI input and output within IQ-Link, is shown in Fig. 21.12. This component, which is in charge of the link- and packet-level protocol for SCI, is a GaAs chip developed by Vitesse Semiconductor Corporation. The elastic buffer can insert or delete idle symbols between packets to compensate for small frequency variations between the sender and the receiver. The stripper recognizes and removes any packet whose destination node label matches that of the local node, sending an echo packet on the output link in its place. The bypass FIFO is needed to accommodate packets that arrive while the local node is inserting a packet on the output link. If the local (destination) node does not have buffer space to accept a packet, it sends a negative echo, thus forcing a retransmission according to SCI's retry protocol. The chip operates at 500 MHz, handling 2 bytes of data and 2 control bits (a flag and a clock) in each cycle. It

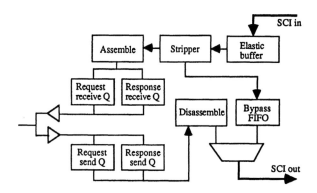

Figure 21.12. Block diagram of IQ-Link's interconnect controller.

needs eight clock cycles to route the first 18-bit symbol of a packet to the assemble block or bypass FIFO and a single clock cycle for each subsequent symbol.

PROBLEMS

21.1. Carnegie-Mellon University's C.mmp

    a. Study the C.mmp multiprocessor system mentioned in Section 21.1 and prepare a description of its shared-memory architecture in a way that could form a section in this chapter.

    b. Contrast C.mmp to the BBN Butterfly described in Section 21.2.

    c. Contrast C.mmp to Stanford DASH described in Section 21.5.

21.2. CC-UMA parallel processors
Identify an example of a CC-UMA parallel processor (see Fig. 21.1) and prepare a description of its architecture in a way that could form a section in this chapter.

21.3. Routing in the BBN Butterfly

    a. Given the description of the routing algorithm on the butterfly network of Fig. 21.4, derive the assumed ordering of the processor labels from top to bottom.

    b. How should we modify the routing algorithm if the processors are to be labeled 0, 1, 2, . . . , 15, in order from top to bottom?

    c. Draw the interconnection network for a 64-processor BBN Butterfly.

    d. Repeat part (a) for the network of part (c).

    e. Repeat part (b) for the network of part (c).

21.4. Robust BBN Butterfly network
Study the structure of the redundant network used in the BBN Butterfly to provide the capability of routing around failed switches. In particular, state the effect of redundancy on the routing algorithm. Relate your answers to the discussions of Chapter 19 on reliable parallel processing.

21.5. BBN Butterfly and NYU Ultracomputer
Compare BBN Butterfly with NYU Ultracomputer. Outline their similarities and differences in a table.

21.6. Cray X-MP vector processor
The Cray X-MP vector processor [Robb89], a predecessor of Cray Y-MP, had floating-point add and multiply function units, implemented as six- and seven-stage pipelines, respectively. Vector computations needed three clock cycles for their setup, which included preparing the appropriate function units and establishing paths from/to source and destination registers. At the end of a vector computation, three more clock cycles were needed for shutdown before the results in the destination vector register could be used in other operations. This six-cycle pipelining overhead became insignificant when dealing with long vectors. The output of an s-stage pipelined unit became available for chaining after $s + 5$ clock cycles. Such a unit needed $l + s + 5$ cycles to operate on an l-element vector. A polynomial $f(x)$ of degree $m - 1$ (m real coefficients, stored in a vector register) is to be evaluated for m different values of x (available in a second vector register) using Horner's rule. The m results are to be deposited in a third vector register.

    a. Estimate the number of cycles needed for this computation with no vector chaining.

    b. Repeat part (a) with vector chaining.

c. Derive the MFLOPS rating of the machine for the computations of parts (a) and (b) assuming a clock cycle of 9.5 ns.

21.7. Cray Y-MP's interconnection network
Assuming an interleaved memory organization, in which the memory bank number corresponds to the least significant byte of the memory address, describe the motivation behind the numbering scheme for memory banks used in Fig. 21.6.

21.8. Cray Y-MP's interconnection network
a. Describe an algorithm for routing a memory access request from Processor i to Bank j of memory in Cray Y-MP's processor-to-memory interconnection network (Fig. 21.6). Note the numbering scheme used for the memory banks.
b. How would you build the interconnection network of a 16-processor Cray Y-MP with 256 banks?
c. Describe a routing algorithm for the network proposed in part (b).

21.9. Tera MTA's pruned torus network
a. Find the exact diameter and average internode distance in the $16 \times 16 \times 16$ pruned torus network of Tera MTA computer.
b. Suppose that we use a 2D, rather than a 3D, routing network. Perform a scalability analysis on this 2D routing scheme and determine the number of processors that can be supported by an $m \times m$ network (or alternatively, the size of the network needed to support p processors). Is latency hiding more or less difficult with the 2D network?
c. Repeat part (b) with the assumption that processors and memory modules are only connected to the boundary processors of the 2D mesh. Does this restriction lead to any advantage?
d. Repeat part (b) for a 4D mesh network; focus on special problems related to higher dimension.

21.10. Tera MTA's latency hiding methods
a. Why do you think that a p-processor Tera MTA computer uses $2p$ or $4p$ memory modules?
b. What are the advantages of using the same interconnection network for memory access and input/output? What are possible drawbacks?
c. Is the multithreading method used in the Tera MTA applicable to uniprocessor systems?
d. What additions or changes to the Tera MTA latency hiding mechanisms would be needed if the processor technology improves to the point when the 3-ns clock cycle is reduced to 1 ns?

21.11. Two-level cache coherence protocol
The Sanford DASH multiprocessor uses a two-level cache coherence protocol: a snoopy scheme within clusters and a directory-based scheme between clusters. Why do you think this two-level scheme was chosen over a pure directory-based protocol?

21.12. Directory protocol in DASH
Study the directory-based cache coherence protocol of the Stanford DASH multiprocessor. Describe in detail the various states of a cache line, types and causes of state transitions, and the scheme used for enforcing release consistency.

21.13. Stanford DASH multiprocessor
Discuss the reasons for the following design choices in the Stanford DASH multiprocessor:

a. Including separate request and reply meshes, as opposed to one mesh with higher-band-width links.

b. Using the mesh architecture, as opposed to hypercube or another network with richer connectivity and lower diameter.

c. Using mesh, rather than torus, networks for intercluster request and reply networks.

21.14. Sequent NUMA-Q parallel computer
The quad nodes of Sequent NUMA-Q are interconnected by a ring network. In what sense is the use of the term *scalable* justifiable for this architecture (or for SCI for that matter)?

21.15. Comparing UMA and CC-NUMA
Pick one of the UMA (Sections 21.2 and 21.3) and one of the CC-NUMA (Sections 21.5 and 21.6) machines discussed in this chapter and present a detailed comparison of the two with regard to performance, scalability (in time and space), cost-effectiveness, and ease of application development.

21.16. Further developments
By the time you see this book in print, changes may have occurred in the architecture, commercial availability status, or key design/performance parameters of some of the systems discussed in this chapter. Pick one of the machines for which you can find information on recent developments or follow-on systems and prepare a report on your findings.

REFERENCES AND SUGGESTED READING

[Adve96]   Adve, S. V., and K. Gharachorloo, "Shared Memory Consistency Models: A Tutorial," *IEEE Computer*, Vol. 29, No. 12, pp. 66–76, December 1996.

[Gott83]   Gottlieb, A., et al., "The NYU Ultracomputer—Designing an MIMD Shared Memory Parallel Computer," *IEEE Trans. Computers*, Vol. 32, No. 2, pp. 175–189, February 1983.

[Harr94]   Harris, T. J., "A Survey of PRAM Simulation Techniques," *ACM Computing Surveys*, Vol. 26, No. 2, pp. 187–206, June 1994.

[Hord93]   Hord, R. M., *Parallel Supercomputing in MIMD Architectures*, CRC Press, 1993.

[Hwan98]   Hwang, K., and Z. Xu, *Scalable Parallel Computing: Technology, Architecture, Programming*, McGraw-Hill, 1998.

[Kusk94]   Kuskin, J., et al., "The Stanford FLASH Multiprocessor," *Proc. 21st Int. Symp. Computer Architecture*, pp. 302–313, April 1994, pp. 302–313.

[Leno92]   Lenoski, D., et al., "The Stanford Dash Multiprocessor," *IEEE Computer*, Vol. 25, No. 3, pp. 63–79, March 1992.

[Love96]   Lovett, T., and R. Clapp, "STiNG: A CC-NUMA Computer System for the Commercial Marketplace," *Proc. 23rd Int. Symp. Computer Architecture*, 1996, pp. 308–317.

[Mori96]   Morin, C., A. Gefflaut, M. Banatre, and A.-M. Kermarrec, "COMA: An Opportunity for Building Fault-Tolerant Scalable Shared Memory Multiprocessors," *Proc. 23rd Int. Symp. Computer Architecture*, 1996, pp. 56–65.

[Mori97]   Morin, C., and I. Puaut, "A Survey of Recoverable Distributed Shared Virtual Memory Systems," *IEEE Trans. Parallel and Distributed Systems*, Vol. 8, No. 9, pp. 959–969, September 1997.

[Prot96]   Protic, J., M. Tomacevic, and V. Milutinovic, "Distributed Shared Memory: Concepts and Systems," *IEEE Parallel & Distributed Technology*, Vol. 4, No. 2, pp. 63–79, Summer 1996.

[Robb89]   Robbins, K. A., and S. Robbins, *The Cray X-MP/Model 24: A Case Study in Pipelined Architecture and Vector Processing*, Springer-Verlag, 1989.

22

Message-Passing MIMD Machines

Like shared-memory parallel computers, message-passing systems can be based on different interconnection topologies and provide various logical user views. In this chapter, following a survey of topics pertaining to the implementation and performance of communication structures for message routing, we review several parallel computer systems that use explicit message passing. One of the systems chosen is a product of university research (Berkeley NOW), two were built by companies that were pioneers in the fields of transaction and multimedia processing (Tandem NonStop and nCUBE3, respectively), and two utilize high-performance scalable switching networks (Thinking Machines Corporation CM-5 and IBM SP2). Chapter topics are

- 22.1. Mechanisms for message passing
- 22.2. Reliable bus-based Tandem NonStop
- 22.3. Hypercube-based nCUBE3
- 22.4. Fat-tree-based Connection Machine 5
- 22.5. Omega-network-based IBM SP2
- 22.6. Commodity-driven Berkeley NOW

22.1. MECHANISMS FOR MESSAGE PASSING

Message passing is becoming the dominant paradigm in modern large-scale parallel systems. Like shared-memory implementations, message-passing parallel computers vary greatly in the hardware architecture that they use and in the programming model (logical user view) that they support. In this section we review the most common hardware architectures for message passing, and also discuss the various logical user views and their performance implications, to set the stage for the case studies that follow in Sections 22.2 through 22.6. Ideas and terminology introduced in Section 4.5 are relevant to our discussion here, as are the data routing topics covered in parts of Chapters 10 and 14.

The trend in building parallel computers in recent years has been to use commercial off-the-shelf (COTS), rather than custom-designed, components. High-performance processors are readily available from several manufacturers. Various types of interconnection and routing hardware have also emerged as COTS components. The use of COTS components reduces the hardware development cost of parallel machines and allows for relatively simple updating of the resulting designs as faster processors and interconnections become available. An additional benefit is that software becomes more portable and less expensive for COTS-based systems in view of the development cost being borne by a larger user base. The loose coupling of message-passing architectures makes them ideal candidates for implementation with COTS components, as we will see in the rest of this chapter.

Message-passing parallel computers are built of processing nodes and interconnection elements. Processing nodes are typically complete computers with storage for programs and data, instruction execution logic, and input/output. Depending on the complexity of processing nodes, three categories of message-passing MIMD computers can be distinguished:

1. *Coarse-grain parallelism.* Processing nodes are complete (perhaps large, multi-board) computers that work on sizable subproblems, such as complete programs or tasks, and communicate or synchronize with each other rather infrequently.
2. *Medium-grain parallelism.* Processing nodes might be based on standard micros that execute smaller chunks of the application program (e.g., subtasks, processes, threads) and that communicate or synchronize with greater frequency.
3. *Fine-grain parallelism.* Processing nodes might be standard micros or custom-built processing elements (perhaps with multiple PEs fitting on one chip) that execute small pieces of the application and need constant communication or synchronization.

Like any other classification that is based on the imprecise notions of "large," "medium," and "small" (e.g., for clothes or automobiles), the above categories have fuzzy boundaries and one can easily identify systems that could fit in two classes. Most existing message-passing systems fall into the medium-grain category. In spite of not being very discriminative, the classification is still useful in providing perspective and pedagogical help. Perhaps categories such as "medium-coarse" and "medium-fine" (analogues of cooking levels for steaks) or "medium-medium-fine" and the like (analogues of direction specifications for wind or sailing) should be envisaged!

Note that we have defined *granularity* (or grain size) by considering both the processing node complexity and the complexity of subcomputations performed by processing nodes in

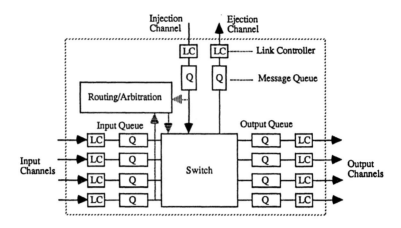

Figure 22.1. The structure of a generic router.

between communications or synchronizations. In theory, it is possible to run coarse-grain computations on fine-grain hardware, and vice versa, but neither is advisable from the standpoint of efficient hardware utilization as measured, e.g., by the FLOPS performance per unit cost.

The interconnection network architecture needed to support message passing is strongly dependent on granularity as discussed above. For coarse-grain parallelism, neither network latency nor bandwidth is critical in view of the light communication load. Early message-passing architectures, such as the pioneering C.mmp (Fig. 21.2), were of this type. We will examine one example of such architectures in Section 22.2 (Tandem NonStop, using a bus system for message transmissions). For fine-grain parallelism, the heavy communication load placed on the network makes its aggregate bandwidth a critical performance parameter. The network latency is also quite important in this case, unless latency hiding or tolerance methods are used. You do not have to be a genius to guess that the communication loads, and thus the network performance requirements, for medium-grain parallelism fall between the above two extremes. All of our remaining case studies in Sections 22.3 through 22.6 (hypercube-based nCUBE3, fat-tree-based Connection Machine 5, omega-network-based IBM SP2, and local-network-based Berkeley NOW) fall into this class.

Interconnection networks for message passing are of three basic types [Duat97]:

1. *Shared-medium networks.* Only one of the units linked to a shared-medium network is allowed to use it at any given time. Nodes connected to the network typically have request, drive, and receive circuits. Given the single-user requirement, an arbitration mechanism is needed to decide which one of the requesting nodes can use the shared network. The two most commonly used shared-medium networks are backplane buses and local area networks (LANs). The bus arbitration mechanism is different for synchronous and asynchronous buses. In bus transactions that involve a request and a response, a *split-transaction protocol* is often used so that other nodes can use the bus while the request of one node is being processed at the other end. To ease the congestion on a shared bus, multiple buses or hierarchical bus networks may be used. For LANs, the most commonly used arbitration protocol is based on conten-

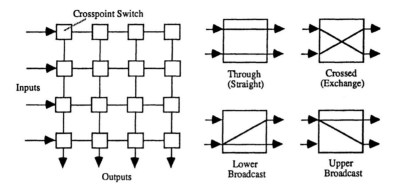

Figure 22.2. Example 4×4 and 2×2 switches used as building blocks for larger networks.

tion: The nodes can detect the idle/busy state of the shared medium, transmitting when they observe the idle state, and considering the transmission as having failed when they detect a "collision." Token-based protocols, which implement some form of rotating priority, are also used.

2. *Router-based networks.* Such networks, also known as *direct networks*, are based on each node (with one or more processors) having a dedicated router that is linked directly to one or more other routers. A generic router is shown in Fig. 22.1. The local node(s) connected to the router inject messages into the network through the *injection channel* and remove incoming messages through the *ejection channel*. Locally injected messages compete with messages that are passing through the router for the use of output channels. The link controllers handle interfacing considerations of the physical channels. The queues hold messages that cannot be forwarded because of contention for the output links. Various switching strategies (e.g., packet or wormhole) and routing algorithms (e.g., tag-based or use of routing tables) can be implemented in the router. The router shown in Fig. 22.1 has in- and out-degree of 5; 1 for the local node's messages and 4 for in-transit messages. By interconnecting a number of such routers, one can form a 2D mesh or torus network, a 4-cube, or any other network with node degree of at most 4. Example routers include the Cray T3E router (3D torus, 14-bit data in each direction, 375 MHz, 600 MB/s per link) and the Chaos router (2D torus, bidirectional 8-bit links, 180 MHz, 360 MB/s in each direction).

3. *Switch-based networks.* Such networks, also known as *indirect networks*, are based on crossbars or regularly interconnected (multistage) networks of simpler switches. Typically, the communication path between any two nodes goes through one or more switches. The path to be taken by a message is either predetermined at the source node and included as part of the message header or else it is computed on the fly at intermediate nodes based on the source and destination addresses. Figure 22.2 shows a 4×4 crossbar and a 2×2 switch that is capable of broadcasting as well as simple forwarding. Such switches can be used for synthesizing networks of arbitrary size. However, the number of switches on the message path, and thus the network latency, will grow with its size. Switch-based networks can be classified

	Shared-Medium Network	Router-Based Network	Switch-Based Network
Coarse-Grain	Tandem NonStop (Bus)		
Medium-Grain	Berkeley NOW (LAN)	nCUBE3	TMC CM-5 IBM SP2
Fine-Grain			

Figure 22.3. Classification of message-passing hardware architectures and example systems that will be studied in this chapter.

as unidirectional or bidirectional. In unidirectional networks, each switch port is either input or output, whereas in bidirectional networks, ports can be used for either input or output. By superimposing two unidirectional networks, one can build a full-duplex bidirectional network that can route messages in both directions simultaneously. A bidirectional switch can be used in forward mode, in backward mode, or in turnaround mode, where in the latter mode, connections are made between terminals on the same side of the switch. Example switches include the Myricom Myrinet (8×8 crossbar, 9-bit full duplex channels, 640 MB/s per link) and IBM SP2 (crossbars for building omega networks, 16-bit bidirectional channels, 150 MHz, 300 MB/s in each direction).

Routers and switches are becoming increasingly similar and in fact there are products on the market now that can be used to form both direct and indirect networks. An example is the SGI Spider that supports both multistage interconnection networks and irregular topologies.

Combining the two classification schemes discussed above, we get nine categories of message-passing parallel computers, as shown in Fig. 22.3.

22.2. RELIABLE BUS-BASED TANDEM NONSTOP

The first Tandem NonStop, a MIMD distributed-memory bus-based multiprocessor, was announced in 1976 for database and transaction processing applications requiring high reliability and data integrity. Since then, several versions have appeared. The Tandem NonStop Cyclone, described in this section [Prad96], was first introduced in 1989. A main objective of Cyclone's design was to prevent any single hardware or software malfunction from disabling the system. This objective was achieved by hardware and informational redundancy as well as procedural safeguards, backup processes, consistency checks, and recovery schemes.

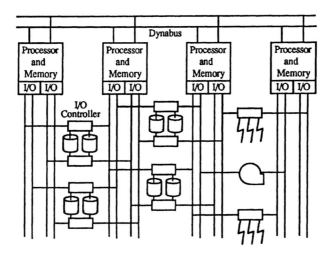

Figure 22.4. One section of the Tandem NonStop Cyclone system.

A fully configured cyclone system consists of 16 processors that are organized into sections of 4 processors. Processors in each section are interconnected by a pair of 20 MB/s buses (Dynabus) and can each support two I/O subsystems capable of burst transfer rates of 5 MB/s (Fig. 22.4). An I/O subsystem consists of two I/O channels, each supporting up to 32 I/O controllers. Multiple independent paths are provided to each I/O device via redundant I/O subsystems, channels, and controllers. Up to four sections can be linked via unidirectional fiber optics Dynabus+ that allows multiple sections to be nonadjacent within a room or even housed in separate rooms (Fig. 22.5). By isolating Dynabus+ from Dynabus, full-bandwidth communications can occur independently in each 4-processor section. Other features of the NonStop Cyclone are briefly reviewed below.

Processors. Cyclone's 32-bit processors have advanced superscalar CISC designs. They use dual eight-stage pipelines, an instruction pairing technique for instruction-level parallel processing, sophisticated branch predication algorithms for minimizing pipeline "bubbles," and separate 64-KB instruction and data caches. Up to 128 MB of main memory can be provided for each cyclone processor. The main memory is protected against errors through the application of a SEC/DED (single-error-correcting, double-error-detecting) code. Data transfers between memory and I/O channels are performed via DMA and thus do not interfere with continued instruction processing.

System Performance. Performance estimates published in 1990 indicate that, after accounting for cache misses and other overhead, the custom-designed Cyclone processor can execute each instruction in an average of 1.5–2 clock cycles. Thus, with a clock period of 10 ns, the peak performance of a fully configured NonStop Cyclone system is about 1000 MIPS. Because each of the two I/O subsystems connected to a processor can transmit data at a burst rate of 5 MB/s, a peak aggregate I/O bandwidth of 160 MB/s is available.

Hardware Reliability. Use of multiple processors, buses, power supplies, I/O paths, and mirrored disks are among the methods used to ensure continuous operation despite hardware malfunctions. A "fail-fast" strategy is employed to reduce the possibility of error

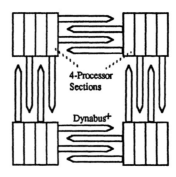

Figure 22.5. Four four-processor sections interconnected by Dynabus⁺.

propagation and data contamination. Packaging and cooling technologies have also been selected to minimize the probability of failure and to allow components, such as circuit boards, fans, and power supplies, to be "hot-pluggable" without a need to interrupt system operation. When a malfunctioning processor is detected via built-in hardware self-checking logic, its load is transparently distributed to other processors by the operating system.

Software Reliability.   The GUARDIAN 90 operating system is a key to Cyclone's high performance and reliability. Every second, each processor is required to send an "I'm alive" message to every other processor over all buses. Every 2 seconds, each processor checks to see if it has received a message from every other processor. If a message has not been received from a particular processor, it is assumed to be malfunctioning. Other software mechanisms for malfunction detection include data consistency checks and kernel-level assertions. Malfunctions in buses, I/O paths, and memory are tolerated by avoiding the malfunctioning unit or path. Processor malfunctions lead to deactivation of the processor. For critical applications, GUARDIAN 90 maintains duplicate backup processes on disjoint processors. To reduce overhead, the backup process is normally inactive but is kept consistent with the primary process via periodic checkpointing messages. On malfunction detection, the backup process is started from the last checkpoint, perhaps using mirror copies of the data.

Related Systems.   In addition to NonStop Cyclone, and the more recent RISC-based Himalaya servers, Tandem offers the Unix-based Integrity S2 uniprocessor system that tolerates malfunctions via triplication with voting. It uses R4000 RISC processors and offers both application and hardware-level compatibility with other Unix-based systems. Commercial reliable multiprocessors are also offered by Stratus (XA/R Series 300, using a comparison- and replacement-based hardware redundancy scheme known as *pair-and-spare*) and Sequoia (Series 400, using self-checking modules with duplication). Both of the latter systems are tightly coupled shared-memory multiprocessors.

22.3. HYPERCUBE-BASED nCUBE3

The approach to parallel processing taken by nCUBE is to develop a custom high-performance processor with built-in communication capabilities. Processor chips for nCUBE1/2 were introduced in 1985 and 1989, respectively. The more recent 2.7M-transistor nCUBE3 includes 16 DMA channels and 18 bit-serial interprocessor or I/O links, thus theoretically allowing an 18-dimensional, or 256K-processor, hypercube to be configured. Alternatively, a smaller hypercube, with multiple or folded interprocessor links as well as I/O links, can be constructed. At present, nCUBE's parallel computers are targeted toward multimedia server applications. For example, the MediaCUBE 3000 system, which is comprised of server modules of varying types (media server, Ethernet server, native SCSI, interconnect, and media control) can be scaled to handle from 90 to over 20,000 concurrent 1.5 Mb/s MPEG video streams.

The nCUBE3 processor is a custom single-chip computer, designed for a message-passing MIMD system architecture. It couples directly to banks of synchronous DRAMs (SDRAMs) and interconnects to other nodes in a hypercube network via bidirectional links. It integrates onto one chip an instruction and data pipeline, a 64-bit integer unit, a double-precision floating point unit, a 64-bit virtual memory management unit, instruction and data caches (8 KB each), an SDRAM controller, an adaptive message router with 18 communications ports, and 16 DMA channels. The nCUBE3 processor connects to the SDRAM via a 72-bit data interface (64 bits data + 8 bits error-correcting code) and a 14-bit multiplexed address interface, along with control signals and clocks. Up to 1 GB of physical memory is addressable by a single processor.

The communications unit of the nCUBE3 processor serves to directly connect a large number of nCUBE3 processors together in a hypercube topology (Fig. 22.6). Within each processor, bidirectional ports, at least one for each dimension of the hypercube and at least one for I/O transmissions, transmit and receive data packets (flits) that make up messages directed through this node from one node in the network to another. Eight "send" and eight "receive" DMA channels move message data from memory to an output port, or from an input port to memory. Routing logic selects the next internode segment of a message's path and obtains a cut-through path from a send channel or an input port to the selected output port or, if the message has arrived at the destination node, from an input port to an appropriate "receive" DMA channel. Several fault detection and recovery, as well as diagnostic, features are implemented, including parity, message flushing, port disabling, and a "node reset" message.

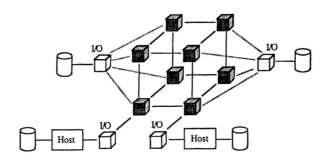

Figure 22.6. An eight-node nCUBE architecture.

The DMA channels are buffered for both control and data, so that software overhead can be overlapped with data transmission in order to maximize that memory bandwidth. Scatter-gather capabilities are also implemented at both "send" and "receive" channels. DMA operations snoop the data cache to ensure cache-memory consistency.

The 18 input/output ports can be used to connect the processor to its hypercube neighbors and/or to system I/O channels. Any number of ports can be configured as I/O channels, and hypercube connections can be duplicated on otherwise unused ports to create a partially or fully "folded" hypercube, thus making full use of the available network connectivity and bandwidth.

The nCUBE3 communications architecture also provides an end-to-end reporting mechanism that ensures reliable messaging, whereby both the sender and receiver of a message can know quickly whether that message was delivered reliably, and the receiver may deliver status information back to the sender before the established path is broken. End-to-end messaging is accomplished via an end-to-end reporting network, which pairs a "back-track" path with the corresponding parallel transmission path. The message transmission network and the back-track network are implemented as virtual networks sharing the same physical communications network of internode links. The end-to-end hardware mechanisms have the advantage of providing reliable messaging without additional message transmissions and the corresponding CPU and software overhead. In addition, these end-to-end mechanisms provide the back-track network on which an adaptive routing protocol can be built.

The previous generation of hypercubes, including the nCUBE2 family, implemented wormhole routing, using an oblivious, deterministic routing scheme that avoids deadlocks. In addition to the oblivious wormhole routing of the nCUBE2 architecture, the nCUBE3 architecture provides an adaptive routing mechanism as well, called the *maze router*. This router routes messages around blocked or malfunctioning nodes and hot spots in the hypercube network, by implementing an adaptive routing algorithm that makes use of the end-to-end back-track network. Simulations show this algorithm to perform substantially better than the oblivious wormhole router in both latency and network bandwidth usage.

An nCUBE3 message can be routed using any of seven methods. These routing methods are specified according to three characteristics: oblivious or adaptive route selection; progressive message transmission or otherwise; and minimal-path routing or allowing misrouting. The two main routing methods are oblivious wormhole routing (like nCUBE2) and adaptive maze routing. The other five are derivatives or combinations of these two, in conjunction with a couple of misrouting techniques. The derivatives include the "helix," "hydra," "misrouting maze," and "oblivious hydra."

Maze routing is an adaptive routing scheme devised for the nCUBE3 architecture. For a message from Node A to Node B, all minimal-length paths between the two nodes are searched one at a time (actually, paths in which the first leg is nonminimal may optionally be tried also) by a single-packet scout (or "circuit probe"), starting with the lowest uphill path and doing a preorder traversal of the minimal-path graph until a free path to the destination is found. The successful arrival of a scout packet at the destination establishes the path. Then, once a "path acknowledge" packet is delivered back to the sender, this reserved path is used to transmit the message. If no free path is found, however, an interrupt is generated at the source node, whereupon the software may retry the path search after an appropriate delay (and/or using a different set of first-leg paths). This scheme is deadlock-free.

nCUBE is now part of Oracle, a database company. In fact, applications in data warehousing, data mining, decision support systems, and multimedia (e.g., of the type associated with the film and entertainment industries) are projected to be important market drivers for future high-performance and parallel processing systems.

22.4. FAT-TREE-BASED CONNECTION MACHINE 5

The Connection Machine 5 (CM-5) parallel computer was introduced by Thinking Machines Corporation in 1991. CM-5 represented a significant departure from TMC's previous machines in virtually every respect: It constituted TMC's first MIMD machine, was built of commodity RISC microprocessor chips, contained built-in floating-point pipelines, and worked under a Unix-like operating system. The largest CM-5 shipped by TMC, before it filed for Chapter-11 bankruptcy protection in the United States in 1994, had 1024 processing nodes.

As shown in Fig. 22.7, CM-5's components include three types of nodes (processor, control, and I/O) that are interconnected via three separate networks (data, control, and diagnostic).

The control processors are standard computers with CPU, memory, I/O, LAN connection, and interfaces to the data and control networks. Each control processor is in charge of a partition of processing nodes, the size and membership of which are set at system startup time. This allows multiple user programs to run within disjoint partitions on CM-5; however, communication between such partitions is not prohibited. The control processor broadcasts blocks of instructions to the processing nodes. The nodes execute instructions independently (e.g., they may take different control paths within the code block) and synchronize when required.

Each processing node is composed of a SPARC CPU, four vector units with attached memories, and interface to the data and control networks (Fig. 22.8). The vector units execute instructions that are issued to them individually, or to groups of two or four, by the SPARC

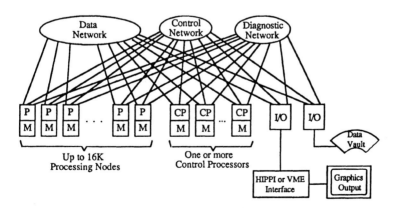

Figure 22.7. The overall structure of CM-5.

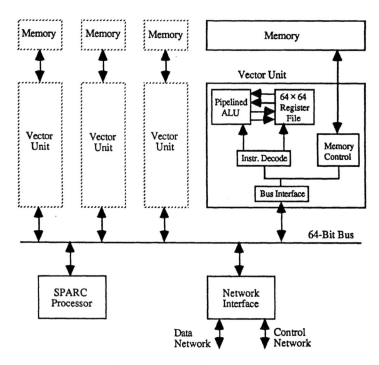

Figure 22.8. The components of a processing node in CM-5.

microprocessor. The four vector units together provide 128 MFLOPS peak performance and 0.5 GB/s memory bandwidth.

The register file within the vector unit can be viewed as consisting of 64 long-word (64-bit) or 128 short-word (32-bit) registers. Scalar instructions are executed on the vector unit by setting the vector length parameter to 1. A register operand for a vector instruction is specified by a starting register number (7 bits) and a stride (7 bits). Usually, a default stride of 1 (for 32-bit operands) or 2 (for 64-bit operands) is used. Some instructions allow the specification of arbitrary strides, including negative strides that are encoded as large positive strides. Every vector unit instruction includes four register addresses: two for source operands, one for destination, and one for an independent, concurrently executed, memory operation.

CM-5's control network allows all processors to communicate efficiently in performing broadcasting, global reduction, parallel prefix, synchronization, and error signaling functions. The diagnostic network is itself an easily testable tree that has the machine entities to be tested at its leaves and one or more diagnostic processors at its root.

The data network, which provides high throughput for point-to-point messages, has a fat-tree or hypertree architecture depicted in Fig. 22.9 for a 64-node configuration. This network is optimized for data-parallel applications and may not perform as well in an asynchronous MIMD environment. A message is routed to its destination by routing it up the tree to the node representing the least common ancestor of the source and destination nodes and from there down to the final destination. Multiple paths are available for both the

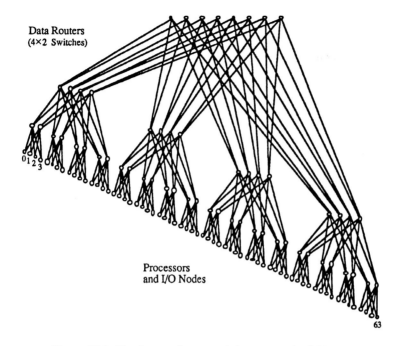

Data Routers
(4×2 Switches)

0 1 2 3

Processors
and I/O Nodes

63

Figure 22.9. The fat-tree (hypertree) data network of CM-5.

upward and the downward movement phases. Random routing decisions are used to distribute the data traffic evenly and to reduce congestion. The data network's high bandwidth allows each processor to sustain a data transfer rate of 5–20 MB/s, depending on the degree of locality in message destinations. The small factor of 4 difference between best- and worst-case communication performance is one of key characteristics of CM-5's data network.

When a message is delivered through the data network, the receiver finds out about it by polling a flag within the network interface module. With proper setting of the message tag, the arrival of a message can also be optionally signaled by an interrupt. In the latter case, the interrupt handler notifies the user process by way of a signal.

22.5. OMEGA-NETWORK-BASED IBM SP2

IBM launched its scalable POWERparallel (SP) project in 1991. The first machine resulting from this project, the IBM SP1, was delivered in 1993, with the SP2 emerging a year later. An interesting fact about this series of parallel machines is that they formed the processing power behind IBM's Deep Blue chess program when it beat the world chess champion Garry Kasparov in a series of matches in 1997 [Hami97].

The architecture of the IBM SP series is shown in Fig. 22.10. Each compute node consists of a processor (66.7-MHz POWER2 microprocessor, with a 32-KB instruction cache and a 256-KB data cache), up to 2 GB of main memory, a network interface controller that links the node to the high-performance switch, an Ethernet adapter, a micro channel

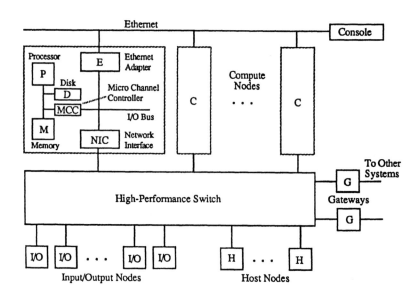

Figure 22.10. The architecture of IBM SP series of systems.

controller (80 MB/s, 8 slots), and a local disk. The Ethernet link is used for system control functions and program development in addition to being a backup for the high-performance switch. A copy of AIX (IBM's Unix) resides in each node. The detailed characteristics of a node differ according to which of the three available node types is chosen for configuring the machine. Our description here relates to "wide" nodes, which are more powerful than "thin" nodes or intermediate nodes code-named "thin2."

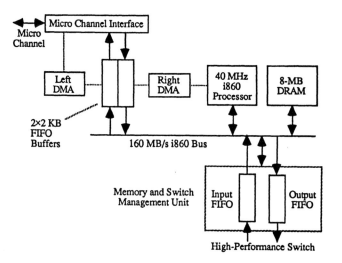

Figure 22.11. The network interface controller of IBM SP2.

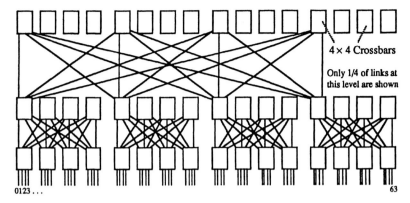

Figure 22.12. A section of the high-performance switch network of IBM SP2.

The POWER2 microprocessor is superscalar with a 128-bit instruction bus that can specify six instructions per 15-ns clock cycle: two load/store operations, two floating-point multiply–add operations, an index increment, and a conditional branch. The two floating-point units, along with the ability of the four-way set-associative data cache to supply them with four 64-bit operands per cycle, give each node a peak performance in excess of 0.25 GFLOPS.

The network interface controller within a node has a special memory and switch management chip, with input and output FIFOs that sit between the unit's internal bus and 8-bit unidirectional links to the high-performance switch. The unit has its own 40-MHz i860 processor, an 8-MB memory for meeting the buffering requirements of various protocols, a 4-KB FIFO (2 KB in each direction) between the internal i860 bus and the micro channel interface, and two DMA engines that transfer data between the FIFO buffers and node's memory via the micro channel and between the FIFO buffers and input/output buffers via the unit bus.

The high-performance switch of IBM SP2, partially depicted in Fig. 22.12 for a 64-processor configuration, is a multistage bidirectional omega network that uses buffered wormhole routing and is driven by a 40-MHz clock, providing a per-port bandwidth of 40 MB/s. In the absence of contention, an 8-bit flit is routed through each stage in five clock cycles or 125 ns, implying that, under light communication load, the network latency can be below 1 μs for the largest SP systems. Of course, because of the software overhead for message initiation and reception, the latency seen by application processes is much higher (on the order of tens of microseconds).

22.6. COMMODITY-DRIVEN BERKELEY NOW

The "network of workstations" (NOW) project at the University of California, Berkeley, aims at building a distributed supercomputer from commercial workstations that are linked together via switch-based and high-bandwidth networks [Ande95]. With the use of commodity hardware and operating systems, NOW should be able to efficiently support sequential, parallel, and interactive jobs. Thus far, the NOW project has laid claim to the world's fastest Web search engine and disk-to-disk sorting routine and its working prototype is rated among the world's most powerful supercomputers based on benchmark results.

As part of the NOW project, research is being conducted in the following areas:

- *Network interface hardware.* NOW represents an emerging trend to use system-area network (SAN) interconnection, a middle ground between LANs, which typically have higher latencies, and specialized interconnections used in massively parallel computers. The networking hardware itself is relegated mostly to commercial developers of gigabit networks. The core of Berkeley NOW includes 100 Sun Ultrasparc workstations and 40 Sun Sparcstations (running under Solaris), 35 Intel personal computers, and up to 1000 disks, all connected by a Myrinet switched network. A large number of other workstations may also be integrated into Berkeley NOW in the future.

- *Fast communication protocols.* Many aspects of communication protocols and their performance implications are being studied. Berkeley NOW offers competitive values for the parameters in the LogP model (see Section 4.5) when compared with tightly integrated routing or switching networks in massively parallel computers. For example, the L, o, and g parameters of NOW (in μs) are around 5, 3, and 6 compared with 6, 2, and 8 for the Intel Paragon and 7, 2, and 14 for the Meiko CS-2 [Mart97]. Research is also being pursued on *active messages* that carry, as part of their headers, control information that point to, and invoke, user-level subroutines. These *message handlers* extract the message data from the network and integrate them into ongoing computations.

- *Distributed file systems.* A key component of the NOW project is the xFS server-less network file system. Data files are distributed among the nodes and there is no central data warehouse or arbitration authority. In such an environment, a number of cooperative file caching strategies, which require each node to allocate a portion of its memory as a file cache and to participate in data accessing and forwarding of file pages when needed, might be implemented. The implementation aspects and performance implications of various alternatives are being actively investigated. The xFS file system is in effect a software-implemented RAID (see Section 18.5).

- *Global resource management.* The NOW project is experimenting with GLUnix (global-layer Unix) that is built on the philosophy of a two-layer operating system for clusters. The lower layer is a kernel-level commercial operating system and the upper layer is a user-level operating system that provides all of the additional features needed by the cluster. A prototype implementation of GLUnix provides parallel program coscheduling, idle resource detection, process migration, load balancing, fast user-level communication, remote paging, and support for availability.

Several projects at other universities and research organizations are experimenting with this approach and have comparable agendas. Here is a partial listing:

- Argonne Globus: metacomputing platform formed by ATM-connected sites
- NSCP metacomputing: local clusters linked through the Internet
- Princeton SHRIMP: various types of interconnections via special network interfaces
- Rice TreadMarks: software-based distributed shared memory on workstation clusters

- Syracuse WWVM: worldwide virtual machine using commodity technologies
- Virginia Legion: metacomputing software for a national virtual computer facility
- Wisconsin Wind Tunnel: distributed shared memory on workstation clusters

Although some of the above projects aim at providing a shared-memory view to the user, they all have an underlying message-passing mechanism based on modern communication technologies.

     Anecdote.   Both NOW and SHRIMP violate the four-letter acronym/abbreviation rule stated at the end of Section 1.4. What has caused the deviation is unknown at present (David Patterson of Berkeley gave us both RISC and RAID). *Cluster of workstations* (COW), used as a generic name for such systems, represents another nontraditional term. I propose the generic name *cluster of loosely assembled workstations* (CLAW) as a contribution toward correcting this unwelcome trend.

PROBLEMS

22.1. Router-based networks

    a.   Under what conditions can we eliminate the input queues from the router depicted in Fig. 22.1?

    b.   Repeat part (a) for the output queues.

22.2. Switch-based networks

    a.   In the 4×4 crossbar switch of Fig. 22.2, can one remove some of the crosspoints without compromising its capability to route any permutation? How or why not?

    b.   For the 2×2 switch of Fig. 22.2, assign 2-bit codes to the four possible states shown in such a way that the switch can be implemented using only two multiplexers.

22.3. Classification of message-passing systems

    a.   Which of the five blank boxes or categories in Fig. 2.3 would you say is least likely to represent an actual parallel system and why?

    b.   Choose one of the blank boxes in Fig. 2.3 and fill it in with the name of a parallel machine. Briefly discuss the main features of the selected parallel machine.

22.4. Fine-grain message passing systems
Identify an example of a fine-grain message-passing system (see Section 22.1) and prepare a description of its architecture in a way that could form a section in this chapter.

22.5. Carnegie-Mellon University's C.mmp

    a.   Study the C.mmp multiprocessor system mentioned in Section 21.1 and prepare a description of its message-passing architecture in a way that could form a section in this chapter.

    b.   Contrast C.mmp to Tandem NonStop described in Section 22.2.

    c.   Contrast C.mmp to IBM SP2 described in Section 22.5.

22.6. Machines with multistage interconnection networks

    a.   Compare the multistage interconnection networks shown in Figs. 22.9 and 22.12 with respect to implementation cost and communication bandwidth.

> b. Find the numbers of nodes and links for the next larger configuration for each of the two networks in Figs. 22.9 and 22.12.
>
> c. Study the IBM SP2 and Meiko CS-2 networks and discuss their differences.

22.7. **Reliable bus-based multiprocessors**
Consider the particular Tandem NonStop Cyclone system configuration depicted in Fig. 22.4.

> a. Of the components shown in the diagram, which appear to be the most critical for the continued system operation and why?
>
> b. What types of processor malfunctions are most easily tolerated by this system? What types are likely to create the most difficulties?
>
> c. Relate the handling of disk storage in this system to redundant disk arrays of Section 18.5.

22.8. **Hypercube machines**
The Intel iPSC (personal supercomputer) hypercube-based parallel system was quite popular in the 1980s. Study the iPSC and contrast it to the nCUBE3 architecture of Section 22.3.

22.9. **Hypercube machines**
Consider the eight-node nCUBE3 architecture in Fig. 22.6.

> a. Describe possible reasons for including two host computers in the configuration.
>
> b. Explain possible reasons for the way in which I/O nodes are configured.
>
> c. Suppose we have to double the size of the system in order to be able to use more advanced algorithms on the incoming MPEG video streams. The volume of the data being processed does not change. What would the new configuration look like? Justify your answer.
>
> d. Repeat part (c), this time assuming that quadrupling of the processing power is needed.

22.10. **Processing nodes in CM-5**
In CM-5, the SPARC microprocessor fetches vector instructions and issues them to the vector units while also fetching and executing its own instructions. Estimate what fraction of SPARC's time is spent servicing the vector units. Where you cannot find needed data, proceed with reasonable assumptions.

22.11. **CM-5's data network**
The CM-5's data network performance is 20 MB/s per processor if all source–destination pairs are within the same 4-node group. This corresponds to an intragroup bandwidth of 80 MB/s. Between different 4-node groups belonging to the same 16-node group, an aggregate bandwidth of 40 MB/s into or out of each group is available. Thus, all 4 processors of a 4-node group can communicate at 10 MB/s or only 2 at 20 MB/s. The bandwidth into or out of a 16-node group is 80 MB/s, allowing each of the 16 processors to communicate at 5 MB/s, 8 at 10 MB/s, or only 4 at the maximum 20 MB/s. Show how to map an 8×8 mesh onto the processing node of a 64-processor CM-5 so that nearest-neighbor communication in one direction for all processors can be performed at the maximum rate of 20 MB/s.

22.12. **IBM SP2**
Study the IBM SP2 interconnection network architecture. Prepare a short report that outlines its main properties and answers the following specific questions:

> a. What is the internal structure and performance of the switching modules used in its implementation?
>
> b. How are the top-level switches configured, given that the processing nodes are all at the bottom?

    c. What is the routing algorithm used and how much of it is implemented in hardware or software?

22.13. TMC CM-5 and IBM SP2

    a. Compare the interconnection network architectures of TMC CM-5 and IBM SP2, described in Sections 22.4 and 22.5, respectively, with regard to complexity and performance.

    b. Consider the scenario described in Problem 22.11 for a 64-processor IBM SP2. Derive an efficient mapping for the nodes of the 8×8 mesh.

    c. If you have solved Problem 22.11, compare the results obtained in part (b) with those of TMC CM-5 and discuss.

22.14. Networks of workstations

A network of workstations consists of workstations in a number of adjacent offices linked together by 10-m optical cables in which light travels at two-thirds of the free-space speed of light. If each workstation executes instructions at the rate of 100 MIPS, how many instructions will be executed during the signal travel time? What type of limit does the above observation impose on the granularity of parallel computation on such a network of workstations?

22.15. Other router-based architectures

In this chapter, we have studied two switch-based parallel computers (TMC CM-5 and IBM SP2) and one router-based system (nCUBE3). To balance the coverage, study one of the following machines and prepare a description of its architecture in a way that could form a section in this chapter.

    a. Intel Paragon system, which uses routers configured into a 2D mesh.

    b. Cray T3E parallel computer, which uses routers configured into a 3D torus.

22.16. Further developments

By the time you see this book in print, changes may have occurred in the architecture, commercial availability status, or key design/performance parameters of some of the systems discussed in this chapter. Pick one of the machines for which you can find information on recent developments or follow-on systems and prepare a report on your findings.

REFERENCES AND SUGGESTED READING

[Ande95]   Anderson, T. E., D. E. Culler, and D. Patterson, "A Case for NOW (Networks of Workstations)," *IEEE Micro*, Vol. 15, No. 1, pp. 54–64, February 1995.

[Atha88]   Athas, W. C., and C. L. Seitz, "Multicomputers: Message-Passing Concurrent Computers," *IEEE Computer*, Vol. 21, No. 8, pp. 9–24, August 1988.

[Bokh96]   Bokhari, S. H., "Multiphase Complete Exchange on Paragon, SP2, and CS-2," *IEEE Parallel & Distributed Technology*, Vol. 4, No. 3, pp. 45–59, Fall 1996.

[Bonn95]   Bonniger, T., R. Esser, and D. Krekel, "CM-5E, KSR2, Paragon XP/S: A Comparative Description of Massively Parallel Computers," *Parallel Computing*, Vol. 21, pp. 199–232, 1995.

[Dong96]   Dongarra, J. J., S. W. Otto, M. Snir, and D. Walker, "A Message Passing Standard for MPP and Workstations," *Communications of the ACM*, Vol. 39, No. 7, pp. 84–90, July 1996.

[Duat97]   Duato, J., S. Yalamanchili, and L. Ni, *Interconnection Networks: An Engineering Approach*, IEEE Computer Society Press, 1997.

[Duze92]   Duzett, B., and R. Buck, "An Overview of the nCUBE 3 Supercomputer," *Proc. Symp. Frontiers of Massively Parallel Computation*, October 1992, pp. 458–464.

[Hami97]   Hamilton, S., and L. Gerber, "Deep Blue's Hardware–Software Synergy," *IEEE Computer*, Vol. 30, No. 10, pp. 29–35, October 1997.

[Hill93]Hillis, W. D., and L. W. Tucker, "The CM-5 Connection Machine: A Scalable Supercomputer," *Communications of the ACM*, Vol. 36, No. 11, pp. 31–40, November 1993.

[Hord93]Hord, R. M., *Parallel Supercomputing in MIMD Architectures*, CRC Press, 1993.

[Hwan98]Hwang, K., and Z. Xu, *Scalable Parallel Computing: Technology, Architecture, Programming*, McGraw-Hill, 1998.

[Mart97]Martin, R. P., A. M. Vahdat, D. E. Culler, and T. E. Anderson, "Effects of Communication Latency, Overhead, and Bandwidth in a Cluster Architecture," *Proc. 24th Int. Symp. Computer Architecture*, 1997, pp. 85–97.

[Prad96]Pradhan, D. K., "Case Studies in Fault-Tolerant Multiprocessor and Distributed Systems," Chapter 4 in *Fault-Tolerant Computer System Design*, Prentice–Hall, 1996, pp. 236–281.

23

Data-Parallel SIMD Machines

Data-parallel SIMD machines occupy a special place in the history of parallel processing. The first supercomputer ever built was a SIMD machine. Some of the most cost-effective parallel computers in existence are of the SIMD variety. You can now buy a SIMD array processor attachment for your personal computer that gives you supercomputer-level performance on some problems for a workstation price. However, because SIMD machines are often built from custom components, they have suffered a few setbacks in recent years. In this chapter, after reviewing some of the reasons for these setbacks and evaluating SIMD prospects in the future, we review several example SIMD machines, from the pioneering ILLIAC IV, through early massively parallel processors (Goodyear MPP and DAP), to more recent general-purpose machines (TMC CM-2 and MasPar MP-2). Chapter topics are

- 23.1. Where have all the SIMDs gone?
- 23.2. The first supercomputer: ILLIAC IV
- 23.3. Massively parallel Goodyear MPP
- 23.4. Distributed Array Processor (DAP)
- 23.5. Hypercubic Connection Machine 2
- 23.6. Multiconnected MasPar MP-2

23.1. WHERE HAVE ALL THE SIMDs GONE?

In Section 4.2, we briefly reviewed the main properties of SIMD and MIMD parallel architectures, justified the inclination to use the SIMD paradigm in early parallel machines, and hinted at the economic factors that have led to the trend toward building and marketing more flexible MIMD systems since the early 1990s. A natural question thus is: Is SIMD spending its final days on life support or will we see future parallel architectures of this type? In this section, after discussing the origins and types of SIMD processing, we review the designs of five SIMD machines that are representative of the various generations of, and approaches to, SIMD processing.

As argued in Section 4.1, associative processing is the earliest form of parallel processing. Associative memories (AMs), conceived in the 1940s, were offering processing powers at the level of million bit-operations per second (mega-bit-OPS) in the 1950s. This was well before any reference to "parallel processing" in the technical literature. It may seem strange that we talk about the processing power of a memory, so let us justify this briefly.

Figure 23.1 depicts the functional view of an associative memory. There are m memory cells that store data words, each of which has one or more tag bits for use as markers. The control unit broadcasts data and commands to all cells. A typical search instruction has a comparand and a mask word as its parameters. The mask specifies which bits or fields within the cells are to be searched and the comparand provides the bit values of interest. Each cell has comparison logic built in and stores the result of its comparison in the response or tag store. The tag bits can be included in the search criteria, thus allowing composite searches to be programmed (e.g., searching only among the cells that responded or failed to respond to a previous search instruction). Such searches, along with the capability to read, write, multiwrite (write a value into all cells that have a particular tag bit set), or perform global tag operations (e.g., detecting the presence or absence of responders or their multiplicity), allow search operations such as the following to be effectively programmed [Parh97]:

- Exact-match search: locating data based on partial knowledge of contents
- Inexact-match searches: finding numerically or logically proximate values
- Membership searches: identifying all members of a particular set
- Relational searches: determining values that are less than, less or equal, and so forth
- Interval searches: marking items that are between limits or not between limits
- Extrema searches: min- or max-finding, next higher, next lower
- Rank-based selection: selecting kth or k largest/smallest elements
- Ordered retrieval: repeated max- or min-finding with elimination (sorting)

Additionally, arithmetic operations, such as computing the global sum or adding two fields in a subset of AM cells, can be effectively programmed using bit-serial algorithms.

Associative processors (APs) are AMs that have been augmented with more flexible processing logic. From an architectural standpoint, APs can be divided into four classes [Parh73]:

1. *Fully parallel* (word-parallel, bit-parallel) APs have comparison logic associated with each bit of stored data. In simple exact-match searches, the logic associated with each bit generates a local match or mismatch signal. These local signals are

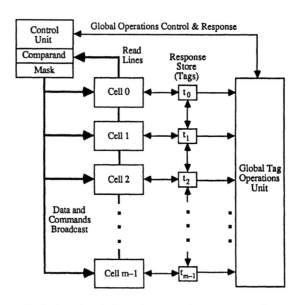

Figure 23.1. Functional view of an associative memory/processor.

then combined to produce the cell match or mismatch result. In more complicated searches, the bit logic typically receives partial search results from a neighboring bit position and generates partial results to be passed on to the next bit position.

2. *Bit-serial* (word-parallel, bit-serial) systems process an entire bit-slice of data, containing 1 bit of every word, simultaneously, but go through multiple bits of the search field sequentially. Bit-serial systems have been dominant in practice because they allow the most cost-effective implementations using low-cost, high-density, off-the-shelf RAM chips.

3. *Word-serial* (word-serial, bit parallel) APs based on electronic circulating memories represent the hardware counterparts of programmed linear search. Even though several such systems were built in the 1960s, they do not appear to be cost-effective with today's technology.

4. *Block-oriented* (block-parallel, word-serial, bit/byte-serial) systems represent a compromise between bit-serial and word-serial systems in an effort to make large systems practically realizable. Some block-oriented AP systems are based on augmenting the read/write logic associated with each head of a head-per-track disk so that it can search the track contents as they pass underneath. Such a mechanism can act as a filter between the database and a fast sequential computer or as a special-purpose database search engine.

These four basic architectures, along with intermediate or hybrid schemes, provide AP designers with a vast design space and speed–cost trade-offs. Examples of the available cost–performance trade-offs in the design of a class of VLSI-based search processors have been reported by the author [Parh91].

The next major idea after the development of AMs/APs was the notion of array processing. A key paper in this area introduced the Solomon computer [Slot62] that served as a model for the University of Illinois's ILLIAC IV (see Section 23.2). Various architectural advances, coupled with dramatic improvements in technology, produced a steady stream of SIMD designs. These designs vary in the processing node structure and complexity, the amount of memory per node, interprocessor communication facilities, and the instruction set implemented in hardware. Sections 23.3 through 23.6 contain descriptions of some of the key SIMD machines built over the years. Goodyear MPP and Distributed Array Processor (DAP) represent direct descendants of the AM/AP approach, while Thinking Machines Corporation's CM-2 and MasPar's MP-2 can be viewed as more modern router-based implementations.

It is worth mentioning at this point that mixed-mode SIMD/MIMD parallelism has also been considered. A well-known example is the partitionable SIMD/MIMD (PASM) system designed and implemented at Purdue University for image processing applications. Figure 23.2 depicts the architecture of Purdue PASM [Sieg96]. Midlevel controllers allow PASM to be partitioned into multiple SIMD (M-SIMD) machines working on independent tasks. The interconnection network is an omega (multistage cube) network. A prototype with $p = 16$ processors has been built and is used for research and education.

So, where have all the SIMDs gone? One answer is that they are quietly executing parallel applications at numerous installations [Parh95]. Vector SIMD using time-shared as opposed to, or in addition to, parallel hardware is alive and well in Cray, Fujitsu, and Hitachi vector computers. As for parallel SIMD, even though current technology and implementation considerations seem to have shifted the balance in favor of MIMD, it is still true that parallel SIMD machines provide more performance per unit cost for a vast collection of pleasantly

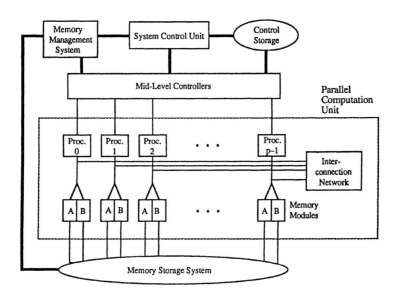

Figure 23.2. The architecture of Purdue PASM.

parallel problems that are of considerable interest to the scientific computation, embedded control, and database communities. SIMD architectures also offer advantages in ease of programming, hardware testing, reliability, and speed/precision trade-offs. These advantages may well lead to greater prevalence of SIMD architectures, if not in the form of full-blown parallel computers, at least as array-processor attachments to workstations or even personal computers.

23.2. THE FIRST SUPERCOMPUTER: ILLIAC IV

ILLIAC IV, widely recognized as the first supercomputer, was conceived at University of Illinois as a research vehicle for advancing the state of the art in digital system technology, architecture, and performance. Prior to ILLIAC IV, research at Illinois had led to several innovative computer systems, including ILLIAC III, which embodied significant advances in computer arithmetic algorithms and implementation methods. Besides producing the world's first supercomputer, the ILLIAC IV project led to many advances in component/manufacturing technologies, parallel architectures, and computation-intensive applications. Hord has written fascinating histories of the ILLIAC IV project, its difficulties, and many triumphs ([Hord82] or [Hord90], pp. 17–30).

As an experimental SIMD computer system, ILLIAC IV was envisaged to have 256 processors, organized in four quadrants, each consisting of an 8×8 twisted torus. Each of the quadrants was to have a separate control unit, allowing the machine to be partitioned into four smaller array processors for applications that did not require the computational power of the entire system. Eventually, only one quadrant was built, becoming operational in 1975. Its 64 processors were comparable to the fastest CPUs at the time (80-ns clock cycle) and operated on 64-bit words. Each processor had six registers and 2K words of local memory. The Burroughs 6700 host computer was responsible for input/output, network connection, and a number of supervisory functions (Fig. 23.3).

In ILLIAC IV, sequencing and control instructions were executed by the control unit, concurrently with data manipulation functions in the array. Three data paths were available for interprocessor communication. First, the control unit, which had access to all processor memories, could move data between them. This word-at-a-time route was simple and flexible, but relatively slow. Second, the control unit could broadcast one word of data to all processors. This second approach was quite effective for performing arithmetic operations between scalar and vector operands. Third, the processors could communicate via a ROUTE instruction that allowed data in one processor's register to be sent to another processor's register. Because Processor i was connected to Processors $i \pm 1$ and $i \pm 8$, routing to Processor $i + 5$, say, was done by the software figuring out that the best way would be through one step of $+8$, followed by three steps of -1.

ILLIAC IV processors could be individually enabled or disabled via commands from the control unit or based on local data-dependent conditions. Only enabled processors executed normal instructions that were broadcast by the control unit. A disabled processor ignored all instructions, except for the ones that could change its mode. The mode link in Fig. 23.3 allowed the control unit to examine a status bit in each of the 64 processors and to perform conditional operations based on the values received.

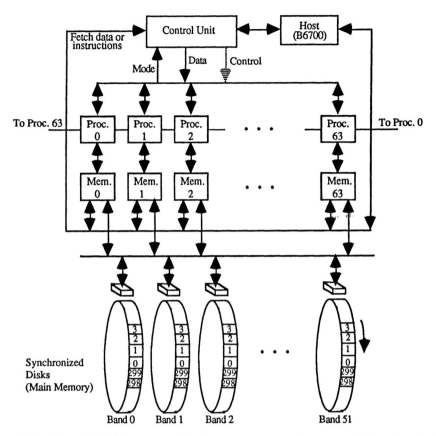

Figure 23.3. The ILLIAC IV computer (the interprocessor routing network is only partially shown).

Besides 8 Mb of memory associated with the 64 processors (2K 64-bit words per processor), ILLIAC IV had a main memory of 16M words. This 1-Gb memory was implemented using 13 fixed-head magnetic disks in synchronized rotation. The disk storage space was organized as 52 bands, each holding 300 pages of 1024 words. The half-rotation time of the disks was 20 ms, some 10^5 times longer than the access time of the memory within processors. However, the data transfer rate of 0.5 Gb/s allowed large blocks of data to be read out or stored fairly efficiently.

A conventional Digital Equipment Corporation PDP-10 computer controlled the main memory, directed the I/O peripherals, and performed all other system management functions. A Burroughs B6700 computer compiled submitted programs into machine language.

23.3. MASSIVELY PARALLEL GOODYEAR MPP

The MPP system, built by Goodyear Aerospace Corporation and delivered to NASA's Goddard Space Flight Center in 1982, was one of the earliest massively parallel processors.

It contained 16K bit-serial processors and was aimed for applications involving the processing of satellite imagery. Prior to MPP, in the early 1970s, Goodyear had built the STARAN associative processor, which contained up to 8K processors and was promoted for applications in air traffic control and radar signal processing.

Figure 23.4 shows the architecture of Goodyear MPP. The array unit consisted of a 128×128 mesh of single-bit processors under three levels of control: the array control unit, program and data management unit (PDMU), and a VAX 11/780 host computer. PDMU, a key component of MPP, consisted of a PDP-11 minicomputer running the RSX-11M real-time operating system. It was used for program development, machine diagnostics, and controlling the flow of data into and out of the array. Array input and output was performed via special I/O interfaces or links to the staging memory, each 128 bits wide. The opposite edges of the array could be connected together to form a horizontal cylinder, a vertical cylinder, or a torus. A tree of OR gates, to which every processor was connected, provided information on the global state of the array to the control unit.

The staging memory had some interesting features. Besides buffering the array input and output data, it could provide various data rearrangement functions needed to convert byte- or word-oriented data into the bit-slice form for processing by the array. In addition, it allowed multi-dimensional access to data, i.e., reading out array data with various ordering of dimensions (row-major, column-major, and so on).

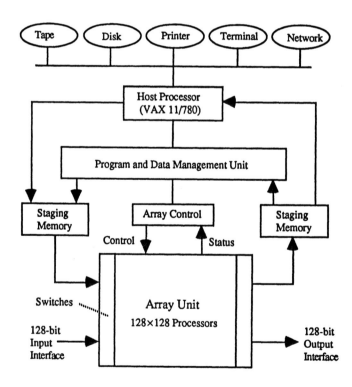

Figure 23.4. The architecture of Goodyear MPP.

The bit-serial MPP processors contained six single-bit registers plus a full adder, a comparator, a logic unit capable of forming any two-variable Boolean function, a variable-length shift register, and 1K bits of memory (Fig. 23.5). Registers A, B, and C, along with the shift register, were used in arithmetic operations. Register P was interconnected to the NEWS neighbors of the processor, received the results of logical operations from the attached logic unit, and supplied one input of the full adder. The G register determined if the processor should execute or ignore the broadcast instruction. The S register was used primarily for shifting data into and out of the 2D array through its row links, with the leftmost and rightmost columns of processors serving as input and output points, respectively. This shifting of data into and out of the array could be done concurrently with other array operations, thus allowing computation and I/O to be fully overlapped.

A 2-row by 4-column section of the MPP processor array was placed on one chip, with the processor memories occupying another chip. Thus, the MPP array needed a 64×32 matrix of processor and memory chips. In fact, 33 columns of chips (132 columns of processors) were used to allow processor malfunctions to be tolerated through bypassing of the chip column holding the malfunctioning processor. Of course, if the malfunction was detected during MPP operation, the computation was restarted or was rolled back to the last checkpoint.

With a cycle time of 100 ns, MPP could perform 8-bit integer array additions at 6.6 GOPS and multiplication (yielding 16-bit products) at 1.9 GOPS. Addition of floating-point arrays (32-bit format) was done at 0.4 GFLOPS and multiplication at 0.2 GFLOPS. Finally, the peak performance for the multiplication of a scalar by an array was 2.3 GOPS for 8-bit

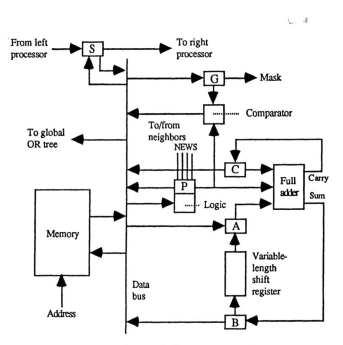

Figure 23.5. The single-bit processor of MPP.

integers (yielding 16-bit results) and 0.4 GFLOPS for 32-bit floating-point numbers. All in all, this was quite impressive for the early 1980s.

23.4. DISTRIBUTED ARRAY PROCESSOR (DAP)

The SIMD Distributed Array Processor (DAP) was originally developed in 1976 by International Computers Limited in England and was initially known as ICL DAP. Later, Cambridge Parallel Processing, with branches in England and the United States, was formed to build and market DAP-based systems. Recent products in this series have included 1K- and 4K-processor systems configured as 32×32 and 64×64 meshes, with each processor having up to 16 and 64 MB of memory, respectively. The smaller model fits under a desk and the larger one is housed in a standard EIA rack cabinet. Both DAP models are typically hosted by a Sun workstation.

DAP's processors are bit-serial and can thus perform variable-length arithmetic with software support. Processors operate in lockstep and have nearest-neighbor mesh connections as well as row/column data highways to allow efficient global fetches and broadcasts. More expensive models of DAP come with an 8-bit coprocessor per PE to speed up floating-point and integer operations. Code and data stores are separate, and the processors have access to a high-speed data channel. The control structure consists of a Master Control Unit (MCU) that reads instructions from a program memory and issues them to the processors. The MCU also acts as a high-speed scalar processor. An application consists of two parts: one running on the front end and a separately compiled part running on the DAP itself.

DAP's architecture is similar to that of ILLIAC IV, with major differences being bit-serial processors, row/column highways, much larger memory per processor, and high I/O capability. Figure 23.6 shows the structure of each bit-serial processor. The interconnection is to the four nearest neighbors in a 2D grid, together with an additional bus system connecting processors by rows and columns. Each processor has its own part of the array memory. Processors access data of neighboring processors by carrying out hardware-implemented shift operations. Array memory can also be addressed conventionally by the MCU. A fast channel is provided to allow data to be fed into one edge of the square torus of processors.

The five single-bit registers in each processor serve for activity control (A), carry storage (C), accumulation (Q), data input/output (D), and storage data buffering (S). Register S does not appear in the programmer's view. The remaining registers are viewed as four planes as shown in Fig. 23.7. Once data are loaded into the D plane, they can be clocked out asynchronously without interrupting the processing functions. I/O node processors can return data to the broadcast processor along fast data highways for collation and return to the front end. In addition, a fast bus along one edge of the processor array can drive disk units or a high-resolution graphical device.

The variable-length arithmetic capabilities of DAP make it well suited to both nonnumerical and numerical applications involving large volumes of data. Major application areas include scientific and engineering computing, image processing, signal processing, defense information processing, and data storage and retrieval functions in large databases (particu-

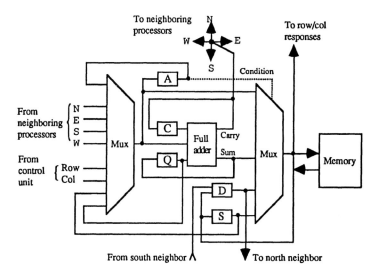

Figure 23.6. The bit-serial processor of DAP.

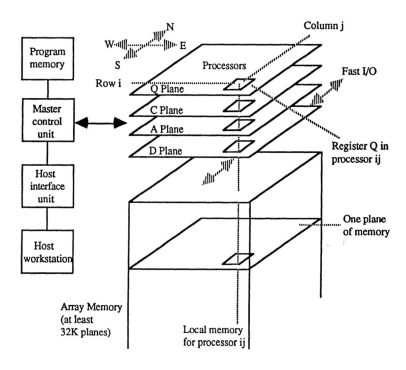

Figure 23.7. The high-level architecture of DAP system.

larly searching of text databases). A standard operating system, typically Unix, is run on the host computer. The internal DAP operating system, which interfaces the control unit and the processor array, is not normally visible to the user. A parallel version of Fortran (Fortran-Plus), which is similar to Fortran 90, is used for application program development.

So far, at least four generations of DAP systems have been built. The latest models available are DAP Model 510 (32×32) and 610 (64×64). The bit-serial processors of these models have been augmented with 8-bit coprocessors in Models 510c and 610c. This significantly speeds up integer and floating-point arithmetic computations. DAP 510c has a peak performance of 140 MFLOPS, while that of DAP 610c is 560 MFLOPS. Per 1992 performance data, DAP 610 can achieve 40 GIPS for Boolean operations.

23.5. HYPERCUBIC CONNECTION MACHINE 2

Thinking Machines Corporation was founded in 1983. The company's first product, the 1-GIPS Connection Machine 1 (CM-1), was based on the MIT doctoral thesis of W. Daniel Hillis, one of the founders of TMC. Less than a year after the first commercial installation of a 16K-processor CM-1 system in 1986, the 2.5-GFLOPS CM-2 was introduced, which had 64 Kb of memory per processor (instead of 4 Kb), a faster clock, and hardware-implemented floating-point arithmetic capability. The design philosophy of both CM-1 and CM-2 was that using a large number of slow, inexpensive processors is a cost-effective alternative to a small number of very fast, expensive processors. This is sometimes referred to as the *army of ants* approach to high-performance computing. Each bit-serial processor of CM-2 was so simple that 16 processors, plus a number of other components, fit on a single integrated-circuit chip. The processors were bit-serial because otherwise their parallel input/output and memory access requirements could not be satisfied within the pin limitations of a single chip.

Figure 23.8 depicts the overall structure of a 64K-processor CM-2. Up to four front-end computers are connected to the array sequencers via the 4×4 programmable bidirectional Nexus switch whose setting determines the machine configuration. With a single front-end computer connected to all array sequencers, the operation mode is simple SIMD. On the other hand, if each front-end computer is connected to a different array sequencer, CM-2 operates as four independent 16K-processor SIMD machines (M-SIMD mode). Other configurations are also possible. Programs execute on one or more front-end computers that issue instructions to the parallel processing part as needed. These instructions, which include integer and floating-point arithmetic, interprocessor communication, sorting, and matrix multiplication, constitute CM-2's Paris machine language. Paris instructions are not directly handled by the processors, but rather by the sequencers, which break them down into streams of processor instructions.

The array part of CM-2 is built of four chip types: a chip that holds 16 ALUs, along with their associated flags (4-bit register) and router/grid connections, commercial RAM chips for memory, a floating-point interface chip, and a floating-point execution chip. The floating-point chips are shared by 32 processors (two processor chips). Each processor has 64 Kb of bit-addressable local memory and a bit-serial arithmetic unit. With all of the processors performing 32-bit integer additions in parallel, CM-2 operates at about 2.5 GIPS. Using the floating-point unit associated with every 32 processors, a peak performance of 3.5

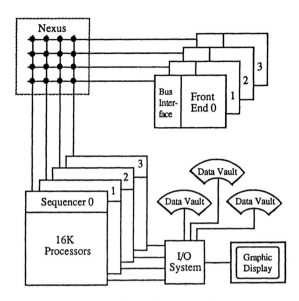

Figure 23.8. The architecture of CM-2.

GFLOPS (single-precision) or 2.5 GFLOPS (double-precision) is available. Because the memory of each processor can be accessed at the rate of 5 Mb/s, the aggregate memory bandwidth is about 300 Gb/s.

CM-2 offers two mechanisms for interprocessor communication. One is a programmable NEWS grid that allows the 64K-processor CM-2 to be viewed as a 256×256, 1024×64, $16 \times 16 \times 16 \times 16$, or other grids of various sizes and dimensions. The other mechanism is through the routers that have been provided for the processor chips. The 4096 routers of a 64K-processor CM-2 are interconnected as a 12-cube via bit-serial channels. Messages destined for the same processor can be combined in hardware using sum, OR, overwrite, max, or min rule.

The ALU of a CM-2 processor essentially consists of two 8-to-1 multiplexers, each implementing an arbitrary logic function of three single-bit inputs (Fig. 23.9). Two of the input bit streams of the ALU, say a and b, came from the processor's 64-Kb memory and are read out in consecutive clock cycles. The third input, c, comes from the processor's 4-bit flags register. Thus, $16 + 16 + 2$ bits are required to specify the addresses of these operands. The f output is stored as a flag bit (2-bit address) and the g output replaces the memory operand a in a third clock cycle. Another flag bit can be specified to conditionalize the operation, thus allowing some processors to selectively ignore the common instruction broadcast to all processors.

To perform integer addition in the ALU shown in Fig. 23.9, we proceed as follows. The a and b operands are bits of the addends, which are stored in memory, and c is a flag bit that is used to hold the carry from one bit position into the next. The f function op-code is "00010111" (majority) and the g function op-code is "01010101" (three-input XOR). Note that the op-codes are in effect the truth tables for the three-variable functions f and g. A k-bit integer addition requires $3k$ clock cycles and is thus quite slow. But up to 64K additions can

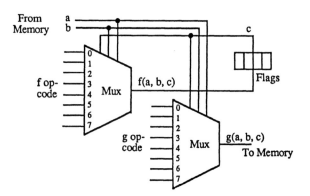

Figure 23.9. The bit-serial ALU of CM-2.

be performed in parallel. Floating-point arithmetic can be implemented similarly and this is the way it was done in CM-1. In CM-2, the hardware floating-point units lead to significant acceleration for both single- and double-precision ANSI/IEEE standard floating-point numbers.

23.6. MULTICONNECTED MASPAR MP-2

The design philosophy for MasPar MP-1 and MP-2 was to use a high level of parallelism with simple processors, implemented in nonaggressive (and thus inexpensive) CMOS VLSI technology, to achieve good performance/cost ratio. MasPar MP-2 can have from 1K to 16K processors, with the largest configuration achieving a peak performance of 68 GIPS, 6.3 GFLOPS for single-precision floating-point numbers, and 2.4 GFLOPS with double precision.

The architecture of MP-2 is depicted in Fig. 23.10. The array control unit, which occupies one printed-circuit board, is a 12.5-MIPS RISC-type processor with demand-paged

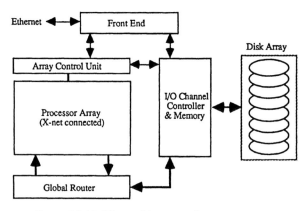

Figure 23.10. The architecture of MasPar MP-2.

instruction memory. It fetches and decodes MP-2 instructions, computes addresses, operates on scalar data (usually requiring one 80-ns clock cycle per instruction), issues control signals to the processor array, and monitors the array status.

The processor array (Fig. 23.11) consists of one printed-circuit board for 1K processors and their associated external memory units. There are 64 clusters of 16 processors on each board. Processors in a cluster are interconnected by the X-net (eight-neighbor mesh) topology, with X-net links provided between neighboring clusters. Processor chips are custom-designed, with each chip containing 32 processors (two clusters). The 14-mm by 14-mm die uses 1-μm CMOS technology and contains just under 1M transistors.

The processor has no instruction storage, fetch, or decode logic but rather receives decoded instructions from the array control unit (Fig. 23.12). Each processor has 52 bit- and byte-addressable registers (32 bits wide) of which 40 are available to the programmer and 12 are used internally to implement the MP-2 instruction set.

In addition to the register file, which accounts for roughly half of the transistors on each chip, the processor has a 16-bit exponent unit, a 64-bit significand unit, a 32-bit barrel shifter, a 32-bit ALU, a 1-bit logic unit, and a flags unit. Both 32- and 64-bit floating-point operations can be performed, as well as 8-, 16-, 32-, and 64-bit integer arithmetic. The processor overlaps memory access (load/store) with computation. Up to 32 load/store instructions can be queued and executed while computation proceeds. A hardware interlock mechanism is used to ensure that registers are not read before they have been loaded and not modified before they have been stored. Optimizing compilers move loads to earlier points in the program and delay the use of registers that receive operation results.

The X-net connectivity is provided by using only four wires per processor. All processors have the same direction controls so that, e.g., they all send an operand to the northeast neighbor and receive from the southwest neighbor. The processor chip has two 4×4 processor

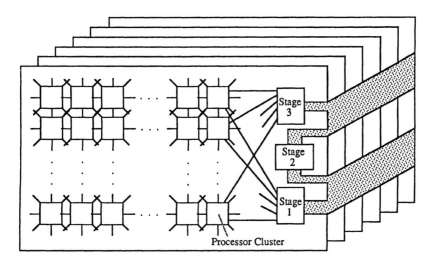

Figure 23.11. The physical packaging of processor clusters and the three-stage global router in MasPar MP-2.

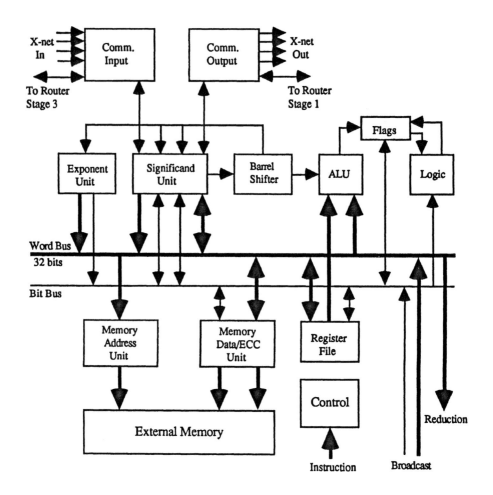

Figure 23.12. Processor architecture in MasPar MP-2.

clusters and 24 pins for their bit-serial X-net connections. The aggregate bandwidth of the X-net in a 64K-processor MP-2 system is 20 GB/s.

In addition to the X-net, a three-stage 1024×1024 crossbar network (Fig. 23.11) connects every processor cluster to every other cluster and also forms the basis of the I/O system. The crossbar is built of 64×64 crossbar chips, 3 of which are placed on each processor board. When a processor wants to send a message to another processor, it transmits it through the router's Stage-1 port. From there, the appropriate connection to the next stage is chosen based on the target processor number. Once a connection is established, data can be exchanged between the two processors in both directions. The target processor returns an acknowledgment once the connection is closed. Because each cluster of 16 processors has one router port, an arbitrary permutation requires 16 routing cycles to complete. A 16K-processor MP-2 has an aggregate router communication bandwidth of 1.3 GB/s.

PROBLEMS

23.1. Membership search in associative memories

   a. We would like to identify all associative memory cells that contain one of the bit patterns 0101, 0110, 0111, 1101, 1110, or 1111 in a particular 4-bit field. What is the minimum number of search instructions that are needed for a fully parallel associative memory?

   b. Formulate a general procedure for doing membership searches of the type given in part (a) with the minimum number of instructions.

   c. Show how the membership search of part (a) might be programmed on a bit-serial system.

23.2. Systolic associative memories
   It has been argued that the requirements for broadcasting instructions to all cells and combining the tags in a global operations unit have a negative impact on the scalability of associative memories [Parh92]. Show how small AMs can be combined into a pipelined configuration to achieve good performance when multiple searches are performed in the same data set (batch searching). What are the implications of such an architecture for other types of searches? In particular, what can you say about max-finding or membership searches of the type defined in Problem 23.1.

23.3. Goodyear STARAN processor
   The Goodyear STARAN associative processor was perhaps the first massively parallel computer ever built. It had several interesting features that were subsequently copied in other designs.

   a. Study the Goodyear STARAN and prepare a description of its architecture and applications in a way that could form a section in this chapter.

   b. Compare STARAN with both MPP and DAP, identifying their similarities and differences.

23.4. The twisted torus network of ILLIAC IV
   Draw a diagram showing the 8×8 twisted torus network of ILLIAC IV. How should the matrix multiplication algorithm for a torus (Fig. 11.4) be adapted to run on ILLIAC IV?

23.5. The twisted torus network of ILLIAC IV
   Determine the diameter, average internode distance, and bisection width of the twisted torus network in the 8×8 ILLIAC IV configuration. What is the bisection bandwidth of this configuration?

23.6. The main memory of ILLIAC IV
   From the information given in Section 23.2 about the synchronized disks that form the main memory of ILLIAC IV, derive as much information about the physical characteristics of the disk units used as possible. When two or more parameters are interrelated but there is not enough information to determine their values, take reasonable guesses for some and determine the other ones.

23.7. Goodyear MPP
   The variable-length shift register in the processor of MPP (Fig. 23.5) could be configured to have a length of 2, 6, 10, 14, 18, 22, 26, or 30 bits.

   a. Try to find out why these lengths were chosen.

   b. How can such a variable-length shift register be implemented?

23.8. Comparison of MPP and DAP

Present a detailed comparison of MPP and DAP. In particular, discuss the relative efficiency of the two architectures in performing integer and floating-point arithmetic. Assume a DAP model with no arithmetic coprocessor.

23.9. Connection Machine 2

Discuss how 2's-complement addition can be performed on CM-2 in such a way that a flag bit is set on overflow. *Hint:* The next-to-the-last carry is needed.

23.10. Arithmetic on DAP and CM-2

Compare the speed of standard 32-bit integer arithmetic operations of addition, multiplication, and division on DAP and CM-2 bit-serial processors, assuming the same clock rate for both.

23.11. Image smoothing on MP-2

Consider a 1024×1024 gray-scale image for which the brightness of each pixel is represented by an 8-bit unsigned integer. In image smoothing, we replace the value of each pixel with the average of its own value and those of its eight nearest neighbors. The edge pixels do not have eight neighbors and are thus not modified.

    a. Show how the smoothing algorithm for the above image should be mapped onto a 4K-processor MP-2 in order to minimize interprocessor communications.

    b. How many interprocessor communication steps on the X-net are needed for this problem?

    c. Develop an efficient computation scheme for image smoothing. *Hint:* Dividing by 9 can be done efficiently if one notes that $9^{-1} = (2^3(1 + 2^{-3}))^{-1} \approx 2^{-3}(1 - 2^{-3})(1 + 2^{-6})$.

23.12. Hybrid SIMD/MIMD architectures

The M-SIMD (multiple SIMD) class of parallel architectures is defined as one in which subsets of processors can operate in SIMD or SPMD mode within the subsets and in MIMD mode between different subsets. Study the PASM project [Sieg96] as a representative example of machines in this class, focusing on special implementation problems and performance advantages over pure SIMD or MIMD. Prepare a description of PASM in a way that could form a section in this chapter.

23.13. Geometric Arithmetic Parallel Processor (GAPP)

GAPP was developed in the early 1980s at Martin Marietta for image processing applications.

    a. Study GAPP and prepare a description for it in a way that could form a section in this chapter.

    b. Compare GAPP with MPP, DAP, and CM-2.

23.14. Conway's game of life

In the Game of Life, conceived by John Conway, the world of microorganisms is modeled by a Boolean matrix. A 1 represents the presence and a 0 the absence of a living organism. Discrete time is assumed and the new state of each matrix cell at time $t + 1$ is determined by three rules based on the number of living organisms in the eight neighbors of the cell at time t: (1) Any living organism with two or three neighbors survives. (2) Any living organism with four or more neighbors dies of overcrowding. (3) Any living organism with zero or one neighbor dies of solitude. (4) An organism is born in any empty cell with exactly three neighbors. Compare the SIMD machines described in this chapter with regard to their ability to simulate the Game of Life on a 256×256 matrix for thousands of time steps (generations).

23.15. The editor's parallel processor

The editor of a scientific journal on parallel processing has decided that he must practice what he preaches. He has, therefore, developed the following parallel processing scheme for paper evaluation and selection. He asks each of five referees to rank a paper on a scale of 0–100 and attach to their reviews confidence levels in the same range (both 7-bit numbers). The five referees of each paper always return their evaluations promptly (remember, this is just a textbook problem) and an aide enters the 14 bits of information from each referee into the memory of the editor's parallel computer. At the end of each month, the editor processes the data by running his paper selection program. The program computes a 16-bit composite score for each paper by multiplying each referee's ranking and confidence levels and adding the results. Each composite score is compared with a randomly chosen acceptance threshold (determined in a drawing each month). Which of the architectures described in this chapter would you say best matches the requirements of this application and why? Assume that millions of papers must be evaluated each month.

REFERENCES AND SUGGESTED READING

[Batc80]   Batcher, K. E., "Design of a Massively Parallel Processor," *IEEE Trans. Computers*, Vol. 29, No. 9, pp. 836–844, September 1980.
[Cyph94]   Cypher, R., and J. L. C. Sanz, *The SIMD Model of Parallel Computation*, Springer-Verlag, 1994.
[Hill85]   Hillis, W. D., *The Connection Machine*, MIT Press, 1985.
[Hord82]   Hord, R. M., *The ILLIAC IV: The First Supercomputer*, Springer-Verlag, 1982.
[Hord90]   Hord, R. M., *Parallel Supercomputing in SIMD Architectures*, CRC Press, 1990.
[Jurc96]   Jurczyk, M., and T. Schwederski, "SIMD Processing Concepts and Systems," Chapter 22 in *Parallel and Distributed Computing Handbook*, edited by A. Y. Zomaya, MaGraw-Hill, 1996, pp. 649–679.
[MasP92]   MasPar Computer Corporation, "The Design of the MasPar MP-2: A Cost Effective Massively Parallel Computer," November 1992.
[Parh73]   Parhami, B., "Associative Memories and Processors: An Overview and Selected Bibliography," *Proceedings of the IEEE*, Vol. 61, No. 6, pp. 722–730, June 1973.
[Parh91]   Parhami, B., "The Mixed Serial/Parallel Approach to VLSI Search Processors," *Proc. Hawaii Int. Conf. System Sciences*, January 1991, Vol. I, pp. 202–211.
[Parh92]   Parhami, B., "Architectural Tradeoffs in the Design of VLSI-Based Associative Memories," *Micro-processing and Microprogramming*, Vol. 36, No. 1, pp. 27–41, November 1992.
[Parh95]   Parhami, B., "Panel Assesses SIMD's Future," *IEEE Computer*, Vol. 28, No. 6, pp. 89–91, June 1995. Unabridged version of this report under the title "SIMD Machines: Do They Have a Significant Future?" appeared in *IEEE Computer Society Technical Committee on Computer Architecture Newsletter*, pp. 23–26, August 1995, and in *ACM Computer Architecture News*, Vol. 23, No. 4, pp. 19–22, September 1995.
[Parh97]   Parhami, B., "Search and Data Selection Algorithms for Associative Processors," in *Associative Processing and Processors*, edited by A. Krikelis and C. Weems, IEEE Computer Society Press, 1997, pp. 10–25.
[Sieg96]   Siegel, H. J., et al. "The Design and Prototyping of the PASM Reconfigurable Parallel Processing System," in *Parallel Computing: Paradigms and Applications*, Edited by A. Y. Zomaya, Thomson, 1996, pp. 78–114.
[Slot62]   Slotnick, D. L., W. C. Borck, and R. C. McReynolds, "The Solomon Computer," *Proc. AFIPS Fall Joint Computer Conf.*, 1962, pp. 97–107.
[Tuck88]   Tucker, L. W. and G. G. Robertson, "Architecture and Applications of the Connection Machine," *IEEE Computer*, Vol. 21, No. 8, pp. 26–38, August 1988.

24

Past, Present, and Future

In this final chapter, we present a brief overview of the history of parallel processing, discuss the current trends in system architecture, and look at some promising technologies and research areas that are likely to shape the future of this field in the coming decade. Chapter topics are

- 24.1. Milestones in parallel processing
- 24.2. Current status, issues, and debates
- 24.3. TFLOPS, PFLOPS, and beyond
- 24.4. Processor and memory technologies
- 24.5. Interconnection technologies
- 24.6. The future of parallel processing

24.1. MILESTONES IN PARALLEL PROCESSING

Many interesting parallel computers have been built or proposed. It would be impossible to devote even a single paragraph to each interesting parallel machine that has been built or proposed since the early 1960s. Lerman and Rudolph [Lerm94] survey some 200 parallel computers built by universities, industrial research laboratories, and commercial vendors from around 1960 to 1992. An appendix in their volume provides a brief listing of the architectural features for each of the machines surveyed. More detailed descriptions for a smaller number of parallel computers can be found in two books by Hord, respectively devoted to SIMD [Hord90] and MIMD [Hord93] machines. In the remainder of this section, we review a few key ideas and developments in the history of parallel processing.

The desirability of computing multiple values at the same time in order to speed up repetitive computations, such as those needed for the formation of numerical tables, was noted as early as 1842 in connection with Babbage's Analytical Engine ([Hock81], p. 7). In 1952, von Neumann showed that a 2D array of processors with 29 states could simulate the behavior of a Turing machine and thus could be considered universal. A few years later, Holland [Holl59] described what can be viewed as the forerunner of modern MIMD-type parallel computers: an array machine in which the instructions of multiple subprograms were distributed in space, with data and control transferred among the processors as required by the subprograms' control flow. The history of SIMD-type parallel processing can be traced back to the SOLOMON (simultaneous operation linked ordinal modular network), which was itself based on Unger's 1958 computer design for spatial problems, and later led to the design of 8×8 mesh-connected ILLIAC IV (see Section 23.2).

In a sense, the ILLIAC IV project was a failure in that it cost several times as much as planned and delivered a small fraction of the expected performance. However, these reflected in part the ambitious goals of the project and a mismatch between its technological requirements and what was available in the 1960s. The project provided valuable lessons in computer design and led to many advances in software and algorithm development. The ILLIAC IV legacy has continued with a host of SIMD-type parallel processors. The number of processors gradually increased from a few tens in ILLIAC IV, to hundreds in PEPE (developed by Burroughs for the U.S. Army), and to thousands in STARAN (Goodyear's associative processor), DAP (see Section 23.4), MPP (Section 23.3), TMC CM-1/2 (Section 23.5), and MasPar MP-1/2 (Section 23.6) computers. The increase in the number of processors was not only related to advances in IC technology but also to a trend toward using simpler processors compared with those in ILLIAC IV.

Concurrent with the development of SIMD architectures, progress was being made on two other fronts. One was the design of vector supercomputers, which can be viewed as implementations of SIMD-type parallelism with shared (pipelined) hardware. Cray super-computers and, later, machines by Fujitsu, Hitachi, and others fall into this category. Subsequently, multiprocessor versions of these machines were offered for even higher performance. The second type of intraprocessor concurrency was pursued by Control Data, Amdahl, and IBM, among others, and consisted of providing multiple independent functional units within a CPU. Several functional units could be made concurrently active by multiple instruction issue, instruction lookahead, and out-of-order execution. With the steady increase in the number of transistors that can be put on a single microchip, these pipelining and instruction-level parallelism techniques were gradually incorporated into the designs of advanced microprocessors and, eventually, in ordinary micros.

On the MIMD front, we can trace the development of two classes of machines. Early bus-based multiprocessors, which were introduced primarily to increase the throughput of a computer installation in running many independent jobs and for sharing of expensive peripheral and network resources, were the forerunners of the class of bus-based MIMD multiprocessors that cooperate in running parts of a single large application. A MIMD machine of this type was the five-processor prototype PRIME time-sharing system developed at the University of California, Berkeley, in the early 1970s. PRIME was developed as a fail-soft, highly available system and thus incorporated information coding, error detection, and reconfiguration logic in addition to multiple buses that could be used for interprocessor communication.

Many bus-based MIMD machines have since been developed. Examples include the Carnegie-Mellon Cm* multiprocessor, MIT Concert, Encore Multimax, Sequent Balance and Symmetry, Sun SPARCserver, Alliant FX, HP Apollo, Sequoia Series 400, Intel iAPX 432, Synapse N+1, and Tandem NonStop (see Section 22.2). The second MIMD class, based on specialized (point-to-point or multistage) interconnection networks, has more variety. A large number of different interconnection topologies have been proposed and implemented in such systems. An early, and highly influential, system of this type was the Carnegie-Mellon C.mmp multiprocessor, which was built of 16 PDP-11 minicomputers in the mid-1970s (see Fig. 21.2). It has both a crossbar and a bus for interprocessor communication via shared variables or message passing.

In view of the limitations of crossbars and their poor scalability, research intensified on other interconnection schemes for larger numbers of processors. Caltech's Cosmic Cube was the first hypercube multicomputer ever built (see the introductory paragraph in Section 13.1 for prior history). It was built in 1983 and had 64 processors that were interconnected as a 6-cube. Subsequently, commercial hypercube multicomputers were offered by Intel (iPSC introduced in 1985, with 16–128 nodes composed of an 80x86 processor and 0.5–4 MB of memory) and by nCUBE (see Section 22.3).

Again, scalability concerns were raised and using constant-degree networks was deemed as the only feasible way of scaling beyond the few thousand processors afforded by hypercube-type networks with their logarithmic node degrees. New York University's Ultracomputer (scalable to 4096 processors) was the first general-purpose computer to be based on the butterfly (omega) network. Thinking Machines Corporation's CM-5 computer used a fat-tree (hypertree) interconnection network to connect up to 256K processors (see Section 22.4), but the largest configuration ever built had 1K processors. The KSR-1 computer by Kendall Square Research used up to 34 rings of 32 processors in a ring of rings architecture. Neither of the latter two machines, both introduced in 1992, became successful, in part because of an economic downturn in the United States and in part to renewed interest in mesh architectures, as discussed below. IBM's SP series and Meiko's CS-2 belong to this class of scalable machines and use small custom crossbar switches to synthesize the interprocessor interconnection network (see Section 22.5).

The widespread use of wormhole routing made mesh topologies more attractive. With wormhole routing, network diameter was no longer as important as with store-and-forward routing, which induces significant per-node delay for storing the entire message in intermediate nodes en route to the final destination. The adoption of, and improvements in, wormhole routing led to reasonable routing performance, at least at the scales of up to several thousands of processors. Many 2D and 3D MIMD mesh architectures have been designed and built (even several systolic linear array architectures, such as Intel's iWARP, were built).

Examples of mesh-connected parallel architectures include Ametek Series 2010 (announced in 1988, 4–1024 processors), Stanford DASH (Section 21.5), MIT J Machine (1992, up to 64K processors, 3D mesh with virtual channels and deterministic e-cube routing), Intel Paragon (known as *Touchstone Delta* in its research stage, 1991, up to 4K processors), Cray T3D (32–2048 processors interconnected as a 3D torus) and its successor Cray T3E, and Tera MTA multithreaded parallel system (see Section 21.4).

After several major MPP vendors went out of business in the mid-1990s in view of market saturation and severe budget cuts in organizations using high-performance machines (the in joke was that in computer architecture texts, parallel processing should be covered in Chapter 11), emphasis was shifted to building highly parallel machines from commodity processing and network products in order to minimize research and development costs. Examples of systems and projects in this area include Berkeley NOW (see Section 22.6) and Digital's Alpha Farm. Virtually all major computer vendors now offer parallel processing products in this cluster-of-workstations (COW) class.

24.2. CURRENT STATUS, ISSUES, AND DEBATES

The state of parallel processing today is aptly summarized by David Kuck ([Kuck96], p. 41) in his highly perceptive treatment of high-performance computing problems and trends:

> Today the parallel computing field is in a state of turmoil as various computing architectures struggle for market share and users are presented with a wide range of programming models, new languages, and compilers. In the midst of this, system designers must be constantly aware that the ultimate competition is not with some other parallel architecture or new parallel language; the competition is with sequential computing as it has evolved since the mid-1940s. Inexpensive personal computers that can be used without programming for a wide range of applications, make sequential computing a formidable competitor for emerging parallel systems, as do other systems, ranging from workstations to vector supercomputers, which offer users relatively friendly and powerful environments for problem-solving.

The cost–performance edge of workstations and personal computers is related both to the mass market and to intense competition. This is best understood by examining a pricing model for products in these categories ([Patt96], pp. 14–17). Taking the list price as a basis, a typical product in these categories has a component cost of 25–30%, direct production and marketing costs of around 10%, a gross margin of 15–35% (this is what covers the personnel, research and development, taxes, and, of course, profits), and is sold at 35–45% below the list price (volume discount, incentives, seller's cut, and so forth). For parallel processors, on the other hand, the high R&D costs must be recovered from a relatively small number of sales, making the component cost a very small fraction of the final price. This explains the disparity in MIPS or MFLOPS per unit cost.

But even the fastest personal computers can only do so much in 1 second or 1 hour. Operating systems, compilers, and application programs are growing fatter to incorporate more functionality, appeal to a wider group of users (mass-market economics), maintain backward compatibility, provide more appealing user interfaces (the bells and whistles), and survive all sorts of abuses (be fool- or villain-proof). The clock rates and performance of microprocessors continue their dramatic improvements (see Section 24.4), but the perceived need for performance seems to be always one step ahead. It is inconceivable that this chase will end some day, with contended users saying "OK, we have all the performance that we need." On the contrary, the quest for higher performance appears to be accelerating.

Of course, the processor clock rate and performance are not the only determining factors in the design of parallel processors. Memory access latency and bandwidth, interprocessor communication, and input/output are also important. While the access speeds for both main and secondary memories continue to improve, the rate of improvement is not as dramatic as for processors (see Section 24.4). This worsening of the performance gap between processors and memories has brought about the need for advanced data caching and concurrency techniques, with the attendant increases in complexity, development costs, and power consumption.

And it is not just a matter of architecture and technology; progress is slowing down on the algorithmic front as well. Discovery of an algorithm (sequential or parallel) that leads to substantial speed improvements is now quite rare. This is especially true in the general-purpose domain where the algorithms have to deal with data sets of greatly varying, and unpredictable, characteristics, as well as a multitude of hardware platforms. Algorithm designers and researchers are now talking about percentage-points, as opposed to orders-of-magnitude, improvements in performance. However, the potentials of special pairings of algorithms and architectures have not yet been exhausted, and this forms a compelling argument for designing special-purpose systems.

Despite the recent dwindling of interest in building massively parallel processors, the future of parallel processing now looks brighter than ever. On the design side, the accumulated know-how about interprocessor communication structures, data routing schemes, performance–cost trade-offs, parallel algorithms, data layout in parallel memories, and high-performance I/O makes the implementation of efficient parallel systems relatively straightforward. On the technology side, increasing integration levels (billion-transistor chips are on the horizon), combined with emerging building blocks such as smart memories with internal processing power, single-chip multiprocessors, and gigabit per second communication channels, will make the synthesis of parallel machines from commodity products feasible and painless. Finally, on the application side, expanded focus on data- and computation-intensive applications such as modeling, digital libraries, and multimedia will necessitate parallel processing even at the level of workstations and, perhaps, personal computers.

In-depth comparisons of the myriad of design alternatives in parallel processing, based on the vast collection of published work as well as hands-on experience with commercial and one-of-a-kind parallel systems, have only just begun. Ongoing debates in the following areas of parallel machine design will no doubt continue within the parallel processing research community:

Architecture	General- or special-purpose systems? SIMD, MIMD, or hybrid?
Processing	Custom or commodity processors? Coarse- or fine-grain?

Interconnection	Shared-medium, direct, or multistage? Custom or commodity?
Routing	Oblivious or adaptive? Wormhole, packet, or virtual cut-through?
Programming	Shared memory or message passing? New languages or libraries?

There are strong opinions on each side of these issues and a dearth of empirical evidence as to which schemes work and why.

With regard to architecture, general-purpose MIMD systems appear to have the upper hand now, but SIMD has maintained a niche market within the domain of special-purpose real-time systems (see Sections 4.2 and 23.1). Today, the development of one-of-a-kind circuits is extremely expensive and is likely to lead to noncompetitive products. Building special-purpose systems from commodity components, on the other hand, appears to be getting easier and presents itself as a valid way to achieve higher performance for time-critical applications.

The raw processing power of commodity processors is hard to beat. Thus, the use of custom processors is becoming harder to justify on the basis of performance. However, size, environmental requirements, and power consumption are still valid reasons for pursuing custom designs. This is, to some extent, being addressed by commercial vendors who offer different versions of their chips, which are based on the same overall architecture, to satisfy specialized needs. Coarse-grain processing nodes in parallel systems essentially correspond to the capabilities of the current top-of-the-line microprocessors. These processors all contain more or less the same functionalities and leave little for us to argue about. On the other hand, whereas we can now easily put 4–16 simpler processors on a chip [Kogg94], difficulties arise as soon as we begin to discuss which features of a full-blown microprocessor are candidates for removal or simplification. Thus, at least for now, *fine-grain* is synonymous with *custom*.

The communication revolution, fueled in part by the exploding use of the Internet, has led to significant advances in the performance of commodity interconnection technology. This technology is now driving the parallel processing industry. As with processors, custom interconnection components are very expensive to develop and at best offer limited performance benefits. All three alternatives of shared-medium links, router-based direct topologies, and switch-based multistage networks offer data transfer rates in excess of 1 Gb/s (see Section 22.1), making them natural candidates for use in parallel processors. The asynchronous transfer mode (ATM) communication technology has the potential to merge the data transfer needs of both parallel and geographically distributed computing systems (see Section 24.5).

Data routing has been one of the most contentious points of argument in recent years among the designers and researchers in parallel processing. For example, it is often taken as a fact that the advent of wormhole routing has made packet routing obsolete. Yet, many current and planned high-performance machines are based on packet routing [Magg96]. While raw communication bandwidth is no longer viewed as a limiting factor in the development of massively parallel processors, efficient use of communication resources and adapting their use to data traffic patterns is still an important area of study. A fundamental point is the choice between the simplicity of oblivious routing, leading to smaller/faster switches and lower end-to-end latency when there is no conflict or malfunction, and the flexibility of adaptive routing that often goes hand in hand with more complex protocols to enable routing decisions and to avoid resource deadlocks.

Parallel machines have traditionally been hard to program and remain so even today [Kuck96]. There are two basic reasons for this state of affairs: economics and need. The relatively small number of parallel systems of any one kind makes it unattractive for commercial software vendors to invest in developing software for them. Also, users of parallel machines have usually been large companies and government entities with substantial in-house programming expertise, and, given the high prices of the machines they were buying, they could easily afford to keep a competent programming staff on their rolls. However, this strategy has resulted in a host of one-of-a-kind, inefficient, nonportable, and unmaintainable software systems. The endless debates about which parallel programming language is better mirrored those in the early days of digital computers about the relative merits of the available options: Fortran, Cobol, and Algol. With the prospects of the language debate being settled quite dim, the use of portable libraries emerged as the paradigm of choice for parallel programming. Software and program development tools for parallel computers might start showing greater improvements now that parallel system designers have been relieved from worrying about hardware development and circuit design.

24.3. TFLOPS, PFLOPS, AND BEYOND

We all seek simplicity and like the idea of putting things in order. We rank-order sports teams, record albums, movies, popular books, and many other things; so, why except computers and parallel processors? Just as the high ranking of a book or movie according to total sales volume is no guarantee that you will like it, the peak performance of a parallel processor in GFLOPS or TFLOPS might be a poor indicator of how it would fare if applied to your computational problems. Ranking machines based on their performance on benchmarks is somewhat better, but still not free of pitfalls. For one thing, benchmarks may not be completely representative of some applications. For another, parallel machine vendors have been known to tune their systems to do well on certain popular benchmarks, sometimes to the detriment of performance, or even correct operation, in other areas; see Patterson and Hennessy ([Patt96], pp. 44–50) for an informative discussion on the fallacies and pitfalls of performance comparisons and benchmarks.

The above disclaimer nonwithstanding, there is a certain usefulness to numerical performance indicators, for even though they may be misleading in micro-level comparisons, they do provide fairly accurate macro-level views of technological advances and trends. For example, the very fact that today we are talking rather casually about TFLOPS performance, and looking ahead to the PFLOPS level, is quite significant in itself. Looking back at Fig. 1.2, we note that the upward trend will be marginally affected by small adjustments in the data points. Thus, using GFLOPS or TFLOPS for monitoring performance trends over time is much less dangerous than using them for performance comparisons in space.

In order to push the development of TFLOPS supercomputers for both military and civilian applications, the U.S. Department of Energy launched the Accelerated Strategic Computing Initiative (ASCI) in 1994 with a budget of U.S. $ 1 billion spread over 10 years. Figure 24.1 shows the goals and milestones of the ASCI program. ASCI started when TFLOPS peak performance was within reach, but still rather expensive and, thus, not implemented. The first step of the program was thus to achieve a performance in excess of 1 TFLOPS in a machine with 500 GB of main memory; this goal was achieved in 1997 when Intel installed and tested its 1.34 TFLOPS Option Red machine at the Sandia National Laboratories in New Mexico. The Intel/Sandia Option Red parallel computer, which uses a 38 × 32 × 2 mesh topology for interconnecting two-processor nodes, is comprised of 9200 Pentium Pro processors with a clock frequency of 200 MHz, 573 GB of system memory, and 2.25 TB of disk memory. Most of the nodes are compute nodes, but there are also 32 service, 24 I/O, 2 system, and several spare nodes. The components of this parallel machine are housed in 86 cabinets occupying 160 m^2 of space (including aisles and access walkways), consume a peak power of 850 KW, weigh 44 tons, and require 300 tons of air conditioning equipment.

Two parallel projects are under way to realize the next ASCI milestone of 3 TFLOPS by the end of 1998 (Option Blue in Fig. 24.1). Silicon Graphics is developing the Blue Mountain, a CC-NUMA machine with 3000+ MIPS processors. IBM is in charge of Blue Pacific, a cluster architecture using 4K POWER3 processors. Cray T3E Model 1200, announced in November 1997, has already laid claim to a peak performance of 2.5 TFLOPS with 2K 600-MHz processors.

Looking at the microprocessor performance trends (Fig. 1.1), it appears that ASCI's various performance milestones will be attainable by using no more than several thousand processors. Speed and bandwidth requirements of the communication network are also well within the range of current technology, when projected performance improvements are factored in. Dealing with power dissipation may turn out to be the hardest technical obstacle to overcome. Current processors consume of the order on 50–100 W/GFLOPS. So, a 100-TFLOPS machine might need 5–10 MW of power just for the processors.

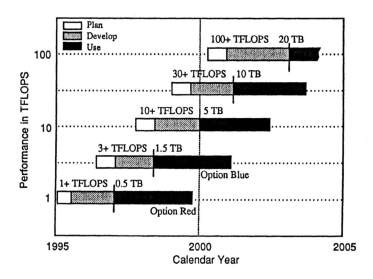

Figure 24.1. Performance goals of the ASCI program.

The pursuit of higher performance most likely will not stop at the current level of TFLOPS, being promoted by the ASCI program, or the next milestone of PFLOPS now being discussed. Much work remains to be done not just to achieve PFLOPS performance for advanced applications but also to make GFLOPS and TFLOPS performance more affordable for everyday use. Given the past performance trends and projections for the future, it is virtually guaranteed that some day we will look back at the Intel/DOE Option Red machine in the same way that we now view the ENIAC, wondering exactly why a machine that is less powerful than our battery-operated laptop computers needed so much space and power.

24.4. PROCESSOR AND MEMORY TECHNOLOGIES

Commodity microprocessors are improving in performance at an astonishing rate (see Fig. 1.1). Over the past two decades, microprocessor clock rates have improved by a factor of 100, from a few megahertz to hundreds of megahertz. Gigahertz processors are not far off. In the same time frame, memory chip capacity has gone up by a factor of 10^4, from 16 Kb to 256 Mb. Gigabit memory chips are now beginning to appear.

Along with speed, the functionality of microprocessors has also improved drastically. This is a direct result of the larger number of transistors that can be accommodated on one chip. In the past 20 years, the number of transistors on a microprocessor chip has grown by a factor of 10^3; from tens of thousands (Intel 8086) to a few tens of millions (Intel Pentium Pro). Older microprocessors contained an ALU for integer arithmetic within the basic CPU chip and a floating-point coprocessor on a separate chip, but increasing VLSI circuit density has led to the trend of integrating both units on a single microchip, while still leaving enough room for large on-chip memories (typically used for an instruction cache, a data cache, and a Level-2 cache).

As an example of modern microprocessors, we briefly describe a member of Intel's Pentium family of microprocessors: the Intel Pentium Pro, also known as Intel P6 (Fig. 24.2). The primary design goal for the Intel P6 was to achieve the highest possible performance, while keeping the external appearances compatible with the Pentium and using the same mass production technology.

The Intel P6 has a 32-bit architecture, internally using a 64-bit data bus, 36-bit addresses, and an 86-bit floating-point format. In the terminology of modern microprocessors, P6 is superscalar and superpipelined: superscalar because it can execute multiple independent instructions concurrently in its many functional units; superpipelined because its instruction execution pipeline with 14+ stages is very deep. The Intel P6 is capable of glueless multiprocessing with up to four processors, operates at 150–200 MHz, and has 21M transistors, roughly one-fourth of which are for the CPU and the rest for the on-chip cache memory. Because high performance in the Intel P6 is gained by out-of-order and speculative instruction execution, a key component in the design is a reservation station that is essentially a hardware-level scheduler of micro-operations. Each instruction is converted to one or more micro-operations which are then executed in arbitrary order whenever their required operands are available.

The result of a micro-operation is sent to both the reservation station and a special unit called the *reorder buffer*. The latter unit is responsible for making sure that program execution remains consistent by committing the results of micro-operations to the machine's "retire-

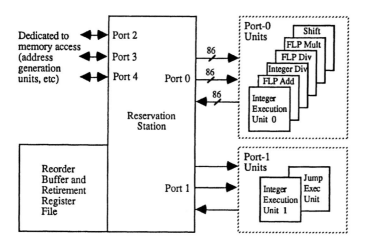

Figure 24.2. Key parts of the CPU in the Intel Pentium Pro microprocessor.

ment" registers only after all pieces of an instruction have terminated and the instruction's "turn" to execute has arrived within the sequential program flow. Thus, if an interrupt occurs, all operations that are in progress can be discarded without causing inconsistency in the machine's state. There is a full crossbar between all five ports of the reservation station so that any returning result can be forwarded directly to any other unit for the next clock cycle.

Fetching, decoding, and setting up the components of an instruction in the reservation station takes eight clock cycles and is performed as an eight-stage pipelined operation. The retirement process, mentioned above, takes three clock cycles and is also pipelined. Sandwiched between the above two pipelines is a variable-length pipeline for instruction execution. For this middle part of instruction execution, the reservation station needs two cycles to ascertain that the operands are available and to schedule the micro-operation on an appropriate unit. The operation itself takes one cycle for register-to-register integer add and longer for more complex functions. The multiplicity of functional units with different latencies is why out-of-order and speculative execution (e.g., branch prediction) are crucial to high performance.

With a great deal of functionality plus on-chip memory already available, a natural question relates to the way in which additional transistors might be utilized. One alternative is to build multiple processors on the same chip. Custom microchips housing several simple processors have long been used in the design of (massively) parallel computers. Commercially available SIMD parallel systems of the late 1980s already contained tens of bit-serial processors on each chip and more recent products offer hundreds of such processors per chip (thousands on one PC board). Microchips containing multiple general-purpose processors and associated memory constitute a plausible way of utilizing the higher densities that are becoming available to us. From past experience with parallel computers requiring custom chips, it appears that custom chip development for one or a few parallel computers will not be economically viable. Instead, off-the-shelf components will likely become available as standard building blocks for parallel systems.

No matter how many processors we can put on one chip, the demand for greater performance, created by novel applications or larger-scale versions of existing ones, will sustain the need for integrating multiple chips into systems with even higher levels of parallelism. With tens to tens of thousands of processors afforded by billion-transistor chips, small-scale parallel systems utilizing powerful general-purpose processors, as well as multi-million-processor massively parallel systems, will become not only realizable but also quite cost-effective. Fortunately, the issues involved in the design of single-chip multiprocessors and massively parallel systems, as well as their use in synthesizing larger parallel systems, are no different from the current problems facing parallel computer designers. Given that interconnects have already become the limiting factor (see Section 24.5), regardless of the number of processors on a chip, we need to rely on multilevel hierarchical or recursive architectures.

Whereas main memory capacity is growing at an impressive rate, memory access times are reaching fundamental limits that cannot be easily overcome. In the same 20-year period when we have seen factors of 10^4, 10^3, and 10^2 improvements in memory capacity, microprocessor transistor count, and clock rate, memory access speed has improved by a factor of less than 10. Use of more, and larger, caches helps to some extent, as do architectural fixes such as wider data paths and multithreading. Nevertheless, the main memory access speed may be the ultimate limiting factor for sustained performance improvements.

Unlike main memory technology whose slower performance improvement compared with microprocessors is a cause for concern, secondary storage devices do not appear to be limiting factors in building even higher-performance supercomputers, despite the fact that data transfer rates from disks are also experiencing slow growth (see Section 18.4). One reason is the disk array technology that allows us to get higher data rates from a large number of inexpensive disks. The other, more important, reason is that with larger main memories, extensive disk caching and the use of log-structured files have become possible.

24.5. INTERCONNECTION TECHNOLOGIES

Various forms of interconnections are needed in a parallel processor. At the lowest level, there are wires that connect components inside a chip. Then we have interchip connections on a printed-circuit board, interboard connections via a backplane, interchassis connections via cables, and intersystem connections via various types of network links.

On-chip interconnects comprise local and global wires that link circuit elements and distribute power supply and clock inputs. Downward scaling of VLSI technologies continuously improves device switching (computation) times. The effect of this scaling on interconnect performance, however, is just the opposite, given the increased current density, chip size, and noise margin, along with reduced width and spacing [Parh98]. To stress the influence of interconnect delay on performance, we consider Fig. 24.3, which depicts the ratio of wire delay to device switching time as a function of the minimum feature size, extrapolated to the point of allowing 1B transistors on a chip (dotted portion). Two scenarios are shown: continued use of Al/SiO$_2$ (top curve) or changeover to less resistive copper wires and an insulator with lower dielectric constant, in order to reduce wiring resistance and capacitance (bottom curve). In the latter case, downward scaling appears to improve the wire

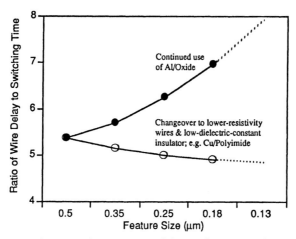

Figure 24.3. Changes in the ratio of a 1-cm wire delay to device switching time as the feature size is reduced.

delay problem, but this may not be the case once other factors such as the transmission line effect (which is largely unknown at present) are factored in.

At the physical level, the dominance of wire delay will necessitate changes in wiring material and circuit design styles [Mein96]. At the architectural level, designs with local data and control flows will become increasingly more attractive. As on-chip wire delays increase, the difference between on- and off-chip transmissions, which is now a determining factor in parallel computer implementations, will diminish. However, these changes only affect the numerical values of the technology-related parameters used in trading off performance for lower cost and realizability. The basic model, based on pin and channel capacity limitations at various packaging levels, remains the same. The effect of architecture on the chip interconnect delay was discussed in Section 4.6.

Beyond the chip boundary, various interconnection technologies are available that offer trade-offs in bandwidth and end-to-end latency. As shown in Fig. 24.4, options range from multi-gigabit-per-second backplane buses offering submicrosecond latencies to much slower wide-area networks with latencies of 1 second or more. Note, however, that with the development of higher-bandwidth geographically distributed networks and the use of common underlying technologies, like ATM, for several of these classes, boundaries between the interconnection classes depicted in Fig. 24.4 are becoming increasingly blurred.

Given a particular on-chip connectivity, two issues must be considered for building larger parallel systems. The first of these, the provision of off-chip links, is really within the realm of the chip designer. However, one must look at the potential overall architectures in order to decide on suitable off-chip connectivity. Perhaps the most general and flexible option is to provide one (or a few) off-chip port(s) per processor. A variety of hierarchical architectures can be built when every processor on the chip is directly accessible from outside [Yeh98]. All routers will be identical, thus leading to manufacturing simplicity (e.g., fault tolerance for yield enhancement) and algorithmic uniformity. In most existing hierarchical architectures, the performance advantage is obtained through the replacement of off-module communications with (a larger number of) on-module transfers. Thus, the communication

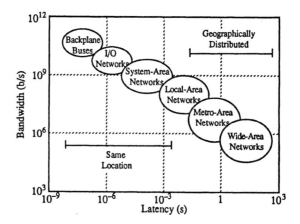

Fig. 24.4. Various types of intermodule and intersystem connections.

performance of the low-level modules (chips) is a determining factor in the overall performance. This points to the importance of research on hierarchical architectures, based on large
building blocks, whose performance is less sensitive to the low-level connectivity.

Above the chip and board levels, the physical media commonly used for computer and
network interconnections are of three basic types (Fig. 24.5):

1. *Twisted pair* of copper wires. Two insulated copper wires, each about 1 mm thick,
   are twisted together to reduce electrical interference. This is because a twisted pair
   of wires does not form an antenna, whereas two parallel lines do. A twisted pair can
   handle data transmission rates on the order of 1 Mb/s over 1–2 Km. Higher
   bandwidths over shorter distances can be accommodated, as long as the product of
   bandwidth and distance is kept the same. Thus, it is feasible to use a twisted pair
   for a 20 Mb/s LAN in one building.
2. *Coaxial cable*. This type of connector was developed for the cable television
   industry in view of their requirements for high bandwidth and good noise immunity.
   Coaxial cable is both more expensive and more difficult to connect than twisted
   pairs. Common connection methods involve the use of a *T junction* (the cable is cut

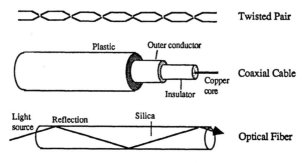

Figure 24.5. The three commonly used media for computer and network connections.

and reconnected via the T junction, which has a third link for connection to the computer) or a *vampire tap* (a hole is drilled to the copper core and a special connector is screwed in). The second option is less expensive and is thus often preferred. Coaxial cables offer a bandwidth of around 10 Mb/s over a distance of 1 Km.

3. *Optical fiber.* Data are transmitted via light traveling in the fiber. The light is produced by a light source (LED or laser diode) at one end and detected by a photodiode at the other. There are various optical fiber types that differ in the light source used, feasible transmission distances, and ease of connection. Transmission rates around or in excess of 1 Gb/s are currently possible. The main drawback of optical fibers is in the need for optical-electrical converters at each interface to an electronic device. Note that because optical fibers are unidirectional, establishing a full-duplex connection requires two fibers.

Given the transfer-rate limitations for communication media, bandwidth can be increased by providing more channels between the sender and the receiver. Various standards have been developed for gigabit networks with the aim of reducing the burden of computer manufacturers in supporting a variety of channels. For example, the *fiber channel* standard has been developed to integrate data transfer methods between computers, storage units, and other devices into a set of channel and network standards.

24.6. THE FUTURE OF PARALLEL PROCESSING

We have witnessed many innovations since the development of early parallel machines. Numerous ideas have been tried and a variety of resolved and unresolved debates have transpired. A few years ago, it was unclear whether the TFLOPS performance milestone would be reached with a thousand or so GFLOPS processors or a million simpler MFLOPS nodes. Just as we found out the answer to this question, the question resurfaced, but with the prefixes changed to P, T, and G, respectively. Either answer to this last question would likely require that the equivalent of one of the current ASCI computers be implemented on a handful of chips. While this is not inconceivable, given the record of past progress, it should not be taken for granted. Microprocessors with clock rates of 1 GHz are expected to arrive around the year 2000. Beyond that, however, there is some agreement in the computer architecture community that subnanosecond clocks might present insurmountable challenges. The use of massively parallel processing appears to be the only reasonable option to overcome this flattening of the performance curve.

In fact, highly parallel processing is not just useful for reaching new milestones in performance but is also critical to lower power consumption. One reason is that power consumption in the currently dominant CMOS technology is proportional to the square of the supply voltage. It is now quite feasible to lower the supply voltage by a factor of 2 or more (say from the present 3.5 V to 1.5 V), thus reducing the power consumption significantly. The problem with this approach to power conservation is that lower-voltage circuits tend to be slower. Thus, to recover the lost performance, we might make the pipelines deeper or use a larger number of parallel units. While this increases the power consumption again, the amount of power increase to recover a performance comparable to that of the original higher-voltage design is much smaller than the factor of 4–5 gained from lowering the supply voltage. The same argument might be made for cost, which, at the leading edge of technology, is a superlinear function of speed.

Two major driving forces in the future of parallel processing are the VLSI and communication technologies. Advances in VLSI design and manufacturing will provide us with more powerful and adaptable building blocks for use in parallel systems (see Section 24.4). The computing components of the twenty-first century will likely contain many built-in capabilities and hooks that facilitate their integration into larger systems. The communication technology (see Section 24.5) appears to be similarly moving in the direction of highly functional and flexible building blocks that can be used at many different levels within a system.

Concurrent with technological developments, changing application characteristics will dictate a shift of focus in parallel processing from high-speed or high-throughput designs in top-of-the-line supercomputers to low-cost and low-power designs for personal, embedded, and mobile applications. These will ensure continued interest in bit-serial and digit-serial processing as mechanisms to reduce the VLSI area (cost) and to improve adaptability, packageability, and testability. High-performance designs, with lookahead and speculative execution, are expensive and often at odds with the goal of reducing power consumption to extend the battery life and/or to facilitate heat dissipation.

Many challenging research problems are being addressed in the above areas and numerous technological and architectural innovations are being evaluated for use in (massively) parallel processors of the future. The following list is intended only as a sample of the many exciting research topics and is by no means exhaustive.

1. *Asynchronous design.* The higher speeds and packaging densities of modern digital circuits are stretching the limits of our ability to distribute a clock signal to all of the required points. Use of a global clock signal throughout a system simplifies the design and verification processes and avoids the overhead of handshaking in asynchronous designs. However, as signal propagation delays over long wires force the designers to modularize the systems, an overhead that is comparable to that of handshaking for asynchronous operation is being introduced in synchronous systems. Novel design paradigms and improved tools for synthesis and analysis of asynchronous systems may change the balance in favor of the latter.

2. *Intelligent memories.* One way to overcome the limitations imposed by the memory-to-processor bandwidth is to merge processing and storage functions into a single chip. Current memory chips have extremely high bandwidths internally, as they read out a row of bits from the memory matrix. However, they then select a portion of this row for output through the limited number of pins available in the memory package. Providing processing logic on the memory chip would allow for all of the row bits to be manipulated at once, leading to extremely high peak performance. The task of translating this peak performance to useful processing power is of course nontrivial. The above concept is being pursued by several research teams using descriptors such as logic-in-memory, processor-in-memory, and intelligent RAM.

3. *Reconfigurable systems.* The ability to reconfigure a computer system in order to match its structure to the needs of the computation at hand, or to adapt to changes

in the availability of resources, is highly desirable. Such reconfigurable systems can be produced in large quantities and then customized for various applications through "programming" of their cells and connections in much the same way that programmable logic devices are now used to implement varied logical functions with standard building blocks. When used with suitable design tools, such programmable "raw" machines facilitate the development of high-performance special-purpose systems and allow the tuning of the machine architecture to computational needs in general-purpose systems.

4. *Network computing*. Inspired by the widespread popularity of the World-Wide Web, new paradigms for computing on a collection of independent heterogeneous networked computers are emerging. Using appropriate software on each computer, the user of a networked machine can view the collection of computers to which she has been granted access as the components of a single powerful computer. This approach was used on an experimental basis recently when a group of volunteers pooled their computational resources to crack an enciphered message. More work remains to be done before the approach becomes more generally applicable.

The emergence of new technologies and the unwavering quest for higher performance are bound to create new challenges in the coming years besides the ones discussed above. Fundamentally new technologies and hardware/software design paradigms (e.g., optical computing, digital neural networks, biological computers) may alter the way in which we view or design parallel systems.

PROBLEMS

24.1. The Holland machine
The Holland machine [Holl59], a forerunner of modern MIMD-type parallel computers, was briefly described in Section 24.1. Study this machine and prepare a description of its architecture and programming model. Did the Holland machine correspond to the shared-memory or message-passing paradigm?

24.2. The SOLOMON computer
The SOLOMON computer [Slot62], a forerunner of SIMD-type parallel computers, was mentioned in Section 24.1. Study this machine and prepare a description of its architecture and programming model. How was the SOLOMON computer similar to, or different from, ILLIAC IV?

24.3. Which came first, SIMD or MIMD?
From the papers cited in Problems 24.1 and 24.2, their references, and additional research, trace the history of SIMD and MIMD parallel computing paradigms, going as far back as possible. For example, note the reference to Babbage's work in Section 24.1. Based on your studies, answer the question: "Which came first, SIMD or MIMD?"

24.4. The great debates in parallel processing
In Section 24.2, the ongoing debates concerning architecture, processing, interconnection, routing, and programming within the field of parallel processing were outlined.
  a.   Choose one of these debates, take a side, and write an essay that justifies your position.

b. Which of these areas of disagreement do you think will be of greatest relevance in the pursuit of PFLOPS performance and why?

24.5. COTS-based parallel systems

The availability of small bus-based multiprocessors as off-the-shelf components, with hooks in place for building larger systems, has made it easier to design and build scalable parallel processors. Using analogies with other areas of engineering and technology, discuss if this trend will lead to more cost-effective products or will stall progress by inhibiting innovation.

24.6. Parallel computer performance

The peak MIPS rating of a machine is often specified by using the execution time of a 32-bit integer add instruction. Similarly, the peak FLOPS rating can be obtained by considering floating-point addition. With benchmarks, the issue is trickier, as various floating-point operations take different amounts of time and library routines for functions such as sin and log are really more complex than individual operations. Study how various operations are weighted in determining the MFLOPS rating of a machine from its running time of a benchmark with a known mix of operations.

24.7. Higher than peak performance

In bit-serial machines, an interesting phenomenon is possible. The peak FLOPS performance of the machine is obtained by considering the time needed for floating-point addition. However, when multiple operations involving the same operands are needed (such as an add and a subtract), it is possible to share some of the computation steps, thus exceeding the machine's peak performance. Present an example to show how this is possible.

24.8. Performance versus the number of processors

Obtain data about the number of processors and performance of at least 100 parallel processors (e.g., from the "top 500 supercomputer sites" page on the Internet). Produce scatter-plots for the number of processors versus performance, number of processors versus year of introduction, and performance versus year of introduction. Use different marker symbols for parallel vector processors, large-scale parallel machines that are still in production, and past large-scale machines. Discuss the observed trends.

24.9. DEC Alpha microprocessor

Digital Equipment Corporation's Alpha microprocessor is among the fastest processors available today. Study the architecture of Alpha and compare it with that of Intel Pentium Pro.

24.10. Machines based on crossbars

It is well known that crossbar switches are not readily scalable. An 8×8 crossbar requires 16×40 = 640 input/output pins, assuming 32 bits of data and 8 bits of control per port. This is already beyond the I/O capacity of a single VLSI chip.

a. What are the problems of implementing a large crossbar switch through bit-slicing (i.e., implementing 1 bit or a few bits of the data path on each chip)?

b. What are the problems of implementing a large crossbar switch through hierarchical composition (i.e., building a large crossbar from a set of smaller ones)?

c. Compare the approaches of parts (a) and (b) for synthesizing a 64×64 crossbar switch.

24.11. Parallel processing in your automobile

Most automobiles manufactured after 1995 have an on-board computer to monitor various subsystems, adjust engine parameters in real time to improve efficiency, and perform on-line as well as off-line diagnostic functions. Discuss future applications for the automobile's on-board computer that might necessitate parallel processing. Then, estimate the total MIPS or MFLOPS of all automobile on-board computers with and without the parallel processing additions in the year 2010.

24.12. The *n*-body problem
A very important problem is physics is the time evolution of a system of *n* bodies interacting by gravitational attraction or some other symmetrical force. For gravitational interaction, exemplified by our solar system, the force between Bodies *i* and *j*, with masses m_i and m_j and located at Points x_i and x_j, is $f_{ij} = gm_im_j(x_i - x_j)/|x_i - x_j|^3$. The total force on Body *i* is $F_i = \sum_{j=0}^{n-1} f_{ij}$. Time is then advanced to $t + 1$ and the new velocities and locations of the *n* bodies are recalculated from $F_i = m_i \, d^2x_i/dt^2$. In these equations, g, m_i, and m_j are scalar values, while x_i, x_j, f_{ij}, and F_i are 3-vectors. The computation continues indefinitely, with the states of the *n* bodies recorded on disk for future reference after every *r* time steps. Discuss the suitability and efficiency of each of the parallel architecture classes reviewed in this book for solving the *n*-body problem.

24.13. Parallel synergy
Consider the problem of moving a heavy piece of furniture from one point in the room to another. The piece is too heavy for one person to lift, push, or drag. Thus, the only option available to a single mover is to disassemble the item, move the pieces separately, and finally reassemble the pieces at the new location. The whole process takes about 1 hour, say. Four movers, on the other hand, can simply lift and move the item to its new location in less than 1 minute. This type of superlinear speed-up is sometimes referred to as *parallel synergy*. Based on what you have learned about parallel processing, propose a computational problem for which superlinear speed-up of this type is observed.

REFERENCES AND SUGGESTED READING

[Bald96]   Baldi, L., "Industry Roadmaps: The Challenge of Complexity," *Microelectronic Engineering*, Vol. 34, No. 1, pp. 9–26, December 1996.
[Bell92]   Bell, G., "Ultracomputers: A Teraflop Before Its Time," *Communications of the ACM*, Vol. 35, No. 8, pp. 27–47, August 1992.
[Burg96]   Burger, D., J. R. Goodman, and A. Kagi, "Quantifying Memory Bandwidth Limitations of Current and Future Microprocessors," *Proc. 23rd Int. Symp. Computer Architecture*, May 1996, pp. 78–89.
[Gokh95]   Gokhale, M., B. Holmes, and K. Iobst, "Processing in Memory: The Terasys Massively Parallel PIM Array," *IEEE Computer*, Vol. 28, pp. 23–31, April 1995.
[Hock81]   Hockney, R. W., and C. R. Jesshope, *Parallel Computers*, Adam Hilger, 1981.
[Holl59]   Holland, J. H., "A Universal Computer Capable of Executing an Arbitrary Number of Sub-Programs Simultaneously," *Proc. Eastern Joint Computer Conf.*, 1959, pp. 108–113.
[Hord90]   Hord, R. M., Parallel Superconducting in SIMD Architectures, CRC Press, 1990.
[Hord93]   Hord, R. M., Parallel Superconducting in MIMD Architectures, CRC Press, 1993.
[Kogg94]   Kogge, P. M., "EXECUBE—A New Architecture for Scalable MPPs," *Proc. Int. Conf. Parallel Processing*, Vol. I, pp. 77–84.
[Kuck96]   Kuck, D. J., *High-Performance Computing: Challenges for Future Systems*, Oxford University Press, 1996.
[Kwai97]   Kwai, D. M., "Pruning Strategies for Deriving Cost-Effective and Scalable Parallel Processor Interconnection Networks," Ph.D. Dissertation, Dept. Electrical Computer Engineering, University of California, Santa Barbara, December 1997.
[Lerm94]   Lerman, G., and L. Rudolph, *Parallel Evolution of Parallel Processors*, Plenum, 1994.
[Magg96]   Maggs, B. M., "A Critical Look at Three of Parallel Computing's Maxims," *Proc. Int. Symp. Parallel Architectures, Algorithms and Networks*, Beijing, June 1996, pp. 1–7.

[Mein96]   Meindl, J. D., "Gigascale Integration: Is the Sky the Limit?" *IEEE Circuits and Devices*, Vol. 12, No. 6, pp. 19–23 & 32, November 1996.

[Parh98]   Parhami, B., and D.-M. Kwai, "Issues in Designing Parallel Architectures Using Multiprocessor and Massively Parallel Microchips," unpublished manuscript.

[Patt96]   Patterson, D. A. and J. L. Hennessy, *Computer Architecture: A Quantitative Approach*, 2nd ed., Morgan Kaufmann, 1996.

[SaiH95]   Sai-Halasz, G. A., "Performance Trends in High-End Processors," *Proceedings of the IEEE*, Vol. 83, No. 1, pp. 18–36, January 1995.

[SIA94]   Semiconductor Industry Association, *The National Roadmap for Semiconductors*, 1994.

[Slot62]   Slotnick, D. L., W. C. Borck, and R. C. McReynolds, "The Solomon Computer," *Proc. AFIPS Fall Joint Computer Conf.*, 1962, pp. 97–107.

[Wood96]   Woodward, P. R., "Perspectives on Supercomputing; Three Decades of Change," *IEEE Computer*, Vol. 29, No. 10, pp. 99–111, October 1996.

[Yeh98]   Yeh, C.-H., "Efficient Low-Degree Interconnection Networks for Parallel Processing: Topologies, Algorithms, and Fault Tolerance," Ph.D. dissertation, Dept. Electrical Computer Engineering, University of California, Santa Barbara, March 1998.

Index